Events Management

A developmental and managerial approach

Events Management

A developmental and managerial approach

Third edition

By
Dimitri Tassiopoulos (editor)

JUTA

Events Management: A developmental and managerial approach

First published 2000
Second edition 2005
Third edition 2010

© Juta & Co Ltd, 2010
First floor, Sunclare Building, 21 Dreyer Street, Claremont 7708

ISBN 978-0-70217-779-8

Project manager: Sharon Steyn
Editing: Wendy Priilaid
Proofreading: Lee-Ann Ashcroft
Cover design: Paula Wood
Indexing: Sanet le Roux
Typesetting in 10.5 pt on 13 pt Adobe Caslon Pro by Mckore Graphics
Illustrations by Mckore Graphics
Printed and bound in the Republic of South Africa by Print Communications

The authors and the publisher have made every effort to obtain permission for and to acknowledge the use of copyright material. Should any infringement of copyright have occurred, please contact the publisher, and every effort will be made to rectify omissions or errors in the event of a reprint or new edition.
Photo credits:
Dimitri Tassiopoulos pp. i, iii, 1, 3, 34, 49, 65, 67, 87, 108, 125, 143, 161, 183, 185, 207, 225, 251, 273, 293, 317, 341, 343, 363, 365, 390, 408, 451, 470, 489;
EIBTM pp. 67, 273, 293, 428, 451;
Gavin Young p. 67;
IMEX pp. 49, 125, 225, 251, 470, 502;
iStockphotoR p. iii;
Juta pp. 343, 489;
MediaClubSouthAfrica.com.
    Chris Kirchhoff p. 365;
MediaClubSouthAfrica.com.
    Hannelie Coetzee p. 291;
MediaClubSouthAfrica.com.
    Mangaung Local Municipality p. 87;
MediaClubSouthAfrica.com
    Rodger Bosch pp. 34, 291;
Razaq Raj and Paul Walters p. 390;
SA Tourism pp. 34, 408;
World Travel Market pp. 67, 185, 207, 249, 273, 317, 428, 451, 470, 489, 502;
Zoë Moosman pp. 34, 87, 451

Contents

About the editor vii

About the contributors viii

Foreword...xv

Preface xix

Acknowledgements xxi

PART I: EVENTS MANAGEMENT: AN INTRODUCTION

Chapter 1 – The world of events (*Dimitri Tassiopoulos*) 3

Chapter 2 – Events strategic development (*William O'Toole*)............................... 34

Chapter 3 – The role of management in events management (*Julia Silvers*) 49

PART II: EVENTS AND ADMINISTRATION

Chapter 4 – Events role players (*Dimitri Tassiopoulos*).. 67

Chapter 5 – Bidding and securing an event (*Graham Berridge, Liz Quick*)...................... 87

Chapter 6 – Events planning and coordination (*Tom Wanklin*)................................... 108

Chapter 7 – Events organising (*Tom Wanklin*) 125

Chapter 8 – Project management for events (*Tom Wanklin*)............................. 143

Chapter 9 – Events accounting and financial management (*Debbie van Oudtshoorn*)..... 161

PART III: EVENTS AND DESIGN

Chapter 10 – Design management of events (*Graham Berridge*) 185

Chapter 11 – Sustainability and events design (*Urmilla Bob*) 207

Chapter 12 – Catering management design for events
(*Jurgen Gasche, Malcolm Ellis*)... 225

PART IV: EVENTS AND MARKETING

Chapter 13 – Events marketing and communication strategy
(*Rita Carmouche, Nimish Shukla, Angela Anthonisz*) 251

Chapter 14 – Events sponsorship and fundraising
(*Brendon Knott, Douglas Turco*) 273

PART V: EVENTS AND OPERATIONS

Chapter 15 – Events operations management (*Matthew Bromley, Conor Moss*) 293

Chapter 16 – Events technology (*Peta Thomas*) 317

PART VI: EVENTS AND RISK

Chapter 17 – Events risk and safety management (*Errol Ninow*) 343

PART VII: APPLIED EVENTS MANAGEMENT

Chapter 18 – Hallmark and mega-events (*Kamilla Swart*) 365

Chapter 19 – Festivals (*Razaq Raj, Paul Walters*) 390

Chapter 20 – Sport events (*Kamilla Swart*) 408

Chapter 21 – Exhibitions, expositions and fairs
(*John Knocker, Howard Pell, Dimitri Tassiopoulos*) 428

Chapter 22 – Political, civic and government events (*Jo-Ansie van Wyk*) 451

Chapter 23 – Banqueting (*Malcolm Ellis*) 470

Chapter 24 – Corporate events (*Paul Walters, Razaq Raj*) 489

Chapter 25 – Meetings (*Deborah Johnson*) 502

References 527

Index 553

About the editor

DIMITRI TASSIOPOULOS (Chapters 1 & 4): Dimitri is an Associate Director at the School of Tourism & Hospitality of Walter Sisulu University, South Africa. Since 1993, he has been involved in various national and international tourism research projects, of a multidisciplinary and multi-institutional nature, concerning agritourism, events, cultural and wine tourism, among others. Dimitri is a board member of a a number international peer-reviewed research journals. He has presented several papers at national and international conferences. Dimitri is the author and editor of the multiple-edition books - *Events Management – a developmental and a managerial approach (Juta)*. He is also the editor and author of *New Tourism Ventures – an entrepreneurial and managerial approach* (published by Juta). Dimitri has written a number of academic articles and chapters on various event- and tourism-related topics. In 2004 he was appointed as a member of the South African Qualifications Authority's Standards Generating Body (SGB) for Travel, Tourism & Events, and as the chairperson of the said SGB. He acts as the vice-president of the Tourism and Hospitality Education Providers of South Africa (THEPSA). This Federation represents further (FET) and higher education training (HET) institutions offering the spectrum of qualifications related to the management of the tourism industry. He is also acts as chairperson of the Tourism and Events Educators Chamber of South Africa (TEECSA), which is an association representing higher education travel, tourism and events-related programme providers.

About the contributors

ANGELA ANTHONISZ (Chapter 13): Angela is a senior lecturer in the Department of Hospitality, Tourism, Leisure and Events Management at the University of Huddersfield, UK. Angela's area of interest is in events marketing, and innovation and creativity within the events industry.

BRENDON KNOTT (Chapter 14): Brendon is a lecturer at the Cape Peninsula University of Technology in Cape Town, South Africa. He graduated from the University of Cape Town with a Bachelor of Business Science (BBusSc), gaining Honours in Marketing and specialising in sport event sponsorship. Brendon was the first candidate to complete the MTech degree in Sport Management at CPUT (*cum laude*, 2008) with his thesis study related to sponsorship of the *Cape Argus* Pick n Pay Cycle Tour event. He also has a Higher Diploma in Higher Education and Training (HDHET) (*cum laude*, 2006) and was awarded the Teacher of the Year Award by the Faculty of Business (2007). Brendon gained industry experience working for a local sport management company focusing on sport event and player management. He has presented research and conducted guest lectures at various conferences and universities internationally. His research consultation work has included projects such as the development of an events strategy for the City of Cape Town, Universal Access implications for sport tourism events in the Western Cape, and other related research for the 2010 FIFA World Cup Organising Committee. Brendon continues to be involved in lecturing and researching areas of sport event sponsorship and tourism.

CONOR MOSS (Chapter 15): Conor is a Workforce Development Fellow for the University of Derby where he works closely with events and tourism organisations to train their staff through innovative work based degree level programmes. Prior to this he managed the BA and MA Events Management degrees for the University of Derby. He recently developed several qualifications in collaboration with key industry bodies that are intended to provide continued professional development for those individuals in industry. The most recent and currently unique of these qualifications is a university diploma in Events Safety Management. Before commencing a career in academia he worked in festival management, sponsorship and public relations. Conor is a member of the Executive Council for the National Outdoor Events Association.

DEBBIE VAN OUDTSHOORN (Chapter 9): Debbie was born in Port Elizabeth and graduated from the Nelson Mandela Metropolitan University (formerly known as University of Port Elizabeth – UPE) with a BCom, majoring in Business Economics and Economics. She has five years' experience in the hotel industry. She was previously employed at Walter Sisulu University (formerly known as Border Technikon), where she lectured in Financial

Management to the Tourism Management and Hospitality Management students, and is currently employed in the private sector in Port Elizabeth.

DEBORAH JOHNSON (Chapter 25): Deborah holds a Master's degree in Post School Education; and recently completed her doctorate in Tourism and Hospitality Management with a specialisation in events management. She worked for SATOUR from 1987–1996 and was involved with marketing, tourism development and event organising. Deborah has been in the event industry for the last 20 years. She worked for Cape Peninsula University of Technology from 1996–2008, and was the Head of Department for Tourism and Event Management. She has been seconded by Cape Peninsula University of Technology to Prince Sultan College for Tourism and Business in Jeddah, Saudi Arabia to serve as vice dean of their Ladies Section. This is the first female college based in Saudi Arabia focusing on tourism, with specialist streams in event and hospitality management.

DOUGLAS MICHELE TURCO (Chapter 14): Douglas is an associate professor of Sport Management at Drexel University, US. He received a PhD from the University of New Mexico, and MS and BS degrees from the University of Wisconsin at LaCrosse. Prior to arriving at Drexel University, Douglas was a professor of sport and tourism at Illinois State University, where he was named the university's Outstanding Teacher in 2002, and at DeSales University, where he received two teaching awards. Turco is also on faculty at the R J Gandhi Indian Institute of Management, IMC FH-Krems (Austria), National Taiwan Sport University, and IESE Madrid. Douglas teaches courses on sport event marketing, sport tourism, international sport management and sport economics. He has authored over 40 articles in journals including *Sport Marketing Quarterly*, the *International Journal of Sport Management, Journal of Travel Research*, and the *Journal of Sport and Tourism*, and has written several books. He consults on sport and tourism planning, economic impacts and consumer market research for organisations worldwide. His current research involves the Commonwealth Games, the US Open Women's Golf Championship, Deaflympics, Pocono 500, the Cricket World Cup, and the Olympic Games. He is founder and director of the i-Team (International Sport Tourism Research co-Laboratory).

ERROL NINOW (Chapter 17): Errol is managing director of Alex Gintan Associates, a business founded in 1980 and specialising in corporate compliance issues such as occupational health and safety, disaster risk management and risk assessments (he qualified at the University of South Africa with a DIP.DIS.Risk.Mngmnt), environmental management, incident/accident investigation and disaster risk management coordination for special events, local and international conferences, concerts, exhibitions, etc. Errol completed his postgraduate (Hons) P.G.Dip.Mngmnt.Prac. – Events at the UCT Graduate School of Business. He is a registered Grade A security provider and instructor registered with the private Security Industry Regulatory Authority in South Africa. He has been in the eventing industry for 28 years, specialising in safety and security, and has served as a director of the Exhibition and Special Events Association (EXSA). Errol served as Chairman of the Special Events Committee with the Security Officers' Board (now PSIRA), setting minimum training standards and making recommendations on regulations and legislation.

Alex Gintan Associates has been a contributor to the South African National Standard for Health and Safety at Live Events (SANS 10366) since inception with the SABS (South African Bureau of Standards).

GRAHAM BERRIDGE (chapters 5 and 10): Graham is a senior lecturer and course leader for Events Management at Thames Valley University (TVU), London. He taught event management from the early 1990s on various tourism and leisure courses prior to developing the event degree at TVU in 2000. He has over 30 years' experience in events spread across the private, voluntary and corporate sectors. He is a founder member of the Association of Events Management Education where he served on the Executive Committee from 2005–2009. He has edited and had published chapters in various Leisure Studies Association volumes and contributed to the CABI Compendium on Volunteerism. He is one of the few academics to focus on the design and experience elements of events and in 2007 he published the ground-breaking book *Events Design and Experience*. He is currently researching for his PhD on the 'experiential characteristics of cyclo sportive events'. In 2004 he was awarded University Teaching Fellowship status for his excellence in teaching and learning; in 2007 he received a Research in Teaching Excellence sabbatical, which was partly served as visiting academic at University of Queensland, Brisbane; and in 2009 he became a Work-based Learning Fellow for developing enterprise links between events and education. Graham remains an active events manager as well as an academic, and is involved in coordinating several cycling events each year.

HOWARD PELL (Chapter 21): Howard came to South Africa in the early 1950s and joined Hortors Limited, a company specialising in printing, stationery and office equipment. In due course Hortors and a leading UK exhibition organiser, Andry Montgomery Limited, formed a joint operation called Specialised Exhibitions to develop the market in South Africa. As Howard had gained substantial sales experience with Hortors and had attended a three-month Business Management course at the University of the Witwatersrand, he was given the role of setting up the company. Over a period of some 30 years Specialised Exhibitions became the largest and most successful exhibition organiser in the country. The company researched and launched exhibitions in the following fields: building materials, mining and engineering equipment, packaging and printing, transport, education and training, electronic equipment, fishing equipment and services, etc. During this time Howard established agents in a number of countries overseas so as to encourage foreign participation in the exhibitions held in South Africa. Howard held the position of MD for 20 years and retired in 1990.

JO-ANSIE VAN WYK (Chapter 22): Jo-Ansie lectures International Politics at the University of South Africa, South Africa. She obtained an MA (Political Science) from Stellenbosch University and is currently a doctoral candidate at the Vrije Universiteit, Amsterdam, The Netherlands. She has published on political event management, international relations, foreign policy, space politics, environmental issues and international political economy. She is Fulbright Alumna and a member of the Suid-Afrikaanse Akademie vir Wetenskap en Kuns. She has served as the review editor of *Politikon* (Routledge/Taylor & Francis) and the editor of *Politeia* (Unisa Press). She regularly lectures at the South African National Intelligence

Academy, the South African National Defence College, the South African War College and the South African Diplomatic Academy. She has completed consultancies for the World Bank, UNESCO, the Institute for Security Studies, the South African Department of Foreign Affairs and Consultancy Africa Intelligence.

JOHN KNOCKER (Chapter 21): John has been involved in selling and managing a team of exhibition managers involved with trade exhibitions since 1985. His experience covers a wide range of exhibitions operating in a variety of industries. As a director of Specialised Exhibitions he has been involved with all aspects of the organisation of exhibitions from concept through to delivery of events, for new as well as for existing shows. His activities have not only covered small shows, but he has also been actively involved with the largest trade show in South Africa. His experience encompasses the full spectrum of activities including marketing, organising and administrative responsibilities. Prior to working in the exhibition industry he had extensive experience in sales and sales management in a leading company in the business systems industry

JULIA RUTHERFORD SILVERS (Chapter 3): Julia is an author, educator and consultant in events management. She has authored two highly acclaimed industry books as well as award-winning training programmes and research. In addition, she is the originator of the Event Management Body of Knowledge (EMBOK) project, an educational resource on her website that illustrates and examines the scope of knowledge and processes used in the events industry. A four-time International Special Events Society Esprit Award winner for Best Industry Contribution for her educational programmes, Julia has served as an industry consultant for the George Washington University Event Management Certificate Program, the Professional Convention Management Association, and the Canadian Tourism Human Resource Council. She is a frequent speaker at industry conferences throughout the world and has served as Adjunct Faculty for UNLV and UNLV Singapore and special lecturer at universities in Colombia, Jordan, Morocco, the Palestinian Authority and Puerto Rico.

JURGEN GASCHE (Chapter 12): Jurgen is a qualified chef and patissier who has worked through the ranks of kitchen brigades in Germany, the Bahamas, Kuwait, Iraq and South Africa. Before joining Walter Sisulu University (formerly known as Border Technikon) as a lecturer in Culinary Studies and Techniques, he worked as executive chef for Sun International. He obtained an MBA and a degree in Management and is also a registered trainer with the UK-based Hotel and Catering Training Company. In 2007 Jurgen returned to the industry as training, development and quality manager for the Corinthia Hotel Group in Libya and is currently employed as director of training for Sofitel Luxury Hotels in Egypt. Planning and executing large events was part of his duties as chef, while maintaining high-quality standards for a luxury brand are his responsibilities today.

KAMILLA SWART (chapters 18 and 20): Kamilla is an associate professor in the Faculty of Business and has headed the Centre for Tourism Research in Africa (CETRA), Cape Peninsula University of Technology (CPUT) since 2003. Her research interests include sport and event tourism, with a specific focus on the 2010 FIFA World Cup and event policies, strategies and evaluations. Her interest in sport tourism, specifically events, ignited as a result of her work at the Olympic Bid Company. She completed her doctoral degree in Education and Sport Tourism, and graduated from Illinois State University in 2001. She worked at Octagon SA (2000–2003) and managed the Durban Events Corporation, and was the lead consultant for the South African National Events Strategy. Recent consultancy projects include reviewing the draft events policy for the City of Cape Town and providing research services to the 2010 FIFA World Cup Organising Committee South Africa. Kamilla co-authored the first US text on sport tourism in 2002 and has published in the *Journal of Sport Tourism, Third World Quarterly* and *Politikon*, among others. Kamilla was chosen as one of the 10 Outstanding Persons in Sport Tourism in the 1990s and recently received the inaugural *BBQ (Black Business Quarterly)* Research and Development Youth Award 2009.

LIZ QUICK (Chapter 5): Liz is a senior lecturer and programme leader for Business Travel and Tourism at Thames Valley University, London. She graduated from the University of London, Goldsmiths College with a BA (Hons) degree in German and Drama. After working for Lufthansa German Airlines for several years, she worked for a number of large events and incentive companies. Liz now successfully brings all her experience to bear as a lecturer and has been studying for an MA in Learning and Teaching in Higher Education. She is a fellow of the Higher Education Academy. Liz has extensive business development and recruitment experience and also trains students at postgraduate level in Event Management Training. She has recently run a number of sessions to train event organisers within specific companies on how to manage their own internal events.

MALCOLM ELLIS (chapters 12 and 23): Malcolm started his career in the hospitality industry in Huddersfield, Yorkshire. He is currently the Head of Department: Hospitality, at the School of Tourism and Hospitality at Walter Sisulu University, where he offers Hospitality Management and Hospitality Accommodation Management as major subjects. After completing his initial studies in Bulawayo in Zimbabwe (then Rhodesia), and at Portsmouth, UK, he returned to (then) Rhodesia where he worked in a number of hotels, both large and small, catering to the tourism and the commercial market. For a number of years, he was general manager of a Casino Hotel catering predominantly to the mass conventions market. Subsequent to working in the Republic of the Maldives, he moved to South Africa and worked in a number of hotel groups prior to joining WSU. He currently holds an MBA and is working on his PhD where his current focus is on the management of the effects of the HIV pandemic upon the tourism industry in South Africa.

MATT BROMLEY (Chapter 15): Matt is the programme leader for Events Management courses at the University of Derby Buxton. He has MA and BSc degrees and is currently undertaking a PhD specialising in event experience. Prior to working at the institution, Matt worked in events and marketing for ten years, managing or promoting over 400 shows. In addition to teaching, he now consults on many areas of the events industry including safety management, strategy and event marketing. His research interests include event experience, employability, safety management and future studies.

NIMISH SHUKLA (Chapter 13): Nimish holds a Master's degree in Commerce and is registered for a doctorate degree in Tourism Marketing at the Cape Peninsula University of Technology, South Africa. He previously worked as the head of the Tourism Management Department at Walter Sisulu University (South Africa), and as industry liaison coordinator at the University of Western Ontario in Canada. He has undertaken various research projects and presented research papers internationally on marketing and consumer behaviour. Nimish currently owns a consulting business to assist small businesses in London Ontario (Canada) with developing marketing plans; and conducts strategic marketing analyses of such businesses. As part of giving back to the community, he is actively involved in organising cultural events within the Indian communities in Canada.

PAUL WALTERS (chapters 19 and 24): Paul is the programme leader and senior lecturer for Events Management at Manchester Metropolitan University and was instrumental in developing the course over the past five years. In doing so he has forged a programme of study that connects with Manchester's international destination status. His teaching profile and industry experience coupled together span over 20 years. While teaching Paul has attended international conferences and presented articles, and contributed to two academic text books published by Butterworth-Heinemann and Sage Publications. Apart from teaching undergraduates Paul also teaches Master's students in Germany and France on the international context of events management. Paul regularly consults and works with industry partners in a professional capacity as event manager, further enhancing his knowledge and experience within the areas of festivals and sports events. With that wealth of knowledge and experience, Paul is currently undertaking his PhD conducting research within politics and international sports events.

PETA THOMAS (Chapter 16): Peta has worked in the South African events industry for the past eight years. She was trained as a COBOL programmer and business systems analyst for information technology and holds a BSc (Hons) degree, a Master's degree in Business Administration, and a postgraduate diploma (Events). She is a South African assessor and moderator for the events industry, conducts recognition of prior learning assessments, and is a member of Meeting Professionals International, Europe-Middle East and Africa region.

RAZAQ RAJ (chapters 19 and 24): Razaq is a senior lecturer in the Events Centre at Leeds Metropolitan University, teaching Financial and Strategic Management, and course leader of the MSc in Events Management. He has published works on special events, financial management in events, information technology, events sponsorship, cultural festivals and events, sustainable tourism and religious tourism. He is editor–in-chief for the *World Journal of Tourism, Leisure and Sport*. Razaq is the author of the text books *Religious Tourism and Pilgrimage Management: An International Perspective* and *Advanced Event Management: An Integrated and Practical Approach*. He is currently editing a book on sustainability and events management. He also sits on a number of voluntary sector management boards. Razaq is a board member of international academic associations, the Centre for International Research in Consumers Location and their Environments (CIRCLE) and the Association for Tourism and Leisure Education (ATLAS). His particular research interests include cultural and community events, outdoor events, impacts and risks, financial management and religious tourism for events.

RITA CARMOUCHE (Chapter 13): Rita is the head of Hospitality Tourism Leisure and Events Management at the University of Huddersfield, UK. She has a background in the social sciences and her specialist area of interest is in consumer behaviour and marketing in the events industry.

TOM WANKLIN (chapters 6, 7 and 8): Tom holds a BSc (Hons) in Town and Regional Planning from the University of the Witwatersrand and has extensive experience as a development planner. After lecturing in Tourism Development and Event Management in the School of Tourism and Hospitality at Border Technikon (now Walter Sisulu University) he returned to full-time private practice, with tourism consulting and project implementation as an additional offering. Much of his work involves physical planning, community development and facilitation. Tourism project implementation has involved establishing heritage tourism routes, leisure and water-based enterprises, and an ecotourism resort.

URMILLA BOB (Chapter 11): Urmilla is an associate professor in Geography (School of Environmental Sciences) at the University of KwaZulu-Natal, Westville Campus, South Africa. She completed her Master's and her PhD in Geography at West Virginia University in the US. She also has a Certificate in Project Management from the Graduate School of Business, University of Durban-Westville. Urmilla conducts research on urban and rural development, sustainable land use and natural resource management as well as socio-economic impact assessments of events and tourism (currently focusing on ecotourism in Kenya and South Africa as well as the 2010 FIFA World Cup). She has published in these fields in both nationally and internationally recognised academic books and journals. She has been involved in collaborative research with national and international academic organisations and NGOS, and has attended several conferences and workshops worldwide. She is also involved in several training programmes and skills development initiatives. Urmilla has supervised several postgraduate students.

WILLIAM O'TOOLE (Chapter 2): William is an advisor to the government of the Kingdom of Saudi Arabia on the development of their events industry. He has worked as an events development specialist for the European Commission, Aqaba Development Authority in Jordan and the Dubai Tourism Commerce and Marketing, developing their events strategy and events management competence. He is a founding director of the Event Management Body of Knowledge (EMBOK). He is the author of three international works on events management that are translated into four languages and are the basis of events management courses. His CD-ROM – EPMS.net – is used by events around the world as the framework for their management system. He has worked with event teams and trained managers from countries as diverse as Azerbaijan and New Zealand. As well as developing the theory of events strategy and event project management, Bill has assisted, created and managed events and festivals in over 20 countries.

Foreword

Events and their producers have been part of humanity's need to mark special occasions since man first dragged a woolly mammoth back to his cave for a catering convention.

No doubt Roman emperors had their Cecil B de Mille equivalents to whom they would turn whenever they tired of the same old lions, Christians and gladiators in the Coliseum but unfortunately the names of those early showmen have not survived. Possibly neither did they – we all know what it is like to have a difficult client.

And those Roman spectacles were simply a highlight in the long history of man's need for bread and circuses, preferably paid for by others. But it is only in the last 20 or 30 years that we have created university courses for practitioners of events that are described as special.

Which makes me a dinosaur in this business, having started producing events before there was even a business and well before any event was being called 'special'. My early years were spent producing shows for television, which I still believe is the best all-round training for an event producer because it requires communication skills that are essential for the planning and execution of any production. Subsequently I moved into the production of major events like Olympic ceremonies, world expos and national bicentennials, and slowly discovered that there were more and more people like me around the world who were producing events on every scale.

Over the past 25 years, while I was producing the opening and closing ceremonies for five different Olympic Games, Dimitri Tassiopoulos was developing his expertise and contacts in the field of events management, and this book is the result, now in its third edition.

Setting up a company and maintaining a successful business in special events is never going to be easy, but as with most human endeavours, it is worth getting the best advice you can before starting out. Clearly, this book has become more and more relevant as the industry itself has become increasingly organised, the events themselves have become more challenging and the budgets have remained, as always, less than you would like. The best producers combine creativity with practicality, so this book provides practical advice for everything that is still left to do when the script outline is ready. The biggest challenge you will face is finding the time to read it between shows!

So thanks to Dimitri and his contributors – it is much easier than ever to find what is required when you decide to enter the events business from the ground up.

Ric Birch
CEO Spectak Productions

Third Draft, May 8, 1998
The Future of Event Management Charter
Researched and Submitted by Leaders in the Special Events Industry
Columbia University's Biosphere 2
May 3, 1998

Introduction
The events industry is one of the world's largest employers, and contributes a major positive economic impact. The events industry is not only our profession but also a personal mission through which we are able to make a positive contribution to the lives of millions of people. Through events, human beings mark important milestones. As events professionals we are responsible for positively impacting people and the environment in which we live. We are humbled by this responsibility and share a reverence for this mission. We give thanks for the heritage that we have received from past generations, and embrace our responsibilities to present and future generations of events professionals.

The events industry stands at a defining moment. A fundamental understanding and commitment to economic, technological and environmental challenges is needed to ensure a sustainable future for this industry and the professions it represents. Foresight and positive use of knowledge and power are the foundations for a successful future of the events industry. We must advance it, finding new ways to balance self and community, diversity and unity, short term and strategic by using and nurturing, preserving and expanding.

In the midst of all of our diversity as a special events industry, we are one humanity and one family with a shared destiny. The economic, technological and environmental challenges before us require an inclusive ethical vision. Alliances must be forged and cooperation fostered at every level, in every profession, and in every community on Earth. In solidarity with one another and the community of life, we the stewards of this profession commit ourselves to action guided by the following interrelated principles.

Mission
To anticipate environmental, technological and economic change in order to ensure a successful and enduring industry we must:
1 **Serve** *as responsible custodians of the natural environment and educate others to understand this value and financial benefit.*
2 **Improve** *our technological capabilities to simultaneously reduce cost and improve quality.*
3 **Establish** *strong mutually beneficial strategic alliances for educational, social and economic benefits worldwide.*

Responsibility and accountability
We believe that in order to achieve long-term sustainability for this profession it is essential that we continually monitor, evaluate, analyse and correct these goals as needed to ensure proper accountability.
1 **Serve as responsible custodians of the natural environment and educate others to follow our example.**

a. Begin to commit ourselves to do well by doing good.
b. Use pre-cycling and other pre-planning strategies to reduce negative impacts on the environment.
c. Develop written environmental policies for our businesses, professional organisations, and industry.
d. Reduce and re-use event materials to promote positive impacts on the environment.
e. Continually monitor environmental changes in order to develop new strategies to lessen negative impacts.
f. Promote positive environmental practices within our businesses and industry to encourage others and newcomers to share this responsibility.
g. Utilise green achievements as a selling tool and a positive public relations opportunity for current and future clients.

2 *Improve our technological capabilities to simultaneously reduce cost and improve quality.*
a. Utilise technology as applicable for every facet of the events industry.
b. Invest in the research and development of software that will improve efficiency, quality, and financial yield.
c. Encourage the development and use of technology (i.e. the World Wide Web) for the production and marketing of events.
d. Reduce technological cost through cooperative agreements.
e. Improve communication and collaboration through encouraging the use of electronic systems by internal and external publics.
f. Provide training for ourselves and those we supervise to ensure educational parity with these emerging technologies.

3 *Establish strong beneficial global strategic alliances and cooperate with one another for mutual economic benefit.*
a. Encourage organisations to increasingly utilise events to convey their mission, or provide competitive compensation schemes to attract the highest-qualified employees.
b. Encourage inclusiveness among all peoples for maximum participation in and benefit from the events industry.
c. Identify systems that determine the actual economic return on each event/investment.
d. Balance the need for qualified employees and economic expansion with realistic forecasting to ensure financial growth.
e. Share, invest and utilise initially quality re-usable goods, emerging technologies and environmental awareness to reduce cost and increase financial yield.
f. Create cooperative buying opportunities with industry partners, e.g. seek out and encourage suppliers who use green practices.
g. Encourage organisations to utilise events to increasingly communicate their mission or cause.

Covenant

Embracing the values in this Charter, we can grow into a sustainable profession that allows the potential of all persons to fully develop in harmony with the events industry. We must preserve a strong faith in the possibilities of the human spirit and a deep sense of belonging to the universal family of events professionals. Our best actions will embody the integration of knowledge with compassion for our fellow human beings.

In order to develop and implement the principles in this Charter, the members of the special events industry should adopt as a first step an integrated ethical framework for lasting and future sustainable policies. This framework should serve as an irrevocable covenant that will remove all previous and future barriers in order to achieve the principles set forth in this Charter.

Adopted by acclamation on 3 May 1998 by the events industry leaders
United States of America

Preface

Events management is an exciting new medium, along with the events sector of most tourism destination industries, which has become a force to be reckoned with around the world. Events are now widely accepted by most tourism stakeholders as a development and marketing strategy from which destinations can gain economic benefits. It goes without saying that events tourism is now increasingly recognised by governments and destinations, and has seen considerable growth in recent years.

When this book was first conceptualised in 1998, there was scant indication as to how large the events management field would become, and few envisioned the profound potential of such an evolution, both in education and in the events industry. The first and second editions became established as the authoritative texts on events management for a developing country context. The third edition remains the first multidisciplinary book of its kind and is guided by internationally recognised key knowledge domains for staging any genre of event professionally. It comes to you as a collaborative approach between experienced events practitioners and academics from a number of academic institutions around the world.

This book is intended as an academic and 'how to' professional text. Although there are numerous books dealing with a variety of applied event disciplines, there is a relative dearth of books that provide the theoretical and methodological management knowledge base which is a prerequisite for establishing and managing events. Further, the need to develop adaptable problem-solving skills, foster professionalism and stimulate event research is seen as an overall outcome of this book.

Events Management: A developmental and managerial approach is about the actual developmental process of understanding what events are, and ultimately planning and managing events for the sustainable benefit of tourism destinations.

The book consists of seven parts

Part I offers a background for the study of events. Chapter 1 provides an overview of events management and sets the scene, so to speak. Chapter 2 is concerned with the strategic developmental impact of events. Chapter 3 deals with the role of management in the area of events management.

Part II deals with events and administration. Chapter 4 discusses the activities of the various stakeholders of events. Chapter 5 deals with the process of securing and hosting an event. This is seen in the light of discussing the process whereby some sought-after international events are subject to international bidding, as required by some event owners. The planning and coordination of events is discussed in chapter 6. Chapter 7 investigates establishing best-practice in event organising. Chapter 8 deals with the principles of project management for events. Chapter 9 is concerned with one of the least-liked but most crucial activities of event management – accounting and financial management.

Part III deals with events and design. Chapter 10 provides a focused discussion on the role design in events. Chapter 11 offers an in-depth discussion concerning the impacts of events on destinations and how this can contribute toward sustainability. One of the main activities at most events is the exposure of event participants to the activities of food and beverage professionals, as discussed in chapter 12. The proper planning of such an activity is critical for a successful experience by event attendees.

Part IV deals with events and marketing. Chapter 13 is concerned with ensuring that the event is properly marketed and communicated to all the stakeholders. Events sponsorship and fundraising, two of the most critical lifelines of organising events, especially in the light of ever-tightening public sector purse strings, are discussed in chapter 14.

Part V deals with events and operations. Event operations management, the subject of chapter 15, is a critical skill all event organisers need to master in order to manage the operational aspects of events. Chapter 16 discusses the importance of technology for events.

Part VI deals with events and risk. Chapter 17 outlines the reasons why event organisers need to be aware of the dimensions of a proper risk management plan.

Part VII is concerned with applying and focusing the theory on some of the better-known segments of the events sector. The overall purpose of this part is to assist the reader with developing the necessary skills and knowledge to be able to organise any such form of event. Chapter 18 aims to assist readers with understanding the bidding and planning process that should be followed when organising a mega-event. Festivals are discussed in chapter 19 to provide an understanding of how to put together such an event successfully. In chapter 20, the process of organising sports events is discussed. Exhibition management, one of the most easily experienced forms of a business event, is dealt with in chapter 21. Chapter 22 exposes the reader to the techniques and skills required to successfully organise various forms of political, civic and government events. Chapter 23 deals with banqueting and chapter 24 with corporate events. And, finally, meetings are discussed in chapter 25.

Dimitri Tassiopoulos
Editor
Walter Sisulu University
South Africa

Acknowledgements

As is the case with all literary ventures, we could not have produced all this work without the assistance, guidance and support of many individuals. Initial ideas and suggestions were generated from round-table discussions involving leading events management practitioners and academics.

We are delighted that Mr Ric Birch was willing to write the foreword to this book. Ric is the CEO of Spectak Productions and has been involved with a spectacular array of mega- and hallmark events around the world, including designing and producing various opening and closing ceremonies of the Commonwealth Games and the Olympic Games, and a number of the Sydney New Year's Eve Celebrations. He is a highly respected professional who intimately understands the complexities and challenges of successfully staging world-class events, qualities which make him an ideal candidate to comment on this work.

We also wish to thank the following:

❒ Edward Grant, University of Derby, Buxton, United Kingdom;
❒ Irene Costa, editor: *Southern Africa Conference, Exhibition and Events Guide*, Contact Publications (Pty) Ltd, Johannesburg, South Africa;
❒ Kiko McBrown, Tshani Consulting, Buffalo City, South Africa;
❒ Louise Roberts, Walter Sisulu University, Buffalo City, South Africa;
❒ Matthew James, Sound and Motion Studio, Cape Town, South Africa;
❒ Sugen Pillay, South African Tourism, Johannesburg, South Africa; and
❒ Tracy Daniels, Nuraan Hendricks and Mushfieqah Salie, Centre for Tourism Research in Africa (CETRA), Cape Peninsula University of Technology, Cape Town, South Africa.

Special gratitude is extended to Ndipiwe Taleni and Headman Sayedwa, for their assistance with the events calendar data processing aspects of this book.

Our appreciation is extended to the production staff of Juta & Company for their excellent handling of our manuscript. Thanks are due to the invaluable contribution of Sandy Shepherd and Sharon Steyn, who project managed this publication.

Finally, there are, of course, other people in our lives about whom we care deeply and who have made enormous sacrifices while we wrote this book.

NOTICE: *Although the internet sites provided for further information are presented in good faith and believed to be correct, the authors, editor and publisher make no representations or warranties as to the completeness or accuracy of the information and make no commitment to update or correct any information that appears on the internet.*

PART I

Events management: an introduction

Photo: Dimitri Tassiopoulos

Photo: Dimitri Tassiopoulos

1

The world of events

Dimitri Tassiopoulos

Abstract

This chapter aims to develop an understanding of the basic concepts and definitions of the events sector and to offer ways of thinking about events tourism, thus providing a framework of knowledge for readers approaching this sector.

Chapter objectives

After you have read this chapter you should be able to:
- ❐ understand of the definitions, history, types and different forms of event;
- ❐ understand of the trends and dynamics of events;
- ❐ explain why destinations concern themselves with hosting events;
- ❐ understand as to why the study of events needs to go beyond a developed-country concept; and
- ❐ comprehend why the hosting of events in a developing country context needs to be understood.

1.1 The world of events

Although increased publicity has been given to the events sector as we have come to know it over the past few years, the phenomenon of events can hardly be described as a new one. Throughout history, events have been an important feature of people's lives. The most well-known and documented event is the Olympic Games which were held in Ancient Greece as from 776BC (Jago & Shaw, 1998; Trigg, 1995). There have, however, been countless other large and small events around the world that have been held throughout the ages. One can only speculate about what procedures, problems and techniques events organisers of the time might have faced and used.

The youthfulness of the events sector, however, does suggest that it does not have some of the characteristics of more established sectors or industries, such as well-developed professional standards which reflect well-defined terminology, adequate market intelligence, appropriate education and training structures, and clear entry routes (Rogers, 1998). This chapter forms a basis for the subsequent chapters in this book and consequently seeks to develop a framework to ensure that the planning and management of events is focused, coordinated and aligned with other areas of tourism development and urban management.

1.2 Introduction

The events sector is relatively young and dynamic but growing and maturing at a rapid pace. From its professional origins in North America and Europe, it is now a truly global sector of the international tourism industry with many

Case study 1.1 The events sector in South Africa

South African events organisations, most of which are meetings organisations (namely conference organisations) started to operate formally (albeit on a small scale) in the 1960s and early 1970s. Furthermore, the South African exhibitions industry, a key sub-sector of the events industry, began to operate formally in the mid-19th century.

The South African events sector, according to South African Tourism (2007), has shown a marked growth since 1994 as the tourism industry has reoriented itself towards the marketing of the country as a business, sports, cultural and lifestyle events destination and in such a way capitalising on the benefits of inbound tourism to the country.

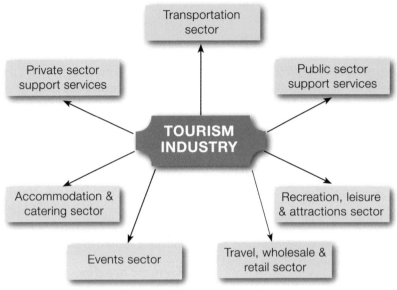

Figure 1.1 Graph of the tourism industry

Sources: Adapted from Jordaan (1994); Cooper et al.(1999)

decision makers of developing countries increasingly recognising the benefits of events management and events tourism for their respective economies. The standard industrial classification (SIC) does not distinguish the tourism industry, including events sector, as a distinct economic division. Nonetheless, the tourism industry, including the events sector, is depicted in figure 1.1.

1.3 Events described (refer to figure 1.2)

1.3.1 Events tourism

Events are increasingly becoming established as an integral and major part of tourism development and marketing strategies. *Events tourism* is a term that could be used to describe this phenomenon, and could be defined as the 'systematic development, planning, marketing and holding of events as tourist attractions'.

The goals of events tourism could be:
❑ to create a favourable image for a destination;
❑ to expand the traditional tourist season;
❑ to spread tourist demand more evenly through an area; and
❑ to attract foreign and domestic visitors.

Events have become one of the most common channels through which visitors can satisfy their desire to sample local foods and culture, participate in games or be entertained. Smaller local events have the advantage that they can make events tourists believe that they are participating in authentically indigenous activities. Local and regional events can have the added advantage of keeping domestic tourism markets active (Getz, 1991).

Event tourists, visitors or *attendees* are those who patronise events. *Events tourists* may be described as those who travel away from home to do so, and who stay overnight at the event destination. However, events tourists may also visit other destinations as visitors (or as same-day visitors) before returning home. *Events visitors* (or same-day event visitors) do not stay overnight after patronising an event. However, they may also visit other destinations as tourists or return home. Such visitors are the most likely to make a more limited contribution to the events tourism economic multiplier.

1.3.2 The tangible product

Events can be described by referring to their tangible components. Getz (1991) proposes that the tangible products of an event are actually presented to the public as a 'façade'– these are the mechanisms by which a visitor experience is partially created. There is a synergistic process involving these products and many intangibles to create the atmosphere that makes events. Further, events are usually produced as a means of achieving some greater goal. Even in cases where they have not been planned with tourism objectives in mind, tourism tends to become a strategic factor once the destination managers begin to market, promote or package the events as part of the attraction mix of a destination.

1.3.3 Visitor experience

Events present the visitor with a unique perspective of ordinary everyday life with an opportunity to participate in a collective experience where novelty is assured because events occur infrequently or at different times.

Targeted benefits

Targeted benefits are those which position events differently and provide a competitive advantage. Events visitors are attracted to particular events that offer something extra in addition to the basic services provided and the general benefits derived from all events. The events theme is therefore critical in sending the message to potential visitors about the benefits that they could gain from attending. The name of an event alone, however, is not enough, and neither are the activities. The presentation of the theme should be such that the unique benefits offered by the event are clear. Each element of the tangible product can provide a competitive advantage – for example ethnic food and activities.

Generic benefits

Generic benefits are those which distinguish events from permanent attractions. Such benefits are likely to be expected by a visitor regardless of the tangible events programme. The relative importance of each of these benefits varies from event to event. Generic benefits, according to Getz (1991), fall into the following categories:

❏ *The spectacle.* The spectacle element of events, especially media-oriented ones, has universal appeal. Raw spectacle can, however, overpower the fundamentals of festivity, ritual and games that the events could embody. Spectacles play an important role in any event by focusing on visual, larger-than-life displays and performances. Events oriented towards television, however, run the risk of having the events programme being subjected to the demands of television programme scheduling.

❏ *Ritual.* This is at the heart of most traditional events, such as festivals, either in secular or religious form. Symbols and themes that may invoke community or national pride and loyalty, often found in parades, are closely linked to ritualistic activities.

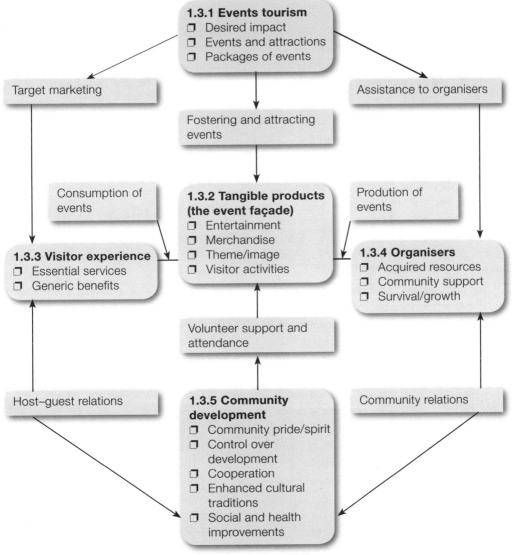

Figure 1.2 Special events perspectives

Source: Getz (1991)

The figure contains the following elements:

1.3.1 Events tourism
- Desired impact
- Events and attractions
- Packages of events

Target marketing

Assistance to organisers

Fostering and attracting events

Consumption of events

Prodution of events

1.3.2 Tangible products (the event façade)
- Entertainment
- Merchandise
- Theme/image
- Visitor activities

1.3.3 Visitor experience
- Essential services
- Generic benefits

1.3.4 Organisers
- Acquired resources
- Community support
- Survival/growth

Volunteer support and attendance

Host–guest relations

Community relations

1.3.5 Community development
- Community pride/spirit
- Control over development
- Cooperation
- Enhanced cultural traditions
- Social and health improvements

- **Games.** Events visitors and volunteers expect to have fun at events. Such expectations can be fostered through a general atmosphere of festivity and through the opportunity to participate in, or witness, various events activities.
- **Sense of belonging.** The sharing of experiences with others in a public celebration or display can be seen as a major leisure motivator. This emotional benefit is usually the main reason why many people participate in events, either as volunteers or visitors.
- **Authenticity.** This subject is much debated in the literature with no clear conclusion as to its significance, and is an issue for continued research and clarification. From an events tourism

perspective, the real issue is ensuring visitor satisfaction and community support. Tourism developers should be sensitive to the goal of protecting events that are primarily cultural and local in nature.

1.3.4 Organiser's perspectives

Once events organisation becomes established, producing the events might, over time, become secondary to the survival of the group, or totally different goals may replace the original ones. Getz (1991) outlines three key processes requiring analysis:

❐ *The environment and the organisation.* The environment for events comprises both the physical and the community setting. Most events have a community impact because they are dependent on community volunteer participation and attendance. The physical impact tends to be less for most events, unless major construction occurs. Events organisers should view the community and physical environments as resources, and thus be mindful of negative impacts that might arise.

❐ *Transforming process.* Most organisational energies should be directed at converting resources, including volunteers, into the events and events outcomes. The outcomes of events should not be the events themselves but what they can do towards achieving broader goals. This leads to the consideration of a whole range of possible outcomes that define events products in terms of their effects on the host community.

❐ *Internal management processes.* Events differ from most attractions in that they rely on volunteers. This makes management more 'challenging', notably because of the lack of professional expertise, difficulty in recruiting and retaining volunteers for long periods, and diffuse goal setting and decision making. Further, the volunteers may not view the events product of equal importance as the prestige, community involvement or socialisation considerations of the events.

1.3.5 Community development

This concerns the enhancement of the host population's way of life, economy and environment. Events can be expected to reflect the needs of the host community, but this cannot be taken for granted. Difficulties can occur when the event is imposed on the host population and is controlled by a narrow interest group.

Events can create linkages between people and groups within communities, and between the community and the world. Research on the socio-cultural impact of events reveals both positive and negative forces. The costs and benefits of events must therefore be carefully considered, with emphasis on the host community's perspective.

Community development can benefit from events if the following objectives are satisfied:

❐ The community must have *control* over the events;

❐ Events *planning* must be *comprehensive*, taking into account the economic, social, cultural and environmental impacts;

❐ *Local leadership* and inter-organisational networks must be fostered; and

❐ The events must be directed at meeting *community needs* (Getz, 1991).

1.4 Towards defining events

The world of events covers a spectrum of planned cultural, sporting, political, life-cycle and business occasions. (Refer to figure 1.3 for a diagrammatic representation of the events sector and its various segments.) Events, according to Getz (1991), are a unique form of tourist attraction, ranging in scale from mega-events such as the Olympics and the Munich Oktoberfest, to community festivals, to programmes of recreational events at parks. Events are, however, increasingly being viewed as an integral part of tourism development and marketing planning, even though the majority of events have most probably arisen for non-tourist-related reasons, such as conducting business, competitions, cultural celebrations or the need to raise funds for charity or government coffers.

Despite the outcomes of events being well recognised, there appears to be a lack of a clear, all-embracing definition for events. Much literature seems to focus on the various characteristics of events and some of the reasons why they are organised are given. The literature does not, however, detail what types of events there are that would enable one to determine the range of events that would be classified as special versus those that are not. Jago and Shaw (1998: 23) testify that 'it is a measure of the adolescence of research on these tourist events that terminology utilised by researchers ... has not yet been standardised'

Figure 1.3 Diagrammatic representation of the events sector and its segments

Source: Adapted from Getz (1997: 7)

and that events 'lack unified terminology'. A typology of clear definitions of the various forms of events is clearly needed if there is to be any chance of research being able to make a contribution towards establishing this sector of the tourism industry as a strategic and developmental tool. An additional complication is that events are not static and that both their *meaning* and *significance* are likely to change in response to changes in society.

A further dilemma that needs to be resolved is whether events should be regarded as part of the leisure field in general or restricted to the tourism industry. A review of published research indicates that most research and publication on events in recent years comes from researchers associated with the tourism industry. Despite this, an event should be regarded primarily as providing a leisure activity that

has the potential to attract tourists (Jago & Shaw, 1998: 24).

Another issue is whether events should be classified as attractions or activities, or a combination of both. As an attraction, events lure tourists to the host destination, whereas it is more often the activities (or offerings) of the events that act as a draw card for the local host destination. Jago and Shaw (1998) propose that events be regarded as hybrid, combining both an attraction and a range of activities.

The following nomological structure is suggested, although there is no consensus about the relationships between various forms of events:

❑ 'Events' consist of two types: *planned* and *unplanned*;

❑ 'Planned events' consist of two categories: *routine, ordinary or common* and *special events*;

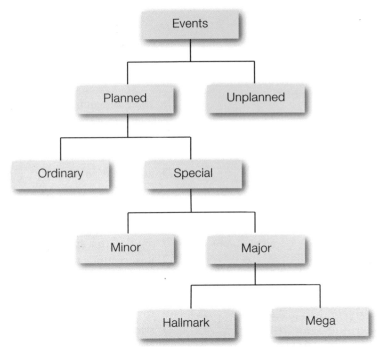

Figure 1.4 Events nomological structure

Source: Adapted from Jago & Shaw (1998)

- ❏ 'Special events' is a generic term used in a touristic sense and includes the following categories: *minor special events* and *major special events*;
- ❏ 'Major special events' contain two categories: *hallmark events* and *mega-events*.

1.4.1 A definitional framework

An extensive literat ure review by Jago and Shaw (1998: 29) confirms that it is unlikely that a single, all-embracing definition of events can be developed as such a phenomenon includes a vast array of types and perspectives of an events that may differ when viewed from a national, international or local level.

Events, according to Getz (1997: 4–11), are temporary occurrences, either planned or unplanned, with a finite length of time.

Planned events have a length of time that is usually fixed and publicised. *Events can thus be described as transient, and every event is a unique blending of its duration, setting, management and people.*

Major events, according to Jago and Shaw (1998), are large-scale (usually national or international) events which are high in status or prestige, and which attract large crowds and media attention. They may be expensive to stage, may involve tradition or symbolism, attract funds to the region and lead to demand for associated services, and leave behind legacies (positive or negative) to the host destinations.

Hallmark events, such as the various national government elections of countries, the Munich Oktoberfest in Germany, the 1976 United States Bicentennial Celebrations, the Tour de France (throughout France and its bordering

on their success or uniqueness, status or timely significance to create interest and attract attention.
Hall (1992a).

In their research, Jago and Shaw (1998) were able to isolate the following attributes as the most representative of hallmark events. They:

- ❏ are large in scale in a relative sense only;
- ❏ can be held on an international or national scale;
- ❏ are tied to a specific place;
- ❏ attract funds to the region;
- ❏ attract large crowds;
- ❏ are of infrequent occurrence;
- ❏ incorporate festivals or other events;
- ❏ stimulate demand for related services;
- ❏ incur large costs;
- ❏ involve prestige and status;
- ❏ involve tradition or symbolism;
- ❏ leave behind legacies or result in urban renewal; and
- ❏ result in the events and destination becoming synonymous.

Mega-events can be described as sport, cultural or business events that can attract very large numbers of event attendees or have a large cost or psychological effect on host destinations. *Mega-events, by way of their size or significance, are those that yield extraordinarily high levels of tourism, media coverage, prestige or economic impact for the host destination.* Mega-events, according to Getz (1997), should have an attendee volume that exceeds one million visits, an event development expenditure that runs in the millions, if not billions, of US dollars (or the equivalent value), generate enormous exposure through media coverage, and should have a worldwide must-see reputation and prestige factor.

countries), the National Arts Festival in Grahamstown (South Africa), the Edinburgh International Festival (UK), the Rio Carnivale (Brazil), the New Orleans Mardi Gras (US) and the various New Year's eve celebrations around the world (e.g. in New York, London, Sydney, etc.) can be referred to as those events that are considered to be iconic and embody the spirit and ethos of a destination; are synonymous with the name of a destination; or mark an important historical anniversary; and can be defined as:

Major one-time or recurring events of limited duration developed primarily to enhance the awareness, appeal and profitability of a tourist destination in the short and/or long term. Such events rely

Mega-events do not necessarily have to be financially successful, but are increasingly expected to strive for environmental, social and economic sustainability. Mega-events ultimately involve political decision making and strategic priorities of governments. Suggested examples of mega-events are world fairs and expos; telethons, e.g. Live Aid; the Olympic Games™; the FIFA World Cup™; and the International Association of Athletics Federation's (IAAF) World Championships in Athletics.

Research undertaken by Jago and Shaw (1998) has indicated the qualifying attributes of mega-events as:

- leaving behind legacies or resulting in urban renewal;
- involving tradition or symbolism;
- involving prestige and status, usually a political approval process;
- incurring large costs;
- stimulating demand for related services;
- incorporating festivals or other events;
- attracting large crowds (usually over a million visitors);
- attracting funds to the region;
- being of international scale;
- being large scale;
- being one-off occurrences; and
- having the reputation of a 'must-see' event.

Spilling (1998) views the concept of mega-events as comparable to that of hallmark events, mega-events being seen as a major one-off or recurring event of limited duration which serves to stimulate awareness of a destination and to enhance its appeal and profitability in the short and/or long term, while hallmark events are related to tradition and iconic attractiveness or image of a destination.

There are, though, no clear and absolute boundaries between the different categories of events as proposed in figures 1.3 and 1.4. It is suggested that the definition of an events depends on one's perspective. For instance, an event held on an annual basis may be regarded initially as a special event because it is so different; however, in subsequent years it may be viewed as a routine occurrence (Jago & Shaw, 1998). Any event can be categorised as 'special' in terms of the previously mentioned criteria; however, *mega* and *hallmark* are concepts that can only be applied to public events.

Festival and cultural events

The most common form of celebrating this type of event is through a festival. Festivals are mostly traditional with long histories. The majority of festivals, though, have been created in recent decades. Heritage events, according to Getz (1994b), are a class of events which have historical themes or which celebrate some dimension of a community's or cultural group's heritage.

Parades and processions are often found in festivals. Festivals can thus be defined as celebrations with a public theme where the social and symbolic meaning of the event is closely related to a series of overt values that the community recognises as essential to its ideology and world-view, its social identity, its historical continuity and its physical survival. This is, in effect, what the festivals ultimately celebrate (Falassi, quoted in Hall, 1992a: 4). Heritage events can be viewed as tools for interpreting community life by bringing people into direct contact with historical facts, objects or ways of life, thereby increasing knowledge and appreciation of traditions. Interpretation, according to Getz (1994a), is an educational activity which aims to reveal meanings and relationships through the use of original objects, by first-hand experience and by illustrative media. Heritage interpretation can make the heritage of a destination come to life for both visitor and resident. This, however, requires a real and authenticated first-hand sensory interaction with the resources of that destination. The term *staged authenticity* is used to describe events which are created with the intention of fooling observers.

Many of the other major events – especially art and entertainment – are frequently found within, or as the theme of, the festival. Sport and recreation are also important festival elements.

Corporate and business (or trade) events

There are numerous types of corporate events, particularly various corporate meetings (e.g. shareholders' meetings, annual general meetings, etc.), training seminars, product introductions and incentive events. The latter, for example, are designed to reward sales and other performance by employees during a specified period in order to meet corporate targets. Furthermore, business or trade events typically include fairs, trade or consumer shows, and exhibitions. Some fairs are called *exhibitions*, according to Getz (1997), reflecting their educational and commercial orientation. The term *exposition* (or *expo*) is also applied to trade and consumer shows:

- ❏ **Trade shows.** These are targeted towards industries or specific professions, some incorporating educational components, to which the general public may have access.
- ❏ **Consumer shows.** These are held for the general public and can cover virtually any topic.

Meetings and educational events

The 20th century saw improved transport-ation and communications technology and with this, according to Mathews (2008), came a rapid growth of various types of meetings that had as their main reason the exchange and presentation of knowledge. Scientific-, medical- and industry-specific meetings have resulted in a burgeoning meetings sub-sector industry that is worldwide. It is a distinct professional specialisation, with a distinct professional designation (namely certified meeting planner or CMP) available through a regulating body. Advocacy bodies include Meeting Planners International (MPI) and the Professional Convention Management Association (PCMA). Various types of meeting that are included under this events genre are, for example, retreats, conventions, seminars, webinars (live web meetings), workshops, conferences, conventions and symposia.

Sports events

The field of sports events management has evolved into a genre of its own. Most types of sport today are organised and competitive, although some games are still played purely for recreation. In the light of the large variety of sports played worldwide, sports events are now big business. It can be argued that sports events have many commonalities with other events, which include their service orientation, a celebration and drama element, media coverage, and similarities in organising and operations (Getz, 1997).

Art events

Art events have their own terminology and associations. Art events are universal, and display considerable diversity in the forms and types of art featured. Art events are classified into the following categories:

□ *Participatory* events, where there is no separation of audience and performer; and

□ *Performing* events, usually involving performers in front of audiences (e.g. *visual* events, including painting, sculpture and handcrafts).

The following criteria are used for the classification of art events:

□ Temporary versus permanent events;
□ Regularly scheduled, periodic or one-off events;
□ Professionals versus amateur artists;
□ Paid or free performance;
□ Mixed or single genre (e.g. a music festival versus a jazz festival); and
□ Competitive versus festive events (Getz, 1997: 11).

Social life-cycle events

Prehistoric evidence (related to elaborate funeral rituals, monumental building erection and destruction ceremonies in various sites around the world) has been found, according to Mathews (2008), suggesting celebratory social life-cycle events dating as far back as about 60 000 years from the late stages of archaic *Homo sapiens* (typically referring to *Homo neanderthalensis*, among others). Modern social life-cycle celebrations, whose economic impact is often underestimated, are typically characterised by festivities, according to Goldblatt (2004), and also commemorate or honour all aspects of the human life cycle. Social (including religious) life-cycle events typically refer to engagement parties; bachelor and bachelorette parties; wedding and civil ceremony receptions; anniversary celebrations; baby showers; baptism and naming receptions; birthday parties; bar mitzvah, bat mitzvah or coming-of-age celebrations; confirmation receptions; graduation parties, memorial events; and funeral receptions.

1.5 An insight into trends and dynamics in the events sector

Knowledge of trends helps events organisers to develop products that are suited to the current needs of the destination and its market (Getz, 1997). The most crucial issues in this regard are now discussed.

1.5.1 Major trends

Strategic events growth

The importance of staging events has increased in a number of destinations; more and more destinations are beginning to realise the potential benefit of using events as a strategic development tool. Destinations, for instance, have created permanent posts for this purpose, while other destinations have created posts contingent on being able to prove sustainability. City events strategies show that differentiation exists in relation to the capacity for bidding for events, the ability to attract major events, infrastructural capacity and institutional arrangement. Specific events dominate certain destinations – it could be indicative of certain destinations developing events niches as well as clear branding and positioning. Some destinations have given themselves events-related titles to accentuate their tourism strategy, for example, positioning themselves as sports or cultural events cities. Some level of competition, though, between destination cities which offer similar or undifferentiated events offerings is evident. Attempts are also being made to utilise events to flatten seasonality or to boost tourism in a destination. The proliferation of events

Case study 1.3 Legacy after the Athens 2004 Olympics, Greece

The 2004 Olympics helped thrust Athens into the 21st century, creating a transportation infrastructure, a can-do attitude and economic stimuli critical to a modern city. That made the scene at the Olympic Athletic Centre of Athens, or OAKA, more jarring.

Throughout OAKA, it seemed the clock stopped after the closing ceremony. Four-year-old cardboard signage at the velodrome identifying Olympic usage of locations was still in place, even if it seemed out of place now.

No major events have been held at the pool complex since 2004, and the lack of effective maintenance was obvious. Tiles were missing on the deck, and rust stains in the pool were signs of slow decay. A crew was trying to remove accumulated grime from the diving well.

In the main stadium, the permanent home field for the AEK soccer team and site of frequent major concerts, seatbacks were dirty, and the concrete aisles and walkways stained. A feeling of benign neglect permeated the 26-year-old stadium, renovated to be the jewel of an Olympics that cost the Greeks billions of dollars for lasting infrastructure and temporary operations.

'It always is a big challenge to make sure the post-Olympic legacy will be used,' said Dora Bakoyannis, Greece's minister for foreign affairs and the mayor of Athens from 2002 to 2006.

Some of the Greeks' challenge undoubtedly came from the shift in national government four months before the Olympics, when the conservative New Democracy Party took over for the socialist PASOK. Long-range planning was abandoned in the new government's rush to get everything done before the opening ceremony.

Gianna Angelopoulos-Daskalaki, the woman whose leadership of the Athens Olympic Organizing Committee turned the 2004 Games from an organisational question mark into an unquestionable success, has been left to 'hope and pray the necessary actions will be taken to make the most out of these venues'.

Angelopoulos-Daskalaki highlights that some venues, through a public tender process, had been turned over from the Greek state to private owners, who have used them for concerts, sports events and exhibitions. 'Other venues have remained in the ownership of the state — and have not been properly maintained or utilised,' she stated. 'I always said careful planning was needed in all stages of preparing for the Olympics and for the maximum benefit after the Games ended.'

The Greeks created a state-owned company called Hellenic Olympic Properties to manage and lease venues in a dozen areas. Constantinos Mattalas, chairman and chief executive officer of Hellenic Olympic Properties, declined repeated requests for comment about plans for the venues under its control. It is impossible to get current or detailed information about the state of the venues from the English version of the company's website, www.olympicproperties.gr

'We had a lot of negative press that said we wouldn't be ready,' Bakoyannis said. 'Well, we were ready, and we paid the price for that, and we know that. It takes time and money. We needed a breath after the heavy financial burden we had to face.' Costas Cartalis, the government's former general secretary for the Olympic Games, told David Owen of the Financial Times it was €5.51 billion, or about $7 billion at the 2004 exchange rate. Other sources have pegged it at €11.2 billion, or some $14 billion.

Most municipal mayors have indicated that they could not afford to pay for the maintenance of these facilities. Most municipalities are financially not prepared to manage such a huge task.

The lingering question, of course, is whether the impact of having the Games justified the enormous cost, which doubled or tripled because Greece wasted years of preparation time and had to pay staggering amounts of overtime in the final push.

'There are people who are sceptical about it, but I strongly believe it was worth it,' Bakoyannis said.

Source: Adapted from the Chicago Tribune (2008)

offerings has created exciting possibilities for public–private partnerships among the arts, environmental and sponsoring organisations. This means that events, to an ever-increasing extent, need to be managed as businesses. Events are beginning to play an important role in destination marketing, the aim being to attract investment and tourism, and even desirable residents.

Sponsorship

Events sponsorship, accompanied by the professionalisation of events marketing, has grown dramatically. Many events have become dependent on sponsorship revenue to be viable. Corporations are increasingly seeking to market their products and image through appropriate events. Events offering public participation (e.g. in sport) are becoming increasingly popular with events sponsors. A trend is for sponsors to target smaller market segments and to aggressively market the niche through relationship marketing.

Special-purpose events venues and legacy

Destinations often require appropriate or special-purpose facilities should they wish to bid competitively for some events. Athens, for example, used the bid to fast-track the construction of numerous special-purpose events venues around the city for the 2004 Athens Olympic Games. Case study 1.3, however, illustrates some of the challenges that such special-purpose events legacies have to face after such events are staged.

There seems to be an increasing trend toward building mega-events venues such as convention centres and exhibition facilities, festival markets and sports stadia. Destinations are doing so to gain prestige or enter into public–private partnerships in order to gain facilities which the destination would otherwise not have obtained. Case study 1.4 hereunder illustrates how the Sydney Olympic Park Authority is planning for the venues of the former Sydney 2000 Olympic and Paralympic Games.

Case study 1.4 Sydney 2000 Olympic and Paralympics Legacy, Australia

The Sydney 2000 Olympic and Paralympic Games were the catalyst for the creation of Sydney Olympic Park. Although the Games have moved on, the legacy of the Park with its extraordinary natural environment and state-of-the art sporting and events facilities is now integral to the life of the city of Sydney.

Since the Games the Park has further evolved and is now a place of lively community interaction and a must-see attraction for increasing numbers of Australian and international visitors. Each year more than 8.5 million visitors come to the Park to enjoy its diverse range of leisure, entertainment, cultural and educational activities.

Sydney Olympic Park Authority has developed the Draft Master Plan 2030 as a blueprint for the future development of Sydney Olympic Park. This Master Plan is designed to facilitate the Park's continuing evolution into a vibrant specialist economic centre and urban parkland.

The vision for the Park is unprecedented. The aim is for continual enhancement of an urban park to enrich the lives of all those who live, work, play and learn here – a living legacy from the greatest events in Olympic history.

Source: Sydney Olympic Park Authority (2009)

The evaluation of events, states Getz (2007), often has to consider their long-term, indirect and often subtle impacts. 'Legacy' applies to all that remains, or is left over, from the events as a positive inheritance, or as challenges to deal with by future generations. Mega-events are usually sold to the public on the basis of their many benefits plus the creation of a permanent legacy and, according to Casey (2008), acts as a catalyst for economic regeneration or some other social, environmental or

---

Case study 1.5 The legacy of the 2010 FIFA World Cup™, South Africa

Throughout its bidding process, according to Van Wyk and Tassiopoulos (2009), South Africa has placed an emphasis on 'making [the 2010 FIFA World Cup™] an African event, one that would help spread confidence and prosperity across the entire continent': 'South Africa stands not as a country alone – but rather as a representative of Africa and as part of an African family of nations' and 'the successful hosting of the FIFA World Cup ™ in Africa provides a powerful, irresistible momentum to [the] African renaissance'.

In constructing it as an African Cup, the South African government has stated that the event was intended to have a clearly defined legacy and social impact:

❐ 'An event that will create social and economic opportunities throughout Africa'. In fact, South Africa's hosting of the event as an African event is strongly supported by the African Union (AU), which 'seeks to promote sport as an instrument for sustainable economic development and poverty reduction, peace, solidarity and social cohesion.

❐ 'To ensure that one day, historians will reflect upon the 2010 World Cup as a moment when Africa stood tall, and resolutely turned the tide on centuries of poverty and conflict. We want to show that Africa's time has come'. (Republic of South Africa, 2008a: internet)

In November 2006, the African Legacy Programme, a joint responsibility of the local organising committee (LOC) and the South African government, was announced. For the South African government,

one of the main inspirations behind South Africa's preparations for 2010 FIFA World Cup™ to leave a legacy for the African continent. The objectives of the African Legacy Programme are to:

❐ *support the realisation of the objectives of the African Renaissance such as the programmes of the African Union's New Partnership for Africa's Development (NEPAD);*
❐ *ensure African participation in the event;*
❐ *develop and advance African football; and*
❐ *improve Africa's global image and combat Afro-pessimism.*

Furthermore, the South African government maintains that the legacy of the 2010 FIFA World Cup™ will be

different from that typically associated with other large sporting events for three main reasons:

❐ *The legacy benefits are not to be confined to the host country.*
❐ *The host country itself has made an undertaking to make the continent-wide legacy one of the core focus areas of preparations for the event.*
❐ *The African Union is actively involved in ensuring that the 2010 FIFA World Cup™ legacy agenda is owned continent-wide. (Republic of South Africa, 2008a: internet)*

political imperative of the destination. Benefits of events are usually exaggerated while costs are usually underestimated or underemphasised.

Legacy planning, according to Casey (2008), needs to start from the very moment of deciding to bid – usually ten years before the event is to be staged. It needs to start with a philosophical base: 'Why is a destination bidding?'. Casey (2008) concludes by stating: 'Through effective legacy planning, we are all entrusted with the outcome of the Games for generations to come.'

Events accountability

Donors, sponsors, communities, governments and development organisations are increasingly expecting greater accountability and return on investment (ROI). Owing to the importance of events and the huge costs involved, events (particularly larger ones) usually do not escape vigorous scrutiny. Increasingly, the affected parties expect ROIs to be determined by the event planners during the conceptualisation stage of such (particularly large-scale) events that include determining measurable indicators for the appropriate event design, event management systems, marketing and sponsorship strategies, and operational and risk management, as well as the appropriate information technology platform, in order to be able to evaluate the efficiency of an event investment or to compare the efficiency of a number of different event investments.

Most of the scrutiny in events accountability is inclined to focus on the tendency to exaggerate event benefits and to underplay hidden costs. Many impact studies tend to gloss over the outcomes and real costs by indiscriminately using multipliers and unreliable data on visitor numbers, motives and expenditures. There is an increasing trend to require events organisers to undertake complete impact and feasibility studies and to report all events impacts during the planning stage (Tassiopoulos & Johnson, 2009). This scrutiny is often accompanied by controversy, with concern being focused on the social, environmental and economic ROIs of such planned events.

Continued growth

International indicators show that over the past few decades there has been a substantial growth in events, and all indications are that this growth will continue. Countries with developing economies have much to gain from this trend if they participate in the development of events products. Unfortunately, there are few reliable statistics, and few research findings are available. Few destinations have attempted to monitor the trends and classifications necessary to quantify events growth.

In developing economies, such as South Africa, India and Brazil, there is a greater interest in issues such as the life cycle of events and the possibility of market saturation of events within a destination. It seems unlikely that there is an upper limit to the number of events that can be organised, given the diversity and benefits of events; however, within a given event, type or destination, saturation could occur. New events products entering a mature events marketplace would have to be innovative. Research evidence seems to indicate that events products can continue to grow as attendance and budget sizes have been increasing in many categories of events.

1.5.2 Forces

Economic forces

Most people living in developed economies have sufficient disposable income for a variety of leisure activities, including one or more annual vacations. Developing countries have much to gain from this, provided that they produce the right tourism and events products. The rapid growth and diversification of the international events sector corresponds with the economic expansion throughout the post-war era, especially in the 1970s and 1980s.

In some newly developing market economies, destination managers find events to be a very cost-effective means of developing tourism. Such events prove to be popular with tourists eager to discover new cultures and until such a time when the incomes of the host populations have increased substantially, events may be the only leisure and cultural opportunities in which host residents can partake. Casey (2008) indicates, however, that there are instances where events are staged by a city and/or the country because of mainly economic repositioning strategies. Cities and/or countries use major events to act mainly as catalysts for regeneration or other economic imperatives – they may be less cavalier with initial capital investments, have relatively strong planned legacies, and are set within more relatively democratic (and therefore often critical) public domains. Suggested examples of such economic repositioning event strategies are the Barcelona Olympics in 1992; the Sydney Olympics in 2000; the Manchester Commonwealth Games in 2002; the Glasgow Commonwealth Games in 2014; the Prague Olympic Bid for 2016; and the possible Delhi Olympic Bid for 2020.

There seems, however, to be a trend towards polarisation between events for the rich and those for the poor – some events, even with government subsidies, are priced beyond the reach of the lower- and middle-income groups. Arts events are particularly susceptible to escalating operational and production costs. Government departments are critical role players in creating an enabling legislative environment that will foster the development of free or affordable events for the general public. The challenge is to mix the best of free public celebration with the best of professional events activities without excluding certain sectors of society by reason of income alone. Cutbacks in government subsidies have increasingly required events organisers to compete with other events organisations for the attention of corporate sponsorships, resulting in an aggressive and more efficient form of events management that measures the impacts of events accurately.

Discretionary time

In the international arena, improved productivity has resulted in households experiencing an overall increase in discretionary time. Economic upturns and downturns have in many cases created increased unemployment and not shorter working hours, and as a result, the long-awaited 'age of leisure' has not materialised. Research indicates that time is valued more, and more is expected of free time. In two-job and single-parent families there is less time for family-oriented leisure and the demand for leisure is spreading more evenly over the day, week and year (although the weekends and summer season are still the most popular periods). In developing economies such as China and South Africa, however, these issues are pertinent as many households struggle to meet their basic economic needs.

Population and demographic interests

Socio-demographic forces have a significant impact on leisure travel and events tourism. Factors such as life-stage responsibility, wealth, tastes and physical ability have a critical influence in explaining events preferences and demand preferences. Developing economies are usually characterised by very young and growing populations, while the most developed economies are characterised by their growing aged populations. Industrialised nations are also experiencing growth from immigration and higher birth rates among minorities.

Urban conditions

The majority of people in developed countries live in urbanised environments which are negatively impacted by congestion, pollution, crime, social tensions and a declining sense of community. On the positive side, they experience greater art, cultural, leisure and entertainment opportunities. While the majority of neighbourhood events are celebrations intended to strengthen community pride or a sense of place, others may be linked to ethnicity and special interests. These events present an insight into the lifestyles of the host populations and can be classified as potential tourist attractions. City-wide events usually serve multiple purposes as they are flourishing in cities active in urban renewal and redevelopment schemes.

Political forces

Government departments in developed economies usually support the development and growth of events as policy tools. Government agencies in developing countries such as China, South Africa and India have yet, however, to prove their consistent support in this regard. The delayed commitment of financial guarantees by the South African government to the failed Cape Town 2004 Olympic bid is a case in point. Furthermore, according to Casey (2008), where there is a lack of 'fit' or a mismatch between the major events and the size or capabilities of the city and/or country (and often the events are mainly politically led), there is often a lack of understanding of the true nature of events and their requirements. Suggested examples of such mismatches are the Sheffield (UK) World Student Games in 1991; the Athens Olympics in 2004; the Qatar Asian Games in 2006; and the West Indies Cricket World Cup in 2007 (Casey, 2008).

Sometimes events can be manipulated for party-political purposes: a government might support an event to provide economic stimulation for a depressed area with the aim of re-election. In other cases, major political celebrations and anniversaries can lead to programmes of chauvinistic display by the government. Sometimes events can be used to sidestep normal planning and consultative processes should the political powers wish to remove undesirable groups – especially from the inner-urban areas. Legacy in such instances, according to Casey (2008), tends to be an afterthought rather than planned because the events are used to reposition the city and/or the country on the world stage. In many such instances, money to fund such planned events is not considered a hurdle and events are considered as mainly part

Sanctions are coercive measures adopted usually by several nations acting together against a regime or organisation believed to be violating international law. Measures may be economic, diplomatic, cultural or of some other type. South Africa, because of the then National Party government's system of legalised racial segregation enforced between 1948 and 1994, was systematically isolated from the global economy through international cultural and sports boycotts, and economic trade sanctions and disinvestment, as from the early 1960s. Consequently, the country was also unable to derive much benefit from being able to stage, or participate in, cultural and sport events, particularly from the 1960s to the 1980s. For instance, the cultural boycott of South Africa affected everyone from crooners to authors to movie makers, although during the period, Sun City, an interracial gambling resort located in the then nominally independent homeland of Bophuthatswana, was able to stage various international shows such as Barry Manilow, Frank Sinatra, George Benson, Dolly Parton, Chicago, Queen, Cher and Liza Minnelli, as well as host international beauty pageants.

of a process of change in global or regional politics. Suggested examples of such political event repositioning strategies are the Moscow Olympics in 1980; the Seoul Olympics in 1988; the Kuala Lumpur Commonwealth Games in 1998; the Qatar Asian Games in 2006; the Beijing Olympics in 2008; and the Sochi (Russia) Winter Olympics in 2014. Casey (2008) indicates, however, that there are instances where cities and/or countries bidding for and hosting events have 'nothing to prove'. It is stated that there are cities that bid for events although neither political nor economic repositioning is considered a key motivator, but in which there is some internal catalytic effect where the rationale is a mix of sport, personal aspirations, political ambitions and legacy issues. Suggested examples of 'nothing to prove' cities and/or countries are considered to be the Atlanta Olympics in 1996; the Vancouver Winter Olympics in 2010; and the London, Paris, Madrid, New York, Moscow Olympic bids for 2012 (Casey, 2008).

Technological forces

Technology has permeated every facet of events organisation. Consumers are increasingly expecting events ticketing and packaging to be available over a large area through commercial online booking services, for example Ticketmaster® (US) or Computicket® (South Africa). Ticketing at events and the management of events data is also becoming computerised to an ever-increasing extent, thus enabling better management and more accurate decision making, improved marketing strategies, and improved control and detailed accounting of sales to ensure improved return on investment from staging events. Increasingly, technology is also being used for special effects through a combination of lasers, sound systems and other techniques to attract attention to events.

Values and sustainability

During the last decade, many businesses began to consciously engage in what has been come to be called corporate social responsibility (CSR) – the effort to achieve societal goals while still enhancing corporate profitability (to do good and do well). In turn, non-governmental organisations (NGOs) and international institutions alike have increasingly attempted to harness market forces to the public good (Middlebury College, 2009). Similarly, socially responsible investing (SRI) refers to the integration of personal values and societal concerns with investment decisions, while considering both the investor's financial needs and an investment's impact on society (CSRwire, 2009). *Social responsibilities* are directly linked to business ethics and the former is described by Griffen (as quoted in Van Aardt & Van Aardt, 1997: 203) as 'the obligation of an organisation to protect and enhance the societal context in which it functions'.

Prevailing values are increasingly requiring events businesses and events to be environmentally friendly and proactive about 'green' management and operations. Sponsors want to be associated with 'green' events products and provide funds to improve environmental practices. Government and business downsizing has resulted in a shift towards self-sufficiency and market-driven decision making. This value shift in society fosters more private-sector events with improved accountability. Events organisations are increasingly also expected to be socially and economically proactive so as to meet the needs of the economically and physically disadvantaged and to ensure racial and cultural equality, thus avoiding all forms of discrimination. The principles of responsible events, according to Events Research International (ERi) (2008), are based on the overall objective that events should contribute towards local sustainable development across the 'triple bottom line' representing the economy, socio-culture and the environment. Responsible events contribute to sustainable development through considering local needs; by managing economic, socio-cultural and environmental impacts; and by implementing best practices. Responsible events aim to maximise positive and minimise negative economic impacts within the local host community; optimise positive and minimise negative social and socio-cultural impacts within the local host community; and optimise positive and minimise negative environmental impacts within the local host community.

Consequently, events businesses are encouraged to subscribe to the principles and practices of responsible events tourism in conducting their operations and to strive to minimise the impact on the environment, spread the benefits throughout the local economy and promote community well-being.

Cultural diversity

The marketplace for events cannot be assumed to be uniform. Cultural differences, according to Getz (2007), must be taken into account when considering motivation and the nature of free choice and leisure.

Case study 1.8 Events and sustainable (or responsible) development, South Africa

In 2002, the Department of Environmental Affairs and Tourism (DEAT) developed South Africa's Responsible Tourism Guidelines. These guidelines also provide encouragement to events managers to grow their events businesses while providing social and economic benefits to local communities and at the same time respecting the environment. The main points can be summarised as follows:

❑ Economic guidelines:
  • Assess the economic impacts of events before developing such events;
  • Maximise local economic benefits by increasing linkages and reducing leakages from hosting such events;
  • Ensure communities are involved in and benefit economically from events;
  • Assist with local marketing and events product development; and
  • Promote equitable events business practices and pay fair prices.

❑ Social guidelines:
  • Involve local communities in planning and decision making; and
  • Assess the impact of events on host societies and cultural diversity, and be sensitive to the host culture.

❑ Environmental guidelines:
  • Reduce environmental impacts when developing and staging events; and
  • Use natural resources in a sustainable manner; and
  • Maintain and protect biodiversity when planning and staging events.

Source: Adapted from DEAT (2003: 4–5, 40)

Case study 1.9 Events and celebrating cultural diversity in the state of Victoria, Australia

Australia's state of Victoria is committed to multiculturalism, which is reflected in a variety of events celebrating the state's cultural, racial and religious diversity. There is something for everyone, from Chinese New Year processions to Greek film festivals; Italian folk music performances and Aboriginal dance. The City of Melbourne's Event Partnership Program recognises that events play an important part in the city's well-being by helping to activate precincts, raise the city's profile, assist in building relationships, deliver economic benefits and enliven the city. The event engages a well-defined sector of the community and through the activity fosters a spirit of togetherness and well-being, educating both the community group and the wider population; promoting tolerance and understanding throughout the broader population; encouraging participation; and enabling the essence of the activity to be celebrated and experienced widely. Melbourne's iconic or cultural events are defined as events that are uniquely Melbourne; showcase or support an iconic asset of the city; have cultural importance; or celebrate a historically significant cultural group. This strategy acknowledges the contribution of people from different cultures by celebrating and showcasing their stories, days of importance, festivals and contributions to the ongoing life of the city.

Sources: Melbourne Victoria (2009); City of Melbourne (2009)

Asian and other cultures assign greater value to belonging and maintaining cultural harmony as opposed to being individualistic. Relatedness may be considered more important than autonomy; and free choice and maintaining harmony being seen as more important than individualism, so the assumption can be made that leisure and recreation activities based on free choice is a "western" construct. Thus, cultural difference should be considered when designing events, in communicating their benefits and even when considering their impacts on communities and individuals.

1.6 Why destination managers should bother with events

Events tourism, as with any niche market or special-interest travel segment, according to Getz (2007), must be considered from both a demand (or events consumer) and a supply (or destination) perspective. It appears, however, that until recently very few developing events destinations had focused on events in their tourism development strategies, even though many such destinations may have staged successful events in the past. As the need increases to develop distinct competencies in order to achieve a competitive advantage, it is inevitable that developing events destinations will need to look more to their natural or cultural resources. Getz (1995) indicates that developing country events destinations must take the following into account:

❑ *Support services.* Developing destinations find it difficult to undertake the necessary research and evaluations to successfully capitalise on events tourism. Intelligence and marketing support systems such as marketing partnerships may have to be shared with other destinations.

❑ *Quality.* Providing services and products that are of a world standard is a challenge that all destinations face, and this can be exacerbated when there is little experience in events production. Training is necessary, as is careful planning of the events portfolio and evaluation research. Stressing events authenticity and spontaneity rather than sophisticated events structures could be an effective strategy for creating quality tourist experiences. Minor events can be packaged with high-quality products such as shopping, dining, sports and nature-based tourist products. Developing at least one good-quality hallmark event should be the goal of every destination.

❑ *Organisation and leadership.* The leadership necessary for bidding and

Case study 1.10 Events and cultural diversity, South Africa

In post-apartheid South Africa, the multicultural nature of the country is recognised by the country's Constitution when it states that 'the South African nation consists of a diversity of cultural, religious and linguistic communities'. The biggest challenge for South African events organisers, however, is to organise culturally inclusive event offerings whereby the country's spectrum of cultural groupings, including cultural minorities, feel that event offerings meet their diverse cultural expectations. South Africa is, however, in the process of slowly cultivating multiculturalism whereby unity and diversity of culture can be truly valued as well as lead to sustainable and inclusive multicultural events.

for producing indigenous events is usually a weakness in developing destinations. Management training will be necessary, with an emphasis on building capacity from existing groups. A volunteer recruitment and training programme is essential. It is, of course, possible to develop multi-destination events, thereby attracting tourists into an events tourism cluster. However, this requires the establishment of an events development entity or a strategic partnership.

☐ *Marketing management.* Many developing destinations are usually over-dependent on a single tourism product such as nature-based tourism and should therefore diversify. It is suggested that market segments travelling with the sole purpose of participating in events be targeted. The high cost of long-haul tourism requires careful niche marketing by destination managers; events tourism can be one such niche which provides greater value-added experiences for all visitors.

☐ *Destination attractiveness.* As it is usually more expensive to travel to developing destinations, a special effort is needed to create a positive image and to provide added value. Events can be used to stress unique resources and themes that make the destination worth the cost and effort.

☐ *Capacity.* In addition to accessibility and transport limitations, developing destinations often lack the physical space, services and basic resources necessary to host major events. Accordingly, minor events with strong image enhancement potential might have to substitute for them. This is reinforced by the fear of the negative impact that major events could have on sensitive environments and communities. In other words, because of a low carrying capacity in many developing destinations, it is important that events be carefully planned and managed. Destination managers should develop a portfolio of attractions and events that reflect national values, cultures, institutions and history with dignity and authenticity when developing the destination's distinctive competency.

Research by Ritchie (1996) has shown that events have been found to effectively address seasonality during the troughs of the winter months as well as the peaks of the summer months, if used strategically (through the use of marketing and de-marketing).

If planned and operated effectively through employing environmental, economic and social responsibility, this can ensure sustainable events over the long term.

1.7 Understanding why the study of events should go beyond a developed events destination concept

In the past, bidding for events was usually restricted to cities or destinations in developed economies. Such cities usually possessed the necessary resources, skills, expertise, facilities and infrastructure to bid for and stage events, and may have had previous experience in this regard. Consequently, events owners trusted the capacity of these cities to host events as they may have had successful track records.

Destinations in developing countries are also broadening the concept of legacy from that of mere physical infrastructure provision to include the benefits experienced in preparation of a new vision for a destination city or town.

Developing-country destinations are, however, increasingly learning to bid and win the right to host events in order that they may also take advantage of the multiple direct and indirect benefits of doing so. They are studying the past experiences of other cities, both successful and unsuccessful, and are learning to become more internationally competitive. Consequently, an analysis of the South African events sector reveals both opportunities and challenges for destination managers. The strategic development and use of events products and offerings can benefit destinations by identifying gaps in the events market and proactively developing events products and offerings to fill this gap. In October 2002, SA Tourism and DEAT received and approved the final draft of a commissioned research report regarding the development of a national events strategy for South Africa. The report (2002: 112) concludes that 'a clearly articulated and coordinated events strategy is needed to ensure that the opportunities are maximised and potential pitfalls are minimised. The lack of synergy among various stakeholders, both in the public and private sector, hinders South Africa's ability to become a major player in the global events tourism industry'.

1.8 Summary

This chapter strove to provide an overview of the highly complex, but dynamic, world of events. Events have become one of the most commonly used channels through which visitors can satisfy their desire to sample local foods and culture, participate in games or be entertained. Events are a unique form of tourist attraction, ranging in scale from mega-events such as the Olympic Games and the Munich Oktoberfest, to community festivals and programmes of recreational events at parks. Events are, however, increasingly being viewed as an integral part of tourism development and marketing planning, even though the majority of events have most probably arisen for non-touristic reasons, such as conducting business, competitions, cultural celebrations or the need to raise funds for charity or government coffers.

Knowledge of trends helps events organisers to develop products that are suited to the current needs of the destination and its market. Events tourism, as with any niche market or special-interest travel segment, must be considered from a demand (or events consumer) and from a supply (or destination) perspective. It appears, however, that until recently very few developing events destinations had focused on events in their tourism development strategies, even though many such destinations may have staged successful events in the past. Destinations in developing countries are broadening the concept of legacy from that of mere physical infrastructure provision to include the benefits experienced in preparation of a new vision for a destination city or town.

Case study 1.12 The legacy of Cape Town's bid for the 2004 Olympic Games, South Africa

Destinations in developing countries need to broaden the concept of legacy from that of mere physical infrastructure to the benefits experienced in preparation of a new vision for a destination city or town. In the case of Cape Town's failed bid to host the 2004 Olympic Games, the legacy left to this city's authorities in terms of moving towards implementing the vision for the city's future and proposing frameworks for the future development of strategically located land is rich indeed: the establishment of new partnerships between local authorities, the private sector and communities; and skills training and development of the city's human resources. Cape Town also held a number of smaller international sports events during its bid, which improved the management experience of local firms and the communities' willingness to find practical solutions, encouraging the fast tracking of development applications, and the development of a lasting database for the future. If maintained and updated, this mass of information is an invaluable resource for other developing destinations wishing to host an event.

Case study 1.13 An overview of the current situation of the events industry in South Africa

The events sector of the tourism industry represents a major untapped resource, and much is being done to develop it in South Africa. The challenge facing every regional and local tourism organisation is to determine the extent the events sector can be potentially developed for the benefit of the region and the country as a whole, and the identification of the capacity constraints such an events strategy needs to overcome. The situation is compounded by an events sector that is largely dominated by a fragmented small, micro and medium-sized events enterprise sector. Although local and regional authorities have a major role to play in attracting and facilitating the strategic development of event offerings for their destinations, especially in historically marginalised destinations and through creating enabling environments for such destination attractions to grow in a sustainable manner beyond the initial grant funding that is provided to kick-start such events, the reality is that there are various capacity constraints that need to be overcome (Tassiopoulos & Haydam, 2008). Typically, events organising skills have been concentrated in the hands of business owners of European descent. There is now some effort by government (e.g. the Department of Tourism, the Department of Arts and Culture (DAC), Sports Recreation South Africa (SRSA) as well as the sector education and training authorities (SETAs)) and the private sector to transfer skills across a broader spectrum of the population and to create events entrepreneurs particularly among the population groups that have historically not been able to participate meaningfully in the events sector.

Events statistics

The gathering and analysis of events statistics in South Africa is in its formative stage. At the time of writing, there was no single entity effectively collating a comprehensive national events database and executing comprehensive research and analysis of all planned events in the country. South African Tourism (SA Tourism) has been in the process of institutional transformation for some time, and currently sees its mandate as being to promote South Africa as a preferred international events tourism destination. To this end, SA Tourism promotes South Africa as a destination for business tourism. Currently, SA Tourism is building limited capacity in respect of research and analysis of the events industry. The body has started compiling an annual national calendar, or database, of events being hosted in the country. Contact Publications, a commercial publisher that includes an events data-gathering initiative, collates (raw) data of international and national events that are taking place in South Africa, and publishes this database in the form of the annual SA Conferences and Exhibitions Calendar.

Currently, the entry of events details into both of the aforementioned databases by events organisations is largely voluntary, which makes it difficult to derive an empirically sound analysis of the entire events sector in South Africa, especially from a strategic and long-term perspective. The strategic and long-term significance of both databases, at the time of writing, remains unclear.

Although it is accepted that the SA Conferences and Exhibitions Calendar database is reasonably representative of most national and international events taking place in South Africa, it does not include most local or community special events. Nonetheless, as a point of departure, Contact Publications' 1999–2009 Calendars of Events (mostly meetings, exhibitions, recreational and cultural events) will form the basis of analysis hereunder.

Contact Publications' 1999–2009 Calendars of Events

The overall provincial distribution of meeting and exhibition events in South Africa for the period 1999 to 2009 is depicted in figure 1.5. An analysis of the results suggests that 1999 was an exceptional year for events being staged in South Africa and may be indicative of the end of the post-1994 boom period that the country experienced in respect of being able to attract international events. The period 2000 to 2004 saw a consistent number of national and international events being hosted in the country. It is further noted that 2005 to 2009 saw a rapid increase in such events, especially as a number of world-class event venues became operational around the country. A noticeable drop in the number of events being hosted during 2008, however, is most likely due to much of the industrialised world entering a recession.

The South African events statistics further suggest that the provinces can be grouped into three clusters in terms of events distribution, namely high, medium and low:

- *High cluster.* This cluster consists of the provinces of Gauteng, the Western Cape and KwaZulu-Natal. The period under study indicates that Gauteng has largely led this cluster, which is probably because of its rich array of events-related facilities (amalgam) and being the business hub of the country. The Western Cape has been consistently the second most popular leader of this cluster (probably because of its international reputation as a world-class leisure tourism destination), followed by KwaZulu-Natal.
- *Medium cluster.* This grouping has been consistently led by the Eastern Cape. The other members of this cluster are Mpumalanga and North West (probably deriving much of their events business from their close proximity to Gauteng).
- *Low cluster.* This grouping has been consistently led by the Free State with the other members of this cluster being the Northern Cape and Limpopo.

A more in-depth analysis of the events distribution data indicates that the provincial events distribution is polarised within provinces according to the availability of events venues and the general quality of the events amalgam in the provinces. Most events in Gauteng, for instance, take place within the Greater Johannesburg area; in the Western Cape they are mostly hosted in and around the Greater Cape Town metropolitan area; in KwaZulu-Natal they are found largely in Durban; in the Eastern Cape they are hosted for the most part in and around Port Elizabeth, and so forth. There is seemingly a need for the effective implementation of a national events development strategy that will focus on improving the capacity for bidding and hosting by the 'moderate cluster', and to fundamentally improve the events hosting ability of the 'low cluster'.

An analysis by genre of events, as depicted in figure 1.6, indicates that the business events segment (largely meetings and exhibitions) dominates the current events market in South Africa. This is followed by the cultural events genre (which mostly includes art/entertainment events); this is followed by the recreational genre which largely mostly includes national and international sport events hosted in the country. The recreational events genre has seemingly growing rapidly in popularity with various sports codes, particularly in 2009, probably due to the elevated international status of South Africa being the host of the 2010 FIFA World Cup™.

The monthly events frequencies for the period 1999 to 2009 (particularly in the business, cultural and recreational genres) are indicated in figure 1.7. The findings suggest that the national events season in South Africa is characterised by two peak periods: May and September, with May leading by a narrow margin. There is a general downward trend in events activity after September as business traditionally prepares for the end-of-year festive season. The large volunteer and entry-level employee base that becomes traditionally unavailable during this time further accentuates this trend. The months of December, January and February are considered to be relatively 'slow' events months. The events sector only shows an upward trend as from March, peaking in May. The period June to October is seen as a 'flat' but moderate period for events frequency, with a slight decline toward the month of October. The analysis further suggests that businesses have a particular preference for hosting their events during certain times of the year, with peak periods in May and September. The research further suggests that the period December to March is a more popular period for the hosting of mostly general special (e.g. social life-cycle) events and festivals.

An analysis for the period 2000 to 2009 (refer to figure 1.8) reveals that, except for 2008, there was an overall upward growth trend in the total number of events staged in South Africa with 2008 being considered as negatively impacted by the late-2000s worldwide recession, with particular consequences for Gauteng and the Western Cape. Pereira (2009) described the late-2000's global recessionary period as characterised by 'low cost' and 'green' events, and 'late cancellations', and furthermore recommended that events organisers employ innovation strategies and provide event attendees with value-for-money event offerings and authentic experiences. The events sector was also recommended to employ the right people with the right skills, knowledge and attitudes; make the right decisions based on researching the needs of the market; and to make use of appropriate sales techniques so as to successfully conclude event business negotiations.

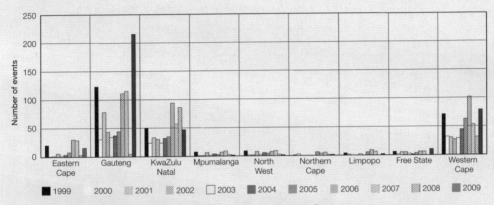

Figure 1.5 Provincial event frequencies in South Africa, 1999–2009

Source: Contact Publications (1998–2009)

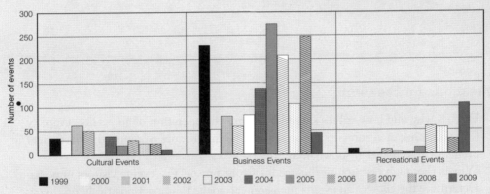

Figure 1.6 Main event genre frequencies in South Africa, 1999–2009

Source: Contact Publications (1998–2009)

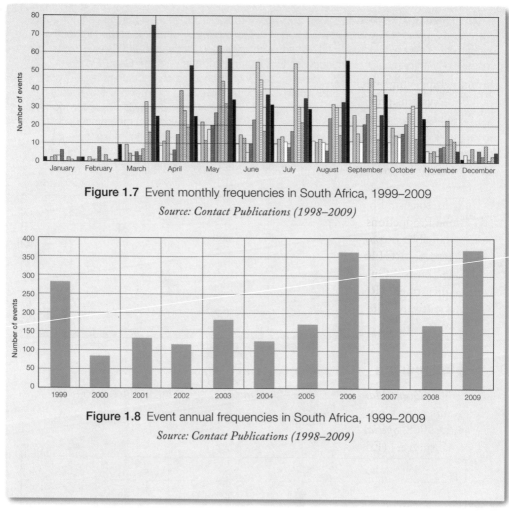

Figure 1.7 Event monthly frequencies in South Africa, 1999–2009

Source: Contact Publications (1998–2009)

Figure 1.8 Event annual frequencies in South Africa, 1999–2009

Source: Contact Publications (1998–2009)

Questions for research

1 Discuss why, and how, values should influence the operation of an events company.
2 Can you think of arguments for or against the importance of return on investment in events management? If so, what are they?
3 Why is thorough research of the needs of your prospective events visitors important?
4 Determine the choices an events manager can make to impact positively on the environment, society and economy of a destination.
5 Evaluate the differences and similarities between mega- and hallmark events.
6 Discuss the implications of the various trends and forces influencing the events sector.
7 Evaluate the role of event destinations in developing multi-culturally inclusive events.
8 Critically evaluate the role of local and regional authorities in attracting and facilitating the development of event offerings, particularly in destination economies that are considered marginalised.

Recommended websites

Browse the following internet sites for interesting and informative information:

Championchips – high-tech time management system: http://www.championchip.com/products/systems.php

City of Melbourne – Event Partnership Program: http://www.melbourne.vic.gov.au/info.cfm?top=77&pa=4482&pg=4487.

Event Manager Blog: http://www.eventmanagerblog.com/

Events Research International (ERi) – The Principles of Responsible Events: http://www.eventsresearch.org/index.php?id=164

Fair Trade in Tourism South Africa (FTTSA): http://www.fairtourismsa.org.za/

Green Globe Productions – produce eco-friendly events which are economically feasible and sustainable: http://www.greenglobeproductions.net/services.htm

MeetingMetrics – ROI:http://meetingmetrics.com/research_papers/White_Papers.htm

Responsible Tourism Guidelines: http://www.icrtourism.org/sa

Return on investment (ROI): http://www.juliasilvers.com/embok/ROI.htm

Web-based software suite that helps increase and accelerate event sales: http://www.a2zshow.com/

Suggested reading

Getz, D. 1997. *Event Management & Event Tourism.* New York: Cognizant Communication Corporation.

Mathews, D. 2008. *Special Event Production. The Process.* UK: Butterworth-Heinemann.

Raj, R & Musgrave, J (Eds). 2009. *Event Management and Sustainability.* United Kingdom: CABI.

Photo: Zoe Moosman

Photo: SA Tourism

Photo: Dimitri Tassiopolous

Photo: MediaClubSouthAfrica.com. Rodger Bosch

2

Events strategic development

William O'Toole

Abstract

As the events industry grows around the world, the tools of strategic analysis and asset management are increasingly being applied to the events portfolio. The strategic development of events, describing the tools, processes and techniques that constitute a model of strategic development are discussed. This includes the governmental return on investment in events, namely, social capital, goodwill and commercial returns. The methods and decision criteria that governments use to guide event development are explored. Finally the rise of the event corporation is described. The use of these tools and techniques represent the next step in the maturity of the event industry worldwide.

Chapter objectives

After you have read this chapter you should be able to:
- ❏ understand the international trend in the development of event strategies;
- ❏ discuss the role of event support in the strategic development of events;
- ❏ describe the development of events and festivals;
- ❏ describe the development of an events strategy in the international context; and
- ❏ understand the central position of objectives and decision criteria in the strategic process.

2.1 Introduction

Over the last ten years the events industry has been recognised by governments around the world as a significant economic and social activity. There is no one study to show the international impact of events and, as pointed out by many authors, the fragmented nature of the current industry has been an impediment to the collection of any verifiable and commensurable data on the impacts. What started as a loose collection of small festivals, conferences, exhibitions and so forth is now seen as a portfolio or an events programme for a region. The high visibility of events and their significant impact have meant that governments need to be involved to address the various interests and concerns of stakeholders. The complexity of government actions and the need for policy decisions have given rise to the need for long-term planning for any government intervention. This led numerous nations, regional and city governments, and authorities to develop an events development strategy. The number of countries that have developed *national* strategies are, to date, quite small. New Zealand, Korea, South Africa and Saudi Arabia were among the first to do this. However, there are numerous regional and city strategies such as the state of Victoria (Australia), the region of North East England (UK), and the

cities Christchurch and Wellington (NZ), Abu Dhabi (UAE), Aqaba (Jordan), and the cities of Casey and Devonport (Australia). The population of these areas ranges from 20 000 to 20 million people. In some cases the events strategy has taken one part of the events industry such as the National Business Events Strategy in Australia 2008 and the Strategy and Action Plan for the Development of the 'MICE' Market in Saudi Arabia 2007.

There is a discernible pattern – a collection of describable interconnecting processes – which is common to all these strategies. In part this is a result of the nature of government planning that needs a structure to its strategies to ensure implementation. At the same time it is a response to the unique nature of the event industry and its development.

This chapter describes the background to the strategic development of events and the strategic planning, and analyses these common processes and their application to the various regions.

2.2 Events as assets

When viewed over a period of five years, a programme or a portfolio of events can be considered as an asset to a region. Although the results of the asset are intangible, the way that it is created or procured, maintained and eventually disposed parallels the management of physical assets such as roads, machinery and buildings. The science of asset management was developed through its application to physical assets. For governments, it mostly concerned the infrastructure assets such as roads, parks and airports, and the decision to commit resources to these assets. In the manufacturing industries, asset management concerned the financial sustainability of the means of production as well as asset maintenance, service, renewal, scheduling, valuation and depreciation. This highly developed management science gives a new perspective on events such as public festivals. A large part of the current event management literature concerns the management of a single event at a single time. Asset management enables the life cycle of single or repeat events, such as an annual festival and a portfolio of events, to be managed. In the view of a large corporation or a government, the asset management must be accountable to the shareholders or the constituents. For this reason an asset management plan is common to all complex organisations. The asset takes up important resources and delivers a return on the investment. Any asset has three types of return on investment (ROI):

1 Commercial;
2 Social capital; and
3 Goodwill.

Commercial returns are measurable financial returns on the asset. In some cases, these are straightforward for events. A ticketed concert, for example, has a measurable return or profit. An event can have indirect financial benefits that may be more difficult to measure, such as the commercial returns of a promotional event for a new tourism development. Similarly,

a product launch, such as a new Mercedes, may increase sales of the car. However, it is not easy to attribute this increase directly to the event. The multiplier and the tourism satellite accounts are examples of how these indirect commercial returns may be measured. Commercial returns often dominate the measurements of economic impact and the benefit part of the cost benefit analysis.

Social capital is a slightly more difficult return to measure. Directly this may be infrastructure built for the event, such as road improvements and stadia. However, social capital includes the intangible networking of the host population. The building of a nation by means of major events is recognised by developing nations such as South Africa and Saudi Arabia. The intangible 'national pride' and loyalty is vital to the functioning of a country. Political outcomes of events should never be underestimated. Mega-events such as the Asian Games, the World Cup and the Olympics are examples of this. From the circuses of ancient Rome to the pageant movement in the US at the beginning of the 20th century, politicians have been aware of the enormous power of public events. Social capital is also found in corporate events. The raising of morale of staff through the end-of-year party or award nights are examples of events with corporate social capital consequences.

Goodwill is the value of the region or company above its physical assets. It can be measured by the share value of a company. A company such as Red Bull is worth far more than its physical assets. Goodwill is often called the brand value plus the intellectual capital. It can be valued exactly when a company is sold. It is not as simple for a region or a city. However, *brand value* is well known in the tourism industry. For example,

Singapore and Abu Dhabi have a strong brand-oriented strategy for their events.

Examples of these ROIs in event assets are found in (refer to case study 2.1) the North Shore City (Auckland, New Zealand) events strategy (as depicted in case 1); the Cape Town Event Policy (as depicted in case 2), stresses the social capital outcomes; and the mission statement for the Abu Dhabi Tourism Authority (as depicted in case 3), for whom event development is a key priority, contains the brand or goodwill dimension and the development of social capital.

2.3 How events develop

To successfully produce an events strategy, the development of an event over a period of time must be studied and compared to other events, and a model developed. Major events and festivals, such as the Olympics, the Festival de Fès des Musiques Sacrées du Monde in Morocco or the Grahamstown National Arts Festival in South Africa do not suddenly appear – they take time to develop over years. Stakeholders must be certain of the stability of an event before they will be involved. Often the inaugural festival is full of problems as the complexity of marketing, operations and finance have yet to be understood and simplified even if planned rigorously. Each annual repeat of the festival assists in reducing the risk in the organisation and marketing. This is the same for all types of events. Exhibitions and conferences can take years before they are fully financially stable and the risks managed.

There is a parallel with the development of any business. The first years of any new business are full of risks, and many start-up companies fail. Unfortunately there are no studies on this aspect of events. However,

Case study 2.1

Case 1: North Shore City, New Zealand
Events celebrate our city. Events help provide a great city in which to live, work, play and learn. They enrich our lives by providing opportunities to engage and interact, explore culture, participate in sporting and recreational activities, and celebrate our city, its people, and foster talent, creativity and innovation. Events provide a platform for collaboration between organisations. This builds the events sector and economic benefits from events. Events also play a key role in developing social capital and volunteerism. Events are a vehicle for contributing to the social, cultural, environmental and economic well-being of the city. Events promote our city and bring economic vitality to it both through direct economic impacts and also by supporting a creative, innovative, exciting city in which to live, work, play and learn (NSC, 2008: 2).

Case 2: City of Cape Town, South Africa
The hosting of events is a significant part of the City of Cape Town's competitiveness strategy. Events have an important role in modern cities to enhance cultural and social cohesion in communities, and support urban rejuvenation and economic growth. Communities are central for making events successful (CCT, 2008: 2).

Case 3: Abu Dhabi, United Arab Emirates
To be a leading tourism authority that is positioning the Emirate of Abu Dhabi as an outstanding, globally recognized, sustainable tourism destination, while enriching the lives of the Abu Dhabi community and visitors alike (ADTH, 2008: 2).

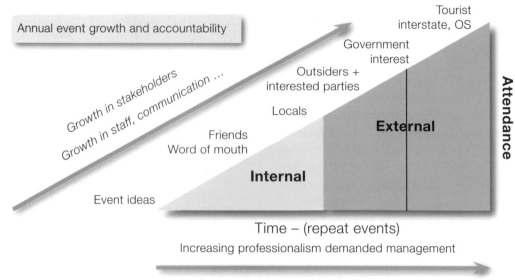

Figure 2.1 Events development

Source: Reprinted from EPMS CDROM (2009)

an informal survey of many public festivals shows that they take at least three years to get on their feet. The authorities, the management team and the sponsors are refining their relationships with each event. Figure 2.1 illustrates the growth of public festivals. Although the diagram was based on the growth of public events, such as music festivals, it can also be applied to other types of events.

Like all good ideas, events start with a person or small group coming up with the initial concept. It can be purely creative or in response to a need – or a combination of both. The Olive Festival in Al Jouf in Saudi Arabia was started by enterprising olive growers in the region and quickly grew to be a public event. The Woodford Festival in Queensland Australia started as small gathering of local people interested in folk music. Innovation and passion for the event are fundamental to all the festivals.

As an annual event grows it is a common problem that staff members find it difficult to let go of all their previous responsibilities. In the early days of a festival, the success is dependent on the very personal commitment of key members of the organising group. Huge sacrifices are made, there is no limit to the work that is done and the festival becomes a personal achievement.

However, the festival becomes bigger than the individuals who created it. It reaches a change of phase, and at this stage, key staff members need to reassess their roles and responsibilities. Taking on the same responsibilities is a bigger risk than not doing the work. It can lead to missing priorities, early exhaustion and disappointment.

The only solution to this is to have an organisation structure that can grow with position descriptions, which can be achieved by employing an integrated management system. A project management approach allows the creation of such a management system. The tasks, timelines, quality levels and responsibilities are delineated and defined. Although not perfect, the project management approach will minimise the very real possibility of staff burnout, confusion and repetition of mistakes.

2.4 The events development strategy

A strategy is a long-term plan of coordinated action designed to achieve a major goal of an organisation. Large organisations have strategic plans that may have three-, five- and ten-year cycles. Government tourism bodies, for example, have these cycles and need a strategy to enable the effective allocation of their resources. The size of the organisation often corresponds to the complexity of its tasks. A strategy enables the organisation to align the tasks into processes that can be delegated to departments, divisions and, finally, individuals.

The government events strategy generally is the responsibility of economic development or the tourism department. This is the case in Coffs Harbour Council in Australia, for example, which has objectives for supporting or sponsoring

Figure 2.2 Hierarchy of objectives

events and festivals which align with its long-term objectives. These strategic objectives fit under the department's policy and objectives, which in turn fit under the government's policy. This may be mapped out as a hierarchy of objectives – such as illustrated by figure 2.2. The outcomes of events and festivals must be supporting these objectives to gain government approval and support.

The importance of an events strategy to the development of events and festivals around the world is demonstrated in table 2.1. In the last ten years numerous events strategies have been produced.

2.5 How governments and companies procure and support events

There are three key policy elements a government employs to develop their events programme: keep out of it, outsourcing and local development.

The 'keep out of it' and leave it to private industry is a common government policy for events that are business focused and have commercial outcomes as their primary purpose. Any government intervention tends to skew the market. By favouring one organisation in a competitive marketplace, the government can damage business development. It is common for the stakeholders in the corporate or business events industry to ask for government funding. This is part of the business principle of reducing costs and increasing income. In many cases around the world, the funding for business events is a political decision. In most countries the government support for business events is found in the construction and maintenance of general infrastructure. In many cities, such as Doha and Singapore, the support

Table 2.1 An overview of the leading countries in the development of event strategies

Note: the list of event strategies in this table is not exhaustive and only deals with a sample of event strategies that are published in the public domain.

Korea	In 1995 Korea had three cultural festivals when the government decided to support and foster the developed of major cultural festivals for each of the eight regions. Through a system of careful support, monitoring and improvement, and through the concerted implementation of a strategy, Korea now has over 1 200 festivals, 36 of which are supported by the Minister of Culture and Tourism. These festivals include the Ginseng, Science, Martial Arts, Butterfly and Icefish festivals.
Singapore	Singapore has followed a highly proactive strategy of festival and event support and development. One of the key aims, according to the Singapore Tourism Board's 2015 – Vision, Targets and Initiatives, is 'Anchoring iconic/major events: Attracting iconic or mega-events that will highlight Singapore as a premier destination for Leisure, Business and Services customer segments' (STB, 2009). The strategy is strongly overseas tourist focused, and its highly targeted market analysis matches the events programme to the market segment.
New Zealand	New Zealand has a sophisticated event strategy system that has been developed over ten years. They have a national strategy related to the tourism strategy (NZ Major Events, 2006). Underneath the national strategy lie the regional and city event strategies. The regional and city event strategies contribute to the national strategy, and constantly refer to it. Events in New Zealand are seen as a way to overcome their problems of distance from the world centres of population.
Australia	Australia does not have a published national event strategy, and the states (or provinces) have independently developed their own. Within the states, the cities and regions have developed their individual strategies. A number of the state governments have set up 'event corporations' to guide their events development through bidding and selective support. In response to the importance of conference and exhibitions, the stakeholders in that aspect of the event industry have developed a business events strategy.
South Africa	South African Tourism established an Events Tourism Unit in 2006 and developed their 'Event Growth Strategy'. This is in response to the future impact of the Soccer World Cup in 2010. There are a number of regional/city event strategies developed under the national strategy. South Africa is particularly interested in events that develop the skills of its population and promote the country as an international events destination in order to meet its economic growth imperatives.
Canada	There is no national events strategy for Canada, but there are number of city events strategies. These tend to be highly localised. However, Canada is leading the way in the development of competencies for the events industry and events education. The recent development of the International Event Management Standard based on the Event Management Body of Knowledge is an example of the strategic planning for their event industry.

UK	The UK has a number of regional event strategies. Owing to the long history of public festivals and celebrations, their strategies often concern the re-energising of festivals and the regeneration of the townships after the decline in manufacturing industries. The following quote from the Stoke-on-Trent City Council strategy paper is an example:
	    The consultants were made aware of the history of Stoke-on-Trent and the fragmentation of the pottery towns and also how strategies for regeneration are focussing on developing the City Centre. It made sense therefore to develop a strong strand of festival activity in the City Centre to support strategies for regeneration and market the transformation of the city, whilst the change is taking place.
	    (Remarkable Productions, 2007: 3)

UK (continued)	The London Olympics has changed the focus of many events strategies to include methods and ideas to maximise the advantages of hosting the Olympics in 2012. The importance of business events is recognised by the government as illustrated by this quote: *Conferences, exhibitions, incentive travel, corporate hospitality, outdoor events and individual business travel account for a growing share of total inbound tourism into the UK. In 2001, for the first time ever, expenditure by business visitors exceeded that of leisure visitors, representing 31.7% of all spend compared with 29% of spend by holiday visitors.* Rogers (2003a: 3)
Kingdom of Saudi Arabia	The Supreme Commission for Tourism has been very active in the development of events, and to date there are two event strategies. The first is for the MICE (meetings, incentives, conventions and events) industry and the other for public events and festivals. The government regards events as a way of nation building and cultural enhancement.
The Gulf	The rapidly developing economies of the Gulf countries of Qatar, United Arab Emirates, Bahrain, Oman and Kuwait have created ideal conditions to guide the development and acquisition of events through government strategies. Abu Dhabi, for example, regards events as vital to their tourism strategy: *To increase creative, unique and diverse tourism products and capacity for the Abu Dhabi tourism economy, utilizing its tourism areas which will enrich the visitors experience.* ADTA (2007: 7).

extends to the government funding for the construction of conference and exhibition centres. Quite a few countries, under their business events support programme, will assist in the bidding for major international conferences and exhibitions.

The second policy is the outsourcing or 'buy in' of events. The numerous countries that host the Formula 1 Grand Prix are an example of the success of outsourcing their events. To the government there are advantages to a policy of 'buying in' events. The primary one is that the events development has already been completed and the country is purchasing a professionally organised package. Case study 2.2 illustrates the advantages and disadvantages of this policy.

Case study 2.2 Advantages and disadvantages of outsourced or 'buy in' events

Events, such as the Red Bull Air Race which was conceived in 2001 (featuring the world's best race pilots in a competition that combines speed, precision and skill) or the 'Night of the AdEaters' (which originated in France in 1981 and is now a global phenomenon of commercials from numerous countries with shows in more than 150 cities across 52 countries) have sophisticated marketing and management systems. Often they have experienced all the mistakes that could appear, and can prepare for them. Their core teams are well versed in the event.

The Olympic Torch relay of the 2008 Beijing Olympics, for example, had commissioned a highly sophisticated core management group, Maxxam, who has honed their skills in a number of Olympics and in the Asian Games. They were able to set up local groups or teams to organise the local participants in cities around the world, from Dar es Salaam to Almaty to San Francisco. However, even the most experienced events organisers are prone to new risks. The protests against China's policy in Tibet and the ensuing bad press resulted in deciding on the possibility of the 2012 London Olympic Torch relay being cancelled or at least consolidated.

The disadvantages of the 'prepaid' event are that the country is getting the same event that is held in other countries. The uniqueness and possible tourism value of such events is diminished. There is an information asymmetry in the negotiations as the event owners or sellers of the event have complete knowledge of it, whereas the client country, the event buyer, may have limited knowledge. This can lead to a high cost for an event to a country as it becomes a seller's market, resulting in bidding wars, driving up the prices and costly mistakes, and cannot be justified as 'good governance' (Banks, 2002).

A major question asked of the outsourcing policy is: 'Is there a positive legacy from the event?'. In some cases stadia and event precincts remain vacant and become a cost to the host well after the mega-event has left the country. The government must watch that it is not imposing the event on the local population. This can have disastrous consequences as the locals can undermine the event or vote against the politicians who supported it.

The last policy is to develop events within the country – that is, 'in-house'. Before the internationalisation of events driven by the sporting industry, the media and the attraction of international competitions, most events were developed in their own communities. These are the local festivals and community events. Many of them develop into hallmark or signature events such as the Rio Carnival in Brazil, the Munich Oktoberfest in Germany or the Kumbh Mela on the Ganges River in India, attracting an estimated 60 million people. These events take years to develop. The advantages of this policy are the following:

❑ The local population is involved;
❑ Unique events are created – such as the Taif Rose Festival, based on the Damascus rose grown in that city;
❑ Sustainability – the support and slow growth allows the local population and businesses to develop at the same time as the event; and
❑ Training – local events mostly employ local people and can be used as training for many types of skills.

The limitations to this policy are that these events take time to develop. The local stakeholders must be gradually convinced to support the event. Also, the event can become a juggernaut that is impossible to stop or change. There are many stories of festivals that have taken a life of their own, absorb a lot of funding and become a financial liability on the community. They keep going due to political considerations.

Many local events are small and therefore 'under the radar' of the government authorities. When these events are added up, they can often have a far larger impact or return on investment than the mega-events. As the saying goes: 'There is one Olympics every four years, but it is dwarfed by the millions of weddings'. The 'micro-events' and local events provide the basis of many larger events – they provide the training and the testing ground to people and ideas. These micro-events are quite common in sport and associations. The street soccer and club cricket ultimately enables the mega World Cup. The local Rotary meetings enable the International Rotary to hold conventions of over 40 000 attendees.

2.6 Events support process

The events support process is an accountable system allowing the events companies, businesses and individuals to apply for government support for their events. Figure 2.3 illustrates the flowchart of the process used by government authorities to guide the development of events. The event can range from business to sporting events, exhibitions and festivals. The applicant may only want to obtain government permission to hold the event. In other cases they may ask for full financial support. In the process illustrated, the applicant applies for support from the tourism authority (TA). One of the roles of a TA is to assist events development, therefore the first official response should be 'How can we help?'

The applicant must understand the objectives of the TA and the events manual. From these documents, the applicant can assess the level of support it needs. It could be advice on the local suppliers or facilitation of permits, for example. The next step is to apply for the support. It may involve submitting the event plans, including a risk management plan. The TA compares information supplied by the event applicant to the decision criteria, which are the core of the process. Depending on the score in the criteria, the TA will approve and suggest a level of support. If the event

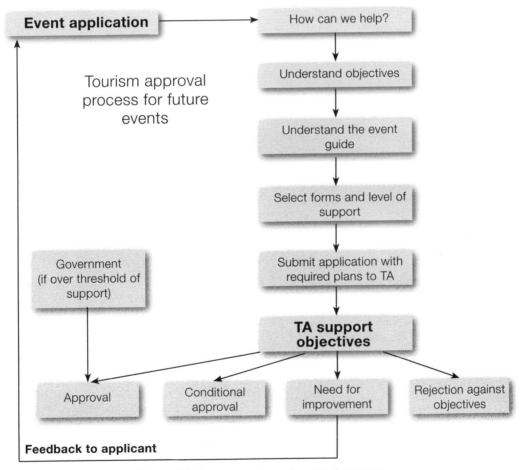

Figure 2.3 Government event support process

Source: Reprinted with permission from EPMS CDROM (2009)

is seen as worthwhile, the TA may suggest areas of improvement so that the event will score higher with the criteria.

This process is similar to the process used by companies in sponsoring events and in countries applying to host events.

2.7 Decision criteria example

Driving the engine of event support are the decision criteria. It is a formal and accountable version of 'making a choice'. For a government to support events, it must have a system that prioritises the use of the public resources. In other words, some events will be approved and others will miss out. Some events do not have any benefits that fit into the government objectives. Most projects within a country compete for government resources. The decision criteria table as illustrated by the example in table 2.2 is a spreadsheet that allows the relevant government department to score the applicant against the strategic objectives of the department. The strategic objectives can be traced directly back to the asset management returns on investment.

> **Case study 2.3 International Olympic Committee decision criteria**
>
> The International Olympic Committee uses a version of the spreadsheet that incorporates fuzzy logic or probability of correctness, to select the next host country for the Olympics (IOC, 2008). Each of the criteria is weighted according to government policy. Referring to table 2.2: *E2. Providing job opportunities* may be a higher priority in government policy than *E4. Improving facilities*. Consequently, it will be given a higher weighting.

The technique of the decision table is used in many event related activities.

Each support application that is passed through the decision criteria also tests the efficacy of the process, hence the decision criteria improve with time. It is a risk that the criteria become an 'end unto themselves' instead of a tool to assist decisions. Not all of the benefits of events can be captured on paper or described in a few words. Given these risks, it is still a very effective tool. The spreadsheet can easily be adapted to any changes in government policy. The decision to support one event and, conversely, not support others is taken out of the hands of one person. The decision to support a particular event becomes defendable and transparent.

2.8 Do or die

Events can pass their 'use-by' or 'sell-by' dates. The events support process thus does not include the actual internal development of the event. It is concerned with the support for the event. The development of an event involves the interventions by the event owner, which in common product development decisions, involves these alternatives:

1 Grow;
2 Consolidate;
3 Devolve; and
4 Cancel.

Quadrant analysis tools such as the Boston Consulting Group (BCG) Matrix for Product Competitive Positioning or the Ansoff Product/Market Growth Matrix may assist with these decisions. Some of the question involved in the development of an event over the years include: are parts of the event programme not working and is there is a need to

Table 2.2 Decision table

Decision criteria for level of event support		Rating	Rating	Rating
Economic objectives				
	E1. Generating income – a net financial benefit			
	E2. Providing job opportunities			
	E3. Generating foreign income			
	E4. Improving facilities			
	E5. Assisting to create private/public partnerships			
	E6. Business networking and mixing with OS businesses			
	E7. Sustainability			
Marketing objectives				
	M1. Promoting local and international tourism to the city			
	M2. Increasing awareness of the brand of the city			
	M3. Increase awareness of the unique qualities of the city			
Social objectives				
	S1. Community development including:			
	Community involvement in event			
	Education in other cultures and mixing with cultures			
	S2. Local culture promotion and development			
	S3. Environment awareness			
	S4. Broadening experience through innovation and creativity			
	S5. Suitable time			

Source: Reprinted with permission of EPMS CDROM (2009)

consolidate the programme? Can the 'stars' of the programme be expanded? Are there new events sites or venues we can use? Are there new markets? Can part of the event be franchised?

The event may be 'sold off' or, in the case of public festivals owned by council, they may be handed over to a private company. The event may not have any return on the investment and lack the positive financial, goodwill or social capital balance needed to continue, in which case it may need to be terminated. For large public festivals, the decision to cancel can have far-reaching consequences as there may be hundreds of stakeholders.

This development has been compared to the product life cycle (PLC). However, the PLC is a descriptive model and not a prescriptive or predictive one. There are some events that have lasted thousands of years and others that are over in a day. The Olympics is an example of a product that has returned. It would, however, be almost impossible to predict their place in the product life cycle with any accuracy that has financial consequence.

2.9 The events corporation

A government's role in the development of the events industry is becoming more active with the creation of government events agencies. Some national, state, regional, city or local governments may have an *events unit* within their departments of tourism, marketing or economic development.

The planning and staging of events span a number of government departments and most industries. In response, some countries and regions have established events agencies. If the agency is moderately independent of the government and uses a private industry business methodology, it is often called an events corporation. Events corporations are allowed to derive their funds from sources other than the government. In other cases they are completely funded and controlled by the government. Overall, their role is to rationalise the events industry, ensure events contribute to the national objectives and further the strategic plan of the government. Case study 2.4 illustrates this

Case study 2.4 The events corporation in Australia

There is a strong trend around the world for the creation of such bodies. Australia began this process early with the establishment of the West Australian Events Corp followed closely by Victorian and Queensland. An illustrative example of their aims is provided by the report to establish Events New South Wales (Events NSW).

The Events Corporation would have as its objectives:
- ❏ To acquire and nurture events for Sydney that will make a major contribution to Sydney in terms of:
  - Economic benefit:
    - – direct economic benefit (e.g. immediate sales and tourism expenditure); and
    - – factors that sustain and enhance Sydney's position as a creative global city;
  - Community benefit:
    - – entertainment of a sort not possible without government support;
    - – social unity; and
    - – community spirit.
- ❏ To acquire and nurture events in other parts of New South Wales that are of significant value to their regions and the State;
- ❏ To foster the development of a consistent, master calendar for events that provides increasing value to Sydney and to New South Wales; and
- ❏ To ensure optimal leveraging of events, including working with other agencies and the private sector to achieve this result

O'Neill (2007: 3)

role of the event corporation in Australia. Similarly there are events units set up in corporations whose role is to sponsor events as well as develop and manage the internal events such as seminars and training.

The initial funding to establish these events corporations is indicative of their importance to a government. For example, in May 2008, the Dubai government announced the allocation of US$40 million for the creation of the Dubai Event Management Corporation, whose role is to assess and actively bid for events to be held in Dubai.

A summary of the roles and responsibilities of the various government and semi-government events agencies are as follows:

1 Discover and bid for suitable events as well as assist the bids of regions and cities;
2 Assess the events and their impacts;
3 Assist the events industry by sharing information on best practice;
4 Oversee the development of a major/mega-event and its opportunities;
5 Assist in the development of the competency of the events teams and the capacity of the country to host major events; and
6 Coordinate the agencies and government departments involved that are affected by major events.

It is indicative of the development of a new industry when the tasks, responsibilities, processes and risks that are distributed across many sectors are placed under one authority. The huge impact of events has been realised by governments as shown by creation of the new events corporations.

Case study 2.5 Scotland the Perfect Stage

In the document 'Scotland the Perfect Stage', the role of EventScotland is described as follows:

EventScotland aims to influence, lead, coordinate, support and bring together people and organisations in order to deliver this events strategy. EventScotland is the lead agency for public sector engagement and investment in events. This lead role is at a national strategy and policy level while other agencies will provide leadership on a geographical or event-sector basis.

EventScotland (2008: 15)

2.10 Summary

The development of the government events strategy is the ultimate proof that events and festival are recognised by governments as a serious contributor to the life and economy of their populations. With two exceptions, the strategies used in this chapter were written recently. Events development is similar to the development of any industry or company. It takes time and the internal drivers of commitment and innovation as well as the external support, or at least non-interference by governments. From the smallest community festival to the massive World Olympics, all events started the same. It was an idea of a person or group of people, who grew with time and learned from their mistakes. The role of the events strategy is to facilitate the events that have benefits to the population. Although the objectives may differ slightly, each country, state, region and city uses a version of the process outlined in this chapter.

Questions for research

1 Compare the various quotes from the events corporations with the concept of asset development. How does each of the objectives fit into three outcomes of asset investment?
2 Create a spreadsheet with decision criteria based on the Events NSW objectives.
3 Discuss the limitations of a government-based event support process to the development of public festivals.
4 List the ways that government support is similar to commercial sponsorship of an event.
5 Event strategies generally have a five-year time frame. Discuss the risks in having a long-term plan.
6 Why does the event strategy of Stoke-on-Trent place an emphasis on regeneration whereas the Abu Dhabi strategy emphasises brand development?

Recommended websites

Browse the following internet sites for interesting and informative information:

Information on event strategies, project management and risk: http://www.epms.net
Organisers of the Olympic Torch Relay, Asian Games (Relay, Queen's Baton Relay and Delhi Commonwealth Games Relay): http://www.maxxamevents.com

Selection of websites with strategy statements, event support process and documents:
NSW, Australia: http://www.eventsnsw.com.au/
Outlines the strategy for Scotland: http://www.eventscotland.org/
Saudi Tourism with their events strategy: http://www.scta.gov.sa

Suggested reading

Getz, D. 2007. *Event Studies: Theory, Research and Policy for Planned Events*. UK: Elsevier.
IOC. 2008. *Games of the XXXI Olympiad 2016 (Working Group Report)*. Lausanne, Switzerland. Available from: http://www.olympic.org/common/asp/download_report.asp?file=en_report_1317.pdf&id=13
Wunsch, U (Ed). 2008. *Facets of Contemporary Event Management*. Bonn Germany: Bad Honnef Series on Services Management.

Photo: Dimitri Tassiopoulos

3

The role of management in events management

Julia Rutherford Silvers, CSEP

Abstract

This chapter considers the nature of management and its role in the context of events by examining the typical functions of management, the scope of responsibilities assigned to event managers, and the importance of experience and leadership in events management.

After you have read this chapter you should be able to:
- ❏ recognise the role and functions of management;
- ❏ identify the skills necessary for event managers;
- ❏ discuss the importance of experience in effective management;
- ❏ describe the scope of responsibilities associated with events management;
- ❏ understand the characteristics of communication and control inherent in events management; and
- ❏ comprehend the nature of leadership and professionalism in the context of managing an event.

3.1 Introduction

Management is a business administration function required in virtually any field of endeavour. A manager plans, organises, directs, monitors and controls resources and operations in order to achieve a goal. The manager is typically responsible for finance, information, sales and marketing, research and development, organisational structure and the delegation and supervision of personnel, and strategic, tactical, and operational planning (PMI 2000). In this respect, events management is the same as general or project management in any other venture. The skills required for management include communication, organisation, negotiation, problem solving, leadership, logistics, time management and human resource management. Here too there is no difference between events management and management in general.

The difference is the context – the unique aspects of assembling the tangible components that create the intangible product of an event experience. Events have a human dimension that is distinctive in that they are heavily reliant on people in order to produce them as well as audiences that become an inherent part of the experience. Events are also unique in that they are short-lived, often one-time occurrences with strict time constraints that require exceptional organisational skills and dynamic decision making. Managing an event is an intense and complex task that requires logic, imagination and experience.

3.2 Management as a science, an art and a craft

Events management authorities Getz (1997) and Goldblatt (1990) both characterise events management as an art and a science, with Getz noting that 'all the theories and methods of management can be applied' and, in addition to generic areas of management in general, the 'functions of programming and event production … combine creativity with operational skills' (Getz, 1997: 11). Mintzberg's model of business management (2005), however, adds 'craft' to form a triangle of characteristics necessary for balanced and effective management, and identifies the potential problems when there is a flawed implementation of or an imbalance in these three aspects. This tri-part model is analogous to Gerber's model (1995) of Manager (pragmatic), Entrepreneur (dreamer), Technician (doer) used to describe the facets of small-business ownership, which is particularly pertinent in the events industry because so many events organisations are small enterprises in which the owner serves as both the company's chief executive and the event manager.

Mintzberg (1994) also examines the correlation between left brain and right brain functions with regard to management tasks and abilities, specifically in relation to the 'science' of planning and 'craft' of management. These correlate to hard and soft data – information versus judgement, and the so-called hard and soft skills – intellect versus wisdom. The interpersonal nature of soft skills will be discussed further later in this chapter. Mintzberg (1994) and Pink (2006), based upon a broad range of scientific studies, state that the function of analysis – the examination of the details – resides in the left hemisphere of the brain, and synthesis – a holistic interpretation in context – occurs in the right. In addition, Mintzberg contends that 'synthesis is the very essence of management' (1994: 37), which is, of necessity, based on analysis. As Gladwell explains, 'when experts make decisions, they don't logically and systematically compare all available options … [they] act, drawing on experience and intuition' (2005: 107) and are able to do so because they have the ability to 'synthesize the whole' (2005: 144). Thus we have a model that combines the science of logic, the art of interpretation, and the craft of wisdom through experience.

3.2.1 Science: Logical examination

Logic is recognised as a foundation of events management, so much so that logistics is one of the primary facets of various competency blueprints for industry credentialling programmes. It is also an important facet of project management, used in determining dependencies, precedence order and the sequencing of tasks. Analysis is characterised by the identification and examination of the details and hard data, often historical and measurable, surrounding an event project. This analysis is vitally important in every aspect of an event project, from feasibility studies to operational plans, especially as events are under increasing scrutiny regarding value – return on investment or return on objectives – as well as the safety and welfare of those in attendance.

The downside, however, is performing a detached or rule-based analysis without regard to the context or consequences (Mintzberg, 2005). Although the science of event management helps to foster the replication and improvement of effective processes and choices, a basis for quality management initiatives (Tricker, 2001), every event is unique even if recurring and longstanding. Choices made in one context may be wholly inappropriate in another, such as the number and deployment of security personnel at a conference when there are no high-profile speakers or controversial topics, and one when there are.

When an events manager has a comprehensive understanding of creating an intangible product that is produced in tangible form, this facilitates the logical examination of data and details in what Pink calls 'rapid sequential reasoning' (2006: 24) and the ability to make quality decisions. Conversely, a stubborn adherence to technique alone and a disconnected reliance on sterile facts and figures inhibits an events manager's ability to make decisions that provide creative solutions and capitalise on opportunities.

3.2.2 Art: Interpretive vision

The visual and performing arts are an integral part of creating an event experience (Berridge, 2007; Getz, 2007). Not surprisingly, the creativity and imagination required in these fields is what often attracts individuals to the world of events management and can provide event managers with valuable skills and inventive techniques. The ability to establish and/or interpret the vision for an event project relies on insight and the synthesis of the details of analysis into a 'big picture' concept. Such aesthetic and strategic perspectives are required from event inception through completion; they foster ingenuity in all management processes.

The problem with an over-reliance on the creative facet of management is that it can result in the pursuit of unrealistic aspirations. When creative vision is not tempered with reality, it often fails to meet the functional and economic objectives of an event project, and/or the needs of those working on and attending the event. This is reflected in the naïve segregation (division of labour) of business administration, design and technical expertise, when in fact all three are required to properly interpret and create the event experience desired.

Innovative thinking and a holistic approach to event design and management provides the comprehensive synthesis an event manager should strive for when conceptualising, planning and producing an event project. However, transforming inventiveness and novelty into an engaging experience for event goers can be a challenge for even the most experienced events designers and managers. Events must be legible and practical in order to be effective and enjoyable, which requires more than a visionary perspective alone.

3.2.3 Craft: Practical wisdom

Although facts and figures may not lie, they rarely tell the whole story. Standard techniques and tactics may be effective but there are always situational nuances that affect their applicability and viability. Keeping a clear focus on the vision for an event helps guide decision making, yet it must be flexible enough to adapt it to the constant variables affecting an event project. This is where the depth and breadth of experience or 'craft' comes in. Expertise is only gained through experience – finding out what works, and works best, through encounters with similar situations – what some refer to as lessons learned or the 'school of hard knocks'.

Experience is a powerful source of practical wisdom, but its drawback can be the formation of an inflexible 'we've always done it this way' mindset resulting in unyielding repetition. Years of experience, and often tradition, can block awareness and consideration of innovative solutions or opportunities that could be revealed through analytical and visionary inputs. Heuristics – rule-of-thumb or experiential (tacit) knowledge – is certainly a valuable commodity in events management, yet must be judiciously employed in accordance with the uniqueness of the circumstances rather than unconditional reliance on the past.

Management, as a practice, requires practice. Mintzberg cautions us not to confuse knowledge with wisdom, noting that the practical wisdom gained through experience, often the foundation of intuition, requires an 'intimate knowledge of the subject … sometimes [taking] years to develop' (1994: 325). Problem solving and decision making are certainly enhanced when hard data and creative insights are carefully filtered through the lens of experience, but the craft of experience needs to be appropriately balanced with the science of logic and the art of imagination in order to prevent short-sighted or tradition-based inflexibility.

3.3 Body of knowledge and body of experience

It is estimated that more than a billion (1 000 million) planned events occur around the world each year (MPI, 2008; Silvers, 2008; Silvers & Nelson, 2005) ranging from small celebrations such as weddings to mega-events such as the Olympic Games. Hundreds of thousands of people are involved in creating and staging these events and thousands of millions of people attend them. And planned events have been occurring for thousands of years. However, events management has yet to achieve status as a true profession because it has not taken the steps necessary for legitimacy, one of which is the establishment of an acknowledged industry-wide body of knowledge that has captured and codified all that experiential knowledge, although initiatives around the world are attempting to do so.

As previously discussed, experience is the foundation of intuition, referred to by Gladwell as 'rapid cognition' (2005: 143), and the ability to make good management decisions. Managers devise strategies and formulate plans, and make decisions based upon the analysis of hard data and creative insight. However, ad hoc planning and decision making are often necessary in events management because, as Silvers notes, 'it is all about change management … there are ALWAYS changes … things NEVER go exactly as planned' (2008: 33). It is primarily experience that provides the event manager with the agility and flexibility to exercise good judgement in the emergent situations that invariably occur.

Capturing the tacit knowledge of experience is critical to the ability to transfer this knowledge in an efficient and consistent manner through formal education and training systems instead of by trial and error or one-on-one apprenticeships (Abbott, 1988; Freidson, 1986). However, internships and the school of hard knocks are valid, even important, facets of learning events management. For students the message is that academic credentials alone do not qualify or fully prepare one to manage events. For practitioners the message is that one's body of experience is unarguably valuable yet it can be enriched by the study of the theoretical foundations to be found in a body of knowledge. Quality management, and correspondingly a quality education in management, may be 'theory led' but it is 'practice driven' (Mintzberg, 2005: 187).

3.3.1 A brief overview of the EMBOK and its applications

Body of knowledge initiatives range from competency outlines for industry certification credentials to 'best practice' models and glossaries such as the Convention Industry Council's Accepted Practices Exchange (APEX) programme (http://www.conventionindustry.org) to occupational standards devised by national skills authorities in various countries including the International Event Management Standard (IEMS) devised by the Canadian Tourism Human Resource Council (http://www.cthrc.ca). These initiatives use job analysis surveys, academic and practitioner experts, project teams and widespread validation activities in their endeavours to capture and structure the knowledge associated with the events management industry.

Bringing all this together into a conceptual framework has been the focus of the Event Management Body of Knowledge (EMBOK) Project and the International EMBOK Executive (Getz, 2007; Silvers, 2004b, 2005; Silvers et al., 2006). The International EMBOK Model includes a temporal dimension (phases), a tactical dimension (processes), a normative dimension (core values) and a functional dimension (domains). The five domains encompass the 35 categories listed below (listed alphabetically to eliminate any suggestion of implied hierarchy or sequential application), which provides a useful framework for analysis in a variety of contexts.

❑ *Administration.* This is the management of finances, human resources, information, procurement, stakeholders, systems and time.
❑ *Design.* This is the management of content, entertainment, environment, food and beverage, production elements, programming and theme.
❑ *Marketing.* This is the management of marketing plans, materials, merchandise, promotions, public relations, sales and sponsorships.
❑ *Operations.* This is the management of attendees, communications, infrastructure, logistics, participants, the site, and technical or equipment requirements.
❑ *Risk.* This is the management of compliance requirements, decision making, emergencies, health and safety, insurance, legal issues and documents, and security.

The EMBOK framework offers a structural arrangement that allows the division of knowledge and heuristics into recognisable groupings that facilitate the collection and aggregation of data, as well as illustrate the full scope of responsibilities assigned to events organisers. In this vein, it supports a disciplined and comprehensive analysis of the needs, opportunities and challenges associated with an event project. The EMBOK framework may also suggest areas of specialisation for practitioners, and provide an agenda for curriculum development for academic programmes and professional development programming created by industry associations to meet the lifelong learning needs of their constituencies. It may also provide competency guidance that may enhance credentialling programmes, training initiatives, and hiring and advancement criteria.

3.3.2 Management is defined by its context

Although the EMBOK can serve as a framework for all types of events, it cannot serve as a guarantee that an expert practitioner in one type of event genre, or in one domain, can claim expertise in another. Events management encompasses a broad range of event genre or types (to be discussed further in part 7), each type ranging widely in scope and nature. It also encompasses and relies upon the integration of concepts from many other disciplines and fields (Getz, 2007). Therefore, a good manager in one context – an industry, an events sector or a specific discipline – does not necessarily have the performance skills in a different context.

As noted at the beginning of this chapter, there are typical functions a manager performs and typical managerial skills one must have. The skills required for events management, as in any management context, encompass organisational, resource management (time, money, materials, space, information and personnel), interpersonal, technological, mathematical, decision-making and strategic-thinking skills. Numerous studies highlight communication skills (speaking, reading and writing) as a priority in the events field (e.g. Nelson, 2004; Nelson, Silvers & Park, 2005; Zevin, 2003), as well as creativity and the ability to multitask, to endure high pressure, and to work long and non-traditional hours, and the flexibility to adapt to rapidly changing needs in a project management style (Nelson, 2004; Silvers & Nelson, 2005).

The functions required within events management typically conform to the five domains of the EMBOK framework but their inclusion, emphasis and specific techniques depend upon the type, scope and nature of the event project – the specific context. One may adopt the theories and techniques from other contexts because they include many of the same functions, but not necessarily in the same form. One may also apply theory and techniques from other contexts, but these must be transposed through proper adaptation. Mintzberg contends that wisdom does not come from formulas or techniques; it comes from adapting them to the unique situations that occur, noting that 'technique applied with nuance by people immersed in a situation can be very powerful' (2005: 39).

Management is a multifaceted process that varies in application according to its context. It requires both a generic and a specific skill set that also varies according to context, yet always focuses on communication, attention to detail and the ability to motivate others. A planned event is first and foremost a social endeavour, bringing people together for a specific time, in a specific place, for a specific purpose. Time, place and purpose are the logistical facets to be managed; it is the human dimension that gives a planned event that social character and its unique context requiring the proper adoption and adaptation of management theories and techniques.

3.4 Management as structure rather than power

A manager is the individual who is in charge – of an enterprise, a division, a project or an event. He or she has the authority and responsibility to direct the planning and oversee the implementation of those plans. As such, this person has the power to make decisions regarding form, function, features and focus, as well as power over those who will participate in their development and execution. However, the event manager, whether event owner or under the auspices of an internal or external client, does this within an organised coalition of people, which requires some form of organisational structure.

Organisational structures and management styles vary widely and are often based upon the nature, scope and complexity of the specific endeavour. Some organisational structures are more hierarchical than egalitarian, some more bureaucratic than entrepreneurial, and some more centralised than dispersed. The larger the scope and complexity of an event project, the more likely a formalised chain of command will be employed. The smaller or less complex the event is, the more likely an informal structure of authority will be used. However, most events organisations tend toward some degree of an 'adhocracy' or 'project structure' (Mintzberg, 1994: 399, 408) in which formal authority is more ambiguous and collaborative, rather than a strict bureaucracy. Yet it must be clearly understood that the event manager always retains accountability even if certain levels of authority are delegated throughout the organisation, therefore the organisational structure must incorporate and illustrate reporting relationships. Collins (2001) recommends the creation of a culture of discipline that encompasses both freedom and responsibility within a framework of appropriate boundaries.

Management styles can range from democratic to autocratic to laissez-faire (Goldblatt, 2002b) with varying degrees within those categories spanning the extremes of tyrannical expert to apathetic amateur (or domineering amateur to ineffectual expert). Here again, these management styles are often based upon the needs and nature of the event being produced, although they are sometimes strongly influenced by the personality of the person instead of the project. As with the organisational structure, a balanced management style of collaboration and control typically provides optimal results.

3.4.1 Change, control, connection, and other constants

In any management context, and especially in events management, the adage that *the only constant is change* should be recognised as fundamental. The very nature of events requires rapid, high-quality decision making because the development and delivery of this product is subject to continual adjustment as problems and opportunities emerge, often with an urgency not found in other ventures. Traditional command and control must give way to a network of distributed intelligence with the event manager as the electrical current that powers that network.

Many conventional organisational structures include a chain of command, either vertical (top down or bottom up) or horizontal (linear phase or chain). These may be useful in delineating a division of labour or committee structure; however, a hub or web configuration, as shown in figure 3.1, best reflects the communication network most often beneficial to events management, although this must be adapted to the hierarchical needs of large-scope or highly complex endeavours. An interconnected network facilitates the collaborative effort often referred to as 'participatory management' in which those doing the tasks – the ones who have the tacit and current knowledge – are active participants in the decision making.

The hub network is a centralised network without explicit or implicit levels of authority or importance except that it clearly defines the event manager as the final decision maker. The web network, on the other hand, does not conspicuously separate the event manager as the final authority or the only communication conduit; rather, it requires the event manager to be involved in all aspects as a semi-equal partner in the choices made. This aligns with Hunsaker and Alessandra's advice that managers 'maintain a consultative atmosphere' (1980:

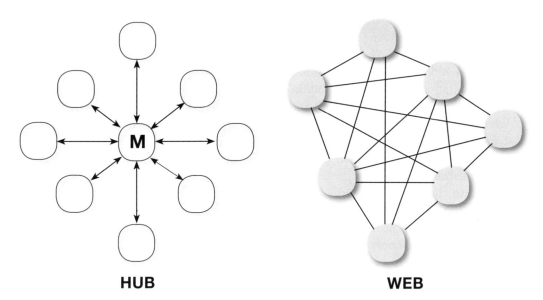

HUB

WEB

Figure 3.1 Hub and web organisational structures
Sources: Adapted from Mintzberg (2005); Silvers (2008)

119) and relies on having good people and letting them use their creativity, agility and best judgement, within, of course, a framework of guidelines and procedures that control those aspects that are critical, such as legal or safety standards.

The web structure also reflects the nature of 'management by walking around' and allows the event manager to take advantage of those 'in the field' and their experience as well as facilitates robust communications and effective decision making. Collins notes that good decisions begin with the 'brutal facts', which can only be ascertained when the organisational structure and culture encourages truth telling (2001: 74), and Silvers (2008) emphasises the need to decriminalise risk messages (e.g. brutal facts) so that accurate and timely identification of problems (or opportunities) are encouraged. Thus, some form of the web format is most likely to create the distributed intelligence network so vital to the safety and success of an event.

The communication network is as important to how an organisation will or should ultimately be structured as any other factor. Effective communication requires that the network touches each individual in the organisation (Leavitt, 1951), and the structure must incorporate how quickly and to whom information must be transmitted. Larger organisations naturally adopt a more departmentalised hierarchy, which requires less information transmission among its parts due to the autonomy granted each department (Simon, 1960). Fayol's (1949) Unity of Command principle contends that individuals should only be responsible to and receive instructions from one superior in order to limit confusion and frustration. Current practice in emergency management suggests that no more than seven subordinates at each hierarchical level provide the optimum for an effective communication network.

The number of communication channels in the network depends on a balance between the line of authority and the need for speed. Event managers typically rely on oral communication due to its efficiency and effectiveness; however, this should be supported by proper documentation to ensure verification and provide evidence. Although an authoritarian chain of command and communication is clearly vital in an emergency situation, autocratic management and message styles stifle creativity and stop important communication due to fear (Collins & Porras, 1994).

3.4.2 The event organisation as a social system

'Organizations are systems of inter-dependent human beings' (Pugh, 1971: 213). An organisation is a social system encompassing a community of individuals with common interests, goals and values, and shared connections. This is particularly pertinent to event organisations due to their typically strong reliance on volunteers and the constituency nature of their audiences. Managing within social systems requires an understanding of human needs, interpersonal relations and politics, and the motivations that drive the organisation as well as the individual. A society needs a set of agreed-upon boundaries including accountability and predictable behaviour among its members (March & Simon, 1958), but the individual members need the freedom to use their skills and pursue their objectives while contributing to the aims of the organisation (see table 3.1).

Management is a form of governance – the framework of authority for an

Table 3.1 Human needs and volunteer motivations

Needs	Motivations
To be accepted	To make a difference
To be part of a community	To use or improve their skills
To be respected	To acquire new skills
To be appreciated	To be with friends or make new ones
To be independent	To have a challenge
To be recognised for achievements	To express their support

Sources: Getz (2007); Herzberg (1966); Maslow (1943); Silvers (2004c)

organisation; there are certain administrative rules and procedures that are necessary, and managers in an organisation are as subject to these constraints as those being managed. However, the umbrella of governance must be adapted by the event manager in such a way that the both social order (a place for everyone and everyone in his place) and esprit de corps (unity and harmony among personnel) may be achieved (Fayol, 1949). Compliance with the rules and regulations comes from understanding rather than enforcement (Hunsaker & Alessandra, 1980), and the system must be able to respond to the situation (Simon, 1960).

Management cannot exist without teamwork (i.e. sustained cooperation) and teamwork cannot exist without a team. Buchholz and Roth (1987) cite empowered interdependency and shared responsibility as critical facets for developing a high-performance team. They contend that managers should focus their energies on the collaborative linkage of roles, tasks and purpose, which facilitates a synergy wherein the whole (the team) becomes greater than the sum of its parts (the individuals). And it is this synergy – establishing mutually agreed-upon expectations and focusing collective efforts – which transitions people from groups of individuals into teams.

The challenge specific to events management is the short-term or temporary nature of the employment of paid or volunteer personnel (Van der Wagen & Carlos, 2005). The familiar forming-storming-norming-performing-adjourning model of team development (Tuckman, 1965) must be accelerated in the context of event organisations that utilise volunteers and transitory workers. The event manager must create a strong organisational structure that can accommodate limited responsibility and short-term assignments, as well as an organisational culture that inspires commitment to the event's objectives and rapidly facilitates relationships building within a diverse workforce (Van der Wagen & Carlos, 2005).

3.5 Management, leadership, and professionalism

Management, at its core, is simply good decision making combined with respectful leadership and professionalism. Managers are decision makers and problem solvers. Leaders are vision guides and influential motivators. Professionals are practitioners committed to attaining and maintaining the highest standards of competency in their field. It is the fusion of these three facets that produces great managers. Those seeking to become great event managers require expertise in both the hard skills associated with planning and analysis and

Table 3.2 Soft skills necessary for great event managers

Active listening	Fairness
Ability to teach	Flexibility
Accountability	Integrity
Adaptability	Leadership
Ambition (for the project, not for self)	Negotiation
	Motivation
Diplomacy and tact	Passion and
Collaboration	compassion
Communication	Reliability
Courage	Respect for others
Empathy	Sincerity
Confidence without	Team builder
arrogance	Tolerance
Consistency	Willingness to learn
Creativity	

Sources: Goldblatt (2002b); Nelson (2004); Silvers & Nelson (2005)

the soft skills associated with interpersonal relations, as shown in table 3.2.

Great event managers can be found and should be developed throughout an event organisation, at every level of hierarchy or realm of responsibility. Hierarchies are established whenever duties and responsibilities are delegated to capable individuals, and within that framework 'leaders arise in context' (Mintzberg, 2005: 334). An event organisation or event manager should seek out or identify those individuals with entrepreneurial instincts who demonstrate the passion to achieve and a willingness to take risks (within acceptable parameters) in order to accomplish goals (Collins & Porras, 1994; Goldblatt & Supovitz, 1999). And managers and managers-to-be at all levels should be encouraged to expand their knowledge and improve their skills throughout their career endeavours.

3.5.1 Managers – decision makers

To summarise the advice given in dozens of popular books on management, a manager's job is determining what needs to be done, finding good people who are willing and able to do the work, getting everyone pointed in the right direction, and then getting out of their way. This requires making good decisions every step of the way. Delegation, however, does not mean abdication – the manager still retains accountability. Good decision making is about not only the most effective ways to make decisions, but also about taking responsibility for their consequences.

Event organisers typically make anywhere from 30 000 to 300 000 decisions regarding an event project depending upon the scope and nature of the event (Silvers, 2006). These decisions range from making choices to solving problems. Decision making typically falls into four categories: *yes/no* – single option; *which* – two or more alternatives; *degree* – value-based choices; and *if/then* – threshold or rule-based decisions (Silvers, 2009a; Yates, 2003). The decision methods, shown in table 3.3, specify how and by whom decisions will be made. Although event m anagers often have latitude in making their decisions, it is important to specify selection method and criteria in order to justify the decisions

Table 3.3 Decision-making methods

Autocratic	Majority or plurality vote
Consensus	Priority based
Consultation	Random draw
Cost/benefit analysis	Rating scale
Delegation	Rule based
Elimination	Scoring system
Logistics based	Threshold based
Negotiation	Time based

Sources: Silvers (2008, 2009a); Yates (2003)

made, as well as prevent unsanctioned decision making by those without authority.

Event managers should be both predictive and reactive regarding problem solving and decision making. One must be able to identify problems in order to make decisions regarding solving them, and the earlier these problems can be identified, the easier it will be to devise effective solutions. Reactive event managers are able to calmly and quickly analyse a situation or occurrence, and act decisively when a problem comes up. Although able to assess the root cause of the problem, they do not become obsessed with the symptoms. Predictive event managers strive to identify potential problems and analyse the reasons they occur and their importance within the overall 'big picture' of the event and the event organisation. They are able to see patterns or conditions that could lead to problems, and implement procedures to eliminate or reduce their possibility or gravity, thus reducing the need to be reactive. Both proactive and reactive problem solving require strong reasoning skills and innovative thinking.

3.5.2 Leaders – motivators

Pugh defines leadership as 'a social process rather than a personality trait' (1971: 213), which recognises the human interactions necessary in team building and teamwork. Leadership revolves around locus of control: who is in control and how they exercise it. Leaders change their viewpoint from 'I am in charge' to 'I am responsible' and not only allow but encourage subordinates to take control over their respective areas of responsibility, under varying levels of supervision as appropriate. Collins and Porras refer to this as 'ideological control and operational autonomy' (1994: 137). They contend that this encourages individual initiative and takes advantage of entrepreneurial instincts that could improve both the organisation and its potential for success.

The quality most often identified with leadership is the ability to motivate people. Leaders 'catalyze commitment to and vigorous pursuit of a clear and compelling vision, stimulating higher performance standards' (Collins, 2001: 20). They see themselves as servant leaders rather than superstars, preferring to apportion credit to the members of their team, and making that clear to their team members. They empower their people as well as serve as their role model. They also recognise the motives of their team members (review table 3.1) and strive to meet their needs as well as be worthy of their trust.

Event managers are often compared to symphony conductors – assembling the orchestra, selecting and interpreting the musical score, and directing the musicians' performance according to that interpretation. Yet this analogy is incomplete because event managers, as leaders, often help their 'musicians' learn how to play their instruments (or play them better). Leaders mentor their co-workers or subordinates at every level; they seek to draw out the skills, talents and initiative of the individual, preparing them for their own leadership roles. Great leaders practise succession planning through competency building, coaching and guiding so that every member of the team has the ability to take on increasing levels of responsibility – even the event manager's job, if necessary, in an emergency.

3.5.3 Professionals – lifelong learners

A professional is often defined as someone who has specialised skills and knowledge that others do not have. This specialised knowledge for events management professionals includes the recognition of the full scope, complexity and responsibilities associated with events. This body of knowledge, as illustrated in the EMBOK, is vast and sometimes overwhelming, and it is expanding at an exponential rate as new tools, technology, tactics and regulatory requirements emerge on an almost daily basis. As with any profession, event managers must keep up with these advancements and continually improve their skills. Event organisations must do the same.

Event managers must become lifelong learners by pursuing continuing education, reading books and trade publications, and participating in industry associations. They should seek out information from other professionals and their suppliers, research trends and best practices from around the world, and pursue credentials that verify their competency. Event organisations must become learning organisations by providing training and encouraging individual lifelong learning activities that support personal growth. They need to establish an atmosphere that makes it safe to be creative, that fosters discussion and dialogue that challenges the status quo, and that is committed to capturing and benefiting from lessons learned, both pleasant and painful (Senge, 1990).

Case study 3.3 Ten Ugly Men Festival

The Ten Ugly Men Festival is a one-day community beer, food, music and sports event organised by a group of ten college friends, now a not-for-profit organisation, that started it as way to have fun, meet eligible women and raise money for charity. Increasing from a crowd of 200 in 1990 to more than 7 000 in 2005, the festival grew into one of the largest summer charity events in Rochester, New York. The 2005 festival, however, included an incident that exposed the lack of experience and professionalism on the part of the organisers, even after 15 years of producing the event. A 22-year-old woman was trapped under and then run over by a shuttle bus as she attempted to board it at the close of the event, and suffered severe injuries with lifelong medical implications.

In the discovery process of the subsequent legal action, the organisers admitted that they had no experience in setting up the shuttle service or its loading area, even though the festival had provided a free shuttle service from two remote parking locations for a number of years (the service had previously been donated and coordinated by the service provider). They had not consulted anyone on the positioning and set-up of the loading area, nor did they have any historical records with which to make any reasonable estimates on the travel demand, especially at the close of the event. There was no evidence that the organisers belonged to any industry organisations, read industry publications, had pursued educational activities regarding festival production or best practices, or had conducted a formal risk assessment or post-event debriefings from which they could learn and improve their event management practices.

Source: http://www.redorbit.com/news/oddities/73862/10_ugly_men_fest_raises_cash_for_charity/; https://www.naz.edu/news/story.cfm?pressID=770

3.6 Summary

Events are fun, exciting and dynamic, and managing them is creatively and emotionally rewarding. Nevertheless, it is imperative that events management be approached with a businesslike perspective – one that recognises the full range of responsibilities as well as their economic, social, environmental and cultural impacts. Events management utilises the traditional theories, tools and techniques found in any business endeavour, but adapts them to the unique context of creating and producing the intangible product of an experience. A manager, in any context, makes decisions based on logic, imagination and experience, avoiding the dispassion of the scientist, the conceit of the artist and the hubris of the craftsman while using the collective experience of those who bring valuable skills and knowledge earned first hand.

Events are inherently temporary – they occur within a short span of time even though their planning may involve months or years of work. They typically rely on large numbers of people and providers that form a temporary organisation, which must have a recognisable and effective structure within which to operate properly.

Public events often start small and grow, allowing an organisation to retain a workforce constituency and develop from an informal to a fully integrated structure of participatory management. Small or one-time events may be ad hoc in nature, yet they may need to delineate roles and responsibilities in an autocratic manner in order to clearly identify lines and levels of authority. However, the larger and more complex the event, the more defined and rigorous an organisational structure needs to be.

Event managers need to understand and fully embrace the social nature of an event organisation, as well as cultivate the leadership skills and attitudes in themselves and those they manage. They need to continually develop their decision-making abilities as well, increasing their personal and external resources by expanding their own knowledge base and extending their network of communication within the organisation. Events have a pulse – their nature as an experience has a rhythm and a progression, their organisations are pulsating in scope and intensity, and their people are the lifeblood that runs through them. And event managers and their managerial approach are at the heart of it all.

Questions for research

1 What are the strengths and weaknesses of the science, the art and the craft of events management?
2 What theories and techniques of traditional business management can be transposed into events management, and how?
3 In what ways can the EMBOK framework be used by an event manager?
4 Why would a manager from another discipline not be automatically qualified to be an event manager?
5 How does the size and complexity of an event affect the ways in which its organisational structure should be set up?
6 What is the difference between leadership and control?

Recommended websites

Browse the following internet sites for interesting and informative information:

APEX site map: http://www.conventionindustry.org/apex
Free Management Library: http://www.managementhelp.org/
MindTools™: http://www.mindtools.com/
SkyMark Management Resources: http://www.skymark.com/resources/refhome.asp
The EMBOK Project: http://www.juliasilvers.com/embok.htm

Suggested reading

Bowdin, GAJ, Allen, J, O'Toole, W, Harris, R & McDonnell, I. 2006. *Events Management*, 2nd ed. Oxford: Butterworth-Heinemann.

Gerber, ME. 1995. *The E-Myth Revisited: Why Small Businesses Don't Work and What To Do About It.* New York: HarperCollins Publishers, Inc.

Silvers, JR. 2008. *Risk Management for Meetings and Events.* Oxford: Butterworth-Heinemann.

Van der Wagen, L & Carlos, BR. 2005. *Event Management for Tourism, Cultural, Business, and Sporting Events.* Upper Saddle River, NJ: Pearson Education, Inc.

PART II
Events and administration

Photo: Dimitri Tassiopoulos

Photo: Dimitri Tassiopoulos

Photo: Gavin Young

Photo: World Travel Market

Photo: EIBTM

4 Events role players

Dimitri Tassiopoulos

Abstract

This chapter focuses on the various events role players and intends to equip the reader with the necessary knowledge to identify the various service and product clients, and providers when organising an event.

Chapter objectives

After you have read this chapter you should be able to:

- ❑ understand the events triangle (the events with its management and performers, the audience and sponsors);
- ❑ distinguish between the various suppliers and buyers of events;
- ❑ show that you have a basic knowledge of the agencies, intermediaries and other important organisations (domestic and international) involved in events.

4.1 Introduction

The events industry is highly complex, comprising a multiplicity of buyer and supplier organisational role players, sponsors and events audiences. For many events organisers – the so-called 'buyers' – the organisation of events is only part of their function. On the other hand, the 'suppliers' include the providers of venues, facilities, destinations and accommodation; transport companies; agencies; and specialist contractors. The suppliers and buyers are linked together and supported by national and international associations and bodies, the trade press and educational institutions, each making a contribution to this industry.

4.2 The events triangle

No event takes place in isolation and each involves a set of interdependent and interacting elements within a system: the event product with its event participants, the audience or customer, and the sponsors. Events benefit from administrative support, planning and marketing, indicating a financial link between the event, its audience and its sponsors. This interdependent relationship is illustrated in figure 4.1.

Schaaf (1995) identifies three underlying principles that interact in the event triangle model:

- ❑ Events management requires sponsors for financial subsidy and publicity.
- ❑ Events performers solicit compensation for their time and talents.
- ❑ Sponsors need events for promotional exposure and opportunities in their target market.

The event attendee audience, according to Schaaf (1995), can have a physical presence at the event venues or an electronic presence via radio and television listener- or viewership, respectively. The event audience can also be represented through the print media such as newspapers, magazines and journals. Sponsorships provide companies access to a variety of promotional packages, including all forms of media advertising, licensing rights, event promotions featuring giveaways, sampling, signage, billboards, VIP receptions and merchandising sales opportunities (Schaaf, 1995).

The organisation of an event and the event itself provide a vehicle for attaining certain goals and have the task of creating certain outcomes such as economic and social benefits. These outcomes can include unintended and negative impacts, which need to be identified through research (Getz, 1997). The financial success of events lies within the framework of this triangle. Each event, performer, audience and sponsor has goals that are satisfied by the other groups. If events maintain their audience, sponsors invest

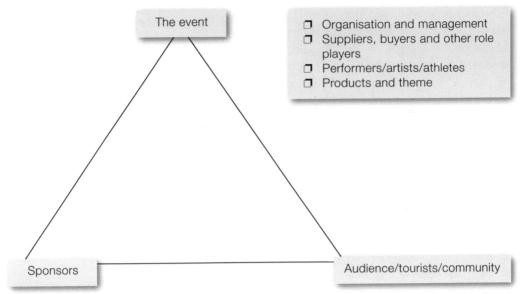

The event
- Organisation and management
- Suppliers, buyers and other role players
- Performers/artists/athletes
- Products and theme

Sponsors

Audience/tourists/community

Figure 4.1 Diagrammatic representation of key events role players
Source: Adapted from Schaaf (1995)

billions to communicate through them (Schaaf, 1995). Furthermore, acceptable economic, environmental, social, as well as marketing returns on investment (ROI) are increasingly expected by the various role players involved with the staging of the event, whether they are government, business, host destinations, host communities or even the event attendees.

In order to gain community support, attract grants and sponsorships, and achieve sustainability, events need to successfully meet a multiplicity of goals. Events are produced by organisations for a variety of reasons. Governments and non-profit-making and community organisations are producing festivals to an ever-increasing extent. Increasingly, profit-motivated organisations are organising events for clients who require economic development through events tourism, such as tourism agencies, resorts and facility managers. Getz (1997) provides a three-sector classification of events:

- *Private, for-profit organisations*
  - Organisations produce events for profit under contract or individually.
  - Corporations create events for marketing and sales purposes.
  - Hotels, resorts and facilities use events as attractions and image makers.
- *Non-profit-making or voluntary*
  - Charities and causes use events to attract revenue and support.
  - Community-based societies and informal groups stage events for multiple community benefits.
- *Government agencies or public–private groups*
  - Leisure and social agencies organise events to foster sports, health or social integration.
  - Economic development and tourism agencies stage events to create employment and income.
  - Arts and cultural agencies stage events to foster appreciation and participation.

Entrepreneurs who produce events set out to generate a profit, normally through admission charges, merchandising, sponsorship, media revenue and rental of service to participants. Historically, such producers tend to be from meeting, planning, hospitality, entertainment and tourism backgrounds. In established events markets, events entrepreneurs compete or bid directly for clients in order to produce many events. Although an event might not be required to make a profit, the event organiser's business has to do so. Corporations that sponsor events are another business entity that create or obtain a share in sales and general marketing activities.

Sponsors are organisations or companies which provide money, services or any other support to events and events organisations in return for specific benefits. Many sponsorship agreements are of a short-term nature, although longer-term relations are desirable. It is usually only with longer-term agreements that a true partnership can evolve, as the partners get to know and understand their mutual goals without sacrificing their individual principles (Getz, 1997).

Clients and audiences may also be called *tourists, guests, customers* and *visitors* – these are the customers who have purchased the events service. A marketing orientation requires that we think of them as having paid a price for a product or a service delivered. Events attendance is predominantly purchased or undertaken by the host destination's residents, with travellers forming an important segment of the events visitor market. In some cases, travellers from outside the host destination may form the larger group at certain planned events such as meetings (Getz, 1997).

4.3 The events suppliers and events buyers

As is common in other industries, the events sector is comprised of 'buyers' and 'suppliers'. For the purpose of this chapter, *suppliers* and *buyers* refer to those role players who play an intimate role in researching and producing events for consumption by an audience. In the case of the meetings industry, the buyers are the meeting organisers and planners who buy or hire venues and related services in order to stage their events.

4.3.1 The buyers

Within the meetings industry, writers such as Rogers (1998) refer to two broad types of buyer: *corporate* and *association*. *Government buyers* are a further category of buyer. All three types of buyer may employ the services of various agencies to assist in the staging of their events.

The corporate buyer

Shock and Stefanelli (1992) refer alternatively to the corporate buyer as the business market. They point out that this market can be divided into three segments: *shallow, mid-level* and *deep:*

❑ The *shallow* segment refers to low-budget events with short lead times. For instance, a caterer (the supplier) might only be required to deliver a few deli platters and salads within a day to a local tourism workshop event organised by a local tourism organisation (the buyer). Clients within this segment shop around for the best price. They are, however, conscious of quality and service, but they are normally on a limited budget and cannot afford the best. The shallow client of today can become a potential good (mid- or deep-level) buyer of the future.

- ❐ The *mid-level* segment is usually planned well in advance. Price is important; clients will not quibble over small amounts of money. It is important that the events are memorable and consistent with the status of the executives in the business community. This segment can quickly lead to repeat business, as events can become a regular occurrence. An events organiser who provides excellent value will be the favoured events provider for the clients. Business executives are trained to shop around for the best value, but will remain loyal when it comes to their personal pleasures and benefits.

- ❐ The *deep* segment involves upmarket events that are expensive and where cost is a secondary consideration. While most large meeting events tend to move around a country, many tend to patronise the same destinations on a regularly scheduled basis. Even though most large events clients are booked years in advance, the events organiser should be prepared to serve at short notice, as the loyal client expects this.

Rogers (1998) describes corporate buyers as events organisers who work for corporations which are established primarily to generate an income and provide a financial return for their owners. These can be manufacturing or service organisations and are found in all sectors of industry.

Very few organisations have dedicated events management departments. In fact, during a recession, corporations often opt to make savings by closing down or downsizing their events management departments and outsourcing this function to events organising agencies. In some cases, employees from former events management departments are re-employed on a freelance basis.

Staff involvement in organising events varies widely. On the one hand their function may be to collate information on potential events venues, while on the other they may be given complete responsibility for planning and running an event. Rogers (1998) estimates that about 80% of corporate organisers have received little training in events planning and organising; such activities account for just part of their overall responsibilities.

Identifying the corporate buyer is therefore a major challenge for organisations wishing to market and promote their facilities and services to these role players. The transient role of such corporate events organisers makes it difficult to provide an effective education and training framework, to develop their expertise and increase their professionalism. The lack of such support systems hinders proper recognition being given to the role of the corporate events organiser as a component of an organisation's communication strategy.

Corporate events vary in size and type; Rogers (1998) lists them as:

- ❐ annual general meetings, board meetings;
- ❐ exhibitions;
- ❐ incentive travel events;
- ❐ product launches;
- ❐ team-building events;
- ❐ technical and sales conferences; and
- ❐ training courses and seminars.

The majority of corporate events are held in hotels. Some may take place in purpose-built events venues; however, few corporate events are attracted to civic venues and town halls because these could be perceived as staid and simple. The same may be said of academic venues, unless these comprise dedicated meeting and events venues with high-quality facilities.

Corporate events usually have a relatively short lead time in contrast to association events, with just a few weeks or months in which to plan and stage them. The majority of corporate events usually involve small numbers of no more than 100 delegates. Frequently delegate participation in such events is not voluntary as participation is part of daily operations. The budget for corporate events, expressed in terms of expenditure per delegate, is usually higher than many association events, as the organisation – and not the individual delegate – pays for the delegates' attendance.

Corporate events are now more intensive business-related events than was the case in the past when they were viewed as a 'getaway'. Return on investment (ROI) is a catch phrase across the events industry, emphasising the need to measure the effectiveness of all investments in all activities – including those made in an organisation's workforce. Despite this, research by Rogers (1998) shows that around one-third of corporate events organisers do not evaluate their events after they have taken place. This calls into question the professionalism of the organisers and the organisations' investment in them as staff.

The association buyer

Association events organisers or 'buyers' represent a wide range of organisations that include:

- ❏ voluntary associations and societies (to further interests or hobbies, e.g. Rotary International);
- ❏ trade unions;
- ❏ religious organisations;
- ❏ professional and trade associations;
- ❏ political parties;
- ❏ charities; and
- ❏ civic groups.

Shock and Stefanelli (1992) refer to this market as the SMERF market, SMERF being an acronym for the social, military, education, religious and fraternal markets, which is usually considered to be a cost-conscience market. This market is alternatively referred to as the 'grunt' events market which, according to *Webster's New World College Dictionary* (2009), owes its origins to colloquialism referring to US infantry personnel (also known as *grunts*) in the Vietnam war, but which now can also be used to refer to those events markets that include executing low-prestige projects involving routine activities for minimal or no reward.

One of the largest segments of this market is the fraternal market, which is made up of organisations such as Rotary International, Lions, Round Table and other similar organisations. These represent a good, steady source of business because they meet at the same location each month and do not move around.

The military segment also represents a prime source of steady business, especially for those cities that have major military bases that house their armed forces (army, air force and/or navy), or even organised paramilitary forces such as the police, constabulary, militia or guards. There are many awards, parades and/or armed-forces days (and social-lifecycle events for the personnel and their families) to commemorate or celebrate. Most local hotels can expect to attract their fair share of this market segment as they represent a welcome change of pace, and offer more space for the staging of such events.

The education segment generates a steady amount of revenue as there are many ongoing seminars, symposia and other events. There are also many high-school functions.

The SMERF market is not as profitable as the corporate market; however, events organisers can use this market to fill their events calendar during the off-peak events season by scheduling them between more lucrative events. Many of the attendees probably are also bona fide corporate clients and their exposure to the events service may convince them to use the same services for corporate events.

The SMERF market is similar to the corporate market in terms of the types of events required. These markets have meetings and educational functions, and attend sponsor training sessions.

Few association events are established mainly to generate a financial return as they are of a non-profit-making nature and exist to provide a service to their members and the community. Association events must, however, be run professionally because often they are in the public domain through media exposure. While association organisations themselves are non-profit making, the planned events must cover their costs and, in some cases, generate a profit which is used in the administrative and promotional costs of planning and organising future events (Rogers, 1998).

Delegates attending association events usually share a number of common characteristics:

❐ They usually choose to attend the events voluntarily.
❐ The accommodation range varies from bed-and-breakfast establishments to five-star hotels.

❐ They often have to pay their own expenses, which require the events organiser to keep the costs as low as possible.
❐ The number of delegates attending a major annual event will typically be higher than that for corporate events.

Association decision-making processes are different from those of corporate organisations, even though many of the larger associations have dedicated events organisers or units. The decision of when and where to hold the events is usually taken by a committee elected by its membership. An events organiser is expected to do much of the research and related work, producing a list of venues and services from which the committee chooses and makes recommendations.

Destinations produce detailed bid proposals outlining how they could help the association stage successful events (similarly with corporate buyers). Such bid documents contain formal invitations (signed by the mayor or an important dignitary), and provide a full description of the destination, highlighting its attractions, access, communication infrastructure and information on support services available together with a list of services provided by the events venue, details of accommodation facilities and full details of the venue being proposed to stage the events. The local tourist office (LTO) acting on behalf of the destination may be required, or invited, to make a formal presentation to the selection committee of the association, in competition with other destinations that have been shortlisted.

Before a final decision is made, the selection committee may undertake an inspection visit to assess the destination first hand. The selection process can be very protracted. Lead times for association events are usually much longer than for corporate events. It is not unusual for association organisers to book venues several years in advance. The reasons for this may be a limited range of suitable venues and the organisational requirements of large events.

Many association events may have both the delegate and his or her spouse attending; this occurs much less frequently with corporate events, unless they include an incentive element. Partner (or spouse) programmes are designed to entertain the delegates' partners while an event is in progress. Often, destinations work with the events organisers to help in the planning of the spouse programmes, as well as the coordination of tours and activities both before and after the event. Because of their large size, association events are often held in purpose-built public venues. Some use town halls and civic venues while others book university and college venues. Hotels are booked over the weekend as the rates then are cheaper (Rogers, 1998).

The government buyer

Government buyers are very similar to association buyers. Local authorities, central government departments and agencies, educational bodies and health services are included here. This form of buyer is also non-profit making and is accountable for the spending of public funds. Delegates for government events are normally not expected to pay their own expenses to participate in such events. It is likely, though, that the events will be run on a tight budget, using less expensive venues and facilities.

There is a trend for public organisations to book more upmarket facilities. Such

trends help to account for the major investments which tertiary education institutions are making in their events venue and accommodation stock to enable them to compete in a highly competitive marketplace (Rogers, 1998).

Market sub-groups

A *market sub-group* is the term used to describe an ancillary or auxiliary market that piggybacks on another market (Shock & Stefanelli, 1992). For instance, guests at one large event may also take the opportunity to celebrate a reunion, hence it piggybacks the larger event. Events organisers should be trained to be aware of such auxiliary events and to capitalise on them. Most hotels generally make a conscious effort to court the market sub-groups forming part of large event audiences.

4.3.2 The suppliers

Events suppliers refer to those businesses that make available for external hire the destinations, venues and specialist services. Relatively few of these suppliers are, however, dedicated exclusively to the events industry.

Venues

Research by Rogers (1998) has highlighted the fact that hotels make up the majority of all events venues and are particularly important to the corporate market. The main types of hotels active in the meeting market are city-centre hotels, hotels near to national and international communications infrastructure such as airports, and game-ranch venues. In addition, hotels that are located close to large events venues also benefit as providers of accommodation when a major event is organised at the venue. Larger association events frequently choose one hotel as their headquarters, and this can hold a distinct public relations advantage with the hotel being featured in national and even international media coverage.

While events can tend to be hosted in destinations with the best facilities, authorities do variously use events strategically in order to kick-start venue development in regions that may been considered peripheral to the events economy of a country.

South Africa's national event bidding strategy has prioritised bidding to a number the major sports federations, according to DEAT and SAT (2005a), including the bidding and hosting of the 2020 or 2024 Olympic Games. The infrastructural investment for the hosting of the 2010 FIFA World Cup™ will set the stage for

For this, the South African government completed the National Transport Operational Plan (NTOP) in 2007. Each host city has received funding to develop its own transport plan (see table 4.1 below). In addition to the NTOP, the Public Transport Infrastructure and Systems Grant (PTIS) for the 2010 FIFA World Cup™ has been increased from ZAR 9.2 billion to ZAR13.6 billion.

The implementation of the PTIS has gathered momentum with most of the infrastructure either under construction or scheduled to start construction this year. In addition, operational transport planning is at an advanced stage. By October 2008, revised *PTIS allocations to host cities amounted to:*

- ☐ Johannesburg: ZAR2.832 billion
- ☐ Tshwane: ZAR2.069 billion
- ☐ Ethekwini: ZAR1.691 billion
- ☐ Cape Town: ZAR1.030 billion
- ☐ Nelson Mandela: ZAR586 million
- ☐ Mangaung: ZAR425 million
- ☐ Mbombela: ZAR421 million
- ☐ Rustenburg: ZAR324 million
- ☐ Intercity buses: ZAR500 million
- ☐ Non-host cities: ZAR414 million

Table 4.1 Selected transport projects in host cities

City	Transport-related project
Cape Town	Upgrading of access roads to the Green Point stadium CCTV installation on major access roads
City of Johannesburg	Upgrading of the NASREC Precinct and OR Tambo Airport Construction of the rapid Gautrain
Ethekwini	Improve transport linkages to stadium and CBD precinct Upgrade of airport roads and major highways
Mangaung	Elizabeth Street pedestrianisation
Mbombela	Improved access to stadium precinct access Upgrade of railway station and platform
Nelson Mandela Metro	Rehabilitation of airport access Rehabilitation of Motherwell to Addo road
Polokwane	Widening of streets to upgrade stadium precinct
Rustenburg	New Provincial ring road around Phokeng via N4 Sun City upgrades New ring road around Royal Sports Palace Improved access to airports

the successful bidding and hosting of other mega events in South Africa.

Apart from hotel facilities, other principal types of venues include the following:

❐ *Civic centres.* These include town halls, council chambers and committee rooms that are available for hire.

❐ *College, university and other academic venues.* Many of these venues are available for residential conferences during student holidays; some can stage non-residential events during term times.

Increasingly, academic institutions are investing in venues which are available throughout the year.

❐ *Purpose-built centres (residential and non-residential).* These are designed to host various types of events, ranging from very large events with hundreds or thousands of event delegates to smaller, day or residential events.

❐ *Unusual venues.* This describes a wide range of venues available for the staging of events. The attraction of an unusual venue can give events a special appeal.

Case study 4.3 Green Tourism Business Scheme (GTBS), United Kingdom

Event consumers, according to GTBS (2009), are becoming increasingly aware of sustainability-related issues. In particular, demand has grown for simple labels that allow consumers to make purchasing decisions based on environmental and ethical grounds

GTBS is a tool, which reduces environmental impacts; identifies cost savings through efficiencies; improves public image; offers a credible sustainable choice for consumers; and links quality with the environment.

The scheme's flexibility reinforces the GTBS policy of inclusion, and allows participation from a wide range of tourism and event businesses. Allied to quality assurance, GTBS can promote quality and the environment, two themes at the heart of sustainable tourism.

By choosing a Green Tourism Business Scheme business, an event client is guaranteed:
❐ *that the business:*
  • is committed to sustainable practices and minimising its damage to the environment; and
  • is operating in accordance with the relevant environmental regulations.
❐ *that the site:*
  • meets minimum standards of good practice across a range of sustainable development indicators;
  • has been audited by a qualified professional to ensure standards are maintained; and
  • is committed to providing at least a reasonable quality of service between one and five stars.
❐ *that GTBS will:*
  • reassess the venue every two to three years based upon a set of regularly updated sustainable development standards; and
  • investigate any complaints received about the environmental performance or commitment of the venue.

Some venues may have high-quality facilities, others may be quite limited. Possible venue options include sports venues, cultural and entertainment centres such as museums and theatres, tourist attractions such as theme parks, and transport venues such as steam trains (Rogers, 1998).

Destinations

Events organisers place more importance on the location than on any other single criterion when selecting the events site. The location (destination) may be expressed in terms of town, city or region of a country, or even a whole country, and the atmosphere or ambience it creates for the events. Each event destination must contain a range of venues, facilities, attractions, support services and infrastructure to assist in attracting events business. Cooper et al. (1999) indicate that most destinations comprise an amalgamation of:

❐ **attractions** – natural and artificial (or man-made) offerings (including cultural offerings);

❐ **amenities** – accommodation, entertainment, and food and beverage businesses, among others;

❐ **access** – local transport infrastructure; availability of information, among others; and

❐ **ancillary services** – local service organisations, including, the provision of health, safety and security services, amongst others.

The amalgamation of the events destination components – the amalgam or the so-called 4As – comes together to form the events destination. The quality of the events destination components and associated service delivery system (the so-called *events destination amalgam*) will determine the quality an events organiser perceives, and ultimately will determine the suitability and desirability of a particular destination for conducting prospective events business.

Destination management, according to Srinivas (2009), is complicated by the fact that a single, recognisable destination may include national or several local or regional authorities or municipalities, provinces or other government entities. Participating governance structures led by local authorities, with the involvement of local non-governmental organisations (NGOs), community and indigenous representatives, academia and local chambers of commerce, make up what are known as destination management organisations (DMOs). Often, DMOs take the form of national or local tourism boards, councils or development organisations. The network of domestic tourism and events businesses (hotels, attractions, transportation services, service providers, etc.) is also a significant part of a destination. DMOs frequently provide a one-stop service to a prospective events organiser on what their destination has to offer. They are usually also involved in events product development, identifying weaknesses in venues and facilities and general infrastructure, and working towards eliminating them (Rogers, 1998). Managing tourism destinations, according to Srinivas (2009), can also include controlling and managing the social, economic and environmental impacts of planned events and ensuring an adequate return on investment (ROI) by such events. Destination management can include land-use planning, business permits and zoning controls, environmental and other regulations, business association initiatives, and a host of other techniques to shape the development and daily operation of events and tourism-related activities.

4.4 Events agencies, intermediaries and other important domestic and international organisations

4.4.1 Events agencies

'Agencies' is a generic term used to describe a range of different organisations supplying services to events organisers. They act as both suppliers and buyers – they undertake a buying role on behalf of their clients, who may be corporations or associations, and they may act as intermediaries contracted to assist in the planning and running of events. According to Shock and Stefanelli (1992), such intermediaries are sometimes referred at as 'ten-percenters'. This derives from the fact that their fees are generally 10% of the total bill. If the event is large, the fee may be reduced.

Clients frequently use intermediaries when the event is large and represents a major undertaking. For instance, it may be multi-functioned and multi-venued, and have many outside contractors. Intermediaries are often used in civic and political fundraising events where it is necessary to solicit financial support and to sell tickets. Fundraising fashion events, theme events, charity auctions and art events are also mostly organised and implemented by professional intermediaries.

Intermediaries tend to be more astute buyers than the average events buyer and to drive a hard bargain. They sometimes want more control over the events than the typical events service provider wants to surrender.

Communicating events proposals through a third party such as an intermediary can be difficult and inefficient. It may prove difficult for the events service provider to determine if the proposals are consistent with the wishes of the client, as some intermediaries do not allow contact with the client concerned.

Problems can also occur if the client decides to approach the service provider directly instead of through the intermediary. If discussion involves prices, the service provider faces an ethical dilemma if the intermediary was marking up the prices and rebilling the client. In such a case, before talking to the client, the service provider should rather meet with both to avoid potentially troublesome occurrences.

Agencies have a variety of forms and names, and this can be confusing. The principal types of events intermediaries within the events sector are outlined below.

❒ **Business travel agencies**. These agencies seek to cater for the needs of business clients rather than the general public. They are also involved in sourcing venues for various business events and may contribute to the planning and organising of such events (Rogers, 1998). A recent trend in the industry has been the merging of travel agencies and professional conference organisers (PCOs). The former have the transportation expertise and the latter the meeting management know-how. This gives the buyer a one-stop service (Shock & Stefanelli, 1992).

❒ **Convention and visitor bureaux (CVBs)**. Although approaches and structures vary, according to DMAI (2009), official DMOs, which are variously called CVBs (convention and visitor bureaux) or tourism boards, promote the long-term development and marketing of a destination, focusing on convention sales, tourism marketing and service. Successful DMOs are the mastermind behind the marketing campaigns of destinations to events organisers, business travellers, tour operators and individual visitors. DMOs promote the destination amalgam of hotels, facilities, attractions, restaurants and other providers serving travellers to a destination. Convention and visitor bureaux can generally provide various information and services for:

- promoting and building attendance at events;
- events housing services, especially in the case of multi-property events;
- on-site registration and information; and
- on-site registration staffing (Polivka, 1996).

The CVBs are mostly non-profit-making umbrella organisations that represent a destination in the solicitation, servicing and marketing of the destination to all types of travellers to the area. These bureaux do not actually organise events but serve to:

- ❑ encourage groups to hold events in the destination they represent;
- ❑ encourage visitors to enjoy their visits and the historic, cultural and recreational opportunities that the city or destination provides; and
- ❑ assist groups with event preparations and implementation.

CVBs are primarily not-for-profit organisations that represent a specific destination such as a city or region. CVBs serve as the 'official' contact point for their destination for meeting professionals, tour operators and individual visitors.

Local CVBs can deliver some of the events services, provided by other intermediaries, free of charge. The CVBs provide useful information about destinations that can be used by clients to evaluate a destination's suitability for an event and can be a useful one-stop shop for general and events-specific information about a destination. The most tangible benefit for clients is the time saved. In addition, these bureaux can also provide suitable alternative selections for the client, and logistical support at the local level (Shock & Stefanelli, 1992).

Most CVBs operate on a lead system, whereby the sales manager circulates meeting specifications to facilities and lodging entities that can accommodate the requirements. Basic information required by the CVB is usually indicated on the events lead sheet, which will customarily be distributed to all lodging members capable of handling an event. The events manager may decide to limit the lead distribution and may establish certain parameters. Specifying a particular location or proximity to a major transportation node, such as an airport, may effectively limit the distribution of the lead. Some events managers who may be familiar with the destination's properties may indicate certain facilities by name. In this case only these facilities should receive the lead, unless otherwise indicated (Polivka, 1996).

Once the event is concluded, the relationship between the CVB and the events manager should continue. The CVB will request registration statistics and a critique of the events experience to evaluate the manner in which the facilities and communities responded to the events organisation's needs. The post-event evaluation assists the destination in improving the destination facilities and services for the next event. The final housing report provides critical information obtained from the hotels on actual pick-up, cancellation and no-show percentages (Polivka, 1996).

☐ *Corporate hospitality companies (CHCs)*. Corporate hospitality and entertainment often involve the exploitation of major sports and cultural events to improve links between the organisation and its clients or potential clients. Frequently events are arranged specially for the company, and involve drinks reception, dinners and banquets, dances and discos. Formal presentations or short speeches are often included in the event to ensure that the company gets the message across. Corporate hospitality companies are often involved in corporate team-building events aimed at clients and/or employees. Such events can include golf days, off-road driving or paint ball games (Rogers, 1998).

☐ *Destination management companies (DMCs)*. DMC is a term used for professional services companies possessing extensive local knowledge, expertise and resources, specialising in the design and implementation of events, activities, tours, transportation and program logistics. Most DMCs earn on a commission basis (Rogers, 1998).

Destination management companies range from those which provide highly specialised services to full-service firms capable of handling all group logistics. DMCs provide ground services based on local knowledge of their given destinations. Some organisations may only act as specialised ground handlers operating in the incentive market. They have a specialised knowledge of the specific destination (city, town, region or even country). They may also have access to unusual venues such as private houses that may not normally be open to the public. They have considerable buying power and this makes them very useful to incentive houses that may not be from the specific destination. There is a very close relationship between DMCs and incentive travel houses. It can be seen that there is an overlap between the work of a PCO and a DMC, as well as the work of a convention and visitor bureau. DMCs are employed by the client to locate a venue, handle accommodation, assist with transport arrangements, and put together itineraries and programme arrangements.

While some DMCs can provide only ground transportation such as buses, limo and van services, others can subcontract or handle personally everything a client requires. For instance, full-service firms may book entertainment, plan themed events and coordinate spouse and tour programmes. Full-service firms may provide staff, for example to exhibitors who require local models to work exhibition booths or who need trained registration personnel. The DMCs are often used to secure props for themed events; this may include appropriate

balloon art and pyrotechnic displays. A DMC can be considered as incoming tour operators catering for both corporate and leisure clients. DMCs differ from tour operators in that they do not usually deal directly with end clients, but trade through agents, which may be tour operators.

Many out-of-town clients are willing to pay local DMCs to provide guidance in an unfamiliar destination as it is difficult to judge the quality of services available if the client has never visited the destination before. Client events that are held in different destinations every time prefer to work with DMCs (Shock & Stefanelli, 1992).

❑ **Events production houses.** These organisations specialise in the actual staging of the event – designing and building event sets, providing lighting, sound systems and special effects. They have creative and theatrical skills that are used to produce professionally stage-managed events that should be a memorable experience for the delegates (Rogers, 1998).

❑ **Exhibition organisers.** Many exhibitions have a conference programme as a way of adding value to the exhibition and making it more worthwhile for companies to attend. Some conference organisers organise the exhibitions themselves. Others prefer to employ the services of specialist exhibition organisations (Rogers, 1998).

❑ **Ground transportation.** A typical ground transportation company handles primarily guest baggage. The company can be hired by the events client to pick up guest luggage and bring it to the hotel and to return the luggage to the airport at the end of the event. Some ground transportation firms specialise in transporting clients' personal property. A local transport operator may pick up events material such as equipment and product samples, and deliver them to the events venue. Some ground transportation firms specialise in providing limousine services for picking up and dropping off guests. They can also be on call for personal needs during events. This type of service is often used, as it is in many cases a cheaper alternative to using taxis. Some ground transportation companies specialise primarily in entertainment. Some trips, such as charter boat rides and trail rides, are planned strictly for the entertainment value (Shock & Stefanelli, 1992).

❐ *Incentive travel houses*. Incentive travel is an international management tool that uses travel to motivate and/or recognise staff for increased levels of performance in support of organisational goals. This has given rise to incentive travel houses or agencies. Incentive travel programmes often involve travel to overseas destinations and there is a need to continually discover new destinations and create programmes that are more memorable. Incentive travel houses charge a fee to their clients for the work done on their behalf (Rogers, 1998).

❐ *Professional conference organisers (PCOs)*. A professional conference (or congress) organiser is a company which specialises in the organisation and management of congresses, conferences, seminars and similar events of the meetings genre. PCOs are alternatively known as contract planners, meetings organisers and multiple management companies. Sometimes, PCOs are erroneously described as events managers. The PCO is employed to assist in the organisation of *meetings*, researching and recommending a suitable venue,

helping to plan meetings programmes, booking accommodation for delegates, and handling financial arrangements and the registration of delegates. The PCO is normally paid a fee by the client organisation and may charge the venue a commission. Commission may also be charged on accommodation bookings and other services provided (Rogers, 1998).

❐ *Special events planners*. These agents are sometimes commissioned by corporations to plan and implement company events. They usually have a select client list that is contacted on a periodic, predictable basis. Professional sports teams use special events planners to coordinate after-

Case study 4.7 IAPCO (International Association of Professional Congress Organisers)

The International Association of Professional Congress Organisers (IAPCO), a non-profit organisation founded in 1968 and registered in Switzerland, is the professional association for professional organisers, meeting planners and managers of international and national congresses, conventions and special events.

IAPCO is committed to raising standards of service among its members and other sectors of the meetings industry by means of continuing education and interaction with other professionals. IAPCO is the universally accepted benchmark for quality within a congress organisation and is the global branding of excellence for the meetings industry. Thus, IAPCO membership offers a unique quality assurance recognised by congress clients and suppliers all over the world.

game parties, half-time events, parades, etc. (Shock & Stefanelli, 1992). Major events such as the Olympics and presidential inaugurations usually use special events planners. If several such planners are used, one of them may be responsible for overseeing and coordinating all the other planners through drawing up a master plan for the events and deciding how each planner will be utilised.

☐ *Venue-finding agencies.* Such agencies offer a limited service restricted to researching and recommending suitable venues for events. They normally present a short list of three potential venues to their client and usually receive a commission on the value of the bookings from the venue. Venue-finding agencies may also get involved in booking accommodation for delegates and can expect to charge the accommodation providers a commission. The services of the agency are provided free of charge to the client (Rogers, 1998).

☐ *Other agencies.* Some organisations may play a role in organising an event, or part of an event, for their clients, although this may not normally fall within their usual day-to-day activities. Such organisations are public relations and advertising consultancies, management consultants and training companies (Rogers, 1998).

4.4.2 Other important organisations

As the events industry matures, it requires other organisations to function professionally and establish a code of practice. Below is a list of various organisations that play a supporting role within the events industry.

☐ *Consultants.* They undertake projects on a fee-paying basis for clients who normally operate on the supply side of the events industry. Such consultants may be involved in determining the potential market for a proposed new venue, the specification of a new events venue or the major renovation of an existing venue; advising on marketing strategies for a venue or destination; and undertaking feasibility studies to establish and operate new venues (Rogers, 1998).

☐ *Educational institutions.* The education and training of the events industry's future workforce is critical for the future growth and development of the industry. Tertiary institutions are increasingly devoting attention to the events industry in their syllabi (Rogers, 1998).

☐ *National, regional and local tourism organisations.* Most countries now have national tourism organisations (NTOs) which have been established to promote the country internationally. A number of countries have established national events bureaux to specifically research, market and promote this sector. There is no standard format for such national bureaux – each operates differently (Rogers, 1998).

☐ *Trade associations.* These organisations are formed to serve the interests of the members, and their activities include lobbying and representation, establishing codes of practice, marketing and promotion, education and training, research and information.

☐ *Trade media.* The events industry trade media are primarily magazines published on a regular basis, and may contain articles on new developments and ways to improve the quality of events management. The internet is playing an increasingly important role in this regard. The trade media fulfil the role of keeping the industry informed of the latest developments. Their circulation also provides an advertising and PR medium for suppliers wishing to promote their services and facilities to potential buyers.

4.5 Summary

This chapter strove to focus on the various role players and to equip the reader with the necessary knowledge to identify the various service and product clients and providers when organising an event. The events industry is highly complex, comprising a multiplicity of buyer and supplier organisational role players, sponsors and events audiences. In order to gain community support, attract grants and sponsorships, and achieve sustainability, events need to successfully meet a multiplicity of goals. Events are produced by organisations for a variety of reasons. As is common in other industries, the events sector comprises of 'buyers' and 'suppliers'. For the purpose of this chapter, *suppliers* and *buyers* referred to those role players who play an intimate role in researching and producing events for consumption by an audience. 'Agencies' is a generic term used to describe a range of different organisations supplying services to events organisers. They act as both suppliers and buyers – they undertake a buying role on behalf of their clients, who may be corporations or associations, and they may act as intermediaries contracted to assist in the planning and running of events.

Questions for research

1 Discuss the prime responsibility of a CVB.
2 Explain the purpose the leads process serves during site selection.
3 Explore how a CVB can assist with on-site registration and information dissemination.
4 An excellent event destination amalgam is no longer a competitive advantage for destinations because many competing events destinations now have similar amalgams. Discuss this statement and suggest key factors that destinations need to identify in order to differentiate themselves from their competition.
5 Contrast the difference between association and corporate buyers.
6 Explain why an events organiser should consider dealing with the SMERF market.
7 As an employee of a large trade association that holds an annual event for about 1 000 delegates, with an exhibition alongside the conference (i.e. a confex), you have been tasked to contract out the planning of this event. Describe the types of agencies you would approach, and provide reasons for your choices.
8 Assess the various market segments within the corporate market, and suggest how the events manager should manage these.
9 Discuss the role of the main actors within the events system. Explain their relevance to a prospective events organiser.
10 Discuss the role of events intermediaries.
11 Explain why events managers should take cognisance of the auxiliary events market.

12 Discuss the feasibility of a quality grading scheme for event venues. Conduct research involving event organisers to determine which features and criteria such a scheme could realistically assess and measure.

13 Events suppliers play a vital role in the production of events. Use examples to illustrate your response.

Recommended websites

Browse the following internet sites for interesting and informative information:

BestCities Global Alliance: http://www.bestcities.net/

Business visits & events partnership: http://www.businesstourismpartnership.com/index.html

Destination Marketing Association International (DMAI): http://www.destinationmarketing.org/

International Association of Professional Congress Organisers (IAPCO): http://www.iapco.org/

International Congress and Convention Association (ICCA): http://www.iccaworld.com/

International Festivals & Events Association (IFEA): http://www.ifea.com/

International Special Events Society (ISES): http://www.ises.com/

Meeting Professionals International (MPI): http://www.mpiweb.org/

The International Association of Convention and Visitor Bureaux: http://www.iacvb.org/

The International Olympic Committee (IOC): http://www.olympic.org/

The Southern African Association for the Conference Industry (SAACI): http://www.saaci.co.za/

Tourism Grading Council of South Africa (TGCSA) – Graded Conference Venues: http://www.tourismgrading.co.za/

World Travel Market (WTM): http://www.wtmlondon.com/

Suggested reading

Cooper, C, Fletcher, J, Gilbert, D, Shepherd, R & Wanhill, S. 1999. *Tourism: Principles and Practice,* 2 ed. Essex: Addison Wesley Longman Ltd.

Polivka, EG. 1996. *Professional Meeting Management,* 3 ed. Alabama: PCMA.

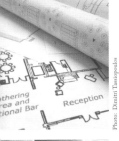

Photo: Zoë Moosman

Photo: Dimitri Tassiopoulos

Photo: Dimitri Tassiopoulos

Photo: MediaClubSouthAfrica.com. Mangaung Local Municipality

5 Bidding and securing an event

Graham Berridge and Liz Quick

Abstract

The concept of bidding is well known for corporate, association and public-sector events where the bid process generally starts with identifying a concept and developing this event concept by means of a formal proposal. The proposal is then submitted to the appropriate organising committee (event owner) and/or delivered by way of a pitch by the interested party (event organiser). This chapter looks at the bid proposal and the required content of the document and presentation, and describes the process that any organisation should follow when considering whether or not to bid to host a major event.

Chapter objectives

After you have read this chapter you should be able to:
- ❐ understand and define the bid process;
- ❐ identify the critical issues determining whether to bid for an event;
- ❐ understand the pitch process and tendering for business in a competitive arena;
- ❐ define the critical aspects, phases and time schedule of a bid document;
- ❐ reflect on the overall bid process;
- ❐ understand the planning and organisation process;
- ❐ know and understand the required content of a request for proposal (RFP); and
- ❐ understand valuation and problem-solving activities.

5.1 Introduction

Having the rights to organise and run events is the result of a competitive process. The times when this is not the case are usually where the event concept has originated by the owner-planners, the event is run by an in-house event team working within a larger corporation, the event resides within the voluntary sector and is committee led and run not for profit and where the event is given to an event agency without any reference to other likely organisers. However, for a lot of public and corporate events the rights to organise are the result of a competitive bidding process and they form an essential part of the events landscape (Berridge, 2007). Competitive bidding ranges from the right to run the Olympics and the World Cup down to private entertainment events for commercial clients, and can be a lengthy process requiring considerable resources. For example, a successful commercial bid results in an event contract between an individual agency and corporate clients, with the event normally running over a single day/evening. There are also those events related to destination development where the successful bidder will be required to spread the event over several days, and requires organisation of travel,

accommodation and leisure planning in addition to the event itself.

5.2 Understanding and defining the bid process

Prior to the commencement of the bid process, the event owner may invite a number of interested parties to express interest in the bid, and then from those interested parties develop a shortlist to invite to submit a formal document and presentation as part of the bid process. The bid process commences when the event agency or organisation is invited to submit a proposal.

Bidding for events is an everyday part of the events landscape, and covers virtually the entire range of event types. The process of bidding applies equally to both public and private events, to corporate companies and destinations, to entertainment and education events and to sports events and conferences.

Within this spread of event types lie significant differences in the scale, shape and size of the bidding process with perhaps the most complex, costly and time consuming being a bid for mega-events, such as the Olympic Games or a World Cup, which could run to millions of dollars and occupy a minimum of two years' preparation for the bid. By contrast, bidding for a bespoke corporate entertainment or business event, while by no means simple, is more straightforward and is likely to cost at most a few thousand dollars, with a preparation of perhaps less than four weeks. As the events industry has blossomed over the past two decades, the value of events to society has become increasingly apparent and events have become an increasing part of strategic and policy initiatives, which has resulted in:

❑ upcoming destinations attracting new business;
❑ new facilities;
❑ increased tourism;
❑ economic benefits;
❑ better infrastructure;
❑ increased standing for the city;
❑ improvement to the area; and
❑ a kick-start for struggling local businesses.

There are a number of terms used within the events industry in relation to securing event contracts, and the boundaries or use of each is sometimes blurred or used as a catch-all to include all processes in winning a contract. Variously, these are procurement, bidding, tendering and pitching.

5.2.1 Event bidding

The term 'event bidding' is more often associated with events that are a one-off, run infrequently or change location each time (Allen, 2005) and can be classed as hallmark or mega-events (Gratton, Dobson & Shibli, 2001a). Most attention, at least academically, has looked at bidding in relation to sports events, possibly because these often involve public bodies and require a high degree of transparency in the process. They are also likely to require considerable resources to organise, and hence carry a high degree of risk with them (Emery, 2002). Such bidding is often carried out annually or bi-annually, apart from mega-events that usually have a four-year cycle. Discussion and analysis of such bids tends to consider the rationale for bidding in the first place, the requirements of the bid, the strategy and policy of the bidding city and the impact a successful bid would have on the economic, social, political and cultural environment (Gratton et al., 2001b). By nature they are competitive and at one time there are likely to be several cities and nations bidding to host major international sporting events. The right to host an international event is now one of the most valuable prizes in sport. The 2007 Dubai International Sports Conference valued the market at US$50 billion worldwide, while UK Sport estimates such events contribute £1.5 billion to the British economy each year (Walmsley, 2008).

5.2.2 Procurement

Event 'procurement' is the most difficult to define because of the range of activities associated with it. Most frequently used within the conferences, conventions and meetings industry where there is a proliferation of corporate, association and public-sector involvement, procurement usually enables a distinction to be made between 'buyers' and 'suppliers' (Rogers, 2003b).

Visitor convention bureaux, for example, act in a procurement capacity by actively seeking and attracting events as part of the wider strategic policy of a region to attract more visitors (Rogers, 2003b; Davidson, 2003) and public and other bodies use the appeal of events to enhance the image of a destination (Gold & Ward, 1994; Smith,

2001; Pugh, 2004). As a management process it can be regarded as the 'sourcing, selection and contracting of the suppliers and vendors from whom goods and services will be procured using accurate solicitation materials and quality criterion' (Silvers, 2008: 173). Procurement is widely interpreted and so difficult to clearly define, but nevertheless it can be seen as 'the business management function that ensures identification, sourcing, access and management of the external resources that an organisation needs or may need to fulfil its strategic objectives' (Silvers, 2008: 173). Events fall within these two areas through the activity of procurement planning when event management companies are invited to bid for an event, or an association or organisation issues a request for proposal (RFP).

5.2.3 Tendering

In cases where the event originates from the public sector or government, this may be called a tendering process. This generally involves a sole provider and a specific process and format that adhere to the event owner's select criteria, which must be submitted to the relevant government body. In a formal tender document the select criteria are sometimes weighted, so that it is clear to the recipient what emphasis should be given to the various criteria detailed in the tender document (Van der Wagen, 2007).

As part of the tendering process, the event owners put together a detailed rationale in the form of a proposal which aims to source the most appropriate location and event management team to implement their event. This formal tendering process allows any number of competitors to submit their proposal for consideration. Usually it

requires bidders to submit a pre-qualifying questionnaire which will be vetted by the event owners and will dramatically reduce the number of potential tenders. In some cases the event tender is presented to a panel or client in person, and it is essential that this presentation is a highly professional summary of the material that has been submitted in the tender document. This is often supported by a multimedia presentation and visual aids; for example, a virtual rendering of the venue or mood boards illustrate the creative concept of the event and provide an excellent opportunity for the event organisation to answer any questions the event owner may have regarding the tender or bid.

5.2.4 Pitching

Pitching is not a term frequently used in academic studies of event bidding, yet is a vital part of the industry. Many event 'bids' conclude with a pitch to the client or event owner, where the concept and ideas for the event are presented. It is a term commonly used by industry professionals and is a key part in persuading the client to offer the contract for managing the event. This is the stage where a bidding team or event organisation need to convey their ideas by using a combination of creativity and psychology to impress the decision makers. For many small to medium-sized events companies, a 'pitch' accounts for anything between 30–100% of their work and is an expression of interest or quotation. A pitch of this type tends to be a more informal process with fewer criteria for success (Van der Wagen, 2007) and the client may select a company on price, reputation or creativity. Even the biggest event, the Olympics, ultimately comes down to a 'pitch' to the IOC members that is the tangible presentation of around two years or more of bid preparation.

5.3 Factors to consider when deciding on whether to bid for an event

There are many reasons why event bidding exists. In the case of mega-events like the Olympics, the bidding process provides a degree of public transparency and it also raises the profile of the event itself. Furthermore, it allows destinations to consult with stakeholders and develop policy towards bidding for events. Even with smaller-scale corporate and association events, event bidding is important in order to select from a potential shortlist of agencies or event organisations tendering the one which has the best credibility, resources and expertise and is therefore most fit for purpose to run the event on behalf of the event owner.

In recent years return on investment

Case study 5.1 Return on investment – bidding, cost and value

The principle that Rouge work on is a round 5–7% of return will be used to bid for an event. So for a recent bid to a major supermarket chain who wanted to put on a huge celebratory event, the budget was $1m. Rouge are transparent in their financial dealings and openly declare that they will take 20% of the budget as their income, in this case $200 000, which absorbs the costs of their pitch, leaving $800 000 to run the actual event. The 20% effectively buys Rouge's expertise, expenses and staff time, and for this event they had a nine-month lead in time. Out of the $200 000 they invested just under $17 000 in the bid. This is the most they had ever spent and was a gamble.

However, the gamble was worthwhile as it took into account other aspects of ROI such as satisfaction and perceived value. Traditionally these are viewed as post-event measurements; however, they are also pre-bid factors. Rouge's satisfaction and value were related to bidding for a major client and the perception value of that, even if they lost. There is an aspect to bidding that is influenced by marketing and the need of the agency to put themselves forward as serious bidders. If not successful now, they gamble that they will be invited to future bids where they might be. Hence satisfaction is drawn from the bid and presentation itself, and the knowledge that Rouge did as a good a job as they could. The perceived value is, of course, met if they win the bid. If not, it is met by their perception of the value of bidding – as a marketing exercise or as a shop window for their skills. Hence it is important that before bidding the agency does its research on the client to be able to make more than just financial judgement on whether or not to bid.

However, satisfaction and perceived value, as indicated, are also post-event measurements, and here Rouge became caught up in a 'satisfaction' conundrum. Out of the $200 000 income, they absorbed the bid at $17 000 and they also set aside a contingency budget of $40 000 for any unplanned for expenses. Owing to the complexity of the event, the contingency was used up fairly quickly and as the time drew closer, decisions had to be made about the how the event would work. Rouge felt it unethical to go back and ask for more money from the client, since the event costing was theirs, and so, once again using a perception value measurement, they elected to add a further $40 000 to fund overrun costs, in effect now using up around 50% of their income. The result: the event was a huge success for the clients and guests, and Rouge subsequently won more event work from the client.

Source: Drawn from interview with Nathan Homan, MD, Rouge Events, UK

(ROI) has become a major factor when considering whether or not to pitch for an event, and it is firstly necessary at the feasibility phase for the event organisation to put together a comprehensive cost-benefit forecast to assess the potential benefits of managing the event against the predicted costs of running it (Masterman, 2004). This process allows event organisations to decide whether there will be sufficient return to make it worth pitching for the business or not. At this stage it is also necessary to identify what the event objectives are and who will be responsible for their delivery in the short and longer term. A further part of the feasibility process is to identify what resources are required, the projected cost of these, stated payment terms and the assessment of longer-term legacies, for example the future use of any new facilities or any regeneration projects.

Further considerations in terms of timing of the bid are the geographical, political and historical background of this event. Event owners prefer to consider geographical spread when selecting event destinations, so that diverse cities that may not have recently hosted other events may stand a better chance than those cities that have recently done so or will be doing so during the same period. It is therefore important to assess these implications when deciding to bid, as although the actual event might only last for a few days, the preparations may take much longer – even years in case of a major event (Maralack & Lloyd, 2005).

Lastly, the feasibility phase requires the evaluation of the event in terms of short- and medium-term social, economical and environmental impacts on the local community. In the case of major events, an existing infrastructure and purpose-built facilities are required before the event can proceed. This requires an initial strategic long-term plan and appropriate legacy planning to ensure that any rise in participation can be sustained after the event has taken place. When such planning works successfully, hosting this type of major event may result in several benefits for the local community such as increased pride of place, social inclusion and increase in geographic identity.

Research on such benefits, however, is not always convincing, and there is evidence to suggest that bidders can overstate the likely benefits prior to the bid. It is also apparent that some of the perceived benefits, especially long-term ones, are difficult to measure. When an event comes to town, the local and regional economy is said to benefit greatly through the spending per head of visitors and participants at the event. There are, however, some historical references from the Olympics that should act as a warning to Olympic bidders that such economic benefit is by no means certain. The example of the economic impact of the 1996 European Football Championships compared with the 1996 World Masters Swimming offers a salutary remainder that high-profile events do not always generate significantly more revenue than those of a lower profile but different attendee characteristics (Shibli & Gratton, 2001). Even with smaller-scale events it is important for the event organiser to consider certain factors in terms of the longer-term benefits to the agency or organisation before deciding whether it is in their interest to tender or not.

5.3.1 Social, economical and environmental impacts

At the root of most rationales is economic impact, as well as social and environmental impacts. When deciding whether to bid for a major event, the event organisation has to monitor the possible impacts and produce evidence in terms of previous evaluation

reports and references to support their bid (Van der Wagen, 2007).

It is essential that as well as meeting the set requirements of the event owner and fulfilling the event objectives, the event organisation also matches the required guidelines in terms of their community and environmental profiles.

5.3.2 Urban regeneration

Many events are associated with having a positive economic impact on host destinations, and sporting and other major events have for some time now been cited as a catalyst for regional economic development and urban regeneration. There is also a belief that hosting such events can promote a city or region as a tourist destination and that the brand identity of the city can be improved.

5.3.3 Environmental development

A major thread in international bidding since the mid-1990s has been the need to incorporate more environmentally sustainable practices. Chernuschenko (1994b) demonstrated the consistent and neglectful waste associated with many major events and the apparent indifference on the part of organisers to address the issues. With such waste getting more and more attention, event organisers have had to adopt more environmentally friendly policies.

5.3.4 Destination image

Destinations are said to be able to enhance their image by association with spectacular, internationally renowned events. Through the concept of events tourism (Getz, 1997), cities can raise their profile significantly and gain direct benefits through an increase in tourism.

Although based on the more established practice of civic boosterism, the practice of city 're-imaging' came to the forefront of urban policy in the 1980s as cities attempted to deal with various economic and social crises. A key part of sports-related regeneration, events have become useful tools for the re-imaging of locations and for developing destination image (Hall, 2004; Ritchie & Smith, 1991). Whitelegg (2000: 3) notes that sport now 'acts as a central, rather than a peripheral component in the restructuring of urban image'. The importance of sport and the images of it that are communicated by the media have therefore become a key factor in developing place identity (Bale, 2003).

Sports tourism events thus become an opportunity for image making (Getz, 1997) and can now be seen as 'an emerging trend that gives the city marketers the opportunity to position their destination while fulfilling specific target markets and stakeholders needs' (Pugh & Wood, 2004: 64). They are deemed by cities to be valuable image or branding tools because of their character

and international recognition, enabling the host community to have a potentially distinct competitive advantage associated with the event's 'significance, in terms of tradition, attractiveness, image or publicity' (Getz, 1997: 5–6). In using popular forms of culture such as sport, it is seen as a 'more legitimate means of representing the city to an external audience' (Smith, 2001: 130). Chalip (2004, citing Kotler et al., 1999) further suggests that the attractiveness of sports events is because the value of the image enhancement extends beyond the time of the actual event, thus deflecting some of the criticism that only immediate benefit accrues with no significant legacy.

Hosting major events presents an opportunity to develop a destination image and also to enhance the lifecycle of the city by using the linked images as an intermediary in development (Boo & Busser, 2006).

From such promotion, local community benefits may emerge, and this understanding of image enhancement and positive representation focusing on community enhancement and positive impact has been explored by several studies (Getz, 1997; Higham & Ritchie, 2001; Jago & Shaw, 1998). Further studies have shown that major events such as the Olympics can demonstrate how a destination's image has been improved (Ritchie & Smith, 1991; Spilling, 2000). Other research has illustrated that hosting community events per se can lead to image improvement (Mules & Faulkner, 1996) and can also result in an increase in the number of visitors (Getz, 1997). This is particularly important for developing countries such as South Africa in the context of events like the Cape Town bid for the 2004 Olympic Games.

Therefore, the decision as to whether to bid for an event or not is dependent on a number of factors including understanding the event objectives, the bidding timelines, other competitors included in the pitch and potential benefits and risks. There is always a hidden cost associated with an event bid in terms of time, resource, marketing and preparation (Allen et al., 2002; Getz, 1997), which may also influence the ultimate decision of whether to proceed with the bid or not.

5.3.5 Planning and organisation of a bid document or tender

The bid document generally covers all aspects of the event concept and planning process and is then submitted to the corporate client or organising committee (Van der Wagen, 2007).

In order to prepare the bid document for submission, it is often necessary to involve a number of third-party suppliers, which may include tourist offices and convention bureaux, venues, airlines, hotel companies, marketing companies, entertainment, and food and beverage companies, etc.

For this reason it is necessary to start the bid process and appoint an agency to manage the event or events well in advance, even several years before the start of the event.

When preparing the bid it is essential that the agency or company adhere to the stated criteria against which they will

---

The typical phases in the bidding process

- **Research and development.** In this phase, organisations consider the merits and risks of bidding before formally announcing their intention to bid. Prospective bidding organisations need to assess the benefits of bidding and the nature of demands that may be placed on them for the delivery of the event. Depending on the scale of the event, this phase may include the destination or city selection, and the appointment of necessary consultants to undertake a cost benefit analysis.
- **Official invitation to bid.** The event owner officially invites organisations or cities to bid, and provides a detailed timetable for submission of proposals.
- **Confirmation of the bid.** Bidding organisations formally confirm and announce their intention to bid for an event. This announcement is usually supported by the necessary political and financial endorsements, and may include the provision of a deposit to the event owners in the case of a major event such as the Olympic Games.
- **Bid preparation.** The bidding entity begins the preparation of a 'candidature file', bid document or proposal, either through the assistance of consultants or the formation of a legal bidding company.
- **Presentation of the bid.** The bidding entities submit and present their proposals to the event owner by a stipulated date.
- **Lobby and evaluation phase.** In the case of international events where the stakes are high, the event owner begins an evaluation of each bid submitted, and the bidding entities, in turn, begin to lobby individual members of the event owner's organisation of the merits of their proposal and for votes in their favour.
- **Final announcement.** The event owner gathers all the candidates and announces the successful bidding entity. In the case of a large-scale or major event, the host city will be announced and a contract signed immediately after the announcement.
- **Hosting phase.** The successful bidding entity enters into a contract with the event owner and begins the preparation for the event.

Sources: Maralack and Lloyd (2005: 56–73)

Case study 5.4 Request for proposal (RFP) by major charity to selected event organisers

A RFP is issued by a major UK charity event to a number of UK business travel agencies to tender for the charity's national travel policy. This RFP requires the agencies initially to submit a proposal, and then three shortlisted agencies will be invited to a formal pitch presentation to select an agency for sole-supplier status. The preferred supplier contract will run for three years with an annual review.

The charity aims to enforce a mandatory national travel policy in order to consolidate spend on all areas of business travel, to include air travel; hotel bookings; all transportation, including car rental, taxis and rail travel; travel air miles and insurance; and conference and meeting spend. They have therefore researched leading business travel agencies in the UK that have the capacity, the infrastructure and the expertise to manage all these requirements with the overall aim of driving efficient travel management practices and making savings through economies of scale purchasing.

Once the preferred business travel agency has been appointed, employees of the charity will have to book all point-to-point air travel through the designated travel agency's online travel booking system. The agency will secure optimum rates with all air carriers, hotels and other travel-related services, and will ensure that a dedicated team is available to book or to answer any queries.

The RFP is designed to assess how the selected business travel agency would propose to best service the travel requirements of the charity. This document includes their objectives and criteria for consolidating their travel policy through one supplier. The RFP also gives details of the charity's organisational structure and locations; their existing travel requirements in terms of their annual room nights, air spend and conference spend; as well as their trading policy, terms and conditions.

The RFP requires the business travel agency document to submit information in the initial proposal regarding their in-house booking systems, staff numbers, company details, company accounts, reporting structure, proposed savings to the charity and payment terms. In addition they need to submit information on internal auditing, quality control and process for queries and complaints.

An important additional requirement is that the agency has the necessary expertise and contacts in the industry to recommend and secure optimum travel solutions and to be able to negotiate individual and group rates with key third-party suppliers on the charity's behalf. A deadline is set in the RFP for the submission of the tender document. During this period a contact person from the charity's procurement division is available to liaise with the selected agencies and answer any questions they may have in order to complete the proposal.

Postscript

Initially eight agencies were selected and invited to pitch for preferred supplier status. Out of this, three were then shortlisted and invited to attend a formal presentation with key personnel from the charity, all of whom were involved in the decision-making process. After this presentation a decision was made, the business agency was appointed and a supplier agreement was drawn up for three years. This was, in turn, subject to an annual review.

be judged. For this reason, on receipt of the brief it is sometimes necessary for the event organisation to seek further clarification from the event owner as to the exact requirements. Following on from this, the next stage is to prepare an action plan or critical path in response to the brief, as the deadlines set are invariably fixed and it is important that the timelines set are achievable and realistic. As well as allowing sufficient time for all third-party suppliers to provide responses in the form of a quotation, to do research and to write the content of the document, it is also necessary to allow time for the print and collation of the documents and any formal presentation that might be required as part of the bid process.

While there are different methods used by clients to entertain a bid, the process is mostly consistent with the pattern described above. Case study 5.4 sets out how a request for proposal (RFP) is issued and then advances into a formal bid and finally the award of the contract.

5.4 Standard contents of a bid document

The initial request for proposal (RFP) often requests details on the event owner's credentials, which may include testimonials or references from previous clients, previous event evaluation reports and full financial auditing of previous company records as well as the necessary licences and insurances to trade.

Standard contents within a bid document may vary according to the size and scope of the bid, but generally information in the following sections would need to be included in the bid document by the event owner:

- ❐ Candidate characteristics;
- ❐ Legal aspects;
- ❐ Finance;
- ❐ Environmental concerns;
- ❐ Security;
- ❐ Medical and health;
- ❐ Transport and traffic;
- ❐ Event requirements;
- ❐ Accommodation; and
- ❐ Telecommunications infrastructure.

5.4.1 Candidate characteristics

Required is information on the political, economic and social structures within which the event hosts will work. Of particular relevance would be the responsibilities of various levels of government that will be involved in hosting the event and will ultimately provide guarantees.

5.4.2 Legal aspects

The agency or team bidding for the event should ensure that the bid conforms to the legal requirements of the event owner, in particular:
- ❐ use of symbols;
- ❐ revenue raising and distribution; and
- ❐ customs and immigration.

5.4.3 Finance

The financial cost of hosting must be clearly identified and should include:
- ❐ capital expenditure on facilities, infra-structure and venues; and
- ❐ operational expenditure for hosting.

5.4.4 Social, economic and environmental concerns

Often event owners require information on location of the city, altitude – as it may affect performance of athletes – temperature and humidity, precipitation, and so forth. Consideration should also be given for any social or economic implications of the event.

Case study 5.5 2015 Rugby World Cup, UK

The International Rugby Board was awarded the right to host the 2015 Rugby World Cup to England. The mainstay of the English bid was financial with a promise that the tournament would generate a $400m (approx.) windfall for international rugby. By contrast the 2011 World Cup in New Zealand was expected to make a $20m loss.

5.4.5 Security

This is often the most critical aspect of a bid document, as the event owner needs to be assured that the event will proceed without any security breaches. Security issues to consider are:
- ❏ crime prevention plans in the host city;
- ❏ security plans for venues and accommodation;
- ❏ emergency and evacuation plans;
- ❏ access control for vehicles and people; and
- ❏ security plan for high-profile or high-risk groups.

5.4.6 Medical and health services

Description of the availability of medical care in and around the venues and accommodation should be provided.

5.4.7 Transport and traffic

These would include:
- ❏ travel to the host city;
- ❏ travelling in and around the host city;
- ❏ travel to and from venues; and
- ❏ transport for people with disabilities.

5.4.8 Event requirements

Whether the nature of the event is sport, cultural or a conference, the host has specific requirements to ensure that the event is well run and will conclude successfully. The event owner usually identifies and determines these specifications and special emphasis must be given to this aspect.

5.4.9 Accommodation

Information must be given on availability of accommodation and its proximity to the venue and places of interest. Often, special requirements are laid down for various levels of competitor, officials and dignitaries.

5.4.10 Telecommunications infrastructure

Mega-events most often depend on media and broadcast coverage. The event owner must therefore be assured that proceedings will be available for broadcasting in the various forms and not be limited by lack of infrastructure.

5.4.11 Event bid checklist

In preparing for the bid process, it is advisable to establish a checklist no matter how large or small or simple or complicated the event. Such a checklist enables clarity of thought and purpose. Table 5.1 is a typical checklist that provides a set of very realistic self-reflective questions that potential bidders should consider.

Table 5.1 Event bidding checklist

THE EVENT
What is the name, nature and scale of the event?
How often is the event held and where has it previously been hosted?
Where will the event take place, with respect to geographical area, city and suburb?
Why does your organisation wish to bid to host the event?
When will the event take place and over what period?
Is there a forecast of impacts and attendance numbers from previous events?
What potential linked events may be organised?
Is there enough infrastructure or do we need to provide new infrastructure?
Will the human resource requirements of the event be met?
Is there clarity on the financial implications of the bid and the event?

THE BIDDING PROCESS
What organisation owns the rights to the event?
Is there a critical path for the bid? If so what are the critical milestones?
What other organisations are bidding to host the event?
Is there a formal lobbying period?
Will an evaluation team visit to assess your potential?
Are there potential competing events occurring over the same period?
Where would the bid headquarters be located?
What are the strengths of your bid?
What are the obvious weaknesses of your bid?
Is there support from the national federation, SASC, and all levels of government?

THE BIDDING MEETING
What are the bidding and hosting requirements?
Is there a specific bidding manual?
Do you have enough time to meet the bidding requirements?
Are there sufficient resources to meet the requirements?
Is there adequate infrastructure to host the event?
If not, what improvements and/or temporary facilities are needed?
Do you have the technical infrastructure to host the event?
Are dedicated training facilities required?
What special transport arrangements will be required?
What additional accommodation arrangements will be required?
What media and IT infrastructure is required?
What accreditation and security measures will be needed?
What specialised equipment will be needed to which you do not presently have access?
Are all venues and modes of transport accessible to disabled people?
What guarantees does the event owner in the bidding process require?

ORGANISATIONAL STRUCTURE & CAPACITIES

What is the nature of your bidding committee?
Who will lead your bid?
Who are the decision makers in your bid?
What is the composition of your committee or board?
Is there sufficient organisational expertise to compete?
Who are the stakeholders in the event at all levels?
What will be expected of them in the bidding process?
Do they have the capacity to assist within the time frames set?
What systems are currently in place to run the bid?
How much public sector input will be required from national, regional and local government level?
What potential is there for South African participants to excel at the event?

FINANCIAL IMPLICATIONS

What budget is required to submit your bid?
What upfront finances exist to compete effectively in the bidding process?
Is there an initial inflow of capital from the event owner?
What funding arrangements are in place or are needed?
Is there private sector interest in the bid and the event?
How marketable is your event in terms of media coverage?
What marketing and sponsorship restrictions apply to the bidding process and event?
What sponsorship arrangements have been secured?
Do you have financial assurance and insurance cover for the bidding process?
Is the event financially and economically viable?

FEASIBILITY STUDY

Have you conducted a feasibility study? If so, please provide the documentation.
What are the potential positive and negative impacts resulting from bidding and hosting the event?
Please provide relevant documentation on the impact of the event. This includes environmental, social, economic and infrastructural impacts.
What legacies will be derived from bidding and hosting the event?
Which geographical area and who in particular will benefit?
Will a post-event evaluation be completed?
What monitoring and evaluation mechanisms will be established during the bidding process?
How will the event fit into national and regional sports and tourism strategies?
Why will participants and spectators want to come to your destination as opposed to any other?
Are the human resources sufficient to meet the requirements for the event?
If not, indicate the measures in place to meet this need.

Source: Maralack & Lloyd (2005: 69)

The event organiser in response to the bid would also provide the following information in their tender document:

- ❏ An executive summary;
- ❏ Company or agency credentials;
- ❏ Programme overview;
- ❏ Destination and venue details – to include general information on infrastructure, accessibility, attractions, etc.;
- ❏ Detailed venue plans, floor capacities, conference facilities, accommodation, etc.;
- ❏ Size of predicted target audience;
- ❏ Marketing and promotional strategies;
- ❏ Financial planning and budgetary control;
- ❏ Proposed use of in-house systems;
- ❏ Event staffing;
- ❏ Staging and logistics;

- ❏ Technical requirements;
- ❏ Health and safety recommendations;
- ❏ Risk management assessment; and
- ❏ Post-event measurement.

5.5 Scheduling a critical path in the bid process

As the timelines for bidding are usually established by the event owners, are generally non-flexible and can be fairly demanding, it is an important factor to consider the feasibility of the deadlines when deciding whether to bid for an event or not. It is rarely possible to secure any extension to the deadline dates imposed by the client or event owner.

In order to assess how realistic these timelines are, it is advisable for the agency to put together a critical path document,

Case study 5.6 A request for proposal from leading pharmaceutical company to selected event organisations

A leading UK pharmaceutical company issues an RFP to a number of events management agencies to tender to handle all their internal and external events. The agencies receive an invitation by letter from the pharmaceutical company inviting them to submit a proposal and providing them with some background information about the company and the four major business sectors that exist.

The pharmaceutical company states that currently off-site meetings are decentralised with few experienced meeting planners involved and that their objective for the proposal is to qualify a limited number of event management agencies, covering both logistics and production, to help manage all meetings and events as generated by UK budget holders within the organisation. They also give statistics on the volume of meetings and the previous year's annual spend on events.

The pharmaceutical company requests that the agencies provide details on their background, fee structure and organisational structure, and to demonstrate their ability and experience to handle meetings, conferences and group air requirements. This information should include a full description of services and a summary list of projects managed over the last two years. They also invite the agencies to explain their vision for the pharmaceutical company's global meetings.

The pharmaceutical company states that they have formed a ten-member team to coordinate the implementation and roll-out of the programme and the task force will evaluate and select proposals that best fit the company's overall business needs and adhere to their corporate culture. They stipulate that seven agencies have been selected to participate in this process and they give a deadline date for submission.

detailing key milestones leading up to the event delivery. Within this critical path document it is essential to consider what trade-offs and compromises will have to be made and whether the timelines are realistic in terms of establishing contact with key suppliers and stakeholders who would be involved with hosting the event. If the event is a mega- or international event, the timelines need to be assessed to determine whether any opportunity exists to host test events in the facilities beforehand. This is particularly applicable to large sporting events.

The work breakdown should be prepared according to the event requirements, and key milestone activities should be prioritised in terms of importance. A Gantt chart can be an effective way of planning key milestones leading up to an event, as it focuses on the sequences of tasks necessary for completion of a project (Van der Wagen, 2007). By plotting tasks on a horizontal and vertical chart, it is possible to view the nature of the task and the time scale over the whole project. This is useful as it shows the relationships between the tasks so that the interdependence of tasks can be clearly seen at a glance.

Contingency plans for unexpected situations should also be included. Schedules for detailed planning, community consultation, design, construction, site preparations and test events must be drawn up so that the event owners can be guaranteed timely delivery, and the local authorities and other groups involved in site planning and development have a clear understanding of their own roles and responsibilities in the process and appreciate how any delay on their part could have implications on the wider schedule plan (Maralack & Lloyd, 2005).

A task scheduling system, such as a computerised project management package or project planning software, is also a useful tool for clustering interdependent tasks together, which allows individual managers to gauge in advance their work responsibilities, the product and resource requirements, and deadlines for completion of each task.

Besides providing relevant information, it is important to remember that the bidding process tests the ability of a prospective host to meet all the event owner's requirements and to host a successful event, therefore detailing the critical path as early as possible enables bid organisers to meet exact requirements within the given timeframe (Maralack & Lloyd, 2005).

5.6 Reflections on the overall bid process

In looking at the key generic features of event bidding then, it is worth reflecting upon the following points as forming the basis for any bid.

Emery (2002) sets out the key phases in a bid process based on major sporting events. However, it is interesting to see how applicable the process is to those considering bidding for much smaller events. Case study 5.7 is drawn directly from a small events management company employing fewer than ten full-time staff. It includes some very specific concerns that such a company would need to address before deciding whether to bid for an event. Comparing the case study to the process set out below, the two are generally very similar, addressing similar concerns but in a different way. The more detailed case study points can be easily fitted in to the e-model process, differing markedly only in the elements of the actual procedure.

Phases of the bidding process

- ❐ *Phase 1: Feasibility study.* This should be carried out quickly and efficiently by the prospective bidder to establish a) if the agency can deliver the event (it has the skill, knowledge and experience and will benefits from the event; and b) if the budget is sufficient to enable the aims of the client to be met.
- ❐ *Phase 2: Strategic planning.* Does the event fit into local/regional/national strategies for events (considering also tourism, leisure and other benefits) and does it bring strategic (marketing and financial) benefits to the agency that can be clearly established?
- ❐ *Phase 3: Event objectives.* What are they? Are they realistic? What purpose does the event serve?
- ❐ *Phase 4: Venue selection.* What is relevant and appropriate for the client, and what type of venue should be considered?
- ❐ *Phase 5: Bid procedure.* How is it being managed and by whom? Is it transparent? Does it seem like the client is interested in ideas or simply wants someone to fulfil basic organisational tasks only?

For major governing body sport rights, there is an extra dimension to be added that makes the bid much lengthier and time consuming. This would consist of the following:

- ❐ *Candidate city/venue presented to the International Federation.* Any candidate city needs to present its credentials in the first place in order to gauge the response of the rights holder. For example, some events rotate continents on a cyclical basis, or rotate between the major federations involved in the sport, and it is important to know what planning is already in place. This is also an act of courtesy to the rights holder and may help the city/venue make a better bid. It also starts the dialogue.
- ❐ *Preparation of a bid document.* Depending on the event this can be several years or several weeks, but nearly all such events require multi-agency cooperation and specifically the support of regional and/or national governments.
- ❐ *Political lobbying.* This is an essential part of the process, and something that was set in motion by the opening dialogue established in the initial enquiry. This went spectacularly wrong for England when it tried to bid for the 2006 World Cup, ignoring a previous decision by European's football administrators that they would all support Germany. By contrast in went spectacularly right when Tony Blair was a strong advocate for bringing the Olympic Games to London in 2012.
- ❐ *International Federation Election – the decision.* This is invariably a decision made by vote from those elected to represent the federation. This will be based on a combination of the credentials of the city, the policy of the federation and politics. Committee members can be put under pressure to vote a certain way, such as in the case of Salt Lake City's successful bid to host the Winter Olympics where committee delegates making the decision were exposed to generous offers of personal assistance to try to influence their vote.

Case study 5.7 Submitting a request for proposal (RFP)

A small events organisation agency lists the required information needed from the event owner in order to submit a successful request for proposal (RFP).

Before starting to write an RFP, event owners have to figure out what is really needed, what is wanted and what is possible. For example, a RFP would not be necessary for a machine that can produce 1 500 widgets per hour when you have never sold more than 25 a month. Likewise, there is no point in issuing an RFP for a flying car when a messenger can get through traffic just as fast on a bicycle. An RFP needs to distinguish between needs and wants. If an application is wanted that can transmit pictures between headquarters and the vans at the job site, you may specify the number of images per second, the maximum size of the image and the resolution needed. It might be nice to have the images in colour, but you need to decide if that is necessary. Things that are needed are identified in the RFP but using words like 'will', 'shall' and 'must'. These are the 'requirements'. Those things that are merely 'wants' are identified by works like 'may', 'can' and 'optional'.

The proposals you get back in response to your RFP will vary greatly. Each company that responds will have different strengths and weaknesses. Some will focus on lowest cost; others on best quality; still others on the most complete feature set. You should therefore decide up front whether you are looking for the lowest cost or the fastest delivery, or a combination of both.

It is essential to plan and organise the document well. An outline is a good place to start. You will need different sections, at least, for introduction, requirements, selection criteria, timelines and process. Many of these will have subsections. For instance, the requirements section will also include the optional items. These may be blended into the individual requirements or placed in their own section. This is where you explain to potential bidders why you are publishing the RFP and what you hope to achieve by doing so. The introduction may also include a summary of the key points from the other sections, including due date.

Continuing with the example above of an RFP for an image transmission system, the introduction might read something like this: 'XYZ Company requests proposals for a highly reliable, easy-to-use system capable of transmitting images from the main office to vans anywhere in the metropolitan area. Responsive bids must be received by 12.00 noon on Monday, 5 March 2010 at ...'

Requirements

This section is one of the most important and usually takes the most time. From the example above you would need to specify the size and clarity of the images to be transmitted and the necessary speed. Be sure to specify what you need, not how it is to be done, unless that is essential. You might want to break this up into subsections by system, for example a) image size and quality; b) transmission (which could include both desired speed and any requirements that the transmission be secure); and c) desired options (where you might list colour as a desirable option).

Selection criteria

In this section you tell the bidders as much as you choose about how the winning bidder will be selected. It is a good idea to include a sentence like: 'The winning bidder, if any, will be selected solely by the judgement of XYZ Company.' Some government RFPs are very specific on the selection criteria. Most commercial RFPs are less precise. You may want to create a spreadsheet that awards each bid a certain range of points

⦀▶

in each category and then have a team make a choice of the 'best' bid from the ones with the top three scores.

Timelines
This section tells companies who want to bid on your RFP how quickly they must act and how long the process may take. Be reasonable when you set your deadlines. Do not ask for proposals with complex systems and only give the bidders a few days to respond. The larger your RFP, the more complicated the desired purchase and the more detailed the required response, the longer you should allocate time to prepare the bid. This is also where you tell the bidders how long the evaluation process will take, when the bidders will be notified, whether they were successful or not, and how soon they will have to deliver the event.

Process
In this section you explain how the process will work – from sending out the RFP to awarding the contract and starting the work. This section might say, for example, 'Bids are due on the date specified in step 8 above. All bids will be reviewed to make sure they meet all the requirements, i.e. "are responsive".

'All responsive bids will be scored in X categories [name the categories if you wish], and the top three will be evaluated by the proposal team to select the winning bidder and an alternate. Negotiations with the winning bidder are expected to result in a contract award in two weeks'.

Decide how to send out the RFP
Most RFPs are mailed, but they do not have to be. You can send the RFP by email or post it on your company website. Be sure to specify the name or number bidders should use to identify which RFP they are answering.

Decide whom to invite to submit a proposal
You may already know who the key suppliers are or your company may even have a list of acceptable vendors. If not, you can find possible vendors through your professional network, by searching on line or by asking trusted vendors of other materials for their recommendations. Try not to limit the list of recipients to only 'large' companies or 'established' vendors. You may find better ideas and even better pricing from smaller vendors who are more interested in winning your business.

Finally, send out the RFP!

5.7 Summary

This chapter has set out some of the main elements involved in bidding for events that apply to both small-scale corporate and conference events as well as mega-events such as the FIFA Football World Cup and the Olympic Games. It has established that while the term 'bidding' is commonly used, the actual process of bidding may include procurement, pitching and tendering. Drawing upon real-world examples, readers should now be aware of the need to clearly identify their strategy and rationale for bidding for any event. For an event bid of any kind the key consideration is: is it feasible? Is it financially, organisationally, conceptually and promotionally beneficial to bid? To that, for larger major and mega-events, can be added the considerations of economic, environmental, social and political benefit.

For events agencies regularly involved in bidding, the level of competition is considerable as all clients now expect high-class documentation and presentation that considers external factors (environmental) as well as organisational ones. Agencies who bid on a regular basis can have a success rate of only 10%, although many will hope to have a rate nearer 30%. At this level, bids tend to be prepared in-house and are done so in a relatively short period of time, often running at one or two per week, but they still require a thorough and detailed event concept, complete with full costing and organisational detail. The decision to bid is made for business reasons and, public sector apart, is often at the invitation of the client. As with all clients, bids must be sensitive to the needs, interests and concerns of the client. They are time and resource intensive.

Major international events, especially sport, require more social, political, economic and environmental reflection and they are often driven by regional or national government or organisations reflecting those interests. As such the time-frame is longer and the bid team needs to be set up in the first place and subsequently requires far more wide-ranging expertise simply because of the size and scale involved. Competition here is just as intense, but often works in a cyclical way to the priorities of the rights holder. The political and social landscape needs immediate consideration before an agreement is made to bid, since any bid is likely to cost several millions of dollars.

Both the bidding examples referred to here end up at the same place and that is that any potential bidders need to know what it is that the client wants and what are they looking to get out of the event. Although simple questions, they may produce a multitude of answers and points for consideration that go beyond the straightforward. In fact, in many cases the answers are complex and problematic. It is up to the bidding agency or team to address these as priorities by adopting a strategic and structured approach to bidding, as suggested in this chapter.

Questions for research

1 Consider what the main factors are that an event owner looks for in a successful bid document and what expertise is expected from an event organisation.
2 Imagine you are an event organiser who has been invited to tender for a bid. What issues would you need to consider before deciding whether to do so?
3 What are the typical phases in any bid process?
4 Produce a script for a 'pitch' presentation for a selected event. It should detail in 30 minutes exactly how you would present your ideas to a client.
5 Visit an event – conference, sports event, festival, etc. In a role-playing exercise, imagine that you will be bidding for the contract to run that event the following year. Critically analyse the event and make a comprehensive list of notes that highlight

(i) the things that you liked and that worked;

(ii) the things you disliked, and specify exactly how you could improve upon them when it comes to producing a bid document.

Recommended websites

Browse the following internet sites for interesting and informative information:

Business Events – a website with information on conference bidding: http://www. businesseventssydney.com.au/bid-for-an-event/your-bidding-partner/how-conference-bidding-works/how-conference-bidding-works_home.cfm

Games Bid – web portal containing information on bidding for events, including specific links to reviews on Olympic Games bidding: http://www.gamesbids.com/eng/other_news/1176296664.html

Sport Business – link to recent report on background history and recent bidding for major sports events (UK bias): http://www.sportbusiness.com/reports/163935/sports-event-bidding

Sports City – the Sports Business Portal provides guidance for opportunities across sports events worldwide: http://www.sports-city.org/bidding.php

Tenders Direct – UK public sector website with information all local authority tender & bid opportunities. Specific section on events: http://www.tendersdirect.co.uk/Ourservice/Search_Results.aspx?Keywords=events

Suggested reading

Gratton, C & Henry, I (Eds). 2001b. *Sport in the City: The Role of Sport in Economic and Social Regeneration*. London: Routledge.

For corporate, conference and destination bidding, see:

Allen, J. 2005. *Event Planning: The Ultimate Guide to Successful Meetings, Corporate Events, Fundraising Galas, Conferences, Conventions, Incentives and Other Special Events*. London: Wiley.

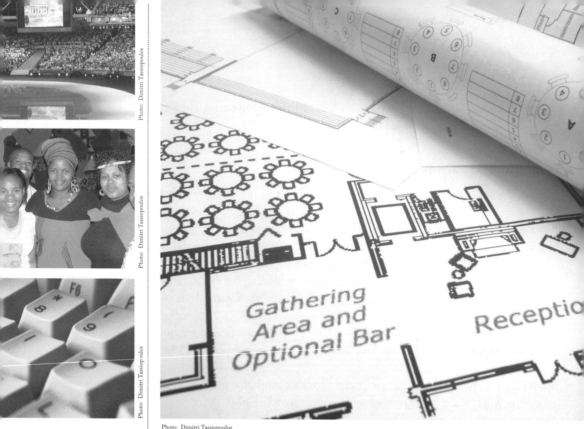

Photo: Dimitri Tassiopoulos

6

Events planning and coordination

Tom Wanklin

Abstract

A successful event is dependent upon comprehensive, effective and detailed planning and coordination between the various event stakeholders. This chapter sets out the planning activities and procedures necessary to assist in achieving a successful event, whether large or small. In addition, the chapter explains how to coordinate the event-planning activities being conducted by many different stakeholders so as to ensure that the event achieves the intended goals and objectives of the various interested and affected parties.

Chapter objectives

After you have read this chapter you should be able to:
- ❒ understand the event-planning process, assess and identify opportunities and constraints and formulate creative event plans;
- ❒ formulate and plan activities with sequencing to meet objectives, budgets and defined outcomes;
- ❒ conduct a site inspection, analyse the site or venue and prepare an event plan;
- ❒ understand the various role players responsible for planning and enable them to achieve the best planning results;
- ❒ identify the various authorities involved in the planning and approval processes so as to achieve necessary approvals for the event; and
- ❒ identify and coordinate the various stakeholders with an interest in planning the event to ensure they achieve their intended goals and objectives.

6.1 Introduction

People engage in planning activities every day of their lives. Planning what one would like to achieve is usually carried out through a rational and deliberate set of actions ranging from day-to-day living, working and leisure, to numerous technical activities such as financial planning, economic planning, human resource planning, event planning, etc. Planning can also vary according to levels of detail, ranging from local events to mega national or international events. Having an event plan helps in coordinating various activities in order to achieve a particular vision.

Planning is one phase of the event management process which determines the specifications, activities, resources and assumptions affecting the nature of the event project (Rutherford Silvers, 2009). Accordingly, in the context of events management, event planning and coordination could be defined as the process by which the event is designed and shaped, resources are allocated and various actions are specified in order to achieve a successful event of a certain type, size,

financial return, socio-economic benefit and agreed purpose.

Unless events organisations plan and coordinate the events they are responsible for, they will not take place when they are intended or required to occur. In addition, the ongoing management and sustained quality of an event or events will not easily be maintained if a well-thought-out plan is not in place and continually reviewed. Figure 6.1 depicts the typical steps involved in planning and coordinating an event.

6.2 Who is responsible for planning and coordinating an event?

In simple terms, any group, community, organisation or collective can plan their event to suit their requirements and priorities. The event planning process is directly linked to the persons organising the event and having the mandate to plan for it. The planning and coordination process can be the responsibility of a number of different role players, including:
- ❒ National, provincial and/or local spheres of government;

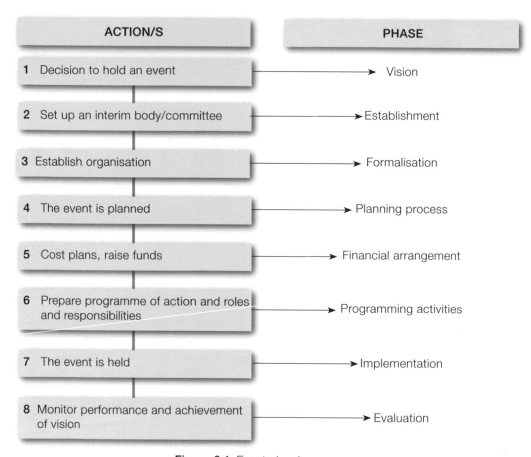

ACTION/S	PHASE
1 Decision to hold an event	Vision
2 Set up an interim body/committee	Establishment
3 Establish organisation	Formalisation
4 The event is planned	Planning process
5 Cost plans, raise funds	Financial arrangement
6 Prepare programme of action and roles and responsibilities	Programming activities
7 The event is held	Implementation
8 Monitor performance and achievement of vision	Evaluation

Figure 6.1 Event planning process

❏ Government entities and parastatal institutions such as tourism boards;
❏ Community groups, associations (such as welfare groups, arts and craft clubs), civic organisations, political parties;
❏ Non-government organisations;
❏ Academic institutions; and
❏ Professional events management teams – such as Olympic Bid organisations, FIFA World Cup organisations, etc.

Case study 6.1 describes one example of an organisation which plans and coordinates an annual event as a voluntary body.

Event planning and coordination requires an integrated approach between those organisations responsible for event planning and the local authorities which are responsible for the overall development of the area or region within which the event is to take place. A considerable number of institutions and event-planning specialists have also stressed the importance of community participation in the tourism and event-planning process.

In many instances, however, event planning is a specialist function, and community consultation or 'partnership' does not necessarily mean control or management involvement. Communities do, however, require that they are in support of the vision, goals and objectives involved in the event because of the benefits it could offer them and also the possible negative impact or costs that could result. Very often, mega-events or hallmark events are nationally driven and the local community is not given much of an idea of the costs they can have on their quality of life in the short and long term. The marketing hype associated with major events can often overshadow negative impacts to the detriment of the local host community, and consultation will assist in reducing problems in this regard.

6.3 The steps taken to plan and coordinate an event

Each event-planning process is managed by the event organiser which is part of a group, committee, organisation or partnership. The organiser invariably determines the broad *vision* of the event and this is used by the event planner as the *planning brief.*

The planning brief is an essential guide to the planning team because it sets out the details of the focus of the planning exercise and the issues to be addressed, and guides the limits of the data collection exercise to be undertaken. In addition, the brief provides a clear instruction on how the work is to be done, the time to be used and the target dates for achieving various milestones. Any planning exercise which does not have a brief setting out the parameters of the work to be undertaken is doomed to failure or, at the very least, a waste of time and funds.

The event organisation, committee and event planner would undertake a planning process involving the following steps:

- ❑ Prepare a concept which describes the *vision* for the event, its purpose, the envisaged date, size and type of event (as detailed in the planning brief);
- ❑ Conduct a *site analysis* and *feasibility study* to identify a possible event venue, conduct a study (situation analysis) and site inspection of that venue and an environmental appraisal of the likely impact of the event;
- ❑ Prepare an *event framework plan* according to more detailed objectives and strategies and, with detailed layouts of the site or venue, associated plans for event activities, such as administration and operations, financial arrangements, institutional issues, transport and parking, communications marketing/ promotions, health and safety, risk management, catering and human resources/volunteers and so on;
- ❑ Prepare an *event programme* setting out the event activities, sequence of events and timeframes; and
- ❑ Review the event plan on a regular basis to *monitor* how relevant the plan is in relation to reality and changed

circumstances, and amend the plan where necessary.

There are several different styles which have developed over time to suit the circumstances of particular needs of communities engaged in planning to achieve certain objectives. The most common planning and coordination style is the *incremental* approach whereby a series of small planning activities and implementation is carried out in order to achieve an end goal. Through this process of numerous small steps, the plan evolves until the preferred result or vision is achieved. The second style of planning, which is more suited to event planning, is called the *systematic* approach, whereby the planning and coordination process follows a rational, pre-established step-by-step process to ensure that each planning participant is part of the process and is able to give input. Systematic planning seeks to integrate the event activities more effectively, and takes into account the environment, finance, human resources and the plans of associated stakeholders, such as the local municipality and government departments. This integrated and systematic planning approach is more suited to the highly complex special and mega-events where a large number of stakeholders are involved. The planning process is also continually monitored with reality so as to ensure the plan can be updated to accommodate changing circumstances.

The steps involved in preparing an event plan are described in greater detail below.

6.3.1 Event concept

When an individual, a community or organisation decides to hold an event, it is essential to understand the *type, size*

and *purpose* of the event. This constitutes the overall *event concept* (or vision) which they wish to achieve. Having a common vision among the stakeholder group is also very important so as to coordinate activities and achieve a successful outcome. In an increasingly complex environment with more individualism in thought and activities, planning by consensus among different role players is vital in order to achieve satisfactory results.

A conceptual vision statement involves a broad outline of what is hoped will be achieved and does not necessarily include details of quantity, size or cost of the event. The vision statement is often also called a goal and it is essential to the planning exercise because it gives the organisation something to work for and a means to measure performance or the event outcomes in future.

6.3.2 Selection of a venue

Appraisal of the proposed event site or venue needs to be carried out to gain an understanding of what venues are available as far as the various buildings, the town, city or region concerned. Site analysis can assist in reaching a better understanding of the potential of the venue to create a unique event which will be memorable to the participants. This understanding is crucial because it ensures that the event plan is relevant and deals effectively with the identified needs, opportunities and market demand. Any venue has an intrinsic character or 'atmosphere' where 'the event site must be functional, meeting the requirements for fulfilling the function of the event – its purpose, goals and objectives' (Rutherford Silvers, 2004).

Perhaps the most critical component in the planning of any event is to find a venue which ensures that the event has a high profile, maintains a good image and is easily seen by prospective participants. This important issue is described as the 'technique of interpretation' (Cooper et al., 1999) and means that events and destinations should maximise the opportunity to be noticed. This can be done by the use of imaginative and visible signs, buildings, towers and audiovisual media. In addition, themes can be a potent tool which will make an event more visible and more appealing in an ever-growing and competitive environment. Regardless of the unique locality requirements of each event, the fundamental consideration in choosing a particular locality is access to the market (namely the participants). These participants would include the people and organisations participating in the events, the spectators and the service organisations supporting the event.

A study is conducted at the outset to ascertain information about the site or venue and its characteristics, the opportunities for holding the event and the constraints which may affect the event success. This study should include collecting information about the venue, for example the size in relation to the proposed event; the layout and topography (physical shape); the entrances and exits; availability of parking and arrangements for special needs of the participants, spectators and competitors; the availability of infrastructure and transport, and so on. Any suitable site should have sufficient land and flexibility to accommodate the event; vehicle parking; readily available infrastructure; an absence of conflicting adjacent land uses or communities which may be detrimentally affected by the event (or alternatively may affect the event); suitable slopes and orientation of the site

to take advantage of views, vistas and prevailing winds, and be suitably orientated to avoid conflict with sun (as required by most sports activities) and poor weather conditions.

Accessibility needs to be considered in terms of proximity to major transport corridors or at least primary routes including road and rail. More efficient movement of visitors would be achieved through integration of modes of transport (i.e. different types of transport) which enables easy, efficient and economic movement through common destinations (e.g. arrivals and departures of taxis, trains and buses). The site or venue selection process needs to consider affordable, adequate and efficient access to bulk infrastructure including sewerage, water, electricity, telecommunications and roads, with ease of access to airports, railway stations and, if appropriate, harbours. Event planners need to consider how the proposed event relates to other events, accommodation, facilities and service activities which could help to achieve a successful cluster of event and tourism products.

Having chosen alternative sites or venues which suit the proposed event from an accessibility point of view, it is necessary to refine the choice of alternative in terms of additional features, such as the cost of the venue, the ease of acquisition of the land and/or buildings (either by rental or purchase); the likely comparative cost of acquiring land at different localities; the alternative costs of connecting to bulk infrastructure and the capacity of the infrastructure to accommodate the event; the current zoning and land use development restrictions pertaining to the land and, if these restrictions are not supportive of the event, the likely time period to change the restrictions (and possibly the likelihood of the local authority supporting such changes); and the findings of a preliminary environmental assessment which provides comparative appraisal on the suitability of each venue.

The venue should preferably be suitably secured to control access and also prevent external vantage points from overlooking the event. Depending on the locality of the site, any sensitive fauna and flora need to be identified and protected. Similarly, the natural drainage areas across the site need to be protected, and development of these areas needs to be avoided to prevent flooding and environmental degradation. Finally, an appraisal of potential risks associated with the site needs to be conducted to mitigate against any problems, hazards and risks.

It is recommended the site analysis makes use of a checklist to ensure nothing is left out. The data collection and analysis stage of the planning process is a key point where the communities interested and affected parties and relevant stakeholders have an opportunity to participate. This can involve individual contributions and group meetings or workshops. Effective *consultation* with all affected parties is critical, because if any groups or individuals are left out of the process, their input might be lost and/or the exercise will be discredited because it is considered exclusive rather than inclusive.

Prior to preparing a detailed event plan, it is often useful to undertake a *feasibility study* which can guide the decision makers (the event organisers) as to whether or not it is appropriate and viable to continue with the event. Analysis of the data collected in the analysis should enable a preliminary assessment of the event feasibility to be undertaken at an early stage, before large sums of money or time are expended.

6.3.3 Event framework plan

Having formulated the event concept, it is possible to formulate *objectives,* which are detailed statements of what it is hoped to achieve by a particular date and certain targets. The ability of a planning team to set meaningful objectives is emphasised by Bell and Vazquez-Illa (1996) who state that '[s]uccessful planning requires that management have a clear understanding of where it wants to go and how it plans to get there, in both the short and long term. Without a clear set of goals and objectives, the organisation could become paralyzed'. It is necessary to formulate the *strategies* or *actions* by means of which you intend to achieve that vision. These describe who has to perform an activity, how they are to work and the programme they will need to follow. The use of various strategies in a careful way can set the tone of an event and have a very important influence on how it is structured and designed.

An event framework plan will require that all the objectives, actions and programmes are linked together in an integrated way so that the event works successfully and no one section operates exclusively and without reference to the others. For example, the event plan needs to synchronise the transportation proposals with suitable site access, parking and traffic management measures, which at the same time take into account the human resources capacity of the traffic management department within the local authority. An integrated event plan must also contain associated or supporting plans dealing with all the elements of the event, including administration, operations, finance, human resources, health and safety, risk management, marketing and promotion, sound, lighting, special effects and so on.

The growing importance of the events industry as a potential source of economic and social benefit to communities, organisations and countries means that the relative return on investment of the planned event needs to be considered right from the inception of the event framework plan. This is particularly relevant in the context of global financial pressure and the need to channel scarce resources for the greatest benefit possible. While the financial implications of the event and the resulting economic rate of return on investment can be measured, it is not often easy to measure the social impact and social return on investment. The event planners need to find ways to evaluate the extent to which the event framework plan will ensure the proposed event has socio-economic spin offs and creates opportunities for communities who would not have benefited had the event not taken place.

6.3.4 Planning event spaces

A critical component of the event is the environmental character, setting, layout and image associated with its design, construction, materials and façade, and appearance of signs, buildings and vegetation. All these components contribute to the event 'experience' and determine the context within which all the activities operate. 'You can have the best publicized, programmed and sponsored event – however, if your site is not well laid out, and visually pleasing, the event will not be perceived as successful ... Ideal site layout should combine artistry and practicality into a design that stimulates revenue' (Citrine, 1997: 17). Considerable scientific and technical expertise comes to play in the planning, design and construction of various event facilities. Such expertise includes urban designers, landscape architects, quantity surveyors, architects, civil and structural engineers, traffic engineers, interior designers, sound engineers, graphic designers and artists. Certain fundamental planning hints are recommended for consideration below; however, readers are referred to specialist planning and design manuals and expertise for more details should this be required.

The wide variety of events and their activities demand a similar diversity of spaces, buildings and facilities. Getz (1997) highlights how most events have a 'special physical dimension' or 'setting'. These can be aggregated into six basic types:

❒ *Assemblies.* These include concerts, conferences, conventions, spectator sports, religious or education ceremonies;

❒ *Processions.* These concern the linear passage of people, vehicles and/or mobile exhibits in a hall, stadium or street;

❒ *Circuit or track.* These involve racing activities where spectators are accommodated along the route or at strategic points (such as the start and finish);

❒ *Public places.* These are open spaces which are often used for events and can include parks, playgrounds, sports fields, plazas, closed-off streets;

❒ *Exhibitions/fairs.* These are situated in warehouses and on large tracts of land which can accommodate a variety of stalls, equipment, trade exhibits, activities and entertainment; and

❒ *Specialised facilities.* Specific and custom-built facilities are required for sport and for certain specialist activities.

All the above event spaces require fundamental facilities and support services which are positioned creatively to ensure that the event can be successfully managed. Basic requirements, according to Getz (1997), include the following:

- ❏ Vehicular access, parking, loading/unloading areas;
- ❏ Emergency vehicle access and parking;
- ❏ Emergency first-aid facility;
- ❏ Administration office;
- ❏ Information/customer care/enquiries;
- ❏ Entrance/exit/fire escapes/reception/waiting rooms;
- ❏ Change rooms and ablutions;
- ❏ Breakaway rooms/preparation and re-hearsal facilities;
- ❏ Toilets, ablutions and powder rooms;
- ❏ Communication room/media facilities;
- ❏ Designated seating or parking for spectators;
- ❏ Refreshment and dining facilities;
- ❏ Catering, kitchens, storage, repair and maintenance facilities;
- ❏ Security booths and accommodation;
- ❏ Solid waste storage and management; and
- ❏ Accommodation, ramps and parking for physically challenged participants and spectators.

Planning the event spaces involves preparation of an event layout plan which is important for coordination of the efforts of all role players in the event production and implementation process (Rutherford Silvers, 2004). This can involve a simple floor plan of the room or building the event is going to use, or a line drawn map of a site and even an aerial photograph of the event spaces (if a large site is involved). The arrangement of the above elements on the layout plan needs to follow the style or character of the event; for example a circuit or track event as distinct from an assembly or an exhibition. Each site is different and it is difficult to prescribe how best to achieve the most suitable layout of functional areas. Kevin Lynch (quoted by Getz, 1997) highlights the necessary organisational tools to set out an event space so that people do not get lost, crowds are channelled to follow a logical route and various functional areas are clearly demarcated by signage.

There are a few examples of the various techniques which can be used in site planning to make the event unique and to 'dazzle' the public. These include making the venue or site inviting with clearly demarcated entrances and pathways. Signs and other methods of demarcating main routes such as focal points, towers, banners and archways can direct the movement of people. In addition, attractive walkways can be created using trees, grass and booths. Decorations can make an area attractive, and special-effects lighting can turn an average venue into an exciting one. Citrine (1997) suggests that one could 'use the environment ... It is much less expensive to use the natural environment than to create one'. These measures could include using outdoor breakaway venues and dining arrangements near an attractive garden feature, and so on. Rutherford Silvers (2004) highlights the versatility of using tents to extend building spaces, creating additional rooms and linking these to the main event, with technological aids such as digital viewing screens and sound systems.

Site planning needs to take into account the fact that people appreciate a convenient venue which is easy to move about in, with a smooth, integrated flow. The most attractive venues and events should be in the outlying areas so that people are lured past the smaller venues or exhibits (Citrine, 1997: 18). The site layout needs as far as possible to allow plenty of space to prevent congestion, and also to create a flow in the pedestrian movement and a free-flowing vehicle traffic system.

Continued growth in the events industry is resulting in the construction of massive multiple-venue facilities in certain city centres resulting in multiple events taking place in the same venue and increasing management complexity due to larger crowds, overlap of venues/facilities and catering demands. The events industry will benefit from such growth, but there are certain essential measures which must be taken to reduce conflict, confusion and a decline in the quality of the experience. Lenhardt (1998) lists these as follows:

❑ *Easy Access – The building should provide a separate entrance and registration area for each group.*
❑ *Lots of Signage – Banners and signs with the name of the association or show create a sense of personal space.*
❑ *Contiguous Space – Make sure all the areas you would be using are in close proximity to one another. Attendees should not have to race from one end of the center to the other or pass through another group's space.*

Making sure the event is secure and access is under the control of the event organisers is a priority. In the case of a building, the access and emergency exit points need to be planned carefully to ensure that participants are able to clearly see them. In the case of open land for large and new events, it is essential that the property in question be securely surrounded by fencing, walling or any other suitable barrier. CCTV camera systems are becoming a growing security tool for managing site security.

Emphasis needs to be placed on enhancing the environment of the site through landscaping, the establishment of gardens and vegetation features. Enhanced visual effects can also be achieved by using strategically placed lighting in and around vegetated areas. Various other landscaping tools can be used to reduce noise from adjacent major transport routes (e.g. grassed earth embankments), wind intrusion (e.g. trees and shrub belts), and other degradation problems (e.g. pathways to prevent soil erosion, dust and crowd damage).

6.3.5 Transport

The importance of integrated transport to support an event cannot be overemphasised. Transportation plans will depend on the size and complexity of the event, the extent to which the participants (spectators and competitors) need to be transported to and from the venue (or rely on their own transport arrangements), the need to transport goods and services to the event, and the extent to which the site is accessible to existing transport services. The transport plan needs to explain in detail how the various elements of the event requiring transport are to be accommodated. The plan needs to list all elements involved in the event that need access to transport facilities and explain what is to be done, who is required to do what by when, and how it is to be done. The plan also needs to set out emergency measures in the event of any problems, and health and safety incidents.

It is easier to prepare a transport plan with the use of checklists which include all the factors requiring planning to achieve an integrated transport solution (Rutherford Silvers, 2004). Such items or elements include making travel arrangements for delegates (reservations, charters, special group bookings, customer care and hosting), addressing all transport needs (supplies and equipment, public and private contractors, specialist vehicles, spectators, employees and competitors) and integrating as far as possible all transportation modes (ships, ferries, shuttles, buses, cars, trains, aircraft, trucks, taxis, etc.).

6.3.6 Parking

There is a need to ensure adequate parking for spectators, loading/unloading areas for suppliers, access and parking for emergency vehicles, and parking for buses and taxis. Most events are characterised by peak parking demands which result because of certain activities which may attract a high attendance for a specific period. Parking capacity should ideally be geared to meet the peak demand.

A variety of parking provision standards are available in technical manuals which provide a guide as to how many parking spaces to provide per number of seats in the auditorium/stadium or premises. Parking demand for festivals, fairs, processions and parades is extremely difficult to ascertain because the attendance potential is impossible to calculate beforehand. Invariably, parking will occur on an informal basis outside the venue, and close liaison and planning with the traffic management authorities will be necessary to accommodate this.

Most authorities require on-site parking for events and have regulations regarding standards of access, type of road surface, signage, and size and number of spaces. Invariably, the local authority's permission to hold the event will hinge on parking formalities. Traffic congestion due to inadequate parking facilities can be highly disruptive and dangerous; accordingly realistic and practical measures are required to address this component.

6.3.7 Event programme

Of vital importance to planning and coordinating an event is the event programme. This element of the plan is the 'rationale' for the meeting or event (Krugman & Wright, 2007) and sets out the order of activities and their duration, and the responsibilities of the participants and event organisers. Creating a favourable image of the event through an attractive programme relates to the arrangement and organisation of the activities according to imaginative themes with the use of logos, mascots and various symbols to enhance the excitement and experience of the event. The event can also be enhanced by the use of rituals, emotional stimulation, great spectacles, entertainment, commercial merchandising and side shows (such as buskers, street performers and animateurs).

The sequence of activities during the event needs to be organised in such a way that the participants are entertained and want to return the next time it is held. In this regard, it is beneficial to have supporting events ahead of the main attraction, so that the event experience rises in excitement to a grand finale. In a similar way, exhibitions and festivals need to arrange their programme to attract attendance over an extended period rather than over a short interval. This can be achieved by having key attractions interspersed with support activities to keep the participants entertained on a regular basis.

Long delays between activities can frustrate crowds and, as a result, crowd management can become a problem, so event programmes need to be prompt and activities evaluated on the basis of their relevance (in the case of a theme), performance and professionalism. Un-rehearsed activities or incomplete exhibits must be taken off as quickly as possible to avoid creating a poor image.

Allowance should be made for food breaks, rest and recuperation. Crowds cannot sustain high levels of excitement for long periods, and peak entertainment needs to be interspersed with alternative acts to extend the experience. Programmes for meetings and conferences differ greatly from those for jazz festivals, sports meetings and opera shows. In most cases the formulation of a programme is basic common sense, and organisers need to use the 'core' or main attraction element as the anchor around which other activities can be clustered.

A determining factor in the success of the event can be the date chosen during the year and the day of the week, the time of day and duration. The seasons and the weather can be a factor affecting the event as well (Allen, 2000) and very often the choice of venue will be affected by these factors. Selection of the date for the event is crucial because it can mean the difference between success and failure. In all cases, whether a regular or a one-off event, it is important to consider the factors which will affect attendance (Whale, 1997), including the impact of public holidays, academic calendars, political activities, days of the week, periods of the month, and arrival and departure times.

Events which depend on outdoor venues or which require particular weather conditions (such as winter sports) have to be held at times determined by the seasons. The advance weather forecasting techniques available can provide trend data which will help determine the most favourable period to hold the event. In selecting the dates for an event it is important to consider the timing in relation to popular television programmes which can influence attendance figures (Richards, 1992). Finally, the availability of broadcasting time on various media can influence both sponsorship interest and viewership support. International events also need to consider international time variations and select optimum time slots to achieve maximum exposure.

In order to ensure that the event is held at the correct time and on the correct date, it is essential to liaise with the project management team who are responsible for programming and managing the development (setup) process. The critical path in the development schedule will indicate the shortest possible time for construction and therefore the most likely completion date of the construction or preparation phase.

The length of time over which an event is held can sometimes be determined by the nature of the event itself. For example, a sports event would be played according to the rules and time allowed by the referee. Other events, such as a festival, can, however, be more flexible, and their duration could be determined by the capacity of the venue to accommodate the activities over a period of time or by the perceived duration of interest which is expected of the attendees. The length of an event can also be influenced by the comfort of the participants. For example, it is well known that the average span of attention is approximately 30 to 40 minutes. As a result, it is important to have a varied programme which allows for breaks when people can stretch and visit the ablution facilities. Also, a varied programme prevents monotony and helps to keep the audience entertained. Care should also be taken to build the programme of events towards the main attraction. This holds the attendance figures up and serves to foster a successful outcome.

'Maintaining awareness and excitement at fever pitch over long periods can require substantial stamina and financial resources. A conservative view has to be taken of the actual levels of programming and awareness that can be maintained to attract a target audience over a period of days or weeks,' according to Richards (1992). Care must be taken not to extend an event beyond its maximum exposure, particularly when the cost of rental of premises and/or payment of artists and performers could bring about a loss of profit. It is often the case that audiences reach saturation and attendance tails off before the main event/attraction is held.

The agenda of an event needs to be prepared at an early stage in order that all role players have a clear understanding of the sequence of events. This ranges from the organisers knowing which activity is to start and finish where and when, to the local authority traffic officers knowing the likely traffic congestion periods due to event programmes and, finally, the mayor knowing when to arrive and perform the appropriate civic duties. As part of setting an agenda, provision needs to be made for the rehearsal of participants so as to ensure that equipment works correctly and performers know what is required of them.

Whale (1997) suggests several useful tips to be followed when preparing a suitable events agenda, including determining the main attraction and using this as the event 'pivot', deciding when refreshments and meals should be served, considering the timing of entertainment, and arranging the programme to suit availability of transport. Generally, an event programme is influenced by the scheduled arrival of special dignitaries, key performers or speakers. In the case of a conference or meeting, allowance needs to be made for the registration of guests or participants and for a welcoming procedure. The opening event sets the tone for the remainder of the event, and the closing event also can influence the level of experience and enjoyment.

6.3.8 Facilities

Organising an event can involve an enormous amount of work in terms of the assembly of facilities to ensure success. Various fundamental requirements need to be taken into account, whether the event is a meeting or a rock concert, a small event or large one. Moxley (1995) recommends these include an event map or model showing the distribution of activities and key facilities such as toilets; information and customer assistance; entrances and exits to main attractions (this can also involve a computer-generated service); facilities for television cameras, including lighting, camera positions and control room (usually an external mobile room); radio and television broadcast/commentators; telephones for the general public, media and the organisation (such facilities should allow for fax and modem linkage as separate direct lines); parking, taxi and bus drop-off zones and separate taxi/bus waiting areas; loading/unloading areas separate from general public access and general parking areas; and finally, event venue facilities, including changing facilities; stage and performing areas; seating auditorium;

assembly areas; catering, dining and toilet facilities; equipment storage; refuse storage areas; maintenance rooms; and security facilities.

Planning and coordinating an event relies a great deal on equipment, technology, sound, lighting, special effects and décor to create the exciting atmosphere which will make the event a unique experience for the audience. Having a good understanding of the special effects and technology needs of the event assists greatly in deciding which venue is most suitable (Allen, 2000) and ensuring that the event framework plan encompasses all the necessary activities and resources to cater for the required atmosphere and effects.

6.4 Planning and coordination tools

There are a few useful tools which event planners use to assist in their work in various planning and coordination activities. Computers and information technology are obviously an important component; however, there will always be important thought processes which aid the planning process. These include the *exchange of views* between all the interested and affected parties involved in an event, *brainstorming* or *mind mapping* of the ideas of the participants, and the use of various planning aids or *technical tools*.

The *exchange of views* between planners, participants, stakeholder organisations, representatives of communities and interested and affected persons is a critical component of successful planning and coordination. This is achieved through one-on-one discussions and focus group sessions (or *workshops*, as they are often termed). For any of these meetings to be effective they need to be structured

with an agenda (which is prepared through group consensus) and a clear understanding of the outcomes expected from each session.

In a more intensive process than an exchange of views in a meeting, the planning process can also utilise the technique known as *mind mapping*. This technique was developed by Tony Buzan and is defined as 'a whole brain, visually interesting version of outlining' (Wycoff, 1991). The technique involves an individual or group of people brainstorming a set of issues, ideas and proposals in such a way that they are drawn in an informal picture with linkages shown to a central theme. Mind-mapping techniques are useful planning tools because they allow uninhibited contributions of ideas by members of a group, and display the ideas and their interrelationships visibly in an interesting and pleasing way. 'Mind mapping and brainstorming work together to further encourage creativity and idea generation' (Wycoff, 1991). However, brainstorming differs from mind mapping because it generally results in random lists of ideas rather than the collective, linked approach of mind mapping.

Apart from hands-on drawings and maps, plans, designs and sketches, computer technology provides various tools such as computer-aided draughting (CAD), drawing/publishing software and geographical information systems (GIS) which can be used in the drawing, design and graphic aspects. Event planners can access several useful drawing aids, site design drawing software and meeting facilitation systems through the internet. These tools enable any planner to prepare simple but effective diagrams, site and room drawings, and layouts showing important information relating to the event. Data analysis for simple to very complex events makes use of various information technology and computer software involving mathematical modelling, matrix analysis techniques and spreadsheets for planning data, estimating, budgeting and preparing action plans.

6.5 Achieving planning compliance for the event

Obtaining permission to hold an event will vary according to the nature, size and locality of the event. Organising permission to hold a meeting in the local sports club would be relatively simple compared to obtaining all the permits and approvals for a mega-event like the FIFA World Cup tournament, for example. The tourism industry is growing in complexity as is the extent of permits and approvals. Compliance and approvals in terms of all the legislation and local rules is essential for the event to proceed safely, and meet insurance requirements and health and safety bylaws. Rutherford Silvers (2004) explains that there is a wide range of items requiring permissions and approvals, which are the responsibility of the event coordinator. These include liquor licences; times of trading; noise levels; use of fireworks; catering; gaming and or gambling activities; licences for playing music and films; access to streets for parades or processions; parking arrangements; access and exit points onto busy streets; meetings of crowds and assembly in public places; display of posters, signage and banners; closure of streets; leases for premises; and solid waste/refuse management.

Depending on where the event is proposed to be held, there is invariably a local authority and law enforcement agency who could advise on the procedures and where to apply for necessary permission. In some areas the approval process is simple and under one roof, but elsewhere it can involve a complex set of procedures with more than one organisation (Rutherford Silvers, 2004).

6.6 Summary

Event planning determines and shapes the nature of an event project according to the vision, objectives and requirements of the event organiser. A well-thought-out, clear, concise and imaginative plan is crucial for there to be a successful event. Planning is undertaken by a variety of people, groups, event management professionals, organisations and government bodies. Small and large events are planned according to a set of straightforward steps starting with preparing a concept or vision of the event, then formulating detailed objectives describing the detailed intentions of creating the event, selecting a suitable venue, preparing an event framework plan and an event programme, and finally, carrying out regular checks to monitor how the event plan fulfils the needs of the organisers and compares to reality.

There are several factors which will determine whether or not the event is planned effectively and held successfully. Factors which must be taken into account to ensure success include the following:

❏ Local community participation and thorough consultation;
❏ A clear and detailed planning brief which is systematic and effective;
❏ An experienced organisation or organising committee with effective leadership;
❏ A multidisciplinary planning team with a principal agent who is responsible for overall coordination and performance;

□ A well-balanced event programme with attractive elements and at least one unique, outstanding main attraction;

□ Contingency planning ('what if' scenarios); and

□ An adequate planning budget.

Questions for research

1 Describe the steps in the event planning and coordination process.
2 Critically discuss the important factors which determine the suitable locality (or site) of an event.
3 Describe how you would prepare an event framework plan.
4 Explain how you would address the transport needs of your event.
5 Describe how you would obtain the necessary approvals for the event you intend to hold.

Recommended websites

Browse the following internet sites for interesting and informative information:

Case studies:
http://www.academic.sun.ac.za/sajrsper/30.2/Ntloko%20641.pdf
http://www.doh.gov.za/department/foodcontrol/docs/specialevents/case.pdf
http://www.hrr.co.uk/pdisp.php?pid=5

Planning guidelines:
http://www.herstmere.gov.uk/environmentplanning/environmentalhealth/dnld_200040/
    GUIDE_SAFE_EVENTS_A5.pdf
http://www.bracknell-forest.gov.uk/environment/env-emergency-planning/env-safety-
    advisory-group.html
http://www.insidesbts.edu/forms/legacy/stepstoplanningasuccessfulevent.pdf
http://geocities.com/heartland/pointe/9385/events.html

Planning process:
http://www.personal.usyd.edu.au/~wotoole/epmspage1.html#EPMS_Schema
http://www.davislogic.com/event_management.htm
http://www.juliasilvers.com/embok/EMBOK_structure_update.htm

Planning tools:
http://www.smartdraw.com/specials/ppc/smartdraw.html
http://www.visioncatcher.co.za/pdf%20folder/canberrastadium.pdf

Suggested reading

Allen, J. 2000. *Event Planning: The Ultimate Guide.* Ontario: John Wiley & Sons, Canada Limited.

Getz, D. 1997. *Event Management & Event Tourism.* New York: Cognizant Communication Corporation.

Rutherford Silvers, J. 2004. *Professional Event Co-ordination.* Ontario: John Wiley & Sons, Canada Limited.

Photo: IMEX

Photo: IMEX

Photo: Dimitri Tassiopoulos

Photo: Dimitri Tassiopoulos

7 Events organising

Tom Wanklin

Abstract

This chapter provides an overview of event organisations, how they are established, their different characteristics and their working relationships with other organisations. In addition the chapter reviews how successful events require leadership and stakeholder commitment. Using total quality management and advanced systems, organisations effectively manage highly complex and fast-moving events. This chapter also reviews the organisational aspects of management, service quality, human resource organising, recruitment and training of event workers.

Chapter objectives

After you have read this chapter you should be able to:

- ❏ understand the different types of organisations involved in holding events;
- ❏ set up an event organisation;
- ❏ identify leadership – 'the champion' to ensure successful events;
- ❏ manage different types of organisations and committee structures to meet event objectives;
- ❏ implement effective event coordination;
- ❏ understand systems management;
- ❏ understand stakeholder management;
- ❏ understand and apply labour legislation and employment condition regulations in terms of human resource management principles;
- ❏ manage, design and implement a volunteer plan, which will enable working with volunteers, volunteer duties and training; and
- ❏ conduct mid- and post-event evaluations.

7.1 Introduction

Every event has an organisation which is behind it: managing activities, organising funding, administering staff and voluntary personnel, undertaking marketing and public relations, organising security, printing leaflets and tickets, hiring performers, arranging decorations, sorting out parking, and many, many other activities. Each event organisation is unique to the event and the characteristics of the people and environment within which it exists. An organisation 'encompasses the creation, structuring and internal coordination of the management system, all with the purpose of fulfilling the organisation's mandate' (Getz, 1997).

The event organisation's structure and key personnel are fundamental to the successful outcome of an event. This aspect is called 'organisational design': the structure of the organisation and its organisational design need to be carefully devised to provide the correct kind of authority, responsibility and accountability relationships for its managers, staff

and service contractors (Cleland, 1999). Further to this, the organisation structure and type of organisation can fundamentally influence the philosophies and policies by which it functions. For example, a charitable institution which is raising revenue for a worthwhile cause may operate with different monetary policies from a profit-oriented company which is privately owned and which is accountable to its shareholders.

There are two distinct types of event: the single event which is held once and for which an events organisation is established specifically for it (almost like a one-off project), and a regularly held event which is held each month or each year (for example sports events, beauty pageants, etc). The types of organisations which organise these different events can differ as a result of their short-term or long-term nature. For example, a single event could be organised by a voluntary association or committee, whereas a regular event could be organised by a more established formal company or institution. This chapter discusses these characteristics and the different organisations used to manage and coordinate events.

7.2 Different types of organisation

The trend in management today is towards more flexible organisational designs due to the establishment of more temporary organisations which have 'modified the traditional concept of organisational design' (Cleland, 1999). Cleland indicates further that 'many organisations of all kinds are starting to abandon the revered "chain of command" where authority and responsibility were placed, in favour of empowering employees to manage themselves …' and the role of supervisors has changed to that of 'teachers, mentors, facilitators, coaches and the like, where they work with the teams rather than supervising them in the traditional sense'.

Events are very often project based in their nature and makeup. Accordingly the changing management approach towards empowering employees to manage themselves in 'alternative teams' (Cleland, 1999) and project-focused teams under a dedicated project/events manager will affect the events industry and organisational design of the future, where organisations are likely to be smaller, more flexible and less bureaucratic.

Determining what type of organisation is appropriate and getting it formally organised is, according to Getz (1997), a matter of forward planning, consultation with experts, and possibly trial and error. There is also no doubt that most events start with a small, core voluntary group of organisers (a committee or association), and as the event process takes off, the organisation evolves into a larger structure with more formal characteristics.

There are seven basic types of organisation (refer to figure 7.1) which are usually found in the events industry.

Figure 7.1 Types of event organisations

Figure 7.2 Functional organisation

Source: Adapted from Getz (1997)

7.2.1 Organisational structures

It is likely that most events are small scale and community based. These are usually organised by members of the community using a simple committee structure to ensure that everyone is involved and coordination of activities succeeds. In the case of larger events, typical organisational companies or structures are usually based on departmental, functional or programme-based approaches. For example, the functional structure usually results in different departments or committees being established to perform a particular function or activity (refer to figure 7.2) and different products or activities.

On the other hand, events organisations can be arranged on the basis of projects or programmes. This is particularly suited to one-off events and the project team approach, and enables a variety of events to receive programme input (refer to figure 7.3). This is also referred to as a *matrix structure* (Getz, 1997).

The matrix organisation offers the greatest flexibility because there is easier interaction between programmes, and the various support services can give

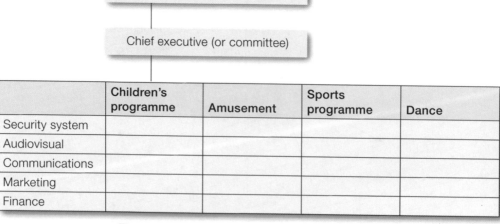

	Children's programme	Amusement	Sports programme	Dance
Security system				
Audiovisual				
Communications				
Marketing				
Finance				

Figure 7.3 Programme-based or matrix structure

Source: Adapted from Getz (1997)

more efficient input. This enables greater productivity and keeps the size of the organisation to an optimum level. The functional organisation can result in duplication of services and less interactive management between the different parts of the organisation.

7.2.2 Corporate company

The decreasing involvement of government in the events industry generally has sponsored the involvement of the private business sector in the organisation and ownership of events. The private sector often collaborates to set up an event through the establishment of a temporary partnership of organisations, subcontracting of different companies or through several events (each with its own management structure) joining together to create a larger event comprising several smaller ones (Getz, 1997).

In the corporate company model, the organisations are formal structures which are created in terms of the Companies Act and have established management boards with senior management, employees and shareholders. The shareholders elect a board of directors at each annual general meeting, which is responsible for engaging the services of a chief executive officer and employees. Such organisations are driven by profit and tend accordingly to be businesslike, efficient and very focused. Each company is governed by its memorandum and articles of association, which are the formal rules and procedures by which it must work.

There are various types of companies which differ according to shareholding and liabilities. A private limited company, or section 20 company, essentially limits shareholding to a certain number of persons with limited personal liability. Should the company acquire debts, the shareholders must meet them and invest to keep the company going. Should the company fail, the shareholders can liquidate the company and their liability is limited to the extent of their shareholding (unless unlimited surety has been given by the shareholders to cover all debts of the company).

A close corporation (CC) is a company which is owned by members (compared to directors and shareholders in a private company). A CC is less expensive to establish and does not normally require an annual audit, provided that the annual financial statements are prepared by a registered accountant. An incorporated partnership (Inc) is a registered partnership between two or more people. This type of company is usually formed by professional event operators or practitioners. Such a company requires an annual audit by law.

An unregistered partnership usually has an agreement (even a handshake) between people who agree to cooperate. Sometimes these organisations can be called a consortium, which can cooperate for the duration of one or more projects. A sole proprietor is the other type of company, where an individual operates a business in his or her own capacity without partners or a formalised structure involving shareholders.

A public company involves the same type of company except that its shareholders are not restricted to specific people or organisations. The general public can own shares in such a company. A company can be sold to (or bought by) another company or group of shareholders. In addition, a company can be listed on the stock exchange to secure investment funding through selling shares to the general public.

7.2.3 Associations not for gain

These organisations are often called 'non-profit making' or 'utility companies' and are established in terms of section 21 of the Companies Act. This type of company was originally formed in the US for the primary purpose of providing utilities (such as electricity, telephones, water, etc.) where the local authorities were unable or not prepared to provide such services. In other countries these companies have also been formed to manage the delivery of social services, accommodation and facilities for communities.

A number of events are organised by associations not for gain because they involve a very effective organisational structure for different people and groups working in association to achieve a common purpose. For example, a local authority, civic structure, church organisation, arts and culture society, and volunteer charity workers could establish an association not for gain. This will be formally registered, and have its own bank account, a dedicated set of audited accounts and an event programme under the joint management of a board of directors representing all the associated organisations.

The 'non-profit-making' aspect of these companies is related to the fact that there are no shareholders in a section 21 company. Any person or organisation working for the company may receive payment for work done, but any revenue (profit) generated by the event must be reinvested in the work of the association. Revenue (or profit) cannot be distributed among the association members or employees.

The members of the association not for gain are responsible for electing a board of directors (a minimum of seven) at the annual general meeting. The board is responsible for administering the affairs of the company during the year, and each member is accountable for the performance of the company. A section 21 company cannot be listed on the stock exchange, and its memorandum and articles of association usually limit the circumstances by which it could change hands. Usually, if an association not for gain has completed its work, it is wound up and closed. However, the articles could also provide that the company and its reserves be donated to a similar organisation having the same intentions and objectives.

7.2.4 Trusts

Most organisations which are established as trusts usually work in education, training and charity fields. Trusts are registered in terms of the Trust Act and each has a trust deed which sets out the objects of the trust, its organisational structure, working arrangements and procedures. A trust is administered by a board of trustees which must comprise at least three people (usually an accountant or attorney, and at least two others).

Traditionally the credibility of trusts is carried by the standing of its trustees, who are usually prominent and respected members of the community. Trusts also establish a high level of community support because they are not 'driven' for the sole benefit of shareholders, but rather by the needs of the community itself. A trust cannot be listed on the stock exchange or bought and sold like a private or public company.

7.2.5 Project team

Usually a specific team of people is assembled for the purposes of getting an event off the ground. A one-off event can be organised by a formal company using its own full-time staff or it can engage the services of part-time workers, specialists and/or volunteers.

Maintaining control and accountability are often difficult within project team organisations, especially for large-scale projects like the Olympics. There is also a difference between establishing an event and running or organising it (i.e. the development and operational stages). Quite often the development stage involves a project team which is disbanded on completion of the task. The operational phase is usually conducted by the event organisation which ensures continuity, especially in financing and marketing (Getz, 1997).

7.2.6 Government

There are a number of instances where events are developed and organised by government, particularly in high-profile situations such as national and international conferences and conventions. Government departments also organise and participate in local events, festivals and conferences. Government involvement in events can result from a policy of supporting local economic development and injecting expertise and funding sponsorship into less-developed regions. Government can also work closely with non-government organisations and the private sector to provide support for events.

Local authorities are perhaps the most proactive governments which organise events. City and town councils very often get involved in festivals and sports events in partnership with local clubs and societies.

Many local authorities, for example, actively pursue the holding of regular sports events, arts exhibitions and cultural and heritage events in cooperation with the various sports codes and the business sector.

7.2.7 Institutions

A variety of institutions organise events, ranging from educational institutions (like schools, colleges and universities) to community-based organisations (like churches, welfare groups, charitable clubs and clubs and societies) to hospitals, houses for children with disabilities, the elderly and the homeless; and environmental pressure groups.

These institutions are often structured as trusts, section 21 associations, welfare organisations and informal associations of members. They are usually comprised of a board of directors or trustees with a number of committees comprising voluntary workers.

7.2.8 Event committees

The final type of event organisation is perhaps the most common – the event committee. Such a body is usually established to organise and run the event by members of the community holding it, whereafter the committee disbands. Although similar to a project team, it differs in that its membership is of a voluntary nature and such committees do not usually receive payment for services rendered. In addition, event committees usually do not comprise paid specialists. Case study 7.1 relates the use of committees in establishing and organising the Souk Okaz festival in Saudi Arabia.

Case study 7.1 Souk festival planned for July

TAIF: The Makkah governorate is planning to make the annual festival at Souk Okaz, a location 40 kilometres north of Taif, a major cultural attraction. Custodian of the Two Holy Mosques King Abdullah is expected to inaugurate the festival, which begins next month...Makkah Gov. Prince Khaled Al-Faisal, himself a renowned poet, is keen on reviving the historic glory of the Souk Okaz festival, which is associated with the development of classical Arabic poetry...The prince heads several committees set up to make the festival a great success. The organising committee sent out invitations to more than 2 000 eminent Arab thinkers, writers, poets, historians, and other cultural activists inside and outside the kingdom. The committee has also fixed 100 road signs and welcome boards to the venue where the festival is being held. Luxury buses will transport the visitors to the souk and back.

Source: Arab News (2008)

7.3 Setting up and managing event organisations

7.3.1 Founding members

Having considered the organisational design and chosen the particular organisation model which suits the event to be organised, it is necessary to take appropriate steps to establish the organisation. Schmader (1997) states that 'a successful event is no different from a successful business and will function best if treated as such; the most successful events are usually independent, with a clear chain of command, strong leadership and a clearly defined mission statement, just as a successful business'.

In establishing an event organisation, it is vital to select a founding group (or interim committee) of people who have credibility and high regard in the community. This group needs to have a 'champion' or 'champions' who will pilot the development and organisational process through all the ups and downs along the way. Very often the founding members will comprise the first members of the board, and it is vital that they all have a common vision and purpose.

The founding members also have an important role in deciding whether other people become involved, why they are needed and the extent to which they should contribute to the event. Founders also influence the way the organisation is structured, how power is controlled and the way in which the organisation is constituted. In a step-by-step process (or evolution) an event organisation grows and gathers members, staff and facilities (Getz, 1997) (refer to figure 7.4.).

7.3.2 Organisation articles

All organisations (even informal committees) are best structured on a set of articles which explain the characteristics of the organisation, what it is to do and how it intends to operate. Formal companies have sets of documents called the memorandum and articles of association. Trusts have a trust deed, and voluntary committees usually have a memorandum or association agreement. These documents are usually prepared by attorneys or accountants who can assist in arranging for the registration of the organisation with the Registrar of Companies or the High Court (in the case of trusts). The memorandum usually covers the following details:

❐ The vision of the organisation;

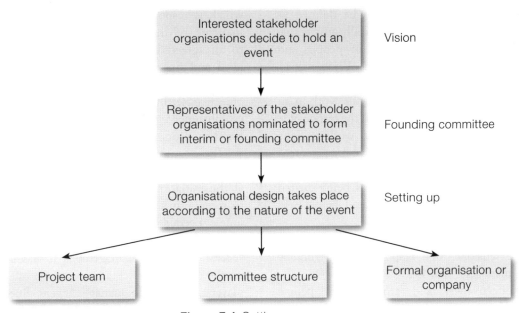

Figure 7.4 Setting-up process

- The main purpose of its activities;
- The structure, size, composition and terms of election of directors and trustees;
- Membership requirements;
- The procedural rules, including the meetings to be held, quorum for voting and decision making;
- How vacancies are filled, and resignations and retirements;
- The responsibilities and liability of members;
- The management of finance, and auditing requirements;
- The financial year and the appointment of auditors;
- The procedure for amending the articles; and
- The procedure for winding up the organisation, and the distribution of assets and funds.

7.3.3 Organisational accountability

For a successful business or event to occur, there needs to be clear definition of accountability, responsibility and authority. Cleland (1999) indicates that failure to perform can often be ascribed to the following factors:

- Failure to define and specify authority and responsibility with people who are solely and jointly responsible;
- Failure to overcome negative attitudes in the organisation;
- Inadequate documentation setting out procedures;
- Inadequate team development;
- Failure to introduce flexible interactive management procedures; and
- Failure to promote synergy and unity so that resources, results and rewards can be shared.

A responsible person can be defined as 'one who is legally and ethically answerable for the care or welfare of people and organisations' (Cleland, 1999: 261). This does not mean that the responsible person necessarily does all the work in an organisation, but rather that the responsible person sees to it that the work is done through delegation, effective management and following up. Responsibility relates to being able to make decisions, being trusted to make those decisions and being held liable for them.

The matter of accountability is an extension of responsibility whereby managers 'are held accountable for the effectiveness and efficiency of people who report to them' (Cleland, 1999). Successful events organisations need to have responsible people, clearly understood authority and accountability so as to ensure that efficient management is achieved.

One of the most severe problems in developing countries is the shortage of skills capacity and experienced personnel. As a result, it is difficult to engender a culture of responsibility and accountability among management staff. Lack of experience and skill often results in managers denying responsibility and assigning blame to co-workers or subordinates, and outside organisations. Events organisations accordingly can benefit from introducing a skills transfer and/or mentorship programme, using experienced managers to uplift and advise emerging events managers.

7.4 Principles of human resource management

7.4.1 Board of directors

Most organisations (event owners) establish a board of directors or an executive which is responsible for formulating the mandate of the organisation (according to an agreed vision and objectives), the legal and financial responsibility for the organisation's activities, event planning and objective setting, conflict resolution, the establishment of priorities and securing event sponsorship.

These directors are expected to interface very closely with event projects at the initiation and planning stages, but to remain at a distance during execution unless needed for setting priorities and resolving conflict. The achievement of success in events management is based on the successful integration of three role players: the events manager, event line managers and the senior management of the events organisation. It is believed that the reason why event executives often meddle during execution of the event is that they do not get accurate information from the events manager as to the status of the project. Accordingly, it is important that the stakeholders be informed on a continual basis.

The most critical node is the relationship between the events manager and the event line manager. These two need to view each other as equals and be willing to share authority, responsibility and accountability (Kerzner, 1998).

As a result of the overriding importance of the board of directors in assuring the creditability of an event, the selection of members is a vitally important process, sometimes involving consultation with stakeholders; national, provincial and local authorities; politicians; community leaders; business; and labour. The lack of credibility of members can result in an event being delayed or even prevented from taking place.

7.4.2 Chief executive officer (event administrator)

Some event practitioners prefer to be known as event administrators or leaders. However, according to Kerzner (1998), the use of such terminology lies in the traditional hierarchical management style which ill equips event practitioners to deal with making quick decisions. This type of organisation results in no one individual being responsible for the entire event project, leading to a failure to provide the necessary emphasis to complete the project as coordination is complex and conflicts arise when activities need to be coordinated in more than one department. Further, decision making favours the stronger functional groups and there is no focal point for customers as response to customer needs is slow. Finally, event ideas tend to be functionally oriented with little regard for ongoing projects.

Because of these problems in the past, event practitioners began searching for methods to coordinate the flow of work between the functional event units. The coordination of events was achieved through several integrated mechanisms such as rules and procedures of the organisation, planning processes, hierarchical referral and direct contact.

The need for event coordinators or managers soon became apparent as it was realised that the control of a project needs to be given to personnel whose loyalties lie in the completion of the project. Managers from the classical management school seriously questioned the amount of authority given to a project manager.

Out of this was born the *matrix event* organisational form. Each event project manager reports directly to the event owner, and each such project represents a potential profit centre, according to Kerzner (1998). The events manager in this case has total responsibility and accountability for the success of the event project. The functional departments have functional responsibility to maintain technical excellence on the event project. Thus, while event project management is a coordinative function, matrix management is a collaborative functional division of event project management. In project coordination, work is assigned to specific people or units. In matrix organisations, information is shared and several people may be required for the same piece of work to ensure adequate capacity and expertise.

A successful event is dependent upon the character, calibre and leadership of the chief executive officer of the event organisation, the chairperson of the interim event committee and/or the project team leader. Watt (1998) stresses that 'it is impossible to overemphasize the crucial need for an effective, charismatic leader for any successful event'. The leader/s of the event organisation must possess several leadership qualities and must be capable of motivating the company to perform at its peak at all times. In addition, the leader needs to be enthusiastic, decisive, analytical and well organised. The successful chief executive officers are invariably opportunistic due to their inherent entrepreneurial nature. However, to inspire the team they also need to be diplomatic and democratic to get the best out of people.

The chief executive officer and/or team leader needs to be capable of choosing an appropriate leadership style commensurate with the situation, taking into account the ability and input of the rest of the team. Watt (1998) suggests that 'the key leader will also be required to provide vision, direction and an awareness of the external environment to ensure success'.

7.4.3 Employees

A one-off special event will invariably depend on the goodwill and services of volunteer workers. However, a recurring event, hallmark or mega-event will necessitate the employment of key full-time personnel. It is most important to ensure that the recruitment of key full-time staff be conducted professionally and according to systematic procedures of advertisement, shortlisting, interviews and appointment. Advertisements need to state clearly the nature of the position, work involved and qualifications/expertise required. This will help the committee to shortlist applicants and invite them to attend an interview.

In certain instances, it may be felt appropriate to engage the services of a professional personnel recruitment company to find the appropriate member of staff for an organisation. This is often necessary for senior management and specialist staff, such as accountants, project managers, sound engineers and security personnel. The personnel consulting business is most efficient and can fast-track the recruitment process. However, it must be remembered that the consultants require payment of commission based on the member of staff's salary, payable on appointment of that person. In addition, the use of personnel consultants for the recruitment of employees for a charitable or public events association is not always popular in the public's view because 'transparency' and open advertising are seen to be preferable and in the interests of giving everybody a fair chance of gaining employment.

Many developing countries have an acute unemployment problem, and events offer the opportunity to provide a certain number of jobs for the unemployed. Affirmative action in the employment process is a national policy in certain countries and the employment of previously disadvantaged people (PDPs) and people with disabilities has to be actively accommodated. Labour legislation requires appropriate affirmative employment for all organisations having 50 or more employees. However, research indicates that the employment benefits of events are often overstated because they are reliant mostly on short-term and volunteer workers.

7.4.4 Volunteers

By far the vast majority of events are small community-based activities, organised by committees and volunteer workers. Recruitment often involves a process of 'word of mouth' within the ranks of the member organisations involved on the committee. In addition, it is sometimes possible to access volunteer databases maintained by community organisations, municipalities and events managers. If recruiting volunteers, it is useful to distribute flyers calling for people to volunteer, use local radio stations to create awareness and place notices in local newspapers (North East England Toolkit).

Often the volunteer workers have just as much responsibility as full-time employees. Accordingly, it is just as important to have clearly defined job descriptions for these workers as it is for the staff. It also helps to have an induction programme to ensure volunteers fit in with the employees and know what they are required to do, the structure of the organisation and the objectives of the event programme. The North East England Festivals and Events

Toolkit's *Working with Volunteers* suggests that a volunteer action plan is essential to managing volunteers. Such a plan needs to identify their tasks, allocate responsibilities, define training and orientation requirements, provide role outlines for identified volunteers with skills, and set out the milestones and timeframes they need to adhere to.

The important difference between a volunteer and an employee is the fact that in most developed countries a volunteer's commitment to the event is on a charitable level. An employee is getting paid and has contractual obligations. Volunteers usually do not have a contract of employment and their interests end immediately the event is over or when they are no longer involved. However, in some underdeveloped countries, volunteers offer their services in return for training and some form of nominal payment for their services. They can sometimes volunteer in the hope of obtaining more permanent formal employment through becoming involved in the event. Case study 7.2 relates how important volunteers were to the Beijing Olympics held in 2008.

Accordingly, working with volunteers requires that their special contribution to the success of the event be acknowledged and shared. Working with volunteers requires consideration, flexibility and enthusiasm because volunteers often work 'for the fun of it' or for charitable purposes. Crayton (1997) explains that 'you will find that the majority of volunteers come back year after year if they have specific assignments, direction and appreciation'. Volunteers require just as much management and coordination as employees. Crayton (1997) adds that 'all it takes is a little imagination, organisation and a lot of enthusiasm'. The North East England Festival and Event

Case study 7.2 Olympic volunteer roundup

Philip Sen relates how the 2008 Beijing Olympics involved the largest number of volunteers in history, estimated at 500 000 people: 'On every street corner and in every venue, there's an army of volunteers meeting, greeting, translating, giving directions and helping visitors in every way imaginable'. The importance of their contribution was recognised by senior United Nations and government officials, including the under-secretary, General Achim Steiner, who saluted the volunteers for 'making a difference in development work worldwide'. CBN News alluded to the high level of effort made by volunteers, referring to their 'gruelling training, stiff competition and dreams of glory'.

Source: Sen (2008)

Toolkit suggests various ways of thanking volunteers, including providing them with a memento of the event (such as an article of clothing, T-shirt or uniform); asking after their welfare and thanking them for work done; organising a dedicated event for them; giving priority treatment to their friends and family in gaining entrance to events; and publicly recognising their efforts through the media and event documentation.

7.4.5 Training

The events industry often requires multiskilled workforce and as a result employees could lack sufficient skills and/ or experience for the work to be carried out. It is advisable to conduct a skills audit among the employees and volunteers, and allocate them responsibilities closely allied to their interests or skills. It also helps to assign a coordinator or mentor to a group of staff to provide training and guidance. In situations where full-time skilled employees are not available and the event has to depend on volunteer workers, it is advisable to introduce an orientation and training programme to ensure that all personnel are capable of executing their duties during the event.

Watt (1998) suggests that there should be two different levels of training, namely *desirable training* – improving skills (catering, bookkeeping, etc.) and *essential training* – ensuring awareness (such as legal rules and requirements; health and safety). Training can involve routine duties, such as ushering and ticket selling, to more specialist responsibilities, such as crowd management and first aid. There is no doubt that training is time consuming and costly. However, adequate preparation and the use of older, more experienced employees or volunteers to train younger recruits can assist in keeping costs down. There are also a number of associations and charitable institutions which can provide training free of charge (e.g. the disaster management department of the local authority, the Red Cross Society and non-government organisations).

7.4.6 Unions

The events industry is, by its very nature, multisectoral. Accordingly, every event depends on the services of a variety of service industries such as caterers, transport, security, accommodation, maintenance, etc., and as a result many unions will be indirectly and directly involved in an event.

Each organisation needs to have a workers' forum which enables the em-

ployees to communicate their needs on a collective basis to management. In many areas of industry, transport and commerce there are well-established union organisations representing the rights of permanent employees.

In a situation of subcontracting it is possible to think that the caterer's employees are the responsibility of the catering contractor and not the problem of the events manager or organiser. However, any union difficulties within the subcontractor organisations will have a domino effect on the outcome of the event. It is accordingly essential to have a good working relationship with the unions associated with the event that is being organised. Unions are a good source of large numbers of labourers for big projects and when working with a union it is necessary to have the proper foundation for a successful worker/employer relationship. A successful event depends on the effective involvement and cooperation of all role players (Sivek, 1996).

The event can only benefit from a constructive and cordial relationship with all unions that come into contact or work with that event. After all, any special event is a team effort. Should it happen, however, that a conflict situation arises, Sivek's (1996) advice is to 'discuss the situation with the proper representatives. A calm dispassionate discussion of the details should resolve any problems'. In a situation where a subcontracting organisation encounters problems with a work stoppage or dispute, it is essential that the event organisers play an active, supporting role to facilitate a solution to such problems, without necessarily getting directly involved between the employer (the subcontractor) and the employee.

Figure 7.5 Organisational role players

7.5 Stakeholder management

7.5.1 Role players

There are several fundamental role players in most organisations, including the board of directors or trustees, managers and employees. These various role players (see figure 7.5) all have a function to perform and must interact effectively to do their work.

Usually, the management of an organisation is responsible for ensuring efficiency and productivity in order to fulfil the policies, objectives and vision of the board of directors. The board is also responsible for ensuring that a suitable environment is made available for the functioning of the organisation, including premises, facilities, resources, equipment and personnel.

Large organisations are usually structured in a hierarchy which places the board of directors at the top of a pyramid (refer to figure 7.6).

Smaller organisations, project teams and committees are usually less complex and have fewer tiers in their structure (refer to figure 7.7).

7.5.2 Organisational culture

The process by which an event organisation becomes established is gradual and

Figure 7.6 Large organisation: hierarchical structure

Source: Adapted from Cleland (1999)

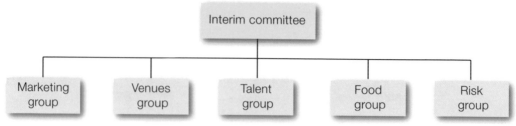

Figure 7.7 Smaller organisation structure

dependent on the ability of the participants to work together for a common vision. As the event process gathers momentum, the event organisation grows from an interim committee of volunteers to a more formal, registered organisation and, finally, to an established or professional institution (Getz, 1997). This process has been described as the change process in developing the cultural characteristics of an organisation. Getz (1997) relates this process to the social process of group development, ranging from founders organising the event, leaders taking control and the ups and downs of leadership struggles, to eventual stability. However, as the organisation becomes large and formal, it can also suffer from becoming stagnant and can deteriorate as a result.

Care therefore needs to be taken to continually focus on the purpose of the organisation to ensure the continued enthusiasm and commitment of the participants. This is because organisations (and particularly committees) can stifle the momentum of an event if allowed to do so.

7.6 Summary

There are several different types of organisation which organise events, ranging from the commonly used local organising committee, to a project team, an association, a non-government organisation and a registered company, to a government or municipal department. The essential elements to successful events organising relates to the people, skills, commitment and expertise in organising the event according to that organisation's capacity. Therefore the management structure, accountability and responsibility of all involved need to be structured and well understood.

There needs also to be appropriate human resource management with training and support to enable teamwork, flexibility under rapidly changing conditions and an understanding of how to foster the commitment of volunteers. Finally, management of the event stakeholders is a special skill to ensure the sponsors are satisfied with the return on investment, participants achieve full benefit, event organisers are satisfied and spectators obtain an exceptional experience, which makes the event special, unique and memorable.

Event organising is a challenging activity which is dependent upon several critical success factors:

❐ An appropriate event organisation which is suited to the nature and complexity of the event;
❐ Support of the stakeholders in the area, including the politicians, local authority, community, local leadership (champions) and event sponsors;
❐ A clear understanding of who in the organisation is accountable and

responsible for each element of the event;

- ❑ An experienced, proactive and committed event organiser (manager, chief executive, etc.) with the support of an organised and able group of staff and volunteer workers;
- ❑ A skilled team of employees with a clear understanding of their employment mandate, what they have to do, and by when;
- ❑ A well-managed team of volunteers with commitment to the event and its overall purpose; and
- ❑ An appropriate training and skills transfer programme.

Questions for research

1 Describe the various types of organisation and indicate those which are more suited to charitable and welfare event activities.
2 The process of setting up an organisation follows a number of steps. Explain these steps.
3 There are functional and project-based organisational structures. Explain the difference between these structures and describe how they work.
4 What would be the difference between accountability, responsibility and authority?
5 The recruitment of personnel is a crucial element in building an organisation. Indicate the differences between full-time employees and volunteer workers, and explain how the recruitment process may differ as a result.
6 The management of volunteers requires careful consideration of workers' needs. Explain why this is so.
7 Explain why training and skills transfer should be an integral part of event organising.

Recommended websites

Browse the following internet sites for interesting and informative information:

Additional reading material:
http://www.blackbaud.com/solutions/raisersedgemodules.asp

Management process:
http://www.personal.usyd.edu.au/~wotoole/epmspage1.html#EPMS_Schema

Organising guidelines:
http://www.crowdsafe.com/taskrpt/toc.html#TOC
http://www.sheffield.gov.uk/out--about/parks-woodlands--countryside/gettinginvolved/
    organising-community-events.html
http://www.themat.com/eventfliers/eventorganising.pdf
http://www.inside.sbts.edu/forums/legacy/stepstoplanningasuccessfulevent.pdf
http://www.tourismnortheast.co.uk

Suggested reading

Crayton, C. 1997. Managing volunteers. In *Event Operations.* Washington: IFEA.

Getz, D. 1997. *Event Management & Event Tourism.* New York: Cognizant Communication Corporation.

Kerzner, H. 1998. *Project Management,* 6 ed. New York: John Wiley & Sons.

Photo: Dimitri Tassiopoulos

Photo: Dimitri Tassiopoulos

Photo: Dimitri Tassiopoulos

Photo: Dimitri Tassiopoulos

8

Project management for events

Tom Wanklin

Abstract

Achievement of a successful event, which is held on time and within the prescribed budget, is of critical importance to event organisers and sponsors. This chapter describes the essential elements, activities and processes of programming and managing event development from inception to the final closing moments.

Chapter objectives

After you have read this chapter you should be able to:

❒ understand the nature, processes and activities involved in programming and event development;

❒ identify all the elements involved in establishing the event, organising and scheduling those activities in terms of the time involved and the budget necessary to implement the event development process;

❒ identify and manage event stakeholders and role players in order to achieve a successful event;

❒ become acquainted with project management techniques and procedures;

❒ understand how to project manage the event to achieve teamwork and cooperation among participants;

❒ monitor the progress of the event, understand the event lifecycle and intervene to ensure a successful outcome before problems occur; and

❒ understand the critical success factors in event programming and project management.

8.1 Introduction

When setting out to hold an event (whether small or large), it is essential that all the activities and arrangements are implemented at the correct time and that everybody knows what they are required to do at a particular time and date. Whether it involves a wedding reception, a meeting, a sports competition or an international conference, the effectiveness of the organisation and the management of the event is critical to its success.

The process by which the implementation of a plan and the development of an event are managed is called *project management*. This can be defined as 'a philosophy and a process for the management of ad-hoc activities in organisations, characterised by a distinct life cycle and a management system that uses a matrix organisational design' (Cleland, 1999). In the context of project management, a *project* can be defined as 'a combination of organisational resources pulled together to create something that

did not previously exist' (Cleland, 1999). This chapter aims to describe the project management process and the tools and techniques used to achieve successful events in the process.

Project management aims to achieve a particular event within the budget and timeframes available and, according to the project management body of knowledge (Haughey, 2009), typically follows a five-step process, namely initiating an event or project; planning, executing, monitoring and controlling it; and finally closing it down. The aim of such a management process is often displayed in a diagrammatic form as shown on page 145.

8.2 Event project management and how it works

The main person usually responsible for the coordination of the event programming and implementation process is the project manager (or, if it is a mega-event, usually several project managers). A typical event

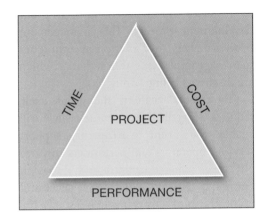

or project generally has six characteristics, and a project manager needs to facilitate the implementation process on this basis (Harris, 1998):

- ❒ A start and a finish date;
- ❒ A timeframe;
- ❒ A unique operating period;
- ❒ The involvement of several organisations and/or individuals;
- ❒ A prescribed set of resources; and
- ❒ A scheduled number of activities and phases setting out their sequence of occurrence.

The major intention of project management is to meet certain agreed targets, within budgets and within the timeframes that have been stipulated by the event organiser. In order to achieve this, it is essential to undertake the following activities, regardless of whether the event is a small local community event or a mega-event:

- ❒ Establish a clear project goal;
- ❒ Determine the project objectives;
- ❒ Establish milestones and tasks to be undertaken, and the relationship between tasks and timeframes;
- ❒ Prepare a diagram of the project programme;
- ❒ Direct people individually and as part of a team;

- ❒ Support the commitment and enthusiasm of the team;
- ❒ Distribute information to all role players;
- ❒ Motivate and build a project team;
- ❒ Empower the team to perform effectively; and
- ❒ Manage the risks and encourage creativity to find new solutions and ideas (Harris, 1998).

Project management teams are usually different from conventional organisations in that they are usually multidisciplinary, small and highly focused. The team requires a stable working environment, with clear lines of reporting to senior decision makers, efficient and high-quality equipment and adequate budgets to get the work done. It is the responsibility of the project manager to effectively manage the project implementation process, including planning, organisation and motivation, and directing and controlling all the activities, role players and stakeholders involved.

There are several areas which require careful management and expertise, including stakeholder involvement (particularly a host community), risk management and evaluating performance. In addition, it is useful to be aware of factors which can result in project failure. Cleland (1999) indicates that there are 12 reasons why projects fail. These include a lack of understanding of the project complexity; a lack of access and internal communication; failure to integrate key elements of the project; inadequate control; subtle changes in the requirements; and an ineffective execution strategy. In addition, there can be too much dependence on software; different expectations between customer and the contractor; no shared win-win attitudes; inadequate education or training; a lack of leadership, commitment and sponsorship; and the event not being viewed as a start-up business (Cleland, 1999).

8.3 Project management activities

8.3.1 Introduction

Having formulated a plan for the event (refer to chapter 6), it is necessary to put that plan into action and to stage the event. This will require a lot of coordination, because each event comprises a large number of individual activities which need to be carried out successfully, at the correct time and in the correct order. Many of these activities are dependent upon other actions being taken beforehand or at the same time. Should this process not take place smoothly, there could be delays, which could be costly to the event organisers, the host community and the sponsors.

Management of the development of the event involves four main activities: firstly, *event development programming* or *project scheduling* (as it can also be called); secondly, managing and coordinating the *event development programme* itself (when the event is held); thirdly, managing the *stakeholders* involved in ensuring the event is a success; and fourthly, the *shutdown* or *decommissioning* activities which come about after the event has been held.

The first activity involves the process of setting out in detail those actions which need to be implemented; determining who should take those actions; detailing the timing of such actions to achieve the objectives, targets and milestones; and coordinating the activities of the teams, contractors and role players during the event development process. These time and action programmes form an essential part

of the successful management of an event development process. This management process makes use of a variety of techniques to manage implementation activities, which are discussed below.

The second activity, the event itself, requires a detailed programme which will enable the event participants, support services, operators and performers to carry out their required actions and duties in harmony, thereby achieving a successful event. The third activity involves ensuring the needs and expectations of the interested and affected people and organisations are met. This also means that the project manager must ensure the actions of all the people involved are coordinated properly, and all people understand what they have to do, when it is to be done and how much money is involved in that activity. The fourth and final activity involves the decommissioning process, whereby the facilities and venue are either closed down or renovated in preparation for the next event.

8.3.2 Event development programming/scheduling

There are six basic steps or activities involved in event development programming, which are set out in figure 8.1. The process of rapid change and the increasing complexity of activities have a growing influence on the management of events. Event organisers are experiencing an environment of ever-increasing competition, rising costs, funding constraints and greater diversity of thought and objectives in both individuals and organisations. An event manager has to be highly skilled and professional to draw every component of a plan together in as short a time as possible to reduce risk, retain financial viability and manage a complex situation. The role of information

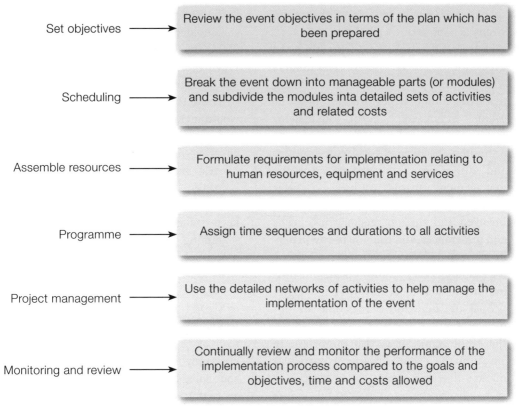

Set objectives	Review the event objectives in terms of the plan which has been prepared
Scheduling	Break the event down into manageable parts (or modules) and subdivide the modules inta detailed sets of activities and related costs
Assemble resources	Formulate requirements for implementation relating to human resources, equipment and services
Programme	Assign time sequences and durations to all activities
Project management	Use the detailed networks of activities to help manage the implementation of the event
Monitoring and review	Continually review and monitor the performance of the implementation process compared to the goals and objectives, time and costs allowed

Figure 8.1 Event development programming activities

technology has grown enormously in assisting the project management process, especially with more complex and larger events.

8.3.3 Managing the event stakeholders

The technical team which is responsible for implementing the event in consultation with the community and event stakeholders would invariably comprise a professional project manager or managers with experience in programming and implementation. Being the key focus of responsibility, it is the project manager who integrates and coordinates all the activities and role players. Under these circumstances, the project manager

can influence the success or failure of an event (Burke, 2007). The larger the event, the more complex the programme management process and the higher the risks involved. Accordingly, event organisers are urged to use competent expertise in this process.

Project managers require special qualities to handle complex and stressful work situations, and should have diverse qualities and capabilities, including be able to lead a project team; anticipate problems; make decisions promptly; network effectively with stakeholders; be flexible; review, monitor and assess performance; administer contracts and manage the scope of work to be done; be proactive and get things done; create a positive working environment within a situation of constant change; and, finally, be able to ensure the 'client' is happy (Burke, 2007).

Successful events entail meeting the expectations of the many stakeholders who have an interest in them, ranging from the audience, performers, sponsors, event organisers, event managers, contractors, suppliers, marketers and promoters, financiers, local communities and authorities. It is essential for the management team to have a clear understanding of the stakeholders involved and their characteristics, needs and preferences, and the role they will play in the event. With regard to audiences, for example, Allen (2000) points out how important it is to ensure that the 'right' people are there and that people are not merely invited for the sake of filling the event venue. It is also important to 'position the event' towards a particular market that the event seeks to serve so as to ensure that it is successful, makes money and leaves the participants with a memorable experience.

Managing the event stakeholders as a project manager necessitates preparing a stakeholder management plan. This plan identifies all those stakeholders involved, and clusters them into groups of primary and secondary categories. The primary stakeholders invariably are those who have a direct impact or interest in the event and could determine the success or failure of the proceedings. The audience, for example, would be a primary stakeholder, as if they do not attend, the event would be a failure. The secondary stakeholders would have an indirect impact on the event but their exclusion from the event would not be a determining factor in the success or failure of the event. Such stakeholders could include the media, for example.

Having categorised the stakeholders it is then useful to create a profile for each stakeholder group or constituency (Silvers, 2004) to fully understand their needs. Having understood the nature of the stakeholder groups, it then helps to work out how the project management process would include them in the event planning and development. This would include ensuring regular meetings with different interest groups, obtaining permission to hold the event, consultations, operating an information distribution system to keep stakeholders apprised of progress, marketing (including advertising and promotions) and operating an event website which is regularly updated.

The ever-growing power and usefulness of second generation internet or Web 2.0 technology is opening up opportunities to manage stakeholders more quickly and effectively through information sharing and collaboration with the use of user-centred social network applications such as Facebook© and Twitter©. Managing volunteers, attendees and participants by personalising the distribution of information about events and activities can enhance event success. On the other hand, such technology also enables participants to share experiences (both positive and negative) with others almost immediately, hence management of stakeholder experiences, perceptions and access to information is becoming more and more critical in stakeholder management activities.

8.3.4 Event closure

In the case of a one-off event which has to be wound up, or should it be decided to close down a regularly held event, care should be taken to programme this winding-down process in a deliberate way. Often this aspect of the programme can be handled poorly because the organisers have lost interest or energy. A poorly managed closure process can result in wastage of resources (through poor controls, theft, mismanagement and delays). Events can also be closed down – with as much fanfare as the launch (Getz, 1997) – to avoid costly overheads and to allow reduction of resources (people and funding) to other events or new activities. Alternatively, it may be appropriate to shut down an event and phase in a new one to replace it.

To avoid confusion and antagonism in those communities which may be dependent on a regular event for employment or charity, the organisers may decide to close down an event on a phased basis over time. However, very tight controls are needed at all times to prevent rising costs and wastage.

There are several termination strategies which need to be followed, including ensuring that all work has been completed. The project manager needs to make a review of all contracts to ensure that all their clauses have been fulfilled, and to monitor the shutdown process to ensure that all activities are being conducted satisfactorily. It is necessary to advise all stakeholders that the event is shutting down and make sure that all financial commitments are fulfilled. If appropriate, the management team should help employees to secure alternative employment.

Prior to closure, the project manager needs to prepare a project history report so that a record is available for future events of a similar nature. This gives future managers an opportunity to learn from the mistakes of others. As a final component of the project history report, conduct an audit to highlight strengths and weaknesses, and to show how mistakes could be avoided in future.

When events are brought to a close, it needs to be remembered that certain activities must be carried out (either in expectation of future events or the revival of the event in the forthcoming year). Such activities can include maintenance of services and facilities, revamping the products and activities, and rejuvenating the marketing process.

8.4 Programming tools and techniques

In the discipline of project management there are several different programming tools or techniques which are used, ranging from simple lists of work to be done to complex computer project management software. Information technology plays a critical role in enabling project management activities to be performed quickly and efficiently. In addition, the growing importance of events in creating economic and social benefits for communities, districts and even countries makes it essential that appropriate information technological systems and tools are used to ensure the event maximises the return on investment. The most common programming tools are:

- ❒ Work breakdown schedules (WBS);
- ❒ Bar charts (such as the Gantt chart);
- ❒ Network schedules;
- ❒ Critical path analysis (CPA);
- ❒ Programme evaluation review technique (PERT); and
- ❒ Time and cost analysis.

These are described in greater detail below.

8.4.1 Work breakdown schedules (WBS)

A work breakdown schedule simply involves the unpacking of the overall project into lists of individual activities, requirements and resources (Silvers, 2004) or 'into work elements that represent singular work elements, assigned either with the organisation or to an outside agency such as a vendor' (Cleland, 1999). These work elements need to be in packages which can be allocated to accountable operators, builders, subcontractors, etc. This will enable the project managers to control activities, productivity and the quality of work more effectively. Work breakdown schedules also facilitate the management of risk, resources and outputs through the display of all tasks to be performed in sequence on a chart. This system is popular because it is user friendly, inexpensive and simple to develop. However, more complex projects require more sophisticated tools, such as bar charts and network schedules.

8.4.2 Bar charts

One way of displaying activities and events in sequence is in the form of bar charts, which are linear pictures representing the various activities which have to be performed over time. A bar chart for a typical carnival development is provided in figure 8.2.

These bar charts are sometimes referred to as *Gantt charts* (after Henry Gantt) and are a widely used 'non-mathematical technique' (Render & Heizer, 1997), being simple, user friendly and inexpensive. The bar chart is useful but cannot adequately show the relationship between activities and time.

8.4.3 Network scheduling

In order to be able to effectively control the implementation process, it is essential

Task name	Jan	Feb	Mar	Apr	May	Jun	Jul	Aug	Sept	Oct	Nov
Carnival start	■										
Stall bookings	■	■	■	■	■						
Confirm vehicles	■										
Land-scaping			■	■							
Official launch				■	■						
Press release					■						
Stall con-struction						■	■	■			
Event HQ									■		
Event wrap up										■	■

Figure 8.2 Bar chart for a typical carnival development

to have a detailed breakdown of all the activities that need to be carried out and the time that each should take to be completed. Project or network scheduling involves determining the project's activities in the time sequence in which they have to be performed (Render & Heizer, 1997). One can also devise schedules of the human resources needed, and the equipment and materials required to fulfil those tasks.

Scheduling charts, which combine the list of activities to be performed, the time sequence of the implementation of tasks, and the manpower, money and materials required, are used to help manage the project development process. The scheduling activity is very simple and merely requires every single element of the project to be identified. Then the actions or activities required to achieve them must also be listed in detail.

After listing all the elements and activities, it is helpful to write them up in a chart which shows the sequence of activities and the way in which they relate to each other. In scheduling jargon, the elements are usually called *events* and they are usually represented by a number in a circle. This number would correspond to the detailed list referred to earlier. These should not be confused with the special events which are the subject of this text.

The activities which are required to achieve the 'events' are shown as an arrow or a line, which links the events (e.g. event 1 to event 2).

Hildreth (1990: 64) describes each *event* as an objective and 'the work necessary to accomplish an objective is called an *activity*'. It is also customary for there to

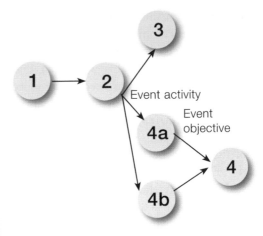

be only one activity between each element or 'event'. As the list of elements (*events*) and *activities* is transformed into a chart, it can become a very detailed and complex diagram, full of arrows and circles with numbers.

It has been found useful to include the estimated completion time for each *activity* in these charts. By doing this, the performance of the implementing team, the builders or carpenters, etc. can be monitored. More importantly, the implementing team can be informed of the expected duration of each task so that they can ensure that their productivity is enhanced accordingly.

The length of time to be taken for an *activity* is usually shown in numbers (days, hours, months, etc.) above the activity time, between the *events*:

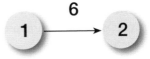

The use of time in a scheduling chart is beneficial because it is possible to calculate the likely date by which the project can be completed. In certain situations, it may be necessary to calculate backwards from the date when the event is to commence, because the commencement date of the event has been decided beforehand and cannot be changed. This will mean that the implementing team needs to produce a scheduling chart which allows for all the elements and *activities* to be achieved within a predetermined timeframe. Examples of this would be the Olympic Games or the FIFA World Cup Tournament. In such situations, the scheduling charts will highlight those activities which need to be carried out simultaneously to save time and achieve better productivity. Also, the chart would highlight instances where additional resources would be required: double shifts, overtime and additional equipment could help the process to be 'fast-tracked' to achieve fixed deadlines.

The availability of computer technology has greatly enhanced the ability of scheduling and, as a result, also project management. There are a variety of different techniques which are useful tools in this regard.

8.4.4 Critical path analysis (CPA)

Apparently, this network schedule technique was devised in 1957 by JE Kelly and MR Walker in the US to 'assist in the building and maintenance of chemical plants' (Render & Heizer, 1997). It is different from the network scheduling description above, because it identifies those activities which have a critical effect on the event implementation process. These critical activities are represented as the 'longest time path through the network', referred to as the *critical path* (Render & Heizer, 1997). Critical path analysis has enhanced project management by enabling more strategic monitoring of the project process. It also allows for an implementing team to intervene at critical moments to avoid delays. Such critical elements and activities are not easily identified with the use of bar charts.

8.4.5 Programme evaluation review technique (PERT)

The programme evaluation review technique (PERT) is a similar system to critical path analysis and was evidently invented by the US navy in 1958 (Render & Heizer, 1997). This technique differs from CPA because it uses different terms and three time estimates for each activity, namely 'optimistic time (the shortest duration likely), most likely time (the average expectation of the majority of people) and the most conservative estimate, taking into account the likelihood of setbacks and restarting the project' (Hildreth, 1990).

These three estimates of time for an activity can be aggregated statistically to achieve an expected time, which is effectively an average of the optimistic, most likely and pessimistic times. Hildreth (1990, 66) describes the equation for this calculation as follows:

$$t_e = \frac{a + 4m + b}{6}$$

Where
t_e = expected time
a = optimistic time
m = most likely time
b = pessimistic time

The calculation of expected time enables the CPA network to be more informed and realistic. This is because the estimated time has been modified by influences of both a positive and negative nature and the event management team has a more realistic idea of the likely duration of the event implementation process.

8.5 Linking event project management to time and money

The critical factors influencing every event involve ensuring it meets the expectations of the event organisers and sponsors, is held on time and is completed within the budget. Accordingly it is extremely important to link the event activities to time and money. The growing importance of the events industry in the economy of most countries is also leading to greater significance in the financial impact of events and increasing complexity of their activities. Accordingly, event programming and project management play an increasingly crucial role.

The comprehensive project management technique using total quality management (TQM) has emerged over the last few years as an effective way of maintaining the importance of the client, achieving continuous improvement of the team, teamwork and continuous effective management through the entire project life cycle (Burke, 2007). With regard to major events, it is important to stress the huge odds that are at stake and how 'large, often one time projects (such as mega events) are difficult challenges to operations managers. It is becoming more important for events to be successful business ventures and ensure they achieve a beneficial return on investment. The stakes are high and millions of dollars in cost overruns have been wasted due to poor planning of projects. Unnecessary delays have occurred due to poor scheduling, and companies have gone bankrupt due to poor controls' (Render & Heizer, 1997). Accordingly, the linkages between time and money

need to be achieved in each event, whether small and community based, or large and international in nature.

8.5.1 Duration of event programmes

All events have a life cycle which varies according to their unique characteristics. Obviously, those events which take place only once have a programme duration which lasts over a short period. The single event cycle is as follows:

❑ Conception of the idea to hold an event;
❑ Feasibility study;
❑ Detailed planning;
❑ Implementation; and
❑ Shut down

Figure 8.3 depicts the above process in a time-related manner.

Events which are held on a regular basis (e.g. perennial or annual events) have a cyclical programme and these are much more difficult to sustain. The regularly held events can often suffer from repetition within their event programme, which can ultimately affect their viability. In addition, the programme cycle needs to take into account the requirements of maintenance of equipment and facilities, marketing, promotion and development of new activities in order to ensure that the event remains fashionable and exciting. Figure 8.4 depicts this process in a conceptual form.

Getz (1997) points out that '[p]rograms should be planned to have a life expectancy and if it is not a planned process there is a risk that the event will lose popularity or money'.

Continual reappraisal of the fashionability of the event, its image and

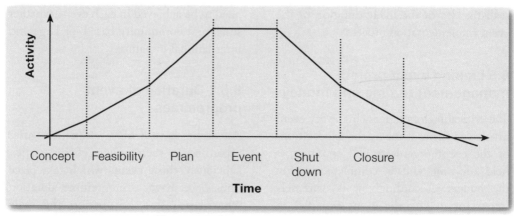

Figure 8.3 Single event duration cycle

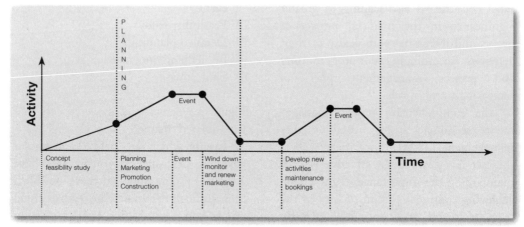

Figure 8.4 Cycle of perennial events

relevance in the context of trends and current events is a crucial component of sustainability. In a number of towns in the Eastern Cape, for example, the events tend to exhibit similar (or the same) craft stalls every year. This fails to achieve a sustainable attendance because the market becomes saturated or at worst bored. This is an area of events design which relates to theming. Often the image and attractiveness of an event can be stimulated by introducing exciting themes (such as fantasy, current events, fashions and cultural issues).

There are programme cycles which relate to the stages that events go through: growth, motivation and rejuvenation or, alternatively, decline and closure (Getz, 1997). Event programmers need to continually take this cycle into account, and intervene to achieve rejuvenation based on market research, innovative trends and new activities.

8.5.2 Time/cost management

An organising event committee and project manager need to have the ability to pay attention to every detail of the event activities, the order or priority by which activities take place (Silvers, 2004) and the time it takes to get the job done. It is essential to create a critical path of all the activities, working backwards from the intended date and identifying what has to be done and when (Allen, 2000). The art of project management is strict adherence to the programme, making sure the critical path is followed and adjustments made as circumstances change. Allen (2000) highlights the importance of looking over all the event contracts and making them part of the critical path in such a way that all the contracted cut-off dates are met. Then as the implementation process develops, the critical path, the cost spreadsheets and expenditure record can be updated regularly. This will ensure that the project manager is able to keep a constant reflection of what has been achieved and when, and how much has been spent.

Effective and clear communication with all the role players in the event process is critical so as to ensure everyone knows what is expected of them. This means the project manager must hold regular meetings with the teams of people involved in the event. Thereafter, minutes of meetings need to be circulated, and managers must ensure that all participants receive the correspondence and act on them. In this increasingly busy world, there is a tendency for people to become dependent on email as a means of effective communication. Unfortunately, email can be a one-sided exercise because the person on the other side of the link does not necessarily receive the email or read the message, or may not implement the tasks required. Accordingly, project managers cannot assume anything and have to continually monitor and check that the actions are being implemented at all times.

A further tool used to link time and costs together in project management relates to function sheets which serve as an operating manual for all the role players in the event itself. Function sheets are prepared as an information guide explaining in fine detail how the event is to be arranged and operated, with detail (for example) on where equipment is to be set up, who is to wear what uniforms, the nature of the décor in specific venues, the sound system, the catering arrangements, how the dignitaries are to be hosted and where they are to be seated, and so on. Allen (2000) explains that function sheets 'make sure that everything is in place with no surprises'. Poorly prepared function sheets invariably mean the event is less successful or even a failure.

Management of resources can have a profound influence on project implementation; for example, additional construction teams could be brought onto site, or a 24-hour construction programme could be introduced. Sometimes the introduction of certain equipment rather than using labour-based methods can result in the construction programme being shortened, compressed or 'crashed' (Render & Heizer, 1997). This simply means that the implementation process is executed more quickly by using more people and/or equipment to speed up production. Activity crashing can be a useful technique if there are penalties payable for late completion of a project. It may be more efficient or economical to pay for more labour rather than suffer penalties. Render and Heizer (1997) explain that 'the objective of crashing is to reduce the project completion time at least cost'. Careful analysis of the critical path of a project schedule can reveal areas where additional resources could reduce the path and project deviation. However, it needs to be acknowledged that undue 'crashing' can place the project at greater risk should unforeseen events or delays occur.

Both CPA and PERT are totally dependent upon the clarity of project activities, timing and precedence. Time estimates are usually subjective, and forecast on the basis of the expectations of clients, managers and event owners, and sometimes over-optimistic estimates can result in failure in the performance of network programmes. Caution is also suggested by Render and Heizer (1997) with regard to 'too much emphasis being placed on the longest, or critical path' and as a result 'near critical paths need to be monitored as well'.

8.6 Monitoring the event and ensuring success

Effective implementation of the event programme requires a methodical evaluation and review of several components of the event. These would include systematic evaluation procedures before the event is held (i.e. during the establishment/development phase), during the event itself and, finally, after the event has been held. A key element in event monitoring and review is *project auditing*. Cleland (1999) describes this as 'a formal independent evaluation of the effectiveness with which the project is being managed'.

Project auditing can involve four elements: firstly, identifying those activities that are performing correctly, and why; secondly, identifying what is going wrong, and why; thirdly, determining those factors affecting the achievement of the objectives; and fourthly, evaluating the efficiency of the project management team, organisers and participants (Cleland, 1999). Monitoring

and review not only seek to measure how the event is doing in terms of expenditure, budget and performance, but also need to canvass visitor and participant views regarding how well the event meets their expectations. Such information is vital for planning future events and is also essential for report-backs to sponsors and financial institutions in order to establish the extent to which the event was a success and value for money. Silvers (2004) recommends appropriate evaluation criteria be prepared at the outset to ensure the monitoring process is meaningful and adds value. In this regard, monitoring criteria need to help measure performance in terms of a 'baseline', assess changes or trends over time, assess how the event is meeting expectations and at the same time comply with legal and safety requirements.

8.6.1 Pre-event monitoring and evaluation

These processes are normally conducted by the project management team which is responsible for the planning, programming and development phase. The monitoring process seeks to achieve an understanding of *expenditure* against the budget during construction; *quality* in terms of the specifications and expectations of the organisation, and *progress* in terms of time, meeting expected milestones timeously and the impact of any delays on the critical elements of the event itself.

8.6.2 During the event

The organisers of an event need to take the opportunity to monitor the achievements of the event while it is taking place. Monitoring event achievements involves measuring and evaluating the performance

VISITORS ATTENDING 3-DAY FESTIVAL IN TOWN XYZ

Day .... Time .... am/pm

1. Where is your residence?
   Town/City.. Region/Province...................................

2. *(a)* Are you staying overnight in the XYZ area? Yes/No
   (b) If so, what accommodation are you using?

   ☐   ☐   ☐   ☐   ☐

   Hotel/   Bed &   Friends/   Camp-   Flat/
   Motel   Brkfst   Relatives   ground   Timeshare

3. Number of people in your group.
   Adults .... Children 12 years and under.........................

4. How much do you plan to spend at the festival (excluding accommodation and travelling costs)? R ....

5. How much do you plan to spend in areas other than on the festival site? R ....

6. How long do you plan to stay at the festival? ....days

7. How did you hear about the festival? (Mark as many as apply)

   ☐   ☐   ☐   ☐   ☐   ☐   ☐

   Newspaper   Internet   Radio   TV   Brochure   Poster   Magazine

   ☐   ☐

   Word of mouth   Other describe ....

   ....

8. Please rate how well the festival met your expectations.

   ☐   ☐   ☐   ☐   ☐

   Excellent   Good   Average   Below average   Poor

9. Please give your comments or suggestions (to improve the festival)

   ....

   ....

Thank you

Figure 8.5 Sample festival questionnaire

Source: Adapted from Leibold (1990: Appendix D)

of the activities in terms of budget, expectations and quality specifications; monitoring visitor perceptions, attendance statistics and expectations; and monitoring the extent and nature of media reports and promotional exposure given during the event. An example of a practical way to measure visitor perceptions is in the use of a simple single-page questionnaire (refer to figure 8.5). The questionnaire uses the opportunity of monitoring to obtain various statistics about the visitors. These statistics can include questions about the origin and destination of visitors; accommodation type used; the number of attendees; their age, characteristics, expenditure and length of stay; their perception of their enjoyment of the event; and the success of the marketing. Not only are these statistics useful for future planning, but they also provide a useful basis for ongoing event-planning research, of which there is a limited amount available, especially in developing countries.

8.6.3 After the event

Monitoring and review at the end of an event is becoming increasingly important (Cleland, 1999) because it enables project outcomes to be evaluated relative to the actual costs incurred. This evaluation stage can be difficult to execute if it involves participants, because at the end of the event people are usually in a hurry to leave, perhaps have a distorted perception of the event (due to excitement, fatigue or emotion) and lack the time to answer a questionnaire (Hildreth, 1990). One possibility is to mail questionnaires to a sample of the visitors to obtain their views after the event. This can improve the quality of the response (because people will have been able to reflect on the event

at leisure) but could also be difficult to execute as there is usually a low response rate to mailed questionnaires.

Monitoring and review after an event would accordingly seek to consider the actual cost incurred for the event and the level of enjoyment, perceptions and views of participants in the event (e.g. the exhibitors, sportsmen/women, actors, etc.). The views of people who attended are important for the organisers and sponsors not only in order to plan for the future but also to enable the organisers to arrive at conclusions regarding the attainment of the objectives. An event-monitoring process also needs to assess what went well and why, what went wrong and why, and what amendments should be made to the plan, the programme and the event itself.

8.7 Summary

Successful events depend upon a well-managed process of implementation to ensure the event fits with the original plan, is held on time and meets all the stakeholders' expectations. Small events usually involve voluntary members and committees who organise the process and hold the event according to their expertise and capabilities. As events become larger, more complicated and costly, it becomes sensible to assign a project manager to assume the responsibility of managing and programming the implementation process.

In order to meet the agreed targets, timeframes and budgets of larger events, various project management methods, techniques and tools are used. These vary according to the needs of the project manager and the event itself. It is important that constant monitoring is carried out of the implementation process so that progress can be evaluated in terms of the original objectives of the event plan, costs can be overseen and the quality of the event activities can be assessed to ensure all stakeholders are happy with the outcome. Event programming requires attention to detail and careful project management to ensure success.

There are several critical factors which need to be accommodated in the programming phase:

☐ Commitment from the events organisation and its management;
☐ A realistic, achievable and firm schedule of activities aligned to the critical path;
☐ Clearly defined decision-making lines of communication and authority;
☐ A well-motivated and cooperative team;
☐ Flexibility in the organisation to accommodate unforeseen changes;
☐ Involvement of the project management component as early as possible (preferably in the formulation and planning stage);
☐ Well-prepared and detailed function sheets;
☐ Continual review and monitoring of performance, quality and budget;
☐ Involvement of stakeholders with effective distribution of information, regular meetings and clear, concise action plans.

Questions for research

1 Explain how the life cycle of single events differs from perennial events, and describe the various measures needed to sustain the life of events.
2 Describe the scheduling process. Explain how this process could help managing an event and the steps involved.
3 Project management/programming seeks to achieve a successful project with three parameters. Name these and explain how you can assist in meeting these objectives.
4 There are various network scheduling methods. Name these and describe how they differ from each other.
5 What is meant by 'stakeholder management'? Describe how you would best achieve this.
6 Describe the skills required by a project manager with reference to programming an event.
7 Explain the various factors which can result in project failure, and indicate how these can be avoided.
8 The monitoring and review process has certain specific components. Describe these for the full event life cycle.
9 Monitoring activities should take place before, during and after an event. In your opinion, why is this the case and how should these activities be performed?
10 What are the critical success factors of event programming? Explain why these are critical to the success of the event.

Recommended websites

Browse the following internet sites for interesting and informative information:

Additional reading material:
http://specialevents.com/

Event project management tools:
http://www.webex.com/services/event-center-features.html
http://www.strategicevents.com/services.htm

Guidelines:
http://www.jisc.ac.uk/uploadeddocuments/jisc-event-programme-example.doc
http://www.paconsulting.com/industries/travel_tourism/services/private/event+planning/
http://www.premiers.qld.gov.au/library/office/Event%20management%20plan.doc

Project management process:
http://www.juliasilvers.com/embok.htm

Suggested reading

Burke, R. 2007. *Project Management Techniques,* college ed. Burke Publishing.
Cleland, DT. 1999. *Project Management,* 3 ed. New York: McGraw-Hill.
Rutherford Silvers, J. 2004. *Professional Event Co-ordination.* Hoboken, NJ: John Wiley & Sons, Inc.

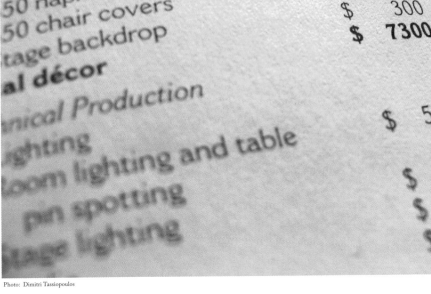

Photo: Dimitri Tassiopoulos

9 Events accounting and financial management

Debbie van Oudtshoorn

Abstract

The aim of this chapter is to enable the reader to prepare, maintain and understand a complete set of accounting books for an event enterprise. The financial goals of an enterprise are achieved by using standard generally accepted accounting principles (GAAP), budgets, costing, capital expenditure (CAPEX) and cash flow management.

Chapter objectives

After you have read this chapter you should be able to:
- ❑ distinguish between management and financial accounting;
- ❑ demonstrate an understanding of cash flow management;
- ❑ list the reasons why budgeting is of importance; and
- ❑ explain how an income statement may be used to better manage an event.

9.1 Introduction

It is necessary to keep track of how all event projects or enterprises are performing, and the following questions need to be answered:
- ❑ Who owes money and how much?
- ❑ How much money is owed and to whom?
- ❑ What items of property (assets) are owned?
- ❑ Is a profit or a loss being made?

Event managers need to be professional about accounting, especially when large budgets are involved. Financial accounting involves the preparation and presentation of the financial statements (income statement and balance sheets) as required by law or other external parties. Generally accepted accounting practices (GAAP) are used by accountants to compile and present the reports. Management accounting involves preparing and internally using the financial reports to assist in management decision making (Getz, 1997).

9.2 Accounting

There is a continuous flow of activity in every business day in an event enterprise. The finance department produces a report for each month on a monthly basis. Businesses have a financial reporting calendar which states the start and end dates for their financial year. In order to produce these monthly reports, the financial activity is halted, but business carries on as normal.

Three disciplines are found in accounting. They are management accounting, financial accounting and cost accounting.

- ❑ *Management accounting* is responsible for providing internal reports for management only. These reports are useful for planning and controlling routine or daily functions and making non-routine decisions (capital expenditure or establishing a new line of business, formulating plans and policies). *Financial accounting* is responsible for external reporting to shareholders, creditors, government, potential investors and money lenders.
  - Internal reports need to be relevant for immediate decision making. Management accounting does not need to follow strict accounting rules because the process differs from one business to the next, depending on the needs of each.
  - External reports need to follow uniform rules as applied nationally and internationally. Shareholders and other outside parties need information which they can compare, on the same basis, with other businesses.
  - The internal and external reports need to be reliable. This is achieved by using internal controls and auditors reports.

❏ **Cost accounting** is used to accurately determine the precise cost of the product or service the business enterprise produces or sells. In order to determine the cost, access is needed to information such as labour costs for each part of the process, overhead costs and inventory costs. This information is used to determine what to charge when a ticket is purchased. A successful enterprise is one which keeps a very close check on the expense of an item and adjusts the selling price in order to maintain some level of profitability.

9.2.1 Project management accounting

The process of planning, organising and managing resources in order to complete, successfully, project goals and objectives is called project management. A project is a temporary goal, with a defined beginning and end, and it is undertaken to meet specific goals and objectives. Project management accounting is thus a projected budget for an event project. Sometimes an event owner will have to put in a bid for an event and this bid is calculated by means of a projected budget.

9.3 Budgeting

A budget is necessary for control purposes. It is a document that compares expected revenue with actual revenue, and expected expenses with actual expenses. This assists the event manager to keep control of the event. A budget is a plan in financial terms of the event enterprise's activities for a future period (Faul et al., 1993). Budgets are management tools and plans that involve process and control, and are

indicators of performance. Thus budgets are performance management tools, their purpose being to allocate limited resources to unlimited needs. Budgets are the planned financial activities for the year ahead and indicate strategic priorities for the period. The act of preparing a budget is called budgeting. The use of budgets to control an event enterprise's activities is called budgetary control.

The ideal profile is to consider what you want to generate for both your enterprise and your local economy. A finance committee should be appointed. Develop a budget according to necessity, and then add extras that will enhance the event. Balance the income with anticipated expenses, always keeping the financial goal in sight. If sponsorship does not cover upfront costs, a fundraising drive may be necessary. This should all be taken into account when planning an event.

Some of the expenses that will need to be considered before the event will be publicity, food and beverages, printing and postage, site fees, licences and permits, labour costs, insurance, deposits, decorations and prizes.

Planning and control are the two most important tasks of management. These two processes occur during the budgeting process (Faul et al., 1993):

❏ **Planning.** There are three levels of planning in an event enterprise, namely strategic, operational and financial planning. Strategic planning is the process in which the event enterprise decides on its broad objectives and the scope and nature of its business. Operational planning involves the detailed planning of the activities which are necessary to attain the objectives of the event enterprise. Financial planning deals with planning the financial implications of the operations. There needs to be planning for income, expenditure, assets, cash flow and liabilities. Financial planning takes the format of a budget. It will include a budgeted income statement, a budgeted balance sheet and a budgeted cash flow for a future period (Faul et al., 1993).

❑ *Control.* Specific persons in the event enterprise accept responsibility for specific functions and therefore the financial results thereof.

A person who accepts responsibility for a specific function should also budget for the implications of that function and ensure that budgeted results are met (Faul et al., 1993). Standards are set in a budget. Actual results should be compared to the budget on a regular basis in order to exercise control. Corrective action may be taken for any variances.

The accounting system needs to be designed in such a way that budgetary control is possible through the reports generated (Faul et al., 1993). Thus, budgets lead to prioritisation. In addition, budgets demonstrate the vision of the event enterprise and guide it in that direction. Budgets, according to Goldblatt (1997: 106), are based on:

❑ the financial history of previous identical or similar event businesses and/or events;

❑ the general economy and forecasts for the future; and

❑ the income and expenses that can reasonably be expected with the resources available.

The initial budget shows the results which may be expected, including the assumptions used in obtaining that budget. If the objectives are not met, the budget will need to be re-looked at and further calculations done until they are.

A budget is a financial plan as it is expressed in monetary terms – it is used as a guide for operating an event. The budget is based on available information and consists of revenue and expenses. Before any event is considered, a budget should be prepared in order to determine whether the event will be feasible or not. The bottom line of any event is profitability and there has been plenty of money lost and even bankruptcy due to budgets not being prepared. Conditions do change and the budget needs to be flexible in order to accommodate them. What all event managers and staff must strive for is for expenses to be kept to a minimum. Revenue cannot be predicted exactly. Expenses may be controlled and kept to a minimum (Getz, 1997: 230–232).

Some of the benefits associated with budgeting:

❑ Budgets communicate management's plans;

❑ Budgets force managers to think about and plan for the future;

❑ The budgeting process may uncover potential problem areas before they occur;

❑ Budgets coordinate the activities of the event enterprise as the various departments' plans are integrated; and

❑ Budgets define goals and objectives which may be used for evaluating subsequent performance.

Budgets normally cover a one-year period corresponding to the fiscal year of the organisation. The annual budget may be detailed by week or month. Event managers use budgets to plan for the future. There are many different kinds of budgets that may be prepared. Examples of budgets are the income and expenditure budget, capital expenditure (CAPEX) budget, cash flow budget and the personnel or payroll budget.

The income and expenditure budget shows the income and expenses of each week or month, and the resultant net profit or loss.

The CAPEX budget shows the weeks or months in which capital expenditure (purchasing of assets) is to occur, while the cash flow budget plans for the incoming (receipts) and outgoing (payments) cash. The personnel or payroll budget shows the expenses associated with employing staff on a permanent and a casual basis.

It often happens that the actual results from an event vary considerably from budgeted results. This is quite prevalent as regards revenue. The economy may be in a recession or a boom, which will definitely have an effect on the revenue of an event. The variances between budgeted and actual figures need to be identified, the causes determined and corrective action plans put in place. Perhaps ideas need to be pursued for increasing income or reducing expenditure, and this information and any decisions need to be communicated to those affected:

❐ Identify opportunities for improved budget performance;
❐ Proactively source new suppliers and revenue streams;
❐ Discuss desired budgetary outcomes with colleagues; and
❐ Present recommendations to appropriate individuals or departments

Actual results from an event will be used to prepare the budget for the next year. It is taken for granted that the previous year's budget will be used as a baseline for preparing the following year's budget. By using historic information, event managers will be able to prepare a more realistic budget than if no historic information is available. Historic information will obviously not be available for an event to be held for the first time. Rather, a method of zero-based budgeting will be used. This means that managers will be required to justify all expenses and not just changes in the previous year's budget. This means that a zero cost is used as a starting point, and expenses which can be justified are added. Considerable documentation is required for zero-based budgeting.

The success of any budget depends on top management's acceptance of the budget as well as the way in which top management uses this budgeted data. In order for the budget to be successful, there needs to be support from key management. Budgeting is hard work and if top management is not enthusiastic or committed to the budget, then it is unlikely that anyone else will be either. The budget should be used as a positive instrument to assist in establishing goals, measuring results and identifying variances.

People need to understand the concept of variance (the difference between the budget and the actual amount). Each variance can be explained in some way (the work was not done, the money came in late, more was spent because the budget was not prepared properly, etc.).

Give people a chance to look at the variance report in depth. Ask them to identify which variances would worry them, what the underlying reason might be for the variance, and what the organisation should do about it.

A variance that is larger than 10% (whether it is a negative or a positive one) should be explained. Most organisations set their own limits. Some variances are due to

Example 9.1 The weekend getaway: Budgeted income statement

Background

You have been contracted by a local company as a professional conference organiser (PCO). You have been requested to organise a one-day weekend function from Saturday 9 January to Sunday 10 January 20xx for 50 delegates.

The following must be assumed:

- ❐ You are responsible for organising a one-day weekend function.
- ❐ There will be 50 delegates, staying one night in twin rooms.
- ❐ Three meals and tea, coffee and beverages will be provided on Saturday.
- ❐ All equipment (including OHP, computer, microphone, flipcharts) must be supplied.
- ❐ The function on Saturday night must include music.
- ❐ Breakfast on Sunday is included.

The following would need to be budgeted for:

Conference room hire	2 000
Equipment hire	750
Accommodation per delegate	750
Breakfast per delegate	75
Lunch per delegate	120
Dinner per delegate	150
Tea, coffee per delegate	25
Beverages for the function	1 000
Saturday night function music	1 500

The cost for the weekend conference can be calculated as follows:

	Quantity	Amount
Conference room hire		2 000
Equipment hire		750
Accommodation per delegate	50	37 500
Breakfast	100	7 500
Lunch	50	6 000
Dinner	50	7 500
Tea, coffee	50	1 250
Beverages		1 000
Saturday night function music		1 500
TOTAL COST		**65 000**

The cost per delegate can be calculated as follows:
Total cost divided by number of delegates = 65 000 divided by 50 = 1 300

Budgeted income statement of the weekend getaway ended 10 January 20xx:

Total sales	0.00
Less expenses	65 000.00
Loss	65 000.00

a timing problem and not to overspending, but they may reflect a problem with the way the organisation is run.

9.4 Management of cash flow

The core of working capital management is to monitor cash flow. Cash is constantly moving through an event enterprise. Nearly all transactions recorded involve a flow of cash into or out of the event enterprise. It flows in when customers purchase tickets for an event, and it flows out as payments are made to suppliers. The typically uneven nature of cash inflows and outflows makes it important that they be properly understood and regulated.

An event manager must be able to monitor cash flow. Cash flow is the net result of cash inflows and cash outflows, where cash inflows deal with receipts and cash outflows with payments. The cash budget is thus important. The revenue from events is received on the day of the event while expenses have been incurred prior to receiving this income. The cash outflows will exceed the cash inflows prior to the event being held. This is called a negative cash flow or a deficit. Once the event has been held, the cash inflows will be received, which will exceed the cash outflows. This is called a positive cash flow or a surplus.

The cash flow is a forecast of monthly expenses and revenue. Danger months will be identified. By being able to do so, the event manager will be able to make necessary arrangements, if possible, with the bank manager and suppliers. It might be arranged that the bank account may go into overdraft while the suppliers might extend their credit terms until the event is over. This is known as back-ending. Sponsors and donors might advance money to help alleviate the negative cash flow.

When the cash flow is drawn up, it is important to get the timing of the expenses and revenue correct as this has an impact on the available cash. Are all

---

Example 9.2 The weekend getaway: Budgeted cash flow

Budgeted cash flow of the weekend getaway for January 20xx

	Dec 20xx	Jan 20xx
Opening balance	0	(65 000.00)
Cash inflows:		
Cash sales	0	
Cash from debtors		
Other receipts		
Total cash inflows	0	
Cash outflows:		
Cost of sales		
Salaries and wages		
Promotions		
Judges' fees		
Equipment rental		
Other payments	65 000.00	
Total cash outflows	65 000.00	
Closing balance	(65 000.00)	

expenses going to be incurred before the event, or most before and a few after? Have grants been applied for? When can the funds be expected to be received? (Getz, 1997: 233)

The cash flow consists of four sections, namely cash receipts, cash payments, cash excess or shortage, and financing. The receipts section consists of all the cash inflows expected during the event. Cash received from financing does not form part of cash receipts. The payments section consists of all the cash outflows expected during the event. If there is a cash shortage, the event enterprise will need to borrow funds. If there is a cash excess, funds borrowed in a previous period can be repaid or the excess funds may be invested. The financing section details the borrowing and repayments projected to take place. It also lists interest payments that will be due on money borrowed.

9.4.1 Internal control over cash

It is very easy for cash to disappear, so there needs to be a control system in place. Cash is the most liquid form of money and therefore it is an event enterprise's most active asset. Because it is the most liquid asset, it is also the most abused, therefore every event enterprise must have an effective internal control system for cash. The policies and procedures for cash handling need to be communicated to staff and volunteers, and steps taken to prevent theft.

In smaller event enterprises, the owner or manager usually exercises personal control over all cash transactions. In larger event enterprises, however, it is impossible for one person to exercise individual control, hence these duties are segregated.

A sound cash control system should meet the following requirements:

❏ Employees' duties and functions must be segregated in order to ensure that those persons who receive, pay out or handle cash in any way are not involved in the recording function. This prevents a person misappropriating funds and concealing the fact by forging entries in the books. The functions must be segregated in such a way that an error by one employee will be revealed during normal business activities by another. This means that at least two employees need to be involved if funds are to be misappropriated.

❏ Cash receipts must be recorded in such a way that the actual cash received can be checked against an independent daily record. A source document must be recorded as soon as cash is received.

❏ All cash received must be banked daily. No payments must be made from the receipts. The bank deposit slip will serve as a control of the cash received.

❏ All payments, except for petty cash payments, must be made by cheque. Cheques must be countersigned and the supporting documentation must be provided. The functions of the employees handling cheques must be segregated from those who record the transactions.

❏ Cash must be verified. The actual cash on hand must be compared with the source documents. The cash received must be checked daily by an independent person – someone who is not responsible for receipting or handling cash. The manager or supervisor needs to check the deposit slip for banking.

❏ The cash records must be compared with the bank statement (Tassiopoulos, 2000).

❏ Floats should be checked regularly

as there is temptation when they are not checked at all. Should there be a petty cash float, it should have all the necessary backup documentation supporting the petty cash vouchers for any petty cash paid out. The person who is being reimbursed from petty cash needs to sign the voucher on receipt of the cash.

9.4.2 Ensuring a positive cash flow

While the basic financial statements (income statement and balance sheet) contain a great deal of information which is useful to management and investors, they do not answer the questions that could be raised by users of financial statements. Such questions may include the following:

❐ How much cash was generated in the enterprise's operations?
❐ Why did the enterprise, although being very profitable, pay only a small dividend?
❐ How much was spent on new plant and equipment and where did the enterprise get the cash to finance the purchase thereof (Faul et al., 1993)?

Cash inflows concern the ways in which incoming cash is received. Cash inflow thus represents all the receipts. A cash sale is when money is received at the time of the sale. Some sales may not be cash and are made on account or credit. This means that although an item or items have been sold, no cash is received at the time of the sale, and is received at a later date. This receipt of cash at a later date from someone who purchased on credit, called a debtor, is therefore called 'cash from debtors'. Receipts made of all other forms of cash received that do not form part of

the main business are called 'other receipts'. Total cash inflow represents the total of all the above-mentioned cash receipts for the month.

Cash outflows consist of all the reasons why cash is paid out of the event. Salaries and wages represent the salaries and casual wages paid to staff employed on a permanent and casual basis. Any promotional expenses are reflected here. There might be judges for certain events, and the fees to be paid to them are shown under cash outflows. Any equipment that is rented needs to be paid for and this is also reflected here. Other payments are made up of any other sundries. Total cash outflows represent the total cash paid out in a particular month.

The closing cash balance will be the opening balance for the following month, and can be either positive or negative.

9.5 Financial accounting statements

The income statement and balance sheet make up the financial accounting statements.

9.5.1 Income statement

The income statement shows the financial result of the event. It shows whether a net profit or loss was made. Financiers, sponsors and directors are able to see from this financial accounting statement how well management performed. Did it make a profit or a loss? The bottom line for any event is profitability, and it is the income statement which is going to reflect this. Income statements can be prepared after the event has taken place and/or after the audit has been completed. Only revenue and expense accounts are taken into account when drawing up the income statement.

$$\text{Profit} = \text{Revenue} - \text{Expenses}$$

Revenue is obtained from normal selling before/at the event. An example is the sale of tickets. Expenses are those which are incurred in the day-to-day running of the event and are not bought with the intention of reselling. Purchases are the only expenses that are bought with this intention.

The following is a list of possible accounts that may appear in the general ledger:

Revenue	Expenses
Food	Food cost of sales
Beverage	Beverage cost of sales
Vendor	Vendors' cost of sales
Music	Musicians' cost of sales
Entertainment	Entertainment cost of sales
Equipment	Equipment cost of sales
Décor	Décor cost of sales
Advertising	Salaries
Concession	Wages
Donation	UIF
Gifts	Medical aid
Exhibit booth rentals	Pension or provident fund
Interest from investments	Leave pay
Merchandise	Bonus
Registration fees	Advertising
Special events tickets	Promotions
Sponsorship fees	Audit fees
Vendor commissions	Bank charges
Other revenue	Credit card commission
	Commission paid
	Data processing
	General expenses
	Insurance
	Judges' fees
	Legal fees
	Licences and permits
	Printing and stationery
	Professional fees
	Repairs and maintenance
	Subscriptions
	Depreciation
	Rates and taxes
	Rent paid
	Other cost of sales

Example 9.3 The weekend getaway: Income statement

Income statement of the weekend getaway for the day ended 10 January 20xx

Revenue:	
Food and beverages	0.00
Less expenses	
Cost of sales	65 000.00
Net income before taxation	(65 000.00)
Less taxation at 30%	19 500.00
Net income after taxation	(45 500.00)

Note that this income statement does not take capital repayments, debt or finance charges into account

Should the management of an event decide to hold back some of the income made from the event for expansion purposes or for any other reason, such income is called *retained income*. The income which is made from the event is added to the opening balance of the retained income at the beginning of the year. The total retained income at year end will thus represent what was made in total from the lifespan of the event so far.

As a company grows, it can have an appetite for cash. As its sales increase, so do the firm's asset requirements and its need for financing. The retention of profits is a primary source of financing for small but growing firms (Longnecker, Moore & Petty, 2006).

Sometimes it is these retained profits that have ensured the solvency of an event.

Cutting costs

Controlling expenses is extremely critical. While expenses must be kept to a minimum, revenue must be maximised. There are different types of expenses associated with events. There are fixed expenses, direct expenses and indirect expenses or overheads. Fixed expenses must be paid for irrespective of whether the event is held or not. Examples are capital expenses associated with equipment and buildings (rent), insurance, salaries for permanent staff, and telephone equipment and line rental. Variable expenses are those expenses which increase or decrease with a corresponding increase or decrease in event revenue. Event revenue depends on attendance. An example of a variable expense would be cost of sales, casual wages, postage, decorations and telephone calls. Direct expenses are those expenses which are associated with a specific event. Overheads or indirect expenses are those such as the office rent and the general manager's salary (Getz, 1997: 233).

Certain events managers can employ one or more employees on a permanent basis. These employees are paid regardless of the volume of sales. They are salaried employees and their costs are fixed. The problem with salaried employees is that when business volume decreases, they are still paid. These costs quickly erode profit and create big losses.

Every events manager should aim to keep payroll costs in check by keeping permanent employees to a minimum, which is achieved by using part-time casual workers on an ad hoc basis.

Many events rely on volunteers and if it

was not for their help, some events would not succeed at all. Volunteers are not paid for their services. Rather they are given vouchers, complimentary tickets or some other package. The package may take the form of T-shirts, name badges, food and beverage vouchers, free transportation from the event to parking areas, tog bags and peak caps.

The aim is to take control of the event, to minimise risk, to optimise revenue and to use resources efficiently.

9.5.2 Balance sheet

The balance sheet shows how all the assets have been or are being paid for; it shows the financial position of the event. The balance sheet is drawn up according to the accounting equation, as follows:

$$A = OE + L$$

where:
A = assets
OE = owner's equity
L = liabilities

There are three categories of assets, namely fixed assets, investments and current assets. Assets are something of value. Fixed assets consist of land, buildings, motor vehicles and equipment. Assets depreciate due to wear and tear. This loss in value is called depreciation. Assets are shown in the balance sheet at their net book value. This is equal to their original cost price less accumulated depreciation. Investments represent money that has been deposited for a fixed period of time. Current assets are those which are also of value, but the difference between fixed assets and current assets is

that the value of current assets changes during the year. Current assets are more variable in nature. Examples of current assets are stock, debtors and bank.

The money, cash, assets or whatever the owner has contributed towards the event business represents owner's equity. Owner's equity thus represents the owner's interest in the business. Owner's equity may be increased by further contributions, and is regarded as the permanent investment by the owner.

Owner's equity may be broken into:
$$OE = Capital + Profit - Loss - Drawings$$

Drawings represent what the owner has taken from the event business for own use. Drawings may be in the form of cash or stock.

Total liabilities are made up of owner's equity, long-term liabilities and current liabilities. Liabilities show the creditors of the event enterprise – i.e. owner, finance houses and suppliers. Long-term liabilities are creditors of the event enterprise, their debt being settled over a period of time (anything from five years and more). Current liabilities represent the shorter-term creditors of the enterprise. These creditors need to be repaid within the year.

9.6 Measuring financial performance

9.6.1 Solvency
Many small event enterprises have a cash flow problem. The reason for this is due to expenses being incurred prior to any revenue being generated. There is therefore the need to calculate the solvency (the ability to settle its debts or obligations) of

Example 9.4 The weekend getaway: Actual balance sheet

Balance sheet of the weekend getaway as at 10 January 20xx

Employment of capital		Capital employed	
Fixed assets:		Owner's equity:	
		Capital:	
Current assets:		Loss	(45 500)
Revenue Service	19 500	Current liabilities:	
		Creditors	
		Bank overdraft	65 000
	19 500		19 500

The loss of 45 500 can be obtained from the example. There are no sales, therefore no funds can be deposited into the bank account. The function was paid for by cheque, therefore the bank overdraft is 65 000.

The sum of 19 500 represents the liability in favour of the company by the Revenue Service for taxation of 30% of the loss.

the event enterprise. Solvency is calculated by means of the current ratio:

$$\text{Current ratio} = \frac{\text{Current assets}}{\text{Current liabilities}}$$

Current assets represent those assets that can be converted into cash within one year, while current liabilities represent those liabilities that need to be settled within one year. It is a measure of solvency, alternatively referred to as the liquidity or quick ratio.

This ratio calculates that for every one unit in any currency an event organisation owns, it owes x. A ratio of two is normally desired, as this would represent two units owned for every one unit owed (Getz, 1997).

Using example 9.4, the calculations are as follows:

$$\text{Current ratio} = \frac{\text{Current assets}}{\text{Current liabilities}}$$
$$= \frac{19\ 500}{65\ 000}$$
$$= \frac{195}{650}$$
$$= \frac{39}{130}$$

This ratio has calculated for every 39 units in any currency an event organisation owns, it owes 130 units.

The acid-test ratio is also a solvency ratio. It is calculated as follows:

$$\text{Acid-test ratio} = \frac{\text{Current assets} - \text{Stock}}{\text{Current liabilities}}$$

The difference between the current and the acid test ratio is stock because stock is excluded from the total of the current assets when calculating the acid-test ratio.

By comparing the current and acid-test ratios, it can be calculated how much the value of the stock contributes towards the solvency of the event organisation. If the stock holding is very high, then the current ratio will be much higher then the acid-test ratio.

Using example 9.4, the calculation is as follows:

$$\text{Acid-test ratio} = \frac{\text{Current assets} - \text{stock}}{\text{Current liabilities}}$$
$$= \frac{19\,500 - 0}{65\,000}$$
$$= \frac{195}{650}$$
$$= \frac{39}{130}$$

This ratio has calculated that for every 39 units in any currency an event organisation owns, it owes 130 units.

9.6.2 Return on investment and return on expenses (ROE)

Return on investment (ROI) has become popular in the world of events management as a tool to evaluate events. Historically, ROI was a measure of profit gained through an investment. This was a quantitative measure and calculated whether the owner, or manager, was getting value from the event.

The formula for ROI is as follows:

$$\text{ROI} = \frac{\text{Profit}}{\text{Total investment}}$$

Profit is represented by the total profit of the event. Total investment consists of capital plus any further contributions such as retained income plus any debt that was incurred; the objective is to achieve a high ratio of profit to investment. The owner of the event organisation will want to be able to calculate whether there is a good return on any investment made in the business. If a good return on the investment is not being made, then why not take the financial resources and place them in a bank?

9.7 Price administration and producing profit

Richards (1992) states that the event manager should ask the following questions:

❏ Has the product been priced to match the visitor perception of good value?
❏ Will the event income cover all fixed and variable overheads, depreciation, future capital investment and all marketing costs to yield a profit?

Other questions might include:

❏ Can the event be provided at a price acceptable to customers?
❏ Can price packages be put together to support group attendance or tourist rates?

One of the main responsibilities is the understanding of the financial goals of the sponsoring organisation. Once this is determined, market research will illustrate the competitor's pricing patterns. Who is offering a similar product, to whom and at what price? The demand for the product and economic indicators such as economic climate in a particular city or region or even globally need to be taken into account or considered. The bottom line of some events is to make money, while for others it is to break even. The price must reflect the total cost of goods and services.

What are the financial demographics of the audience? The market's ability to pay must be analysed. An event designed

Example 9.5 Calculating ROI for an event project

Calculate the ROI using the following information:

Revenue	10 000
Expenses	8 000
Capital	10 000

Calculation:
Profit equals revenue less expenses = 2 000

$$ROI = \frac{Profit}{Total\ investment}$$
$$= \frac{2\ 000}{10\ 000}$$
$$= \frac{1}{5}$$
$$= 20\%$$

This means that for every one unit of profit, five units of capital were invested.

Should a bank be offering 10%, it would be better not to invest the money with the bank as the return of 10% is less than the return on the above event project (20%).

The primary objective is to measure the success of the event in quantitative terms, i.e. in currency. ROI may also be measured qualitatively. Some examples would include making contacts at exhibitions, the level of enjoyment and participation at festivals.

Example 9.6 Calculating ROE

Calculate the ROE using the following information:

Expenses	8 000
Capital	10 000

$$ROE = \frac{Expenses}{Total\ investment}$$
$$= \frac{8\ 000}{10\ 000}$$
$$= \frac{4}{5}$$
$$= 80\%$$

This means that for every four units of expenses, five units of capital were invested.

---

for company executives who have access to a credit card and can charge their participation as a business expense is likely to be priced more highly than one designed for those who must pay out of their own pocket. Market research will help determine the ability and willingness of attendees to pay ticket prices at various levels. This will influence the planning of the event.

In practice, revenue maximisation is the key to ongoing success.

Yield management, also known as revenue management, is the process of understanding, anticipating and influencing consumer behaviour in order to maximise revenue or profits from a fixed perishable resource (such as seats for an event). The challenge is to sell the right resources to the right customer at the right time for the right price. This process can result in price discrimination, where an enterprise charges customers consuming otherwise identical goods or services a different price for doing so.

There are three essential conditions for revenue management to be applicable:

❐ That there are a fixed number of resources available for sale;
❐ That the resources sold are perishable. This means that there is a time limit to selling them, after which they cease to be of value; and
❐ That different customers are willing to pay a different price for using the same number of resources.

Industries that use yield management include airlines, hotels and stadia, and other venues with a fixed number of seats. It is particularly suitable when selling perishable products, i.e. goods that become not saleable at a point in time (e.g. tickets after the show has ended).

The following are ways in which to maximise revenue for an event:

❐ *Admission fees.* This requires research. If the event is a fundraiser, the more visitors have to spend on admission, the less they will have available to spend in the grounds. What needs to be remembered is that if the admission fee is too low, it might attract an unwanted element. If the fee is too high, it might attract too few people. For slow days, offer free admission or discounted rates at the time the business is needed. No discounts are to be offered to price-insensitive clients at peak times.
❐ *Concessions.* These may be offered to families in order to lure them to the event. Complimentary tickets may be offered to sponsors and donors to say thank you.

❐ *Donated goods.* When goods or items are donated, it does not mean that the selling price should be unrealistically low. An estimated purchase price of donated goods or items needs to be taken into account.

9.8 Introduction to financial controls

The purpose is to provide a basis for financial stability and sustainability. Financial stability guides the operations and plans. Financial control is a critically important activity to help the business ensure that it is meeting its objectives.

9.8.1 Accounts receivable and payable

Credit decisions impact on working capital and particularly on cash flow. The most important factor in managing cash well within an event enterprise is the ability to collect accounts receivable quickly. Granting credit to customers directly affects an event's cash account. By selling on credit and thus allowing customers to delay payment, the event enterprise delays the inflow of cash. *Accounts receivable* refers to a sale on credit. Although the item has changed hands, the cash is not yet in the bank, and a sale has not taken place until it is. This cash is a current asset. A debtor is someone who has purchased goods on credit, or who was sold goods on credit, and thus owes money for them. This will be settled at a later date. An enterprise usually has a specific credit policy governing the amount of credit that may be granted to clients and the time they will be allowed to meet their obligations. These requirements may vary from client to client – some clients may be required to pay immediately, while others may be granted 30 or 60 days to pay a particular invoice. The number of days for which this debt is outstanding needs to be limited. This is referred to as debtor days. An example of credit terms may be 30 days from date of statement. This means that debtors need to settle their debt by no later than 30 days from the statement date. The receipt book needs to be numbered and it needs to run in sequence. A receipt sequence that is used for one month cannot be the same for the next month. For example, if the receipt books are numbered from 1 to 100, perhaps the first book could be A1 to A100, the second book, B1 to B100, etc. This would alleviate the problem of having receipts issued with the same numbers. Should a large volume of cash be handled on the premises, a safe could be installed, or use could be made of cash pickups by a security company.

Cash flow management and accounts payable management are intertwined. As long as a payable is outstanding, the buying event enterprise can keep cash equal to that amount in its own cheque or current account. When payment is made, however, that event enterprise's cash account is reduced accordingly. Although payables are legal obligations, they can be paid at various times or even renegotiated in some cases. Financial management of accounts payable therefore hinges on negotiation and timing. *Accounts payable* refers to a purchase on credit. Although the items have been received, they have not been paid for. A creditor is someone who is owed money. Suppliers want to be paid within 30 to 60 days of supplying goods and/or services. Some services require cash on delivery (COD). Supplies that are paid for COD will affect the cash flow of the event. It would be advisable for the event manager to arrange credit facilities with the supplier. A relationship can be established with the supplier if it is based on honesty, fairness and frankness. The number of days for which this debt is owed should be extended as it is to the benefit of the event. If the event can reduce debtor days and delay payment to creditors, the cash flow will be better. There need to be at least two signatories on cheques issued. This ensures that there is a control system in place as two people have to give the approval on a payment being made.

Any business is subject to emergency situations and may find it necessary to request of its creditors postponement of its payable obligations. Usually, creditors will cooperate in working out a solution because they want the enterprise to succeed.

When goods are delivered, a tax invoice (if the supplier is registered as a VAT vendor) is supplied, or in the case of a non-vendor, it would be an invoice. The person who receives these goods onto the business premises must sign either the delivery note or the invoice to indicate that he or she has received them. This is what is termed proof of delivery (POD). Should there be a number of items on the invoice, it must be clearly marked what has and has not been received.

The saying 'buy now, pay later' is the motto of many enterprises. By buying on credit, a small enterprise is using creditors' funds to supply short-term cash needs. The longer the creditors' funds can be borrowed, the better. Payment therefore should be delayed as long as acceptable under the agreement.

9.8.2 Stock control

Stock is an example of a current asset. It is something of value, the value of which changes during the year. Stock can go missing rather easily if it is not monitored properly. Stock needs to be counted on a regular basis in order to check whether there are any variances between what is in the books of the event and what is actually there. Examples of stock are crockery, cutlery, glassware, goods and tickets.

9.8.3 Asset control

There are three categories of assets, namely fixed assets, investments and current assets. Assets are something of value. Fixed assets consist of land, buildings, motor vehicles and equipment. Assets depreciate due to wear and tear. This loss in value is called *depreciation*. Investments represent money that has been deposited for a fixed period of time. Current assets are those which are also of value, but the difference between fixed assets and current assets is that the value of the current assets changes during the year – they are more variable in nature. Examples of current assets are stock, debtors and cash in the bank. What applies to stock control applies to asset control. Assets need to be safeguarded and controlled, and they need to be numbered for identification purposes. Assets need to be counted on a regular basis to check whether they can all be accounted for. Should any equipment be borrowed, this must be noted somewhere. Somebody needs to be given the responsibility for controlling assets.

Examples of internal control over assets are as follows:

❐ Assets are numbered;
❐ Assets are entered into a register;
❐ Assets are properly maintained;
❐ Assets are kept in a safe place; and
❐ Assets are regularly compared to the register (physical verification is to be carried out).

Another example of an internal control is the common practice of allowing managers to sign off on smaller purchases up to a pre-authorised limit, above which the manager must obtain senior management's approval.

9.8.4 Petty cash

Petty cash refers to any small payments made. There should be a policy as to what expenses can be claimed and what cannot be claimed. The person receiving the payment must sign that he or she has received payment. The necessary supporting documentation needs to be attached to the petty cash voucher.

9.8.5 Tickets

Some events require tickets to be sold and the counterfoil or stub of the ticket must have the same number sequence as the ticket itself. These tickets and stubs need to be numbered for there to be a control system in place. Any complimentary tickets given out should be noted. There might also be unsold tickets of which there needs to be a record.

9.9 Auditing

Auditing is the process whereby an external auditor will check the financial records. An event enterprise will make use of an external auditor to give his or her opinion as to whether the books have been recorded using generally accepted accounting principles (GAAP). Audited financial statements are required when financing or additional financing is required by an event enterprise. Should an event not be audited, there might be the suspicion that the event is trying to hide something (Getz, 1997).

Auditors are independent from the people producing the reports. They examine the controls and reports, and issue an auditor's report on the reliability of the system controls and the reports compiled by the finance department.

There are two types of auditor, namely internal and external auditors. Normally, large event businesses employ internal auditors who are part of their staff complement. Small community-event projects may appoint external auditors to perform the audit. They are not employees of the business and charge a fee for their services.

9.10 Breakeven

All event managers must be aware of what level of turnover is necessary to cover all costs, and at what point a profit will start being made. This is called the breakeven point.

9.11 Event financial challenges

Events are faced with financial challenges. They may be big or small, but they are challenges nonetheless. The following are ways in which to reduce or limit the financial challenges which may be faced by an event enterprise:

- ❑ Pay all bills on time. Never pay them before they are due unless there is a discount offered for early settlement. There is a disadvantage to paying early if no discount is earned – interest could be earned on your money.
- ❑ Deposit excess cash into an interest-bearing account. Take every opportunity to place extra cash in institutions where interest rates are favourable. This is more advantageous than having the cash just sitting in the petty cash box.

- ❑ It is rarely advisable to extend credit to clients. Provide large organisations with a pro-forma invoice before the date of the event so that the necessary arrangements may be made regarding settlement of the account.
- ❑ Do not issue cheques when it is possible that there are insufficient funds in your account. Approach creditors if there could be problems with settling their bills. Rather make other arrangements than issue a cheque that could be 'returned to drawer' by your bankers.
- ❑ Establish a personal trusting relationship with the banker.
- ❑ Reconcile all cheque accounts once a month, as soon as the bank statements have been received. One of the worst things to do is let these bank statements accumulate, and then try to reconcile many months.
- ❑ Make deposits on a daily basis. Money should be deposited as soon as it is received. Accounts should rather be settled by cheque or petty cash than by deposit money. This allows for better audit trail (Hansen, 1995).
- ❑ Give clear guidelines to salespeople about what business is required, at what time, from what market segment and when.
- ❑ Avoid business being secured that blocks out better pieces of business.
- ❑ Gather the correct data.
- ❑ Update and review the model, taking into account changing market conditions and trends.
- ❑ The economic climate may result in fewer sponsorships and donations being made available. Companies may be scaling down.
- ❑ The potential losses associated with bad weather may be cancellation and the consequent financial loss; potential

Example 9.6 Festival popcorn wagon: Breakeven analysis

A popcorn wagon serves between 100 and 150 customers per day over the weekend at a festival. The average amount spent per customer is 5. Variable costs are estimated at 38% of revenue, while fixed costs amount to 380 for the weekend, including labour cost.
- ❐ The revenue figure is calculated by multiplying the average spending power by the number of customers.
- ❐ The variable costs are calculated by finding 38% of the revenue figure.
- ❐ The fixed costs of 380 remain constant.

Number of customers	Total revenue	Variable costs	Fixed costs	Total costs	Net profit (+)	Net Loss(-)
100	500	190	380	570		70
115	575	218.50	380	598.50		5.50
130	650	247	380	627	23	
140	700	266	380	646	54	
150	750	285	380	665	85	

electric shock from unprotected cables and the resulting lawsuits; viability of the event; safety and health.

Financial risks include insufficient sponsorship to sustain a bid; insufficient funding to construct the needed infrastructure and facilities; inaccurate capital and operating cost estimates; inaccurate estimating of possible revenue flows; lack of public money needed to make good shortfalls in private-sector revenue generation; and thorough underestimating. Financial planning and budgetary controls are crucial to all business ventures. The event industry has many non-profit-making or voluntary associations that aim to hold an event in order to break even. Should profit be generated, this is often passed on to charities. There is a growing trend towards private-sector investment in events with profit being a driving force. This is due to the fact that government departments are reducing monetary involvement in events throughout the world. Accordingly, the risk of financial loss is one which needs to be constantly in the mind of event owners, organisers and managers.

There is a need for professionalism in the events industry and the following principles should be adhered to:

- ❐ *Events are businesses and should be managed as such;*
- ❐ *Event organizations should aim to make a profit (i.e. surplus revenue) to ensure financial self sufficiency; without a surplus there will be no reserve fund and little possibility of capital investment for expansion; and*
- ❐ *Events must establish a comprehensive financial planning and control system, including full cost revenue management, budgeting and standardized accounting and reporting (Getz, 1997: 230).*

By adopting the above principles, all event organisations should be able to continually review their position in relation to net worth, solvency and the return on investment (ROI) of each event.

Financial risk management should involve the introduction of strict control policies and procedures on the following matters:

- ❐ Cash management and receipting;
- ❐ Signing authorities for bank accounts;
- ❐ Authorisation for drawing of stock and equipment;
- ❐ Expense perks, complimentary tickets and credit facility policies;
- ❐ Ticket numbering and security;
- ❐ Charitable donations and associated receipting; and
- ❐ Written contracts to be financially and legally sound.

9.12 Summary

It is essential that events managers, at all levels, understand the financial aspects of the events business. Such managers would have a better chance of succeeding in their events business venture than those managers who have no financial knowledge. This financial knowledge embraces budget preparation, producing accounting records, analysing financial reports, implementing cost control measures, dealing with finance houses or banks, and limiting tax liabilities (Hansen, 1995).

Questions for research

1 What is the relationship between an income statement and a balance sheet?
2 Why are cash flow and profit not equal?
3 What determines an event or event enterprise's profitability?
4 Distinguish between owner's equity capital and debt capital.
5 What is the importance of budgeting?
6 Explain why the flow of incoming and outgoing cash needs to be monitored.
7 Why must revenue be maximised and costs minimised?

Recommended websites

Browse the following internet sites for interesting and informative information:

Blackbaud – Financial management: http://www.blackbaud.com/solutions/acctg.asp
EventManagerBlog: http://www.eventmanagerblog.com/category/budget
Festivals and events toolkit – planning your finances: http://www.tourismnortheast.co.uk/pages/home
Fundamentals of cost accounting: http://www.moneyinstructor.com/art/costaccount.asp
MeetingMetrics – ROI: http://meetingmetrics.com/research_papers/White_Papers.htm
Return on investment (ROI): http://www.juliasilvers.com/embok/ROI.htm
Web-based software suite that helps increase and accelerate event sales: http://www.a2zshow.com/

Suggested reading

Getz, D. 1997. *Event Management and Event Tourism*. New York: Cognizant Communication Corporation.

Mathews, D. 2008. *Special Event Production. The Process*. UK: Butterworth-Heinemann.

PART III
Events and design

Photo: Dimitri Tassiopoulos

Photo: World Travel Market

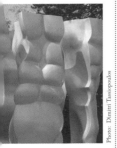

Photo: Dimitri Tassiopoulos

Photo: Dimitri Tassiopoulos

Photo: Dimitri Tassiopoulos

10 Design management of events

Graham Berridge

Abstract

Design plays an integral part in all planned event experiences. It ranges from initial concept and pitch through to programme and content design and onto theatrical and staging design. All elements within an event are infused or enhanced by design to create memorable event experiences. This chapter looks at what design is, the different stages of design input required for different event types and the creation of event experiences.

Chapter objectives

After you have read this chapter you should be able to:
- ❏ define and explain design;
- ❏ understand the nature, processes and activities involved in event design and creativity;
- ❏ familiarise yourself with the creative process for event design;
- ❏ see how design fits into the events framework;
- ❏ understand the planned event experience;
- ❏ understand the relationship between design and the event experience; and
- ❏ appreciate the value of experiential foresight

10.1 Understanding and defining design

Design is one of the key knowledge domains of events management and it is the key area that enables one event experience to be different from another. The design domain consists of seven specific classes where design is said to typically occur in an event. These classes are as follows:

- ❏ *Catering design.* Food and beverages are nearly always present at events, and the production and service of food allows for creativity. Examples where design can be a prominent feature include food stations, edible centrepieces, menus, dessert shapes, drink mixes.
- ❏ *Content design.* Creativity can challenge preconceptions. Designing an event with content that differs from the norm can be risky but also gives the opportunity for surprise. A wedding, for example, can include the bride and groom's preferences on format and structure, and include special content such as poetry, musical performance and ceremony.
- ❏ *Entertainment design.* This can be formal or informal, and can be linked to 'surprise guests'. Such things as look-alikes have become popular as have roving street entertainers or magicians. Reference to popular culture and television shows appeals to many

people as does the inclusion of musical acts, comedians or extravagant shows.

- ❏ *Environment design.* A key element in the creation of experiences, designed environments can surprise or reassure a guest or audience. Environment design is the purposeful use of a specific space that enables the event experience to take place.
- ❏ *Production design.* This is an area where the event borrows from theatre and performance, where design produces spectacle and show, for example the production of multiple settings within an event environment, or a stage design such as the U2 heart-shaped stage used during their half-time performance at the US Super Bowl. One international conference presenter used to insist on using two separately managed screens.
- ❏ *Programme design.* Events often have an order of occurrences or a format. This is sometimes based on written rules or guidelines, at other times on past references that have now become a standard format. For example, many academic conferences do not have designed interactions beyond food and wine gatherings. Inserting something like a speed dating research session into the programme creates a new experience.

- **Theme design.** This is where a visual spectacle is created by symbols and artefacts that imaginatively reinforce a special theme. Themes themselves can be inspirational, and opportunities arise to be creative both in reference to a theme and to its interpretation. A venue and its service staff would be decorated to reflect a main theme such as *Cabaret, Star Wars, Art Deco, Casino Night*, and so on.

Events cannot exist in and of themselves; simply put they have to be designed and created, whether it be for education, escapism, absorption, aesthetic appeal, an exhibition, a conference, for entertainment, a meeting, a sporting event, etc. Events management is the business of designing planned occasions, and such planning is done purposefully with the intention of meeting and creating event experiences for a variety of stakeholders.

Designing special events requires creativity so that those attending them feel they have experienced a special moment. Design is mostly seen, therefore, as a skilled action or an act of creativity that gives something a visual identity or recognition: 'event design is the creation, conceptual development and design of an event to maximise the positive and meaningful impact for the event's audience and/or participants' (Brown, 2005).

What most sources on the study of events agree on is that designing an event requires a conceptualisation of an idea. This can then be linked throughout the event by a specific theme, such as a casino night, and then the event space itself requires decoration, the craft of producing the idea physically, to give a tangible existence to the design and concept ideas. As Monroe (2006:4) explains, 'event design is the conception of a structure for an event, the

Case study 10.1 Production design: Hugo Boss fashion show, Berlin

The client, Hugo Boss, asked for an 'outstanding and surprising show' to be produced by agency *villa eugenie*. Situated on the 'Buhne' of the German Opera House, 1 000 people were treated to a show that combined fashion and opera. The entrance to the event held a surprise in itself as guests were ushered in through the back door and not the main foyer entrance. This was further enhanced by the seating arrangement which rather than use the house seating was in fact set out on the empty opera stage facing the invisible audience. The producers also chose to twist tradition in other ways by separating the audience from the performance space with a black velour curtain and omitting any sign of a catwalk. Instead there was just a glistening black floor. In an effort to create the tension, suspense and drama associated with opera, the fashion show was split into several acts. With scenery changes between each act, guests were plunged into darkness at each set changeover before the next group of models emerged.

Structures were used to infuse each act with a special element. Act 1 started with a lowering of a 14m-high steel staircase for the models to enter the stage, while Act 2 saw an 82m glistening white walkway emerge that then folded into nine tiers to create a suspended catwalk operated by hydraulic lifts for perfect timing and safety. The finale, Act 3, featured 25 000 gem-like components reflecting a dazzling light that created a tunnel for models to walk through. The aim was to produce a show that was 'illusion', creating surprise, appearance and disappearance.

Source: Happening Design for Events, Birkhauser

expression of that concept verbally and visually, and, finally, the execution of the concept'. He concludes that events that combine design and decoration successfully produce synergy and result in a practical, successful event.

A person can be designing something – say a ticket entry system to an event – but, they may not necessarily be creative about it. However, for most people in events management, designing an event, especially one for entertainment or celebration, results in acts of creativity. This is because

design is viewed as a skilled, creative endeavour that produces some element of artistic interpretation for anything from clothes to cars. Understanding and interpreting the meaning of design is, for most of us, not always the easiest of tasks since the difficulty lies in analysing or extracting meaning from the design. When we talk about design though we can usually describe something that has been designed and mostly we can refer to design as being creative (Berridge, 2007: 36).

Design can be associated with a host of different activities and different contexts, for example graphic design, software design, interior design, engineering design, industrial design (Bayley, 1985). Writing on the need for education on understanding design, Archer (1973) explains that design should be regarded as skill and knowledge that is concerned with a person's ability to create an environment that would meet certain spiritual and material needs. This suggests a link with the more commonly held understanding for design today that it is a purposeful activity that is intended, planned and conceived to meet a particular purpose or solve a particular problem (Markus, 2002). Berridge (2007), citing

research work undertaken at Princeton University, has suggested that the following list indicates the central and recurring explanations and activities for design:

- ❏ The act of working out the form of something;
- ❏ A plan – making or working out a plan for; devising;
- ❏ Designing something for a specific role or purpose or effect;
- ❏ An arrangement scheme;
- ❏ A blueprint – something intended as a guide for making something else;
- ❏ Creating the design for; creating or executing in an artistic or highly skilled manner;
- ❏ A decorative or artistic work;
- ❏ Making a design of; planning out in a systematic, often graphic form;
- ❏ A purpose – an anticipated outcome that is intended or that guides your planned actions;
- ❏ Answering immediate needs;
- ❏ Creating designs;
- ❏ Conceiving or fashioning in the mind; inventing; and
- ❏ A preliminary sketch indicating the plan for something.

Therefore, what now becomes apparent is that the activity of design embraces actions that are purposeful, systematic and creative. By being purposeful, design is providing for both functional and aesthetic needs; by being systematic it is analysing problems and finding usable solutions to them; by being creative it is using expertise to give visual form to those ideas and solutions. So when a client expresses a desire to have an event that is 'fantastic, enchanting and memorable', the event management team will start to put together one or more conceptual ideas that they hope will meet the client's expectations.

Case study 10.2 Event ConneQion Expo 2008, Brisbane Convention and Exhibition Centre (BCEC)

BCEC basic facts:
- ❐ The Great Hall has a plenary capacity of 3 958 persons;
- ❐ There are four exhibition halls with a combined space of 20 000 m² ; and
- ❐ It has 24 multifunction rooms.

There is some irony in this case study since it involves an event developed as a showcase for industry practitioners. Pre-event promotional literature read as follows:

When you come to the 2008 show, there will be no doubt about what's hot in the event and incentives industry this year! So, whether you are a professional event planner or are responsible for just one major show a year, Event ConneQion will provide you with– creative concepts – inspired solutions – ingenious idea.

As a research exercise, 65 students were asked to visit the event and make observations and comments on the design. A summary of their views reads as follows:

The expo was sited in one of the four main halls. Unfortunately little or no design concepts had been applied or utilised in the entrance, reception or exhibition areas. While it was functional it was not especially captivating for a guest. In fact it was truly uninspiring and boring. Inside the hall the layout of the exhibition space seemed to have been given little thought other than a basic grid approach to stalls and stands. While individual exhibitors demonstrated some creativity with their own display areas, the overall concept of the event was very flat and uninspiring. There were not enough exhibitors to fill the hall floor space, and as a result a lot of empty space was evident. No attempt had been made to reduce the space down to fit the exhibitors and so in turn create a more vibrant setting. So the emptiness detracted from any sense of ambience or community as it was easy for the visitor to meander aimlessly. Minimal attempts had been made to theme the exhibitors and create hubs of similar interest or expertise. Some effort had been made to create a performance space and this did act as a central point at times, but it was sectioned off from other areas by a few basic service features. No sense of expectation or 'happening' was created around the space and most visitors largely wandered past it without interest.

Conclusion
This approach to exhibiting is, sadly, not uncommon, where space is simply sold and little or no design is applied to the environment itself. Hence many such events are lifeless, listing along hour by hour with visitors trudging around hoping for some inspiration rather than having it created and presented to them.

10.2 Reflecting on design's role in event management

Based on the understanding of design put forward above, it can now be seen that when discussing events, design should be regarded as a fundamental part of the process since the very nature and practice of event management is 'purposeful, systematic and creative'. For design to work effectively in an event, it should follow some basic guidelines. There are now several excellent sources on various aspects of the event design process that identify the principles and elements of design, and the resources and creative ideas that can be used to create events (Goldblatt, 2008;

Malouf, 1999; Monroe, 2006; Matthews, 2007). In general these principles can be characterised as follows:

❐ That design should have a focus;
❐ That design must consider the use of space; and
❐ That design must consider and reflect the flow of movement (Monroe, 2006).

With these principles in place, Berridge (2007) suggests that the aesthetics of design advocated by Malouf, Monroe and Matthews can then be further addressed and that consideration should then be given to technical awareness and application and, importantly, the tangible expression of ideas that gives rise to the event experience.

Therefore the elements of design should include the following:

❐ **Space** – three-dimensional space and how to fill and use it so that décor fits in with it;
❐ **Colour** – often provides meaning since

it affects us psychologically, and choice of colour combinations is important;
❐ **Line** – often used to reinforce a message or draw attention to some point of a setting, or to use objects to separate one area from another;
❐ **Composition** – the placement and arrangement of artefacts (décor) that tend to give a view of the whole concept;
❐ **Form** – the shape (e.g. curved, square) of decorative props and objects that show the importance of the design and theme;
❐ **Texture** – the feel of materials used in the décor: lush or basic furnishings designed to evoke feelings or moods;
❐ **Pattern** – using triangular, oval, circular, rectangular and diagonal patterns with the event space to create settings;
❐ **Scale** – size and shape: the proportion of a prop, usually related to a dominant theme or sub-theme within the event;

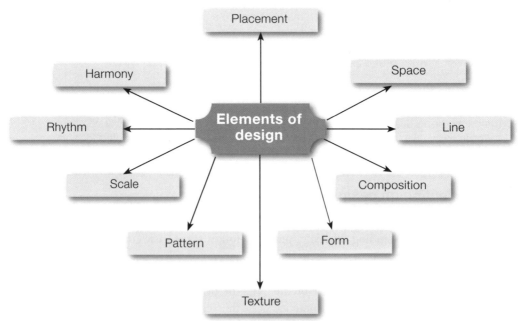

Figure 10.1 Design elements

- ☐ **Rhythm** – movement of words or music, or arrangements such as flowers to create a rhythmic impact gradually or suddenly;
- ☐ **Harmony** – creating unity within a setting, reinforcing the message or the ambience; and
- ☐ **Placement** – décor in the right place and context, as a focal point or as a subtle message.

Using such approaches will give the basis of a blueprint for designing and creating event environments. In fact it has been suggested that the very basis of events management itself is, simply, the 'design management' of an event and that to ignore or marginalise design is to neglect the very heart and soul of an event (Brown, 2005). In this view, design should then be considered as a critical tool for events management as it relates directly to developing the event concept and the event experience. Furthermore it enables the event manager to envision and implement the event. Event managers should therefore see themselves as not simply logistical and organisational problem solvers but as 'experiential engineers' who are able to piece together the overall picture of the event. Remember event environments are produced on the basis that the majority of those attending will receive a fulfilling experience, no matter what type of event it is or what purpose it serves, therefore event managers should regard themselves as 'packaging and managing an experience' from start to finish and imagine all aspects and details of that experience (Silvers, 2004).

An important part of many events is guest interactions, and these need to be carefully designed and not just left to chance. Interactions can be designed to introduce people to one another, to engage with a product or service, to sample a food or beverages, to participate in an activity, or to contribute in some way or other to the experience. Interaction can also be used to 'animate' an event in order to help create an atmosphere or ambience. In such cases 'plants' within the environment, such as look-alikes of celebrities, are designed to encourage communication between and with guests. Such design interventions help ensure an event works effectively. Equally, some of the rituals and symbolic features associated with an event (a winner's podium, for example) should be part of an integrated designed experience. These aspects are created in just the same way as the more observable and recognised features of an event such as the thematic framework, the props and décor, the lighting, the food design or the flower arrangements. What is also apparent is that the level of design input varies enormously from event to event, and that variation is a by-product of the event type and concept. Consequently, events that have a more celebratory or entertainment remit tend to be the ones that attract the most attention and where the 'design' element is more visibly seen as the added ingredient that takes the event onto another dimension and gives it that something special. Here design is apparent in the themed elements and message of the event, and is inextricably linked with, for example, audiovisual production, entertainment and music (Sonder, 2004).

To summarise, (Goldblatt, 2004) stresses the importance of design in events by advocating a design blueprint as one of the keys for success and stresses at the outset the importance of creating the environment.

When creating the environment the special events professional must again return to the basic needs of the guests.

The final design must satisfy these needs to become successful. Lighting, space, movement, décor, acoustics and even the seemingly mundane concerns such as rest rooms all affect the comfort of the guest and so play vital roles on creating a successful environment

Goldblatt (2004:5)

10.3 Design and pitching for the event

Event bidding is dealt with in chapter 5, but it is important to note that many event contracts are won by the company pitching directly to the client. Pitching is a presentation whereby the concept and ideas for the event are mapped out for the client. At this stage the pitching company needs to verbally and visually convey the experience they intend to create. Hence strong design ideas, visual themes, clear messages and mock-ups of the environment and some of the features to be incorporated may all be required to convince the client that the concept will be a good one. Many events management companies use design software to produce a computerised image of how they see the event. In addition, storyboards might be used to show different components within the event, such as stage settings or food-service areas. As well as these mock-ups, samples of colour swatches, say for service uniforms or for table decoration, may be required. Images of food design, light design and backdrops could also be shown. While clients clearly want to hear what the company has to say, they also want to see how the company visualises the event, and here design ideas have to come across in a strong, clear manner. For events with a strong promotional message, the client will want to see how the event will express

the experience associated with the product or service. For entertainment the theme associated with the event will need to be carefully researched to ensure that the right images, symbols and artefacts are portrayed so that the client is left with a clear impression of what will happen on the night.

10.4 Creativity and event planning and production

Creativity is the one thing that really can make an event stand out from others of a similar kind.

But what is creativity? In the previous sections, discussion of design has taken place, but the process of creativity also requires some attention. Matthews (2007) suggests that there are key attributes to being creative, namely intelligence and personality. The former is now less pre-occupied with IQ than with the influence of parents and the belief that intelligence manifests itself in many ways – in other words not just through academic tests. Personality is regarded as dispositional where people have a behavioural and cognitive flexibility that helps in risk taking. These are in turn affected by lifespan development and the different influences we encounter as we go through our personal life cycle and the social environment we operate in. Matthews concludes that the more exposure someone has to creative concepts in a socially relaxed environment, the better chance they will have of coming up with creative thoughts.

Welded to this are the cognitive process and the act of knowing, perceiving and conceiving (Matthews, 2007). Factors that now influence creativity are based around perception and how individuals respond to problems. The precepts used help

Table 10.1 External environment

Quantity equals quality	Think, repeat, think again, and consider the widest range of possibilities, not just the first thing that comes to mind
Suspend judgement	We've always done it this way! Creativity is about new ideas, so judgement on an idea is a creative killer. Allow ideas to flourish and see where they lead to
Relax and have fun	Stream of consciousness while doing other things, e.g. riding a bike, swimming, listening to music. Ideas can pop into the mind at any time. Think about recording them on a cellphone or in a notebook for later use
Continue to learn	Stay in tune with new developments, and exposure to new concepts; keep a note of initiatives and ideas elsewhere that may influence in the future. Some creative people keep records of things they encounter
Practice	Like a musician, learn to be creative, maintain ideas for all things and always consider how they can be changed

Source: Matthews (2007)

make sense of things acting as a constant reference for them, but they can alter and change as new information is acquired. In a wide-ranging chapter on creative thought, Matthews considers the different ways of seeing things as providing crucial armoury for its emergence. He reflects on the way people organise any stimulus, how they view familiar sites in a constant frame, the level of depth perception they have and the awareness of motion in relation to objects. Underpinning such responses is the experience and context that the recipient has been exposed to. As a logical stage in this creative awareness, the external environment can play a major part in shaping creativity. Table 10.1 draws attention to Matthews' (2007) key points to consider when creating an environment.

A way to start thinking about design and creativity is to take an event right back to the very basics and ignore all previous iterations of it. So, thinking of an event as starting out with four bare walls or a blank canvas encourages scope for creativity since it is not anchored by what went on in the past. This is especially helpful if the event is outdoors but it applies equally to large multipurpose venues where there is a need to create an environment. In stark contrast are the historical or unique venues that are uniquely different due to their architecture and interior design, in which case the question is whether to use or complement the interior or to mask it from view. From this starting point it is possible to begin to envisage how this 'empty space' will be filled and with what. What types of decisions have to be made in order to create an event? What are the actions that need to be undertaken in order to fill the space or transform the bare walls into the created event experience?

A number of design or creative actions have been identified that establish a blueprint of the sorts of things to be done to produce an event. Not all of them occur equally at every event, and so their application is dependent upon the type of event to take place. A common way of thinking about an event at this stage is to develop the event concept or to conceptualise what the event will be for and about, and begin to develop a blueprint (Goldblatt, 2008). The factors that need to be addressed include the range of elements that need to be considered when an event concept is first being developed. This should begin with the purpose of the event, and move on to the event theme, the venue, the needs of the audience, the available resources to make it happen, the timing of the event, and the skills of the team (Van der Wagen & Carlos, 2005). Using design ideas and practices will then enable each of these aspects of the event to be fully developed. Once this has been established and agreed, it needs translating into physical reality. So it is appropriate to begin to think about the physical elements needed to fulfil the concept. A popular approach to achieving this successfully is to give the event a 'theme' where design of the environment revolves around a common thread. The theme then requires a series of decorative elements to characterise the message (Monroe, 2006) and with that, a series of props and artefacts that embody and reinforce it (Malouf, 1999). These can be extravagant and sensational, using the aforementioned design tools to piece together the whole ensemble. This, in turn, should help to begin to create an appropriate ambience that reflects the theme (Shone & Parry, 2004) and this might mean consideration of the entertainment experience to be provided for the guest (Silvers, 2004). Ultimately, the whole package needs to be produced and staged (Matthews, 2007).

Within the above considerations, design is regarded as an implicit aspect of the event planning since it enables the event manager to understand and envisage the characteristics of things like ambience, service and personal interactions. By designing these features carefully, the right environment for the specific event can be produced. An 'event with the right ambience can be a huge success. An event with the wrong ambience can be a huge failure' (Shone & Parry, 2004: 15). The question of how the right ambience is designed and created may not seem so straightforward to answer, but there are signposts that can be used in order to understand and design ambience. The practicalities of creating ambient settings is discussed by authors such as Sonder (2004), Monroe (2006) and Matthews (2007b), all of whom offer design specific approaches or, as in the case of Silvers (2004), place it as the central core of event management practice.

As all planned events run to some kind of programme, ensuring that the programming also fits into the environment can be the key to an event having a successful outcome. This can be seen in the way sports podium presentations are designed, combining the different elements of the event to ensure a successful finale. In most cases there is a programme that enables the event to follow a specific path, and this programme directs various stakeholders at the event towards a culmination moment where the winner's presentation is made. Spectators, media, participants, organisers, team personnel, etc. are purposefully moved into position. The Tour de France is a good example of this where the podium is visually designed to reflect the iconic yellow jersey of the race leader and some of the key sponsors (Credit Lyonnais, Michelin). The ambience of celebration and euphoria on success is created as a direct result of the path the event programme takes to get to this point, and where the event focus moves from the uncertain outcome of the competition to

Case study 10.3 Red Nose Day, charitable fundraising event, UK

Event: A charity event for a major UK supermarket's suppliers. This case uses a heritage building as a venue; however, design ideas within it are applicable internationally

This event had a two-fold aim – to raise money for a charity (Red Nose) and to provide an entertaining evening for the guests. There were 300 guests invited from the different regions throughout the UK. The event company managing the event made a bold and creative decision to use a National Trust property that had not previously held large-scale entertainment events. As a heritage-listed property this created some restrictions on the use of the main building, so this required some creativity to ensure the event design worked effectively. However, the venue had lavish gardens and so rather than base everything indoors the event team decided to use the main building as a 'stage and backdrop' and created the main event environment within the landscaped grounds

Originally the concept had been to create a Moulin Rouge spectacle as an obvious reference to the Red Nose charity. However, once it became known that the venue had some links to Queen Elizabeth 1, they decided to develop their design concept around the work of William Shakespeare. Drawing on references to the works and writing of Shakespeare, the team was able to pool together a wide array of performers and actors to augment the entertainment. On entrance to the main gate, guests were escorted by carriage around the side of the main building and into a huge marquee situated behind it. Inside the marquee various characters from the plays of Shakespeare served drinks and, later, food. Throughout the grounds and in the marquee, lighting was provided by flames set on 2m-high columns and as the event started in twilight the impact of the flames increased as darkness descended. The marquee had a stage in the centre of it, an interpretation of the famous Globe Theatre where Shakespeare's work was originally performed and where it is recreated today since the theatre's lavish period refurbishment. At various junctures in the evening, actors would perform selected extracts from different plays. Decoration inside was period furniture and props. Interactive elements were created by having several characters from the plays appear as guests at the event. For example the character of Puck was to be found roaming a part of the grounds where drinks where served, while a moody and slightly mad Macbeth could be seen wandering around the ground muttering and mumbling to imaginary foes.

A series of images were projected against the side of the building and facing the marquee was another stage-like setting, set about 3m off the ground. As the evening wore on, Queen Elizabeth 1, plus aides, made an appearance and mingled with guests, passing comment on their attire and preparing them for a charity auction. At 10pm a band of trumpeters appeared, unannounced, and this was the signal for the fake Queen to climb the stairs to the stage and announce, in imperious fashion, the start of the charity auction. Then, at her side appeared Shakespeare who acted as auctioneer, and a 'prosecutor' who looked not dissimilar to a hangman. His job was to liaise with the Queen and identify people who were not bidding and contributing to charity. The Queen would occasionally stop the auction and make a comment or two at specific members of the audience, threatening them with 'consequences' if they did not submit a bid.

the plaudits for the winner. The podium is designed to engender celebratory ambience by its location at the finish, its visual characteristics and its physical size and shape that allows all spectators to gaze upon it and share in the winner's joy. Such an outcome does not happen by chance – it is designed and planned purposefully and it gives closure to the event. The alternative is to allow the end of the event to stumble to a vague conclusion when the winner crosses the line, and simply hand them a trophy/cheque while they are changing or when they go back to their hotel. It is this act of designing and creating the environment that is the central point that makes events so different from other activities, and is a central component of any attempt to understand them.

Therefore the decisions that are made about how to fill an event space and how to create an active space for guests, attendees or participants are crucial in determining how the event environment will appear and how the event experience itself will occur. This suggests an emphasis is mostly placed on event guests as the recipients of the active event rather than on those who are contributing to its delivery or administering it. Creating this environment requires an awareness of guest requirements and therefore events managers have to consider mind mapping, flow, tempo and even psychographics in order to perceive what those requirements might be (Goldblatt, 2008). Some of the considerations that design and creativity might address in pursuit of this include the following:

- **Soundscaping.** This is the use and distribution of sound at an event. Sound can be central to the event (speech or music) but it can also affect ambience by creating suspense, attention, excitement or even distraction.

- **Visual cues.** These are references to a theme or other identifying element in an event. For example, a themed event would use specific artefacts and imagery to create a visual spectacle. An *Alice in Wonderland* theme would perhaps have waiters dressed as large playing cards, or staff dressed like the Mad Hatter serving drinks, and it might have fake-looking glasses as display items.
- **Smell.** This refers to the olfactory sensations that can enhance an experience.
- **Taste.** This may take the form of a creative blend of food or drink that surprises, e.g. lavender wine and ice cream.
- **Blending.** This is the combination of different elements that make up a whole event – mostly they complement each other to create a theme.
- **Amenities.** The experience should be re-affirmed in all areas, such as the toilets.
- **Reception areas.** The first impression is important, and greetings for guests can be a moment to set the standard for the remainder of the event.
- **Function areas.** These can include rest areas, games areas or hospitality areas designed to be 'functional' or have a twist to them.
- **Innovative sites.** This can be venue based or be a special section with an overall site.
- **Edible displays.** This is where culinary skills come to the fore, and flower arrangements, table centrepieces and even napkins or invitations can be made from edible ingredients that allow guests to consume the display.
- **Decoration.** This refers to the use of props, backdrops, colours, materials to create overall settings.
- **Interactive décor.** This can be clever and

Case study 10.4 BlackOut Dining Experience, UK

This case study draws on an example from a UK events and catering company but is applicable to international audiences.

In this case the event client was looking for a totally different dining experience and gave carte blanche to the company to be as creative as possible. Taking up the challenge, the company decided to go with a concept based on a single unifying idea and came up with a theme based on the colour black. They had considered some of the more obvious themes of dining such as a specific food type and décor (Indian) or using popular culture references (the film Casablanca) but felt they really needed to give the event a unique 'edge'.

In order to create the required impact meant the total dining experience had to embrace the colour black in the food and beverages, utensils and drinking vessels, décor and props, and clothing for staff. Everything as much as was practicably and safely possible had to be in black. The only exception to the black theme was the need to have some lighting as a blacked-out room would be unusable. So LED lighting in purple, deep green and deep blue was used to create mood, layout and lines for movement. While crockery, napkins, utensils and glasses could be easily made, food was a more problematic issue. Creating a balanced menu seemed a problem simply because so very few foods are black in colour or appearance. However, research produced a range of international foods that could be made in black using either food colourants or black/dark ingredients such as chocolate, squid ink, soy or blackseed. Food that could be made black included spaghetti, pizza along with interesting variants such as chocolate ravioli, chocolate-hazelnut spread, tortillas and caviar rolls. Black pudding also made an appearance, as did Schwarzbrot bread. Drink was a slightly easier option to offer in the shape of tea and coffee but also included Guinness, black root beer and Coca-Cola, which provided the perfect mixer for clear spirits. Staff wore black trousers, long-sleeved black T-shirts, black socks and shoes and, as an added touch, black gloves.

witty, designed to be non-static and so perhaps surprise guests.

❑ *Parades and float design.* These are usually for outdoor events but some larger exhibitions allow for creative approaches. A typical example would be the Tour de France sponsors' procession that precedes the race.

❑ *Theme.* This is a unifying concept, perhaps drawn from history or some recognisable aspect of culture such as cabaret.

❑ *Environmental sensitivity.* A hugely prescient element is to avoid the waste associated with many events. A simple example is to use re-usable materials where possible (such as water jugs and glasses) rather than disposable plastic articles.

❑ *Timeline.* This refers to a running order for activities to occur, often to build suspense at an event or to lead to an unveiling of something.

❑ *Security.* It is preferable to adopt a discreet almost invisible security policy rather than one that is highly visible.

Several design and creative solutions are linked to food and beverage operations, a feature of the vast majority of events and in many cases the main attraction for guests. Food and beverages can be highly visible (e.g. a chocolate fountain) and can clearly create an aroma and obviously produce a sense of taste when consumed. They can be used to provide decoration in the form of props and can be a centrepiece of a display, edible or not. Culinary arts skills are always in demand as clients and guests seek new and interesting ways of being wined and dined. It is not so long ago that the presence of a Smoothie bar at an indoor event was something of a novelty and there is a cyclical factor that sees the use of cocktail bars go in and out of fashion. Themed banquets offer a real sense of identity to events and invariably borrow ideas from restaurants and bars. Replacing standard Western chairs and tables with half-height tables and assorted cushions enables Asian cuisine to be offered in a much more relaxed and informal way. Indeed, in taking up this theme some UK entrepreneurs have begun to deconstruct the traditional curry and replace ingredients.

10.5 Designing communication

A part of any event is the ability to communicate to the guest or audience beforehand through a marketing communication strategy. Event marketing relies heavily on communication by trying to establish shared meanings with the event's target stakeholders (Masterman & Wood, 2006). Designing the message to be conveyed is crucial at this stage as it is the key representation of how the event will appear. This pre-experience phase is about communicating the prospect of the event to an external audience and enticing them to the event with the promise of something special. To a large extent it is about creating the anticipation and a sense of excitement, therefore the theme and 'look' associated with the impending event will act as a powerful attraction. Strategically designed communication will convey this to a likely audience and instil in them an inner need to want to attend.

10.6 Understanding the planned-event experience

Planned-event experiences are then what events management is all about. People attend or participate in an event often seeking something specific from the experience and this is, initially, based on what pre-event communication they have had. They might be looking for something extraordinary, unique or special, or they might be seeking something educational or transformational. The idea that they are looking for an 'experience', though, is central to their decision to attend, and that applies not only to public, private and business events but equally to conferences, festivals and fundraising events. Therefore, argues Getz (2008), experiences and the meanings attached to them should be identified as the core phenomena of events and consequently 'if we cannot clearly articulate what the events experience is, then how it can be planned or designed? If we do not understand what it means to people, then how can it be important?' (Getz, 2008: 170). Getz is arguing that if event practitioners do not themselves understand the significance and importance of experiences then their capability in creating the right ones for guests has to be questioned.

This idea that we are seeking experiences has become prominent in the last 20 years largely because the corporate sector has adopted the concept of experience as a tool to make their businesses more competitive. In marketing, the old 4Ps have been replaced by a more psychographic approach to the consumer with 'experiential marketing' taking over and the emergence of more complex approaches to marketing (Schmitt, 1999; Shukla & Nuntsu, 2005). In explaining what an experience is, Schmitt indicates that they are private events, the result of stimulation prompting a response, and they affect the entire living being. Furthermore, they are a result of direct observation or participation in events, and are not self-generated but induced. He argues that there are five types of customer experience that form an experiential marketing framework, namely sense, feel, think, act and relate. Experience providers then tap into these via 'implementation components' including spatial environments, communications and people.

Adopting a similar view but with a different approach, O'Sullivan and Spangler (1999) suggest that experiences are infused with special or novel qualities, that they are enhanced via personal and individual care, and that ultimately they are made by providers (or event managers) who are looking to immerse people in the experience that has been created. For them, experiences involve participation and involvement; a state of being physically, mentally, socially, spiritually or emotionally involved; a change in knowledge, skill, memory or emotion; a conscious perception of having intentionally encountered, gone to or lived through an activity or event; and an effort that addresses a psychological or inner need. They promote the idea that for something to be called an experience it must consist of the following five components or parameters of experience (O'Sullivan & Spangler, 1999: 23)

1 The stages of the experience – events or feelings that occur prior, during and after the experience;
2 The actual experience – factors or variables within the experience that influence participation and shape outcomes;
3 The needs being addressed through the experience – the inner or psychic needs that give rise to the need or desire to participate in an experience;
4 The role of the participant and other people involved in the experience – the impact that the personal qualities, behaviour and expectations of both the participant and other people involved within the experience play in the overall outcome;
5 The role and relationship with the provider of the experience – the ability and willingness of the provider to customise, control and coordinate aspects of the experience.

A further approach to planning and understanding experiences is the notion of the 'experience realm' (Pine & Gilmore, 1999) which suggests that experiences are either passively or actively consumed and consequently offer a level of immersion or absorption. Within these dimensions an individual will more than likely seek and receive an experience realm that is then either educational, escapist, aesthetic or entertaining. It is possible that all four dimensions and realms can be designed within a single experience; however, such events are infrequent and highly complex. Thus it is argued that 'staging experience is not about entertaining customers; it's about engaging them. An experience may engage guests on any number of dimensions' (Pine & Gilmore, 1999: 30). By utilising the framework of the experience realm, events can be subsequently designed to purposefully engage guests in the dimensions appropriate for the event. This enables the event manager to develop a rationale for designing certain event elements. For different events, each of the 'realms' or 'parameters' will have a different emphasis placed upon them, dictated by the event concept. So where the event is more participatory than active, the focus for designing the experience will be stronger in that aspect, and the event manager will need to address how and in what way that should occur.

10.7 Further tools for experience design

Designing event environments to engage guests in an experience requires foresight as to what type of experience is required and how it can be created. Designing and creating environments is a predictive skill based on the concept of the event. By anticipating the experience, design is able to predict the future (Morello, 2000). The previous section offered some suggestions about how an experience could be framed but perhaps more specific tools are needed. Failure to understand or appreciate these central concerns of experience will lead to a poorly designed event. Events thrive on promise since, unlike products or even services, guests cannot try them out before making a commitment to attend. The first and usually the only time an event is experienced is when it takes place. So the promise that the event will live up to its billing is paramount, and therefore what is called experience foresight is needed to ensure that the promise is kept. Designing experiences involves foresight and interpretation on the part of the designer to reflect the aims of the event and those of the client/organiser, and to try to ensure that guests interpret the experience as it was intended. There is no doubt it is a challenge to do this and design successful event experiences but equally there is no doubt that events management requires that deliberately designed experiences

are created. Events must be designed to provide meaningful experiences that people value from their engagement. There are 15 recurring types of experience valued mostly by participants and guest that have been identified (Diller et al., 2008). The list includes a sense of freedom and of wonder, a sense of validation, an understanding of enlightenment, a pleasurable feeling inspired by beauty and a sense of oneness and compatibility with everything around and associated with the event. Consideration of these value experiences and their relationship to a specific event can therefore give designers some basic and meaningful ideas to work with when they are creating the event.

Other existing tools for experience design have emerged out of the digital media field, and there are obvious synergies with models for understanding experiences. Berridge (2007), referring to the 'experience matrix' developed by Zoels and Gabrielli (2003), argues that adopting a clear human-based strategy for events management will enable event experiences to become ever more predictable. The experience matrix (see table 10.2) suggests therefore that foresight of experience can be also designed when consideration is given to the following human centric concerns:

Table 10.2 The experience matrix

1 Sensory
2 Tactile
3 Visual
4 Photographic
5 Auditory impact
6 Intellectual
7 Emotional
8 Functional
9 Informative
10 Cultural
11 Core

To further illustrate the application of this foresight of experience design, the following examples have been used in conjunction with some of the seven design classes, previously referred to in section 10.1, that make up the design domain. These examples show how some of ideas of experience design can be specifically applied in practice to event design:

❑ *Accomplishment through programme design.* Many events offer guests the opportunity to achieve goals and gain a sense of satisfaction, such as sports events where participants can try out a range of sports, conferences, network events, and outdoor adventure and challenge events. How do guests leave an event with this feeling? One way to create such an experience is to design a varied programme of achievement, perhaps based on levels of ability or age, as is often done for sports events. Academic conferences often include 'new blood' presentations or works-in-progress or poster displays. At one teaching conference, for example, there was a 30-minute speed dating research session designed to get colleagues to discuss one another's research aims and ambitions, and to develop collaborative work.

❑ *Community through catering design.* These are events that require a sense of connection with others such as those that are network, charity, educational or issues based. Creative network sessions need deliberate design interventions and interactions. If left to chance there is likelihood that a portion of the guests will feel excluded or disenfranchised. A network experience designed by one UK catering company was to serve food at four stations in a room where no single station had a complete menu, so guests had to visit another station. To add to the flow of movement and the connection with people, no tables and minimal rest zones were provided for guests to place their plates. The idea was to encourage assistance from other guests to find space or look after each other's food while someone else went for drinks, etc. This arrangement made it virtually impossible for individuals to acquire their food and drink without assistance.

❑ *Wonder through production design.* This refers to a feeling of being in the presence of great creation, more commonly referred to in events as the 'wow' factor. Many events are supposed to have this large element of surprise (Allen et al., 2005). Here again, this is not an easy element to quantify or describe. At many events and festivals, the right 'wow' can be the difference between success and failure. Traditional project management depends on the asset or deliverable being defined during the initiation phase. The surprise aspect of the event is often difficult, if not impossible, to describe. For some events, describing the 'wow' or surprise may lessen its value. It would be similar to describing the plot of a 'whodunit' mystery before reading the book. This means designing something that the guests can marvel at and look on, literally, in wonderment. Memorably, the opening to mega-events like the Olympics provides this. In Sydney 2000, Cathy Freeman, wearing a NASA all-in-one heat-protective suit stepped into a pedestal bowl high above the stadium seating to light the Olympic flame, seemingly setting herself alight as well. In 2008 in Beijing a performer appeared to be literally floating as he ran round the upper tier of the stadium to deliver the final phase of performance before the flame was lit. An international knitwear company once presented their catwalk show at the London Fashion Show by building an ice-rink on a large cylindrical pedestal at the end of the traditional catwalk and dropping ice-skaters onto it who then modelled their new clothing range.

❑ *Sensory, visual, cultural and auditory impact through content and entertainment design.* In the week prior to the start of the 2009 Tour de France, the German techno-pop band Kraftwerk performed a concert at an unusual venue, the velodrome in Manchester, England. The velodrome is the base for Great Britain's indoor cycling track team and was an interesting venue for the hypnotic and metronomic rhythms associated with the music and also with track cycling itself, which creates a low reverberation as the bikes go round the banked ends. A more than usually momentous event was enhanced by the appearance of a quartet of Team GB Olympic cyclists racing around the banked track in tandem with Kraftwerk's performance of its stellar composition, *Tour de France*.

10.8 Event meanings and memorable experiences

As has been explored, event design is concerned with creating experiences that, by and large, should be memorable. Inevitably this raises the question of whether or not that has been achieved and the process for evaluating that achievement. Events are given meaning by the experiences encountered at them and by the images associated with them.

Guest and participant experiences are a result of having emotionally encountered interactions at the event. Images, conveyed through the media or other communication platforms, act as a message to an external audience (non-attendees, business, tourists).

What the images say is dependent on the event, and its size and scope, but both the corporate sector and municipal authorities have found that hosting events with strong imagery presents an opportunity to develop a destination image and also to enhance the life cycle of a city. An example of how carefully designed event experiences can transform the image of not just a city but a nation was witnessed at the 2006 World Cup in Germany. In an attempt to create a festival-type environment for all nations competing and all the various nationalities visiting Germany, the government, football authorities and city councils created a series of festival environments in and around the venues and cities staging the tournament matches. Using nearby parks and open space, including town squares, Germany offered a celebratory environment to visitors in an effort to combat its perceived image among overseas tourists as a dull, uninspiring destination. Employing carefully designed uses of technology, space, culture and entertainment, a series of festival events was created to supplement the football matches in an attempt to create a celebratory environment to offset the often tense environment that surrounds international football and the teams' respective fans. Consequently there were far fewer incidents of hooliganism compared to past events, and further research by the German tourist agency revealed that the perception of Germany among tourists was far more positive than before the World Cup.

Case study 10.5 Designing experiences and animation

Resorts, museums, heritage sites, markets, stadia and shopping centres, for example, are all developing programmes of events. Attractions and facilities are increasingly realising the advantages of 'animation' – the process of programming interpretative features and/or events that may make a venue come alive with sensory stimulation and an appealing atmosphere (Getz, 1997). Animation describes a role played by people within a providing organisation that expands the range of provision. Animation is concerned with the experience of motion from a single purpose to a multifaceted one whereby guests and visitors are offered 'extra' activities or programmes. Rossman & Schlatter (2003) explain that in designing 'leisure services' the role of the animator can help extend visitors' experience dimensions. Typically, animators have become a feature of the hotel or tourist experience, providing additional guest experiences through a programme of activities and events. The aim of tourism animation is to satisfy the contemporary visitor's needs, desires and expectations considering active holidays. Nowadays, it has become a demand of the visitors that the holiday destination should offer extra advantages for the money they paid. Emphasis is placed on harnessing local creativity in developing new and engaging experiences for tourists which are characteristic of the destination in order to diversify the tourism product (Fernandes & Brysch, 2009).

Ski resort and travel operator engagements – generic

Ski holidays are a popular tourist activity where the supply of animation (or fun and entertainment) in the form of 'après-ski' activities is regarded as essential to the experience, and ski travellers are frequently exposed to boredom or unfulfilled promise by both resort and travel operator (Muller et al., 1997). Therefore two aspects to animation experiences emerge. On the one hand are the travel operators who have representatives in resorts dedicated to looking after clients who have booked their holiday with the operators. On the other hand are the resort representatives – people employed by the resort or region and who help provide services for all visitors to the resort.

Example A: Travel operator animation

A typical ski holiday package could be said to consist of two parts:

❐ Part 1 includes travel, accommodation, equipment hire, ski lift passes, ski tuition and the skiing itself;
❐ Part 2 includes food, beverages and entertainment – the so-called 'après-ski' experience.

Part 1 is largely functional and is seen as the core product of the holiday. Part 2 is a variable and is reliant on the ski experience becoming animated through a series of extended engagements. Such animated extras can include general après-ski activities that are non-specific to a resort, whilst others can be more specialised and based around specific resort characteristics. Travel representatives act as a fulcrum for the transmission and delivery of such opportunities which are exclusive to their clients. Such activities and events include:

❐ *Catering animation.* This refers to afternoon specials, often offered in hotels and larger chalets as a relaxational and social networking session after a day's ski. These invariably feature local pastries and desserts, plus drinks including locally mulled wine. Hotels and chalets also offer a 'themed evening meal' once a week – for example local or ethnic cuisine. Sometimes this is accompanied by music or similar entertainment.

- *Programme animation.* This is for skiers who wish to explore the parameters of their resort. Travel company mountain guides take clients to quieter or remote sections of the resort ski area, often introducing them to undiscovered routes and trails. In a similar vein, they also organise day trips to nearby resorts. For example, skiers at La Plagne, France, may visit nearby Courcheval or Tignes.
- *Entertainment animation.* This includes guided tours of local pubs, as well as evening games sessions such as outdoor/indoor curling, quiz nights and group night rides on snowmobiles. In family-based accommodation, activities for children are arranged almost daily and include things like pool or table tennis events (for adults as well).
- *Content animation.* Chalet groups or hotel client groups may be invited to take part in special ski events. A common offer here is a timed and filmed slalom run that is then screened back at the hotel in the evening.

Example B: Resort animation

This can be a feature of a 'lively' resort such as Verbier in Switzerland or Val d'Isère in France where the range and level of built amenities provide plentiful opportunity for extended attraction. Many ski resorts seek to expand the range of visitor services they now offer, and this is apparent in the style and type of recent new developments in the French resorts of Arc at 1950 and Flaine at Monsoleil, where premium-style accommodation has been built along with shops, fitness centres and other amenities to create a mini-resort village within a larger resort complex. These and similar resorts offer visitor engagements designed to enhance their image as winter ski towns. There is often a range of provisions available to all visitors to the resort, such as ice-rinks, outdoor pools and tubs, cinemas, leisure centres, bowling alleys, shopping malls, paragliding, ski bikes, snowmobiles and so on.

- *Programme and entertainment animation.* Ski resorts now offer a calendar of events and activities that all visitors can attend. Obvious celebration events based around public, local and national holidays abound, with many providing, for example, firework displays to celebrate New Year. Some resorts where the ski area is only accessible by gondola (Mayerhofen, Austria) provide special evening 'stargazing' for guests, as well as a catering element. In other resorts (Plagne Bellecote), the main retail area is lit in the evening and offers 'donut' sledge riding and ice-car rally racing. Furthermore, many resorts act as host to winter sports events such as winter car rally championships and international ski competitions. In the latest trend, winter music festivals are becoming popular attractions for visitors with the Snowbombing Festival in Mayrhofen, Austria, the market leader.
- *Content animation.* Resorts such as Davos (Switzerland) position themselves as world-class conference and events centres as well as ski resorts, and offer a glittering array of services to attract delegates. They also promote themselves to the corporate event market, offering bespoke ski services and events to companies. For example, Whistler, Canada, has hosted a medical conference during its ski season while others are happy to lay on competition events and team-building challenges for larger clients.
- *Themed animation.* It is obvious that snow-themed activities proliferate. Almost every resort includes at least one end-of-season snow festival when ski guides and instructors perform a series of shows and tricks, as well as racing and jumping competitions. These are very much appreciated by resort guests who turn out in numbers to watch a showpiece event that is a combination of skill and pantomime.

Frameworks that can be used to explore the meaning of designed experiences include research with participants recording their feelings and thoughts at a different moment throughout an event. Using ethnography enables an understanding of what is taking place by direct observation, and recording participant interactions with each other and with the event objects. Interpretation of these actions is made in order to understand them, and interviews are usually conducted with various stakeholders to see if the experiences match the interpretation. This, though, is not a quick method for extracting meaning and while valuable, it is often impractical. Latterly, some experiential event companies such as Jack Morton Worldwide have developed their own analytical tools to measure 'experience' at events. Naturally enough, these tools are not freely available but they have lead to much discussion about the nature of experiential events in the industry so that most 'industry' conferences in the past few years have included forums or panel debates on event experiences. As buzzwords go, in a developing industry, combining 'design and experience' is currently in favour and so it is paramount that events managers understand the relationship between the two and, importantly, how this translates into an actual event experience.

Questions for research

1 Using the seven categories of design discussed in 10.1, consider each in turn and design the event experience for that category based on one of the following suggested event themes. You can repeat the process again and again for the different themes, and compare and contrast the creative ideas you come up with:

Suggested themes

Art deco	Classic film or film genre
Classical music	Architecture
Brand experience	Fashion
Active adventure	Transport
Religion	Theatre
Gothic	Historical incident or event
Royalty	Music (any style, e.g. 1970's glam/heavy/punk)
Literature	Dance (any style, e.g. tango)
Sport (any)	Art (any period or idea, e.g. cubism)
Television (any programme)	

2 Pick a colour: red, yellow, green, blue, purple, brown, white, etc. Now design an event entirely around that colour. It does not have to be a dining experience and it does not have to be a total colour concept like the example in the chapter, but try to incorporate the colour as the overwhelmingly dominant theme. Alternatively you can attach the colour to known objects or symbols that are normally seen in that colour and incorporate those into your design.

3 Imagine you were asked to produce a 'design experience' survey to obtain guests' response and reaction to the event that could be quickly and relatively easily completed at an event. What types of things would you want include in it? Would you make the survey applicable to all events, or would you make it adaptable for different event types?

4 Visit a selection of, say, three public venues of a similar size. Where possible take photographs of the main space and make notes on the interior design. Now, drawing on the list of event types below, develop (a) a creative concept for the event at each venue, and (b) clear design ideas for creating the experience in that specific venue:

❑ A themed product launch
❑ A wedding celebration
❑ A sports-award dinner
❑ A 'taste of' event based on a specific country, e.g. Spain, France

Recommended websites

Browse the following internet sites for interesting and informative information:

This site has lots of archive discussion on experiential marketing, podcasts and industry interviews:

Event Design Research Network – this is a new site and under development. It is a useful link to academics interested in research events and design: http://fhrc.flinders.edu.au/research_groups/edrn/edrn.html

EVENTS: review: http://eventsreview.com/

Experience design – a very useful and regularly updated website from Nathan Shedroff. Nathan explores a series of theories and thoughts on experience and design: http://www.nathan.com/ed/

International Special Events Society (ISES) – mainly in the UK/Europe and the US, ISES often includes presentations from its conferences and has a list of industry members, many of whom work on creative events: http://www.isesuk.org/

Jack Morton Experiential Marketing Agency has published a number of *White Papers* on experiences, available to download by request: http://www.jackmorton.com

Suggested reading

Berridge, G. 2007. *Events Design and Experience.* Oxford: Elsevier.
Getz, D. 2008. *Event Studies.* Oxford: Elsevier.
Pine, J & Gilmore, BH. 1999. *The Experience Economy: Work is Theatre & Every Business a Stage.* Boston: Harvard Business School.

Photo: Dimitri Tassiopoulos

Photo: Dimitri Tassiopoulos

Photo: Dimitri Tassiopoulos

Photo: World Travel Market

11

Sustainability and events design

Urmilla Bob

Abstract

This chapter provides a critical examination of events in relation to economic, social and environmental impacts and concerns pertaining to sustainability imperatives. The focus is on highlighting issues and concerns that are relevant to small-scale and large-scale events. However, an attempt is made to underscore aspects that are likely to be unique to specific contexts and types of events. A key focus of the chapter is to examine current strategies and approaches to integrate economic, social and environmental considerations in the planning and design of events. To this end, the FIFA World Cup's 'Green Goal' and Olympic Games' 'Green Games' programmes are used as illustrative examples. Additionally, specific tools and techniques that can be used to promote sustainability at events are discussed. These include seven steps to a waste-wise event, environment education programmes, environmental impact assessments (EIAs), social impact assessments (SIAs) and economic impact assessments. The chapter emphasises the need to incorporate and integrate sustainability issues into the conceptualisation and design of events.

Chapter objectives

After you have read this chapter you should be able to:

❐ provide a critical examination of events in relation to economic, social and environmental impacts and concerns over sustainability;

❐ recognise key social, economic and environmental (triple bottom line) impacts and sustainability concerns that are associated with the hosting of events;

❐ understand current strategies and approaches to integrate economic, social and environmental considerations in the planning and design of events; and

❐ identify specific interventions and techniques that can promote sustainability at events.

11.1 Introduction and background

A well-organised event has the potential to deliver a range of benefits related to return on investments and triple bottom line imperatives to localities or communities, including the following (adapted from Turco et al., 2003):

❐ Reinforcement of a locality's profile and the creation of a positive image for the region as a tourist destination;

❐ The instillation of community pride and confidence;

❐ An increase in community support for events;

❐ Indirect advertising for the region, perhaps to a wider community through the media coverage of events;

❐ Maximum use of existing facilities, thus increasing revenue;

❐ Better maintenance of facilities, even for use by locals;

❐ The creation of entertainment opportunities/experiences for locals (mega-events provide a once-in-a-lifetime experience);

❐ Enhancement of the organisational, marketing and bidding capability of local event organisers;

❐ Improvement in the institutional and infrastructural capacity of the region;

❐ A decrease in negative elements, e.g. crime;

❐ Encouragement of public/private partnerships;

❐ The possibility of being used as part of regeneration strategies; and

❐ An increase in environmental awareness.

There are several intended and unintended impacts of hosting events that relate to economic benefits, increased destination awareness, an increase in investor potential, infrastructural development, social aspects, etc. Numerous studies indicate that event-driven tourism has the potential to be a powerful social and economic force (Auld & McArthur, 2003; Turco et al., 2003). Additionally, there is an increased awareness on sustainability imperatives in relation specifically to minimise and mitigate against negative environmental impacts. Notably, the focus on the 'greening of events', among others, as well as ensuring economic and social legacies has gained prominence. Weed and Bull (2004) assert that in recent years, the necessity to use events to drive long-term developmental plans has popularised the concept of appropriate 'event legacies' as an aspect of event planning and design. As Shaw and Williams (2002) indicate, events have the power to contribute towards negative, social, economic and environmental impacts, especially in the host destinations. Thus the triple bottom line (addressing and balancing social, economic and environmental concerns) has become increasingly central to the design and planning of events. Therefore, the integration of social, economic and environmental sustainability in relation to the planning and design of events is critically important.

The events industry and related activities often attract significant numbers of people (especially hallmark and mega-events) and interact with the environment in numerous ways. However, in the past, environmental concerns have been largely ignored in relation to event planning and design as well as impact studies. Huggins (2003) asserts that there is increasing recognition that the development of events' infrastructure and the events themselves have significant impacts on the environment. Ahmed, Moodley and Sookrajh (2008) state in relation to sporting events that as these events are getting bigger and bigger, the negative effects associated with them are growing. Furthermore, Ionnides (1995) indicates that there is abundant literature which indicates that any event attracting large numbers of visitors to a relatively small area is likely to create noise, cause heavy traffic and overcrowding, result in large amounts of waste and energy use, compromise water quantity and quality, disturb natural environments and processes, and disrupt local activities.

This chapter discusses the different aspects of sustainability in relation to events design. The first section briefly examines the concept of sustainability in the context of the continuum of events ranging from community-based, small-scale events to mega-events. The increasing importance of sustainability in relation to event planning and design is emphasised. This is followed by a more detailed examination of the three main components of sustainability, specifically social, economic and environmental aspects. Each dimension is discussed in terms of implications for event design, how to leverage related benefits and minimise disruption, and specific strategies and approaches (including tools) to integrate social, economic and environmental considerations.

11.2 Sustainability in the context of events design

Golusin and Ivanovic (2009) assert that sustainability does not only emphasise the quality of life in a society in which economic, social and environmental systems provide an opportunity for a healthy, productive and meaningful life for all at present and in the future, but that its significance lies in the links between and achieving the balance among social and economic components of society. In relation to events, this entails ensuring that the event itself achieves sustainability outcomes in terms of ensuring the viability of smaller-scale events that take place regularly, and leveraging the legacy and long-term positive impacts of one-off hallmark and mega-events. Additionally, the event itself, irrespective of its size, should be sustainable in terms of maximising positive economic, social and environmental impacts while minimising or mitigating against potentially negative ones.

The fields of sustainable development, and sustainability science more recently, have increasingly focused on identifying appropriate and effective tools and specific indicators to monitor impacts and to assist in centralising sustainability considerations in planning and design. Yunus (2004) states that sustainability indicators are formal sets of information which are carefully selected to measure aspects of sustainable development. In relation to events, key aspects that need to be considered are the size of the events (both in terms of attracting attendees and geographical spread) and the objectives of the event (what it hopes to achieve). Singh et al. (2008) assert that sustainability indicators report on sustainability or on the capacity of any system or process to support itself indefinitely.

The relationships between an event and the social, economic and natural environments include the impact of the event on the environment and vice versa. It is important to note that social, economic and environmental aspects often overlap, and that these intersections and interactions need to be considered when planning and designing events, especially in relation to ensuring that a positive impact pertaining to one component (e.g. maximising economic benefits) does not have a negative impact on another (e.g. harmful environmental consequences). The next sections examine social, economic and environmental aspects.

11.3 Social issues

The social environment in relation to events could include the following aspects:

- The way events respect, enhance and promote local social systems as well as cultural values and resources;
- Disruptions and negative impacts on local communities related to the hosting of an event such as noise pollution, increase in the cost of goods and services, and traffic congestion;
- Opportunities for nation/community building and building unity – events are often used as a catalyst for social change

and promoting cultural understanding and tolerance. Saayman and Rossouw (2008) state that boosting local residents' national pride and morale serves to increase corporate involvement and generate public support;

- The 'feel-good effects' of hosting events. Allmers and Maennig (2008) assert that this refers to the 'experience value' and benefits for the host country's population from the event taking place in their neighbourhood, even if they themselves are not directly involved or do not have access to the venues where the event is being held;
- Skills development and training, which is often associated with voluntarism and specific programmes targeting individuals from historically disadvantaged backgrounds. This includes development of skills related to the type of event being hosted, for example sport programmes linked to sporting events;
- An increase in safety and security measures for both locals and visitors;
- Access to event infrastructure by local communities post-event; and
- Philanthropic projects associated with an event that benefits local communities, especially disadvantaged and vulnerable groups.

The core elements of social sustainability are safeguarding existing and future members of society, the maintenance and development of social resources, equity in terms of access to resources and opportunities, participation in decision-making processes and investments in social capital.

It is important to note that communities are socially differentiated and not homogeneous, therefore events are likely to have varying effects on individuals and

INCREASING LEVEL OF PUBLIC IMPACT				
INFORM	**CONSULT**	**INVOLVE**	**COLLABORATE**	**EMPOWER**
Public participation goal				
To provide the public with balanced and objective information to assist them in understanding the problem, alternatives, opportunities and/or solutions	To obtain public feedback on analysis, alternatives and/or decisions	To work directly with the public throughout the process to ensure that public concerns and aspirations are consistently understood and considered	To partner with the public in each aspect of the decision including the development of the alternatives and the identification of the preferred solution	To place final decision making in the hands of the public
Promises to the public				
We will keep you informed	We will keep you informed, listen to and acknowledge concerns and aspirations, and provide feedback on how public input influenced the decision	We will work with you to ensure that your concerns and aspirations are directly reflected in the alternatives developed, and provide feedback on how public input influenced the decision	We will look to you for direct advice and innovation in formulating solutions, and incorporate your advice and recommendations into the decisions to the maximum extent possible	We will implement what you decide
Example techniques to consider				
Fact sheets Websites Open houses	Public comment Focus groups Surveys Public meetings	Workshops Deliberate polling	Citizen advisory committees Consensus building Participatory decision making	Citizen juries Ballots Delegated decisions

Figure 11.1 Public participation spectrum

Source: International Association for Public Participation – IAP2 (2005)

groups within a community. This implies that event organisers during the design of an event need to understand the range of social impacts and how these are likely to be dispersed across a community. Every effort should be made to ensure that benefits are equally distributed and that vulnerable groups are targeted.

Ohman, Jones and Wilkes (2006) state that there are likely to be several social costs associated with the event, such as an increase in crime and prostitution as well as alcohol use and drug abuse. Other possible negative social impacts include cultural exploitation, social exclusion of certain groups and individuals, and displacement of local residents.

There is a range of strategies and approaches to integrate social considerations into event planning and design.

A crucial aspect is to ensure that relevant stakeholders (including local communities and businesses) are integrated into the design process and that their concerns and needs are addressed. A key component to facilitate this is public consultation and participation. Public participation and consultation processes need to be undertaken in accordance with the principles of integrated environmental management, and meet the requirements of environmental impact assessment regulations (to be discussed later) for larger events that are likely to have significant environmental impacts. These regulations call for the meaningful and open participation of stakeholders and other interested and affected parties during a number of key stages of planning an event, including the inception and review phases. Stakeholders and other interested and affected parties are invited to provide inputs and comments. Abelson et al. (2001) undertook a comprehensive overview of public participation and consultation methods including citizen juries, workshops, focus groups, surveys, visioning and consensus building exercises. They underscored the importance of developing an effective communication and information dissemination strategy.

The International Principles for SIA (Vanclay, 2003: 6) considers that SIA:

> ...includes the processes of analysing, monitoring and managing the intended and unintended social consequences, both positive and negative, of planned interventions (policies, programmes, plans, projects) and any social change processes invoked by those interventions. Its primary purpose is to bring about a more sustainable and equitable biophysical and human environment.

Moon (2007) states that a social impact assessment (SIA) is a stand-alone report or a subfield of an environmental impact assessment (EIA). In relation to events, SIAs provide a systematic appraisal on the likely impacts of an event on persons and communities whose environment is affected by the hosting of the event in a particular locality. These include disruptions, which can have short- or long-term impacts, on the day-to-day lives and activities of local community members as a result of the event. A SIA therefore is a method of analysing what impact a proposed event will have on the social environment.

SIAs need to be undertaken during the event design and planning process. For events that require bidding, it is imperative that SIAs be conducted during the bidding stages of a proposed event. The SIA will highlight intended and unintended social impacts. The findings need to be considered in the actual design and implementation of the event if the bid is won. Furthermore, the pertinent issues emerging from the SIA need to be communicated to affected stakeholders, the event organisers and other decision makers. As Moon (2007) states, SIAs provide a realistic appraisal of possible social ramifications and suggestions for project (in this case, event) alternatives and possible mitigation measures.

The main SIA steps are as follows (adapted from Becker & Vanclay, 2006):

❑ **Public involvement** refers to the development of an effective public plan to involve all potentially affected parties (see public participation above);

❑ **Identification of alternatives** describes the event and related impacts to identify alternatives aimed at informing data/information requirements;

- ❒ *Baseline conditions* describe the relevant human environment/conditions prior to the event;
- ❒ *Scoping exercise* identifies the range of probable social impacts including the probability of the event/impact occurring, the number of people likely to be affected, the duration of impact, and the extent to which impacts are reversible or can be mitigated, etc.;
- ❒ *Projection of estimated effects* estimates probable impacts;
- ❒ *Predicting responses to impacts* determines the significance of the identified social impacts and how local communities are likely to respond;
- ❒ *Indirect and cumulative impacts* estimate subsequent impacts that are likely to be experienced at a later stage;
- ❒ *Mitigation plan* includes avoiding the impact by not taking or modifying an action; minimising, rectifying or reducing the impacts through the design or operation of the project; and/or compensating for the impact by providing substitute facilities, resources or opportunities; and
- ❒ *Monitoring* means assessing the success or failure of interventions in relation to specified indicators.

Tassiopoulos and Johnson (2009) highlight that in the case of community events (or small-scale events), most communities neither have the time nor the resources to conduct feasibility studies on a number of different event proposals. They assert that, in reality, most ideas for events are generated by an individual, or a group within the community, who has identified the concept for an event that is suited for that community. Small, Edwards and Sheridan (2005) indicate that undertaking impact assessments in such cases is considered resource intensive, time consuming and inappropriate. While a standard SIA may not be relevant nor possible, given the various constraints, for small-scale events, the principles and steps identified above can be adapted in 'a flexible but logical framework that incorporates practical tools for evaluating the socio-cultural impacts of the event so that valuable feedback can be input into the organisation of future events', as proposed by Small et al. (2005: 68). Specifically, they assert that the alternative to pre-event impact projection is to 'learn from mistakes' and document the socio-cultural impacts during and after the event. The retrospective approach, Tassiopoulos and Johnson (2009) indicate, can serve to clarify what has already happened and help impact projections for the future. Tassiopoulos and Johnson (2009) further state that for any event, it is imperative that local communities or stakeholders are consulted and due consideration is given to potential impacts.

A main concern that needs to be considered during the design of the event is local community access to it. If the event is not an open-access or free event, event organisers need to consider how to facilitate access, if possible. Attempts could be made to provide tickets via schools so that community members are given some opportunities to attend the event. When this is not financially possible, organisers could create other spaces for locals to 'participate' in the event. For example, the Fan Parks in Germany during the 2006 FIFA World Cup provided venues for locals to feel as if they were part of the mega-event taking place in their country. If it is a community, ticketed event that requires local support, the event organisers could assess 'willingness to pay' to examine whether the event will be viable.

Social impacts of events are generally neglected during the design phase with a significant focus on economic benefits. However, failure to adequately consider the needs and concerns of local communities may have negative penalties which can range from lack of support for the event to antagonism towards it. Event organisers need to, therefore, consider social impacts and ensure that these are integrated into the design of the event. It is worth recounting the factors identified by Fredline (2004) that inform residents' reactions to events:

❏ Financial benefit from the event (through employment or ownership);
❏ Identification with the event theme;
❏ Contact (usually defined by residential proximity);
❏ The social and political values of residents;
❏ Their perception of their ability to participate in the planning process;
❏ Residents' level of attachment to the community; and
❏ Their perception of justice in the distribution of the costs and benefits of the event.

These aspects need to be considered by event organisers. They should create opportunities for local communities to raise concerns as well as provide information in a manner accessible to communities. It is important to consider appropriate mechanisms of consultation and communication with communities.

11.4 Economic considerations

The events industry globally and in developing countries such as South Africa, Brazil and India is growing but faces several challenges. A crucial one for event stakeholders and managers is to develop economic development strategies, more especially a local economic development strategy for cities or regions, as well as ensure that events do not have negative economic impacts. Some of the negative impacts include economic leakages, price hikes, increased taxes and limited economic opportunities for local communities. Additionally, in some instances local communities bear the huge cost of hosting the event. Sookrajh (2008) states that it is likely that the spatial and temporal concentration of events leads to a similar pattern in the distribution of the available jobs and because of the seasonal nature of employment, only people who are close by are able to benefit from it. He also indicates that economic benefits leveraged from events tend to be concentrated in the hands of a few rather than distributed among the general populace. Specifically, the accommodation and hospitality sectors tend to accrue direct benefits associated with tourism events. Economic 'spill-over effects' can spread opportunities, especially at the local level, if well planned.

Cornelissen and Swart (2006) argue that infrastructural development associated with hosting events can enhance a prospective bidder's prospects of hosting an event or maximise the investment impetus that generally characterises the general build-up to events. Thus, infrastructural development is aimed at leveraging economic interest and investment in a destination. However, large-scale infrastructural projects (such as stadium and transport development) can have significant negative social and environmental impacts. For example, the Centre on Housing Rights and Evictions (COHRE) (2007) notes that mega-events in particular are primarily used as a means to promote economic development and modernisation as well as improving the image of the host city, with little attention being given to the negative impacts of these events. They assert that, more often than not, the benefits of mega-events are not reaped by all and the negative impacts experienced by many people are in direct violation of human rights laws. In relation to the FIFA World Cup specifically, COHRE (2007: 29) states that despite FIFA's attempts to embrace socially responsible ideals and its commitment 'to protecting and promoting human, social and economic development', FIFA World Cup events have had a significant negative impact on housing rights. They use illustrative examples of how 'clean-up' programmes associated with World Cup events have led to the displacement of homeless people, especially near stadium venues.

A key technique to examining economic impacts is economic impact assessments. Direct expenditure categories usually considered in economic impact assessments are as follows:

❐ Spend at the event (especially tourists, if applicable);
❐ Spend at the destination (can be calculated at different geographical scales, i.e. locally, provincially and/or nationally) by visitors (e.g. attendees, teams/participants, VIPs, sponsors and the media). Main expenditure items considered are transport costs, accommodation, food and beverages, and entertainment;
❐ Spend related to sponsorship, merchandising and concessions; and
❐ Capital expenditure on infrastructure (including overrun and maintenance costs), rentals, catering, etc.

Direct income categories generally included are the following:

❐ Jobs created by the event (it is important to consider how many of these jobs will be permanent or temporary/seasonal, and the levels of the jobs created); and
❐ Government taxes/revenues generated (including contribution to the gross domestic product).

It is important to use appropriate income and employment multipliers and taxation rates to calculate the overall economic benefit of the event. However, it is imperative that economic projections are realistic, and this has become an important challenge for event economists.

Linked to the economic impact assessment is the cost-benefit analysis. A cost-benefit assessment highlights the direct and indirect costs with respect to hosting an event, compared with the economic and social benefits. The direct/tangible costs and revenue streams are indicated above (direct expenditure and income categories linked to economic impact assessments). Examples of intangible/indirect costs are negative impacts on traffic flow, residents and local governments; increase in crime and violence (safety and security concerns); and tourism displacement. Examples of intangible/direct benefits are enhancement of a destination's profile, an increase in tourism, the fostering of confidence and pride in locals, and hosting similar events in the future. Bohlmann (2006) notes that although limited in its application, the cost-benefit analysis remains one of the easiest and most understood methods of measuring potential economic impacts of events. However, he cautions that the income and employment multipliers tend to be over-optimistic.

11.5 Environmental issues

David Chernushenko's (1994a) book *Greening our Games: Running Sports Events and Facilities that won't Cost the Earth* was a seminal text that highlighted the importance of integrating environmental considerations and applying principles of ecologically sustainable development (ESD) to sporting event management. The Olympic Green Games and the 'Green Goal' experiences (see case study 11.1) with the 2006 FIFA World Cup in Germany have centralised the importance of promoting environmental awareness and education. These programmes underscore

---

Case study 11.1: FIFA Green Goal and Olympics Green Games Programme

To ensure ecologically friendly events, many countries and events organisations are institutionalising legislation and guidelines to green events. The Sydney Olympic Games in 2000, hailed as 'the Green Games' was an attempt made to consider the environment in all aspects of planning and staging of the games including design, construction and operation of venues, remediation, transport, catering and waste management. The David Suzuki Foundation (2009) highlights that the Sydney Green Games lived up to their name with legitimate environmental achievements. Specific examples cited were the showcasing of the use of solar energy where electricity for several events was powered by the sun through photovoltaic panels, the Athletes' Village was designed to maximise energy efficiency and use sunlight to provide electrical power and hot water, much of the water used was recycled, and the first car-free Olympics was planned where parking lots were not paved for spectators who were encouraged to walk or cycle, or use the expanded rapid transit system.

The Local Organising Committee (LOC, 2006) of the 2006 FIFA World Cup Germany states that in June and July 2006 the world experienced a breathtaking football festival, and for the first time in the history of the World Cup the environment was on the programme. The 2006 Football World Cup held in Germany was the first Cup that developed and embraced the concept of the Green Goal. The Green Goal, the LOC (2006) asserts, is an innovative and ambitious environmental programme which was successfully carried out at the 2006 FIFA World Cup in Germany, which pursued new paths for large sporting events and intended to reduce to the greatest extent possible the adverse effects on the environment that are often associated with large-scale sporting events. The Green Goal programme focused specifically on water, waste, energy and transport. It also provided an opportunity to sensitise broad sections of the public about environmental and nature conservation beyond the World Cup, and that environmental protection can also be economically worthwhile (LOC, 2006). LOC (2006) further asserts that the integration of the Green Goal into the planning and organisation of the 2006 FIFA World Cup was an important step for acquainting the football fraternity with ecological issues as well as providing the environment with a secure long-term foundation in national and international football. The Green Goal programme is a major aspect of the 2010 FIFA World Cup to be hosted by South Africa and is clearly an environmental legacy of the event in Germany.

The International Olympic Committee (IOC) acknowledges the importance of sustainable development and social responsibility, and developed the Olympic Games Impact programme (OGI) in 2003 (VANOC, 2007) which measures the long-term impact of the Olympic and Paralympic Games through a consistent and comparable reporting system across all future Games. The OGI programme includes a series of indicators

---

(126) that measure the status of a range of environmental, socio-cultural and economic dimensions of the host city, region and nation (VANOC, 2007). The OGI programme is integrated into Games management, is presented in a series of four reports and spans a period of 11 years. The first report provides the baseline against which indicator data in future reports will be compared and analysed (prepared three years prior to the Games). The second report is prepared one year prior to the Games and the third of the four reports is the required volume of the Official Report of the Olympic Games, which is mandated by the Host City Contract (VANOC, 2007). The final report is completed three years after the Games.

The 2008 Beijing Olympic Games specifically is an example of how a mega sporting event can embrace an environmental thrust. The IOC requires all cities bidding to host the Games to have a comprehensive environmental programme which is followed through during the preparatory phase of the Games (Beijing Olympic Committee of the Olympic Games (BOCOG), 2007). Each Games is expected to leave a sustainable legacy. Furthermore, the Games needs to promote environmental awareness, policies and practices which are monitored by the IOC. The international significance of greening the Games is the signing of a Memorandum of Understanding in November 2005 by the United Nations Environmental Programme (UNEP) and the BOCOG aimed at making the 2008 Olympic Games environmentally friendly – the Green Olympics.

and promote the mutual relationship between mega sporting events and environmental sustainability, which are applicable to the events industry generally. Ahmed et al. (2008) state that mega-events and many other sporting events have opened up a new industry to the scrutiny by environmental management tools. Huggins (2003) indicates that generally there is increasing pressure for organisations globally and locally to manage and improve their environmental performance, with opportunities and benefits potentially being large and the risk of non-compliance high. Huggins (2003) further asserts that environmental considerations are increasingly likely to become a determining factor in the future and success of sporting events. The environment is clearly an issue which organisers of events, especially larger-scale ones, must carefully consider and integrate into the event design.

The United Nations Environmental Programme (UNEP, 2007) states that activities and facilities associated with events (they refer mainly to sporting events but the issues are also applicable to other events) have an impact on the environment, creating an ecological footprint whose cumulative impact can be extremely significant and can include pesticides, erosion, waste generation and habitat loss. UNEP (2007) also shows that it is important for events to be pursued in an environmentally sustainable manner, given that the deterioration of environmental conditions reduces the health, well-being and living standards of individuals and communities, as well as their level of physical activity. Sookrajh (2008) states that a cleaner environment encourages people to be more connected to the natural environment and to be more physically active, which promotes healthy lifestyles and improves general well-being.

The greening of events (case study 11.1) refers to the growing importance of incorporating environmental issues in event planning and implementation. The

International Symposium on Green Events (2004: 1) states:

> An event can be considered 'green' if it is designed, organised and staged in accordance with sustainability principles, with a special focus on environmental, health and social concerns. The goal is to use as few resources as possible, reduce waste to a minimum, and protect biodiversity and human health. At the same time, opportunities are used for rehabilitating land, improving living conditions, designing sustainable post-event use, saving financial resources and raising awareness among citizens and visitors.

The symposium asserts that events that adopt a green approach utilise as few resources as possible which are adapted to available local resources, and they provide ideal opportunities to promote green technologies and innovations. Specifically, waste is minimised and/or recycled and nature, biodiversity, water, air quality and soil are protected. The Green Goal and Green Olympic programmes indicate that events are increasingly being judged by their ecological standards, especially larger-scale events. Schmied et al. (2007: 12) state: 'The environment and event organisers benefit equally from energy savings and waste avoidance, particularly since the protection of resources also means cost savings and represents a contribution to sustainability'. This also applies to small-scale events. Case study 11.2 illustrates key issues that Melbourne's council highlights in relation to the impacts in relation to sustainability considerations of events held in parks.

Event environmental impacts may be direct or indirect, immediate or cumulative, short-term or long-term. Additionally, while some impacts may only impact the

Case study 11.2: Impacts of events on parks: Sustainability

Issues pertaining to sustainability of holding events in parks are regarded as important, especially given drought and water restrictions. The parks and gardens accommodate approximately 8 000 events ranging from small activities such as weddings to major festivities such as Moomba. These events include both community and commercial activities. To achieve sustainability, events are only permitted in accordance with the Guidelines for the Sustainable Management of Parklands Supporting Events Staged in Melbourne's Parks and Gardens, unless authorised by a specific council decision. Event organisers are required to comply with a number of other specific guidelines including the Guide to Holding an Event in Parks and Gardens and individual site requirements. Various aspects are addressed which include road usage and treatment, infrastructural requirements (if any), portable toilets, vending/food preparation and water usage. The guidelines stipulating sustainability requirements are provided to event organisers. Additionally, every event (irrespective of its size) is rated.

Source: Council report (2007)

vicinity where the event is held, others could have impacts on entire ecosystems. Gossling (2002), for example, indicates how coral reefs can be damaged through trampling, buying or collecting reef species (a direct impact occurring locally) as a result of tourism events occurring in fragile coastal environments. Events can also alter landscapes directly because of infrastructure development requirements associated with larger-scale events. This may contribute to substantial erosion and loss of natural environments. Hallmark and mega-events which attract relatively large numbers of people over short periods and in specific localities can have long-lasting impacts in relation to dealing with the waste generated. Sewer contamination of natural water sources is also a chronic problem worldwide associated with tourism events (Ahmed et al., 2008). Specifically, the World Bank (1987 cited in Ioannides, 1995) indicates that in Cyprus, sewage commonly seeps into the sea because the high volume of waste exceeds the soil absorption capacity during the peak tourist season, making its waters a serious health hazard from a bathing point of view. Thus, environmental degradation is a key possible negative environmental impact. Other negative environmental impacts include noise pollution, poor management of waste and excessive use of resources.

Mathieson and Wall (1982 cited in Garrigos, Narangajavanab & Marques, 2004: 277) define carrying capacity as 'the maximum number of people who can use a place without an unacceptable alteration in the physical environment and an unacceptable decline in the quality of the recreational experience'. Several authors (see Davis & Tisdell, 1995; Garrigos et al., 2004; Saveriades, 2000) describe some of the negative impacts of tourism developments and events, and propose the carrying capacity framework for addressing them. Lindberg et al. (1998) illustrate that measures that shed light on carrying capacity include issues and concerns identification; developing indicators for each of these concerns; establishing a desired level of each indicator; and lastly, identifying the relationships between the number of visitors and each indicator. Furthermore, Lindberg et al. (1998) underscore that there is no standard scientific panacea for establishing these criteria, but that it needs to be context specific. This implies that the type of event and the location/s where it is held need to be considered.

Urry (1995, cited in Gossling, 2002) states that the loss of knowledge about ecological limits, the alienation of lifestyles from the capacity of ecosystems to provide goods, services and functions, and the decreasing attachment to place are interacting processes which are seen as the major factors in the global environmental crisis, and are considered detrimental to sustainable development. Education initiatives, media focus and travelling (especially to protected areas) have contributed to the increase in environmental consciousness. Natural landscapes often provide ideal locations for events, entertainment and leisure. Simultaneously, events provide ideal opportunities for environmental education. UNEP (2007) argues that the inherent link between a clean environment and participation in sporting events specifically is part of what makes sport a powerful tool for communicating environmental messages and encouraging action to clean up the environment. Schmied et al. (2007) indicate that events are attracting more and more participants, spectators and media attention and therefore 'if event organisers actively address the topic of environmental and climate protection they can reach target groups that either have little interest in or are insufficiently informed about ecology' (Schmied et al., 2007: 21).

Events, especially those held within or in close proximity to natural areas such as beaches, dams and conservation reserves, provide an ideal opportunity to educate attendees about the natural environment and the importance of taking care of it. Integrating environmental education programmes in the design of an event is therefore important. In this regard, it is critical to understand the levels of environmental awareness among event attendees and the types of activities that they are likely to be interested in. Linked to environmental education is the need to identify and mitigate against the various types of potential and likely negative environmental impacts associated with events which need to be understood by event organisers/managers, business activities associated with the event, attendees and nearby communities. Environmental education programmes at events could include environmental guided tours, nature displays, information dissemination and non-certified courses. The challenge faced by event organisers will be to find common ground between the event themes/activities and the promotion of conservation and environmental education values. Sookrajh (2008) indicates that in relation to centralising and funding environmental education and awareness programmes, the key issues that need to be addressed are defining whose responsibility they are and what the effective and appropriate education mechanisms are.

Undertaking environmental impact assessments (EIAs) is critically important for large-scale events that require infrastructural investments, as well as any event that is likely to have significant negative impacts on the natural resource base. EIAs are generally undertaken to modify and improve the design of an event, ensure efficient resource use, enhance social aspects (often SIAs are part of EIAs), identify measures for monitoring and managing impacts, and inform decision-making processes. Environmental impact assessments should include research aimed at measuring direct impacts on the natural environment as well as pollution and carbon emissions attributed to the event. The EIA guiding principles identified by the United Nations (2003) are participation, transparency, certainty, accountability, credibility, cost effectiveness, flexibility and practicality. Typical EIA steps are similar to SIAs (with a bias towards environmental considerations) and include project screening and scoping, project description and consideration of alternatives, impact assessment and mitigation measures, reporting and review, and decision making (United Nations, 2003).

Linked to EIAs are strategic environmental assessments (SEAs), and according to Verheem and Tonk (2000), most SEA practitioners agree that a SEA is a structured, proactive process to strengthen the role of environmental issues in strategic decision making. SEAs emerged as a subject of deliberation of and in response to the limitations of project-level EIAs, especially their tendency to be reactionary (examining already pre-determined development undertakings), narrow (falling short of addressing cumulative impacts), and poorly integrated into broader political and economic processes (Stinchcombe & Gibson, 2001). SEAs of policies, plans and programmes (PPP) present a tiered approach – a policy provides a framework for establishment of plans, plans are frameworks for programmes, programmes lead to projects (Glasson, Thérivel, & Chadwick, 1999). It can be applied to three main types of actions (Thérivel & Partidário, 1996): sectoral PPPs (e.g. community-based events); area-based or comprehensive PPPs which cover all activities in a given area (e.g. land-use or development plans) that are likely to be impacted by a mega- or hallmark event; and actions that do not give rise to projects but nevertheless have a significant environmental impact (e.g. the introduction of new technologies). The comprehensive framework of the SEA process makes it an approach particularly well suited to provide the overall methodological framework for addressing the triple bottom line of events, including benefits, risks and EIA studies. This approach is particularly useful during the bidding stage since it provides information that underscores the likely impacts of the event as well as the relevant issues that need to be considered when managing the hosting phase. Table 11.1 provides a suggested indicator list for assessing the triple bottom line impacts of the event, which can be positive, negative or neutral. While most of the indicators listed are

relevant for larger-scale events, some may also be useful in examining the impacts of smaller events. The table clearly shows that economic impacts are more relevant in relation to larger events, while social and environmental indicators are likely to be associated with small-scale events.

The management of waste is a key problem associated with events. The City of Port Phillip (n.d.) identifies seven steps for a waste-wise event, which are illustrated in case study 11.3.

Several recommendations are forwarded by the International Symposium on Green Events (2004: 12) for the greening of events that are useful for event organiser and managers to consider:

❒ Be aware of the (limited) capacity of

Table 11.1 Suggested indicators to assess triple bottom line impacts

Economic	Social	Environmental
Number of jobs created ❒ Number of new businesses created ❒ Event leveraging in terms of cash and in-kind sponsorships, naming rights, ticket sales, media rights, participant fees, merchandise sales, etc. Visitor attendance (specifically tourists for larger-scale events) and spending Capital expenditure, e.g. investments in infrastructure, facilities and equipment Operational expenditure, e.g. salaries/wages, PR costs, catering expenses and administration costs ❒ Outside investment to the local economy due to the event ❒ Accommodation occupancy capacity and rates ❒ Amount of public debt created as a result of the event	Demographic profile of attendees Number of volunteers Number of training programmes/opportunities Number of charities supported ❒ Image enhancement of destination (media tracking) Entertainment and social interaction opportunities Level of accessibility to disadvantaged groups such as the disabled Extent to which the lives of local residents are disrupted Increase in crime, prostitution and alcohol/drug abuse Increase in price of goods and services	Pollution (e.g. air and noise pollution) associated with the event Extent of environmental degradation ❒ Number of environmentally linked conflicts Amount of waste generated and how disposed of (including recycling) ❒ Application of greening principles in design infrastructure Number of conservation efforts associated with the event

existing sewage systems, and limit additional event created pressure on the facilities;

❏ Always respect restricted and protected areas, and isolate them from any new installations or entrances (event infrastructure);

❏ Protect nature from brief but massive influxes of people:

• Ensure only minimal impact is caused to flora and fauna during all phases of an event (pay special attention to indigenous plants and wildlife, especially in the case of sensitive ecosystems)

• Be especially careful when water-based natural resources (such as rivers, lakes and dams) are being used; and

• Use the event for making visitors and the general population aware of the beauty (and importance) of nature and biodiversity.

These are points to consider, irrespective of the size of the event.

11.6 Summary

Events, especially larger-scale ones that utilise significant resources and can have major impacts, need to be assessed in relation to sustainability considerations. This chapter reveals that events have a range of potentially negative and positive social, economic and environmental impacts that event organisers need to consider during the design process. These impacts are linked in part to the type of event, the size of the event, the location, and the legislative and regulatory requirements. Events provide an ideal opportunity to leverage economic and social benefits as well as promote environmental education and ecologically friendly practices.

The eventing landscape is becoming increasingly competitive with the bidding and hosting of mega- and hallmark events, in particular, being considered part of 'big business' in the international arena and a key component of several countries' tourism strategy. Additionally, destinations compete to host national events and continue to host established annual events which are considered part of a destinations eventing calendar (e.g. the SA Tourism Indaba held in Durban, the Cape Town International Jazz Festival, and national regularly held conferences and exhibitions). In this context, sustainability legacy planning and design become crucial components in ensuring that longer-term benefits are realised and sustained. Furthermore, an examination of sustainability indicators can inform and guide key decision makers locally, nationally and internationally in deciding which events and/or destinations to support. Thus, examining sustainability in relation to event design can be a key decision-making tool. Ensuring that due consideration is given to the various components of sustainability has become a discourse which is becoming entrenched in the way in which the design and planning for an event takes shape. However, hosting a sustainable event requires careful planning and design, which includes setting clear targets, securing stakeholder buy-in, developing appropriate mitigation strategies, and monitoring and evaluating key sustainability indicators. Furthermore, effective coordination between a range of stakeholders such as event organisers, relevant local government agencies, local businesses, sponsors and community representatives is needed. Additionally, securing sustainable events requires attentive planning and event managers who are responsive to the significance of the range of impacts.

If designed, managed and coordinated effectively, a well-thought-out event strategy and plan that integrates sustainability considerations has the potential to bring numerous economic, social and environmental benefits. These benefits include promoting environmental education, encouraging integrated and sustainable management practices, attracting visitors, promoting the event and/or the destination, leveraging economic development opportunities and improving the quality of life of local communities. By linking sustainability to events design, strategies and management practices can be developed that conserve environmental resources and make a significant contribution to economic and social development.

Questions for research

1   What are the key components of a sustainable event plan?
2   What are the key indicators related to events that can be used to assess the triple bottom-line?
3   Who is responsible for developing and managing sustainable events?
4   What are the key steps of undertaking EIAs, SIAs and economic impact assessments? What criteria should event organisers use to decide which assessments should be undertaken?
5   What sustainability legacies (both positive and negative) are likely to be associated with hosting larger-scale events?

Recommended websites

Browse the following internet sites for interesting and informative information:

Abelson, J, Forest, PG, Eyles, J, Smith, P, Martin, E & Gauvin, FP. 2001. *Deliberations about Deliberation: Issues in the Design and Evaluation of Public Consultation Processes* (McMaster University Centre for Health Economics and Policy Analysis Research

Working Paper 01-04, June 2001): http://www.vcn.bc.ca/citizens-handbook/compareparticipation.pdf

International Association for Public Participation. 2005. *Spectrum of Public Participation*: http://www.iap2.org/associations/4748/files/spectrum.pdf.

International Symposium on Green Events. 2004. *Greening Events and Leaving Positive Legacies* (results of conference on Local Governments Implementing Sustainability Principles as Hosts of International Events held in Barcelona, Spain): http://www.iclei-europe.org/index.php?id=1012

Interorganisational Committee on Guidelines and Principles for Social Impact Assessment. 1994. *Guidelines and Principles for Social Impact Assessment*: http://www.nmfs.noaa.gov/sfa/social_impact_guide.htm

Moon, G. 2007. *Social Impact Assessments*: http://www.enviropaedia.com/topic/default.php?topic_id=216

United Nations Environmental Programme (UNEP) 2007. *Sports and Sustainable Development*: http://unesdoc.unesco.org/images/0015/001508/150845e.pdf

United Nations. 2003. *Environmental Impact Assessment Principles and Process*: http://www.unescap.org/drpad/vc/orientation/M8_1.htm

Suggested reading

Gursoy, D, Kim, K & Uysal, M. 2004. Perceived impacts of festivals and special events by organisers: an extension and validation. *Tourism Management*, 25(2): 171–181.

Singh, RK, Murty, HR, Gupta, SK & Dikshit, AK. 2008. An overview of sustainability assessment methodologies. *Ecological Indicators*, 9(2): 189–212.

Photo: Dimitri Tassiopoulos

Photo: IMEX

Photo: Dimitri Tassiopoulos

Photo: Dimitri Tassiopoulos

12

Catering management design for events

Jurgen Gasche and Malcolm Ellis

Abstract

The aim of this chapter is to examine the event design fundamentals involved in organising the supply of food and beverages and delivering the experience through catering management for events. The chapter covers both controlled and uncontrolled events. In addition, it analyses the harmonisation of entertainment, such as dancing and other components, into the catering function of a controlled event.

Chapter objectives

After you have read this chapter you should be able to:

❏ discuss the artistic interpretation and expression of event catering design management and its experiential dimensions to create the event experience;

❏ explain food and beverage planning for events, with particular reference to fundamental planning principles and the selection of the menus, quantities and service styles to meet the food and beverage requirements of an event;

❏ discuss the level of service and staff requirements for specific events;

❏ describe the working relationship with the caterer and the need to take into account both religious and cultural requirements when designing meals for events;

❏ identify costs and profits associated with a catered event;

❏ identify the basic health and safety regulations including the specific requirements associated with the serving of alcohol;

❏ evaluate the catered event and keep accurate records; and

❏ incorporate entertainment and other elements into the catering function to ensure a seamless event.

12.1 Introduction

The organisation and planning of events (regardless of the type and size) will involve fundamental planning and design principles, but as each event remains a special case, it will impact on certain project areas that form part of the organisation and planning strategy.

One of these project areas involves food and beverage catering design for an event. The type of event to be organised will largely determine the type of catering offered. The food choices that are made, either by the client or by the caterer, will be influenced by many interacting factors. For most persons, and in ordinary circumstances, food must be palatable or have appetite appeal. The basic challenge for the organiser is to satisfy everyone's taste – for a controlled event, such as a national or international conference, this could be anything from 500 to 5 000 people. The task becomes rather daunting in an uncontrolled event such as the Standard Bank National Arts Festival held annually in Grahamstown, South

Africa, where up to 20 000 people a day could call for various types of nourishment. The same principles apply to the provision of beverages.

This chapter deals with both the controlled (limited access) and uncontrolled (unlimited access) events. The biggest challenge undoubtedly lies with uncontrolled events. Here, circumstances beyond the control of the organiser could ruin all efforts. While the controlled event is mainly in a composed environment, the challenge here lies more in the total satisfaction of all guests. Once more, things can go awry, for an extended speech can ruin a perfectly baked supreme of salmon, or an unexpected (or garrulous) speaker just before dessert can destroy the flame-grilled *crème brûlée*.

Regardless of the size of the event or the number of guests to be catered for, be it 10 or 10 000, the same fundamental and detailed catering design planning has to take place. It is neither easy nor simple to orchestrate an event from concept to conclusion, and even if most of the work is contracted to professional services, the overall coordination of all contracted services remains with the event organiser.

Record keeping is yet another factor that is discussed in this chapter. This function is essential – not only for tax purposes, but also for future events. From the very day that a catering business is established, every caterer should keep detailed records of the types of function, food consumed, drinks served and customers catered to. Further, a record of entertainment used at an event (musician, band, DJ, etc.) will be helpful for future reference.

It must always be remembered that the catering and service at a function can be of the best, but the overall event can be spoiled by an injudicious choice of and inauspicious timing of the entertainment, which will ultimately reflect negatively on the caterer.

12.2 Event catering design management and its experiential dimensions

Events encompass numerous activities, including the need to nourish the bodies of attendees. But from the perspective of event management and catering design, a more common but under-acknowledged motive is to provide some form of pleasurable culinary experience that complements the event. It might well be that the attendees are buying a quick snack to keep hunger from the door while watching a sporting event, for instance, but if the snack is found to be unpalatable, the experience at the event might well be spoiled.

For instance, if the catering at a wedding reception is part of a wedding ceremony, consequently the meal and service experience are a vital aspect of that event. Once again, a poor dining experience will detract hugely from the memories of the occasion. There is some justice in the belief that many wedding guests will forget the ceremony itself, but will remember the accompanying meal and celebration for a much longer time.

It is also a truism that food is often involved with celebration. Given this, it follows that the organiser serving to such a celebration (be it an engagement party, a festival, a wedding, a christening, a *bat* or *bar mitzvah*, a 21st birthday, a graduation celebration, an anniversary, promotion congratulatory party, retirement celebration – the list is endless) should be designed not only to provided sustenance, but also to enhance the occasion by giving people a reason to meet and socialise. A well-planned and designed catering event will not only appeal to the senses of the guests (sight, scent, smell, taste, for example), but will also embed itself in the subconscious of the guests as reinforcing a memorable event.

This appeal to the senses of the diner, the ability to associate, for example, a scent or aroma with favourable experiences and events is well known to marketers. The appeal to the senses of a well-designed, effectively serviced and catered event cannot be underestimated. When designing the event, opportunity must be created for this appeal to sight, scent and, above all, taste to be allowed to create the memories of an enjoyable social occasion.

12.3 The working relationship with the caterer

Food, beverage and celebration are inextricably mixed. From social life-cycle events to mega-events such as the Olympic Games, the relationship between food, entertainment and fun has always been a close one. As Goldblatt (1997) implies, this is not to suggest that this relationship is not serious business also. As will be seen, catering to large numbers of people who are enjoying themselves eating and drinking can be a very serious business indeed.

Rich Benninger, quoted by Rutherford (2002: 264) says that '[c]ustomers are the number one component to a successful catering operation. Without customers, the grandest ballrooms, the most spectacular cuisine, and the best service are all moot points. So every day, [the caterer] must work to fill the pipeline with customers'. When a potential client approaches a caterer for the organisation of a controlled, limited-access function, then it is the caterer's duty to collect as much information as possible from this client, probably at an informal interview or consultation. Even if the caterer delegates

this interview to someone else, this first meeting should include general questions to ultimately provide the caterer with a fairly good idea of the client's vision for the event. Lillicrap (1971: 167) in his seminal work *Food and Beverage Service* pointed out that at 'the initial meeting of the ... manager and client a file must be opened recording all points mentioned concerning this particular function and to hold all correspondence received'. The file mentioned was formerly some form of standardised paper document which could subsequently be translated into a working plan for the staff concerned. In contemporary catering, it may now be an electronic 'document', and the correspondence is now most likely to be found as emails and faxes, but the principle of keeping records, of recording the decisions made and agreed holds good – even in the fast-moving 21st century.

Following are a few points that should be determined at the first meeting with the customer:

❑ *Estimated attendance.* This refers to the number of people who are expected to attend the event. Often the organiser may have no accurate figures at this stage and it may be necessary to work on a 'best estimate'. This estimate needs to be finalised to an accurate number before pricing the catered event.

❑ *Meal service requirements.* Depending on the style of service required, more or fewer staff will be required for the function. The greater the degree of formality, the greater the number of service, supervisory and catering staff that will be required.

❑ *Ceremonies performed during meals.* Any interruptions to the flow of service during the meal – such as speeches, prizegiving, special announcements and the like – will have to be well coordinated with the catering and service staff. It is possible for over-long speeches to lead to food being overcooked. Consequently, the event planner and the caterer need to schedule, for example, the dessert parade to occur between two segments of an event programme so that it happens right on time.

- ❐ *Religious meal requests.* Many religions have their own restrictions on what may and may not be served at a meal. Provision has to be made for these restrictions and to give acceptable substitutes.
- ❐ *Special diets.* Increasingly, guests at events are likely to be subject to any one of a number of allergic reactions to foodstuffs. Allergy to shellfish is fairly common, and allergic reactions to peanuts are becoming increasingly common. Diabetes too is becoming a common condition that must be allowed for.
- ❐ *Client's budget.* This usually determines the lavishness or stringency of the meal or catered event.
- ❐ *Security measures.* Catering for dignitaries from public life such as politicians, musicians and actors or actresses can pose a challenge to the caterer. Since the events of 11 September 2001, security has become ever more of an issue for the caterer. Frequently, access to whole areas is closed off for long periods prior to an event, making it difficult for urgently needed supplies to reach the caterer. Occasionally, a vital member of staff may be refused access to the environs. The presence of well-known or 'superstars' as entertainers may prove to be a challenge for the catering staff.

After the first meeting, the caterer should have a fairly good idea about the client's vision for the event. The success of the catered event often depends upon the ability of the catering team to make the client's imagination a reality. This is particularly true of the birthdays of elderly people where usually two or three generations (with widely differing expectations) of the same family are participating.

In addition to the above, the caterer will make suggestions about the meals served by providing the client with dated menus and a current price list. This practice is often found when dealing with conference organisers. In her book, *Planning Successful Meetings and Events*, Ann J Boehme provides a food and beverage checklist for organisers of events. The caterer can use the following abridged form of this checklist in order to determine the client's prerequisites (1999: 74–75):

- ❐ Make dated menus available;
- ❐ Ascertain the client's food and beverage budget;
- ❐ Have the chef meet with the client;
- ❐ Discuss the event style and options with the client; and
- ❐ Finalise the menu.

After this first meeting, the caterer should now have a very good understanding of the client's needs. The caterer must now secure supplies and enquire about prices and availability of certain products. The identification of appropriate suppliers that can handle the caterer's needs adequately is next on the list. A long-lasting and good relationship with the main suppliers will have a positive impact on the overall outcome of the event. Often, new suppliers promise clients the impossible just to get their foot in the door – this can be detrimental to the outcome of the event

(Shock & Stefanelli, 1992: 340). Here are some of the techniques that could be followed to control product costs and ensure supply of requested goods:

❏ Seek long-term competitive bids from suppliers and maximise purchasing power;
❏ Qualify for purchase price discounts, such as volume discounts;
❏ Make use of stock discontinuation sales;
❏ Seek out new-on-the-market convenience products to benefit from introductory prices;
❏ Use raw-food products rather than pre-manufactured products; and
❏ Always have a contingency or emergency plan on hand, i.e. a second supplier.

Food and beverage sales are an essential service at most events and can generate a targeted profit. Whether planning the catering for an uncontrolled or a controlled event, Getz (1997) suggests a number of key principles that must be considered:

❏ The types of food to be served;
❏ The number of meals to be served; and
❏ The size of meals and product availability, which need to be planned in harmony with revenue goals, theming and availability of staff to do the job.

Suppliers can sometimes provide information or advice on what volume of food and beverages is desirable. Monitoring sales and keeping records will help the caterer next time around when a similar event is catered for (Getz, 1997: 209).

Each event designer and each caterer will almost certainly design their own template. Users of computer-based systems will undoubtedly find themselves using templates printed by the system. These can sometimes be customised by the computer programme developer to the client's own requirements.

The cost of sales is an important calculation. Cost here usually refers to both direct costs (those involved specifically in production) and of indirect costs (often referred to as overheads). In order to generate revenue while keeping customers happy, the caterer has to carefully calculate the expenses and profit margin. The outcome should give a price that will satisfy both the caterer and the client. To provide value for money is vital.

Once a menu has been drafted, supplies are secured and the event priced, it is time to have a second meeting with the client. At this stage, the client has the opportunity to make minor changes, or to make sure that the choices presented by the caterer are in accordance with the client's wishes. However, when catering for the sometimes extravagant events of leading organisations, the caterer sometimes has to deal with more than one function coordinator, or even with members of the executive management of the organisation who wish to stamp their influence on the planning of the occasion. In cases of this kind, it is most advisable to insist on written instructions from the official, designated function coordinator and, wherever possible, have all interested parties at the same table when having a planning meeting. Always ensure that the most responsible person is the one giving the final instructions.

Health and safety concerns

Health and safety can be detrimental to the caterer in two ways. Society is becoming increasingly health conscious, and the demand for light and healthy meals is on the increase. More and more people are declining to eat fatty foods such as deep-fried fish and chips. The caterer needs to be

Example 12.1

14 hit by food poisoning at popular restaurant

Plettenberg Bay – At least 14 people suffered food poisoning after dining at a popular Plettenberg Bay restaurant over the New Year, forcing it to temporarily suspend operations. Samples from both the restaurant and the supplier have been sent to the National Health Laboratories in Cape Town to ascertain the break in the 'cold chain' which led to the appearance of the bacteria.

Source: The Herald (7 January 2003)

Example 12.2

Boy, 5, dies from food poisoning

East London – A five-year-old boy has died and seven people are still in hospital after being admitted to hospital with food poisoning over the weekend. An estimated 100 people were admitted to hospital with food poisoning on Sunday and Monday. They are thought to have drunk contaminated ginger beer or eaten contaminated meat.

Source: Daily Dispatch (7 August 2003)

aware of the latest food fashions and fads. In addition to the above, the caterer has to carefully observe health laws and local bylaws affecting food preparation, service and storage. Occasionally, newspapers report of mishaps which have occurred during large catering events. Although meals can be prepared in large numbers in advance, hygiene becomes an all-important factor in the production of large-scale food operations. If food is prepared in advance, it must be stored in almost-sterile conditions and at the correct temperatures. The suspected food poisoning of 14 diners at a popular Plettenberg restaurant (illustrated in example 12.1) was, in fact, a direct result of a break in the cold chain. The culprit was a bacteria-generated poison called scombrotoxin, which itself generates histamines. The bacterium typically appears when fish is frozen and allowed to thaw before being refrozen. There are many factors that lead to the spoilage of precooked food:

❐ An unsanitised storage container;
❐ Mixing hot and cold foods together in storage areas;
❐ Long-term storage of food in a warm environment;
❐ Contamination of food from incorrect food handling techniques; and
❐ Poor hygiene standards of ill-trained staff.

The caterer and catering staff must understand how food poisoning develops and so be able to eliminate the dangers. There is much literature available that deals with these issues, and most of the reputable suppliers of cleaning materials and chemicals are very ready to give assistance, training and advice.

Sporting events are always a particular challenge to the caterer. Auguste Escoffier (1965: 12) knew that '[t]he extremely active existence we lead does not leave us leisure to devote the necessary care to the upkeep of our bodies ... Nature supplies the raw materials in their simplest forms, so we must know how to make the best use of them'. Depending on the level of the event, be it a local soccer match, a national cycling tour or the Olympic Games, a carefully balanced nutritionally sound menu must be presented. This is when a catering firm should seek the services of a qualified nutritionist. The athletes participating in an ultra marathon require a very different diet from that of a defender in a soccer squad. While the ultra marathon runner requires a carbo-loaded breakfast at midnight, the soccer player will need a regular breakfast at the more usual time. The planning of such highly specialised meals is best left to nutritionists, since they have a greater insight into the nutritional requirements of sportsmen and sportswomen. In addition, digestion time plays a vital role in the food intake of competing sportspeople. Imagine the 23 000 starters at an annual marathon being fed a breakfast a mere one hour before the start of the race. Within two hours of the start, these runners would be desperately seeking toilets!

The menu should always be the focal point of the caterer for a controlled event. A menu which is well presented and which meets the client's highest expectations will be the deciding factor in granting the caterer the contract for the function. The caterer for an uncontrolled event – be it a food stall at a festival or the catering for a sporting event – must ensure that the menu offered is suitable for the event.

Generally, in order to ensure success, whether catering for an event with controlled or uncontrolled access, every caterer should prepare a checklist around the topics listed below:

Menu planning

The menu will determine the following:

- ❏ Food to be purchased;
- ❏ Staffing;
- ❏ Equipment needed;
- ❏ Layout and space utilisation for off-premises catering;
- ❏ Décor for buffets, food stalls, and sometimes even for the venue itself;
- ❏ Food production plan; and
- ❏ Beverages.

Menu categories

The various categories include seated or served meals, in general:

- ❏ Breakfasts, luncheons, dinners and gala dinners;
- ❏ Buffets, including those for breakfasts, themed lunches or dinners;
- ❏ Food stations, which are used when a variety of food is offered, or at an uncontrolled event;
- ❏ Cocktail parties, which are always a stand-up affair where *hors d'oeuvres* are customarily served.

Planning guidelines

Usually there are no rules when planning off-premise catering menus. The client's requests for innovations should never be ignored, provided that they are within the abilities of the caterer and the staff. Planning for the event always depends on the ability of the service team to deliver on the commitment to the client.

Food trends

Popular foods, foods that are in fashion and even food garnishes must not be overlooked (Hansen, 1995: 34–55).

When catering for a controlled event, the caterer must also take into account the level of activity delegates have had during the day. If a delegation has a team-building exercise filled with a number of physical activities, then these guests will be much hungrier at dinnertime than those who have been inactive the whole day. So, how much food should be prepared?

There are a number of factors to be considered before ordering food supplies:

❑ **Cultural background.** Are the guests from a modern suburban environment or from rural areas? In general, the suburbanite has greater access to health food – and perhaps a greater desire for such – than the rural person does.

❑ **Buffet style or sit-down menu.** People will consume more food if eating at a buffet. However, if the room is crowded, guests will eat less since it will be difficult for them to reach the food tables. There is also the requirement that a buffet should not run out of food or appear 'stingy', hence a degree of over-catering will always be required if the event organisers are not to appear miserly. It is far easier to calculate the quantities required for a sit-down, waiter-served menu where the portions are controlled by the staff and the opportunities for abuse of the food supplies are minimised.

❑ **Type of menu.** Often, the organiser requires help when choosing an appropriate type or style of menu. Coordinators will sometimes request a menu more suited to be served with pre-dinner cocktails to be served as a lunch or dinner menu on the first day of the event. Delegates may be disappointed with this, particularly if they have had a long and tiring trip to the event.

Once more, record keeping becomes imperative. If a record of a similar previous event is available, the caterer can calculate the portion sizes and quantities to be ordered far more precisely. Information on the calculation of food portions, and the costing thereof to achieve a profit, is readily available. A rule of thumb is given by Hansen, and this appears to have broad applicability. In general, the smaller the number of guests, the higher will be the percentage of over-catering, as shown below:

Attending guests	Over-order %	Order for
20	20	24
100	10	110
200	7.5	215
400	5	420

Source: Hansen (1994: 49)

The catering team must also remember to account for the losses in quantity during cooking itself. This will vary according to the cooking method used, but depending on how well cooked the meat has to be, the caterer must allow for up to 20% loss in quantity when determining the cooking yield. This percentage 'loss' could increase to as much as 50% of raw weight if the caterer has to trim and bone the meat. Even though suppliers will usually deliver portioned meat, poultry or fish, the caterer must still be aware of the loss during the cooking itself. Large joints of beef that are cooked for buffet service and are usually served well done can lose up to 20% of their raw weight during the cooking process.

> Remember, too that no one became a chef in a day, or stopped learning. The fun of cooking is adapting, developing, experimenting.

Jean-Christophe Novelli, entrepreneur and chef

The beverage service for a controlled event also needs to be considered. Above all else, the catering team must comply with the law of the land. In many countries there is a legal age below which no one may be served any alcoholic beverage. But in yet other countries, anyone can drink alcoholic beverage provided such drinking takes place as part of a meal. Conversely, in other countries, no alcoholic beverages at all may be served. If the event organiser is not familiar with the legislation of the country being worked in, it will be necessary to find authoritative advice.

Employees of the caterer who are to serve guests with both food and beverages must be made aware of the applicable laws, as the caterer is usually held liable if alcoholic beverages are sold (or provided) to minors. But regardless of whether the customers are minors or legal adults, the provision of beverages can be problematic for the caterer. Following are some pointers that will assist in controlling the sale of alcoholic beverages at a controlled event (Hansen, 1995: 58–59):

- ❐ *Encourage short cocktail hours.* Shorten the length of time that pre-dinner drinks are available. Where the organiser provides a cocktail hour before a gala dinner, attempt to encourage the provision of wine and malt liquors rather than spirits;
- ❐ *Serve attractive hors d'oeuvres.* Cheese, fried foods and food with a high fat content serve to retard the absorption of alcohol into the drinker's system;
- ❐ *Serve attractive non-alcoholic beverages.* These could include freshly squeezed fruit-juices, non-alcoholic fruit punches and, increasingly popular, a variety of mineral waters, both sparkling and still;
- ❐ *Pour wine.* Having wine poured by service staff as opposed to leaving open bottles for guests to help themselves helps to control the rate of consumption and allows some control over the size of the drinks served;
- ❐ *Close the bar.* Although this is frequently a source of contention with 'thirsty' customers, it is helpful to liaise with the organiser to permit the bar to be closed some time before the event is over;
- ❐ *Serve coffee.* Encourage the service of coffee, in any one of a number of guises, towards the end of the event. When the service of coffee coincides with the main speaker of the event, consumption of alcohol is noticeable reduced. Even so, it may be necessary to allow discreet refreshing of the glasses of VIPs;
- ❐ *Be aware of religious restrictions.* Although non-alcoholic beers and wines are available, the service of these must be cleared with the organiser of the event. Special beverages are available for certain religions.

Figure 12.1 provides a planning schematic that can be used for both uncontrolled- and controlled-access events. The first three stages of the structure have been discussed above.

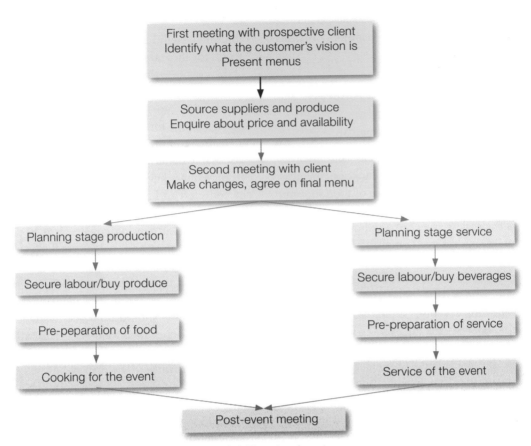

Figure 12.1 The planning stages

The remaining stages will be elaborated upon in the sections to come. During all of the stages, record keeping is important. It is important that a database of information is kept of such information as the names (and contact details) of service and kitchen staff, and of reliable suppliers that can be called upon for future functions.

Additionally, it is a very good plan to (confidentially) record interactions and experiences with the client before, during and immediately after the event. These will not only be helpful if the client brings repeat business as the caterer will have prior knowledge of the client's vision, likes and dislikes, but these records may also be useful when dealing with subsequent queries or complaints.

Small businesses are constantly hunting for ways to distinguish themselves from their competition. A good way to separate their offerings from those of anyone else is to touch their customers with kind, thoughtful gestures as often as possible (Trotter, 1999: 186). Not only will the guests appreciate them, but the goodwill generated will reflect favourably on the event organiser. This goodwill in turn can confidently be expected to reflect on the catering team. Such gestures do not have to be extravagant or expensive. The provision of a chocolate mint on the saucer of the coffee cup, wrapped toothpicks, warm (not hot!) moist towelettes, either before or after the meal, holding back the chairs of women guests as they sit – these and many other actions all reflect favourably on the caterer.

12.4 Various types of catered event: uncontrolled- and controlled-access events

It may be true that as 'all catering involves food, and almost every function involves the production and service of food in some form or other, it may be thought that this is the easiest aspect of any function for any practising caterer' (Small, 1976). However, experience has shown that this is not always the case. The type of event being organised will largely determine the catering. The following section deals with planning the catering for an event with unlimited access. There are many details that have to be considered during the planning stage, the foremost being the weather. Although the organiser cannot control this, arrangements for food and beverages have to be made to suit the weather conditions. In addition, public and religious holidays, major sporting events in the vicinity, the academic calendar and the season of the year will all affect the catering, and thus the success of the event.

> *Many entrepreneurs have gone into business using their wits and their imagination. Most have a taste for success, and scores have a viable vision. The key ingredient is passion – true passion for excellence.*
> Trotter (1999: 3)

12.4.1 Uncontrolled-access events

The unthemed event

Three factors that are often overlooked or ignored when planning the catering for a large uncontrolled-access event are ablution facilities, waste disposal and access for incoming supplies. The provision of disposable eating utensils and containers has to some extent alleviated the burden of cleaning up. But there still remains the necessity for cleaning work surfaces, utensils, equipment – and hands! If disposable materials are used, it follows that arrangements have to be made for them to be collected and stored, and later disposed of. Often the owner of a stall encounters shortages of certain ingredients. It is both time consuming and nerve-wracking to have to carry these supplies back to the stall through thousands of visitors.

A plan or diagrammatic layout of the event premises should be made available to each tenderer for a food stall. This will enable the operator to plan the shortest routes to the outlet. The disposal of waste will have to take place, preferably out of sight, and certainly without coming into contact with the *festinos*. There must be ablution facilities available in close proximity to the outlet, if not actually in the outlet itself. For hygienic reasons, there must be ample numbers of toilets available, but not in close proximity to food outlets.

What then does it take to successfully organise the catering for an event such as the Standard Bank National Arts Festival at Grahamstown? Prior experience will positively affect the overall outcome. Additionally, the following should be taken into account:

❑ *Location.* The catering area must be easily accessible to visitors, caterers and the municipality. There must be easy access for delivery, for loading spaces and for parking reasonably close to the venues.

❑ *Vendors.* Public holidays or school holidays falling during the event could

Case study 12.3 The Standard Bank National Arts Festival (SBNAF), South Africa

The Standard Bank National Arts Festival (SBNAF), which takes place annually at the beginning of July in Grahamstown in the Eastern Cape province of South Africa, is a good example of an unthemed event. During this time, the streets of the sleepy little university town are flooded with festival-goers known almost universally as *festinos*. In addition to the crowds of *festinos,* there are the performing artists, fine artists, musicians, street performers, security personnel (both public and private), the stallholders, large numbers of small-time entrepreneurs, sponsor's representatives, – as well as the permanent residents of the town – sooner or later all seeking food and beverages.

The challenge for the organiser is to make provision for this nourishment. It is most unlikely that the organisers of such a large event will become involved in the catering side. Tendering for food stalls is the norm, where semi-professional and professional caterers will apply to the organisers (or the local authorities) for the appropriate permits and licences.

Hotels, guesthouses and restaurants usually provide for overnight visitors. Food stalls at the outdoor craft markets, and pubs, restaurants, takeaways and hotels make provision for day visitors.

While overnight customers are usually predictable with regular meal intakes, it is the day visitors that have the greatest impact on the food stalls as well as on the restaurants in the town. In Grahamstown, the food stalls are found in many streets, but increasingly they are found in a common area at the outdoor craft markets. This latter arrangement, derived somewhat from the food markets of Asia, is becoming increasingly popular with large events. It can also be noted that in very many shopping malls a number of outlets, each catering for a different taste and style in food and food service, can found together in one section of the mall (i.e. a food court). As the customers become more cosmopolitan in their outlook, the range of foods available has expanded from the ubiquitous hamburger 'joint' or pizza place to restaurants offering Thai-, Hawaiian-, Chinese-, Italian- and Middle Eastern-themed restaurants.

As a caterer at such an event, it is important to accurately forecast the number of people who are likely to visit. Before any tender is made, penetrating research must be undertaken to see how caterers performed in previous years. This information may be available from the event organisers. It may be useful to determine from the previous year's caterers if they intend to apply this year, and if not, why not? A good contact at the local weather forecasting bureau may prove invaluable, for the weather is perhaps the largest single factor affecting any food business at a largely outdoor event such as the SBNAF. As the meal plans cannot always accommodate changes in the weather, it is important that the meal provider can accommodate unexpected changes by planning for shelter from rain, providing braziers for heat, or offering shade away from the sun. The successful catering tender must be very flexible and readily adaptable to changes. After all, it might be the flexibility to adapt to changes that makes the difference between a popular (and therefore profitable) venue and an unpopular one.

bring unexpectedly large numbers of guests.

- ❏ *Sporting events.* Sporting events in the vicinity can do two things – on the day of the sporting event, visitor numbers may decrease, but they may increase immediately prior to and post the sporting event as visitors to the region may try to visit both events in one trip.

- **Season**. The menu chosen must complement the season unless regional or national specialities are being sold. In general, though, salads and light meals are less popular during the winter months, but would be essential during hot summer days.
- **Weather**. Accurate weather forecasts, updated frequently, will enable the alert caterer to change the type of menu on offer appropriately. Fortunately, easy access to the internet now makes this quite simple.
- **Equipment**. The reliable availability of utilities at the venue required to power the equipment will determine what equipment is transported. Electrical equipment is easy to use, simple to clean and efficient to operate, but if there is no electricity, an alternative must be found.

Case study 12.4 Planning to operate a food stall at the Grahamstown National Arts Festival, South Africa.

The caterer should immediately start with the planning of the event on issue of the permit to operate a food stall at the Grahamstown National Arts Festival, which is 90 days prior to the event. It is always extremely difficult to plan for an unthemed event like this. An important issue is the location of the food stall. Will it be in the streets of Grahamstown or at the craft market on the village green? This information is usually obtained from the municipality office granting the permits or from the organiser. With it will come a layout of the location, indicating water supply, electricity, access roads, etc.

- **Menu**. The chosen menu should be easy to prepare at the venue. Baking should be avoided as baked goods become unstable in the oven. Frying in deep oil should also be avoided because of the odours produced. Specialised equipment is available, however, that could minimise this latter issue.

The caterer now needs to know what the surrounding stallholders will be serving in order to avoid duplication (and unnecessary competition). In general, it is a good idea to find out how many competitors, both direct and indirect, can be expected. This information can be obtained from the event organisers. Many organisers are aware of these challenges to the smaller entrepreneur and will limit the types of food offerings (no more than 20 hamburger stands at the event) as well as their location (no more than two hamburger stands at any location and not within 20 metres of each other).

Researching the events of previous years will now become the most important task facing the caterer. Obtaining information about the previous performance of competitors and accurately forecasting the number of expected customers for the next event are crucial to the caterer's overall success. An easy way to investigate the competition's performance is simply to ask them! Of course, the resulting information may or may not be accurate. For this reason, a second source of information is most useful, and suppliers are often good for this. They are often willing to provide general information in the hope that this will encourage business from the enquirer. The event organiser may be able to give figures of guests, turnover and the like. Another option might be to contact universities who often see large numbers of people in a relatively contained area, at leisure, and can be a wonderful research resource. The amount and types of information that can be extrapolated from research reports are most useful.

The calculation of expected guests can be done in a number of ways. Statistics obtained from previous years giving the number of visitors who attended and the number of meals served can be obtained from the organisers. Sometimes these figures are somewhat speculative, and sometimes they can be very accurate. From the figures thus obtained, an estimate can be made of the numbers of visitors likely to be expected in the forthcoming period. Is the number of visitors increasing? Or decreasing? If decreasing, are any efforts being made to counter this trend?

Another source of information would be the archives of the local newspapers. Again, it is quite easy to determine whether a festival is growing or shrinking in attendance. If research reports are available, these may well indicate the average number of visitors, the number of meals served, the average spend per meal, the average spend per visitor, whether attendance is expected to grow, at what rate the attendance is growing year on year, and other useful data.

The caterer now has most of the information necessary to plan the venture. The caterer already knows that the area where the food stall is to be sited, and what the immediate, and not-so-immediate, competition will be. Information received from any number of sources has revealed the average number of meals served on any given day. It is known that the organisers expect the festival to grow by a given percentage. They have given the number of competing outlets they expect to allow. From this point the forecasting of the number of meals to be sold, thus the amount of food required, becomes an arithmetical calculation. See the example below.

Arithmetical calculation of expected business

A caterer may have obtained the following information:
- The festival will be running for 11 days, four weekend days and seven weekdays;
- In the past, there were eight competitors. This year, two more have been added;
- Information received indicates that the competition sold 900 meals per day on weekends, and 550 meals per day during weekdays; and
- The caterer has a menu with a choice of ten main items.

Expected meals during weekends

900 meals × 8 competitors last year = 720 meals × 6% = 763 meals per day
10 competitors this year

Expected meals during weekdays
550 meals × 8 competitors last year = 440 meals × 6% = 466 meals per day
10 competitors this year

Total meals expected to be sold
(466 × 7) + (763 × 4) = 3 262 + 3 052 = 6 314 meals in total during the festival.

Unfortunately, the planning process cannot end at this point.

The caterer does not, and cannot, know at this stage which of the ten items on the menu will be sold. It is unlikely that each of the ten menu items will be responsible for one-tenth of the caterer's sales. So then, how many of each are to be bought in order that the caterer will not run short of any given item – but will have none left unsold at the end of the period? Again, there are other factors that will affect the success of the venture. Petrol prices may increase enormously, deterring visitors from visiting the festival. The competing vendors may decide that they want to cut prices, and thus adversely affect the caterer's business levels. An unscheduled international rugby match in a nearby town can draw visitors away from the festival. The list is endless, but the astute caterer will have a plan in place to deal with each of the above.

Catering for events with specific themes

This item refers to events with specific themes that attract visitors because for those themes.

With all off-premises catering, it is vital that controls be in place to minimise losses. Every item that leaves the home base should be listed. Recipes should be simple to minimise ingredients so that control is simplified.

When catering for an uncontrolled-access event, the caterer should pay attention to the following items to help assure success:

❏ *Event theme*. It is important to determine for whom the event is likely to cater. Once this has been done, a suitable menu can be compiled.

❏ *Duration of event*. An event that only operates for a certain number of hours

> **Case study 12.5 Red Nose Day, South Africa**
>
> Red Nose Day used to draw thousands of people with their families to hotels, shopping malls and showgrounds to take part in events designed solely to take money from the public for a well-known charity. Supermarkets hold food and wine festivals. Schools and religious organisations have fêtes and bazaars. DIY stores hold tool demonstrations. Public service organisations such as Rotary International, Lions and Round Table hold fêtes, fun days and many other events, all aimed at getting people to enjoy themselves while giving (generously, it is hoped) to charity. Recently in South Africa, entrepreneurial competitions have been organised by a major television operator aimed at children with substantial prizes on offer.
>
> Organisational talent is needed to make these events a success. Since the purpose of the activities is to attract entire families, the catering must be geared to satisfy both young and old consumers. This means that the entrepreneur must cater to two quite different markets. Light desserts and sweets must be included to cater to the desires of the youngsters while the adults would perhaps require something more savoury. The theme of the day will give a clue to the way caterers should direct their menu.

daily for limited day or days requires a set-up that can quickly and easily be installed and subsequently dismantled. It is trite but true that potential customers will leave an outlet if it does not meet their needs promptly.

❏ *Research.* It is advisable to research previous or similar events to gauge their success. Information should be available from the organisers, suppliers, the internet and local newspapers. When dealing with 'occasional' street markets, local shopkeepers will often give their opinions quite freely.

- ❑ *Pricing*. Pricing should be fair and must allow a margin of profit, but items should be neither over- nor underpriced.
- ❑ *Controls*. Control must be exercised not only over liquid assets such as cash and production stock, but also over equipment inventory.
- ❑ *Personnel.* In all cases, front-line catering personnel must be friendly and professional. It is very easy for a sharp word to a child customer to turn into a confrontation with the parent, and adverse word-of-mouth reporting can severely damage a business.

Of course the success of catering to a themed event does not only depend on the above factors. First-time caterers in particular should be guided by the following advice when planning a themed event with unlimited access.

- ❑ *Research*. The recipe for success starts with research. The more that is known about the event, what happened in the past, what is planned for the future and what happens at similar events, the better. The more that is known, the easier will be the shaping of contingency plans. Research will sometimes lead to the discovery of similar events in the near vicinity that will have the effect of halving the potential custom.
- ❑ *Location*. Plans of event premises must be available in order to accurately and appropriately plan equipment placement and the layout of the food stall. Staff members and suppliers need to be informed of the exact location.

- ❑ *Visitors and duration*. Any event is likely to draw greater numbers of visitors if it takes place during school holidays, after hours, or on weekends or public holidays. The caterer's task is to provide a steady flow of quality food during the entire period of the event. It is very easy for the quality to fall when the outlet is under severe pressure of numbers, or to tail off towards the end of the event.
- ❑ *Weather and season*. Weather forecasts can be obtained from the weather bureau or online. Flexibility is essential when it comes to sudden weather changes. This is obviously much more applicable to outdoor events, but the effect of adverse weather should not be underestimated, even for events under cover. The menus chosen should complement the season. There is likely to be little demand for thick, hearty soups during the height of summer. This said, it seems that the demand, particularly in South Africa, for curry and rice appears to be constant despite the weather.
- ❑ *Menu and pricing*. Most catering companies work on a tight budget and small profit margin. Nevertheless, the temptation to overcharge (or to undersupply) the customer to create greater profits must be steadfastly resisted. Prices should be fair, possibly in line with those of the competitors. However, where a clear quality differential exists, it may be possible to charge a premium for the higher-quality product.
- ❑ *Controls.* It is in the interest of the caterer to prevent all forms of theft and fraud. Control sheets and systems have to be designed, implemented and rigorously enforced. It is not unusual for temporary staff to over-portion and undercharge their friends and relatives.

The menu items should be designed in such a way that this is deterred.

❑ **Personnel.** As stated previously, the front-line staff of the catering outlet must always appear friendly and professional. This does not exclude the management of the catering business. Each member of the front-line staff should have had some training in customer relations.

Case study 12.6 Researching and planning – a food stall at the Munich Oktoberfest

In this case, the caterer is one of four other stall owners participating in the Munich Oktoberfest. The duration of the festivities is over four days, starting on a Thursday with the finale on Sunday. The event opens on Thursday and Friday at 17:00 and on Saturday and Sunday at 12:00. Closing on all four days is at midnight. Since this is the first time that this event is being held, the caterer has no means of gathering information on turnover from suppliers or competitors. However, these figures are required in order to plan for the event. An estimate could be made by making enquiries with the tourist office and organisers of similar events in the region. If the event is a continuation of previous festivities, the same calculation as in the previous example can be used. The caterer also has only limited knowledge about German food and its preparation, and therefore needs to improve this knowledge. Purchasing books on the subject, visiting a library or consulting a specialist could assist in this regard. Although the Oktoberfest is a German invention, menu items could include local specialities. It is also vital to know what competitors will be offering at their stalls.

The planning of the menu should take into account the preferred tastes of the customers most likely to visit the event, but at the same time should be in line with the overall theme of the event. Since traditional German cooking involves mostly fatty foods, it is not advisable to prepare this type of food in hot conditions. However, traditional German cooking also includes the preparation of sausages, which is also a favourite dish among local patrons.

The caterer, with this newly gained knowledge of German food, can adapt traditional German food to local requirements such as sausage (or alternatively known as 'barbecue sausage') in a roll, apple pie instead of *apfelstrudel*, and cheeseboards using local cheeses served with German bread. The caterer must make provision for the preparation of the food items on the menu as well. Peak periods of sale will most likely be between 12:00 and 15:00 during the day, and 18:00 to 22:00 in the evening. It is also likely that when visitors start to get intoxicated the sales of food will increase! Cold-meat platters, cheese boards and apple pies can be pre-prepared away from the event and pre-plated. An item such as *boerewors* can be prepared slightly ahead of time and kept warm on the side of the grill or can be prepared by order. It is important for the caterer to keep a record of sales, especially if no previous sales numbers were available.

The caterer's research has revealed the following information: at a similar event in the region 250 people were served during the first day at all stalls during the lunch period. This number increased by 20% on each subsequent day. The sales per stall during the evening started on Thursday with 350 meals per stall but only increased by 10% for the following evenings. In addition, sales during the off-peak period (15:00 to 18:00) started with 80 served meals on Thursday but increased by only 6% until Sunday. A total of 3 317 people were served meals during the entire event. That event drew a total of 15 000 visitors over the same period. This indicates that 22% of all visitors made use of the food stalls. The caterer should now plan his or her menu and preparation around these figures.

12.4.2 Controlled-access events

A controlled- or limited-access event is somewhat easier to organise than an uncontrolled-access event. Such an event could range from a cocktail party to a lavish wedding or even a presidential inauguration. However, if the caterer is not careful, mistakes can easily occur. How elaborate the catering will be depends entirely on the budget of the client and the professionalism of the caterer. Planning the catering for any such event will require a good basic knowledge and understanding of foods.

Catering for any controlled-access event such as a gala banquet, conference luncheon, tea break or working breakfast is more predictable than catering for an uncontrolled-access event. The advantage is that the number of clients to be catered for is already known to the caterer, be it through limitations of seating space at the venue or the number of attendees provided by the organiser. As already mentioned, the budget of the client and the professionalism of the caterer will determine how elaborate the catering is to be. The caterer will obviously require a basic knowledge and understanding of food. Ingredients will have to be sourced from reliable suppliers, and the seasonal availability of food has to be followed up. Often a client will demand a food, for example strawberries, that is not available all year round. If the caterer is not fully aware of the availability of these ingredients at local marketplaces, he or she will end up paying a high price, thus eroding the potential profit margin. Banqueting menus should therefore be based on foods that are available throughout the year.

This may lead to a certain degree of predictability in the food offerings and so some caterers will prefer to draw up menus based on the seasonal availability of foods. This, of course, can lead to challenges if an offered foodstuff should, for whatever reason, be unavailable at the time required. Menus would always be drawn up to appeal to the client, and a variety of banquet menus, cocktail menus, and lunch and dinner menus are usually available. However, this availability will not prevent the caterer from accommodating certain client-specific requests, such as vegetarian meals or religious restrictions. Professionalism of the caterer is shown when a client's expectations and wishes are included in a menu, rather than denied because of logistic or personnel problems. This becomes particularly important when the function to be catered for is a wedding.

The organisation of such an event begins at the first meeting with a client. It is important for the caterer to learn about the delegates or participants who will be attending the function. Gathering as much information as possible will help in compiling a group analysis of history of the client. Then, too, if the client is a repeat customer, the caterer may already have previous records of dealings with the client leading to a better understanding of the client's needs and wants.

The points following should be considered when meeting the client (Hildreth, 1990: 20–31):

- ❑ *Age and gender of attendees.* This will enable the caterer to form an accurate idea of portion size as well as the degree of health-food requirements;
- ❑ *Food and beverage preferences.* The food for tea or coffee breaks and luncheons during a conference, for example, should be kept light, with alcoholic beverages usually served only at dinners;
- ❑ *General preferences.* These can be

Case study 12.7 Planning a wedding reception

A family would like to organise a wedding reception at their house. The caterer has a first meeting with the family and investigates the estimated attendance, the meal service requirements, ceremonies that are planned during the meal service and the client's budget. Since the caterer is catering for the entire event, he or she will need to know about all festivities on the premises and the timing of them. In the case of a wedding, menus are usually drawn up completely to the client's specification, since it is a special occasion.

The caterer now has a fairly good idea what the client expects, and also knows that there will be 150 guests attending the outdoor wedding ceremony, which will have a cocktail party prior to commencement. In addition, the main function, a sit-down wedding dinner, will be held in the evening for 100 invited guests only. Fortunately for the caterer there is a fairly large budget to work from. However, the caterer is only involved in the food and beverage planning of the function. This means that he or she has to liaise closely with the company that is involved with the decoration and set-up of the entire function. The planning of the event after the first meeting should be organised as follows:

❒ **Produce menu for cocktail party.** This should be upmarket, for 150 people, served by waiters and should consist of both hot and cold snacks. Service should begin with the service of the first guest and must continue until the wedding ceremony starts.

❒ **Produce cocktail list for cocktail party.** This should also be an upmarket menu, once more, for 150 people and should consist of light alcoholic and non-alcoholic beverages.

❒ **Produce menu for dinner.** This should be a four-course menu for a sit-down dinner for 100 people.

❒ **Produce beverage menu for dinner.** This must complement the four courses of the menu. All beverages will be served by waiters, culminating with the service of coffee.

---

broken down into the preferences of the attendees or those of the organiser;

❒ **Origin of delegates.** Knowledge of the country, province or city from which the attendees originate can provide indications of cultural affiliation;

❒ **Organisation data.** This would include information on previous functions the client has held.

This data can be obtained through questionnaires, computer searches or evaluation data stored from previous dealings with the client. Even so, the best way of obtaining necessary information from a client is undoubtedly a personal interview. The most frequently used method, however, is through a questionnaire. For conferences, these are usually sent out to prospective delegates at the beginning of the planning phase of the event. Most conference organisers incorporate this specific information requirement with their registration forms that will be completed by the prospective delegates. Catering remains the focal point of any event, be it a refreshment break, a set-menu meal, or any food and beverage provision. No matter how beautifully the venue was decorated, no matter how smooth the food service was, it is the food itself that leaves the longest-lasting impressions on the perception of the attendees.

This is the time for the caterer to call upon his or her suppliers to investigate the availability of certain foods and beverages.

The supply of these products should preferably be secured. The menu should now be priced and a second meeting with the organiser should be held. During this final meeting, the caterer will clarify if there are any speeches during the dinner service and how long they will take. In addition the caterer should investigate the equipment that is at his or her disposal for the preparation of both meals. This is needed for the planning of the cooking stage.

Once the menu has been agreed upon, the caterer has to meet with the decorator and investigate table plans, entrances for waiters, areas for the washing-up and collection of used plates and glassware, and so on. After this the caterer will plan the production of the food and the service of both meals. There are many examples of menus and wine lists that can be sourced. Many caterers will happily give them to any sincere enquirer, often regarding them as marketing tools.

12.4.3 Planning of food production

Suppose that the client has chosen *Suprême de canard fumé garni* (smoked breast of duck with garnish) as a starter. The caterer now has to break down each item on the menu into production units. The production units for the starter could look like this:

SMOKED BREAST OF DUCK

❑ *Smoked duck breasts* – pre-portioned from supplier; slicing and plating at event premises;
❑ *Oak leaf lettuce* – pre-packed from supplier; washing and plating at event premises;
❑ *Raspberry vinaigrette* – production at caterer's premises; pre-produce, bottle and store;

❑ *Plate garnishes* – production at caterer's premises on day of event.

After the production has been planned and supplies have been secured, the caterer now has to secure the necessary labour. This labour can be hired from a local hotel school or, if the caterer has a database of names of reliable workers, the workers can be drawn from there. According to the planning schedule, certain foods can be pre-prepared. Considerations of hygiene have top priority during the pre-preparation of food. The storage of food has to be monitored carefully. Staff not only has to be made aware of correct food handling and safe food production but also of the implications that personal hygiene can have on food production.

The final planning stage is the actual cooking for the event. In the above example the caterer has already set times for speeches with the organiser and made it clear what implications unexpected speeches can have on the outcome of a cooked meal. Certain items still have to be

> **Case study 12.8 South Africa – catering to satisfy religious and cultural diversity**
>
> The April 2004 Presidential Inauguration gala dinner of the country's third democratically elected President involved over 6 000 guests, among them heads of state, international icons, diplomats and statesmen at the Union Buildings in Pretoria. The buffet menu was a blend of African and modern produce involving a lavish southern African spread of delicacies including mopane worms (*Imbrassia belina*) and other cultural specialities. The caterer also had to provide meals for a number of religious minorities.

cooked and prepared at the event premises; however, the caterer has prepared a menu that has not only satisfied the client but is also easy to prepare.

Sometimes the caterer cannot provide for specific religious requirements because of strict regulations. One example of this would be the provision of meals for strict adherents to the Jewish faith, as meals can only be prepared in a certain kitchen, using designated utensils in designated manners under the auspices of the Jewish rabbinate. Fortunately, however, food that can be reheated and served to delegates of this faith can be obtained in sealed containers from specialised companies. Catering for other religions too requires the caterer to have at least a basic knowledge of the food requirements of the religion.

Cultural catering is very similar – the same basic knowledge of food production is required as for religious catering. When assessing food and beverage requirements with the organisers, the following aspects need to be considered:

❑ *Number of people attending.* It is important to have an exact number of attendees. An indication of the number of vegetarian or special meals for a particular religious group that are required should also be obtained at this stage.

❑ *Available budget.* This will always determine the extravagance of a function. If the budget for a conference is tight, meals during the day should be inexpensive, but dinners should be memorable and rather lavish.

❑ *Religious restrictions of delegates.* This is important because some require longer notification periods as specially prepared food has to be obtained.

❑ *Break times.* This allows the caterer to set up just in time. If times are

adhered to, absolute freshness of food is guaranteed.

❑ *Speeches during main meals.* This is a nightmare for every caterer – the beef fillet is at its best waiting to be served and the host gets up to give an unscheduled speech! Organisers must be made aware of the implications of unexpected speeches during the meal service.

These are the basic determining factors for food and beverage provision. The more important aspect when planning the catering for an event is the type of delegates attending the event. Every delegate or attendee needs to be considered – being insensitive to their needs will lead to an unprofessional event. An organiser should never forget who pays the bills, and every effort should be made to attend to any special needs. The provision of standard menus by organisers and caterers is acceptable, but provision always needs to be made for special requests.

Imagine that three guests of the Jewish faith are attending the wedding in case study 12.7, in addition to three Hindus and eight Muslims. Five people are strict vegetarians and one is diabetic. In order to cater for these special-case people, the caterer needs to have a good knowledge of the faith and beliefs of their religions or health groups. For example, the food for guests of the Jewish faith may have to be ordered in from a company that specialises in the production of kosher meals. The Hindus would not be able to eat the beef, and the main course would have to be substituted with lamb or pork. The latter choice would, however, not be suitable for the eight Muslims, who are not allowed to consume pork; even then, many Muslims insist their meat to be slaughtered according to Halaal requirements. Absolutely no meat, fish or poultry products are acceptable to strict vegetarians – this includes both butter and cream. A sugar substitute may have to be provided for the diabetes sufferer. These are only a few examples of the challenges a caterer could be faced with during the planning of an event. It is not unusual to be faced with the special dietary requirements of a delegate after the meal has started. The caterer cannot afford to relax his or her attention until after the meal has been served and cleared away.

12.5 Summary

The purpose of an event designer or planner and caterer is, in essence, very simple. It is to produce an event that when the clients are reviewing their experience believe that they received value for money, a memorable event (for all the right reasons) and favourable reviews from their guests – and yet believe that the process was 'easy'. If those goals have been achieved by the event designer or planner and caterer, then the task has been successfully completed, and repeat business, or referral business, will surely follow.

Lillicrap and Cousins (2008: 11) most aptly state that '[t]he main aim of food and beverage [service] operations [is] to achieve customer satisfaction'. This aim must also be that of the event designer or planner and caterer.

Questions for research

1   Why is it important for the caterer to know if there are to be speeches in between meals at a sit-down dinner or buffet dinner for 500 people?
2   The meat supplier you chose for a wedding function has failed to deliver the correct amount of portioned meat for the main course. What would your immediate response be and what long-term action should you take?
3   Your kitchen workers are preparing a chicken stew for 800 people that is to be used for a buffet dinner in two days' time. Is this kind of pre-preparation acceptable? Are there any other factors that have to be observed by the workers?
4   A client would like to entertain 150 guests for dinner, but has a very limited budget. Which type of menu would you suggest and why?
5   You are the caterer at a function for rural municipality workers. There are 200 people attending this function. The only meat on the buffet menu is well-done topside of beef. How would you calculate your meat order to avoid running out of meat during the function or having too much left over?
6   In the finalising stages of a meeting for a function, your client mentions that he or she would like to have a cash bar as opposed to waiters freely serving alcoholic beverages, since the guests have to attend an important conference the following day. You happily accept since this could generate additional revenue. Would you encourage your waiters to offer speciality coffees such as Dom Pedro after the main meal?

Recommended websites

Browse the following internet sites for interesting and informative information (some discretion will be needed):

Affinitus Group – Affinitus is a leading provider of IT software to the catering industry: http://www.affinitus.co.uk/index.html

DeAngelo's, of Portland, Oregon, offers services to the convention, conferencing and catering industry: http://www.cateringbydeangelos.com/

Events Planners Australia is a large company that specialises in the organisation and full servicing of events throughout Australasia: http://www.eventplanners.com.au

Food and Celebrations is an Australian governmental website providing information regarding the links between good food and health: http://www.betterhealth.vic.gov.au/bhcv2/bhcarticles.nsf/pages/Food_and_celebrations

nfs Hospitality and Leisure IT solutions is a provider of fully featured IT property management solutions: http://www.nfs-hospitality.com/

Redcliffe Event Management is a 'one-stop shop' that offers a complete event management service to the client: http://www.redcliffe.com/event_management_services.asp?event_management.asp~mainFrame

Reserve Interactive is a multifaceted provider of software: http://www.reserveinteractive.com/event-management.php

The Aleit Group is a well-known South African full-service event management organisation: http://www.aleit.co.za/

The University of Nevada, Las Vegas, has a very well-regarded and active tourism and convention department, operating as the Harrah Hotel School: http://hotel.unlv.edu/departTour.html

Suggested reading

Craven, RE & Johnson Golabowksi, L. 2001. *The Complete Idiot's Guide to Meeting and Event Planning*. USA: Alpha Books (Penguin).

Ernst & Young, Caterwood, DW & Van Kirk, RL. 1992. *The Complete Guide to Special Event Management*. New York: John Wiley & Sons.

Fisher, WP (Ed). 2008. *Case Studies in Food Service Management: Business Perspectives*, 2 ed. East Lansing: Educational Institute of American Hotel and Lodging Association.

PART IV
Events and marketing

Photo: World Travel Market

Photo: IMEX

Photo: Dimitri Tassiopoulos

Photo: IMEX

Photo: IMEX

13

Events marketing and communication strategy

Rita Carmouche, Nimish Shukla and Angela Anthonisz

Abstract

Marketing plays a central role in identifying the needs of various event stakeholder types and for which plans for the events must be developed (or planned). Marketing tools are important for identifying potential markets, for assessing the competition and for selling and promoting events to potential event markets. Regardless of the type of event that is planned, if marketing tools and concepts are not used, the event risks failure. Event organisers cannot rely on tacit knowledge – gut feeling – or their own evaluations of what might have worked in the past. They need now to increasingly employ analytical situational assessment. In the increasingly competitive world of events, systematic market research, well-constructed marketing plans and a sound knowledge of promotion and communications strategies are crucial for developing events that have a competitive edge and that ultimately are sustainable and successful.

Chapter objectives

After you have read this chapter you should be able to:
- ❏ define events marketing;
- ❏ identify approaches to market research and list the principles of marketing research for events;
- ❏ illustrate the value of a SWOT analysis;
- ❏ illustrate the six Ps of events marketing;
- ❏ identify the five Ws of events marketing
- ❏ appreciate the role of public relations in events marketing;
- ❏ devise a marketing plan for an event;
- ❏ devise a promotional plan for an event;
- ❏ explore the use of electronic marketing in event promotion;
- ❏ employ the full communications mix to effectively promote the event, and establish and maintain relationships;
- ❏ identify ethical considerations in marketing; and
- ❏ identify approaches to measuring the effectiveness of events marketing.

13.1 Introduction

Events marketers need to consider how the event's goals and objectives will be achieved in relation to attracting attendees to it. Events are designed and planned for people, and they have to be sold and communicated to the intended target audiences. Although events are diverse in their objectives, type, size and scale, they all need a means of informing, persuading and attracting potential markets. More and more, events are being used to increase the sale of goods and services and to promote good causes, and generally as an important marketing communications tool. One of the reasons for the growth of events is that they allow face-to-face communication with an organisation's target market (Goldblatt, 2008). Marketing is a key function within all types of event, and it runs in parallel with the event cycle (Getz, 1997). Within the planning process of the event, marketing plans need to be developed to cover all aspects of the event, from pre-event research through to measuring the

effectiveness of the marketing tools and communication channels. This chapter will cover the key role of marketing and communication strategies through the stages of the event.

13.2 Events marketing defined

Event marketing is the function of event management that can keep in touch with the event's participants and visitors (consumers), read their needs and motivations, develop products that meet these needs, and build a communication programme which expresses the event's purpose and objectives.

Hall, 1992, as quoted by Watt (1998: 61)

Events marketing is always undertaken in the context of fulfilling the event's mandate and goals, whether they are for public service or profit. The more comprehensive the goals, the more challenging the marketing of events become.

13.3 Conducting market research for events

The starting point for the event marketer is to develop a marketing strategy for the event. A strategy is a plan of action aimed at achieving a particular outcome (Stokes, 2008). The marketing strategy will include the aims and objectives for the event and the budget, and will then lead to the development of a marketing plan, which should set a range of quantifiable objectives for marketing and communicating the event to the intended market(s). In order to develop an effective marketing strategy for the event, the event marketer must first of all undertake market research.

Conducting market research prior to the event is important to its success. The best-quality event can be developed by events organisers but if it does not meet the needs and wants of the intended market, it will not succeed. A useful starting point in the market research process is to use Hoyle's (2002) approach. As an event marketer there are a number of factors that need to be identified as part of the event screening process. These are referred to by Hoyle (2002) as the five Ws (Why? What? Who? Where? When?):

❏ *Why and what?* (These have been combined as they overlap.) Why is the event being held? What is the purpose of the event? Events are held for a range of purposes, which include entertainment, education and training, launching and promoting products and services, to benefit good causes, for fundraising, as incentives, etc. Goldblatt (2008) notes that events may combine more than one objective and that holding an event can satisfy a range of objectives.

Questions the event marketer may want to ask include:

- What are the event's objectives?
- What is the event designed to achieve?
- How will the event's objectives impact on how it is marketed?

❏ *Who is the event for?* Different events may attract different target audiences depending upon their size, scope and purpose. For example, the Olympic Games are aimed at a global audience, which consists of spectators at the event, athletes and the television audience. A national convention may be aimed at the entire membership, past and potential exhibitors, past and future potential sponsors, and related organisations. A rewards or incentive event would be aimed at internal members of the organisation.

❏ *Where?* Decisions must be taken as to where to hold an event. This relates to location and venue type. The location for a business event may be decided by the client in relation to access for company personnel and key speakers, while in the case of a sporting event, the availability of the facilities may be the main factor in the decision. The choice of venue can be used to reflect the event theme and purpose, and this can be reflected in the marketing and communications strategy.

❏ *When?* It is also important for the event marketer to consider the timing of the event in relation to any activities which may be competing for the same target market. This would require the marketing team to think through the use of the marketing mix. As part of the planning process of the event, the marketing team needs to consider the timing of the promotional activities prior to the event, for example when to schedule the advertising and press release(s); when to make tickets available; where to offer ticket promotions; and when to schedule PR and post-event activities. All of these factors should be considered as part of the events marketing plan.

13.4 Market research techniques for events

Once the type of event to be held has been decided upon – for example an exhibition or a conference – the next step is to conduct market research to assess the potential demand for the event. There are many ways of conducting market research. Ideally, this should be done with the intended target market. There are many sources of information that can be of value to event marketers in the context of market research. For example, the organisation may have held this event previously and the market research may be able to draw upon previous data in relation to sales, visitor numbers, demographics and consumer mix.

No event should proceed without first conducting market research, as this can help to reduce uncertainty and therefore the risk of failure. The extent of the market research required will be determined by the complexity of the event. As far as the marketing plan is concerned, the purpose of market research is to identify quantifiable goals for the events marketing programme (Goldblatt, 2008).

Market research is a complex area; however, when it is conducted well it can be invaluable to event marketers (Proctor, 2005). Undertaking market research in the planning stages of the event can help to determine the demand or potential level of interest in the event; the individuals or groups that might be potential markets; how much they may be willing to pay to attend the event; the channels of communication that the marketer should use to reach the potential market; and much more.

As part of the market research for the event, market research should be undertaken in the following areas:

❏ **Market segmentation:** Market segmentation involves the event marketer identifying groups or individuals, i.e. the target market/s, who have similar demand patterns and interests in attending a particular event.

❏ **Trends and demographics:** Essentially, demographics are concerned with the study of population trends, and include age, gender and family composition. The event marketer can use demographics to identify the potential market for different types of event.

❏ **Identification and evaluation of the competition:** Market research can assist the event marketer to identify other events which may be competing for the same target market. Competition analysis can allow the event marketer to develop a unique proposition for the event to differentiate it from the competition.

❏ **Opportunities to identify new markets for the event:** Market research can reveal the opportunity to identify new previously untapped markets; for example individuals interested in a new product or the inclusion in the event of facilities for families.

❏ **Demand for the event:** This relates to the potential number of people who might be interested in the event and in the case of commercial events, their ability to pay to attend. Demand may be linked to the prevailing economic conditions and the proposed pricing strategy relative to similar types of event being held at the same time.

13.5 Market segmentation: how to identify target markets for events

When the decision has been taken on the type of event that will be held, the next stage is to identify the target market. Different types of event will appeal to different individuals and groups. Some events may be designed to appeal to specialist interest groups such as the medical profession, while others such as the carnival in Rio de Janeiro may attract a wide range of groups, including international tourists. The task for the event marketer is to identify which events will appeal to particular groups, or who the target market/s will be. Event markers use market segmentation to assist with identifying target markets. In general terms, the approaches in table 13.1 are commonly used as a starting point.

13.6 Assessing the internal environment – situational analysis

A SWOT analysis is normally used by a company to identify its strengths and weaknesses, and to respond to threats and opportunities in the external environment. An example of a SWOT analysis and the types of issue that may be identified using it are shown in table 13.2. SWOT analysis can also highlight opportunities and threats which the company faces in its external environment. Conducting a SWOT analysis in relation to the events marketing plan can allow managers to

Table 13.1 Approaches to segmenting the market for events

Segment	Type	Value
Geographical	Identifies consumers on the basis of residence: local, regional and/or international markets	Identifies the catchment area of the market. Includes time and distance the event attendees might travel. Useful for promotion and distribution
Socio-economic	Identifies consumer income and often social composition of markets	Helps to decide pricing strategy of the event, although delegates may not pay themselves for business events
Demographics	Identifies size, type and structure of the market, including age composition, types of household, families, males and females	Different events may have different combinations of demographics – helps with targeting markets
Family life-cycle stage	Individuals go through different stages in their life cycle. Markets include, for example, the youth, singles, couples, families with young children, families with teenagers, childless households	It is useful to understand the types of event that may appeal to individuals in different stages of their life cycle, which is important for promotion and targeting
Psychographics	Individuals have different values, attitudes, beliefs and lifestyles which can influence buying decisions	This is useful for developing niche markets for events, for example the growth of green consumers. Cause-related events may appeal to particular groups

Source: Adapted from Evans, Jamal & Foxhall (2009)

Table 13.2 A SWOT analysis for an event company

	Positive factors	Negative factors
Internal factors	STRENGTHS ❏ Technological skills ❏ Strength of brand (s) ❏ Distribution Channels ❏ Customer loyalty/relationship ❏ Service quality ❏ Economies of scale ❏ Management capabilities ❏ Strength of leadership	WEAKNESSES ❏ Lack of skills ❏ Weak brand image ❏ Poor channels of distribution ❏ Little customer loyalty ❏ Poor service quality ❏ No economies of scale ❏ Management capabilities ❏ Strength of leadership
External factors	OPPORTUNITIES ❏ Changing consumer tastes ❏ New market opportunities ❏ New technology ❏ Changes in government legislation ❏ Changes in demographics ❏ Changes in taxation levels ❏ New distribution channels	THREATS ❏ Changing consumer tastes ❏ Reduced market opportunities ❏ New technology ❏ Changes in government legislation ❏ Changes in demographics ❏ Changes in taxation levels ❏ New distribution channels

Source: Adapted from Johnson, Scholes & Wittington (2008)

effectively allocate resources and convert threats into opportunities.

Having conducted a marketing audit of the external and internal environments, the event marketer can then progress to address more specific considerations such as market segmentation and the marketing mix for the event.

13.7 Preparing and managing the event marketing plan

It is difficult to sell an event without a marketing plan, and all events, regardless of their size and scale, need one. The marketing plan should be closely linked to the event cycle in order to identify the types of marketing activity which will be required at each stage of the event (Shone & Parry, 2004), and it should be continually reviewed in the light of the event's objectives.

Part of the marketing plan is the marketing schedule. The purpose of the marketing schedule is as follows:

❏ It allows the event marketer to know what has to be done and when;
❏ Lead times for preparing marketing materials can be identified;
❏ It assists with identifying promotion and communication opportunities;
❏ Brand awareness opportunities can be maximised;
❏ Promotional materials can be targeted depending on sales volume; and
❏ Marketing effectiveness can be compared against the plan.

Figure 13.1 contains the marketing plan for a leisure event and indicates the types of promotion which are used at different stages of the event schedule, including the lead times. Managing and monitoring the marketing plan is a key function of the event marketer. The marketing plan will also include the budget for marketing and

The Home & Garden Show 2008 marketing plan	
Date	
12 months	Print: Exhibitors' packs
11 months	Print: Flyers
10 months	
9 months	
8 months	Print: Exhibition stand
7 months	Events: Great Days Out – group bookers' exhibition
6 months	Print: Updated flyer National press: Monthly ads commence in *Concept for Living* magazine
5 months	Print: Pop-up banners Local/regional press: City council Christmas campaign – *What's On* magazine
4 months	Print: Flyer for branded ticket outlets Local/regional press: Royal Agricultural Society of England newsletter ticket promotion
3 months	Print: Posters Direct mail: Grosvenor Garden Centre *Seasons* magazine
2 months	Print: Tickets Street presence: Banner city centre Local/regional press: *Chronicle* ad campaign and editorial; Chester Food and Drink Festival brochure ad, 10 000; two months' ads in *Chester Welcome Guide* National press: *Concept for Living* subscribers' ticket offer Direct mail: Arighi Bianchi mailer – 17 000 Events: Retirement show – Manchester; Chester Food and Drink Festival Branded ticket outlets: MasterCard ticket offer
6 weeks	National press: BBC *Good Homes* editorial and competition
4 weeks	Street presence: Billboards; taxi doors × 4; bus street liners × 4 National press: *Design* magazine Web: Best of Chester – ticket offer; Charisma – ticket offer; Chester.com – ticket offer; wherecanwego.com – editorial Branded ticket outlets: Chester City Centre window competition
3 weeks	Local/regional press: *Echo* editorial; *Post* editorial
2 weeks	Street presence: Sheet poster sites × 6 Radio: Silk FM campaign; Manchester Sound campaign; Dee coverage Local/regional press: *Chester Standard* editorial; *Manchester Metro* editorial National press: *Mail on Sunday* feature Branded ticket outlets: Ticket offer for key Chester businesses/employers
1 week	Street presence: Corex boards; banners at venue Television: BBC coverage; Granada coverage
	National press: *OK* magazine feature

Figure13.1 Marketing plan for a leisure event (courtesy of White Events)

Source: http://www.whiteevents.co.uk

promoting the event, and decisions will have to be taken as to the most effective allocation of resources. Additionally, the plan must be monitored in relation to the objectives, and this could lead to changes being made in the response to changing circumstances. For example, discounts may need to be introduced to encourage ticket sales.

13.8 The six Ps of events marketing (marketing mix)

The marketing mix is a useful tool for the events marketing manager to use in making decisions about the event. Hoyle (2002) identifies the five Ps of events marketing as product, price, place, public relations (PR) and positioning. Promotion is also an important aspect of the marketing mix and therefore it is more appropriate to consider the marketing mix in terms of six Ps. The effective event manager will balance the six Ps to produce a good marketing mix.

13.8.1 Product

Events are increasingly operating in a highly competitive market, and it is important that the marketing and communication strategies are designed to make the event stand out from the crowd. To achieve this, marketing approaches require creativity and innovation (Goldblatt, 2008). In the context of events, the *product* is the end result – the event, tournament, exhibition, seminar or show. It also involves all the ancillary contributions like programmes, presentation, quality production and customer care. It may be an educational programme, a country fair, or a fully-fledged convention. It may be a reunion for a fraternal organisation or a corporate product launch. A key issue for the event

marketer is to identify the unique features of the event product. What makes this event different from others? Why should one choose to invest time and money in this event as opposed to the competition that surrounds it? The unique proposition must be emphasised in the marketing materials and communication strategy. This could include a popular headline band at a music festival, a government official opening a conference or an opportunity to try or see new products.

Additional features of the product may be the events history linked to a celebration or, alternatively, the opportunity to participate in a new, first-time event. Depending on the type of event, these aspects can be used in promoting its unique character.

13.8.2 Price

Establishing an appropriate pricing strategy for the event is important to ensure its success (Shone & Parry, 2004). The first point to make in this regard is that not all events are designed to be profit orientated. This means that the event marketer must understand the event's objectives and the goals and financial philosophy of the organisation. Some events are designed to make money, pure and simple. Others are strategically developed to break even financially. And there are some that are positioned as 'loss leaders' – expected to lose money in an effort to gain greater assets elsewhere, such as membership development or community goodwill (Shukla & Nuntsu, 2005). Corporate meetings are typically expensed not as profit centres but rather as 'costs of doing business' in order to build employee loyalty and pride, and to learn how better to sell products and services. Product launches do not expect to be profit making. Expenditure on marketing is undertaken in anticipation of future sales (Hoyle, 2002).

The event marketer must clearly understand the financial mission of the organisation, and design a financial strategy appropriate to the events goals.

Price must reflect the total costs of goods and services, including the cost of marketing itself. Marketing is often relegated to a secondary role in event production because the costs of printing, postage, advertising, public relations and other basic marketing expenses may not be considered part of the event budget. Instead, marketing costs may be treated as part of the organisation's general overhead and operating expenses. The marketing will be considered an integral part of event production when that event's budget provides for marketing as a primary event function and income–expense centre (Shukla & Nuntsu, 2005).

Where the event is designed to generate a profit via sales, key questions need to be considered and these include identifying the demand for the event; assessing the demographics of the target audience, which includes their ability to pay; identifying competitors' pricing strategies; and positioning the product appropriately in order to reflect the added value that may be gained from attending the event.

13.8.3 Place/location of the event

The location of an event can dictate not just the attendance, but the character and personality of the event as well. This is a consideration for the earliest part of the planning stage. Depending on the type of event, it can be useful to work with the local tourist authorities to promote the event in conjunction with tourist promotions to the area. The event venue can also be used as a key feature of the promotion. Conferences, for example, may be held on cruise ships or at unusual venues, and this can help to establish a unique feature for the event. The decision to choose a location is based on more than the appearance of the facility. Selection must be made with the audience and its profile in mind. Hoyle (2002) provides a useful list of logistical elements that are important in marketing place, for example ease of access for visitors.

13.8.4 Place of distribution

The issue of place also encompasses the channels of distribution that the marketing manager selects as a means of allowing the consumer to gain information or purchase tickets for the event. Place is generally used to describe those distribution channels the event uses to make its product available and accessible to prospective customers (Davidson & Rogers, 2006). The most common approaches for distribution within a ticketed-event context include those directly to the consumer via an intermediary such as a ticketing agent; via technology such as telephone or the internet; or face-to-face at a box office or retail outlet. With the growth of live events as a means of marketing communication, channels of distribution can also include trade shows, exhibitions and product launches.

13.8.5 Public relations (PR)

The marketing plan should also include how the PR for the event will be managed.

The public handling and public image of the organising group are pivotal components of a project's success. PR policy effectively combines all the relevant issues like advertising, image, logo and media relations, with the foremost factors of customer relations and customer care (Shukla & Nuntsu, 2005). Managing PR for an event requires careful analysis of the project's purpose, audiences and benefits, and the media available to deliver the appropriate message (Hoyle, 2002).

Skinner, Von Essen and Mesham (2001), as quoted in Shukla and Nuntsu (2005), argue that PR helps an organisation and its public adapt mutually to each other. It is an organisation's efforts to win the cooperation of groups of people. Thus, whatever individuals and organisations may think, their image is in the marketplace and the public's perception of them is all important, whether based on fact or fiction. PR has a key role to play in developing understanding and support for a particular event.

Clearly, PR is a major part of the marketing mix. The PR exercise may be as bold as a team of press agents distributing releases to newspapers or staging press conferences to extol the virtues of the event, or it may be as subtle as a trade publication interview with a leader of the organisation, when the interview includes references to the event and its benefits (Shukla & Nuntsu, 2005). One need not be a PR professional to practise effective PR. A media release, feature article or simply a phone call to the editor of a trade publication can result in invaluable publicity for the event. Getting a positive image is a high priority for many PR projects. By their very nature, events are often designed to achieve an increased awareness of the activity involved and to create a focal point for interest. Hoyle (2002) produces a useful list of PR requirements for events. Hoyle's text also includes a list of tools which can assist with PR, for example videos, familiarisation tours, press releases and news conferences.

13.8.6 Positioning the event

The event marketer must decide on a positioning strategy for the event. Positioning is the process of designing an image and value so that the consumer within the target segment understands what the company or brand stands for in relation to its competitors (Goldblatt, 2008). The marketing mix can be seen as the tactical details of the positioning strategy. In developing a positioning strategy the event marketer can consider the following:

❒ Positioning the event against the competition;

❒ Emphasising a unique benefit of the event; and

❒ Affiliating the event with something the consumer knows and values.

Positioning also relates to the target market, and different events may be positioned to appeal to different groups. For example, festivals may be positioned to appeal to the community or to a specialist audience, such as an arts festival. An event may also involve co-branding where the event is linked to a well-known product or company. For example, the event marketing may include the name of the sponsoring organisation in order to create additional prestige.

13.9 Marketing communications

Marketing communications involves how the event will be promoted to the intended target market. Marketing communications consists of a range of marketing tools that the event marketer can blend together to promote the event and to develop a marketing communications campaign. The marketing communications mix should be integrated into a coherent whole and will normally include both traditional forms of communication such as advertising and public relations and e-marketing (Goldblatt, 2008; Masterman & Wood, 2006).

The *communications mix* consists of all the methods by which the event communicates with its various constituencies and markets, including advertising, cross-promotions, street promotions, stunts, sales promotions and PR (Hoyle, 2002). Sponsorship is also considered to be an arm of communications, from the sponsor's perspective (Shukla & Nuntsu, 2005). Promotion is a key part of the communications mix. Regardless of the nature of the event, its success will largely depend on promotion. Promotion is vital in creating awareness of the event, a desire to participate, and a feeling by the potential participant that the investment of time and money validate the benefits the event offers. This has several aspects: advertising, pamphlets, media relations, posters, publicity, logo, merchandising and displays (Watt, 1998). Getz (1997) states that although many managers use the term 'promotion', it is but one of several forms of communication. Hoyle (2002) maintains that the promotional campaign may include a wide range of marketing tools, or as few as one, depending on the event. A marketing strategy must include the communications tasks necessary to influence the consumer-buying process: informing, educating, persuading, reminding. PR has the added function of fostering community support and sponsorships, but that too is part of ensuring demand for the event (Shukla & Nuntsu, 2005).

13.9.1 Sales promotions

A sales promotion is a non-recurrent action intended to generate sales or increase attendance. A sales promotion seeks to add value to the decision to purchase or attend, and to convey a sense of excitement and urgency. It can also stimulate a first visit, encourage repeat visits, and generate positive word-of-mouth discussion. Sponsors can be found to create the promotions or participate in those invented by the event marketer.

Getz (1997: 310)

Events have to be sold to the potential market and this involves ensuring that the sales team is trained and briefed about the event.

Another aspect to selling takes place at and around the event: merchandising, souvenir sales, franchising and trading. These are the direct financial sales which can make measurable sums of money and contribute massively to event income. For some of the bigger events, franchising (selling all or part of the sales rights for a fee or percentage) is the most convenient way to produce sales returns without significant work by the organising committee. It is not likely to yield the highest possible return, except in events like the Olympic Games. The franchisee gets a share of the profit, partly at the expense of the event organisers (Watt, 1998).

Most often franchised are catering and souvenirs. It may be more appropriate for the organisers to merchandise the goods themselves, realising all possible profits by undertaking all sales. Event souvenirs and other related sales can be lucrative for any event (Shukla & Nuntsu, 2005). They must be carefully considered because the choice of the wrong logo, image or souvenirs can cause a severe financial loss.

At all levels, these sales are absolutely vital to financial viability and must be carefully deliberated. Rash decisions can be permanently regretted. It will take courage to venture perhaps limited money on buying goods to resell, but the profits are often a financial lifeline (Shukla & Nuntsu, 2005). These sales can also help to convey an event image for present and future events. A good range of souvenirs will certainly be appreciated; they will remind visitors of an enjoyable experience and encourage them to return (Shukla & Nuntsu, 2005). They can also be an important source of revenue for the event.

13.9.2 Media relations and publicity

Media relations and publicity should be given a lot of attention. A well-planned publicity campaign should run alongside any advertising campaign. Ideally this drive should be spread over a period of months, building up to a peak shortly before the event. Early warning allows potential participants and spectators to diarise the event, and prevents potential clashes with rival attractions. Some publicity will have to be paid for, but there are ways of obtaining a good deal for little or no cost (Watt, 1998).

There are some well-developed approaches to gaining media attention and publicity, which include holding press conferences and providing photo opportunities. Regular communication with journalists, especially those who specialise in the area of interest of the event, can also be used to gain media attention (Watt, 1998).

13.9.3 Event advertising

A successful advertising campaign (Watt, 1998):
☐ promotes awareness of the event;
☐ passes on knowledge of relevant details;

☐ encourages the desire to participate in or attend the event;
☐ promotes the conviction that the event is worthwhile;
☐ aims to establish attendance patterns in the long term for future events;
☐ encourages the decision that turns the interest into attendance or participation;
☐ promotes the event image and logo; and
☐ should be positive and interesting to attract attention.

How does one decide on the right advertising instrument for the event? Firstly, identify the audience you wish to attract, then investigate the demographics reached by the advertising media you wish to consider. For example, marketing executives for larger events may consider broadcast media, which may reach a regional or even a national or international audience. More localised events will likely be promoted through community newspapers, local flyers or brochures and posters, and co-promotion with supporting groups and facilities (Shukla & Nuntsu, 2005).

Advertising approaches should be tested in advance for effectiveness. Many professionals use a 'split approach', mailing a limited number of advertising pieces featuring different colours, design and paper weight to two control groups and then evaluating the response. Focus groups are also an effective way to judge messages, design and positive acceptance (Shukla & Nuntsu, 2005).

13.9.4 Electronic marketing and internet promotions for events

There are many excellent sources available that cover the technical aspects of designing websites. This section will focus on the

Table 13.3 Advantages and disadvantages of different types of marketing materials

Type	Advantages	Disadvantages
Television advertising	Can reach a wide audience	Expensive Consumers can avoid it via new digital media
Radio	Can be used to target niche markets by targeting specialist programmes	Expensive
Flyers/posters	Cheap and easy to distribute	Paper adds to environmental damage Billboards can be intrusive on the environment
Press articles	Low cost and can be targeted at appropriate media	Depending on publication, they may not reach a new audience
Brochures	Can establish a good image for the event	Expensive and may not be read by the intended market
Association directories	Target the key market	Compete with other event advertising in the directory
Specialist advertising – can include a wide range of event merchandising such as key rings, tote bags, cups, hats, etc.	Increases awareness/interest the event Serves as a memento of the event	Fake and counterfeit goods can be produced
Stunts	Attract attention and may allow the event to gain extra media coverage	Must be appropriate to the event objectives or could damage the image/cause of the event
Internet	Can reach a wide audience	Increased traffic does not always lead to increased sales

Source: Adapted from Hoyle (2002)

value of electronic marketing for events. The internet has quickly become known as the fourth medium of advertising, next to radio and TV broadcasting and print media. Note that although the online community is large, the reach of the internet is far less than TV, radio and other advertising media. This means that although the internet has a wide reach it may not be accessible in all parts of the world (Shukla & Nuntsu, 2005). Despite this, there can be no doubt of the importance of the internet within the context of events marketing. Indeed, Goldblatt (2008) has argued that the internet must now be considered as a central part of any events marketing strategy. Because of the dynamics of the internet as an ever-changing and growing medium, there are a variety of reasons for its use as the ideal marketing tool.

The internet can reach millions of people, while also being used to target marketing at a smaller group of individuals. The 24/7 availability is appealing, and there are few geographic boundaries. Traditional marketing is often more expensive than online marketing, which makes using the internet more cost effective. In addition, receiving instant results is very appealing (Stokes, 2008). This not only allows immediate statistics, bur also allows marketers to review and adjust their campaign on a timely basis (Goldblatt, 2008).

Advantages of web marketing

Unlike traditional marketing, electronic marketing deals with 'real time'. Customers experience the most up-to-date information. By keeping the event website up to date, customers may revisit it over and over again. Following are the advantages of web marketing (Goldblatt, 2008):

- ❐ **Brand building** establishes an instantly recognisable brand by raising awareness of the event site;
- ❐ **Direct marketing** eliminates the costs associated with printing and mailing. The web gives the event marketer the ability to constantly make appropriate changes to target the audience, and allows individualised messages to reach specialised audiences;
- ❐ **Online sales** allow immediate order processing in an interactive environment;
- ❐ **Customer support** gives the public easy access to frequently asked questions;
- ❐ **Marketing research** provides valuable information about consumers – event marketers can use demographics to tailor the site;
- ❐ **Content publishing services** make information on the organisation available to a wider internet audience;
- ❐ **Online bookings and payments** take care of many of the event functions;
- ❐ **Shopping for products** gives information about event suppliers and services;
- ❐ **Access to competitors' websites** makes it easy to identify competition;
- ❐ **The opportunity to target niche markets** is facilitated through the many websites

dedicated to special interest groups, for example in sport, and events may be marketed on these sites.

The use of electronic marketing for events

The value of the internet in promoting events cannot be underestimated. At the same time the event marketer must consider the value of the internet in the communication mix. All forms of electronic marketing should be evaluated to ensure that they are appropriate to fulfilling the events aims and objectives. Some of the issues to consider when using electronic marketing are listed in table 13.4.

13.9.5 Preparing marketing materials

Having considered the advantages and disadvantages of using the various marketing tools to promote the event to the intended target market/s, the marketing and communication materials must now be prepared. Events require a range of visual materials and, as previously stated, marketers have a wide range of marketing tools at their disposal in order to communicate with the potential market (Goldblatt, 2008). The types of promotional materials that are selected will depend on a variety of factors such as the purpose of the event, the available budget, the reach of these materials and the target market. Different marketing materials may be used at different stages of the event. For example, advertising may be used to arouse awareness of a concert in the pre-event period, while offers and discounts may be introduced to increase sales during a festival.

Regardless of the types of marketing tools that are used, the event marketer must

Table 13.4 Electronic marketing tools

Tools	Advantages	Issues
Banner ads include space sold on websites for use by other people. Can be placed on associations', affiliates' and sponsors' websites	Can be used to direct traffic to the event website	Content must be relevant and be able to attract attention of intended markets. Banner ads should open within the host web page to encourage traffic to read them. Marketers can pay for ad-words, e.g. Google©, which will help optimise the search for the web page
Electronic newsletters	Allow potential targets to sign up to receive promotions. These can also be syndicated to reach a wider audience	It is important to allow receivers the option to opt out of these as this avoids unwanted communications
Online advertising	Can be used to increase awareness and sales	Can purchase words that a user may search on, but there is no guarantee that target markets will be reached
Search engines	Can gain traffic to your site. Events should be promoted to popular search engines such as Google©, Yahoo© and AOL©	Can be expensive to purchase top positions
Hyperlink	A programme insert that allows links to the event site to be linked to other sites, and vice versa. Can be linked to affiliate sites, association sites and tourist authority sites for international events. Can be used to create email	Needs to be linked to the appropriate sites to bring traffic to the event site
Email	Cheap and personal, and can be targeted directly to intended market. Messages can be customised and followed up. Online surveys can be attached to email. Events marketers can tell if email has been read – unlike direct mail	Can be intrusive and access prevented by spam filter
Social networking sites	Entire social networks are on line, e.g. Twitter©, Facebook© and MySpace™. These sites can be targeted for promotions. Viral marketing (in which messages are spread via social networking sites) can be used to promote events	The cost of the internet may be prohibitive in developing countries. Access links may also be difficult Viral marketing can be damaging to an event as the organisers have no control over the content of such message utilities

Tools	Advantages	Issues
Blogs, wikis and podcasts	These originate with consumers and are referred to as consumer-generated content. Podcasts can be event-driven content created from event to person. Event marketers can create blogs, for instance, to promote their event. For example, many music festivals allow consumer-generated content. This can increase interest in the event	Event companies have little control over the content of consumer-generated content and this could potentially damage the image of the event
Mobile phone marketing	Can be used to promote events. Text messaging as a form of marketing communication is widely used. Mobile phone marketing is personal – people usually carry their mobile, and mobiles include a payment system	Sending messages to mobile phones can be intrusive and invade individuals' privacy. This may result in a negative response to the event

Sources: Adapted from Stokes (2008); Goldblatt (2008)

choose the marketing materials that will be most effective for communicating with the target market. Secondly, we must bear in mind that consumers also use multiple channels to find out about events and this can include word of mouth (Smith, 2008). Consumers may also use different types of information for different components of the event, for example hotels and transport. This point strengthens the need for market research of the target markets. Gitelson and Kerstettel (2000), as quoted in Smith (2008), in their study of search behaviour for the Taste of the Valley Festival in western Australia, found significant differences in the search behaviour of attendees based upon age and place of residence.

In preparing the marketing materials the following general factors are important to consider (Goldblatt, 2008):

❏ The company/client's message should be reflected within the materials that are produced;

❏ The event theme should consistently recur in marketing materials;

❏ The company's brand should be presented consistently on all of the marketing materials, including staff uniforms, badges, tent cards and giveaways. The brand must be used throughout the event cycle;

❏ Competitions can be used to stimulate interest and attendance; and

❏ Creativity and innovation should be used to attract attention in a crowded marketplace.

13.10 Event merchandising

An important part of promoting and communicating the event to the public is to develop merchandising for the event.

Event merchandising can play an important part in marketing an event. Different types of merchandise can help to promote the event, and merchandising can be an important source of revenue. Decisions on the type and costs of merchandise have to be taken at the planning stage. (Shukla & Nuntsu, 2005)

13.10.1 Logo

An appropriate logo can be a crucial part of any image. It is important to give it careful thought and to consult relevant agencies and authorities before finalising the design. Its impact on merchandising and souvenirs can have a sizeable effect on income (Shukla & Nuntsu, 2005). For larger events this can be a goldmine, but smaller events should be wary of buying in too much stock of items they may not sell. A good logo should reflect the event; portray an event image; pass on what it is about; give relevant messages; be attractive and eye-catching; and be colourful (preferably) (Watt, 1998).

13.10.2 Mascot

Also related to image, any event of any size should have its own mascot, as long as it can afford one (Shukla & Nuntsu, 2005). A mascot can help to promote the event in various ways, especially with certain target groups (compare the mascots that were used for the Olympic Games and the All Africa Games). The mascot must be closely identified with the event; it should be appropriate, relevant and attractive; it should portray the project image; and it should be saleable (Watt, 1998).

13.10.3 Licensing and copyright

Mascots and logos produced by organisations are protected by copyright and may not be used without a licence and payment. Sponsoring organisations often pay large sums of money to use logos, for example the Olympic or the Soccer World Cup logo. Merchandise (cups, stickers, T-shirts, etc.) can be copied, and fake or counterfeit goods may be produced. These can be inferior to the original and therefore damaging to the event image. Furthermore, they lead to a loss of revenue for the event. It is not always possible to take action against this; however, the event marketer may have access to legislation to discourage counterfeit goods.

13.11 Experiential marketing

This approach may be seen as an alternative to electronic marketing. Experiential marketing is now gaining popularity within events marketing and it is closely linked to the use of live events in marketing communications. Many authors believe that allowing consumers to experience the product is the most effective way of marketing (Schmitt, 1999). Within the context of the event industry, many companies are using live face-to-face interaction with consumers in order to promote and sell brands. Furthermore, experiential marketing and live events are replacing print media in many organisations as this is considered to be a more effective way of engaging consumers (EventView, 2008). Experiential marketing is likely to increase within the events sector, and this approach is very appropriate for particular types of event.

13.12 Evaluating the success of events marketing and measuring return on marketing investment

Measuring the effectiveness of the marketing strategy for the event is a key function for the event marketer. What has been the return from the marketing efforts and how has the marketing function performed in relation to meeting the events objectives? These are key considerations for the evaluation of the events marketing. There are many approaches to measuring the return on marketing investment (ROMI) and many tools and instruments have been developed for this purpose. The event marketer can use a range of both *quantitative* and *qualitative* indicators in order to determine the ROMI for the event. Good event evaluation will usually include both of these indicators. The approaches that will be used to measure the ROMI should have been included in the events marketing plan. As discussed previously, good events marketing plans set quantifiable objectives.

To measure the ROMI of the event, according to Goldblatt (2008), each of the marketing tools used in the event must be monitored and tracked. The event marketer will have put in place systems to achieve this. In terms of measuring the effectiveness of the marketing efforts, quantifiable indicators usually include aspects of the event which can be measured statistically, for example:

❑ the effectiveness of the promotions in increasing visitor numbers (this can be compared with the previous year where appropriate);
❑ the number of ticket sales generated by the ticketing agency (where appropriate);
❑ the value of the sales of event merchandising in relation to costs;
❑ the amount spent on advertising per head of visitors;
❑ the value of discounts for early booking in increasing bookings;
❑ the number of sales leads generated from online advertising;
❑ the cost per click of online advertising (divide the number of clicks by the cost of the advertising);
❑ the number of hits received from search engines (note that this will not necessarily result in sales but it will indicate if this has increased traffic to your site);
❑ the number of column inches generated from press releases, articles, press conferences (PR companies offer clipping services for this purpose); and
❑ the value of the sales generated from the product launch in relation to costs (Goldblatt, 2008).

In addition to the quantitative or statistical measures, the event marketer may require an evaluation of the events marketing tools that are not easily quantified by generating statistical data, for example the perceptions of the value of the marketing tools by the event attendees, delegates, clients and other stakeholders. This will require the use of more qualitative approaches and these can include interviews or surveys of delegates or focus groups. The types of evaluation that are usually undertaken using qualitative indicators may include conducting surveys or interviews to assess the event goer or non-attendee's recall of the event advertising. The results of such a survey may assist the event marketer to determine the appropriateness of the advertising media and also the communication channels.

In the case of product launches, surveys may be conducted after the event in order to test the consumer's recall of brand name, slogan or tag line. The results of the survey can be used to assess brand awareness of the product or service after the event.

Interviews may be conducted with a sample of event attendees to gain their views on the pricing strategy and perceived value of the event. This information can be used to analyse the appropriateness of the event's positioning strategy.

In cause-related events, focus groups can be conducted with attendees and the public after the event to test recognition of the name of the charity or cause and the extent to which the event increased awareness of it.

Finally, exit surveys using questionnaires can be conducted among delegates or attendees in order to measure the consumer satisfaction levels with the event information mix.

By using a range of both qualitative and quantitative measures, the evaluation should enable the marketer to assess which of the marketing actions has been the most effective in terms of meeting the event objectives. This information can be transferred to other similar types of event, and can assist in developing future marketing strategies. It is often the case that event resources and marketing budgets are limited and therefore measuring the ROMI on marketing is crucial to demonstrate the value of marketing events. Sponsors and stakeholders will also require information related to the return on investment.

13.13 Social, ethical and environmental issues in events marketing

Marketing is an integrated communications-based process. Events management companies do not work in isolation from the rest of society. Instead they find that greater opportunity exists if the organisation is visibly accessible and involved with the public, which is especially important when staging public and community events. Events marketing tends to operate as the 'public face of the event' so when issues are raised by the public, marketing is often at the centre. The types of issue raised by the public in relation to events have included cultural commoditisation, noise levels, pollution, increased crime and vandalism, environmental damage from disposable promotions and carbon footprints. There is a growing perception among the public that marketing organisations are not just sellers of products (CSR Europe, 2009) but that they also have an inherent responsibility for their actions, including being more responsive to addressing environmental, economic and social concerns – the triple bottom line. Triple bottom line (TBL) responsibility of marketers is the key marketing activity that can ensure events are more sustainable.

Events marketing can contribute to environmental damage as part of the marketing function involves processing, packaging, advertising and distributing the event product. Sustainable marketing involves the event marketer developing strategies that reduce the economic, environmental and social impacts of the marketing campaign, and sourcing products and services that are sustainable. Sustainable marketing relates to all aspect of marketing practices and involves the event marketer assessing the impact of the marketing and communication mix on the environment, society and the economy, and taking steps to minimise it. Developing a sustainable marketing strategy is not a gimmick or an attempt to appease 'green' consumers. It must be seen as a part of the ethos of the event business and be implemented from the beginning stage of the marketing plan through to event evaluation. Within the UK context, the environmental concerns raised by the public have been addressed through the development of the BS8901 standard. Increasingly, those who organise and promote events are questioned by clients about their 'green' credentials. Similarly in Europe, organisations such as CRS Europe have produced guidelines for sustainable marketing practices (refer to http://www.csreurope.org for their useful toolkit for developing sustainable marketing practices).

There is a wide range of factors that event marketers should consider as part of developing a sustainable marketing strategy, and these environmental considerations should be applied at all stages of the event cycle. Some of these are as follows:

❐ That all of the marketing materials should be recyclable or replaceable, including packaging and paper-based materials;

❐ That promotional items and free gifts should be valued by the target market and not items that can be disposed of and thrown away. A key question may be for the event marketer to consider if the promotional item is really needed. Suppliers should be questioned on the sustainability of their products and recyclable alternatives sought;

❐ That paper should be sourced from sustainable forests. Increasingly in the conference market, the amount of paper is being reduced in favour of using more online communications;

❐ That the necessity of travel may be replaced by video conferencing and online forums within the context of business events, thereby reducing the environmental impact of travel; and

❐ That the environmental impact of the events marketing tools needs to be taken into consideration by event marketers. Posters, leaflets and advertising boards not only add to environmental pollution, but can also be intrusive on the environment (CRS Europe, 2009).

Spending money on large, lavish events can have a negative impact on brand image, especially during periods when attendees and communities may themselves be negatively affected by economic downturns. It is advisable for event marketers to also use events to invest in their local communities. For example, attendees participating in charity events for local communities might help to rebuild a playground or volunteer at an orphanage. Ultimately, events marketing should impact positively on societies, environments and economies.

Ethical sourcing of products and labour should also be considered as part of sustainable marketing. This includes sourcing Fair Trade goods that have been produced for a fair price for the producer. There are a number of general ethical issues that marketers need to consider in terms of ethical marketing of events (adapted from Percy & Elliot, 2009). Some examples of these are depicted in table 13.5.

13.14 Summary

Marketing and communications play a key role in assisting event organisers to meet their objectives for the event. By using a variety of marketing and communication tools, the event marketer can conduct market research to ensure that the event is appropriate to the intended market and that they develop appropriate promotional tools and can sell the event to the public. Using return on marketing investment measures, the event marketer can also demonstrate the value of investing in events marketing and communications strategies in order to reduce the risk of the event failing. Finally, adopting a sustainable marketing strategy will be crucial in ensuring long-term success.

Table 13.5 Some ethical issues related to the marketing mix within events

Issue	Example
Product Product information	Failing to disclose the risks associated with an event – the event does not deliver the event elements that were promised
Place/distribution Ticketing	Counterfeit tickets or the failure of tickets to arrive from a ticketing agent – the internet may have facilitated the distribution of counterfeit tickets
People Customer service	The use of volunteers in events management – this requires a commitment to training in order to avoid negative interactions between employees and customers
Promotion Advertising	Deceptive advertising – false claims made about events in relation to aspects like headline bands, celebrity presence at the event, etc. Failure to assess the impact of marketing tools on the environment, e.g. limited attention to recycling, environmental pollution caused by posters and flyers
Pricing Capacity	Providing (complementary) corporate hospitality – this can result in tickets being unused and event goers being unable to gain access

Source: Percy and Elliot (2009)

Questions for research

1 Discuss the value of market research for events.
2 Evaluate the types of marketing tool you would use to promote a music festival. Justify your choice.
3 Produce a marketing plan and schedule for an event of your choice.
4 Show how you would use market segmentation to identify the markets for a sports event.
5 Take the six Ps and consider them in relation to an actual event. Suggest how they affect the event you have chosen and how they would be 'mixed' by the skilled organiser to ensure a quality event.
6 Give a brief summary of public relations and communications tools for events.
7 Discuss the advantages and disadvantages of electronic marketing. Identify how you would use electronic marketing to launch a new product brand.
8 Evaluate the approaches used to measure ROMI in events.
9 Discuss the ethical factors to consider when developing a marketing strategy for a special event.

Recommended websites

Browse the following internet sites for interesting and informative information:

CEMA – Corporate Events marketing Association – premier community for technology events marketing promotions: http://www.cemaonline.com
CSR Europe. 2009. The European business network for CSR: http://www.csreurope.org.

DMA – Destination Marketing Association – the world's largest association of destination marketing associations: http://www.destinationmarketing.org

eMarketing Association – the world's largest association for internet marketing: http://www.emarketingassociation.com

EMI – a global authority on the role of live events in business: http://www.eventmarketing.com

ICEEM – the international Centre for Exhibition and Events marketing: http://www.iceem.net

Suggested reading

Goldblatt, J. 2008. *Special Events: The Roots of Celebration*, 5 ed. New Jersey: John Wiley & Sons.

Masterman, G & Wood, E. 2006. *Innovative Marketing Communications: Strategies for the Events Industry.* Oxford: Butterworth Heinemann.

Meerman Scott, D. 2009. *The New Rules of Marketing and PR: How to Use Blogs, Podcasting, Viral Marketing and Online Media.* New Jersey: John Wiley & Sons Inc.

Stokes, R. 2008. *E-Marketing – Free Online Marketing Book*, 2 ed. Available from: http://www.quirk.biz/emarketingtextbook

Photo: EIBTM

Photo: Dimitri Tassiopoulos

Photo: World Travel Market

Photo: Dimitri Tassiopoulos

14

Events sponsorship and fundraising

Brendon Knott and Douglas Turco

Abstract

This chapter introduces the reader to the main concepts and issues relating to events sponsorship and fundraising for small and large scale events.

Chapter objectives

After you have read this chapter you should be able to:

☐ define sponsorship and distinguish it from fundraising;
☐ demonstrate an understanding of the favour and growth of the global events sponsorship sector;
☐ identify the main objectives of events sponsors;
☐ distinguish between different sponsorship levels and opportunities;
☐ demonstrate an understanding of events sponsorship activation and leverage;
☐ develop successful events sponsorship proposals;
☐ demonstrate an understanding of the rationale for evaluation of sponsorship as well as measurement techniques for evaluating sponsorship effectiveness; and
☐ critically discuss the challenges and opportunities facing the events sponsorship sector.

14.1 Introduction

The proliferation of events in today's society has led to the growing importance of events sponsorship internationally. Sponsorship forms the major component of the revenue stream for most new and continuing events. The sponsor-event relationship is regarded as 'symbiotic' or reciprocal, as corporations promote themselves through events while events are dependent on the revenue and services that they derive from the sponsors (see figure 14.1). Sponsorship is one of the fastest-growing forms of marketing activity, and has demonstrated an annual growth of approximately 10% for a number of years to the current level of about US$43 billion globally (Morris, 2008). However, despite this significant growth, global economic downturns can put pressure on companies to cut back on all forms of marketing, including sponsorship. When companies are battling to stay financially viable and to keep their employees, it is unlikely that many would be willing to take on the added financial burden of paying events, teams and athletes large sums of money or donating money to worthy causes. While this challenge is discussed later (see section 14.9), some industry analysts have suggested that even when all around has been doom and gloom, the sponsorship business has enjoyed the very opposite – a boom (Koenderman, 2009).

The largest global sponsorship markets are the Americas (42.5%); Europe (33.3%) and Asia (28%), while the individual countries contributing the largest amounts to the overall sponsorship spend are the US (33.3%), Japan (12.5%) and Germany

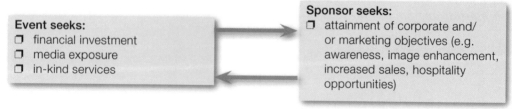

Event seeks:
☐ financial investment
☐ media exposure
☐ in-kind services

Sponsor seeks:
☐ attainment of corporate and/ or marketing objectives (e.g. awareness, image enhancement, increased sales, hospitality opportunities)

Figure 14.1 The reciprocal event–sponsor relationship
Source: Adapted from Allen et al. (2002: 225)

(9.4%) (SportBusiness International, 2001). Sponsorship is categorised as 'below-the-line' or 'non-traditional' advertising.

Across the globe, the top sponsoring industries are telecommunications, sports clothing, financial services, cars/automobile and soft drinks (Sports Marketing Surveys, 2005). Internationally, the top sponsored sports are soccer, American football, the Olympics, golf and motor sport (Sports Marketing Surveys, 2005). It is sometimes argued that there is little sponsor interest in developing or smaller-segment sports (Paul, 2002; Mlangeni, 1999). The bankruptcy and/or merger of some businesses in the automobile and financial services sectors have led to significant changes in events sponsorship for 2009. General Motors, for example, severed ties with Tiger Woods and dramatically reduced its sponsorships from collegiate basketball and automobile racing.

While these factors are generally true for all sponsorship types, growth patterns differ for each sponsorship sector. Sport has traditionally been the largest and most widely used sector. Although the figures will vary for each country, sport often accounts for as much as 80% of total sponsorship spend. The remaining 20% is made up of broadcast sponsorship (mainly sponsored television and other media programmes), arts and culture, and other smaller sectors such as education, the environment and wildlife (BMI Sport Info, 2004; Thwaites, 1994). Although the sport sector remains the most popular, other sectors such as music, theatre, dance, art, the environment and education are becoming increasingly popular sponsorship sectors (Duffy, 2003). Within each sector, there are different sponsorship types. Although figures vary by country, events sponsorship (46%) is the largest sponsorship type, followed by team

(27%), organisation (18%) and personality (9%) sponsorship, as illustrated in figure 14.2.

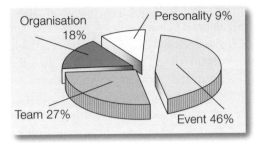

Figure 14.2 Share of sponsorship sector by sponsorship type

Source: Sports Marketing Surveys (2005: 13)

It is clear that events sponsorship has been growing in favour and use. The following section defines events sponsorship and distinguishes it from fundraising and donations.

14.2 Defining events sponsorship and fundraising

The changing views on the nature and use of events sponsorship have led to difficulty in developing a single, enduring definition. For the purpose of this text, events sponsorship can be defined as *an investment/provision of assistance, in cash or in kind, by an organisation (sponsor) to an activity or event (sponsee), for the purpose of achieving specified corporate or marketing objectives through exploiting the commercial potential associated with the event, to the mutual benefit of all parties involved.*

This definition clearly views sponsorship as a business transaction by the sponsor, who is seeking a quantifiable return on the initial investment, namely in the form of an exploitable commercial opportunity. The increased business focus of events sponsorship has led to an emphasis on return on investment (ROI). This emphasis is what distinguishes sponsorship from fundraising, charitable donations, or patronage/corporate philanthropy or grants, which do not have this focus. These are defined below:

- ❐ *Fundraising.* Mostly used by charitable organisations, fundraising involves the organised activity or an instance of soliciting money or pledges. Most often, events are used as fundraising tools, for example sponsored runs/swims/walks, raffles and car washes. Creative ideas are especially successful.

- ❐ *Charitable donations.* These are activities where corporations decide as a matter of policy or as part of a social responsibility programme to give certain funds to charitable causes, often in a set ratio to corporate profits. Publicity is rarely sought and neither is any form of return on investment. Where the contribution is deliberately publicised, the motivation is similar to that for sponsorship (ASOM, 1997).

- ❐ *Patronage/corporate philanthropy.* Sponsorship is often confused with patronage. However, it is the expectation of ROI that is the main distinguishing factor between the two. No commercial advantage or ROI is sought or expected for the support of a patron (Meenaghan, 1983).

- ❐ *Grants.* Often governments, charitable bodies, development agencies or lotteries provide access to financial grants (Shone & Parry, 2004). It usually requires a significant amount of research time to identify, apply and follow up on potential grants.

Sponsorship may include in-kind support as opposed to cash. Sponsors may be able to provide goods or services which are a large cost to the event in lieu of cash. For example, drink suppliers, and communication, transport and computer companies can often become major event sponsors without contributing anything in cash. Local authorities can prove useful sponsors by providing facilities, catering or organisational assistance free of charge.

These days, the business of events sponsorship is in most cases not charitable, and sponsors are looking for the best ROI for their money/in-kind support. Sponsorship can deliver measurable ROI for many events. It is possible to gauge the ROI of the sponsorship through, for example, the measurement of the effect on sales; through comparing the relative ROI of events sponsorship in terms of sales with other marketing mix elements (e.g. television, magazines, promotions); and through understanding the interactions between sponsorship activation (the advertising that promotes a brand's relationship with its target market to that of sponsorship) and other marketing investments. See section 14.8 for more measurement techniques.

However, it is not only the sponsor that benefits from the sponsorship, but also the sponsee, for, in the case of most major events, without the support of the sponsor, it is doubtful that the event would exist at all. The benefits of events sponsorship accrue to the sponsor and the sponsee, as well as to other parties, such as participants, spectators and the broader community. Having defined sponsorship, the following section now looks at reasons for the growth and favour of events sponsorship.

14.3 Reasons for the favour and growth of events sponsorship

There are several factors that may account for the significant increase in sponsorship activity over the last two decades:

- *The prohibitive and escalating cost of media advertising.* Sponsorship has been viewed as an attractive and cheaper alternative to conventional advertising for the purpose of capturing attention and creating awareness. However, increasing competition for sponsorship rights has also raised the costs of sponsorship and media coverage rights.
- *Public indifference to conventional forms of communication.* The conventional media forms have cluttered the marketing arena with messages, leading to a decreasing efficiency of these media. Sponsorship has the ability to cut through this clutter, providing opportunities for the sponsor to create a special relationship with consumers and potential customers. However, the increasing use of sponsorship leaves one questioning the prevalence of 'sponsorship clutter'. Sponsorship is viewed as a means to target today's increasingly sophisticated and media-sceptical consumers, avoiding the irritation factor of advertising bombardment (Erdogan & Kitchen, 1998). Sponsorship allows an organisation to deliver its message to a consumer who is relaxed and naturally receptive to viewing that sport event.
- *A global trend towards increasing leisure pursuits.* In many nations there has been an increased demand for leisure events, but public funding for such activities has often been reduced or limited. The increased demand for leisure events and activities cannot be catered for by public funds. The lack of available public funding creates a need for commercial sponsors. Today, most major events would not exist if it were not for commercial sponsorship.
- *Government policies on tobacco and alcohol advertising.* Restrictive government policies on tobacco and alcohol advertising in many nations forced such companies to seek alternative marketing media, with many investing heavily in sponsorship. However, government policies in many countries now also restrict or prohibit the use of sponsorship by tobacco and alcohol companies, although legislation varies between countries.
- *Greater media coverage of sponsored events.* The increased media coverage of events has attracted a larger audience, offering increased exposure for event sponsors. As such, media publicity backing is regarded as an essential part of the leveraging of events sponsorship. Technology innovations have also enabled the use of new media to transmit live coverage of events, such as the internet (audio and/or video streaming), satellite television and radio (satellite, cable or pay-to-view) and cellular telephones.
- *Sponsorship benefits from a uniquely positive image compared with other communications media.* Sponsorship has the ability to create a feeling of goodwill by delivering real benefits and offering a payback to the community. The event participant is more favourably disposed to anyone who has made the occasion possible or better. When the public is aware of the sponsorship, they tend to approve of it even if they do not benefit directly from it. The sponsor is seen to be taking a commitment on behalf of a cause outside of its own operations which is important to the community and 'earns' goodwill for doing so.
- *Events sponsorship offers access to a live audience.* An event sponsorship allows the sponsor to reach participants or spectators directly in an

environment in which they will be more open and receptive to marketing communication.

☐ *Sponsorship, through the event, crosses boundaries through the sharing of common values.* Events sponsorship has a substantive non-verbal component. Universal messages of delight, hope, pain or victory can transcend language and national boundaries. Sponsorship crosses all barriers of bureaucracy, national prejudice and languages in the same manner as the sponsored activity (ASOM, 1997). As a result, sponsorship can facilitate the building of trans- or multinational brands, a notoriously expensive and difficult process. Sponsorship can thus also be used as a catalyst for building corporate image and brand prominence on a global scale (Quester & Farrelly, 1998). For example, Coca-Cola justifies its sponsorship of football events, claiming that 'football is one of the few activities that truly transcend boundaries, such as culture, language and age. Enemies and rivals have recognised their commonalities through sport' (Becatti, 2006).

Noting the reasons for the favour and growth of sponsorship, the following section now focuses on the objectives of event sponsors.

14.4 Understanding the objectives of event sponsors

Event organisers need to remember that potential sponsors expect a return on their investment, i.e. they want to achieve specified corporate or marketing objectives. The event organisers should make every effort to assist sponsors to achieve their objectives. From the sponsor's perspective, a sponsorship is required to perform a multitude of tasks and contribute to a wide range of objectives at both corporate and brand level. Sponsorship offers sponsors the possibility of achieving several objectives in a single campaign. The following are some of the most common objectives of sponsors:

14.4.1 Awareness

Events provide an excellent platform to increase public awareness of the organisation and/or its services/products. Media coverage and exposure is one of the primary objectives for sponsorship use. Sponsorship is favoured as a low-cost-per-exposure medium. Certain types of media coverage may be valued more highly than others. Television and daily newspaper coverage is usually preferred to radio and the local press, but this depends on the intended target market.

> ### Case study 14.1 MTN Gladiators, South Africa
>
> Cellular telecommunications provider MTN's sponsorship of the 'Gladiator' television sports game show in South Africa achieved spontaneous awareness of its sponsorship that was measured at 55% of the national adult population. This made it one of the most recognised sponsorships in the country. The sponsorship generated R6.9 million through the use of MTN phone lines and the sale of ring tones. Illustrating the value of media exposure, the 'Gladiator' sports game show in South Africa generated television exposure for MTN valued at one and a half times the amount paid for the broadcast package.
>
> *Source: Duffy (2003)*

14.4.2 Image

For the event sponsor, image creation or enhancement often involves the desire to influence general society as well as specific groups among the organisation's many publics. The sponsorship may be used as a medium for community involvement. The mantle of 'good citizenship' is acquired by many companies who have involved themselves directly in improving the life of the community, either at local or national level. Sponsorship of this kind assumes much the same role as public relations, as seen in case study 14.2.

Case 14.2 HSBC Global Education Challenge

HSBC identified the Around Alone yacht race as a suitable sponsorship platform for its Global Education Challenge, a US$1 million investment in online education. HSBC hoped to communicate and raise awareness around its support for education, help raise funds for local education projects and provide a free, internet-based learning tool to supplement curriculum activities for children aged 9–12 years. The website received excellent feedback from teachers and pupils, with over 4 400 registered users of the education programmes from 30 countries. HSBC generated global interest and awareness of its education initiatives while also creating an interesting, fun and exciting learning environment for children.

Source: Duffy (2003)

Events sponsorship may be used to alter public perception of the sponsor. A sponsorship programme linked to a particular set of attributes can be used effectively to create a particular image, which can reinforce or change public perception of the company (Meenaghan, 1983). For example, car manufacturer Hyundai's association with the world's largest sporting event, the FIFA World Cup™ (which attracts an accumulative audience of over 35 billion people), alongside other truly global corporations like Coca-Cola and McDonald's, has allowed the company to create the impression that it is a mega-brand with a larger global reach than might actually be the case (Duffy, 2003).

The sponsorship of particular events or activities provides companies with opportunities for goodwill creation among influential individuals or groups in the business world (Meenaghan, 1983). Many companies use the high visibility gained through their sponsorship as a means of reassuring their shareholders and policyholders.

Sponsorship can also be used to deflect negative publicity by improving public confidence in the company through proving it a useful asset to the community (Meenaghan, 1983). For example, sporting goods company Nike embarked on a wide variety of sponsorship and corporate responsibility activities under the umbrella of 'NikeGO' in an effort to counter the negative publicity and subsequent damage to its reputation from the company's association with exploited young labourers in developing nations.

Sponsorship allows the organisation access to the specific target market attracted to the event, as well as the opportunity to identify with the lifestyle of this market. The sponsorship is used as a positioning statement, where the aim is to align the company with the lifestyle that followers of these events or activities are assumed to have (see case study 14.3). Red Bull sponsors high-adventure sports including freestyle skiing competitions and airplane races to reach a thrill-seeking, young adult market.

14.4.3 Employee relations and recruitment

A key benefit of sponsorship is its ability to assist employee relations as well as to influence the perception of potential recruits. This is often achieved by sponsoring activities and events with which the staff and potential recruits can identify. A sponsorship can encourage a sense of pride among staff in a company. The allocation of event tickets or access to corporate hospitality for staff can be used as staff motivation, or reward or recognition incentives. The Cone/Roper Corporate Citizenship Study showed that the majority of American employees expect their employers to play an active role in supporting social needs (Duffy, 2003). Such involvement has a positive impact on staff morale, with employees more likely to be proud of their company. The most effective employee-focused efforts are those that provide employees with opportunities to become actively involved in the sponsorship campaign. For example, the South African life insurance company, Metropolitan, involved their staff in competitions and performance rewards linked to its sponsorship of the South African Olympic Team in 2000. Prizes and performance incentives for staff included trips to attend the Olympic Games and the chance to win official Olympic merchandise.

14.4.4 Sales

Although it is often argued that sponsorship's impact on sales is more indirect and longer term, there has been a general shift in the sponsorship industry toward more direct and interactive, sales-led marketing motivations (SportBusiness International, 2001). Both existing and potential customers can be targeted. Every sponsorship campaign should contain opportunities to drive direct sales of products and services to the event spectators/participants themselves, either at the event venue or through other media. Direct and exclusive merchandising opportunities at the event may generate significant sales. Events also provide opportunities for product launches or product sampling. Sales promotions programmes are often linked to a sponsorship. The sponsorship can also be used as an opportunity to motivate and strengthen relationships with the distribution channel members.

14.4.5 Hospitality

Sponsorship of events may provide sponsors with opportunity for guest hospitality in an appropriately informal environment. These guests typically include opinion leaders and decision makers within the business environment, trade acquaintances, dealers, wholesalers and retailers. For example, J&B whisky uses corporate hospitality very successfully with its sponsorship of the J&B Met race day, one of South Africa's leading annual social events. The event has become J&B's biggest sponsorship worldwide. An invitation to the J&B VIP marquee, an exclusive hospitality offering, is much sought after and proves to be a valuable incentive for the J&B sales team to use in ensuring that relationships with the trade are strengthened (Duffy, 2003).

The most common objectives of sponsors are to obtain awareness, followed by image creation or reinforcement, although most sponsors are looking to achieve two or three primary objectives through their sponsorship opportunity (Hooper, 2003). Noting the varied sponsorship objectives, it is also important to know that there are distinctions as to the levels of sponsorship involvement and opportunities which will impact or regulate the activities of the sponsor and the effectiveness of the sponsorship. This is now discussed.

14.5 Sponsorship levels and opportunities

The purpose of this section is to illustrate that there exist different levels of sponsorship within an event. The following distinctions are agreed upon, although the exact names given to the opportunities would differ from event to event.

14.5.1 Primary/naming rights sponsor

A naming rights sponsor would pay for the right to include its corporate or brand name in the event title. This maximises the name exposure and links the company/brand with the event more substantially. Traditionally there has been a sole major sponsor along with other secondary sponsors. Today the trend is toward joint primary sponsorships, which may or may not include naming rights to the event. Many mega-events or events steeped in history, such as the Olympic Games or the FIFA World Cup, would not offer naming rights opportunities, but would still have primary sponsorship opportunities.

14.5.2 Secondary sponsors

The distinction between primary and secondary sponsors would be particular to each event, with specific right entitlements depending on the specific sponsorship contract for the event. Secondary sponsorship may include the rights of technical sponsors and/or official suppliers mentioned below. Sponsors in this level may also be referred to as 'presenting sponsors'.

14.5.3 Technical sponsors

A technical sponsor would be entitled to supply official equipment to be used in the event. For example, a watch manufacturer may buy the right to supply the timekeeping devices. This has the advantage of a credible link between the brand and the sport. This level of sponsorship is especially favoured for events which can act as a showcase for potential customers to see what the equipment can do.

14.5.4 Official suppliers

This type of sponsorship would be similar to the technical supplier, except that it would not supply equipment or other products linked directly with the event, but more generic products such as soft drinks. There may also be a number of other categories of sponsor unique to each event that fulfil a role similar to official suppliers. It is also common for events to include links with affiliated associations that assist with the production of the event, often referred to as 'event partners' or 'partner sponsors'.

14.5.5 Broadcast sponsors

As mentioned previously, sponsoring the broadcasting rights to particular events sometimes achieves higher levels of exposure than sponsoring the event itself (see case study 14.4). A distinction has developed in recent years between the event sponsor, who owns the rights to the event itself, and the broadcast sponsor, who owns the rights to the broadcast of the event. The most likely reason for this is that broadcast sponsorship is usually the most expensive component of the total sponsorship cost. Broadcast sponsorship is appealing to marketers because of the perceived benefits of communicating to consumers via the media, seen as an independent third party. Broadcast sponsorships can apply to all genres of television and radio programming, although most commonly sport, music and entertainment. A broadcast sponsorship package is usually negotiated with the official media broadcasters and not with the event organisers. A typical broadcast sponsorship package could include opening and closing billboards; on-screen corner logo displays; picture squeezebacks;

> **Case study 14.4 Guinness Rugby World Cup 1999, UK**
>
> Guinness, one of the world's truly global beer brands, aligned itself with the 1999 Rugby World Cup as a global sponsor and the 'official beer' of the event. Held in the UK and France, the event was broadcast to 135 countries around the globe. This allowed Guinness to reach most of its target priority markets, with Guinness beer available in 150 countries. Guinness recognised early on that broadcast sponsorship would be a significant and critical component of the sponsorship deal. Guinness negotiated a broadcast sponsorship deal in Great Britain, Ireland, South Africa and Canada, and on Eurosport. A post-event survey showed that Guinness achieved a 94% awareness rate in the UK as an event sponsor, which is largely believed to be attributed to this broadcast sponsorship deal.
>
> *Source: Duffy (2003)*

'top-and-tails' stings leading to and from commercial breaks; classical advertising during commercial breaks; mention in the television guide; and branding in the television studio (Ives, 1998; Duffy, 2003).

Each event would use its own set of designations for sponsorship categories. For example, the FIFA World Cup 2010 uses three tiers of sponsors: FIFA partners (long-term global sponsors), 2010 FIFA World Cup sponsors (sponsors with a one-event commitment) and 2010 national supporters (local, one-event-only sponsors) (Koenderman, 2009). Understanding that there are different sponsorship levels/opportunities, our attention now turns to looking at how the sponsor can maximise the benefits from its sponsorship opportunity.

14.6 Sponsorship activation and leverage

From the definition given earlier, the main benefit a sponsoring organisation gains in exchange for its support is the access to the exploitable commercial opportunity associated with the event. There are a number of marketing opportunities available to sponsors to exploit or leverage their sponsorship more effectively. Leverage can be defined as the strategic efforts that are designed to support and enhance the sponsorship (Fullerton, 2007). These activities are also sometimes referred to as 'sponsorship-linked marketing', 'collateral' or 'sponsorship activation'.

Sponsorship is not a stand-alone activity. A sponsorship needs to be seen in the context of a company's integrated marketing communications plan. It is widely recommended that the leveraging budget should at least equal the cost of the rights fees, i.e. for every dollar spent on the sponsorship acquisition, at least one more dollar should be spent on leverage activities (Fullerton, 2007). There are many innovative activities that sponsors use to leverage their sponsorship. It would not be possible to list all possible leverage activities, but the following are some of the key activities that are widely used:

14.6.1 Corporate hospitality

This provides opportunities for a company to make face-to-face contact with select publics in a prestigious, informal social context, thereby strengthening and personalising relationships with decision makers, trade channels and business associates. In this way, corporate hospitality can be extremely effective in facilitating direct relationship building with a wide array of targeted influentials (Meerabeau et al., 1991). This tool is especially popular with industrial or business-to-business companies, although it is also widely used by consumer companies.

14.6.2 Merchandising

Merchandising of branded equipment, clothing ranges, toys and other promotional items provides a follow-through that would not be possible without the vehicle of sponsorship. As an associated marketing spin-off, merchandising is an effective and cheap value addition to the initial sponsorship investment. In effect, the sponsor is able to turn the general public into 'walking billboards' for the negligible expense of manufacturing the clothes! This helps in creating top-of-mind awareness for the brand and reinforces the link with the respective event.

14.6.3 Signage

The cost-effective brand exposure that can be provided by signage in the form of perimeter boards or logos on the television screens makes signage an important element of any events sponsorship. For example, during the FIFA World Cup™ 1998, a perimeter signage board could provide a sponsor with about seven minutes of exposure per match, shown in 150 countries, during 64 matches. This level of media exposure would be very costly to achieve through traditional advertising. However, it is believed that the use of signage at the event itself is almost reaching saturation point. In addition to rotating perimeter boards, innovations in signage include using three-dimensional signage and inflatable billboards, as well as electronic or LCD perimeter boards.

Ives (1998) suggests that event managers should evaluate the scope for the use of signage and carefully control the amount of advertising used as well as who advertises. Although signage is obviously an important advertising tool, many industry participants suggest that 'signage is dead', and that sponsors need to be directly involved with the sponsored properties rather than just advertise on them.

Besides these major activities, there are a number of other common sponsorship-linked/activation activities. These might include theme-based advertising; direct marketing; new media promotions (internet and SMS); sales, trade and staff promotions;, cross-promotions with other sponsors; affinity programmes; and product sampling and demonstration.

Having explored the major aspects of importance to sponsors, the following section now focuses on the task of identifying and approaching potential event sponsors.

14.7 Approaching potential sponsors and developing proposals

Once the event owners have decided on what sponsorship is required for the event, their attention will turn to approaching potential sponsors. Initially, the event owners will need to engage in prospecting with the objective of identifying organisations that represent potential sponsors. Often, potential sponsors may be past sponsors, sponsors of similar events, or competitors of sponsors of similar events. Once identified, information needs to be gathered about the prospects and their target markets and corporate/marketing objectives. This information will help the sponsee to tailor the proposal to the needs of the potential sponsor.

The sponsorship proposal is a sales tool designed to convince the prospect that a mutually beneficial relationship will result from accepting the sponsorship opportunity (Fullerton, 2007). It is used to acquire a new sponsor or to re-sign an existing one at the conclusion of a sponsorship agreement. Although it forms the basis for negotiation, the proposal needs to be as detailed as possible. It needs to stand out from other proposals, as potential sponsors may receive many proposals daily. The proposal should therefore demonstrate an understanding of the prospect's needs, tailoring the proposal to the prospect's business, target markets and likely sponsorship objectives (Fullerton, 2007).

There is no one agreed-upon format for a proposal. Though some prospects may require the use of a standardised format for a proposal, the following elements should be covered in a general proposal (adapted from Fullerton, 2007):

❐ *Executive summary.* The proposal may be a fairly lengthy document. Many executives may not read the entire proposal in detail. As a result, the inclusion of an executive summary of the proposal should be considered, usually placed at the beginning of the proposal. All the key aspects of the proposal should be covered in few short paragraphs.

❐ *Introduction.* The opening of the proposal needs to establish interest and rapport, creating a good first impression. It should identify and give a basic description of the opportunity. The introduction may identify the event managers, the event dates, participants and consumer profiles, as well as give a broad overview of the anticipated media coverage.

❐ *Overview of the event.* For an existing event, the objective is to reflect on the event's beginnings and its growth, recalling past achievements and noteworthy successes and developments. A history of past and current sponsors would be useful for prospects. An overview of the event's attendance record and media coverage in the past should be provided. Any historical financial data that may be of interest to the prospect should also be included here. For a new event, a more detailed description of the event format, anticipated participants, spectators and media coverage would be necessary.

☐ *Plan components.* This section should indicate the types of benefits that the potential sponsor could expect. The components should be customised to the anticipated needs of the prospect. The event owner should carefully select the array of components that it will offer. The most important components for sponsors are typically category exclusivity; on-site signage; broadcast and media opportunities; use of trademarks and logos; website presence; access to property database; and tickets/hospitality opportunities (Fullerton, 2007).

☐ *Value enhancements.* This section should highlight any additional areas of benefit for the sponsor, including additional information (such as providing a research/fulfilment report documenting the effectiveness of the sponsorship); action to be taken by the sponsee (such as efforts to discourage ambush marketing); and opportunities for the sponsor (e.g. leveraging and cross-promotional opportunities).

☐ *Terms.* The proposal needs to detail the financial commitment as well as the terms of the agreement. This may include a provision for value-in-kind

payment. The timing of the payments and the duration of the agreement need to be detailed, although this could be negotiated before the acceptance of a contract. Other terms of a sponsorship agreement may include contingencies i.e. event cancellation due to weather or other forces, situations terminating the agreement, and renewal options.

An evaluation of the effectiveness of the sponsorship is of great importance to both event managers and the sponsors. This is discussed in the next section.

14.8 Evaluating sponsorship effectiveness

While the growth in the usage of sponsorship points towards the sponsor's belief in its effectiveness, there is a need to move towards a greater understanding/empirical validation of its effectiveness, and especially its impact on ROI. Industry analyst Koenderman (2009: 120) notes that 'sponsorship has come into its own as a legitimate marketing tool as accountability and worldwide best practice (has been) adopted'. However, a major concern for the sponsorship industry remains to illustrate the ability of sponsorship to provide a ROI for the sponsor that is both identifiable and measurable.

An important aspect of debate is whether sponsorship effects are indeed capable of measurement. The carry-over effect of preceding or ongoing marketing activities makes it difficult to isolate the effect from one medium alone. The synergistic effects of an integrated marketing communications plan will be greater than the effect from one medium alone. The pursuit of multiple objectives makes different types of measurement suitable for different purposes, i.e. there is no one measurement method for all objectives. Some of the effects of sponsorship are subtle and difficult to observe (McDonald, 1991), i.e. enhanced brand image or corporate social responsibility, leading to a larger view in support of a range of evaluative techniques. In general, practitioners agree that post-event measurement and evaluation should be developed from the beginning of the sponsorship programme, focusing on the sponsor's objectives. ROI measurements will have a different value for each sponsor depending on its particular objectives, its internal organisation, its costs and its margin structure.

There is no single recognised standard measurement tool but rather three broad categories used to measure sponsorship effectiveness and ROI:

❒ **Qualitative assessments.** These rely mainly on the judgement of executives or other experts. The success of the sponsorship is subjectively assessed using whatever means or materials deemed to be of importance.
❒ **Market response.** This would include an analysis of the change in the level of sales; the impact on trade participation; and the impact of the sponsorship on the target market (including the influence of the sponsorship on consumer perceptions and attitudes and buying behaviour).
❒ **Media equivalencies.** One of the major attributes of sponsorship is its ability to generate media exposure for the sponsor. The most popular method for evaluating sponsorship effectiveness is that of media tracking (Thwaites, 1994). This method records the number and length of all media exposure (including logos and images on the television screen and commentator mentions), and

compares them to the equivalent cost for advertising. Often this measurement would include an assessment of the quality of the exposure by analysing in which publications or programmes the coverage occurred, and in what tone and by whom it was reported. Linked to this, sponsors may also want to assess the share of the total media exposure that they gained compared to the other sponsors, or even to similar events or other events that they sponsor.

The appropriateness of these measures is questionable on the grounds that the effects of sponsorship cannot be measured in the same way as advertising. Sponsorship, by definition, has further-reaching effects than advertising, as stated earlier. These methods fail to measure the impact of the sponsorship on the target market in general, or the ability of sponsorship to change consumer perceptions on image in particular.

All of the above techniques fail to account for the long-term nature of the sponsorship impact. While spontaneous awareness of sponsor association may be low initially, long-term association effects can exist even years after the sponsorship has ended. It may take time for consumer perceptions and attitudes to be developed, but these impressions can be long-lasting once a meaningful association is developed.

Sponsors and event managers can access sponsorship research and evaluation tools provided by universities, research companies and consultancies. A variety of practitioners' evaluation tools are being developed by sponsorship, advertising and research agencies. The effects of the sponsorship will be greater if the sponsor and event managers are able to guard against potential threats and challenges within the industry, which are discussed next.

14.9 Industry challenges and future developments

This section discusses some of the major challenges facing the sponsorship and events industries, as well as opportunities created by current and future developments.

14.9.1 Global economic downturn

As mentioned in the introduction, a global economic downturn puts pressure on companies to cut back on all forms of marketing, including sponsorship. Globally, the two biggest sponsorship contributors – financial services and the automotive industry – happen to be the sectors that are most vulnerable to economic fluctuations. Developed markets are hardest hit by an economic downturn, and developing markets less so (Koenderman, 2009). Depending on the unique position of each company and each country's economic situation, companies may decide either to axe their current sponsorships or to shelve plans for new ones. However, most major sponsorship deals are bought on long-term contracts, and companies would need to honour them. As a result, the impact of an economic downturn may be more severe for new events rather than existing ones that have sponsorship rights already secured. An alternative for sponsors is to maintain their sponsorship rights, but to spend less on leverage activities.

14.9.2 Ambush marketing

This is defined as the attempt of an organisation to create the impression of being an official sponsor of the event by affiliating itself with that event without having paid the sponsorship rights fee or being a party to the sponsorship contract (ASOM, 1997). Ambush marketing tactics are numerous and can take many forms (see case study 14.5). These tactics create confusion in the market as to who the sponsor is, and hence dilutes the sponsorship investment. As such, ambush marketing can be extremely destructive. This problem has raised questions such as whether sponsorship associations are powerful enough in the consumer's mind to provide a real competitive advantage and whether these associations can be protected and kept specific to the sponsored brand (Quester & Farrelly, 1998). Sponsors can protect themselves from ambush marketing to a certain degree by being fully

> **Case study 14.5 Ambush marketing and the 2000 Sydney Olympic Games, Australia**
>
> The most aggressive of ambush campaigns usually take place at the major world events. For example, at the 2000 Sydney Olympic Games, Nike was an official sponsor of the event as well as a personal sponsor of one of the star athletes, Cathy Freeman. However, Adidas launched an ambush marketing campaign, creating hospitality and media centres that made Adidas-sponsored athletes available to the press. Although these events took place away from official event venues, they were well covered by the international media. In addition, when receiving a gold medal at the official presentation, the Adidas-sponsored athlete, Ian Thorpe, obscured the team's Nike logo on his official uniform by draping an Australian flag over his shoulders.
>
> *Source: Fullerton (2007)*

aware of and taking full advantage of their sponsorship contractual rights. Trademark registration and licensing can also offer some protection.

14.9.3 Restrictive government regulations

Government regulations in many countries, and especially in Europe, restrict sponsorship by tobacco and alcoholic beverage companies to some degree.

14.9.4 The 'chairman's choice' syndrome

Personal motives for the choice of sponsorship projects have long been associated with the industry. While there is undoubtedly evidence of an increasingly commercial approach by sponsors, the personal agenda of decision makers is still a factor in modern sponsorship decision making (Meenaghan, 1991). Many practitioners still agree that most sponsors choose opportunities suiting their own interests or activities, not those that fit their brand personality (Kloot, 1999).

14.9.5 Sponsorship oversupply

The enormous growth of sport sponsorship use has led many to believe that the use of sponsorship may be reaching saturation point. It is suggested that 'clutter', the very problem in advertising that led to the favour of the sponsorship medium, has become a concern in the sport marketing industry, particularly with the increase in joint sponsorships and the proliferation of signage at sport events (Adfocus, 1998). Not only is there competition between different events, but media clutter can also often exist within one major event. For example, the 1998 FIFA World Cup™ in France made use of 12 official partners, eight official suppliers, nine suppliers of official products and services, and 16 official equipment suppliers. However, none of these sponsors noted any disapproval with the situation (Chislett, 1998). For the 2006 event, the number increased to 15 official partners (FIFA, n.d.). SportBusiness International (2001) note that although the global sport sponsorship industry is growing, it may become more appropriate for some companies to find their own niche areas or association with other sponsorship industry sectors, as the majority of mass sport placements may already be considered branded.

14.9.6 Increasing costs of the medium

As sponsorship has grown in favour as a marketing tool, so too have the costs associated with the medium increased. Many traditional sponsors are disillusioned at rocketing costs, especially the price of being sole sponsor of a major event (Adfocus, 1998). Critics agree that it is not good to have only a handful of companies sponsoring the majority of opportunities, and that consumers may become apathetic if the same sponsors sponsor everything (Media Forum: Get with the game, 1999). As a result, there has been a trend toward shared sponsorships. However, this in turn brings its own challenges in trying to standing out from co-sponsors while not alienating them. For each additional co-sponsor, exposure and branding opportunities are significantly reduced.

14.9.7 New media

The emergence of new media and technology forms create both challenges and opportunities for sponsors. Increasingly, events receive exposure and coverage through new media forms, such as the internet (e.g. news updates and live video streaming on websites), cellular telecommunications (e.g. SMS, MMS and live video streaming), and digital communications (e.g. high-definition television and satellite radio transmission), among other emerging technologies.

14.10 Summary

It is clear that events sponsorship has been growing in favour as a marketing tool. Sponsorship is defined as an investment/provision of assistance, in cash or in kind, by an organisation (sponsor) to an activity or event (sponsee), for the purpose of achieving specified corporate or marketing objectives through exploiting the commercial potential associated with the event to the mutual benefit of all parties involved. Sponsorship should not be confused with patronage/corporate philanthropy. Sponsorship has the ability to perform a multitude of tasks for the sponsor, obtaining corporate objectives as well as sales and media coverage objectives. For most large events, there are different levels of sponsorship opportunities available, each with a defined set of benefits and differing rights fees or obligations. Sponsorship should not be viewed as a stand-alone activity. Sponsors can use any number of innovative activities to leverage their sponsorship and maximise its impact. Once the event owners have decided on what sponsorship is required for the event, their attention will turn to approaching potential sponsors. These would be prospected and a sponsorship proposal developed to aid the sales negotiation process. The most contentious issue within sponsorship is the evaluation of its effectiveness. Many measurement techniques abound, but there is a lack of a single, comprehensive measurement tool. Instead, sponsors should focus on developing measurement tools to evaluate their sponsorship objectives. A range of techniques should cover qualitative evaluation and an evaluation of the sales and market impact, as well as the media exposure gained. There are a number of challenges facing the industry including the global economic downturn, ambush marketing and emerging opportunities, such as new media.

Questions for research

1. Define sponsorship, and distinguish it from corporate philanthropy.
2. Explain the reasons for the favour and growth of the global events sponsorship sector.
3. Explain why sponsorship evaluation is a contentious issue. Identify the major techniques for evaluating sponsorship effectiveness.
4. Select an event of your choice that you have recently visited or observed. Identify the levels of sponsorship opportunities and the different sponsors of the event. Selecting one of the 'major' sponsors, identify what you consider to be the sponsor's main objectives for the sponsorship, giving clear reasons for your selection. Describe the major sponsorship leverage activities that you observe the sponsors undertaking.
5. Assuming that you are the event manager for a new event, identify a potential sponsor for it and develop a sponsorship proposal to present to the prospect based on your understanding of effective sponsorship and the objectives of sponsors.
6. Critically discuss the challenges and opportunities facing the events sponsorship sector.

Recommended websites

Browse the following internet sites for interesting and informative information:

International Events Group, Inc. – sponsorship information, news, and resources: http://www.sponsorship.com
Joyce Julius – media equivalency measurement agency: http://www.joycejulius.com
Media Monitors - sponsorship information services: http://www.mediamonitors.com.au/sis/technology.htm
Octagon – global sponsorship consulting agency: http://www.octagon.com
Performance Research – sponsorship market research consultancy: http://www.performanceresearch.com
Scomm – research and sponsorship evaluation: http://www.scomm-research.com
Sponprops – sponsorship proposal company: http://www.sponprops.com/en.htm
Sponsormap – evaluation of sponsorship effectiveness: http://www.sponsormap.com
Sponsorship Advice – careers in sponsorship: http://www.sponsorship-advice.org
Sponsorship Intelligence – sponsorship service provider: http://www.sponsorshipintelligence.com
Sponsorship news – industry news: http://www.sponsorshipnews.com
Sponsortrack – sponsorship evaluation service provider: http://www.sponsortrak.com
Sportal – sport events database: http://www.sportal.co.uk
SportBusiness International – sponsorship news, information and services: http://www.sportbusiness.com
Starfish - sponsorship research and valuation consultancy: http://www.starfishresearch.com

Suggested reading

Duffy, N. 2003. *Passion Branding*. Chichester: John Wiley.
Fullerton, S. 2007. *Sports Marketing*. New York: McGraw-Hill Irwin.
Hoyle, LH. 2002. *Event Marketing*. USA: The Wiley Event Management Series.
Kolah, A. 2007. *Sponsorship Works: A Brand Marketer's Casebook*. London: SportBusiness.
Masterman, G. 2007. *Sponsorship: For a Return on Investment*. UK: Butterworth-Heinemann.

PART V
Events and operations

Photo: MediaClubSouthAfrica.com. Hannelie Coetzee

Photo: Dimitri Tassiopoulos

15

Events operations management

Matthew Bromley and Conor Moss

Abstract

Operational and logistical management is an essential part of events management and is a process which needs careful consideration of spatial, temporal, internal and external factors, while at the same time allowing flexibility to adapt to changing situations.

This incorporates the management of myriad processes, contractors and publics at both the destination and origin, including the precise movement of resources according to schedule.

Integration of such activity becomes crucial, as the staging of the event is imminent and the team pulls together the different operational and logistical strands of the event. It is also essential to understand that the process continues after the event, as the shutdown takes place and the monitoring and evaluation are undertaken.

Chapter objectives

After you have read this chapter you should be able to:

❏ understand the numerous operational dimensions that must be made at each stage of the event and how activity must be constantly monitored in order to ensure the smooth running of an event;

❏ identify the roles and responsibilities of the events operations team, and be able to determine who should be involved across different types of event; and

❏ understand the purpose of the events operations plan and the details it should cover, including what should be in an emergency plan.

15.1 Events operations management

The origination, planning and delivery of events are a complex task involving many different contributors, including authorities, contractors, public services, attendees and other stakeholders. The success of an event is determined by organisation, planning and cooperation, and as events can gain high levels of media attention, it is extremely important that event managers, both those internal and external of a venue, ensure that due consideration has been given to operational and logistical elements of the event. The planning phase of an event could take as little as a few days or up to a few years, as in the case of a mega-event, and resources required will be linked to the scale and scope of the event.

In most events, at least 90% of the work involved in the delivery is done in the planning stages, and this will ultimately determine the success of the event. There are various planning models available that identify many different aspects of the event as a whole (see chapter 7).

To produce the event, an organiser has a multitude of operational considerations including the procurement of suppliers, choosing a site or venue and, most importantly, ensuring that customer's needs are catered for. Operational management requires attention to detail, teamwork and time for consideration.

For detailed management, each component of the event (e.g. transport, catering, queuing) can be considered using the continual event improvement process (see figure 15.1), which allows the organiser to see the event as 'a sum of its parts', in other words, the bottom-up approach. This is an approach typically used in project and risk management, and at this level, the organiser can exert more control over the various tasks.

Using this process, each process can be considered, allowing the organiser the opportunity to review systems or work, and eliminate or negate the impact of any weaknesses that may only become apparent on delivery. This is effectively a risk-based approach to event management and ensures that there is continual development of the event to meet new standards or objectives.

15.1.1 Logistics management

Event logistics concerns the supply of customers, products and facilities to and management of the event venue or site. There are many considerations within this area, and the larger the scale of the event, the more complex the logistical planning will be. Event logistics is closely associated

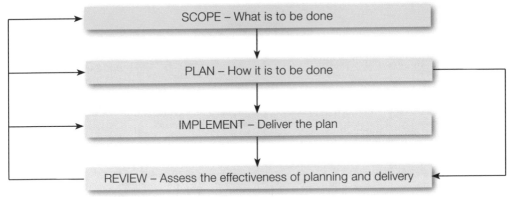

Figure 15.1 The continual event improvement process

with service excellence and customer satisfaction, and will determine the smooth operation of the event. Each area of the event can be broken into tasks (commonly known as a work breakdown structure or WBS) or systems of work, and each system will require scheduling and resources to ensure that the work can be carried out efficiently and effectively.

It is necessary to clearly identify the different phases of an event in order to be able to plan and implement operations effectively. These phases (adapted from HSE, 1999) are:

- ❏ the planning or build-up – suitable selection of venue/site, contracting companies and construction of infrastructure and services;
- ❏ the load-in or move-in – delivery and installation of equipment;
- ❏ the event – management of the event attendees, transport and operational strategies;
- ❏ the load-out or move-out – removal of equipment and non-essential services; and
- ❏ the breakdown – removal of infrastructure and waste.

There is an array of logistical considerations to be made in relation to each period, and splitting the event into chronological sections like this can help enable both the external event manager and those working for the venue itself to ensure the relevant steps are taken to ensure health and safety at all times. It also identifies tasks that need to be carried out in the future in order to allow for preparation. This may involve locating suppliers and subcontractors or applying for any necessary licences. An example of this is the scheduling of contractors arriving at a given event site, and guaranteeing that each one can load in supplies and equipment, and can access on-site amenities. For example, it is important that on an outdoor festival site, infrastructural requirements (power, water, toilets) are in place before contractors arrive. Unlike business logistics, event logistics takes place over a relatively short space of time, and there is rarely time to improve it so this has to be planned correctly in the first instance (Allen et al., 2008).

15.2 Communications management

15.2.1 The events operations team

Given the plethora of contractors, staff and stakeholders on site, it is essential that a clear

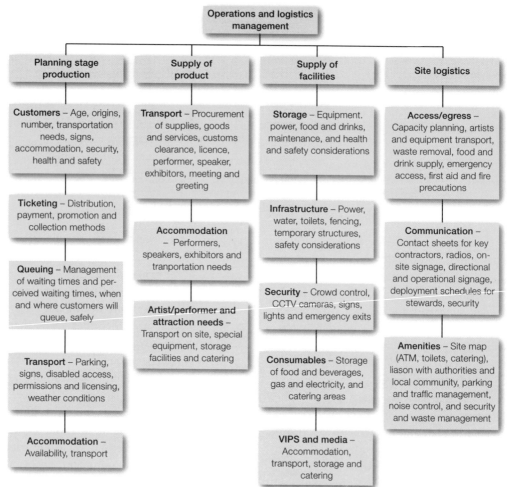

Figure 15.2 Operations and logistics planning for events

Source: Adapted from Bowdin et al. (2006)

structure is established for communications throughout the event. Typically the purpose of an events operations team is to collate knowledge and apply it specifically to individual events to ensure the correct procedures can be effectively implemented in the event of an emergency and to deliver an event successfully.

Members (which may vary) include representatives from:

❏ the events management company;
❏ the venue;
❏ the local authority;

❏ the emergency services;
❏ the client; and
❏ key contractors.

This accumulation of expertise and different perspectives reduces the chance of particular niche issues being overlooked. The strategy requires clear and effective communications at three levels: inter-agency, suppliers and the public. This section looks at how this is achieved.

Communications work at three levels and normally in three periods.

Figure 15.3 Events operations management team

There is, however, the need to consider communication in the event of an emergency. The levels of communication are as follows:

1 Inter-agency communication – local authority/emergency services/environmental;
2 Communication between site suppliers – contractors/subcontractors;
3 Communication with the public – local residents, attendees.

The timelines for this communication are during the planning phase, during the event and after the event. Considerations are required for emergency situations.

Members of the team are also responsible for the production and collation of the events operations plan (see figure 15.4), which details all measures to be taken to reduce any risk factors identified across all stages of an event from build-up to breakdown. This task is regularly subcontracted to a risk management company or specifically to the event management company should it have personnel with the relevant levels of expertise and training.

15.2.2 The events operations plan

Once the organiser has established systems of work, schedules and site-specific details, it is recommended that an events operations plan is produced. Figure 15.4 provides a list of considerations for this document.

The plan only needs to be issued to key members of the event management team, although all personnel should be briefed on the procedures and their responsibilities. It should be regularly updated throughout

The events operations plan

The plan will include **specific details about the event**, including:	1. An assessment of the venue or site including space, surrounding structures and good conditions. 2. Details of the structures to be erected and their locations, who will undertake this task and how it will be done. 3. Profile of the audience, including their anticipated age and numbers. 4. Capacities of the overall site and any separate venues and areas within it. This must take into consideration space accommodated by structures like staging. 5. Duration of the event and opening times if held on multiple days. A timetable of acts may also feature. 6. Food and drink establishments and their locations and profiles. 7. Location and number of toilets. 8. Location of water supplies. 9. Special effects that may feature in the event's entertainment, such as firework displays, and special arrangments made to ensure these are carried out safely. 10. Location of first aid points.
The **site safety plan**. This includes:	1. Site safety rules which must be abided by at all times. 2. Names and contact details of site crew, managers and safety coordinators, and any contractors working on site. 3. Structural calculations and drawings.
The **transport management plan**. This includes:	1. Parking arrangements – location for both staff and attendees to park. A coach park may be required. 2. Highway management issues which may include the enforcement of a one-way system on site to reduce the risks of collisions between vehicles and protect pedestrians. A speed limit may also be enforced. 3. Details of entrances and exits and routes between them. 4. Access for emergency services vehicles 5. Drop-off points for taxis and coaches. 6. Public transport arrangements – routes to and from train stations, bus and taxi drop-off points.
The **emergency plan**. This includes:	1. This will outline a number of scenarios the event could fall victim to, such as fire and bomb threats, and the action that could be taken. 2. Should outline individual roles in the event of a crisis, who should be contacted at what stage and the chain of command.
The **first aid plan**. This includes:	1. Where first aid can be administered on site 2. Names, contact details and locations of personnel trained in first aid. 3. Local hospital arrangements.

Figure 15.4 Events operations plan

Source: Adapted from HSE, GB (1999)

the planning and implementation of the event as new issues arise or changes are made. Meetings should be held before and during the event to assess how it is proceeding. This allows for alterations to be made if the event is held over more than one day.

15.2.3 Communication equipment

The event team usually communicates using either two-way radios with multiple channels or intercom with multiple channels (Matthews, 2008). Channels are often subdivided to teams, such as catering, security, production, etc., and codes may also be used to denote incidents. It is usual to see spare channels used as 'go-to' channels, and one channel reserved for team leaders. It is important that all staff members are trained correctly on the use of these systems to ensure clear, effective communication using established cues and protocols, especially in public areas.

15.3 Site management

15.3.1 Site suitability and selection

The range of features to look out for and ask about when visiting a venue, such as toilets, catering and power supplies, are discussed in earlier chapters. However, it must be remembered that not all venues are permanent. Often a visit may involve inspecting a piece of land for suitability, which may be used for an indoor or outdoor event. In this case some of the factors to assess may be the same, such as availability, location and access. However, it also involves the introduction of a number of new requirements to be considered. In other words, can this venue operate?

❑ *Ground conditions.* It is important the ground is safe to walk on and to assess if it is suitably flat and solid enough for temporary structures like marquees and staging, if necessary. Also, the weather at the time of year and location must be taken into account as this will affect the surface.

❑ *Traffic and pedestrian routes.* Is there suitable access in terms of safety and size? This must be considered in relation to the number of people and vehicles that are expected to attend.

❑ *Positions and proximity of sensitive buildings*. This is particularly relevant if the event will result in a large influx of people to the area and a lot of sound emissions. If there are churches or hospitals in the area it is important not to disturb their operation.

❑ *Location and availability of services.* Is the site in close proximity to motorways? (This is a benefit for access but if too close, noise could pollute the event.) What will the weather be like? Are there sufficient suppliers and subcontractors in the area?

❑ *History.* it is helpful to talk to people who have used the site before and research how successful past events were and if they had any problems. In some cases it may also be beneficial to know the deeper history of the site. For example, more people may be attracted to an event if it is held on the site of a famous battle whereas if it was once an ancient burial ground, some people may be put off.

It may also be helpful to consider some of the requirements of the event and take measurements of the site. Some things to think about include:

❑ occupant capacity;

- the artists' profile;
- the audience profile;
- the duration and timing;
- the venue evaluation;
- alcohol;
- whether the audience is standing or seated;
- the movement of audience between areas; and
- the artistic nature of event.

15.3.2 Site planning

It is essential that effective planning is considered prior to the event (Bowdin et al., 2006), in terms of site preparation it is important to do the following:

- Prepare plans to show the location of stages, barriers, first-aid positions, camera positions, toilets, merchandising stalls, etc. This allows all parties involved to ascertain if there is sufficient space for enough toilets and first-aid points. The recommended number of each per number of attendees can be found in the HSE's *Event Safety Guide*, also known as 'The Purple Guide'.
- Assess if there are going to be sufficient sight lines to the stage with reference to the anticipated number of attendees. This also provides an opportunity to assess if the event will be safe and where barriers and partitions can be used to reduce the risk of overcrowding.
- Obtain plans from the landowner or venue owner/manager for the staging of the event. These will detail the locations of water/gas supplies, etc. that may be installed, particularly if this is an outdoor event on a field or in a park. The location of certain event features can then be decided accordingly. These plans may also include the gradients of the land, thus showing where the

safest, flattest places to erect temporary structures are.
- Roads may be marked, helping to ascertain where emergency access for fire, ambulance and police should be positioned. If an indoor venue, such as an arena, plans can help to position structures and crowd areas to avoid overcrowding and make sure crowd flow will be efficient, especially in areas where emergency exits are located.
- Copies of these plans should be supplied to contractors who are building the infrastructure. Each contractor will have individual expertise in the construction of the feature of the event they are responsible for, therefore allowing them to see the plans provides opportunity to gain different opinions on the decisions made. They may notice risks concerning the position of their feature that have been overlooked, since their experience and specific skills provide them with different criteria with which to look at such plans.
- Contractors and subcontractors must provide copies of their own H&S policies and details of hazards and risks associated with their work.

15.3.3 Managing suppliers and contractors on site

The selection process of companies and contractors to work on an event is extremely important. This section deals mainly with contractor management rather than procurement. This is detailed fully in Tum, Norton and Wright (2006) with an outline of the decision points for purchasing.

Competence

Suppliers, employees, contractors and subcontractors should be competent to undertake the tasks they are given. This means that they should have the necessary qualifications, safety policies and insurances in place, but also that they have prior experience of working within a similar role. For example, a qualified electrician who is experienced in rewiring houses may not be competent enough to install power on an outdoor events site. Organisers must check these details to ensure that a duty of care is provided to other contractors and guests. Competence remains important in less-skilled areas, such as ticketing or car parking, which tend to be the first interaction with customers. If volunteers are used, then the rule of thumb is that they should only be asked to undertake tasks that they are comfortable with.

Control

Establishing and maintaining control is central to all management functions (HSE, 1999). Control extends to address budgetary tasks, schedules and resources, and ensures that the event can be delivered in a timely fashion while adhering to cost constraints. Control also includes the development of an organisational structure detailing the hierarchy of responsibilities, working policies and clear lines of communication. It is essential that all employees and suppliers know and understand their responsibilities while working on the event. A service-level agreement (SLA) is a negotiated agreement between two parties where one is the event client and the other is the service provider, and where the level of service is formally defined and used to refer to the contracted delivery time (of the service) or performance.

Cooperation

Events are often produced under different constraints such as time, scope and cost.

For example, access to a venue for setup may only be available at a certain time, or in urban areas there may be noise-level control at certain periods. Cooperation is important to ensure that all interested parties or event stakeholders are catered for, such as the exchange of information between organisers, venues and local authorities. Cooperation ensures that schedules can be met in a safe manner, especially with events where many different contractors or suppliers are working in the same area.

Communication

Effective communication ensures that all those who are to work on site understand the importance and significance of the health and safety objectives. Make sure that contractors, subcontractors and others are kept informed of safety matters and procedures to be followed on site.

The importance of communication on site is recognised. There needs to be clear and effective communication between the various disciplines and identified lines of demarcation. Agreed and written procedures, roles and specific duties need to be drawn up. For example, for outdoor sporting and music events the police, event management, the local authority and the stewards will need to communicate effectively.

All relevant personnel should use radio communication. It is imperative that all radio frequencies are confirmed and communicated prior to the event in order to prevent crossover. Correct radio procedure and discipline need to be established and then adhered to. It is essential that radio contact within the site is limited to site-related problems. Queries or problems raised must be dealt with by face-to-face meetings where possible to avoid long and drawn-out discussions via radio.

Communication with the public should be carried out when necessary by using the site PA system, allowing clear and audible messages.

Regular meetings between the security manager, medical services, event safety coordinator and the promoter should be scheduled to take place at specified intervals throughout the event (including build-up) to discuss the event to date.

15.4 Infrastructure management

Scheduling is the art of event component breakdown, activity analysis, deciding the order of completing activities, arranging the necessary resources to complete each activity and arranging the timing of activities. Different terms are used to cover these activities. Shone and Parry (2004) describe logistics as being the discipline of planning and organising the flow of goods, equipment and people to their point of use. This is essentially the same as scheduling, and an event is reliant on getting all elements to the right place in time for a range of deadlines.

At the beginning of planning for the event, several activities can be started, but most subsequent activities will be dependent on others finishing. As more activities finish, even more can be started. Some of these activities may include getting special power and utility requirements to the event site (such as telecommunications), and special licences may also need to be applied for. For the majority of events, backwards scheduling activity occurs. This is where the finish date and hour are known, and all the activities are listed with their expected completion times. The schedule is then calculated backwards so that all activities can be sequenced appropriately

and finished by the due date. Tum et al. (2006) describes this technique as one where the time durations of particular activities are subtracted from the required completion date. In certain events the numbers of customers arriving is known, and in some cases also the specific times – for example at a conference or for a dinner dance, or for some other pre-booked event. In these instances the event manager will make the availability of the resources coincide with the start of the event – the manager can control the time of service delivery, and the scheduling can be fairly exact. Efficiency is dependent on customers arriving at the prearranged time. If, however, they are late, service will be delayed or not offered at all. In case of a concert, latecomers may miss the start of the programme. If the organiser agrees to delay the event, this may have an impact on other scheduled services and possibly on other customers. Nonetheless, if customers keep to the prearranged booked times, a high degree of accuracy and efficiency in scheduling of resources will be possible.

15.4.1 Considerations

❐ Plan the arrival and work schedules of contractors to be coordinated and sequential.

❐ Certain contractors will need to work together in the construction of certain features. For example, at a festival those erecting the stage will need to discuss with those providing the sound equipment issues involving places for equipment, access to power supplies and pyrotechnics. Additionally, there are few companies that supply stages, rigging and structures, therefore contractors will need to coordinate and schedule their activities in the planning stages of the event.

- Other construction activities may not be able to proceed simultaneously. For example, it may not be safe for those decorating a venue or laying out seating to work below areas where construction is still taking place due to risks involving falling objects and working at heights (See case study 15.1 on the Henley Festival).

15.4.2 Signage

For safety and quality-assurance purposes the location of and direction to exits, toilets, information points, repatriation areas, first aid, etc. needs to be clearly and conspicuously signed. All temporary signs will be of a suitable type and must conform (where appropriate) to the local health and safety (safety signs and signals) standards.

15.4.3 Traffic management

Traffic management is another complex area of consideration for an event. In most cases, planned events create demand on existing transport provisions through tourism, or may require the closure of certain roads. This usually takes place over an intense period of time, and occurs at local and regional level.

The principles of any traffic management plan for an event are twofold:

- Public safety must be paramount, both for those attending the event and for those going about their day-to-day business; and
- Disruption to traffic must be minimised in terms of area and duration, subject to safety requirements.

It should be noted that traffic management legislation that is intended to deal with major events often exists. Some events will inevitably cause substantial disruption to traffic and require the closure of roads, possibly for considerable periods of time in order to enable the event to take place, and also to allow time for the associated infrastructure and spectators to arrive and disperse. In such cases, there are usually wide-ranging powers available to the respective authority to close a highway or alter any other relevant traffic regulation if it is satisfied it is necessary to do so. This works with respect to road closures and traffic regulation for large sporting events and social events on the public highway and has two purposes:

- To enable closure of public roads to facilitate the taking place of such events; and
- To ensure such events only take place after proper consultation under the authorisation of an accountable and elected authority.

Traffic management plans must also consider the movement of vehicles on or in an event site. It is necessary to identify a red route for emergency vehicle access to key areas, and to set out rules for the movement of vehicles during construction and deconstruction. It is vital to limit vehicle movement within the site when the public is present to essential and emergency users only. All general traffic movement must be stopped. Where possible, essential users must be separated from the public, using stewards as escorts.

15.4.4 Parking

This is often the first interaction between customers and event site, and must be managed effectively. Parking facilities can be monitored for availability, with staff members in place to direct motorists. This provides improved and sustained flow of traffic, and ensures that traffic is moved through a location quickly and without the need to drive around looking for a space, further congesting the local area. Staff members can also communicate the availability of space to members of the public, close car parks when full and reduce the overall number of staff required to run this operation.

15.4.5 Essential services

Access to important services such as gas, electricity and water are paramount to the success of the event. Such services will generally be the first consideration on an event site, as many functions cannot operate without them. For example, power is required to operate machinery and build infrastructure such as tents and stages. Similarly, concession units require power and plumbing, and it is important that the site plan shows where services are located or to be installed to aid contractors on arrival.

15.4.6 Medical and emergency services

At public events medical volunteers are often in attendance to administer first aid, and the number of trained people should be relative to the number of attendees. Members of the event management staff should also have sufficient first-aid training for the type of events they are involved in.

First-aid points must be clearly marked and signposted. All personnel should know their location and be able to escort attendees to them through clear routes that are not obstructed by crowds.

There must also be points for drinking water and sufficient numbers of toilets, and

the general welfare of attendees must be considered in relation to any incidents that may occur, as well as the expected procedure of the event. This includes having sufficient space to evacuate people to if necessary and providing shelter from extreme weather conditions.

15.4.7 Inclusion

Many countries provide organisers with guidance on meeting and exceeding the needs of people with disabilities. At the most basic level, a range of accessible viewing areas must be provided for such spectators with appropriate space and quality of viewing. All reasonable measures should be undertaken to ensure that the organisers do not discriminate against people with disabilities, and it is often best practice to consult local disability groups to ensure that the event meets the correct standard of provision.

15.4.8 Lighting systems

Organisers must provide adequate lighting systems so that customers can enter, exit and move around the event site in safety. This is especially important in non-daylight hours, and organisers must also ensure that important signs such as fire exits are illuminated correctly. A backup or auxiliary power supply should be available, which will power lighting systems for up to three hours should the main supply be interrupted (TSO, 2008: 173).

15.4.9 Waste management and recycling

Events by their very nature are unsustainable and generate large quantities of waste materials left by concessionaires and the audience (ESG, 1999), therefore effective waste management is essential to ensure that customers continue to enjoy the experience and to minimise their exposure to waste materials.

Types of waste generated include the following:

❑ Paper and cardboard packaging;
❑ Food and drink containers;
❑ Left-over food;
❑ Glass;
❑ Plastics;
❑ Metal cans;
❑ The remains of campfires/braais;
❑ Fireworks and pyrotechnics;
❑ Waste food from food concessions;
❑ Other metal waste, e.g. construction materials;
❑ Human waste products (vomit, urine and faeces, sanitary towels and tampons often placed in miscellaneous containers);
❑ Tents;
❑ Medical waste such as needles and bandages; and
❑ Waste water from toilets, showers and hand basins (ESG, 1999: 93).

Waste containers (or skip bins) should be provided for all catering waste in the secure areas to the rear of catering units. This should be monitored to ensure inappropriate levels of waste and combustible items do not build up during the event period. Waste bins of various sizes should be positioned around the perimeter of the venue or site, and also within the venue or site or other areas as appropriate (ESG, 1999: 95). Organisers should also consider reducing the burden on the environment by recycling. This may be done by eliminating waste, such as decreasing the volume of printed materials for an event, or sorting waste and reducing the number of mixed waste collections, thus saving costs and energy consumption.

15.5 Technical management

Once the infrastructure has been built, the production items need to be installed – this includes all technical equipment which will enable the event to happen. Planning is of the essence – this is often the role of a production manager, who has been involved in the planning of all event features and knows exactly which items need to go where, and when they should be installed.

Also, the delivery of equipment to non-performance areas needs to be considered – remember that the performance or activities available to attendees is only one part of their experience. Other features revolve around the main attraction such as food, drink and merchandising. The vendors of such provisions also need to take deliveries of stock. The same safety criteria must apply to this stage as in the build-up. Any additional safety measures that are necessary due to the introduction of new risks at this stage must be included in modified safety procedures and rules. All parties involved must be informed of these changes.

Similar coordination must apply – again, some deliveries must be installed before others. Caterers all located in the same area may need to be flexible to each allow for the delivery of produce for other establishments if there is limited unloading space available.

15.5.1 Temporary structures

A temporary structure can be defined as follows:

Temporary demountable structures [are those] which are in place for a short time, generally no more than 28 days that are designed to be erected and dismantled manually many times. They are usually made from lightweight components and are used for a wide variety of functions at public and private events. They include grandstands, tents and marquees, which may accommodate large numbers of people, and stages and supports for performers.

TDS (2007: 12)

All temporary structures and equipment installations should always be designed, erected and rigged by professional contractors.

In most countries, full details of stages and structures would need to be submitted for approval by the local authority's building control department. Full technical drawings, supporting calculations and any relevant test results should be made available before construction commences. All design loads should be in accordance with the appropriate country standards having regard to their location and use.

Additionally, all main contractors – for example those for staging, lighting, rigging and sound – should submit safety method statements to the events manager in respect of their on-site activity. These will include details of employee/subcontractors' competencies and training in respect of their ability to operate equipment.

The structure should be erected safely in accordance with the Erection Method Statement and drawings provided (documents that detail the way structures are erected the safety of anyone who is affected by the task or process). All kentledge (a system of weights used for load-testing foundations), temporary guying (ropes, cords or cables used to steady, guide or

secure) and other means of temporary support identified in the Method Statement should be properly installed to provide for the safety of operatives.

TDS (2007: 42)

During the construction of said structures the event safety coordinator should ensure that contractors and personnel follow safe working practices and erect the temporary structures as detailed in the specification.

15.5.2 Sound system

The role of the sound system is unique to a given event, but its basic purpose is to achieve louder sound for artistic purposes and/or to enable people to hear sound in remote areas (Davis & Jones, 1990: 348). The sound system must be designed to meet the event requirements, dependent on the type of event, the audience, the location and the size of venue, and whether it is for indoor or outdoor use. A contracted sound engineer will undertake this task, providing a list of equipment to be used and dealing with any event-specific requirements such as those from artists or performers.

15.5.3 Lighting

In addition to general venue or site lighting, the principal use of lighting is to create ambiance and mood, or to add to the theme. Lighting planning and design should be undertaken to determine the type, placement and colour of lights, along with the resources required to operate them, such as power and experienced operators.

15.5.4 Special effects

The level of uniqueness and excitement of an event can be greatly influenced by the special effects used to entertain and create a particular atmosphere. These include smoke, sound, lighting, fog, pyrotechnics, fireworks, laser lights, laser videos, fibre optics, water fountains, robots, moving stages, confetti canons, bubble machines and water screens (Wanklin, 2005: 143). It is important to engage experienced contractors in the use of special effects to maintain safety standards. It is also advisable to discuss some special effects with local authorities. For example, when using searchlight-type lighting effects, an organiser should inform aviation authorities, and in some cities permits must be obtained for the use of effects such as fireworks. Therefore it is always important to consider the use of special effects, audiovisual systems or other event technologies to ensure that it is fit for purpose, and does not lead to the wasting of time, money or resources.

15.5.5 Decor

The theme of an event can be further established with the use of décor. This may include backdrops, props, lighting, table centres, balloons, uniforms and other event-specific décor to establish or reinforce the theme and add to the experience. Companies specialising in this area offer a range of themes or bespoke solutions, and will dress a venue to a given brief.

15.6 Attendee and participant management

There are many facets to managing event attendees and participants, including crowd management, admission, ticketing, registration and seating systems. Tum et al. (2006) suggest the use of flow or customer process charts to help the event manager

anticipate customer choices, enable decisions on the location of facilities or information, and to consider where solutions may be required. Service mapping can also be undertaken to visually display the service by simultaneously depicting the process of service delivery, roles of customers and employees, and the visible elements of the service (Bitner, 1993). This approach, also recommended by Getz et al. (2001), gives the event manager a full understanding of the customer journey, and ensures that the event makes a good first impression. This journey is often overlooked, and it is not unusual to hear of large queues on entry to festivals where customers do not have access to water or sanitary facilities. Similarly, poor parking facilities or customer service as a customer leaves the event may tarnish an otherwise good event experience.

One of the major consideration in events management is crowd management, a complex amalgam of a number of key factors that, when properly managed, enable the safe and comfortable enjoyment of any activity. Crowd management is about understanding and then influencing behaviour using many tools such as design, information and staffing systems. Planning will normally focus on these areas in three time periods, namely ingress (or access), circulation and egress, and is supported by risk assessment to identify and manage the process. Crowd control refers to the subsequent steps that are taken to limit crowd behaviour. This is often linked to disorder and is not to be confused with crowd management (Allen et al., 2008).

To manage event attendees it is recommended that event managers consider the five Cs of crowd management (HSE, 1996):

Case study 15.1 Henley Festival, UK

The Henley Festival of Music and the Arts is a five-day event featuring a wide range of popular and classical music encompassing many styles and also incorporating visual arts including art galleries and sculpture lawns.

The Henley Festival incorporates one main stage for live entertainment, plus smaller, live music venues including the Club Marquee and the Dome. The capacity for the event is 4 500 people per day. The audience profile is estimated at 50:50 male:female split, with an age range predominately between the early 30s to the mid-50s. The event arena is fenced, and access is by ticket only for each of the evening events.

The venue is open grassland crossed by roads. It is owned by Henley Royal Regatta and therefore does not constitute a purpose-built entertainment arena. The regatta infrastructure typically remains in place and is used by the festival. The venue is therefore fixed, and the entertainment designs and crowd management strategies need to be integrated with this infrastructure.

The floating stage

One of the main highlights of the event is the 'floating' main stage, which is built on the riverbed. The stage is built in a period of 2.5 days starting on the Sunday preceding the Wednesday performance. The build is an extremely difficult operational and logistical challenge requiring effective communication, cooperation and scheduling.

Managing contractors

The building of the stage requires the coordination of 60 staff from five different organisations, thus effective operational procedures/plans are needed. Usually a stage of this nature would require five days to erect in a standard open-air festival; however, due to time constraints the team has only three days.

Implications for resources

This means that as the teams are working through the night in three shifts of eight hours, communication is key in the reporting of progress against schedule. Each of the sequential activities requires skilled staff including specialist divers to erect the stage on the riverbed, plant hire such as cranes, rigging staff to build the structure, and sound and lighting specialists to finish the stage. Each of these specialist companies has an implicit cost and should the scheduling of the build slip then the costs will increase, which will impact upon the smooth running of the event and the budget.

Best practice

Competence is shown through necessary training, expertise and established systems of work. The contractors on this stage build have worked together for six years to deliver in a professional and timely fashion, and demonstrate the importance of cooperation on the delivery of events.

❐ Capacity;
❐ Crowd behaviour;
❐ Controls;
❐ Communications; and
❐ Contingency.

15.6.1 Capacity

Capacity is often regarded as the solution to crowd management and can simply be defined as how many people can safely get into, circulate and get out of a specific event space. Capacity is influenced by a number of factors, each of which needs careful consideration:

❑ What is the overall space?
❑ How much of this is viewing area?
❑ How can people get there?
❑ What are the queuing times?
❑ What are the means of escape?
❑ How long to evacuate?
❑ What does the historical data show?

Within a built and established entertainment venue – such as a theatre or concert hall – these figures are usually well known from established historical data. The issues of capacity for an outdoor or open greenfield site, such as a concert in a park, may not be as well known, unless there is previous historical data but in each case, capacity will always require careful re-evaluation. Complexity is further increased in urban and city environments, with many factors such as streets, exits and buildings to consider.

There is much guidance available for calculating capacity, occupant density and evacuation times (HSE, 1999) and the safe capacity of any venue is generally established through a process that deals with the following four elements:

❑ Ingress – the number of people that can arrive and get into the event;
❑ Size of viewing area – the total area that attendees can use to view the event;
❑ Audience profile – the acceptable occupant density; and
❑ Means of escape – the safe evacuation time.

The complex balance of this process is set out in figure 15.5. The process also relies on an understanding and application of historical data, based on the audience profile, and takes a quantitative approach.

The diagram also denotes two separate controls, (P and S factor), the lower of which is applied to the overall viewing area. The P factor relates to terrain/design and its suitability – for example, gradient, drainage and lighting will all form part of the P assessment. The figure varies between 0 and 1, and the closer to 1 the better the suitability of the ground. The S factor relates to the level of safety management, including such factors as stewarding levels and competence, and use of a dedicated crowd/safety manager. The lower of the P or S factor is applied (not both) and can, if circumstances dictate, be given a capacity of 0.

This is a complicated process, but may highlight that an area is unsuitable to hold an event, and is usually one of the first operational tasks that an event manager will undertake.

15.6.2 Crowd behaviour

Each crowd has its own characteristics and drivers that will influence behaviour. The identification and understanding of this behaviour will enable the safety manager to identify and put control measures in place. Each crowd is, of course, made up of individuals and it is important to recognise this when applying broad descriptions to crowds. If people are treated as an individual by management and staff, they are more likely to respond to this level of customer care and through their choices and behaviour be part of management solution.

That stated, one must examine the common drivers behind each audience to put the necessary group solutions in place. Firstly, why is the crowd there? What do they want to see? This will have an impact on the crowd demographics. Secondly,

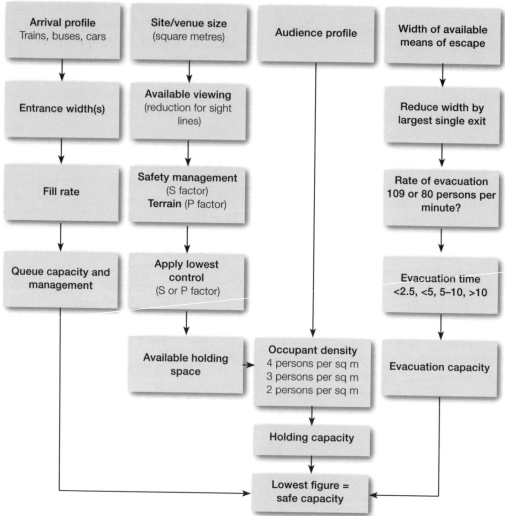

Figure 15.5 Capacity calculation path
Source: HSE (1999)

do they have knowledge or experience of the event? Learnt behaviour can influence choice and groups around them, which is particularly true on ingress and egress – the audience will look to use routes that are familiar to them, which can be a significant factor in an emergency.

15.6.3 Crowd demographics and learnt behaviour

This task looks at the type of audience that is expected, and includes factors such as attendee age, sex, group typology (families, friends, rival factions) which can and will influence how the crowd will behave.

The audience will often have its own expectations over how it will behave, and each type of activity must always be carefully examined as they can change not only from activity to activity but from day to day. The artist or attraction will create an expectation and thus influence behaviour.

Their target audience may reflect a particular demographic that may cause the organiser significant problems. For example, the behaviour of a standing audience at rock concert will be different from that of a pop audience. The front of stage area is where the audience will experience a much higher density, rather than, say, the rear. Members of the audience may choose which type of area they wish to view from. A mature rock audience will understand the behaviour of the pit area and choose based on knowledge, while a teen pop audience will not have the experience to distinguish between the areas, and can gravitate towards the front and try to stay there.

Broadly, the density can be broken into four areas for indoor and outdoor events, as shown in figure 15.6.

The total of these areas must not exceed the capacity, and the event manager must ensure that sufficient controls are in place to monitor the crowd, such as closed-circuit television (CCTV) and stewards.

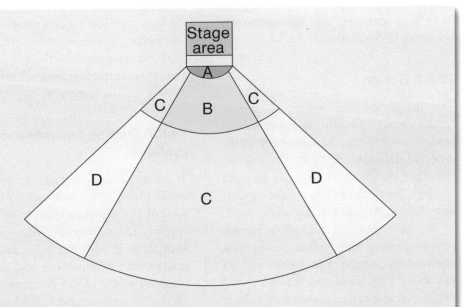

A Very high density front of stage area – probably exceeding occupant density guidance
B High density area behind the front of stage – possibly exceeding recommended occupant density guidance
C Medium density area – meeting recommended occupant density guidance
D Low density area – lower than recommended occupant density guidance

Figure 15.6 Occupant density

15.6.4 Controls

Having identified at the planning stage how it is believed an audience will behave, the application of this knowledge in terms of controls to ensure a safe event is the logical application of the risk management approach. The controls can be implemented in three ways at the design stage by using information and finally by staffing systems. The three methods are not totally distinctive, and link together to ensure that proper crowd management is possible. The controls are designed to influence crowd behaviour and are not to be confused with crowd control, which is forcing a crowd to comply with directives as a result of disorder. These controls are put in place to assist in managing and influencing the behaviour of the audience.

15.6.5 Design

The design of the venue or site is fundamental to establish if the event can safely accommodate the movement of the expected audience.

When designing a site it can be more complex, but the facilitation of the comfort and movement of the audience needs to be the highest consideration. Factors such as queuing lanes, entrances and exits, concessions, services and toilets will all impact on how, when and where a crowd may move, and careful location of services will promote safe crowd migration and reduce the need for intervention.

Many physical control measures exist to support event managers, including barriers, fencing, screens and delay towers, although proper consideration should be given to their use to ensure effectiveness. The final element of design is looking at the soft tools such as the programming of the event, the use of support artists or entertainment, and other methods can be used to manage build-up of crowds, and to facilitate egress at the end of an event.

15.6.6 Information

The planning process should be supported by robust communication channels and this is covered in detail in the section on communication. It should be noted that the timely provision of information not only to the public but also to agencies will enable proactive decision making to take place using known systems of management. Another influencing factor is the ability of the messenger to add or detract from the message that is being provided. Here the beauty of pre-recorded information messages supported by the use of screens and other message systems will assist in the sharing of information.

15.6.7 Staffing and management systems

The correct staffing and deployment of crowd management staff enables the other tools of crowd management to be properly applied. The relationship of an audience with those it perceives as in authority is key, as poor relations can add additional pressures to the crowd management risks. Again, the approach needs to be tailored to the audience profile, but a fair, friendly and firm one is a good starting place.

Staff working on an event should receive full induction training and briefings to understand their role and function, and what should be done in an emergency. This is not only a legal requirement, but also essential if effective crowd management is to take place.

15.6.8 Public information

Communication with the public prior to an event is usually the function of the marketing team. Information about the line-up and the timings will influence how audiences behave. Destinations can be identified by park–and–ride post codes so as to encourage their use.

Directing the public through web links will also ensure that the information is current. They can also sign up to receiving SMS text which can keep people updated without having to go online. This technique can be combined with Bluetooth technology to allow the mobile phone network to be used as one real-time communication tool.

During an event the communication between staff and the public is essential for management to be able to identify and manage situations before they develop. The information helps to continue to understand audience behaviour and allow best use of resources.

15.6.9 Contingency

There is a requirement to have a proper system of management in place to deal and manage with situations outside expected events. This ensures that a decision-making process is established, and accountability can be properly assigned. A contingency plan is designed for the event manager to implement systems to try to revert a situation to normal event conditions. One of the key crowd management tools is to meet the expectations of the audience, therefore to have the ability to continue to operate an event while appropriate measures are put in place is part of an overall strategy. This objective must not, however, be confused with the 'show must go on'-style of management. The overall process that is sought is safe management.

The nature of the event itself may influence what constitutes a major incident and what does not. For example, if a small theatre is evacuated this in itself will not be a major incident, but factors such as audience profile could have further impact. If the audience is primarily made up of children – such as a pantomime audience – their sudden evacuation from the premises, especially if the weather is poor, may actually escalate the problem.

15.7 Evaluation

Evaluation is a critical process within the operational and logistical development of an event. The process of evaluation should be undertaken after each event, with data analysed and improved for following years. Lessons learnt from one event can also be transferred to other events or to the whole events industry (Bowdin et al., 2006).

In this way, events will generally mature over time, as the organisers and other stakeholders become more experienced with working with the unique elements or vagaries of a given event space. Contractors will also develop improved working relationships, ensuring efficiency in their work and that trust is built with key stakeholders.

15.8 Summary

As with all event management processes, the key to success is in planning with the event partners to proper timescales using all of the available data and expertise. This will enable the most effective changes in design and information to be implemented prior to the event, which should allow the management to take a light touch, with crowds effectively 'managing themselves' in what ever zone of the event they are in. In reality, the planning and information provided enables the crowds to manage according to the intention of the management team.

Case study 15.2 Tall Ships, Liverpool, UK

This case study details the infrastructural requirements needed to create an event site in a unique space. Consider the logistical aspects of organising an international event with the many stakeholders outlined below.

Background

The Tall Ships is an international event centred around sailing ships and youth sailing training. When the fleet enters a host port, they are a significant attraction. As part of the 2008 Capital of Culture celebrations, Liverpool was to be the sole host. Coincidently, Merseyside was also host to the British Open Golf Tournament at Birkdale just to the north of the city, thus putting a strain on resources.

Planning

Liverpool's city council (LCC) event team led on planning, closely coordinating with its multi-agency colleagues, namely LCC Highways, Merseyside Police, MerseyTravel, and the Sefton and Wirral councils.

The crowd management plan had three parallel but interconnected elements – movement around the sites, people arriving in Liverpool and how they migrated between the two dock areas where the vessels were berthed.

Crowd modelling

Initial planning began three years before the event, with the Wellington dock being used to host smaller maritime events to enable a slow development of the site and some understanding of how people moved within it.

Initial plans for the layout of the Wellington dock were developed using the multi-agency format. It was very quickly identified that the only solution that maintained crowd movement through and around the site involved the use of temporary bridges. To support this, a raised walkway along one side of the docks nearly 300m long was designed and built. Using crowd management models, LCC were able to show that the site could handle up to 60 000 persons per day.

The other dock, Albert Dock, was an established and well-known visitor attraction; however, previous events had shown crowding issues could prevent migration around the site, and at certain times effectively prohibit all movement. It was felt that a one-way system was required and should be supported by stewards, signage and barriers.

Arriving in Liverpool

Live information feeds were used to determine local, regional and national traffic flows to Liverpool. The aim of the traffic management plan was to direct external visitors to convenient park–and–ride sites to ease the flow of the crowds to and from the site.

The information was shared on a multi-agency basis, with an LCC operational event control being supported by all of the blue-light services and a separate traffic management centre feeding live information to the operations team.

Crowd movement between sites

Using standard crowd management models relating to ingress, queue time and available public transport, a transfer profile was put in place. Efficient transportation relied heavily on public transport – the trains were each able to carry 600+ passengers every seven minutes. Additionally, shuttle buses (up to 22 at a time) on a protected route were able to link Pier Head, the Wellington dock and the Underground.

A truncated radio system with a default back-to-back system was in place for all LCC contractors. CCTV and information technology (IT) also ensured that information was shared and communicated via morning and evening debriefs to highlight action points.

The event was extremely successful with culture company directors claiming over one million visitors. There were no significant crowding issues and all were able to flow at reasonable speed around both sites with queuing times never exceeding 30 minutes.

Questions for research

1 Which local and regional authorities would you communicate with to host a music event for 10 000 people?
2 What should be considered when selecting a site for an event?
3 Consider the Henley Festival case study detailed in this chapter and think about the risks associated with building an event site under time and resource constraints.
4 Consider the role of crowd management at different event sizes. At what size (e.g. 1 000 persons) would an organiser produce a separate crowd management plan and what would it contain?
5 Think about the operational requirements in organising an event in different locations. For example, would there be differing considerations for indoor or outdoor venues, or in rural or urban locations?

Recommended websites

Browse the following internet sites for interesting and informative information:

Event Management Body of Knowledge: http://www.embok.org
Mingus, M – creating an operations manual: http://www.iaam.org/facility_manager/pages/2005_Aug_Sep/OperationsEvents_Manual.htm
O'Toole's Event Management Checklist – event manual: http://www-personal.usyd.edu.au/~wotoole/EPMS_Control/Checklists/manual/manual.html.
The SLA toolkit: http://www.service-level-agreement.net/

Suggested reading

Allen, J, O'Toole, B, McDonnell & Harris, R. 2005. *Festival and Special Event Management*, 3 ed. Milton, Qld: John Wiley & Sons.

Berridge, G. 2007. *Events Design and Experience*. Oxford: Butterworth-Heinemann.

Bowdin, G, McDonnell, I, Allen, J & O'Toole, B. 2006. *Events Management*. Oxford: Butterworth-Heinemann.

Getz, D. 2005. *Event Management and Event Tourism*. New York: Cognizant Communication Corp.

HSE, GB. 1999. *The Event Safety Guide: A Guide to Health, Safety and Welfare at Music and Similar Events*. Suffolk: HSE Books.

HSE publication. 1997. *Managing Contractors: A Guide for Employers*. Suffolk: HSE Books.

Johnston, R & Clark, G. 2001. *Service Operations Management*. Harlow: Financial Times-Prentice Hall.

Tum, J, Norton, P & Wright, N. 2005. *Management of Events operations (Events Management)*. Oxford: Butterworth-Heinemann.

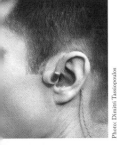
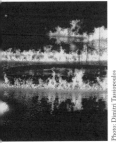

Photo: Dimitri Tassiopoulos

Photo: World Travel Market

16 Events technology

Peta Thomas

Abstract

This chapter illustrates the rationale for using information technology (IT) systems in events from small to large scale by helping the event manager understand the diversity and broad application of information technology to support the overall event. Information technology tools are defined in the design phase of the event to aid in the delivery of event objectives. The tools to be used are chosen for attributes that both enhance the event experience of the event attendees and permit management access to data which will highlight gaps between expected and actual performance. The technology can direct decision making by the event manager as it provides accurate, real-time, snapshots of the event progress. Post-event, the data is critically appraised to improve future event management performance.

Chapter objectives

After you have read this chapter you should be able to:

☐ understand how information technology has useful interventions and value-adding actions at every stage of the event;

☐ understand the term 'information database' and how to design, implement and maintain an information database;

☐ consider which data elements will help manage the event and how the tools necessary to capture this information should be integrated as a framework at the event-planning phase for specific operational areas of an event, such as registration, attendee satisfaction and legal compliance;

☐ consider both paper and electronic document-based information and how each contributes to an event information system;

☐ research and choose appropriate information technology for gathering event data and enhancing the event experience;

☐ appreciate how the quality of the information generated has an impact on service delivery performances through the decisions taken based on this information; and

☐ recognise that the loosely connected network of event stakeholders will be more cohesive in their actions if they communicate pertinent data well.

16.1 Introduction

It is the responsibility of every events manager to decide how best to combine products, processes and the actions of the many support people engaged in an event in a manner conducive to a rewarding event experience. Meeting Professionals International (MPI) (2009a) in their survey *EventView 2009*, notes that events are considered 'experience marketing' so the quality of the experience defines the event success. Choosing appropriate IT tools can augment the event experience from obvious value-adding operational activities such as creating a user-friendly website, to less obvious factors such as including tools that monitor event performance. The latter accumulate data that draws attention to deviations from the expected performance of monitored event variables allowing for strategic management interventions to be made to correct them. Information is 'a collection

of facts organized in such a way that they have additional value beyond the value of the facts themselves' (Stair, 1996: 5). It is up to the event manager to decide what facts are required, what tools will provide them and in what form (written reports, website updates, etc.) to gather and disseminate the collected information. Communicating the right information to the right people at the right time ensures the project momentum is coordinated for event success.

16.2 Planning

The first step in planning an IT strategy for an event is to ensure that the objectives and goals of the event are clearly defined. Examination of the original event brief will highlight the client's needs. If these are not fully understood, undertaking qualitative (open-ended questioning) with selected survey groups within and outside the client company can help. This can involve surveying the potential attendees as to what they believe would offer them a memorable event. The surveyed attendees will be in the range of the client-defined target audience. In the case of exhibitions it would be buyers, trade organisations and exhibitors; for meetings it could be delegates and their association representatives. Using this data, the client and event manager can create a set of objectives for the event that is the expectation of how returns for the investments of time, money and human resources will be gained. These are known as the returns on investment (ROI) objectives. Case study 16.1 illustrates how this works.

Case study 16.1 Event ROI objectives

Annually, a South African government department specialising in reviewing available information technology obtainable in South Africa and internationally organises a conference to showcase the latest technologies, solutions and trends, and to bring together diverse stakeholders across the public and private sector. The main objective of the conference is to deal with the continued education of government employees (who execute IT purchases) through promoting knowledge sharing and fostering dialogue among ICT role players who share a common interest in transforming government. The objectives for the meeting are set by the government department while the method and processes required for delivery of these objectives is decided by the event manager in consultation with the client. The client requires that the success of the event is measured by monitoring the degree to which each objective is successfully delivered. The client and event manager decide how the data that will reflect this will be gathered. Some of the objectives of this event, the processes that helped deliver them and the data they generated are reflected here:

1a. **Objective.** Effective and efficient event registration – online registration with a secure credit card handling facility; promotion of associated sub-events; promotion of keynote speakers; promotion of skills to be learnt;

1b. **Processes to deliver the objective.** By building an online registration website which also links to a promotional marketing plan to which the website responds dynamically;

1c. **Measurement of process quality and effectiveness.** By website statistics; by online questionnaires; by financial reporting (accounting software packages).

2a. **Objective:** Educational event content review – of current government procurement policies; best practice in the management of suppliers; review of current technologies and applicability in an operational environment;

2b. **Processes to deliver the objective.** Investigating and understanding the current skills and future needs of the target pool of government attendees; creation of a speaker programmer with selected speakers and facilitators developing skills; design of sessions for interactive discussion of specialists/lecture/hands-on workshops;

2c. **Measurement of process quality and effectiveness.** Feedback questionnaires on appropriateness of content; quality of speakers; appropriateness of venue to the event using voting software and electronic surveys.

3a. **Objective.** Time-relevant and cost-effective communications about the event;

3b. **Processes to deliver the objective.** Communications processes for delivery by website, SMS, email and fax (fax is the back-up option for less-developed IT areas or for those employees who are not IT literate);

⫸

3c. **Measurement of quality and effectiveness.** Variations on the activity monitored on the website; feedback from attendees as to the appropriateness of the communications using voting software and electronic surveys.

4a. **Objective.** An exhibition in parallel to the conference that displays best-of-breed technology and allows relationships between government departments and suppliers to be nurtured;

4b. **Processes to deliver the objective.** Development of an exhibitor list; integration of a web-based exhibitor support platform; relevant communications to all participants;

4c. **Measurement of process quality and effectiveness.** Feedback from attendees and exhibitors on the appropriateness of the venue; the opportunities set aside during the event for personal networking; the return on exhibitor investment in terms of leads using voting software and electronic surveys.

5a. **Objective.** A confirmation for the government sponsors that the event brings benefit to their many offices and lends in creating superlative technological support within government offices;

5b. **Processes to deliver the objective.** Financial sponsorship plan for the event;

5c. **Measurement of process quality and effectiveness.** A comprehensive report on the degree of fulfilment of the event's stated objectives qualified by actual evaluations of collected data and analysis of reports. This includes recommendations for the benefit gained by repeating the event in the following year while also suggesting improved strategies and policies (normative) management on how stakeholder needs could be better served in the next event – supported by reports created in Microsoft Excel®, and Word®.

Source: Thomas (2009)

Designing systems that ensure that the ROI objectives are met begins with an overall analysis of the current situation of the event. Drawing a picture with computer clipart or by hand (called a rich picture because it should be rich in detail) helps pictorially display these objectives and the stakeholders that have to be satisfied. Figure 16.1 is an example of a rich picture highlighting stakeholders, processes and structures that need to be considered. Rich pictures are easily created in Microsoft PowerPoint® (or equivalent) or by cutting and pasting pictures onto paper. Stakeholders included in the picture will be both internal customers such as the client, organising committee and regulatory bodies, and external customers such as the attendees, the media and the local community. The picture should include potential event threats/constraints relevant to IT usage in this event situation. It can take account of lessons learnt from past experiences with this event from preceeding years or prior events that have similarities. The picture can show what skill competencies are available internally in the event or client company that could be harnessed for the event. These could include, for example, the client's marketing and PR team, or the event company's stage and entertainment designer. Other specialised skills not available internally are reflected in the rich picture, and help identify the external skills that will need to be hired – for instance a specialist registration team. Other aspects of the rich picture could be competitor events that have the potential to take some of the target market share; political aspects that may affect the event; local weather patterns if co-events are planned outside or if the geographic area has threats such as hurricanes; and currency fluctuations if dealing with more than one currency. When doing this situational analysis, it is important to think about the expected and unexpected situations that may need to be dealt with. Lines are drawn between art clips to represent interfaces and relationships across which data needs to flow.

The picture provides a broad overview of the situation for discussion as to how the project can be tackled within the budget available. Discussion around a rich picture can proceed simultaneously with all educational levels of staff. In developing

countries the event manager acknowledges that operational/ground support staff often have key inputs for success and although they may not have the ability to read a written situational scenario, can still understand the concepts pictorially. This discussion will raise many ideas on how each objective can be met. Figure 16.2 shows how the ideas from brainstorming a particular event process – in this example, attendee registration – are grouped through the creation of an affinity diagram. An affinity diagram is a business tool used to show the affinity or relationships between ideas. The headings are chosen to represent broad categories of ideas. They do not have a logical vertical sequence but represent groups of similar ideas. The headings for figure 16.2 were chosen to reflect the main

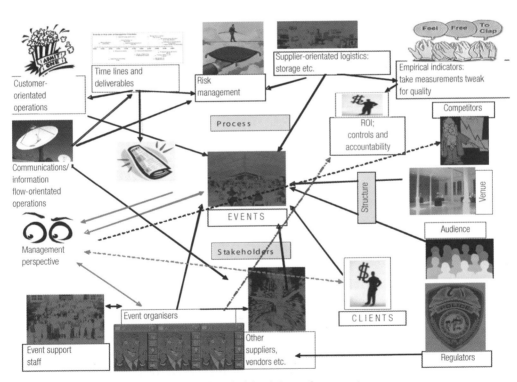

Figure 16.1 A rich picture of an event

Source: Thomas (2009)

What are the issues to be considered on event registration?		
Attributes	**People flow**	**Specialist services needed**
Recall challenges on past events	How many days are required for registration? How many people a day? Opening/closing times at registration	Manual registration or staff trained on IT registration system
Total number of attendees	Registration for consecutive events (sponsor events, gala dinners, workshops)	Interpreters
Categories of attendees: VIPs, media, attendees, disabled, crew, etc.	Currencies to be used	Venue support staff – refreshments; lounge area set-up
Design of badge types: RFID; barcodes; magnetic strips; smart cards (embedded chips); information layout	How many staff required for prepaid, on-site payment, part payment sections, etc.?	Client staff
Collateral each participant needs – where does it come from?	How will money be stored? How will it be banked?	Financial staff
What type of queuing will be used?	Special access – VIPs, the disabled, speakers, media	Event team staff and temporary support staff
How many badges, registration booths required?	Venue layout – ingress and egress	Security
Registration online	Creating pre-populated online registration forms, etc.	Graphic/web design team – website/badge design

Figure 16.2 Example of an affinity diagram for event registration ideas

Source: Thomas (2009)

concepts that a process for registration needed to consider on this particular event. The elements of each row horizontally do not have a relationship. These techniques require no technology, and help to visually construct the process being analysed.

The affinity groupings shown in figure 16.2 reflect elements of the processes that will need to be included in planning when setting up this particular registration service.

It will be found that the discussion around the rich picture and the creation of the affinity diagram will often lead to a clearer understanding of the type of venue required to house the processes so that they will perform optimally. This will be important when choosing a venue as the physical attributes of the venue and its surrounding geographic area can play a crucial role in successful technology implementation.

The type of venue attributes that need to be investigated include the types and number of electrical plugs; IT connection ports; internet connectivity (walls sometimes have structural reinforcing that blocks electronic signals); venue connectivity charges; cellular/public phone accessibility; WiFi facilities; internal wiring (copper cable/fibre optics) dictating the speed of transfer of data; and the venue's internal wiring networks. When choosing the tools to deliver the event it is necessary to consider its unique requirements. Examples of this are event-specific software/hardware (Linux, Microsoft, etc.); different software versions; internet live linking; inclusion of video clips; use of remote pointers, etc. If the event is sending data offsite or receiving it for inclusion in the event, there may be bandwidth limitations, which often requires communicating with local authorities to see if they can provide more. In developing countries a process may be required to handle the needs of speakers delivering presentations in extremely old word editor formats.

Once a thorough understanding of the processes required for the delivery of an event aspect is acquired, it is essential for the event manager to decide on which

---

Examples of performance indicators for event registration

IT performance indicators

Electronic registration of several hundred attendees – possible performance indicators to track:

- ❒ Ease of use of registration website – attendee personal interview or online survey;
- ❒ Time needed online by an attendee to create their registration – website statistics;
- ❒ Webpages of interest to the attendee – website statistics;
- ❒ Attendees registered at critical milestone dates of the event plan – database interrogation to determine the success of the marketing;
- ❒ Pre-event sales special take-up by attendees (early-bird specials) – financial reports;
- ❒ On-site registration time spent in queuing for each attendee – attendee survey;
- ❒ Speed/ease of payment procedures if outsourced before event/on site – internal staff survey and attendee survey; and
- ❒ Currency fluctuations for an international event – financial reports for risk control.

Manual performance indicators

Manual registration of several hundred attendees – possible performance indicators to track:

- ❒ Telephone/fax log book completeness – staff survey;
- ❒ Attendee filing systems rules – quality of attendee experience survey;
- ❒ Manual financial reporting system – financial reports;
- ❒ Manual report of attendees registered – interrogation of attendee filing system;
- ❒ Manual badge preparation – attendee survey of clarity and relevance; and
- ❒ Attendee time in queues – attendee survey.

Source: Thomas (2009)

---

tools will most effectively generate the data that reflects the quality of performance. The box on page 323 reveals the range of performance indicators that could be included in the registration processes to monitor the quality of each process. It is usually up to the event manager to decide where and when to apply the performance indicators over the event from pre- to post-event. It is also up to the event manager in consultation with the event team to choose the most appropriate performance measurement tool to use.

Case study 16.2 reflects some of the IT technology challenges encountered in the delivery of a speaker management process which should have been discovered in the affinity diagram, rich picture exercise and discussion period. It can be seen that there were several unique challenges in this speaker management and if the delivery of the process had not been analysed, this speaker management may well have failed to meet quality objectives set by the client. The processes were planned to operationally support and deliver a high-quality service.

It can be seen that through thorough situational analysis, an IT plan of the complementary strategies that will support delivery of the event emerges. This plan will outline the mix of resources required which includes various IT applications. These applications supplement the entire knowledge pool on the event, and smooth the progressive integration of the skilled suppliers with specialised technical tools (e.g. translation, event registration, etc.) supporting each process. Overall, the plan is designed to deliver an attendee event experience that is memorable for its quality and application to fulfilling stakeholder needs (Getz, 2007). This plan ultimately reflects the Conventions Industry Council's (2005: 51) recommendations which ensure

that the event scope and associated quality of the delivery of each event objective have been individually defined in terms of the:

❑ 'tools' chosen to deliver the objective. These include technology solutions, defined processes and specialist human resource skills;

❑ 'terrain' which is the environment best suited to deliver the objective, such as the venue, the host community and the country; and

❑ anticipated impact over 'time' of the objective which is considered to be the measurement of impact of the event on attendees from their first contact to the post-event legacy that enhances event brand equity.

The integrated processes plan is an operational blueprint for a successful event delivery (Getz, 2007). It reflects all aspects of the information technology required on the event, including the operational processes and performance indicators. Indicators reflect the variation in service quality, illustrating gaps between expected and actual performance. This is important because monitoring and interventions that keep variable performances within acceptable limits help ensure a high degree of satisfaction for the people who receive the services (Scholtes, 1998). Examples of people who receive the service may be the attendees who are trying to buy a ticket online or, the client's accountant trying to report back on event expenditure to-date – it will be their experiences with the processes that the indicators should monitor for quality. The task falls to the event management to motivate the event team to strive for higher service quality levels. This in turn creates an environment where optimised returns on event objectives and investments are made

Case study 16.2 Speaker management

A large not-for-profit association meets annually at an international convention centre. The conference lasts three days and draws in aid workers from HIV clinics working in extremely remote areas across Africa. The meeting's purpose is to consolidate how the past year's fieldwork has proceeded and allow networking between attendees for better solutions to shared problems for the coming year. The speakers are aid workers from doctors to operational staff, and because of their geographical spread they often have minimal IT access in order to prepare in advance for this conference. Approximately 250–300 speakers present over the three days. There are 800–1000 attendees. Pre-event communication to speakers and attendees is delivered by the association through their own website and communications networks. The speaker presentations are received as delegates arrive on site the day before or on the morning of their presentation. Challenges for this conference dealt with annually are as follows:

❑ Many forms of software, i.e. various versions of Microsoft Office Word® word editor, or equivalent word editor software;

❑ Many forms of portable data devices, i.e. 3½ inch stiffie discs (still in use in parts of Africa), DVDs and memory sticks;

❑ Non-standard background to slides – speaker slides need to be reformatted by the IT staff into a standard format look (in PowerPoint®);

❑ Software viruses – choosing virus shields to protect the IT network;

❑ A great need by almost every speaker for last-minute access to computers to make final preparations to their slides. This also requires a great deal of help from competent IT technicians to help incorporate audio and visual clips, and proof printings;

❑ An intellectual property waiver is required from each speaker and for group presentations – the entire group's signatures. The latter is a challenge as often only one representative of a group presentation will be at a conference so care must be taken to ensure no liability falls to the event if only one signature represents the group;

❑ Presentations details as to ownership/creator/presenter and content have to be reconciled on an overall master document of the speaker, presentation, day, track and time of presentation;

❑ Presentations are transmitted from the speaker room to the main plenary room and the breakaway rooms, each manned by an IT technician. The technician needs to know prior to each session in what order the presentations occur and what peculiarities there are, e.g. presentation links to the internet; a video played from a video cassette tape at a point in the presentation, etc.

At the closure of the conference, a legacy DVD of all material presented is required for key personnel (approximately 400). Printed material of specific sessions is prepared for those returning to regions where IT support is unavailable. This collateral needs to be ready by the time the delegates leave the site as shipping to these remote areas is extremely difficult.

Source: Thomas (2009)

possible. The performance-related data is both qualitative and quantitative, telling the event organiser about the 'here and now' of the event for immediate control purposes and the 'there and then' for plotting adaptive and innovation strategies (Espejo, 2003). Performance-related data analysis allows for strategic planning with ongoing adaptive decisions taken to ensure the intended objectives are reached (Getz, 2007).

16.3 Information technology

There is a wide variety of IT services available for events which are continually evolving. Events organisers need to keep abreast of the latest developments in technology to identify the most appropriate technology to attain the IT objectives of the event. Researching international trends helps ensure the most appropriate tool is selected.

Pivotal to the success of the event are IT processes that deliver accurate, relevant data to guide operational efficiencies and strategic decision making. Databases supporting an event store much of this data, so such they need to be well designed and maintained. The databases are integrated into the processes of the event as a whole, so data degradation of any point in this network can affect the performance of the whole system (Warren, 2008). This is because elements of data from a database can be mixed in many ways to generate reports. If some of the data is inaccurate it will affect the entire report quality and any decisions taken based on that report may well be the wrong ones. Good databases reduce the event risk profile by capturing data from many sources and amalgamating it, which ensures a supply of excellent-quality data across the event system. Stair

(1996: 162) notes that '[t]he pool of related data is often shared by multiple application programmes' so errors can have a resonating effect throughout the event system.

16.3.1 Databases

A well-designed and maintained database ensures that data accessed from it is useful, relevant and accurate. An electronic database of event data elements should be designed to store data in simple, standardised formats. Storing several data elements in one field slows down processes such as searches and sorts as shown in the 'wrong format' of figure 16.3. The design of a paper-based database of paper data capture forms needs to apply the same logic. Databases often link each attendee to a unique code, which can be used as a reference in other technology such as RFID tags for sports competitors and conference/exhibition attendees.

Wrong format		Correct format	
Mrs Brown	X	Mrs	Brown
Parkview 2122	X	Parkview	2122
Dietary preference	X	Yes	Vegetarian
John Smith	X	John	Smith

Figure 16.3 An example of data elements format

Source: Thomas (2009)

Use predefined lists of possible variations to standardise data (sometimes known as pre-populated or smart forms).

e.g. '*TITLE*' dropdown list = Mr; Miss; Ms; Dr; Other

e.g. '*BADGE TYPE*' dropdown list = Media; Delegate; Speaker; Security; Staff

An electronic spreadsheet, such as Microsoft Excel®, consists of a grid made from columns and rows much like an old paper-based accounting book as shown in figure 16.4. Useful features of such spreadsheets include the following:

❏ Each cell of the grid can be formatted for numeric/text data;
❏ The spreadsheet can link to a Microsoft statistics suite;
❏ It is a powerful management tool for 'what if ...' scenarios. Cells can be linked by formulae, so changing one cell can highlight the ripple effect through the rest of the system;
❏ It is useful for budget planning, graphs, trend analysis, sorts etc;
❏ The worksheet(s) can be shared by several users simultaneously;
❏ It is relatively easily programmable by most members of the event team; and
❏ There are different levels of access security – different database users will have different privileges (access levels) associated with their jobs on the event. Some will only be able to read the data while others will have the authority to alter and manipulate it in its electronic format.

Limitations can be that the spreadsheets can get very detailed with lengthy columns and rows.

MySQL® is a relational database management system which is used in website-linked database applications and usually requires the services of a programmer. When events databases have many elements, a multi-relational database such as Microsoft Access® or MySQL® can be considered. Multi-relational databases are designed to link several data tables uniquely to each other, reflecting data relationships.

Useful features of such databases include the following:

❏ The ability to import/export data from/to other formats such as Microsoft Excel® and Microsoft Outlook®, which makes sharing data easy;
❏ A multi-user attribute locking a record off from others while one user uses it, but other users can continue to access the rest of the database;
❏ A querying interface tool to display data in various forms for screen/print reports;
❏ Levels of access security; and
❏ Fast access of database data.

The limitations of a relational database's data capacity should be well understood by the event management team before the event begins through discussion with the IT staff supporting the product.

It should be remembered that contents of databases are confidential (personal details

	Budgeted cost	Actual cost	Total expenditure
Registration	10 000.00	9 250.00	c/fwd 13 250.00
Carpark security	5 000.00	7 000.00	
Entertainment	15 000.00 (running total formula)	16 250.00 (running total formula)	29 500.00 (formula: 13 250.00 + 16 250.00)

Figure 16.4 A two-dimensional (row/column) database
Source: Thomas (2009)

of event participants need to be protected) and valuable (this database is important to the event manager for event management and to the client for marketing and future events). Both paper-based and electronic databases should have defined personnel access criteria (passwords associated with levels of access). Databases should have associated change-control processes. Change control is a set of instructions set up by the event management as to when and how changes to existing processes and data can take place. Change decisions need to be documented and signed by the authorised parties before they can be executed to ensure their responsibility for change is established. It is critical for the professional event organiser to create clear and concise evidence trails of IT actions taken during the event life cycle in case of legal action. It is good practice when working with electronic data to make regular back-ups and store them off site to ensure the safety of this important information.

16.3.2 Event websites

Event websites are commercial websites as they are built for the purpose of promoting an event and its associated activities, such as registration/ticketing, associated product sales, etc.

The domain name for an event should ideally belong to the event owner as websites build the financial equity value associated with the event brand. If the event is staged regularly, maintaining the website on the internet and updating the information on an ongoing basis to sustain prominence with search engines is essential. The website can include a content management system (CMS) that allows easy access for uploading new photographs, schedules, etc. by non-programmer staff. Downloadable print material can be available in Adobe Reader® portable document format (pdf) which is a file format created by Adobe Systems, Inc. and is highly portable across computer platforms. Thematic administration, which is the software for the management of speakers' abstracts, papers, etc. for conferences, can also be added to the website. Website content is regulated by intellectual property laws so care must be taken to gain permission for any copyrighted material used.

The event manager and the marketing/promotional team can review the website's statistical package associated with the event website. This software accumulates data about the computers accessing the website. As every computer has a unique identification code, the software accumulates the unique visits under a wide variety of headings useful in directing the decision-making process for website management by the event manager. Since the software collects information on the behaviour of the viewer on the website, it can be used by the management team to decide their next actions to manage the website performance. For instance, since dynamic websites have an associated database that contains data elements that are accessed in different combinations depending on the user request, this can be changed to improve user friendliness. Another example of using the data is to examine online ticket-purchasing behaviour by reviewing the average amount of time it takes to purchase a ticket. This analysis may reveal that the website is performing below optimum speed levels or that the potential attendee is having difficulty completing the registration.

16.3.3 Registration systems

Event registration is usually the first contact point the attendee has with an event. It is often web based, sometimes remote from the event site or can be on site at the event. Registration needs to run efficiently and accurately, collecting and storing all details relevant to that attendee's successful entry to the event. IT software helps in many ways, including ease of financial processing (secure online transactions), personal attendee detail capture (simple, standardised data collection) and sometimes IT hardware such as touch-sensitive screens for selection of data inputs. A well-planned process minimises the attendee's time in queues, reduces the burden of event staff if the system is self-help driven, and maintains an accurate registration database.

Paper-based systems

A paper-based system for small/rural events requires the creation of a standardised, concise registration form. A system needs to be in place to deliver the forms to attendees and receive these back. A date stamp is a useful tool and should be used to date the received papers. Registration documents can be filed in date-ascending order, and sorted alphabetically within date. A master registry of all documents received and the date and financial amounts submitted act as a control. Uniquely numbered receipts, issued for all cash/cheques provide another financial control as the receipts become part of the database for tracking purposes. This is a classic performance indicator that is often overlooked, but gaps in the receipt sequence would highlight an inefficient and inaccurate process. Paper-based systems require performance indicators as errors in their data can have adverse effects on many other aspects of an event. For instance, an inaccurate registration could give the wrong number of attendees, and then meals and accommodation may also be inaccurate, resulting in an unexpected cost to the event.

Electronic-based systems

The Microsoft Office Excel® spreadsheet, or equivalent, can act as the registration database. Alternatively, the services of a specialist event support team offering registration services can be hired for the time of the event. Electronic, web-based registration systems usually have an associated back-end database where attendee details are captured. Websites used for purchases (tickets, promotional items, etc.) require a secure payment platform.

Web-based registration pre-event has the following advantages:

❑ Delegates have a 24/7 opportunity for registration;

❑ Delegates can pay the registration fees while being geographically remote from the event;

❑ Multiple currency types and transactions can be automatically processed;

❑ There is no requirement for event staff to decipher illegible handwriting or copy and paste information out of emails; event staff can be deployed on other tasks; and

❑ The associated database and statistics provide a great deal of managerial information for decision making.

Electronic registration systems can offer the integration of other delegate data, such as travel, meals, spouse programme and accommodation details. Specialised information for the attendee identification badges can be collated – people may be colour-coded into groups (e.g. cyclists linked to their start times); official titles and their organisations in addition to their full names can be captured; photographs, fingerprints and proof of identification can be gathered as event owners often require them for security purposes. A recent development in remotely linking attendees to their personal data held in a database is with the use of radio frequency identification (RFID tags, as in case study 16.3). Sportsmen wear the tag on their arm or leg while at an event and it can be part of the delegate registration badge. This is a good way of monitoring the delegates' movements as they pass through RFID sensors set up along attendee routes – the sensors link to the database and store this data.

The hardware and software IT networks that are set up for the on-site registration area depend on the number and type of people. For example, VIPs would need an exclusive processing routing that detains them as little as possible. In some instances their representative may appear for the process and not the VIP. This needs to be catered for. Media require different event information to a standard collateral pack – they will require VIP and speaker details, and client organisation briefs. Media often do not pay to attend the event so their attendance in the system will be reflected with 'nil' financial data, and a process to handle this needs to have been developed. Aspects such as the time available for the processing and the type of delegate identification to be created need to be considered in the overall time management plans. On-site database and associated software uses the pre-event database as the core information and adds more data to it as more is learnt as the event progresses.

Case study 16.3 Attendee details linked to other technology

August 2007 – The organisers of the *Levene Half Marathon*, held in Taupo, New Zealand, employed ground-breaking timing technology to provide a level of accuracy and responsiveness in recording times unseen at the event before. This year organisers turned to Times-7 Sport, a Wellington-based specialist in sports timing, to provide the sophisticated timing solution. Around 3 000 competitors from around the country had their times automatically recorded using RFID-powered timing tags attached to each competitor's shoes. These RFID tags were used in conjunction with Times-7's Sportscore events management software to record each competitor's start time, half-way split time and finish time.

Source: Times-7 Sport (2007)

16.3.4 Interpretation, translation and transcription

When many nationalities meet for an event there is often a requirement for simultaneous language interpretation systems to enhance the enjoyment and value of the event content to the attendee. Case study 16.4 examines an event using four languages and how IT software and hardware background support added value to the proceedings.

16.3.5 Exhibitions

Exhibitions are an event area for which IT can provide various support tools, especially as exhibition stands become more experiential in an effort to stand out in the minds of buyers.

Case study 16.4 Interpretation, translation and transcription

A large conference whose attendees represented most of the countries of Africa required special support from interpreters, translators and transcribers. Following the guidelines of the organising committee directive on this matter, the event manager designed a support system that ensured event language services were to be available in four languages at the conference – Arabic, English, German and French. The client also requested a specialised mini computer network that linked each attendee to all the others in the room.

The interpretation used specific language specialists who interpreted the spoken word consecutively as the speaker talked. Each language was supported by a pair of interpreters working alternately in the same language, and had a soundproof booth from which the two could observe the speaker and the audience. The booth and its IT support were set up some time before the conference. In this case the IT challenge was to ensure that the interpreters had excellent auditory facilities to hear the speaker and voice link to the audience for interpretation services, which were to be delivered to 300 audience members via audience-linked headphones attached to a software system designed to switch language channels. These systems had the functionality for the delegate to change languages at will to obtain another of the four languages. Additionally, each delegate had a mini computer screen at his or her seat for individual internet linking and email messaging to other consoles in the auditorium. Furthermore, the communication from the floor and by the interpreters was taped to ensure a legacy record and for future back-casting for information that resulted from the conference. The audiovisual links were facilitated through a dedicated computer that was manned by technical staff who monitored the quality of the recordings. The interpreters and the technicians needed to be aware of the IT speaker schedule and to have seen the speakers' slides prior to each session. Venue attributes played a critical part in planning the room set-up for interpretation as pillars affected sound quality of the speaker questions from the floor, while a shortage of electrical outlets meant laying in long lengths of cabling that needed to be covered up to stop people tripping over them.

The speaker's language and the interpreted languages were streamed live to the conference website for virtual attendees, and this needed specialised IT support to ensure that, for example, the speaker's mouth and movements were correctly linked to the voice. Sufficient bandwidth was anticipated to ensure voice audio did not become unlinked from speaker mouth movements. Specialised software allowed the presentation, the speaker video, the agenda, controls for volume and pause, etc., and text messaging to be available to virtual attendees.

Translation required a separate room to have a networked computer system of printers, computers and language-specific software. (Sometimes specialised typing keypads are required.) Translators took printed/electronic documents and translated them to other languages. This network required internet access for research around particular aspects of the translation (context, colloquialisms, etc.) and email facilities to send/receive information pertinent to the translation.

Transcription occurred from speakers' voices taped in conference sessions, and these tapes were transcribed to electronic documents for easy transferral to print/email, etc. These were also stored on DVDs.

Source: Thomas (2009)

For the event organiser the challenge is to conclude sales of floor space and maximise other associated revenue streams from stand sales and stand accoutrements while being as attractive to the buyer and seller as possible. The organiser's efforts are to realise the objectives of the current event and to build positive exposure for the next year. From the exhibitor's point of view, the purpose is to make contacts for sales, so the more attractive the exhibition is to a range of buyers and the more comprehensive the marketing efforts on the part of the event management to attract buyers, the more exhibitors can expect to obtain a better return on their investment by appearing on the show. The same requirement for a return on investment applies from the buyer's perspective – the more they can learn about products on offer and the wider the range of related products to choose from and to learn about, the better they feel the time and cost to attend the event has been realised.

16.4 Communication channels

IT functions can be used to support green events and one of the most successful applications is in reducing the amount of printed materials and collateral circulated. One of the most useful tools is the web and email, which can reduce waste from traditional communication in paper such as flyers/letter/print advertising. Once on site, many communications can be facilitated through the venue's intranet linking with information bulletins, electronic signage and other messaging.

16.4.1 Cellular messaging

Cellular phone text messaging (SMS) is a very cheap, effective way of transmitting information.

The data transmitted can go from one sender to multiple recipients in a single action, and the cost of text messages is low. The SMS travels geographic distance in a very short time. It is reliant on everyone's cellular numbers being previously captured and an associated policy governing usage.

16.4.2 Email

Email communication must have relevancy for the receiver of such communication. The sender should be aware that spam protection on a receiving server may disable the delivery of email messages. Personalisation

---

Case study 16.5 IT support for exhibitions

The annual Tourism Indaba is held in South Africa to facilitate the buying and selling of African tourism products to a global audience. The IT support used includes electronic registration of buyers; exhibitor data collection including payment schedules, stand requirements, peripheral services (catering, lighting, screens, etc); electronic brochure distribution; exhibition service manual; appointment list management for buyers and exhibitors; event communication updates; floor-planning software for exhibitors and associated or concessionary services; schedules of exhibitor equipment delivery to site and off site; lead retrieval systems for exhibitors; and contact retrieval for buyers. As in other events, streaming from the exhibition of special demonstrations or talks by TV and to the website provides interactive participation by wider virtual audiences so creating more value in the event.

Source: Thomas (2009)

is easily done by most automated email systems from an associated database of names. Branding can be set up for all email and signatures, carrying the look and feel of the website and other marketing through the email footer/header. Contact details for event staff must be explicit.

Bulk email and cellular phone SMSs are available through the internet on a hire-as-required basis. These services are generally used to inform attendees of new developments in the event; remind them of important times, places and venues of interest to them; communicate limited opportunities; and discount programmes. The quality of these communications can lead to the building of a strong relationship between the event and the participant. Depending on their planned use in the strategic communication plan, this service can drive attendee sales, and allied sales of co-events (such as tours, dinners, etc).

16.5 Support technology for global participation

16.5.1 Virtual meetings

Meeting Professionals International (2009b: 11), in *FutureWatch 2009*, reported the results of their industry survey of future technological advances in events – that many industry service suppliers see 'virtual meetings as an important trend and many predict a shift to Web-based learning as a way to control meeting and travel costs'. An additional aspect of this trend of virtual attendee participation is that access to the event via virtual connectivity reduces the event carbon footprint by reducing the waste involved in vehicle transportation of attendees to the event and the general waste that would have been created by people attending in person, such as leftovers at meals, paper, washing bedroom linen, etc.

Case study 16.6 Virtual conferencing

Global Linkage over Broadband Links (GLOBAL) is providing a virtual conference centre using advanced communication technologies and concepts to support the promotion of e-infrastructure topics in Europe and around the world.

One of the main goals of GLOBAL is to allow and help research projects to disseminate their results and training events to a wider audience located in multiple geographical locations through the organisation of virtual conferences. GLOBAL provide a user-centric interface for planning, creating, announcing, coordinating, content management and realisation of virtual conferences with open and wide participation. Through these virtual conferences, the participating users will be able to exchange information on e-infrastructure development in their region, identify partners for future collaboration, and exchange and discuss synergies between their running initiatives. The virtual conference events will provide advanced videoconferencing, and collaboration tools and support to the participants. Each event will be recorded and stored on a repository together with documents and outcomes for future consultation. The virtual conference centre will provide three main functions focused on usability: a virtual auditorium for planning, coordination and management of the virtual events; an event repository to store the recordings and outcomes of the events; and a virtual corridor, which will support networking and partnership building among the participants.

Source: European Commissions Global Project (2009)

When several attendees link into the event via the internet, this is known as a webinar or webcast. Webinars can be interactive with participants in the presentation typing their questions to the presenter, or using voice-over internet protocol (VoIP). VoIP is a general term used for a family of transmission technologies used for the delivery of voice communications over networks such as the internet. Case study 16.6 depicts an interesting example of a virtual conference platform that holds virtual meetings throughout the year to aid in the dissemination of information for learning and to advance research.

Case study 16.7 Technology advances – hologram attendees

May 2008 – Sydney, Australia. Leading event services business, Staging Connections, helped to create an industry first when a mobile three-dimensional image of Telstra's chief technology officer, Dr Hugh Bradlow, was beamed from Melbourne to Adelaide to deliver a live business presentation over Telstra's network. The live hologram was created using a video camera which filmed Dr Bradlow in Melbourne. The signal was transmitted over Telstra's network and projected using Staging Connections' latest Christie HD projection system and a Musion Eyeliner optical projection system to create a holographic image for the audience in Adelaide. Dr Bradlow could see whom he was talking to in Adelaide. The entire Telepresence experience allowed real-time interaction, and provided the look and feel of Dr Bradlow being in the same room as the audience.

Source: Staging Connections (2008)

A virtual conferencing technique involving the creation of holograms of people who are not physically present at the event allows access to the event of those who under ordinary circumstances may not have been able to physically attend. Their presence is a three-dimensional holographic image – used successfully several times since mid-2008. Holograms have been used in several trade shows to staff exhibition booths with a repeating pre-recorded message. Case study 16.7 records an interactive hologram appearance by a virtual speaker at a meeting in Australia.

16.5.2 Gap analysis

Gap analysis, according to Wikipedia (2009b), is a tool that helps a company to compare its actual performance with its planned performance. Gap analysis within an event identifies where the event is not making the best use of its allocated resources. Setting tools in place for measuring current event process performance can provide data of where performance can be improved in the future for improved ROI results. Meeting Professionals International in their annual event industry survey, *EventView 2009*, noted that a key concern for companies is measuring their return on investment (ROI). The research reported that in 2008, 25% of companies' marketing budget was spent on events so the importance of measuring the impact to justify the expenditure cannot be understated. Additionally, having proof that the event met set objectives supports the reasoning to repeat similar events in the future. In this chapter it has been seen how the event manager's actions in the process design can help prove the ROI. The chapter has shown how some of the processes such as registration create data about attendees and about financial aspects of the event. The chapter has also shown how applying surveys at pre-designated points in the event life cycle generates data. Case study 16.8 shows how surveys were used in a conference and exhibition event to find out why the event was failing to deliver on the investment made in it. Both types of data can be stored in databases and analysed in many ways using statistical software

---

Case study 16.8 Examples of survey queries

An annual tourism and hospitality conference attracting a local audience found their attendee numbers had been dwindling year on year for the past three years, so the event owner asked for feedback to be gathered to try to establish what needed to be changed to recruit more attendees.

Electronic hand-held voting equipment handed out to every attendee at the conference and exhibition gave the event project manager the opportunity to evaluate the event performance from the following data:

❑ Exhibitors were asked about how many qualified leads were accessed and about their satisfaction with the number of conference attendees visiting their stands;

❑ Attendees at the conference were questioned as to the appropriateness of learning material presented; and

❑ Attendees were asked what they thought of the accommodation; the transport; the speakers; the organisational logistics (in sporting events, this is of high importance); and the networking opportunities presented by the event (for professional growth and learning).

Source: Thomas (2009)

---

packages to see trends in the data collected. Information technology integrated to the event processes is critical for collating data on which to base management decisions.

An audience response system often additionally allows talking (like a walkie-talkie) and texting to others who have a handset. When used for voting, each vote can be instantly presented to the audience in the form of bar graphs by using specialised software that gathers all the individual responses into groups that have similarities (such as the all the 'yes' and all the 'no' answers to a yes/no question), and this is presented on the venue screen. An associated database stores all the responses over the entire interactive period. Data is usually captured in a Microsoft Excel®, or equivalent, spreadsheet, and can include each unique responder (handset) number if these are assigned specifically to an individual to create different groups within the responding audiences. Storing the response data allows further studies of audience reactions after the event. Most audience response systems are accepted as a legal voting method for meetings and board decisions. One of the newer innovations in digital voting packages is an interactive audience response system that reflects the audience mood. For instance, as a political party presentation progresses, a graph will reflect the response of the audience to the speaker. This is useful for qualitative focus groups surveys.

Radio-frequency identification (RFID) is the use of a tag incorporated into or applied to a product or person for the purpose of identification and tracking using radio waves. Some audience response systems can scan RFID tags and collect brief product information and contacts (useful in trade and exhibition environments). The device can be preloaded with the sessions and lectures booked for by the participant so that ingress is easily controlled. In addition, the system can track which attendees went to a pre-booked event activity or if they left the event early. This is powerful quantitative feedback on what participants want. The screens can be in colour for delegate photo ID used for both security purposes and making networking meetings for recognition purposes.

Web-based surveys can be added to an event website. Such surveys are available for hire, as required, as internet software packages offering a user-friendly interface to gather qualitative and quantitative feedback on legacy aspects of a past event, or to use with geographically dispersed focus groups when strategising for the future.

16.5.3 Global media coverage

Many events, especially sporting ones, are now covered live by IT satellite technology which streams content direct to television/the internet from the event. It is possible to determine the number and geographic position of the viewer by collecting data of the unique link-in signature of each satellite decoder. For the event manager in conjunction with a media partner, knowing the interest of the virtual attendee gives a repeating event a potential future advertising revenue stream value to sell in the next year to sponsors or interested market partners.

On-site media need a secluded, private meeting area for interviews, often set up as follows: telephone communication, internet connectivity for email and research, and an IT network of computer and printing facilities. Connectivity for an outside broadcast vehicle may be required.

> **Case study 16.9 Using media as a performance indicator for ROI**
>
> January 2008 – *India's Sony Entertainment Television* network and *Singapore*-based *World Sport Group* secured the global broadcasting rights of the Indian Premier League by paying a staggering (rupee equivalent of) US$87 billion for 10 years.
> *Source: Wikipedia (2009c)*

Web 2.0 refers to what is perceived as a second-generation web development and web design. It is characterised as facilitating communication, information sharing, interoperability, user-centred design and collaboration on the internet (Wikipedia, 2009d). It has led to the development and evolution of web-based communities, hosted services and web applications. Depending on the event type, attendees can create Web 2.0 media interest with home videos by loading such content on social network sites such as Facebook© and YouTube™. Text commentary about an event can also often be loaded on social messaging utility sites such as Twitter©. It is difficult to estimate the real value of these online media but it certainly adds to the indefinable exposure of the event brand. The effect of Web 2.0 activities is often seen in website statistics and ticket sales where a burst of positive promotion of the event by Web 2.0 commentary generated by the social community following that event results in associated activity on the website, seen as increased viewership of webpages, and an increase in online event ticket selling. Web 2.0 can be used as part of a strategised IT promotional plan for events.

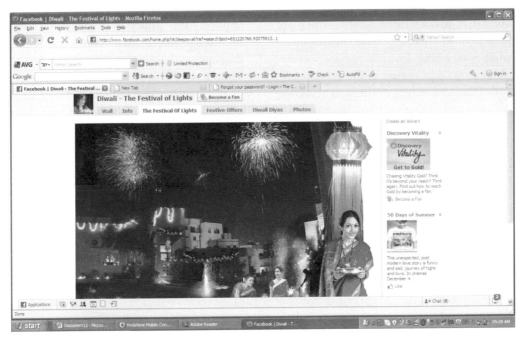

Figure 16.6 Using Web 2.0 – YouTube™ – to drive interest in an event

Source: YouTube™ (2009)

16.6 Summary

It has been seen that the use of information technology for events creates a technological backbone integrated into the processes. The technology can help with the generation of data that reflects the gap between what was planned and what is delivered in terms of the quality and effectiveness sought of that process. It is in this post-event time, often called the event postmortem, that the professional event organiser reviews the heap of data collected from the event in a process that leads to continuous learning and improvement for the event team.

First and most importantly, the event organiser reviews the unplanned-for incidents at the event. These unexpected incidents can often highlight faults in the planned processes or planned application of the specialist skills of people working on the event. The event manager and the event team learn from these unexpected variations about how to plan to avoid a repetition in the next event. The event manager then looks carefully at the audit trail of communications, and decides whether the communications record of the event, reflected in both report (financial, meetings, etc.) and stakeholder survey data, in any way reflects variations in the quality of delivery of objectives that are unacceptable. If the cause of the unacceptable divergence can be pinpointed, the event manager can learn how to avoid this in the future by modifying the event plan.

Analysis of event data guides future event planning, creating knowledge which is the basis for new decisions, and is known as strategic management practice. Additionally, this information is used in normative management actions which are those actions a manager takes to consolidate what was learnt from a previous event. This can be kept as part of the event team's embedded knowledge through creating policies and guidelines on best practice for future events. Creating these policy documents gives the event team a reference to guide decision making on their part. As policy recommends actions to be taken in certain situations, it has narrowed the number of ways that a decision will be applied. The policy statements use the knowledge from past events to guide decision-making actions on future events. The value of this is that the consequences of these actions are known, and so risk of anything unexpected arising from these actions is reduced. This in turn helps secure the future survival and profitability of the event and the event company creating the event simply because past risks and pitfalls will be catered for and in some instances completely eliminated.

Questions for research

1 The event manager has a database of people who attended the previous year. An email and promotional SMS called the 'Early-Bird Special' is sent to potential attendees, inviting them to visit the event website to get a reduced price for registering early for the upcoming event. The promotional message includes the event website registration webpage to advertise the special, and asks recipients to visit this webpage. Discuss how the information in the website statistics could be accessed and used in the promotional campaign decision making.
2 What checklist of features could be created to measure venue suitability when producing an event that is dependent on a good IT backbone (virtual and local audience, media room, electronic registration, RFID tags in the exhibition hall, internet café, speaker room, virtual classrooms) being in place at the venue?
3 What IT performance indicators would you plan and review to measure the quality of an event experience from the perspectives of different stakeholders?
4 The postmortem of an event reviews all the data (surveys, reports, feedback from stakeholders, incident reports, change control forms) collected that has relevance to the event's return on investment in terms of both stakeholder satisfaction and financial outcomes. Determine the reasons why this data can be important in creating policies and procedures to guide the event in the next year.
5 In the case where an event has a limited budget but there is unlimited internet/email/website connectivity, how best can these tools are used to create interest in the event?

Recommended websites

Browse the following internet sites for interesting and informative information:

A free-access social communication tool for sending cellular text messages: http://www.twitter.com
A free-access social networking website: http://www.facebook.com
A free-access web-based video sharing site: http://www.youtube.com

A free tutorial on how to lead brainstorming: http://www.brainstorming.co.uk

An example of a hire-as-required on-line, multi-currency, registration service: http://www.redballoon.biz

An example of an online bulk SMS and email service: http://www.certech.co.za

An example of audience response system software and hardware: http://www.iml.co.za

Creating a web-based survey, quickly and cheaply: http://www.SurveyMonkey.com

Flowchart and brainstorming tools plus venue layout planning tools: http://www.smartdraw.com

More information on online marketing: http://www.quirk.biz

The annual *EIBTM Industry Trends & Market Share Report*: http://www.eibtm.com.

The Meeting Professionals International annual report *EventView* on annual developments in the events industry: http://www.mpiweb.org

The Meeting Professionals International annual report *FutureWatch* for annual technology and event trends: http://www.mpiweb.org

Suggested reading

Phillips, JJ, Myhill, M & McDonough, JB. 2007. *Proving the Value of Meetings & Events – How and Why to Measure ROI*. Birmingham: ROI Institute.

Ramsborg, GC & Miller, B. 2006. *Professional Meeting Management – Comprehensive Strategies for Meetings, Convention and Events*, 5 ed. Iowa: Kendall/Hunt Publishing Company.

Stokes, R. 2008. *eMarketing: The Essential Guide to Online Marketing*. E-Book available from: http://www.quirk.biz/earletingtextbook [accessed on 10 July 2009].

PART VI
Events and risk

Photo: Dimitri Tassiopoulos

Photo: Dimitri Tassiopoulos

Photo: Jura

Photo: Dimitri Tassiopoulos

Photo: Dimitri Tassiopoulos

17

Events risk and safety management

Errol Ninow

Abstract

Risk management is not a highly visible activity and most people are unaware that it has even taken place. All events have elements of risk and it would be futile to think that a 'risk-free' event is possible. It is only when things go wrong and the emergency develops into crisis proportions that the question is asked, 'Why did no one foresee the eventuality and prepare for it?' The level of infrastructural and institutional capacity required to deal with potential personal risks, public safety and security issues, liability risks, potential losses and disasters at planned events, together with the risk reduction strategies to diminish the likelihood of the identified risk condition occurring, is the work that risk management is engaged with. Risk, insurance, security, legal, contractual and ethical issues together with health and safety management need to be integrated into all the facets of the event

organiser's toolkit from the inception of the event idea through the financial risk analysis, where the potential rewards are measured against the risk of loss and all other planning phases of the event. Risks need to be evaluated, controlled and monitored during the implementation phase of the event as well as during the event itself and to the final moment of breakdown/load out. Risk has been identified as one of the key knowledge domains that need to be managed in order to stage any type of event professionally.

This chapter covers the risk domain from a risk management point of view. These risk management guidelines are generic, and are applicable to both small- and large-scale national and international events. The risk domain has been identified in many published papers as it pertains to the world of events and is common.

Chapter objectives

After you have read this chapter you should be able to:

- ❏ understand manage and identify various types of risk associated with events, e.g. financial risk, legal liability, contracts, permits and licences, copyright, trademark and service mark protection, and other intellectual property;
- ❏ provide insight of compliance management and its importance;
- ❏ appreciate the role and necessity of emergency management and the need for disaster risk management and crisis planning;
- ❏ provide knowledge as to why health and safety management is an imperative part of event planning and the impact it has on the event experience and all who participate or attend the event;
- ❏ understand the different facets of security management, the need for it and its role at your event; and
- ❏ analyse the risks and benefits of insurance management, and identify the legal and ethical implications of producing an event.

17.1 INTRODUCTION

17.1.1 What is risk?

'Risk' has different interpretative meanings and depends upon the specific context in which it is used. There are various types of risk and it is generally accepted that the term is associated with and measured in economic loss or probability of loss, or a hazard which may have the potential to cause harm leading to the loss of life or injury, damage to property, social or economic disruption or environmental degradation. In the events context, risk can be measured against the possibility of financial reward or loss, or liability and exposure to possible financial loss measured in both monetary terms and human injury, or loss of life due to exposure to hazards.

A hazard is a potentially damaging physical event which may cause harm, and could include latent conditions such as natural weather (e.g. snowstorms), geological, hydro, meteorological, biological or human-induced or technological processes.

It is commonly accepted that when evaluating a particular risk, the hazard is measured by the vulnerability or probability (e.g. a one in 30 chance) of a particular happening occurring, evaluated by the frequency of the activity (e.g. number of

Figure 17.1 Formula depicting the contributing factors to risk and consequences

times – six per day) on one side of the equation and the severity or consequence of the happening on the other.

17.1.2 What is risk management?

Managing risks is a systemic process whereby there is a gathering of information to assist with the identification of risks and future uncertainties which affect our legal liability and exposure to loss or harm. This identification process includes examining impacts and consequences on the organisation, its reputation, individuals, other people and property. Hazards and unsafe acts are threats to our endeavour and need to be analysed and dealt with. It is generically accepted that risks should be eliminated and avoided as far as possible, and reduction and mitigation strategies introduced to minimise the probability and severity of risks occurring wherever we can. The protection and safety of people and property is paramount in the context of events, and a meeting recognising that some incidents can occur is part of the process of managing risk.

The areas which traditionally pose risks, broadly speaking, in the event and meetings environment are as follows:

❏ Compliance with legislation and regulations;
❏ Health and safety matters affecting workers and the public;
❏ Public safety and security – this includes response plans;

❏ Design (engineering) safety;
❏ Unsafe processes and procedures;
❏ Environmental degradation and impacts;
❏ Lack of adequate research of the project;
❏ Absence of monitoring and feedback systems to enable proper decision making; and
❏ Failure to properly plan and ensure there is no economic loss (loss of business)

The importance of documenting the processes undertaken cannot be overemphasised as these documents not only serve as a blueprint record for future events but also as a documented record of information serving as proof that all reasonable steps were taken in researching and evaluating possible risks for the event. Not to do so could be construed as negligence, with severe personal consequences.

As organisers of events, whether large, small or community based, the two most important processes that are required in risk management are firstly to take the reasonable steps of a reasonable person in dealing with risks and not simply dismiss them. 'Hope is not an action plan' (Silvers, 2008).

The second important process, in the aftermath of incidents, accidents and disasters, is dealing with the question most often asked of the people in charge: whether they can show and prove *a duty of care*. This could entail documented evidence such as minutes of meetings, on-site inspections and other activities which show the efforts, acknowledgement, treatment, decisions and actions taken concerning the potential risk occurrence.

17.1.3 The events risk and safety management domain

Risk and safety management is a key domain that the event manager must deal with, and integrates with all the business domains of events management.

❏ *Administration*
Financial management is an obvious inclusion. As an example in assessing the financial risks of an open air event two basic questions might be posed as follows:
* Can the event and activities proceed if there is inclement weather such as rain or storms?
* Do we have a sponsor or are we dependent on the gate takings (i.e. is there financial risk)?

❏ *Event design*
In deciding on the theme and environment, inflammable materials and open flames in a confined or closed space such as a theatre where multiple performances happen daily increase the chance of an incident.

❏ *Marketing and promotion*
Sponsorship management would include the safety, security and treatment of VIP guests at the event or risk losing the sponsor!

❏ *Operations*
In the area of attendee management, the geographic placement of the event and the nature of the entertainment at a public event should take into account the visitor's profile. For example, a young rock concert crowd in a park will pose different security problems and issues as opposed to a mature crowd attending a classical concert in the same park.

❏ *Risk management*
The domain of risk encompasses every facet of the business and the event project – and this is the heart of this chapter. What constitutes risk is dealt with in more detail in terms of compliance management, decision management, emergency management, health and safety management, insurance management, legal management and security management.

17.1.4 Risk analysis and risk assessment

It is imperative that risks are confronted from the point of view that *the feared threat to the event might occur*. To imagine that the identified risk has not occurred before so it is unlikely that it will happen now would be a naïve assumption. An easy method to help understand where to start in the identification of risks is to ask the questions: 'What is at risk?' and 'What will the consequences be?'

The first order of business is to identify the type of risks the anticipated event could face. The same could be true for evaluating normal business risk. In the business sense we might ask ourselves: 'If we supply the goods or services, and do not receive payment, what is at risk?' If the goods or services rendered cannot be recovered due to the financial default, the consequence will be financial loss.

Why is it necessary to pay so much attention to risks and risk analysis? Cash flows and financial projections are important in business because they serve as early warning systems of impending possible financial loss. They identify possible cash shortfalls, which are dealt with by amending plans and introducing intervention measures, such as cost cutting or other restructuring mechanisms to keep the business profitable. The spreadsheets used for this purpose are a tool to help in analysing and assessing the risks and pitfalls the unknown future may hold, and plans are adjusted accordingly.

It is impossible to begin a preparedness plan for dealing with eventualities until the risk analysis and assessment process has been completed. It must be appreciated that establishing and identifying risks involve the necessity to spend time researching the various risk elements and possibilities. As a general rule, in the modern world it is prudent for very large events where attendance is measured in tens or perhaps hundreds of thousands of people to make use of professional risk consultants as the process can be time consuming, and demands specific and specialist expertise in some areas of risk assessment and compliance.

The identification of risks is therefore the first step, and some examples are shown in a simple table of various risks that may have to be taken into account and planned for by event organisers and emergency management personnel at different types of events (see table 17.1).

❐ **Evaluation and prevention (control).** Once the identification of the risks is complete, the next phase of the risk analysis process involves evaluating the consequences of the risk occurring, and the systems, procedures and measures that will be instituted, preventing the occurrence from having any injurious or harmful effects on the business, people or property. Termination of the risk or total avoidance of the risk is the aim.

❐ **Reduction and mitigation (control).** This term implies that when dealing with some risks we may be able to minimise the chances or severity of

Table 17.1 Sample risk identification

Risk	Cause	Consequence
Evacuations	Fire/bomb threat/building structural collapse	People stampede, causing death or injury
Fire	Combustible materials/carelessness	Loss of life or injury/damage or loss to property
Unruly crowd behaviour	Drunkenness/rioting/fans unhappy with sport result/popular activity or attraction at the event	Loss of life/injury/looting/damage to property
Terrorism	Event is political target and newsworthy	Loss of life/injury/property damage/negative publicity for event
Power failure	Electrical grid down/no standby generators	Injury/darkness/looting/event closure/financial loss
Water failure	Water inlet unserviceable	Possible event closure/no toilets flush/no drinking water/no water for cooking or cleaning
Crime	Inadequate security	Negative publicity/event unpopular due to visitor safety and insecurity/financial loss

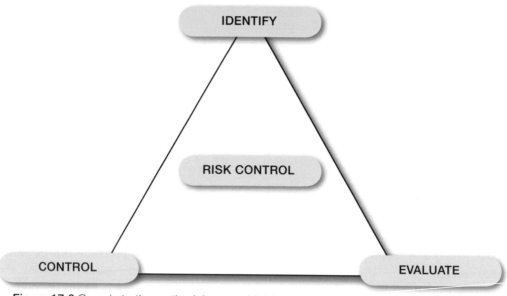

Figure 17.2 Generic to the methodology worldwide for risk assessments showing the links between the identification, the evaluation and control of risk in the risk assessment

Source: Adapted from Koekemoer (2009)

an occurrence or control, and prevent some degree of the risk but not all of the potential effects. Some effects of the risk or possible disaster remain, and all that can be done is to lessen, modify, control or change some factors to reduce the likelihood (probability) of the occurrence.

☐ *Monitoring of risks.* This involves ensuring the effective managing of systems in place that allow for the observation, checking and proper supervision of pre-agreed procedures, coupled to an efficient reporting and communication protocol. This ensures the effectiveness of our early warning mechanisms and is an important enabler for the decision-making processes which may have to follow. A change for the worse in the status of a pre-identified hazard or condition may require a specific response or decision during an event, and the monitoring

process plays a vitally important role in this regard.

☐ *Response.* This refers to the actions and pre-arranged planning and activities involved during an incident or emergency situation. This could be the reaction to a fire or medical emergency. It may require a decision to evacuate, and to notify all the stakeholders and role players to begin with implementation of the plan for this eventuality.

☐ *Recovery.* This is the phase defining the actions and decision-making processes which would enable the event to resume, and assessment of the functionality of all the services required to keep the event going, depending on the scale of the emergency or disaster occurrence.

☐ *Rehabilitation.* In disaster risk management terms and contextualised for events, this may concern permanent or temporary infrastructure replacement, e.g. replacing items such as air-conditioning, lighting, sound systems, fencing, etc., or bringing in generators overnight to provide electricity if the main supply is down for the remainder of the event.

17.2 Compliance management

Compliance management deals with the local legislation, regulations and other applicable statutory laws which may apply to the anticipated event, the permissions, licences and certificates of clearance which may be required for the event by the authorities and other regulatory bodies. These regulations differ from country to country and region to region, and will need to be established as part of the planning phase for the event. Generally they are to do with the regulations and statutory laws

which the activities planned for the event will be subject to and may include the following:

☐ *Fire safety regulations.* These will apply in respect of both permanent and temporary structures. They usually prescribe fire-fighting equipment, assembly points, personnel, exits, aisle widths, inflammable materials and other fire prevention strategies applicable to the event. Pyrotechnics usually require special permission. Safety regulations in most countries have special fire department standby procedures and rules that must be adhered to during fireworks displays. Most countries have compliance regulations in connection with the use of portable liquefied petroleum gas (LPG) and the size of LPG gas cylinders which may or may not be used, and rules regarding the safe storage areas of gas cylinders, which are strictly monitored.

☐ *Floor layout and site plans.* These usually need approval and should be drawn to scale showing exits; passage widths; access and egress points; design details; table and seating layouts, accompanied by information details as to how many people are expected to be in the premises; and the nature of the event being planned. There will be occupancy regulations determining how many people may attend the event, depending on the venue capacity and use. Most venues have multiple uses and this will impact on the number of attendees allowed. An example will be the use of a sports stadium for a football event as opposed to a rock concert, or a ballroom being used for a seminar or lecture with a seated audience. The capacity to host numbers of people will differ depending on the type of event and venue use. Occupancy certificates may be required.

- ❑ *Certificates of compliance and inspection.* These are required in most countries in respect of electrical installations, machinery, temporary installations and structures.
- ❑ *Alcohol consumption and liquor laws.* These must be adhered to. In many countries temporary liquor licences need to be applied for, and there are laws regulating the minimum age of persons who may consume alcohol and restrictions surrounding where, under what circumstances and what kind of alcohol may be served.
- ❑ *Permits or licences.* These may need to be obtained for the playing of music or the display of intellectual property. Other copyright and trademark permissions are required to avoid infringement and illegal use thereof. Foreign performers may be required to have work permits or tax certificates and visas in respect of their performances at the event. Licences to sell alcohol are usually required, as are permits to operate driven machinery.
- ❑ *Environmental regulations.* The environmental impact or 'footprint' of the event will need to be assessed as the world moves more and more towards 'green' events. Waste management compliance with local regulations is essential.
- ❑ *Local council/municipal bylaws.* These need to be considered, for example in relation to noise produced by the event or the impact visitors may have on the local community. Various other regulatory permits and permissions may need to be obtained from councils for the anticipated event.
- ❑ *Food preparation.* This usually goes hand in hand with local health regulations and certification of the acceptability of food vendors involved at an event, and is usually a mandatory requirement. This is an important area of public health with potential liability consequences (food poisoning) and deserves close scrutiny.
- ❑ *Temporary structure inspections.* These often call for structural engineering certificates stating that temporary structures have been inspected by a qualified engineer and are fit for occupancy or use (e.g. marquees, designer-built double-storey exhibition stands, raised staging). Often safety certificates and inspections are required before an event may open to the public, and these will only be granted if all the compliance issues and inspections are met.

Certain events are governed by controlling bodies, and their sanction for the event may be required (such as in motor sport, athletics and other specific sporting codes).

There are other issues to consider, such as suitability of the venue for the anticipated event and available parking, access roads and possible traffic disruption and the nature of the event (in some countries, political gatherings require special permission), all of which influence the compliance management scenario.

Non-compliance in many countries can lead to permission not being granted to continue with the event, especially in cases of public safety and security issues, resulting in financial loss and damage to the reputation of the organiser if initial research was inadequate.

17.3 Legal and ethics management

Legal and ethics management deals with the legal obligations of the organisers and representatives of the event in respect of the specific laws which govern the activities of the event, the contracts pertaining to the event and the ethical considerations of the event and its organisers. These will include legislation and regulations, as well as the contractual obligations of all the parties with regard to issues of, inter alia, confidentiality, liability, taxation, record keeping, performance warranties, privacy, etc., all of which form an integral part of legal compliance.

17.3.1 Contracts and legal documents

Contracts and service level agreements (SLA) form the basis of the business relationship between the contracting parties where the level of service is defined. This can be a legally binding formal or informal 'contract'. An SLA is an essential requirement for the provision or receipt of any important service. The terms and conditions contained in the contract are by definition agreed upon, and any breach of the agreement is enforceable in a court of law. Accordingly a breach of contract by either party may lead to a termination of the contract and, by definition, possibly the event. Accordingly, the importance of sound administrative practices, including documenting all aspects of an event, cannot be overstressed. Non-compliance can lead to legal proceedings and court action in some cases.

A service level agreement should clearly communicate, specify and define the nature and extent of the services to be supplied, and be clear in its purpose together with all relevant information, such as the following:

❐ The expectations of both service provider and the client should be clearly spelt out;

❐ Delineation of roles and responsibilities must be described and understood;

❐ The parameters to measure performance and evaluate key performance areas should be included and agreed to;

❐ Control and communication mechanisms with provision for feedback are also required;

❐ The full scope of the services to be provided should be detailed in the agreement;

❐ Expenditure and budget responsibilities, if appropriate, clearly explained;

❐ Specific timelines and deadlines should be set; and

❐ Terms of payment and any penalties for non-performance are essential.

Unforeseen costs, which could include items such as overtime, accommodation, flights or car hire, should also be dealt with in the service level agreement.

17.3.2 Evaluating ethical implications

A reputation, whether of a business or personal nature, cannot be priced or overvalued, and it should be guarded and treasured at all costs. It should be understood that each individual's ethics are what others perceive them to be and it is a truism in life that individuals usually get exactly what they deserve. In most cultures it is considered wrong and harmful to dishonour agreements or to begin with the wilful intention of causing hurt or loss to those that we interact and do business with.

The uttering of untruths, and cheating and stealing are not a display of personal or business standards but rather a sure way to find oneself on the wrong end of a lawsuit. While ethics may vary among different cultures and are not generally found to be enshrined in the law, our own high standards of behaviour and moral values should be the guiding light in choosing to do what is socially acceptable in the communities we live and do business in.

17.4 Emergency management

Emergency management deals with occurrences which disrupt the planned event possibly resulting in harm, injury or loss of life. The degree of the disruption will define it as an incident (which can be handled through normal procedures) and then as a crisis requiring extraordinary measures to prevent a negative influence on the event.

The process includes the interface with institutional authorities and emergency services such as medical, fire and police departments. Disaster risk management planning includes taking into account response and recovery mechanisms, and also forms part of emergency management. Emergency management has to deal with the identification of hazards, and the hazardous activities and threats to people (and property) attending the event together with the response, planning and mitigating control mechanisms applicable to the identified possible threats. The event organiser must consider the possibility of fire or a medical emergency involving a worker, participant or visitor at the event, or a visitor/spectator disruption that leads to disorderliness at the event suddenly posing a crowd-control problem.

For emergency management to be effective there should be a clear chain of command as to who or which emergency service is in charge of the type of emergency experienced and responded to. A central control room for representatives

from the various emergency services and communication with their support services need to be established. This central control room is sometimes known as a VOC (venue operations centre).

The issuing of statements to the press and appointment of a spokesperson from a public relations perspective is important for maintaining the image of the event and should be known to all the role players. There must be a communication plan that has been pre-communicated to all the role players and stakeholders. Two-way radio procedures and protocols must be in place, and emergency channels must not be used for casual conversation.

Planning should include the procedures and types of response, and by whom, to the possibilities of different types of emergencies.

A sample response planning sheet could be as follows:

Table 17.2 Sample response planning sheet

Type of emergengy	Responder
Medical emergencies	Medical personnel
Crowd control	Security and police
Power loss	Maintenance/electricity department
Water loss	Maintenance/water authorities
Fire	Fire department and evacuation plan
Accident/incident	Safety officer

Other matters that need to be taken into consideration when completing the emergency management plan would also include, inter alia, the following:

Establish what mutual aid agreements (institutional capacity) are in place and what needs to be in place for the emergency management plan to be effective. For example, if the event was an air show, history tells us that accidents at these types of events unfortunately do happen. The questions then are:

- ❑ Can the local or on-site emergency services cope with a potential disaster, or should other emergency services from neighbouring towns or facilities be notified and placed on standby?
- ❑ Should the event organiser contract a private ambulance service?
- ❑ Should an accident occur, what assistance can be expected from neighbouring facilities in the form of medical personnel, hospital beds, fire engines and other essential services needed to deal with the crisis? Where should triage areas be established and what triage procedures should form part of the emergency management plan?

The emergency plan should have built-in early warning systems catering for pre-planned responses to pre-identified situations. Too many people queuing at gates with insufficient cashiers are a classic case of potential trouble and possible crowd crush. Knowing in advance that these situations might occur and monitoring them gives more time for the appropriate response.

Equipment inventories and trained personnel to deal with emergencies must be pre-established and form part of the overall response plan. All the necessary emergency response stakeholders should be engaged early in the planning stages to enable them to adequately deploy and assign their resources. Remember that most events take place over weekends and there are sometimes multiple events on the same

day in the same city, so the more advance warning the different emergency services have the better off the event is likely to be in the area of official manpower and resource requirements. On-site medical services requirements need to be evaluated and included in the overall emergency plan. Numbers of medical personnel and on-site ambulance availability are often legislated in some countries, based on the number of expected visitors to the event.

Hazardous materials always have to be taken into account in the emergency planning as, depending on the crisis, there may be potential exposure to inflammables or harmful gases. Emergency management may have to deal with natural disasters such as earthquakes and floods at or near the event site/venue, all of which impact on the people at the event.

Once an incident has escalated to a crisis, the full-scale deployment of the disaster preparedness plan is put into operation and all the elements and role players swing into action in response. The emergency management plan then needs to deal with the possible recovery phase. This is when decisions are taken as to whether the event can continue or not. Obviously the factors that need to be taken into account will have to do with the venue's serviceability and the severity of the crisis that occurred. In some instances local authorities, who are usually empowered by law, may take the decision arbitrarily if public health and safety are endangered by the continuance of the event.

Medical emergencies may range from an event attendee suffering a heart attack to minor injuries needing first-aid treatment, and the event organiser should ensure that there is an appropriate level of medical assistance available at the event. The total number of visitors to an event will dictate how many medical personnel are required and what on-site back-up facilities such as paramedics, doctors and ambulances are required, taking the type, nature and duration of the event into account. First-aid stations must be established which give easy access to the attendees and swift egress for emergency transportation of patients. Local hospitals and/or clinics should be advised that the event is taking place, including dates, attendance times and expected numbers of attendees.

17.4.1 Disaster risk management planning

Disaster risk management planning involves an integrated and coordinated disaster risk management plan that focuses on preventing or reducing the risk of disasters, mitigating their severity, ensuring preparedness, rapid and effective response to them, and post-disaster recovery – this would include planned events, which may be festivals, fairs, sporting and recreational, entertainment (live acts), educational, cultural, religious, conference, exhibition, community or similar activity hosted at a stadium or venue attended by the public (South African *National Disaster Risk Management*, Act 57 of 2002).

The risk assessment is used as the central advisory documentation, and the planning involves dealing with emergencies on a large scale and possibly of such a nature that it is beyond the scope and ability of the on-site emergency personnel to handle. As much as possible is done to prevent and mitigate any disasters, but contingency plans need to be in place to effectively deal with any manmade or natural disaster which may occur.

There have been well-documented case studies of disasters all over the world where people have lost their lives and scores have been injured in crowd stampedes, collapsing grandstand structures and roofs falling in on top of revellers, resulting in tragedy for the attendees of those particular events. Inadequate crowd control measures can lead to crush and panic, causing multiple cases of serious injury. We often display a predisposition to plan for events and occurrences that have occurred before or some mishap that we previously heard about.

Our planned responses which will most likely include emergency services should include these services in the formulation stages of our planning and include detailed instructions and procedures to follow in dealing with the threat.

17.5 Decision management

Decisions need to be made in a practical way in order to facilitate the correct response to a multitude of possible situations. Different people are usually empowered at different levels of management to make decisions, and this presupposes that they have the necessary correct information to properly evaluate a given situation before making what might otherwise prove to be a bad decision.

Decisions are taken concerning risks right from the first planning and implementation stages of an event. Some risks will be avoided, others tolerated or terminated, and prevention decisions will be taken based on the information researched and available.

Risk monitoring is an ongoing process not confined to the preplanning and implementation phases. During an event proper, certain hazards may require constant monitoring as part of an early warning system decided upon and now implemented. The flow of information must be speedy and accurate, and systems designed to ensure the information reaches the right people without undue delays and filters interrupting the process. This is part of risk control and mitigation, and forms part of normal incident-reporting procedures, which are necessary in order to enable decisions at various management levels of the event.

Planned response and implementation of contingency plans rely upon accurate and reliable information being in possession of the decision makers. This is a key element of the overall event organisational and emergency plan, and decision management must be based on facts in the risk domain after proper consultation and deliberation. Decisions are made with the due authority to do so throughout all the phases of the event, and may impact on resources available to risk control methodologies and finance. Again, it is recommended that all decisions be properly documented and preserved as part of the permanent event record. The transference and communication of this information regarding decisions made at a later stage is very important when the decision-making process starts all over again as planning for the next event begins. It is said that we have only the past in our present to use as our guide for the future.

17.6 Health and safety management

Health and safety management deals with all the issues which may affect the health and safety of everyone involved with the event. This includes the workers during the build-up/load-in phase, and all the participating people. This will be everyone from volunteers, exhibitors, performers, visitors, vendors, etc., and is applicable until

the last worker has removed the last item on the last day of breakdown/load out. The Health and Safety policies, procedures and controls should be clearly documented as they reflect the organiser's duty of care, as well as the world view on public health and safety at events.

17.6.1 Public health and safety issues are generic at events worldwide

Occupational health and safety compliance is mandatory, and while different countries may have different standards and procedures, local legislation and bylaws have to be adhered to. Health and safety encompasses many facets of our lives and the event experience is no different. Some examples of health and safety management are set out below. The reader should, however, note that this list is by no means exhaustive and only serves as an indication in this regard.

❑ *Flooring.* Underfoot conditions can be slippery, and wires left uncovered are considered hazardous due to the possibility of tripping. People with disabilities should be specially catered for.

❑ *Structural defects.* The structure itself, be it a permanent building or temporary structure such as a lighting tower or marquee, poses serious risks in the event of a collapse. Riggers may attach objects suspended from roof trusses which cannot hold the weight causing disaster to strike when the roof caves in.

❑ *Air pollution.* Activities which cause air pollution are deemed to be hazardous to the health of persons in the area.

❑ *Occupational hazards.* Workmen working at heights need to have proper

Case study 17.2 Youth music festival at the Rand Show in Johannesburg South Africa

Bryan Brett, then general manager of this annual event in Johannesburg, South Africa, relates the following story. The main attraction of the Rand Show, held at the showground and Expo Centre south of Johannesburg, is its vast range of entertainment, which is free after paying entrance fees.

In the mid-1990s the Rand Show started a Youth Music Festival, which was aimed at an audience in the 15–25 age group. It was what is known as a kwaito festival. Over the years the Youth Music Festival gained in popularity, attracting attendance of over 22 000 people. The management of the Rand Show became concerned about the amount of underage and illegal drinking. People were arriving under the influence of alcohol and partying in the car parks. For the 2006 Rand Show, management, in consultation with all stakeholders and role players, decided to make it an alcohol-free day at the event venue. Management implemented additional queue shoot systems at all turnstiles and 100 extra stewards to manage them and search every attendee for alcohol, illegal weapons and the like.

The festival was scheduled to start at 14:00, but the festival attendees started arriving in a jovial mood from midmorning, and continued to do so in their thousands throughout the day. All security and related services were constantly on high alert. At 16:00 Bryan went on a specially convened helicopter inspection of the venue and surrounding area. What he saw from the air was tens of thousands of people still making their way to the venue on foot, despite the fact that the festival had started some two hours previously and that the grounds were almost full to capacity.

A venue operations committee (VOC) was immediately convened with all the role players. The metro police sealed off all access routes and extended the perimeter to the venue, and did not allow any further access. However, there were still thousands of people inside the cordoned-off perimeter area still wanting access to the showground. The turnstiles could not handle the unending stream of people, who became annoyed at having to queue for long periods. A crush at the turnstile gates slowly built up, and the threat of injury or worse to patrons had become very real. At 17:30 a decision was taken to open all turnstile gates and allow free, unhindered entry into the venue. After ten minutes the now very happy crowd dispersed into the showground without incident. It was estimated that some 12 000 people gained free access. The gates were then closed and due to the metro police's actions no further people arrived at the perimeter turnstiles.

The VOC functioned as consultative forum implementing their disaster risk management planning, resulting in no serious injuries or loss of life.

Excellent communication as part of the early-warning system to the right people enabled the decision-making process to proceed, based on the information to hand.

This was the last Youth Music Festival held at the Rand Show and the decision was taken that the festival had outgrown the capacity of the main arena and as such had become a public safety risk.

fall protection plans in place which include safety harnesses and hardhats. Workmen may be required to use special personal protective equipment in the course of their work, e.g. welding goggles, asbestos gloves, or safety boots.

❑ *Chemical hazards.* Safe storage facilities and barriers to public accessibility with laid-down written work procedures must be in place. The uses of gases such as LPG, helium or oxyacetylene are usually subject to special permits and approval.

- *Lighting levels (visibility), sound (noise levels), natural light and air flow.* These are all factors which are taken into consideration as part of the health and safety plan.
- *Fire systems.* These should be in place and must be serviceable and in working order. Portable fire equipment such as hand-held fire extinguishers may need to be brought in to the event to bolster existing infrastructure.
- *Facilities management.* The programme will include the number of sanitation facilities available and the condition and acceptability of the facilities provided as far as the health element of the plan is concerned.
- *Food integrity.* This is a vitally important area and deserves attention as it is an activity usually covered by a plethora of regulations governing the food-handling regime, from the peeling process in the kitchen and the hygiene involved with the processes through to the transportation of food, and the heating and re-heating of certain foodstuffs until finally served to the consumer.
- *Disposal of waste.* Many jurisdictions require an environmental waste management plan which includes the procedures and infrastructure surrounding waste disposal.

To cover every aspect and subject on health and safety and all the hazards an event can potentially expose the attendees to would be a library of books in itself, and each event will give cause for the identification of different health and safety hazards specific to the event and the nature of the activities to be undertaken.

Policies and procedures regarding the health and safety of all the people involved with the event should be clearly spelt out and documented with minutes of all safety meetings, deviation reports and details concerning any incidents kept as part of the permanent record of the event.

17.7 Security management

Security management deals with the deployment of protective personnel (security officers or stewards) and equipment as well as the appropriate command and control functions needed to give effect to the security of the event. Police contingents sometimes form part of the security deployment plan. Security is always an important part of risk planning and for big events is usually a large budgetary item. The security officer is the first line of defence against threats, and events can be inviting targets for pre-planned violence, as sometimes happens at football matches. Terrorism also needs to be factored in, depending on where the event is held, the type of event, the international profile of the event, and other intelligence and pertinent factors regarding the event which may trigger a response from activist groups.

Security needs to be visible and accessible but at the same time should not have a negative impact on the attendees' event experience by being overwhelming, which in some situations can create alarm or unease in the mind of the attendee. Choice of service provider (private security) and the image represented at an event should be carefully considered, taking the previous experience and staff-training policies of the service provider into account.

Case study 17.3 Fiery beer fest at a local city sports complex in South Africa

When interviewed, Morné Weyers, a professional risk consultant in South Africa, has this story to tell on an investigation he undertook. In June 2000 at an annual beer fest attracting up to 25 000 people at an all-day open-air venue – adjacent to rugby fields – upon which marquees had been erected, visitors were enjoying the oompah bands and entertainment on a warm summer's day. As part of the catering facilities, a refrigerated truck with a marquee attached to it had been set up on the northern side of the venue and a mini-kitchen established with chip fryers and other gas-operated equipment. At 18:45 there was a huge explosion in the refrigerated truck. The marquee caught fire as well as the vehicle, and security and medical personnel rushed to the scene. A 19 kg LPG bottle had exploded and the situation was exacerbated by the oil in chip fryers spreading the fire and spattering all over the area. The security personnel battled to extinguish the fire as a further gas bottle exploded, going straight up into the air. There were eight people seriously injured, mainly second- and third-degree burns, one had a broken arm and 13 others were hospitalised. At 18:47 the venue operations centre contacted the fire brigade team only to discover that they had left the venue at 18:00. The fire engine could not make its way back to the venue due to the traffic congestion. The medics called for more ambulances to be dispatched from local hospitals but they could also not get through the traffic to the venue. Eventually a medical helicopter was dispatched to transport the injured to hospital.

After investigation it was found that the 19 kg gas cylinder was placed outside the marquee and was accessible to the general public. Someone opened the valve fully, causing the flames to ignite the oil in the chip fryers as well as rupturing the gas pipe, causing the explosion and setting everything alight.

Proper risk management planning was not in place, the emergency plan was ineffective, and no monitoring systems were in effect.

The fire brigade was supposed to be on site for the duration of the event, but this was not communicated to the operational staff or enforced, and they left as soon as their shift ended at 18:00. Inspection by fire safety on gas equipment at the temporary installation was not done. Gas cylinders should not be accessible to the general public.

The event conveners had not taken all reasonable steps to ensure compliance, and the organisers of the event were sued by several of the injured people, who won their respective lawsuits.

The main generally accepted function of security is prevention of loss or harm. There are many other important functions and activities that need to be performed, all of which contribute to the prevention of loss or harm.

Crowd management planning is concerned with queue control, assessing the 'mood' and behaviour of the crowd, ensuring that the exits and walkways are kept free from obstruction, and understanding the dynamics of the evacuation plan should an emergency occur calling for the plan to be implemented. The crowd management plan should include resource allocation and coordination details. The risk assessment will be a great help in establishing the correct personnel deployment numbers at various posts within the site or on perimeters and gates. Equipment requirements such as barriers, fencing, gates, entrances and exits, cashier booths or ticket-selling points – preferably not too near the venue entrances – can also be established as part of the exercise concerned with crowd management and designing a suitable response to situations that may arise.

Access and emergency evacuation control of persons on foot and vehicles to the venue in an orderly and organised fashion with emergency routes kept clear is normally a function of the security force. Control of areas that are out of bounds and not accessible to visitors and the general guarding of equipment need to be decided in the planning phase, and deployment arrangements made accordingly.

Assisting police and other local authorities with the emergency plan and helping visitors to the event by remaining calm and giving directional instructions to assembly points and escape routes are considered privately contracted security force duties which form part of the security plan.

Anti-crime patrols and sometimes physical intervention and even arrests for misdemeanours like public drunkenness and rowdy behaviour and assault or theft sometimes occur. Minor incidents do not always require official emergency services intervention, but it must be part of the contingency planning and acknowledged that incidents all have the potential to escalate.

Scrutiny of accreditation and clear instructions and admission policies including what decisions can be made without referral to the organisers or other higher authority should be spelt out in the security plan. The plan should provide for checking of the venue and its facilities for purposes of possible threats and hazards (bomb, fire, etc.) and general protection of property.

Communication on site with a central control room and procedures for the documenting of communications and seeing to it that information reaches the stakeholders and role players who need it for possible decision-making purposes must be absolutely clear, and the communication plan must be given to everyone participating in it. Communicating with visitors/attendees is also important, and systems in place to be used for this purpose need to have their serviceability and effectiveness checked beforehand.

There may be money to be escorted to and from points within the event or other covert monitoring systems put in place.

The security plan must support the emergency plan as it becomes a key performance area in an emergency. Security personnel must be aware of their specific duties and support roles in dealing with an emergency.

Documenting incidents and information, which can include photographic, video and eye-witness reports, is again of paramount importance and becomes a key enabler for future blueprints for the same or similar events. Electronic security must also not be ignored, and input from suitably qualified information technology professionals may need to be sought.

Enforcement of the rules and regulations, and ensuring the policing of safety procedures are functions that require training and knowledge. The use of volunteers in this capacity without appropriate training or experience is not advisable.

Other aspects of the security management plan could include the VIP protection plan and the protocols that accompany dealing with heads of state, ambassadors or celebrities. Vehicle and car park security are also important as no one wants to leave an event and discover their car is missing. The overall security management plan will only be as good as the initial risk assessment and the efficiency and level of expertise applied by the people charged with its implementation.

17.8 Insurance management

The subject of insurance management deals with possible exposure to civil liability arising from the event, and/or negligence on the part of the conveners, owners or organisers of the event.

The most common type of insurance is called general public liability insurance. It must be immediately pointed out that most underwriters today insert clauses that make it possible for the insurer to repudiate a claim if the cause of loss or harm occurred as a result of non-compliance with legislation, regulations, breach of the contract of insurance or negligence (failure to show a proper duty of care).

Where the event organiser takes control of property, movable or immovable, including buildings, it is advisable to insure against loss or damage. There can be event-specific insurance where failure to meet a contractual obligation on the part of, say, a performer or inclement weather can give rise to a need for insurance against financial loss. Exposure to liability and the negligence of others should form part of the insurance management portfolio. Insurance covering workers should be insisted upon from all appointed contractors working on the building up of the event, be it the erection of temporary structures or signage.

Professional indemnity insurance covering bad or incorrect advice and insuring against errors and omissions can also be considered. Loss of money due to fire or theft, for example, can seriously impact the anticipated income from the endeavour, and insurance against these and

Case study 17.4 Facts from the insurance industry, UK

Slip and fall precautions vital for businesses

Slips, trips and falls are one of the most common forms of public liability claim, which despite many campaigns launched by the Health and Safety Executive (HSE) and councils across the land, show no sign of abating. According to figures released by the HSE, there are more than 1 000 injuries each month caused by a slip, trip or fall from ground level across the UK and while this may seem trivial, the damage that can be done is often extremely serious. For many campaigners, one of the most disappointing things about the number of ground-level falls is the relative simplicity of health and safety risk assessment that could be used to prevent such occurrences.

Lowering the risk

For many companies who deal with large numbers of the public, public liability insurance is a must because no matter how stringent the safety policies in place are, it is impossible to prevent all accidents. But for those companies that have not taken the time to make fully comprehensive risk assessments, the chance of finding themselves on the wrong end of a public liability claim is great.

other eventualities that present possible loss should be investigated and included in the insurance management portfolio.

17.9 Summary

Risk is an inherent part of any business undertaking, and the events and meetings industry is no exception. The financial risk analysis is vitally important, and there is a distinct difference between entrepreneurial risk, where the decision-making processes are made on the availability of solid facts and data, and simply throwing caution to the winds and taking a chance on the hoped-for success of the event, which can be categorised as gambling. The possibility of economic loss must be an early consideration. In conceptualising the event, the potential for personal injury or harm to the participants, visitors and other stakeholders is an essential part of decision making when considering the activities, design and proposed event experience.

Exposure to risk through non-compliance is a threat to the event and could lead to personal prosecution. Public health and safety issues are taken very seriously by the authorities across the globe, and the very nature of the events industry is focused on bringing people together, often in an environment that is strange or different to what they are used to, resulting in the immediate enhancement of the risks from a safety and personal security point of view.

With no understanding of the risks it will not be possible to insure against certain eventualities, thereby nullifying the benefits of insurance where there is a vested insurable interest to protect. Emergency response plans cannot be drawn up unless the risk or potential disaster situations have been identified and are known to the relevant stakeholders and role players. Early identification and monitoring of possible risks and the accumulation of data to enable the analysis of the risks, hazards and threats all contribute to strengthening the knowledge base for the decisions to be made. It logically follows that the risk management process is essential in guiding the conclusions that will be drawn, giving information that is useful in weighing up the pros and cons of what should or should not be done.

The experiences, good or bad, once properly documented, form part of the future risk blueprint.

Questions for research

1   Why is identification of hazards and risks important?
2   What risks can you identify in your own business? Analyse them.
3   Describe the three key elements of a risk assessment.
4   List the areas of compliance in your work or business that need attention or updating.
5   Identify health and safety risks at an event, and design control measures for them.
6   Analyse the legal, ethical and insurance considerations for events.

Recommended websites

Browse the following internet sites for interesting and informative information:

O'Toole, WJ. 2006. *Event Risk Management*: http://www-personal.usyd.edu.au/~wotoole/ EPMS_Control/Control_Areas/Risk/risks.html
Russell, M. 2006. *PCMA REPORT: Crisis Planning for the Meeting, Planning and Convention Industry:* http://www.pcma.org/Convene/Issue_Archives/December_2006/ PCMA_Report_(Crisis).htm

Service level agreement and SLA guide: http://www.service-level-agreement.net/
The Science of Crowd Dynamics: http://www.crowddynamics.co.uk

Suggested reading

Getz, D. 2007. *Event Studies, Theory, Research and Policy for Planned Events.* Oxford, UK: Butterworth–Heinemann.

Tarlow, P. 2002. *Event Risk Management and Safety.* New York: Wiley.

PART VII
Applied events management

Photo: Dimitri Tassiopoulos

Photo: Dimitri Tassiopoulus

18

Hallmark and mega-events

Kamilla Swart

Abstract

The aim of this chapter is to illustrate how event knowledge domains can be used to manage hallmark and mega-events. Specifically, it examines administration, design, marketing, operations, risk and evaluation as they apply to hallmark and mega-events. Best-practice issues in relation to this genre of events are considered, and case studies are used to illustrate key considerations. Attention is also given to developed and developing contexts and how these impact on the organisation of hallmark and mega-events, further demonstrating some of the typical management challenges in relation to this genre of events.

Chapter objectives

After you have read this chapter you should be able to:

❒ define what characterises hallmark and mega-events;

❒ understand how the knowledge domains can be applied to hallmark and mega-events;

❒ understand hallmark and mega-event best-practice issues within developed and developing contexts;

❒ understand what appropriate planning is required for hallmark and mega-events;

❒ understand the key lessons from a number of case studies of a selection of hallmark and mega-events; and

❒ understand the importance of evaluating the impacts and return on investment as well as the importance of knowledge management and knowledge transfer with respect to hallmark and mega-events.

18.1 Introduction and background

There is much overlap between what constitutes a hallmark event and a mega-event. They are both seen as a major once-off or recurring event of limited duration which serves to stimulate awareness of a destination and to enhance its appeal and profitability in the short and long term (Spilling, 1998). Both these types of event are therefore used to promote tourism to a destination, and as such they raise additional concerns for an events manager. They have become prominent in society and are occurring more frequently, especially in developing countries. While they encompass both sport (e.g. the Olympic Games, the FIFA World Cup, the Commonwealth Games, etc.) and non-sport events (e.g. the Rio Carnival, the Munich Oktoberfest and the World's Fair or World Expo, etc.), the significance of the sport mega-event cannot be denied. The intense quest of the growing capital tied to the consumption of sport (Cornelissen, 2005) has made the pursuit of sport mega-events especially attractive to developing countries who are seeking heightened visibility and prestige within the context of

globalisation (i.e. increased opportunities and increased competition). The sheer magnitude of hallmark/mega-events which involve millions of spectators over a couple of weeks, the human resources and financial investments that go along with them and the media concentration to billions of viewers, in addition to the use of primarily temporary systems and logistics operated by a temporary workforce and volunteers in multiple venues, illustrate the significance of applying event-management principles and practices to this genre of events. It is therefore imperative that hallmark and mega-event managers understand how the knowledge domains can be applied to the genre of hallmark and mega-events in order to ensure the development of well-informed, prepared and knowledgeable events managers. Best practice for hallmark and mega-events is elaborated upon in the next section.

18.2 Hallmark/mega-event best practice issues

It is beyond the scope of this chapter to discuss in detail each knowledge domain of managing events in relation to hallmark and mega-events. The approach to this chapter will be to highlight specific aspects that have resonance with hallmark and mega-event planning and management, and are presented below.

18.2.1 Administration

Hallmark and mega-events are planned and managed over a relatively longer period than other events – generally for about six years or more (in addition to taking event bidding into account, which has been covered in depth in chapter 5). Bidding for a mega-event requires very specific event management skills which relate primarily to conceptual planning, demonstrating that the host city or destination has the capacity to host the mega-event and lobbying of the respective members of the international sport organisation to choose the location. This section draws heavily on the Olympic Games experience as it is the most well-documented bidding process.

Four documents are required when bidding to host the Olympic Games (Mallen & Adams, 2008):

❑ A feasibility study, which presents an opinion on the ability of the required resources to host the event;

❑ The candidature document, which outlines the critical path of deadlines and processes to be followed for a bid submission;

❑ The bid questionnaire, which consists of a list of questions that require completion in order for the bid to be considered; and

❑ The bid document, which provides the comprehensive plan, strategy and resources in addition to supplementary detail, plans and testimonials to support the bid.

The Candidate Procedure and Questionnaire for the 2016 Olympic Games includes the candidature procedure, IOC questionnaire (including the 17 themes that need to be addressed) and the instructions concerning the candidature file and guarantees (IOC, 2008).

The themes that need to be addressed are listed in table 18.1:

Table 18.1 The 2016 candidature procedure and questionnaire – themes

1	Vision, legacy and communication
2	Overall concept of the Olympic Games
3	Political and economic climate and structure
4	Legal aspects
5	Customs and immigration formalities
6	Environment and meteorology
7	Finance
8	Marketing
9	Sport and venues
10	Paralympic Games
11	Olympic village(s)
12	Medical services and doping control
13	Security
14	Accommodation
15	Transport
16	Technology
17	Media operations

Source: IOC (2008)

Once the bid submission has been placed on the shortlist, a bid evaluation commission visits the bid committee so they can present the bid dossier in addition to touring the facilities and to demonstrate local community and business support, and why the bid should be awarded. A presentation to the IOC is then required.

Similar to the changes adopted by the IOC in their bidding procedure in recent years, the Federation Internationale de Football Association (FIFA), which is the world governing body for international football, introduced a rotation system (although it has been subsequently reversed) following South Africa's dramatic loss to Germany for the 2006 World Cup (FIFA World Cup, 2006; 2003). Africa was awarded the right to host the 2010 FIFA World Cup, and South Africa won the rights to host this event when they beat Morocco in the first round of voting by 14 votes to ten. As a result of these policy changes, the World Cup will come for the first time to Africa in 2010, and to South America in 2014 (FIFA, 2004).

Similar to sport mega-event bidding, cities and countries also bid for conferences. They too have to demonstrate that they have the capacity host these events successfully. During the United Nations General Assembly 55th session it was decided that a major summit would be held during 2002 in order to assess and continue the groundbreaking work of the United Nations Conference on Environment and Development (UNCED) which was held in Rio de Janeiro in 1992 (United Nations, 2000). The United Nations World Summit on Sustainable Development (WSSD) is considered to be the largest conference held anywhere in the world (Swart, 2005). South Africa and Johannesburg specifically won the bid in December 2000 to host WSSD 2002. This event, also known as the Johannesburg Summit, brought together tens of thousands of participants, including heads of state and government, national delegates and leaders from non-governmental organisations (NGOs), businesses and other major groups to focus the world's attention and direct action toward meeting difficult challenges, such as improving people's lives and conserving our natural resources in a world that is growing in population, with ever-increasing demands for food, water, shelter, sanitation, energy, health services and economic security (JOWSCO, 2002). Further reference to WSSD can also be found in the political event chapter.

Mega-events offer an opportunity to 'open a city to the world often over an extended period of time' (COHRE, 2007: 23). One of the most significant international business mega-events that has been organised and hosted for more than ten years is the World's Fair or World Expo. These events are coordinated by the International Exhibitions Bureau (BIE) and governed by an international convention (COHRE, 2007). From their beginnings as international gatherings of states showcasing industrial prowess and technological innovation, expos have evolved to act as platforms for the international community to debate, share best practices, and explore new solutions for the challenges our planet faces. (BIE, n.d. (a)). They note that there are three main steps an exhibition must follow in order to achieve the essential registration. These are outlined below (BIE, n.d. (b)).

Once a formal nomination of a new project is made (which must specify the date of opening and closing, the theme and the legal status of the organising body), a BIE preliminary enquiry mission conducts an on-the-spot assessment of the project. An enquiry team is thus able to request detailed information, and assess the technical and financial nature of the project. This report is submitted to the executive committee for consideration and subsequently to the General Assembly for approval. If the project is successful in achieving support from these bodies, the Assembly will decide by secret ballot the election of the candidate country which will host the next exhibition. The third and final process is the registration of the exhibition on the basis of the formal review and acceptance of the General Regulations and Draft Participation Contract by the Assembly. The completion of the registration procedure (which may take three years) is marked by the awarding of the BIE flag.

Westerbeek, Turner and Ingerson (2002) developed a survey instrument to identify key success factors of bidding for sport mega-events (which has relevance to other types of mega-events too). The eight key success factors that emerged from their findings are illustrated in table 18.2.

Westerbeek et al. (2002) reported that

Table 18.2 Key success factors in bidding for sport mega-events

Success factors	Description
1 Accountability	The capacity the bid team and the city have to deliver high-quality services to the event promoter and the community stakeholders Must have an established presence in the bidding marketplace Must have a reputation as a city for hosting successful sport events Must be able to showcase a variety of excellent facilities through the hosting of previous mega-events
2 Political support	Increased government involvement in the process of bidding Government involvement enhances the value of the event to the event owner
3 Relationship marketing	The power of the bid committee to influence key decision makers Effective lobbying is critical Built up with experience at bidding and hosting
4 Ability	Organisation and event management skills, including sport-specific technical skills and all the basic requirements to host an event A solid track record in hosting similar events is critical
5 Infrastructure	The city must have the necessary infrastructure to host a successful event Includes the ability to deliver services, accommodation, transportation as well as community support
6 Bid team composition	A mix of talent on the team is essential to the way the team is perceived by the key decision makers as well as to the success of the operation
7 Communication and exposure	The strength of a city's brand image is critical to attracting tourists Communication and IT systems in place to ensure global coverage of the Games
8 Existing facilities	Existence of critical event facilities at the time of the bid Relates to quality facilities provided by the hosting of previous mega-events

Source: Westerbeek et al. (2003: 313–319)

these factors could be further grouped in terms of importance. They assert that the ability to organise an event was the most important factor, followed by a group of factors, namely political support, infrastructure and existing facilities. A second group of factors are at the next level of importance, namely communication and exposure, accountability and bid team composition. The final factor, relationship marketing, was considered to be the least important (Westerbeek et al., 2002), and perhaps influenced by the controversial status of relationship marketing tools. It is evident that most bidding cities are technically competent in terms of the operational aspects of hosting the Games. Nevertheless, as pointed out by Westerbeek et al. (2002), the second group of factors, or supporting factors, may well provide the distinctive edge that cities require to be successful. It is contended that these criteria provide useful guidelines for destinations intending to bid for mega-events.

Rooney (cited by Mallen & Adams, 2008) provides additional guidelines for a bid committee, and includes the following:

❐ Maximise bid confidentiality until the bid is presented;
❐ Clearly define bid committee member roles;
❐ Communicate, communicate, communicate;
❐ Test areas of concern;
❐ Use an external examiner to review the operational plan; and
❐ Be environmentally friendly.

Mallen and Adams (2008) contend that if there is one factor that should be singled out for bid success then it is communication (including both formal and informal and visual communication). It is critical in the bid dossier, the evaluation commission tour, the presentation and the majority of bid activities, including communicating to a network of stakeholders (which will be discussed further in the human resources section).

Once the bid is won, the next phase is signing the host city contract, and the host city/country starts initiating the mega-event concept – the moves towards operational planning, testing, mega-event delivery and evaluation. The compliance, operational and debriefing phases can be applied to any hallmark/mega-event. The financial and human resource elements are key aspects to be considered in the initial compliance phases of the event and will be elaborated upon in the next section.

Financial

The bidding and hosting of hallmark and mega-events are costly affairs and require significant amounts of initial investment investments. For example, the bid for London 2012 was estimated to cost £35 million (ESPN, 2007).

For developing countries, these initial investments are often challenged as it is argued that these resources could be better invested to alleviate poverty (Hiller, 2000) or that these events do little to change the plight of the marginalised (Eisinger, 2000). Moreover, within the context of the global economic crisis, the initial budget for hosting of the London Games was anticipated to cost £2.35 billion (and has since risen about four times the original estimate to £9 billion (Games Bid.com, 2007). Mega-events such as the Olympic Games and the FIFA World Cup require that the bidding city or destination provides financial guarantees to ensure the financing of all major capital infrastructure investments required to deliver the mega-event. In addition, guarantees to cover any potential economic shortfall of the organising committee need to be provided. A case study for the FIFA World Cup is illustrated above.

Revenues and expenditures associated with a hallmark or mega-event usually consist of the elements shown in table 18.3.

As with any event, cash flow is an

Table 18.3 Revenues and expenditures for hallmark and mega-events

Revenues	Expenditures
International Sport Federation contribution	Capital investments directly related to the event (e.g. sports facilities, media broadcasting centre) and not directly related to event (e.g. power/electricity infrastructure, environmental management systems, etc.)
Commercial sponsorship programme (including international, national and local sponsors/suppliers)	Operations (e.g. sport or non-sport venues, media broadcasting centre, workforce, information systems, telecommunications, ceremonies, medical services, catering, transport, security, marketing and administration)
Licensing and merchandising	
Lotteries	
Donations	
Disposal of assets	
Subsidies (national, regional and local government)	

Source: Adapted from IOC budget template (2008)

important consideration. For hallmark and mega-events it is even more critical as cash flow forecasting generally occurs over several years. For example, for the Olympic Games cash flow forecasts take place over a ten-year period (i.e. seven years before the Games as well as two years post-Games) (IOC, 2008).

Human resources

Owing to the size and complexity of hallmark and mega-events, the human resources required is highly complex and involves the collaboration of a number of stakeholders from a broad range of spheres as well as a combination of professional and volunteer staff and subcontractors in the event organisation. Therefore, the key focus of this section will be on the event structure and stakeholder management, and volunteer management.

Hallmark and mega-events, due to their high levels of appeal and complexity, require well-designed event structures that contribute toward successful delivery. For example, stakeholders involved in mega-events include the international sport federations (the rights holders), bid committee (bidding stage), organising committee (hosting stage), commercial partners (sponsors), all spheres of government, the media, sport associations and other volunteer groups, and the general public (local and international). Event structures are developed to aid the governance of an event (Mallen & Adams, 2008). Different events may require different event structures best suited for the management of a particular event; however, there are certain guiding principles applicable to all events. These principles, outlined in the section below, are adapted from Mallen and Adams (2008: 39–40):

❑ *Form follows function.* The purpose of the event and the governance roles required to manage it determine the event structure. It will be necessary to consider and understand the event environment, identify the resources required to deliver the event, and create an event structure that considers the goals and outcomes sought from the event. For example, as per figure 18.1, legacy is an important aspect, and a dedicated legacy manager was appointed which has never been seen in the organisation of previous World Cups.

❑ *Operating specialisation.* Similar or like activities are clustered together into sub-units to enhance communication and interconnectedness.

❑ *Increasing complexity increases both planning and time required for planning.* Hallmark and mega-events require extensive planning, hence operating structures are instituted six to eight years in advance.

❑ *Communications efficiency.* Communication must be formally arranged to ensure efficiency and therefore the required linkages and liaisons for individuals and units within the event structure to communicate is critical, and even more so for complex events such as hallmark and mega-events.

❑ *Synergistic outcomes.* This refers to an event structure that allows agencies to work together and accomplish more as opposed to working as individuals.

The hallmark/mega-event event manager will be required to facilitate the exchange of resources within a web of interconnected constituents (Mallen & Adams, 2008). Managing relationships with event stakeholders is a critical task for the hallmark and mega-event manager. Mallen and Adams (2008) suggest that

Figure 18.1 Legacy – a key priority for the 2010 FIFA World Cup, South Africa

Source: 2010 FIFA World Cup Organising Committee South Africa (2005)

since there are so many event constituents it will be necessary to prioritise the most important stakeholder groups. It is also important to consider that just as there are event stakeholders who are supportive of an event, there are also those who are opposed to them (as illustrated below) and these constituent groups will also need to be considered within the event network.

Volunteers play a critical role in the hosting of hallmark and mega-events. Without their assistance, these events would probably not be able to occur. It is estimated that 100 000 volunteers were used during the 2008 Beijing Olympic Games (70 000 for the Olympics and 30 000 for the Paralympics), while it is anticipated that 25 000 volunteers will be used for the 2010 Winter Olympic Games in Vancouver (Mallen & Adams, 2008). Fifteen thousand volunteers will be required for the 2010 FIFA World Cup (SouthAfrica.info, 2008a). It is necessary for volunteers to be properly serviced and in the case of hallmark and mega-events, there is usually a department

---

Case study 18.2 Environmental group opposes 2010 FIFA World Cup, South Africa

Preparations for the 2010 FIFA World Cup in South Africa have met resistance. The Cape Town Environmental Protection Association (CEPA) has challenged the preparations, opposing the building of a new Green Point stadium in Cape Town to host the semi-finals of the 2010 FIFA World Cup. The city could face legal action as a review application, to be heard in the Cape Town High Court, is still pending, the South African newspaper *Cape Times* reports. The CEPA says it is taking action in the public interest and fights for the environmental and administrative justice rights under the constitution that have been violated. The CEPA's move is the most significant step to date by a civic group opposed to the project. Central to the CEPA's argument is that the approvals for the project have all been inconsistent with the constitution, the National Environmental Management Act, the Environmental Conservation Act, the Promotion of the Administrative Justice Act, the Land Use Planning Ordinance and the National Building Regulations and Building Standards Act. The organisation says while it is in support of the event itself, the building of a new stadium would be a gross misuse of public funds. The Cape Town Civil Society-City-wide forum supports the CEPA's proposed legal action. The group, which represents 179 civic organisations, said in a letter to the CEPA that the decision to build the stadium in Green Point was made in an 'authoritarian and dictatorial' manner without proper and inclusive public participation.

Source: Venø Thesbjerg (2007)

that oversees this function. The volunteer services programme generally includes fundamental personnel management practices such as recruitment, selection, interviewing and database administration (Mallen & Adams, 2008). The following case study serves to illustrate the role of the volunteer programme manager for the 2009 FIFA Confederations Cup in South Africa. The Confederations is considered a 'test' event prior to the FIFA World Cup, which sees the champions of the six FIFA confederations, the reigning FIFA World Champions and the host team competing against each other.

Case study 18.3 Volunteers will be the lifeblood of FIFA World Cup, South Africa

The process to recruit 5 000 volunteers for the FIFA Confederations Cup started on 1 July 2008 and almost 35 000 applications were received. Onke Mjo, volunteer programme manager for the 2010 FIFA World Cup indicated that the volunteers will be the face of the tournament and the lifeblood of the event. Recruitment will take place online, using the fifa.com platform. General and specialist volunteers are required. All the successful applicants, after they have been screened and interviewed, will be provided with comprehensive training from February to April 2009, including general and job-specific training. Volunteers must be 18 years and older.

Sources: FIFA (2008); SouthAfrica.info (2008a, 2008b)

Public Safety Canada (2008) provides the following best practice guidelines for screening volunteers:

1 **Risk management.** Identify the risks of loss or injury to a participant during the delivery of services and put reasonable measures in place to prevent, minimise or eliminate the risk.

2 **Organisational chart and position descriptions.** Use them to identify and manage risk and set the screening standard based on the risk factor. For example, with low-risk positions (minimal or no contact with vulnerable persons), set as a minimum screening standard that volunteers should complete an application form, that the information contained therein is verified, and that supervisors regularly meet with volunteers to provide feedback on their work

3 **Recruitment process.** Be careful of the process and how recruiting is done, and ensure that the organisation is careful about selecting volunteers.

4 **Application form.** This is the first screening tool that potential volunteers and staff will encounter.

5 **Interviews.** These are also an extremely important part of the screening process. Interview questions should encourage responses that allow the interviewer to judge. Past behaviour is a good indicator of future performance.

6 **Reference checks.** This may be the most effective screening step during the selection process.

7 **Police record checks (PRC).** The organisation should decide what type of information is required from the police.

8 **Orientation and training.** A volunteer should be considered as 'on probation' at least until the training is complete.

9 **Supervision and evaluation.** All evaluations should use the position description as a reference point. The right amount of supervision and evaluation is important.

10 *Participant follow-up.* It is important to ensure awareness of any follow-up activities that are required.

Volunteers are generally required for all functional areas of a hallmark or mega-event, and range from accreditation to language support and venue management. Recognising volunteers is a challenge for event managers and should be considered an ongoing service that begins when the volunteer is recruited until the event is over (Mallen & Adams, 2008). They add that volunteers need to be thanked in such a manner that they feel appreciated. Event uniforms, refreshments and a comfortable place to rest are considered important aspects of recognition. In order to ensure a successful event, alignment between the volunteer programme and the overall event is required, and everyone involved in the event should be aware of the purpose, practice and policies of the volunteer programme (Mallen & Adams, 2008).

18.2.2 Design

The design of the event includes consideration for the content, theme, programme, production, entertainment and catering. It will be necessary to review the programme components (both successful and unsuccessful) of the previous year/edition and to research new ideas. In this phase the event theme and logo are decided upon, as illustrated in case study 18.4. For sport mega-events the theme changes with each edition of the event and is specific to the context for the destination as opposed to the other hallmark events whose theme stays the same each year.

In terms of the event programme for sport mega-events, competition schedules are required. It is also important to note that while there is the main event, it is usually accompanied by pre-events (e.g. conferences, preliminary and final draws, and torch relays), peripheral events (e.g. educational or cultural events that accompany sport events such as the Olympic Games educational programme or the public viewing area events commonly associated with football World Cups) or even other major events in their own right (e.g. the opening and closing ceremonies).

Whether the performers and entertainers are being considered for the peripheral events or the opening and

Table 18.4 Hallmark and mega-events themes

Hallmark/mega-event	Event theme
2010 Vancouver Winter Olympic Games	Dream Discover Celebrate (with glowing hearts)
2010 FIFA World Cup	Ke Nako – Celebrate Africa's humanity
2010 Delhi Commonwealth Games	Come out and play
2012 London Olympic Games	Be inspired
Rio Carnival	Farewell to the pleasures of the flesh (samba schools who participate in the Rio Samba Parade choose a different theme each year)
Munich Oktoberfest	Beer and entertainment
Expo 2010	Better city, better life

Source: Official event websites

closing ceremonies, it would be necessary to determine the types of performance best suited for the activities. The performers and entertainers would need to audition and sign contracts for these. For opening and closing ceremonies, these performances are usually subcontracted due to their spectacular nature and magnitude.

Case study 18.4 Olympic Games Opening Ceremony artistic programme

Usually, the content of the Opening Ceremony show is kept secret until the last minute. Over the years, Games organisers have managed to find creative ways to combine Olympic protocol with just the right amount of entertainment, cultural references, technological innovations and festive atmosphere. The Sydney 2000 presentation covered the history, nature and culture of the whole of Australia. In Turin in 2006, the organisers offered spectators and television viewers a ceremony in which the athletes were at the heart of things, with an unforgettable show illustrating the values of brotherhood and dialogue between peoples and cultures, to show that 'passion lives here'. For its part, the Opening Ceremony of the 2004 Games in Athens, produced by Dimitris Papaioannou, offered a memorable mix of Olympic protocol and Greek culture. The various scenes depicted 3 000 years of this historical legacy, highlighting the links between the Ancient Games and this first Olympiad of the 21st century. For the 2008 Beijing Games, 14 000 performers offered the 91 000 people in the National Stadium, popularly known as the 'Bird's Nest', a history lesson in China's contribution to world civilisation.

Sources: IOC (February 2008); Beijing (2008)

The case of the Rio Carnival Samba Parade, Brazil is highlighted in case study 18.5 to provide an example of a non-sporting hallmark event, and more importantly to illustrate that the design feature of this event is critical to its success.

Coordinating food and beverage services forms part of the hospitality on offer. For mega-events, hospitality requirements are especially stringent as they form part of the commercial revenue stream. Sponsors generally buy hospitality packages which combine food and beverage with the sale of tickets. Key consideration will need to be given to the dietary requirements, principles and practices of food safety, transport and storage of food, and the number of people to cater for at each specific function, among others (Canadian Tourism Human Resource Council, 2008). Deliberation should be given to outsourcing of services (and the associated tendering process) as well as compliance with relevant legislation, e.g. liquor laws, and health and public safety. In terms of hospitality, specific plans also need to be put in place for transport and other hospitality services as required.

Accommodation is a particular important consideration for hallmark and mega-events. For example, the FIFA World Cup require 55 000 rooms to be secured for the FIFA family, including sponsors and players. The Olympic Games require the establishment of an athletes' village and is considered as one of the largest projects associated with hosting the Games (IOC, 2008). Athletes and team officials generally number in the region of 18 500 for an Olympic Games (Bovey, 2006). It is also necessary for the athletes' village to serve both the Olympic and the Paralympic Games, so they therefore need

Case study 18.5 The Samba Parade Guide, Brazil

The Rio Samba Parade is very distinctive from all other street parades held at some other places in the world as it entails a competition between the samba schools. The main competition was originally held downtown until the mid-1980s, when the principal parades were moved to the Sambodromo, specially built for this event. Preparation for the Samba Parade starts months in advance, as each samba school mobilises thousands of supporters who will create the various parts of the school's display. The theme of the year is chosen as well as the school's samba song of the year, which is selected through competition, while the school's Carnival Designer creates the costumes and the floats. When ready, the sketches move into production. By December the rehearsals begin. The Rio Samba Parade is a highly orchestrated show of vast proportions. The parade of every school is highly organised and designed. They line up in a unique way to present their pageant. The schools are divided into a number of sections and each section has a number of wings of about 100 people wearing the same costume. In between the wings, there are about 10 Carnival floats separating the sections. Most of them are pushed along by men from the school's community but some are motorised and have mechanical parts. The floats carry special guests along with some young and mesmerising samba dancers in very elaborate, awe-inspiring costume creations.

Source: Carnival in Rio (n.d.)

to meet certain accessibility requirements. It is also necessary to outline existing, planned and additional (not authorised yet) hotel accommodation in the host city. Client groups requiring accommodation for an Olympic Games include the International Olympic Committee, International Federations, National Olympic Committees, host and future OCOGs, marketing partners and media (IOC, 2008).

For the Commonwealth Games about 8 000 athletes need to be accommodated, which also requires the building of an athletes' village (GamesBid.com, 2009). Another example is that of the Rio Festival where accommodation should be organised at least three or four months in advance. This mega-carnival is estimated to attract about 500 000 foreign visitors annually (Carnival in Rio, n.d).

The following section focusing on legacy has been included here as the need

to examine legacies associated with mega-events is increasing in prominence and should be considered as part of the event design. Legacy can be defined as ensuring as many long-term benefits are generated for the host city, region and nation – well before, during and long after the event (Mann, 2008). In fact, it is obligatory for host cities undertaking an Olympic bid to consider legacy in their bid submission. Kirkup and Major (2007) assert that leaving suitable legacies has become a discourse which has left an unforgettable mark on the way in which planning for a mega-event takes shape. When creating legacies it is important to consider the different types of legacies, as described by Chappelet and Junod (2006) below:

❏ *Sporting legacy.* This refers to sporting facilities newly built or renovated for an event, which will serve some purpose after the event has concluded. In addition, they may also play a role in changing local sporting culture by either increasing people's participation in sport, introducing new and different types of sport to the area, or organising more sport mega-events on a regular basis.

☐ *Urban legacy.* This refers to buildings which were built for the mega-event but which serve no sporting functions such as the 'development of new urban districts and specialised areas' (Chappelet & Junod, 2006: 84).

☐ *Infrastructural legacy.* This refers to the different types of network, ranging from transport to telecommunications, which are renovated or developed for a mega-event and maintained after the event is complete.

☐ *Economic legacy.* Mega-events are often associated with increases in the number of tourists and investments to a host city. Other indicators of the economic legacy of mega-events are changes in the number of permanent jobs created and changes in the unemployment rate of the host region or city.

☐ *Social legacy.* Mega-events are symbolic in nature and thus often lead to the creation of many stories and myths, and form part of the 'collective memory' of an event (Chappelet & Junod, 2006: 85). This term refers to local residents' memories and experiences of the mega-event, and can also include the actual skills and experiences which people gain through their direct or indirect involvement in the mega-event.

Sustainability is closely related to building positive event legacies, as illustrated in the following case study of the Vancouver Olympic Games. In order to ensure sound environmental policies and practices, FIFA introduced Green Goal at the 2006 World Cup and has extended this programme to the 2010 World Cup. Minimising the carbon footprint, conservation of water resources, recycling, energy efficiency, indigenous landscaping, green building practices and responsible tourism are key considerations (Western Cape Department of Cultural Affairs and Sport, 2009).

Case study 18.6 Olympic Games Impact Programme

The IOC acknowledges the importance of sustainable development and social responsibility, and therefore developed the Olympic Games Impact (OGI) programme in 2003. The purpose of the OGI programme is to measure the long-term impact of the Olympic and Paralympic Games through a consistent and comparable reporting system across all future Games. Moreover, it is intended to assist cities that are bidding for an Olympic Games and future organisers to identify potential legacies to maximise the Games' benefits. The OGI programme includes a series of indicators (126) that measure the status of a range of environmental, socio-cultural and economic dimensions of the host city, region and nation. The OGI programme is integrated into Games management, presented in a series of four reports and spanning a period of 11 years. The first report provides the baseline against which indicator data in future reports will be compared and analysed (prepared three years prior to the Games). The second report is prepared one year prior to the Games and the third of the four reports is the required volume of the Official Report of the Olympic Games, which is mandated by the host city contract.

Source: VANOC OGI (2007)

Case study 18.7 Negative social legacies – housing displacements and evictions

The city of Shanghai, China, is due to host the next World Expo in 2010 and in an attempt to beautify the city many of its residents are suffering as a result of housing displacement, where 18 000 families have been evicted from the Expo site alone. However, this figure is only a small portion of the 400 000 people who will be moved to the suburbs as part of a comprehensive urban development scheme that includes the Expo, large infrastructural development, and market-rate commercial and residential development. The Expo site is positioned in a densely populated area of central Shanghai, which means many inner-city residents are being relocated while the city is transformed.

One of the most recent examples of forced evictions related to the preparations for a political mega-event are reports of the violent forced eviction of 30 households (affecting 42 families) in Lapu-lapu City in Cebu, Philippines, in September 2006, at the site of the 12th ASEAN (Association of East Asian States) summit scheduled for December 2006. The land on which the families' homes were located was needed as a parking lot for the Shangrila Hotel, the place where the participants in the ASEAN summit were staying. Although the homes were on private land, the authorities did not obtain court orders authorising the demolitions, and instead relied upon building permit violations to evict the squatter families, many of whom had resided on the site for decades. The evictions were violent: authorities used water cannons and truncheons to disperse the human barricade put up by students and members of the Atbang Shangrila Urban Poor Association.

Source: COHRE (2007: 24, 26)

Negative social legacies that have relevance for all types of mega-events include housing displacements and evictions. According to the 1996 Global Report on Human Settlements prepared by the United Nations Centre for Human Settlements (UNCHS), five of the top 34 examples of massive evictions worldwide were related to mega-events (cited by Greene, 2003). In case study 18.7 examples from a cultural and a political mega-event are presented.

Even though there are many cases of forced evictions and discrimination during the bidding and planning process of an event, there are examples of best practices such as the example of the 2006 Commonwealth Games in Melbourne, Australia in case study 18.8.

The Canadian Tourism Human Resource Council (2008) note that in order to implement a sustainable event management plan, it is necessary to review evaluations from previous and/or similar events; determine requirements for sustaining the event; select strategies to create positive outcomes and mitigate negative impacts of an event; and align sustainability practices with existing management structures.

18.2.3 Marketing

Key aspects of marketing in relation to hallmark and mega-events include the marketing plans, sponsorship and PR, broadcasting, licensing and merchandising. The opening and closing ceremonies will also be elaborated upon here as they have

Case study 18.8 2006 Commonwealth Games, Australia

Preparations for the 2006 Commonwealth Games resulted in cooperation between civil society in Melbourne and the Victorian State Government to protect the homeless and low-income earners. This began when an affiliation of community and legal organisations set up 'The Monitoring 2006 project' with the aim of ensuring that the local population, in particular the marginalised residents of Melbourne (such as the homeless), were not discriminated against during the preparation and hosting of the Commonwealth Games. The Victorian State Government worked with the Council of Homeless Persons to create the Victorian Protocol for People Who are Homeless in Public Places, which provides guidelines for respecting the rights of homeless people, focusing on respect, participation, and the provision of information and safety. In addition, the Victorian State Government provided AUS$60 000 to reserve 600 cheap, but safe, accommodations during the period of the Games so that homeless people would not be priced out of the market for a room. Collaborations such as this between community service, interest groups and the local governmental authorities provide one example of the ways in which the homeless and urban poor can be better protected in the planning and preparation of mega-events.

Source: COHRE (2007: 29)

become marketing showcases in their own right.

Hallmark and mega-events provide very effective marketing platforms in the world due to their global reach. Rights holders such as the IOC and FIFA create long-term marketing programmes to build on and support the successful activities developed by each organising committee, thus ensuring the financial stability of their respective organisations.

Revenue generation and distribution for the Olympic Movement is presented as an illustrative case. The Olympic Movement generates revenue through six major programmes (IOC, Beijing 2008). The IOC manages broadcast partnerships, TOP (The Olympic Partner programme), worldwide sponsorship programme and the IOC official supplier and licensing programme. Revenue generated from each major programme managed by the IOC, and the OCOGs, is illustrated in figure 18.2. The IOC distributes approximately 92% of Olympic marketing revenue to organisations throughout the Olympic Movement to support the staging of the Olympic Games and to promote the worldwide development of sport (IOC, Beijing 2008), while it retains about 8% of Olympic marketing revenue for the operational and administrative costs of governing the Olympic Movement.

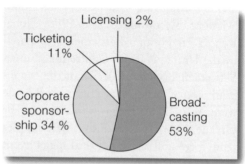

Figure 18.2 Olympic revenue sources
Source: IOC Beijing (2008: 3)

Sponsorship contributes more than 30% of Olympic marketing revenue. Each level of sponsorship entitles companies to different marketing rights in various regions, category exclusivity and the use of designated Olympic images and marks (IOC, n.d).

For hallmark and mega-events commercial programmes are generally developed to meet the needs of different types of sponsor. The commercial programme outlines the benefits to sponsors at each sponsorship level. As these sponsors are secured way in advance of the event, timelines for sponsorship negotiation is significant. The official partners are usually global players. For example, FIFA official partners include Adidas, Coca-Cola and Sony, among others. World Cup partners are also global players but there is room for national companies as well. For example, a South African company, MTN (Mobile Telephone Network), is also one of the World Cup sponsors along with McDonald's, Budweiser and Continental, among others. Mega-events, due to their scale and global stature, are generally associated with extremely high levels of sponsorship. It is estimated that the international sponsorship for the FIFA World Cup has risen from about $2 billion in 1984 to more than $20 billion (Temkin, 2009). Upper-tier sponsors for the FIFA World Cup, including global brands such as Coca-Cola, Adidas, Hyundai, Sony, Visa and Emirates, have been reported to pay in the region of $100 million whereas national supporters for the 2010 FIFA World Cup such as Telkom (telecommunications) and FNB (financial services) are reported to have paid $30 million (Temkin, 2009).

Hallmark and mega-events are generally attractive to a sponsor but it is always important to bear in mind that sponsorship is a commercial promotional technique and therefore the value of the event to the sponsor is important. This is especially important in today's global economic climate. Sponsorship agencies, especially for hallmark and mega-events, are subcontracted by the rights owner to source sponsorship. The rights owner (or sponsorship agency) must be able to service the sponsor upon signing the contractual sponsorship agreement. This generally includes liaising with the sponsor, and ensuring that the sponsorship agreement is fulfilled and that the sponsorship objectives are achieved and evaluated (Shone & Parry, 2004). Return on investment on the sponsorship is critical to its sustainability.

Given the high levels of sponsorship investment in hallmark and mega-events, it is not surprising therefore that ambush marketing, where organisations attempt to capitalise on high-profile events without paying sponsorship fees to the event organiser, is of huge concern to mega-event organisers and their associated sponsors, as highlighted in the risk section below.

Broadcasting is an especially lucrative financial resource for hallmark and mega-events. This has allowed rights holders to ensure that organising committees are able to firm up budgets in advance, thus creating more stable events. A long-term approach to broadcasting also allows the promotional programming to support the event to be concluded between the broadcaster and the rights holder. Broadcast revenue for the Olympic Games has increased from US$1.2 million in 1960 (Rome) to US$1.7 billion in 2008 (Beijing) (IOC, Beijing 2008). Television rights for the 2010 Commonwealth Games in Delhi, India, has doubled and it is expected to reach US$50 million (GamesBid.com, 2009). Television rights fees continue to account for approximately 50% of Olympic revenue (IOC, n.d.). High-definition content and digital media have become important components of broadcasting in recent years. Both the FIFA World

Cup and Olympic Games have started to broadcast in high definition and have also provided opportunities for digital broadcast platforms (internet and mobile platforms) which enhance the experience for the spectator who is able to follow the event at any time and in any format.

In order to safeguard consistent quality and full integration of its event designs, FIFA decided to take control of the TV production of its events (FIFA, n.d.). Consequently, FIFA appointed HBS as host broadcaster for both the 2009 and the 2013 FIFA Confederations Cup, and the 2010 and 2014 FIFA World Cup. HBS will also assist FIFA with host broadcasting matters, the development of host broadcasting requirements and guidelines, as well as the supervision of the host broadcasters appointed by FIFA for other FIFA events during the 2007–2014 event cycle to ensure that FIFA's broadcast operations guidelines and standards are met (FIFA, n.d.).

While rights holders such as the IOC and FIFA do not recognise the opening and closing ceremonies as marketing platforms that generate revenue, they are nevertheless significant marketing platforms for host cities and destinations, as illustrated in case study 18.4, on the artistic programme of the Olympic Games. Case study 18.9 presents the extent of the television coverage of an Olympic Ceremony as well as the spill-over into new media platforms.

Operations

There are many operational details that need to be finalised before the event. These include logistics and infrastructure, participants and attendees, and site and technical components, among others. This section will focus on the site plan, logistics and infrastructural requirements (transport

---

Case study 18.9 NBC: Beijing Olympic Opening Ceremony draws record ratings

NBC's coverage of the Opening Ceremony of the 2008 Summer Olympics drew the largest US television audience ever for a non-US Summer Olympics Opening Ceremony. Some 34.2 million viewers watched the Opening Ceremony, smashing the previous record of 27.3 million for NBC's coverage of the 2000 Summer Olympics from Sydney, Australia. Friday's ceremony from Beijing also drew the highest rating for a non-US opening ceremony – 18.6 – beating the previous record of 18.1 for the 1960 Rome Games on CBS, the first Summer Olympics to be extensively televised in the US. Ratings for most forms of programming have declined in recent years because of increased competition for viewers from cable television, the internet, home video and video games. 'The Olympic Opening Ceremony captivated the American public in unprecedented numbers for a non-US Olympics,' said Dick Ebersol, chairman, NBC Universal Sports & Olympics. 'It was a magical and memorable spectacle and a great way to start the Beijing Olympics.' The heavy amount of interest in the Opening Ceremony also extended to NBC's Olympics website, BCOlympics.com, which had a record 70 million page views Friday, 10 times more than the seven million on the opening day of the Athens Games. NBC reportedly paid $894 million for the rights to broadcast the Beijing Games, and is spending more than $100 million to transmit the games and pageantry.

Source: Xinhuanet (2008)

in particular). As highlighted above, the management of the hallmark and mega-events is highly complex. The key operations will be outlined in this section for illustrative purposes as it is beyond the scope of this chapter to discuss them all in detail. Table 18.6 highlights some of the operational aspects which need to be considered.

Table 18.6 Key operational areas for sport mega-events

Management focus area	Description
Venue operations	Competition venues Non-competition venues Olympic village Accreditation Food services Health services Security
Sports	Doping control Games planning Competition Sports services Paralympic Games
Technology	Information technology Communications
International relations	NOC relations IOC relations Translation services
Broadcasting	Main press centre Venue media centres International broadcast centre
Transportation	Traffic and transport authorities coordination Bus network services

Source: Athens 2004 (2004a)

In terms of hallmark and mega-event operations, it will be necessary to develop a precinct plan before the site development plan. The precinct plan provides a guide to the form and shape of future development parcels on a site and urban design guidelines for these (De Tolly, 1992). The site development plan divides the precinct plan into smaller development parcels, and plans are prepared for groups of buildings. These plans are generally also developed within a development framework. These provide the basic physical organisation for the proposed development of a site and are generally prepared for the larger proposed sites for hallmark and mega-events, as illustrated in case study 18.10. Moreover, the case study further illustrates the operations required for the International Broadcast Centre for the 2010 FIFA World Cup as well as how one of the commercial partners has leveraged its sponsorship.

Van der Wagen (2005: 255) notes that 'logistics is about getting things (and people) in the right place at the right time and pulling everything down'. The logistics department is aimed at providing the attendees (spectators and participants), media, sponsors and the functional areas of the hallmark and mega-event with the best possible logistics services in order to ensure the best possible support of the event within the existing budget (Athens, 2004; 2004b). They note that prior to the Athens Olympic Games, the logistics department was responsible for the receipt, storage, distribution, installation (in some cases), tracking of the assets, and the handling of the equipment and material required for the implementation of all the programmes of Athens 2004.

During the Games, this department was responsible for the scheduling of deliveries to the venues through the management of the master delivery schedule, for providing assistance to all the functional areas through the work orders, for the asset tracking management of the equipment of the venues, in addition to the

Case study 18.10 MTN (South Africa) to build world-class media centre

MTN has partnered with the Johannesburg Expo Centre in the creation of a state-of-the-art media centre, the International Broadcast Centre (IBC), for the 2010 FIFA World Cup. The IBC is the culmination of a multimillion rand development plan for the World Cup, and will host thousands of broadcasters from around the world for the six-week duration of the World Cup. In order to prepare the venue for this influx of media, the MTN Expo Centre will receive some of the most technically advanced facilities in terms of IT and mobile networks on the continent. The cumulative television audience for the 2010 event in South Africa is estimated to reach 30 billion people, and as such needs to be properly equipped. 'The IBC will be the pulse and the nerve centre for all TV operations during the 2010 FIFA World Cup. Through a sophisticated network it will be linking the venues in South Africa to the rest of our football family all over the globe. This way it will also create a legacy far beyond the event in terms of telecommunication infrastructure for the country,' said FIFA president Blatter.

During the 2006 FIFA World Cup in Germany, the IBC was set up in Munich where Germany hosted 13 400 accredited TV commentators, camera crew – members and technical staff. The centre broadcast images and reports of the World Cup to more than 120 television and radio stations in 190 countries to over 26 billion people across the world. The MTN Expo Centre will fuse with Soccer City and turn the grounds into a multi-entertainment area, giving both local and visiting soccer fans a place to go which is safe, attractive and central to the football action. The centre will also serve as the hospitality venue for MTN during the 2010 FIFA World Cup. The entire precinct is a flagship improvement node being developed by the Johannesburg Development Agency to bridge the apartheid spatial planning gap between the south of Johannesburg and the centre of the city.

Source: South Africa The Good News (2009)

management of the procurement in the venue (Athens, 2004; 2004b). Post-Games, the logistics department was responsible for getting back all Athens 2004 property from the venues, while supervising and coordinating the procedures that ensure the protection of the materials and the minimisation of losses. Warehousing and distribution, Olympic family freight forwarding, and venue logistics are some of the responsibilities that fall within the sphere of the logistics department.

Van der Wagen (2005) adds that procurement, transportation, storage, inventory management, customer service and database management are examples of logistical aspects that require consideration. She further notes that many infrastructural requirements are of a temporary nature and may require special licensing requirements. Hallmark and mega-events are of such a nature that they do require significant temporary structures in addition to permanent competition and non-competition venues.

Bovey (2006) notes that it is a remarkable achievement for hallmark and mega-events to achieve operational success for transport requirements as such events need to cope with additional traffic to the magnitude of 200 000 to 600 000 daily spectators, visitors and support logistics over and above normal traffic conditions. 'A highly robust and resilient public transport system is a prerequisite to handle mega-event traffic demands' (Bovey, 2006: 34). A strong public transport system must be accompanied by innovative policies to reduce general traffic on the primary transport network, to avoid congested conditions affecting public transport and to guarantee that accredited vehicles free flow on a designated reserved lane network. In the case of a developing country such as South Africa where the transport network is not as robust, reliance will be on bus services and dedicated lanes as opposed to rail. The only significant rail project, although not directly related to 2010, is the Gautrain, which is a high-speed rail network that will link OR Tambo International Airport with Johannesburg and the country's capital Pretoria/Tshwane (2010 OC, 2008). Hallmark and mega-event transport can be considered a unique opportunity to enhance sustainable transport development.

18.2.4 Risk

All hallmark and mega-event organisers face numerous risks, and some of the major ones encountered will be highlighted in this section. It will be imperative for the hallmark and mega-event organiser to identify, analyse, prioritise, minimise and monitor risks. Some of the major risks that should be considered are the following:

❏ Natural disasters;
❏ Financial risk;
❏ Legal risk;
❏ Technology-related risks;
❏ Mismanagement; and
❏ Safety and security risks (especially terrorism and crime as per the case studies below).

Van der Wagen (2005) observes that risk management involves the following:
❏ Establishing the context (the strategic

> ### Case study 18.11 Security a concern for Delhi 2010
>
> India is being extremely careful about security arrangements for the Delhi 2010 Commonwealth Games, according to Organising Committee chairman Suresh Kalmadi. He told reporters that 'we have to be very careful about the security'. Kalmadi said that the first task for the organisers would be to allay the security concerns of the participating countries, reports Zee News. 'With security becoming an issue in the neighbouring countries, it is important for us to comfort them. We will put up a Beijing-like security bandobust in Delhi. We will put the best foot forward in October and make the right projection so as to satisfy the 71 countries who would be coming for the general assembly meeting.'
>
> *Source: GamesBid.com (2009)*

context, which includes the external environment, and the organisational context for hallmark and mega-events);
❏ Identifying the risk (potential risks that could impact on the success of an event);
❏ Analysing the risk (in terms of what the consequence of the risk is and what the likelihood is of it recurring);
❏ Evaluating the risk (and prioritising a list of risks for further action); and
❏ Treating the risk (avoid the risk by abandoning the activity, reduce the likelihood of the occurrence or reduce the severity of the consequences (contingency planning)).

It is also important to monitor the risk management plan (Canadian Tourism Human Resource Council, 2008).

Complying with legal and regulatory obligations is a critical aspect of managing risk. Hallmark and mega-events are associated with by-laws in order to regulate the hosting of the event. By-laws are especially important to protect the marketing rights of commercial partners associated with the event as well as with respect to the high levels of security required for hallmark and mega-events, given the large crowds that are expected to attend. Careful consideration would need to be given as to how these by-laws are communicated, especially in relation to informal traders and homeless people who generally bear the brunt of them. Case study 18.12 illustrates the importance of by-laws in terms of managing risk by controlling access sites, while case study 18.13 presents the consequences of infringing on the rights of the commercial programme of a hallmark/mega-event.

Case study 18.12 Hardcore by-laws for World Cup host cities, South Africa

In terms of the Municipal Services Act, the 2010 FIFA World Cup by-laws have been passed by South African host cities and towns. The by-laws are identical for all towns which are required to regulate advertising, controlled access, public open spaces and city beautification, public roads and street trading. The by-laws outlaw ambush marketing for the duration of the World Cup and two weeks thereafter. The by-laws demarcate 'controlled access sites' which include the stadiums, the location of the official events, accreditation centres, training sites, fan parks and the hotels hosting FIFA officials and players. The penalties for contravening the by-laws is a fine of up to R10 000 or imprisonment of up to six months.

Source: Chilwane (2009: 3)

Case study 18.13 FIFA is giving the red card to ambush tactics

An application was launched in FIFA's name in the Pretoria High Court claiming interdicts against Eastwoods Tavern on the grounds of infringing the registered trademarks World Cup 2010 and Twenty Ten South Africa, passing off under the common law, and unlawful competition through violating the Trade Practices Act (2001) and the Merchandise Marks Act (2003). The Trade Practices Act makes it an offence for a person to falsely imply or suggest a contractual or other association with a sponsored event, while under the provisions of the Merchandise Marks Act, the Trade and Industry Minister can declare an event 'protected' as in the case of the 2010 FIFA World Cup.

Source: Temkin (2009: 1–2)

Managing risk also take into consideration managing emergencies, complying with health and safety requirements, acquiring insurance and arranging security (Canadian Tourism Human Resource Council, 2008). A hallmark mega-event such as the Munich Oktoberfest which attracts about six million people over a two-week period who consume four million litres of beer (Munich Beer Festival: Oktoberfest, 2009) is high risk in terms of crowd management and medical requirements. Steps have been undertaken to limit the drunkenness and violence by introducing the 'quiet Oktoberfest' in 2005 whereby music was limited to 85 decibels in the afternoon (Johnson, n.d.).

18.2.5 Event evaluation, return on investment, knowledge management and transfer of knowledge

This final section of the chapter will focus on hallmark and mega-event evaluations, return on investment and transfer of knowledge. Gratton, Shibli and Coleman (2006) conclude that event evaluations have evolved and will continue to do so in order to better understand the likely legacies of events, especially in the long term. Cornelissen (2007) contends that within the Olympic Movement there have been more advances to date in establishing knowledge about the effects of the Games in contrast to the FIFA World Cup. The final report is completed three years after the Games. In terms of the VANOC OGI process, the Organising Committee appointed an external advisor to undertake a preliminary review of the initial OGI indicators. Special consideration was given to the following elements (VANOC OGI, 2007):

- ❒ Potential sources of data;
- ❒ Availability of data;
- ❒ Cost implications for data collection and manipulation;
- ❒ Relevance of indicators; and
- ❒ Cross-referencing the OGI indicators with locally developed indicators for the 2010 Winter Games.

Case study 18.14 shows how the impact of Euro 2008 was evaluated.

Event evaluations, especially for hallmark and mega-events, have evolved to undertaking a triple bottom line approach as per the above examples. Furthermore, it is important to underscore that the return on investment (ROI, i.e. a performance measure used to evaluate the efficiency of an

---

Case study 18.14 Euro 2008 Impact Model

The Federal Office for Sport (BASPO) together with the host cities (Basle, Berne, Geneva and Zurich) and supported by UBS and Euro 2008 SA (organisers of Euro 2008), initiated a five-year study (2005–2009) in order to assess the impact of the UEFA Euro 2008 on sustainable development. The project is handled by a research community, and focuses on identifying the most important short-term and long-term effects on the economy, society and the environment, in addition to media and infrastructure impacts. The approach included identifying the relevant target areas within the dimensions of sustainability, developing the indicators and the measurement instruments.

Source: Moesch & Muller (2008)

---

investment) can be viewed very differently, especially since there are so many different stakeholders involved in hosting a hallmark and mega-event. For example, the event organisers (rights owners) would like to ensure a profitable event, the commercial partners would like to ensure an ROI on their marketing spend, and government would like to ensure ROIs with respect to infrastructure spend, visitor attendance (including spend) and destination imaging reach, while it is also important to ensure community support for the hallmark and mega-event. It is therefore evident that, depending on the stakeholders' objectives, different conclusions about the ROI can be reached. In addition, it may be virtually impossible to take into account all the stakeholders' objectives for events as complex as hallmark and mega-events. Hallmark and mega-event stakeholders have therefore opted to use a range of indicators (both qualitative and quantitative) to assess the overall impact of the event, as mentioned previously.

Over and above the hallmark and mega-event evaluation, it is necessary for sport and event organisations 'to successfully capture, share, manage and harness their corporate knowledge to reduce uncertainty of outcomes and co-ordinate and facilitate strategy and policy implementation' (Halbwirth & Toohey, 2001: 91). The Sydney Olympic Games Organising Committee (SOCOG) was able to use an established information infrastructure to grow a knowledge project. Key success factors included the project being championed by senior executive, knowledge management (KM) professionals with a clear vision of contributing to a successful Games, adequate resources, an effective technology infrastructure and a knowledge-friendly culture that supported the project (Halbwirth & Toohey, 2001). The Official Report (post-Games report) serves as one of the enduring legacies and reference tools for future Olympic Games organisers. From a commercial knowledge legacy perspective, SOCOG also sold explicit and tacit Sydney Games knowledge to the IOC for $A5 million. This material was disseminated to both the Salt Lake City and Athens organising committees and formed the basis of the IOC's Transfer of Know How (TOK) programme and established Olympic knowledge as a corporate asset (Halbwirth & Toohey, 2001). Similarly, the Commonwealth Games have also undertaken to develop a knowledge transfer programme, and the Delhi 2010 OC is currently advertising a legacy director position and knowledge transfer is noted as key accountability (Commonwealth Games Delhi 2010, n.d).

Halbwirth and Toohey (2005) contend that academic research concerning the organisation of major sport events have tended to focus on a range of aspects such as impacts, and more recently legacy and other functional activities. However, the success of these functions is significantly grounded in the acquisition, production and dissemination of knowledge and information (Halbwirth & Toohey, 2005). They argue that integrating knowledge into each hallmark and mega-event is critical, just as it is to transfer knowledge across several events.

18.3 Summary

Hallmark and mega-events have become prominent in society and are occurring more frequently, especially in developing countries. They encompass both sport and non-sport events. The enormity of hallmark and mega-events illustrate the significance of applying event management principles and practices to this genre of events. This chapter elaborated upon how the knowledge domains can be applied to the genre of hallmark and mega-events in order to ensure the development of well-informed, prepared and knowledgeable hallmark and mega-event managers. The chapter further attempted to illustrate how key knowledge domains such as administration, design, marketing, operations, risk and evaluation can be applied to the management of hallmark and mega-events. A number of best practice case studies were also elaborated upon to demonstrate some of the typical management challenges in relation to this genre of events. Of significance are challenges related to bidding processes, high volumes of spectators and participants (and the associated logistics), the commercial programme and the protection of commercial partners, sustainable development and creating positive legacies, among others.

Questions for research

1 What are the characteristics of a mega-event? Describe the various types.
2 Select two mega-events, and review and compare their event bidding processes.
3 Why is appropriate planning crucial in preparing to host a mega-event?
4 What are the key management areas that should be considered for hosting a successful hallmark and mega-event in your country or region?
5 Why is it important to evaluate the actual impacts of a hallmark and mega-event, and what are the critical aspects to be measured?
6 How can a knowledge management programme enhance the success of a current and future hallmark and mega-event?

Recommended websites

Browse the following internet sites for interesting and informative information:

Carnival in Rio: http://www.rio-carnival.net/
Federation Internationale de Fooball Association (FIFA): http://www.fifa.com
GamesBids.com - mega events portal: http://www.gamesbids.com/eng/
International Olympic Committee (IOC): http://www.ioc.org
Munich Beer Festival: Oktoberfest: http://munichbeerfestival.com
Resource Guide to the Impacts of Events: http://www.toolkitsportdevelopment.org/
    mega-events/html/resources/44/44AB4690-E2B0-4157-BB9C-4C665F2F7EFF/
    Resource%20Guide%20the_impact_of_events.pdf

Suggested reading

Mallen, C & Adams, LJ. 2008. *Sport, Recreation and Tourism Event Management.* UK: Elsevier.

Photo: Razaq Raj and Paul Walters

19 Festivals

Razaq Raj and Paul Walters

Abstract

The purpose of this chapter is to explain and discuss the planning of festivals and the range of roles they play in society, and investigate some of the objectives they meet for stakeholders. In addition the chapter will provide an opportunity to consider the benefits of festivals and the process for planning and implementation.

Chapter objectives

After you have read this chapter you should be able to:
- ❏ define festivals and their place within the event market;
- ❏ define the role of festivals within society;
- ❏ investigate and discuss planning and managing a festival;
- ❏ compare the festival programming and scheduling the evaluations; and
- ❏ identify and illustrate examples of specific cases of a festivals and events.

19.1 INTRODUCTION

Festivals play an important role for towns, cities or whole regions, and they are often interlinked with local culture and history. In many cases festivals help to stimulate the host city's economy but can also satisfy a range of different other objectives. They can be used to express the relationship between identity and place, and play a very important role in raising civic consciousness. Furthermore, festivals are an important expression of human activity, and contribute significantly to the social and cultural life of their host communities.

Festivals are increasingly linked with tourism in order to generate business activity and income for the host communities. Yeoman et al. (2004) state that festivals can lengthen tourist seasons by extending the peak season or introduce a 'new season' into a community. Events such as festivals do not only serve to attract tourists but also help to develop or maintain a community or regional identity.

Festivals can be divided into single-themed and multi-themed events, as have been identified by Key Leisure Markets (2001). Single-themed festivals can, for example, include music or literature, whereas multi-themed festivals can encompass both themes and several others.

Today, festivals are considered to contribute significantly to and have major impacts on the cultural and economic developmental wealth of host cities. It is estimated that in 2009 alone, music festivals in the UK contributed £450 million to the British economy (King, 2009). Festivals in other geographical locations most likely reflect similar impacts as those associated with UK festivals.

In order to attract visitors and create a cultural image for host cities, festival organisers are now using historical and cultural themes to develop annual events by holding festivals in community settings. The purpose of festivals is not specifically to address the needs for any one particular group. They are often developed because of the tourism and economic opportunities additional to social and cultural benefits.

Festivals have the potential to generate a vast amount of tourism in particular when they cater to visitors from other generating zones. In addition, there is the potential for grants or sponsorships, as identified by Getz (1997), either by direct or indirect intent. Governments now support and promote festivals as part of their strategies for economic development, nation building and cultural tourism. Festivals in turn are seen as an important tool for attracting visitors and building the image within different communities. This stimulus is also linked to fiscal government tax revenue. The Bonnaroo Music and Arts Festival, in case study 19.1, contributed US$412 796 to the local government. The economic impact of tourism, according to Stiernstrand (1996), arises principally from the consumption of tourism products in a geographical area. Tourism-related services, which include travel, accommodation, restaurants and shopping, are the major beneficiaries of the festival, according to McDonnell, Allen and O'Toole (1999).

As far as festivals and tourism are concerned, the roles and responsibilities of governments as well as the private sector and society in general have significantly changed over the last decade. The situations have changed from the state having the key responsibility for tourism development and promotion to a world where the public sector is obliged to reinvent itself by relinquishing its traditional responsibilities and activities in favour of provincial, state and local authorities.

This indicates the growing importance of governments and businesses investing in the general development of the festivals and tourism industries. It further suggests that festivals impact on the host population and stakeholders in a number of impact factors. These factors are primarily concerned with a plethora of impacts – social, cultural, physical, environmental, political and economic – all of which can be both positive and negative.

The people and communities that host festivals provide visitors with a vibrant and valuable culture. Festivals provide an opportunity for the local people to develop and share their culture, which creates a sense of values and beliefs held by the individuals in a local community. Moreover, festivals provide tourists with the opportunity to see how the local communities celebrate their culture, and facilitate the visitors to interact with the host community by enabling people to enjoy and meet their leisure needs.

The festivals also provide support to those who pursue economic opportunities related to sharing community culture with the broader world. UNEP (2002) suggests that cultural tourism is boosted through the development of festivals and events. Tourism can add to the vitality of communities in many ways. An example is the rejuvenation and development of events and festivals, where local residents were previously the primary participants and spectators in order to satisfy tourist interests.

19.2 The role of festivals within society

Previously, festivals were mainly associated with key calendar moments linked specifically to particular seasons and heritage sites. Over the last decade this has changed and festivals have been altered and developed upon so there is now a broad and diverse range of festival events taking place all over the world.

Getz (1997: 1) introduces festivals events as follows: '[e]vents constitute one of the most exciting and fastest growing forms of leisure, business, and tourism-related phenomena'. Goldblatt (2002: 1) introduces festival events as a '[k]aleidoscope of planned culture, sport, political, and business occasions: from mega-events like Olympics and world fairs to community festivals; from programs of events at parks and attractions to visits by dignitaries and intergovernmental assembles; from small meetings and parties to huge conventions and competitions'.

The revolution in festivals has been stimulated through commercial aspects to meet the changing demand of local community groups and increasing business opportunities for the event organisers and local businesses. Festivals play a major part in a city and local community. Such events are attractive to host communities because they help to develop local pride and identity for the residents. In addition, festivals have an important role in the national and regional host community in context of destination planning by enhancing and linking tourism and commerce. Some aspects of this include events as image makers, economic impact generators, tourist attractions, overcoming seasonality, contributing to the development of local communities and businesses, and supporting key industrial sectors.

The case studies within this chapter will explore the development of cultural tourism and multicultural festivals and events within the UK and internationally along with the positive contribution that these events make to solidifying community relations with development of the cultural tourism.

This chapter initially reviews literature related to culture and the role of festivals in the creation of opportunities for community-orientated events and festivals, which contrast with tourist-orientated events that mostly have tenuous links with local communities. Moreover, the chapter will argue that community-based events and festivals provide an opportunity for the celebration of local identity and community empowerment and create tourism for the local area.

Case study 19.3 Edinburgh Festival, UK

The Edinburgh Festival has become major calendar event for the city of Edinburgh by developing cultural tourism and creating cultural image for all groups within the community. The city has also long been world renowned for its rich history, culture and heritage, and for hosting leading international events, giving it an excellent tourism infrastructure.

The Edinburgh Festival has developed since the late-1940s and has become a major hotspot for the artistic and tourists to enjoy multicultural events during the month of August each year. The festival has developed the following programmes over the years to attract visitors from all over the world and to demonstrate a multicultural image. Each summer it is host to the world's largest arts festival, the Edinburgh International Festival, and the Fringe Festival, which are merely the biggest and best-known events from an annual list which includes the Edinburgh Military Tattoo, Hogmanay celebrations, an international science festival, an international book festival, a jazz festival and a film festival.

The Edinburgh Festival provides a phenomenal six weeks of arts and culture in the city. Festival Director Brian McMaster said: 'We are delighted at the response to this year's programmes. Reviews have been excellent, but, more importantly, our audiences are clearly having a very good time, and are trying out a wide range of familiar and less familiar festivals' (http://www.edinburgh-festivals.com).

The Edinburgh International Festival has developed significantly over the years, yet the founders' original intentions are closely reflected in the current aims and objectives. This highlights the point that even though Edinburgh is a successful festival destination at present, to remain competitive in the global marketplace it must continually invest in itself to retain and improve on its position. It has been estimated that tourism is worth over £1.1 billion per year to Edinburgh and supports over 27 000 jobs (Edinburgh Convention Bureau (ECB)). Business tourism and conferencing alone account for around £120 million annually, with their value increasing year on year.

The Edinburgh Festival attracts tourists from all over the world and over the last decade cultural tourism has increased in large numbers. According to official Edinburgh International Festival Audience Research (2002), '43% of the Festival's audience comes from Edinburgh and the Lothians, 18% from the rest of Scotland, 21% from the rest of the United Kingdom and 17% from overseas. Visitors stay an average of eight nights in Edinburgh'.

The success of Edinburgh as a festival destination can be attributed to a combination of factors. The visitors come to Edinburgh either specifically for the International Festival or its unique heritage and cultural history,

Moreover, this increasing value of business tourism to the city can be attributed to Edinburgh becoming the UK's leading conferencing destination, according to the International Convention and Congress Association (ICCA). In 1995, Edinburgh was outside the ICCA's destination league table's top 20, yet jumped to 13th position in 1998 and in 2001 was placed 12th. This steady rise followed the opening of the EICC on 17 September 1995.

A report carried out by the Business Tourism Forum and Business Tourism Advisory Committee also highlights Edinburgh as a strong business tourism destination but detected certain infrastructure weaknesses including:

- insufficient number of direct flights and the lack of a direct transport link into the city centre;
- inadequate exhibition space attached to the Edinburgh International Conference Centre; and
- the need for an additional 400–500-bedroom hotel to act as a headquarters hotel.

19.3 Planning and managing a festival

The following section examines various aspects of professional festival management. The topics covered have been arranged according to the event knowledge domains of staging any type of event professionally. These guidelines are applicable to national and international festivals, on a small or large scale.

19.3.1 Administration

The procurement for human resources and volunteers for festivals follows a number of different avenues. Staffing for the above-line management is acquired by building up a long-term working relationship with competent professional practitioners. The above-line management team can include licensees, event managers, and health and safety operatives, including highway agency. Within that team there is a need to have appointed representatives from all emergency services as well as security. Stakeholder representatives may also be needed in the ongoing decision-making process. If the event is on civic land, city council operatives from various departments all have a role in creating a harmonious festival for the local community, as well as meeting council bylaws and regulations/legislation. They all have a legal remit to supply their own staff members who are competent, qualified and legal in terms of their employment status. Festival organisers have a duty to set up supply chains where procurement of goods and assets flow directly into the festival site during the build and event delivery. The systems put in place must be robust to ensure that contracts with suppliers or contractors work within a legal framework. Upon delivery of goods, invoices are cross-referenced and an inventory list is made of all goods and services, including perishable and non-perishable.

19.3.2 Festivals project management and how it works

Project management in essence is a management function and must be seen and executed in that manner. A festival organiser cannot, nor is able to, handle all elements within the event delivery. To be an effective project manager for a large-scale commercial music festival, delegation is paramount. Delegation, however, does not mean abdication of responsibility. To impart responsibility to a third party, generally known as a contractor, or an individual requires a sound understanding of the type of work/task that is required. With that, one must have a system that can ascertain work/task performance along with a reporting system safeguarded from possible violations. Effective systems do not necessarily mean efficiency in the delivery process. One of the most contentious aspects for customers when attending a festival is the amount of queuing required to access services and amenities. A project manager must consider how customers may use a particular service and at what point that service will become untenable. Therefore continuous monitoring of peak usage is vital to maintain service delivery at a satisfactory level. The project manager will have staff to carry out observation checks on, for example, toilets, shower units and drinking water supply. These basic amenities are essential to the overall experience of customers attending the festival. Part of the project manager's responsibility is to have basic amenities on standby or located on site in the event that demand is significantly higher than expected or a malfunction has occurred leaving replacement/repair as the only alternative.

An indispensable requirement for the festival project manager is a project plan. This becomes a template or backbone against which the management and the delivery of the event can be checked. It outlines in full all the elements that make up the event as well as any person(s) who are responsible for any particular aspect. It also highlights possible issues which, when investigated, may require changes to the plan. It will chart the critical path attributed to the event with 'hotspots' to ensure the correct allocation of resources where necessary. However, the rigidity of the plan may leave the project manager without room to manoeuvre when required. Consequently, flexibility and slippage within the plan aligned to task and activities are essential. When managing a music festival one should be continually aware of the licensing requirement, as this for some managers is an immovable deadline. To contravene the licensing requirement could mean a fine from the licensing authority and subsequently hinder any music licence application.

By definition of the title, the project manager must take a strategic view of the event. Apart from the internal issues, a greater understanding of external situations that could have a negative impact on the event is a prerequisite for an efficient manager. The project manager for a large-scale festival must be supported by competent and qualified individuals. Those persons add to the competence level required to deliver the event. To subjugate the authority of these individuals could leave the project manager open to question from others, and possible investigation. Where key decisions are concerned, the project manager should seek advice from qualified or competent individuals.

Throughout the management of the festival there may be a requirement to have a multi-agency meeting. A meeting of this description involves senior representatives from all emergency services on site, local authority representatives, security, health and safety, and the above-line management team. The rationale behind such a meeting is to bring everyone up to speed on key changes to the project plan and how they may affect operational activities and resources. Therefore, a project manager must have direct communication to all agencies and representatives as and when required.

Where elements of the plan differ from the original documentation, subject to changes by the project manager, there must be a process to amend plus disseminate information accurately to all concerned.

As stated earlier, a project manager is unable to take full responsibility for all aspects associated with a major commercial festival. Therefore, adequate communication across the site to key representatives is paramount and responsible individuals appointed with due diligence as to their level of competence is essential. A robust and flexible plan which documents the entire scope of the festival must be disseminated to all representatives who have a duty to ensure safety, service quality and operational success. This document is commonly referred to as the event manual.

19.3.3 Linking festival project management to time and money

To plan and deliver a successful festival, two significant constraints can have a negative impact on delivery: return on investment and the allocation of resources. The time allotted to carry out a task within the project plan is sometimes based on previous experience and information obtained from the person intended to undertake a task-driven activity. Where that information is not given or potentially inaccurate, the management experience, judgement and advice from others are all necessary

alternatives in building the plan. Therefore, the need for slippage between each task can now be seen as necessary planning criteria for project managers. All festivals have a definite budget requirement; thus financial allocation for contractors should be given consideration, and part payment made to secure commitment. This type of forward planning is a necessary requirement, particularly if the event falls within the summer season when contractors have a high demand for their services and subsequent price increase. Late planning and allocation of resources to the plan can create high cost and/or insufficient time to carry out a particular activity. It is prudent on the part of the project manager to secure enough money for essential services months in advance.

19.3.4 Managing the festival stakeholders

Commercial music festivals cannot operate in isolation and will have a multitude of stakeholders. Some have a greater influence on the project delivery process than others, with sponsors being considered to be the one of the most important. The status given to the sponsors is directly linked to the financial assistance they give to the festival. Without that financial assistance large-scale commercial festivals would find it financially difficult to remain in the market.

Another key stakeholder group is customers; however, due to their number and size at festivals it can be difficult to determine their specific intentions throughout the festival. Unforeseen circumstances or unplanned changes to the project delivery can significantly disrupt and distort the general customer mood.

As stated earlier, a project plan must look at alternative scenarios. For example, if crowd disorder has a history of emerging at a particular music festival, the project plan should factor in a method to identify, secure and isolate any further disturbance. Managing the biggest stakeholder group in terms of size and numbers calls for a plan that leaves no margin for ambiguity like where customers require certain resources to meet their basic needs. The allocation of clean toilets, food and clean drinking water are just some of the necessities not to be overlooked or mismanaged.

All project plans should install a mechanism that allows the project manager to reflect on decisions and the overall process. This can be done via regular meetings with key decision makers and on-the-spot data gathering from all stakeholder groups which can give a snapshot account of the festival. To undertake an approach of evaluation and review during and after the festival demonstrates foresight and engenders an attitude among all major stakeholders that operational delivery is constantly achieving higher levels of quality, thus success. How this information is disseminated to individual stakeholders is absolutely crucial as this can determine future working relationships. To obtain sufficient and sustained performance from major stakeholders and contractors, any negative information should be given with an incentive for improvements or with a method to allow for continual development to meet customer satisfaction.

19.3.5 Festival programming and scheduling evaluations

In 2007, it was estimated, the UK had approximately 500 festivals within one calendar year, with an accumulative attendance figure of five million customers. The majority of these festivals were music related, with a large percentage held within the summer months. Therefore, the programming of festivals, and in particular music-related festivals, compete within a small window of opportunity. It is generally agreed within the live music industry that the festival season commences with the Glastonbury Festival, for which June is the stated and agreed month. The month of September is regarded as the close of the season period for festivals in Europe.

The nature of festival programming

The programming of festivals is planned around a number of variables. Typically a festival organiser will assess the competitive landscape to determine if weekends within the summer months are overbooked with similar festivals. This will not only have an impact on tickets purchased but the time it takes for all tickets to be sold. Revenue from ticket sales contributes significantly to the purchasing power for a festival organiser, thus allowing for early acquisition of contractors and suppliers. Geographical locations and the proximity of other festivals will also have a significant impact on customer attendance.

Festivals within the UK have a geographical spread from the Orkney Islands, Southampton to the Channel Isles, Jersey. On continents which have a bigger geographical land mass, such as the US or Canada, visitors have a tendency to travel as tourists as well as festival attendees. Festival International de Jazz de Montréal is one of Canada's premiere music festivals with a reported audience figure in 2007 of 1.2 million. Coming into its 30th anniversary, the Montreal Jazz Festival is represented by 30 countries performing around 500 concerts thereby attracting a large number of visitors who travel to Montreal every year to attend. In 2009 the government of Canada invested $3 million in support of the festival. This type of investment is not limited to this one festival, as the government has allocated $100 million to what they consider as marquee tourism events, which all fall under Canada's Economic Action Plan. This money will be distributed over a two-year period and through that support it intends to enhance and attract a large number of international visitors and allow the festivals to gain international presence.

One can conclude that festivals are a major contributor to tourism and the economic prosperity for local communities and the wider business sector. The method of local or national government fiscal support has become the cornerstone for many cities that desire to become international tourism and business destinations, and for others to maintain their status as such.

Case study 19.4 Manchester International Festival

This festival is an event of original, new work and special events, and takes place biennially in Manchester, UK. The festival launched in 2007 as an artist-led, commissioning festival presenting new works from across the spectrum of performing arts, music, visual arts and popular culture.

Barcelona, Vienna and Milan also all have their own long-standing and iconic festivals of international stature.

Design

When contractors and suppliers arrive on the festival site the event planning process will already have and determined the full layout of all facilities. This will include not only the build up but also the festival delivery and tear down.

Major music festivals such as T in the Park, Carling Leeds and V Festival, etc. have similar functions and characteristics. For all of them the essential operations must be installed on site to assist in the build process – i.e. the communication network, which could be landline, wireless or both – fresh water supply and sanitary equipment, and the removal of waste. The theme and content of the festival as well as the artists booked are all developed based on the target audience. Within the festival site a number of corporate and individual suppliers are brought in to differentiate the festival from the many that coexist throughout the summer months. An experiential marketing company which has worked with the Strongbow Cider brand for 11 years looks at positioning the brand at festivals. The Strongbow Cider brand has been a feature at V Festival for many years. It has a dedicated temporary structure within the arena site, within which it can serve its branded cider, supported by live music and DJs. The Bacardi B-Live has a 12-year relationship with V Festival, and operates under a similar design and operational arrangement. Merchandising has become a major marketing feature at festivals. The licence for official merchandise is owned by the festival organising team, and branded goods can be purchased online or acquired at the festival site.

Other elements of the festival are also open to licensing, e.g. the sale of alcohol and catering. There are two ways in which catering can be supplied at festivals: the organising team can award caterers the right to operate for a fee, or the licence can be leased for a period of time at a set fee to a catering company, who in turn will hire out the catering plots to independent caterers. However, it should be noted that in legal

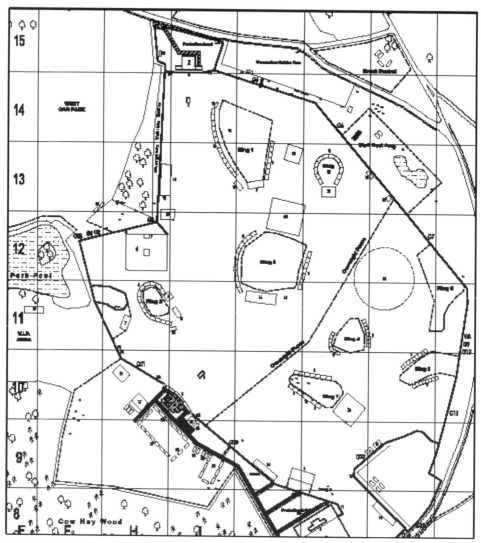

Figure 19.1 The site map of V Festival 2002, Western Park
Source: Unknown.

terms the licensing of merchandising is dissimilar to this type of catering licence, but the principle of extending the rights to a third party remains the same.

Securing the site will be one of the first priorities, and this will coincide with the arrival of heavy equipment and personnel. A clear boundary with a fence line can also help to secure the site and ensure safety to workers and other inhabitants on the land. If the site is within an urban area and owned by the local authority, access by the general public to certain areas continues throughout the build stage. This type of arrangement must be carefully monitored and controlled to ensure that risks are minimised. The build process for a weekend commercial music festival ranges between 2–3 weeks with each contractor or supplier carefully staggered within that time frame to arrive on site with sufficient time to carry out their work.

Scheduling of festivals

Outdoor festivals, such as V Festival, are programmed to fall within the month of August each year in the UK. This festival falls on the weekend directly after the announcement and collection of pre-university examination results for English students. In August 2007 alone, 23 festivals were programmed to take place (*The Times*, 2007). Not all festivals in that month carry the same characteristics as V Festival as many organisations now use the term 'festival' as a generic term that signifies some form of celebration. Of the 23 festivals listed, only 11 have a similar festival design and audience profile.

19.3.6 Marketing

Commercial music festivals have a strong marketing ability, often linked directly to the headline artist. However, some music festivals can have more than one stage or tented structure, and consequently each

---

Case study 19.5 Leeds West Indian Carnival

The Caribbean Carnival is an annual festival celebrated in the city of Leeds since the early 1960s, hereby constituting one of the oldest Caribbean carnivals in Europe. In its earlier days, the Leeds West Indian Carnival used to go into the city centre, a tradition which changed during the 1980s. The carnival has outgrown its original setting since the early 1980s and now it takes place around the local communities of Chapletown and Harehills. The festival has created a multicultural spirit for people of all races and nationalities attending the event during the August bank holiday each year since 1967. Carnival founder Arthur France said: 'This continues to be one of this city's most important and enjoyable family attractions. Our events in the run up to Carnival Day provide something for everyone as well as giving the whole city the chance to come together in one big party' (*Yorkshire Evening Post*, 2002).

Behind the colour – as stated by William Stewart, the founder of the initial Caribbean carnival in this country – the music of the carnival has a deeper meaning which is rooted in the experiences of Caribbean people arriving in England around a time of great change in the late 1950s and early 1960s. So it was a search for identity, for community and belonging that led to the carnival being developed in the early 1960s in the area of Notting Hill in London.

This great festival began initially from the energies of black immigrants from the Caribbean, in particular Trinidad, where the Carnival tradition is very strong, and from people living locally, who dreamed of creating a festival to bring together the people of Notting Hill, most of whom were facing racism, lack of working opportunities and poor housing conditions resulting in a general suppression of good self-esteem.
Notting Hill Carnival (2009)

The carnival has created a platform for the Caribbean people to come together and share their social and cultural differences with the local community from numerous backgrounds. It is about people coming together and having fun.

The attendance at the festival varies throughout the event from 10 000 to 100 000, but at the actual carnival site it is 80 000. However, as the procession leaves the Potternewton Park, the number of carnival watchers grows. Over the last ten years the tourists to the area have increased greatly, mainly because of the festival itself. However, the other element is the image of the carnival expressing an invisible side of local and international culture, developed by the festival over the years.

The carnival has created a very special image for the city of Leeds, because it has brought local communities together and enhanced the local image which has attracted tourism from all over the country.

In the last decade, the Leeds West Indian Carnival has developed as a natural outgrowth and has benefited the local economy. However, the economic development of this festival has impacted on the local small and large businesses during the period leading up to the festival. The festival has become centrepiece event for the local economy each year with local hotels, restaurants, taxis, public transport and small stall traders planning their business activities around it. Moreover, over the last decade cultural tourism to the local area has increased, and visitors are attracted to the festival from as far off as Asia and the Caribbean islands. The festival has increased tourism, which in turn has developed greater economic and cultural benefits for the local areas.

stage could also have its own headline artist. The music festivals T in the Park, Carling Leeds and V Festival all have more than two stages and tented structures. The scheduling of artist/DJs to the various stages or tented structures is based on a number of variables. These include where each artist is positioned within the music charts at the time of booking and the number of record sales nationally or internationally. It could also be linked to an artist's performance on other festivals as well as PR and TV appearances. If the artist is considered to have a high profile and significant fan base, this could ensure top billing as headline artist. However, the status of an artist in terms of the buying public may change before appearing on a festival stage and as a result their fan base may increase or decrease. A headline artist/DJ for any festival is always given the last performance slot on the last night of the main stage. Apart from the marketing issues, this type of scheduling ensures operationally that the largest number of people at the festival is at one particular location at the close of the performance.

Many of the established commercial music festivals throughout the world have no direct marketing strategy other than their official website or online ticket agencies supporting their ticket sales. The need to undertake any form of supplementary advertising/promotion has rendered itself obsolete due to the commercial dominance they have within their established market. For many of the established music festivals, tickets are sold

Case study 19.6 Bonnaroo Music and Arts Festival, US

The 2009 Bonnaroo Music and Arts Festival in the US has 30 partners/sponsors. The main attractions of the festival are the multiple stages of live music, featuring a diverse array of musical styles including indie rock, world music, hip hop, jazz, A, bluegrass, country music, folk, gospel, reggae, electronic and other alternative music. Furthermore, the festival features craftsmen and artisans selling unique products, food and drink vendors, and many other activities including some put on by various sponsors, who are required to provide free activities for attendees. However, the majority of those partners have a specific business relationship with the US and are mainly targeting activities at a national audience.

within hours of going online. V Festival in Chelmsford 2009, with an approximate audience capacity of 70–80 000, sold out within two hours.

Within the marketing strategy, sponsorship plays a major role in the development and continual delivery of the festival year after year.

Within the commercial environment sponsorship deals by and large operate between three to five years. However, this is no longer the standard for many commercial and international festivals as commercial sponsors have established long-term relationships with the festivals beyond ten years. A similar type of sponsorship relationship is widely represented within the sport sponsorship arena.

With such long-term business partnerships comes significant input to the project delivery by way of product interface and further marketing opportunities. This ultimately gives the sponsor, known as the primary stakeholder, a greater degree of influence. It must be noted that the level of influence in most cases does not drive the main operational activities. However, ideal and strategic locations throughout the site will be identified year on year. Primary stakeholders are in essence looking for exclusivity at a festival, particularly if it has broadcast rights attached. With that added extra value, sponsors/stakeholders will insist upon developing greater product awareness where possible.

It should also be noted that the recent introduction of television broadcasters capturing live music festivals also makes them stakeholders. Their contribution to the festival experience beyond the site allows for increased ticket sales, sponsorship allocation and a project plan that runs to schedule. Where live broadcasting is taking place, a project plan must maintain a level

Case study 19.7 Sponsors and events, UK

Festival sponsorship has flourished with brands increasingly eager to benefit from the popular summer season events in the UK. Carling Lager (which took over the famed Reading Festival), Virgin Mobile (which sponsors the V Festival), and Tennent's Lager (which launched T in the Park in 1994) are sponsors of major live music festivals in the UK. All three of these organisations have at least a ten-year history with each festival.

Case study 19.8 Festivals and sponsorships

Mintel (2002) indicated the total value of British sponsorships is $1.3 billion with approximately 55% of the British total devoted to sport sponsorship programmes. This clearly demonstrates the dominance of sports within the marketplace, a trend that remains constant. While sport accounts for the largest amount spent within the sponsorship market, festivals represent the highest number of actual sponsorship deals.

In 2003 the NME, a British national music magazine, signed a three-year deal with Mean Fiddler for the Reading & Leeds Festival, with DF Concerts for T in the Park and with Metropolis Music, SJM Concerts and MCD Productions for V Festival. The deal gave NME exclusivity for signing artists to perform in tents at all three festivals and interviews with bands with an estimated target reach of 500 000 people a year.

of accuracy in delivery. These stakeholders by their representation can have a positive effect on the festival and its long-term sustainability within the market.

19.3.7 Operations

The movement of customers on a festival site is subject to in the main artist scheduling. Furthermore, the facilities are also located in proximity to where large numbers of customers will be located at any given time throughout the festival.

The scheduling of artists can also be seen as a political and PR issue for many festival organisers. Agents, managers and record companies who act on behalf of an artist all consider their performer to be worthy of top billing. A prerequisite for successful political manoeuvring for position within the scheduling is a good partnership relationship with the said practitioners.

While the build process is under way, the festival is subject to many internal and external checks and procedures to ensure it meets with specific legislation and regulations. Internal health and safety checks are carried out on a regular basis to monitor safe working procedures under European regulations. Site rules are also given out to contractors as a means to create a safe working environment and ensure quality build-up. External agencies such as the environmental department, building regulations, fire and safety, and the structural engineer, all have a role to play at various stages within the build-up process. Some contractors must maintain adherence to specific procedures and regulations while constructing and before handover to a festival manager. A qualified electrical engineer has a significant role to play during the build-up process but also remains on call/on site during the festival delivery. Parking, storage and delivery points, as one would expect in any facility, are factors for an outdoor festival.

Crowd management is a logistical and operational requirement for any festival. The location of amenities throughout the site should be linked with the stage location, emergency exit points and amenities for customers. The scheduling of artists on a particular music stage or in a tented structure will have a significant impact

---

Case study 19.9 V Festival

The V Festival, which has been running since 1996 and takes place every third weekend in August during the UK's summer, began spreading out in 2006 – first in Canada and then the US. In March 2007, Virgin Festival was launched in Australia and in December 2008 in South Africa (O'Reilly, 2008).

The V Festival in the UK has a live music stage dedicated to Channel 4 music, a digital channel available on Sky, Freeview and Virgin digital channel. The 'V' represents the Virgin Group, and began as another means of promoting Richard Branson's companies. The event is sponsored by Virgin Media (Virgin Mobile until 2009), with Absolute Radio (formerly Virgin Radio) the official radio station.

The most obvious opportunity for stakeholders to secure more product exposure is by creating a visual backdrop featured when artists are giving exclusive live interviews on site. Apart from Channel 4, BBC 2 and 3 both have a history of broadcasting live from the Carling Reading and Leeds festival, including the T in the Park festival.

on crowd flow throughout the festival. Basic amenities such as water, toilets and food concessions must be positioned so that replenishing stock and necessary maintenance can be undertaken without disrupting the site or customers. The connection between the main music arena and the campsite operates independently in terms of music licensing issues. However, the customers' movements between the two locations at the close of the arena performance will require an adjustment of personnel, equipment and resources to cope with demand. Basic amenities will also have a high usage and should be ready for the large influx of customers as the festival moves over to evening/early morning increased usage. Apart from the crowd aspect, many festivals now have a legal requirement to have emergency services located on site. This becomes a logistical issue, in particular when called upon to respond to emergencies at any given moment, and the festival organising team must ensure that emergency vehicles have priority routes throughout the site at all times. In light of the areas mentioned under section 19.3.7 (Operations), one must also take special care that health and safety considerations remain paramount in any operational task.

19.3.8 Risk

Risk assessment and risk management are two totally different taxonomies; however, they must work together to be effective in any given situation. Risks associated with festivals are plentiful and varied throughout the event, and should be developed from a number of specific parameters. A risk assessment must be developed to enable analysis of customers as they interact with the festival, and contractors and suppliers as they work through the build-up process and carry out their duties during the festival. Employed staff, voluntary workers and agency staff should also be considered in the risk assessment. Under UK law, the festival organiser is also required to request a copy of all risk assessments from contractors and suppliers before commencing work on site. This type of management procedure will help to ensure that a safe working environment has been established and can be monitored by a competent appointed individual on behalf of the festival organising team. The health and safety executive has published a five-step template for developing a risk assessment. One of the key factors in this process is the reporting of incidents and the appointment of individuals to take responsibility for key areas. One must also remember that risk assessment has a direct relationship to insurance, be it public, employers or equipment liability.

The level to which outdoor festivals rely on financial assistance from a number of sponsors and stakeholders is absolutely crucial to the sustainability of the festival within the market. For many festivals, absorbing financial risk is sometimes unavoidable, which leaves the festival open to potential cancellation if ticket sales are slow or insufficient in numbers. To mitigate this fiscal risk, organisations will work together to ensure that all business partners have a shared responsibility in delivering the festival.

A risk plan should not only focus on internal issues but also external problems which relate to unforeseen circumstances. This contingency plan may never be required; however, if needed it must be on hand and able to present a possible solution. A project manager may develop a contingency plan for separate areas throughout the festival. If the allocated field for customers who intend to camp becomes overcrowded, a secondary field is allocated on the site plan to take the overspill. Contingencies for changes in the weather should always be a factor within the project plan when organising festivals outdoors. To disregard potential adverse weather conditions could be viewed as incompetence or negligence. A traffic accident or severe weather conditions can have a major negative impact on crowd movement and the planned start time for elements within the festival.

19.4 Summary

This chapter shows us that the festivals have contributed in the development of local communities. They have a major effect on the local economy, both directly and indirectly, with spending by visitors on local goods and services having a direct economic impact on local businesses. These benefits are passed more widely across the economy and the community.

The study further found that authors such as Yeoman et al. (2004), Getz (1997) and Goldblatt (2002a) argue that the festival organiser and local government generally only take into account the economic impacts and ignore the social implications of festivals, and that greater attention should be paid to the latter.

The programming of events and festivals is planned around a number of variables. Typically, a festival organiser will assess the competitive landscape to determine if weekends within the summer months are overbooked with similar festivals.

The visitors are attracted to these festivals from as far away as Europe and the Caribbean islands. It was found that social and economic factors contributed to growth in festivals. The Edinburgh Festival and Leeds West Indian Carnival have become major tourist attractions for local, regional and international visitors.

Questions for research

1 Discuss and evaluate why festival managers and local authorities target local communities to host festivals.
2 Critically analyse and discuss the role stakeholders play in the operation of commercial music festivals.
3 Evaluate the importance of organising and scheduling outdoor festivals.

Recommended web sites

Browse the following internet sites for interesting and informative information:

Asian Academy for Heritage Management: http://www.unescobkk.org/culture/asian-academy/
Association for Events Management Education (AEME): http://www.aeme.org
Bonnaroo Music and Arts Festival: http://www.bonnaroo.com/
Centre International de Recherches et d'Etudes Touristiques: http://www.ciret-tourism.com

International Council of Tourism Partners USA: http://www.tourismpartners.org/members/IntlMembers.htm

International Festivals Events Association (IFEA): www.ifeaeurope.com

International Sociological Association (ISA): http://www.ucm.es/info/isa

Leeds West Indian Carnival: http://www.leedscarnival.co.uk/

Manchester International Festival: http://www.mif.co.uk/

The Cultural Tourism Research Group: http://www.geocities.com/atlasproject2004

T in the Park: http://www.tinthepark.com/

V Festival: http://www.vfestival.com/

20

Sport events

Kamilla Swart

Abstract

The aim of this chapter is to illustrate how the key knowledge domains, namely administration, design, marketing, operations, risk and evaluation, can be applied to sport events. Best practice issues in relation to this genre of events are considered, and case studies are used to illustrate key considerations and to further demonstrate some of the typical management challenges in relation to this genre of events.

Chapter objectives

After you have read this chapter you should be able to:
❑ understand the prominence of sport events in society;
❑ understand how the knowledge domains can be applied to sport events;
❑ understand what appropriate planning is required for sport events;
❑ understand the key lessons from a number of case studies of a selection of sport events; and
❑ understand the importance of evaluating the impacts of sport events.

20.1 Introduction and background

Sport has become increasingly popular in recent years and been elevated to a level of prominence within and beyond cultural contexts (Turco, Riley & Swart, 2002). As alluded to in the mega-event chapter (chapter 18), sport participation and attendance have become global phenomena, and international sport events have fuelled an ever-increasing tourism market (Turco et al., 2002). They further underscore that sport has increased access to consumer markets via mass information systems and is thus more inclusive to segments previously excluded from participation such as women and girls, and people with disabilities. It is therefore imperative that sport event managers understand how the knowledge domains can be applied to a range of sport events, from the community level to international sport events as well as to various sports (from abseiling to yachting). Pike Masteralexis, Barr and Hums (1998: 328) further note that 'although sport events range in size and scope from local basketball league matches to the Olympic Games, they all share a common element – the necessity for educated and trained sport event managers to ensure success'. Sport event best practice is elaborated upon in the next section.

20.2 Sport event management best practice issues

It is beyond the scope of this chapter to discuss in depth all the knowledge domains in relation to sport events. The approach to this chapter will be to highlight specific aspects that are of significance to sport event planning and management, and are presented further below.

20.2.1 Administration

Whether considering hosting a major national or international sport event, it will be necessary to convince the rights owner that one has the capacity to host the event successfully. This process generally requires a bid submission. It is regarded as the initial commitment one makes on behalf of the city or municipality to the rights holder of the sport event. 'Different sports have different bidding processes and objectives when allocating an event' (Turco et al., 2002: 81). For example, many international sport federations are looking to host events in developing countries to grow the participation of their sport in different parts of the world. Sport events can also be allocated on a rotational basis so depending on the geographical location a bid may (or may not be) recommended. The bid submission generally consists of a proposal in terms of responding to the specific requirements of the rights owner. Written agreements (guarantees) and verbal presentations may also be requested to verify the bid submission (Turco et al., 2002).

For major international sport events, the government can further stipulate processes required before it will endorse a bid, especially when a significant amount of public investment is required. The following box presents the requirements of a government department to a sport event manager who is seeking endorsement for a Formula 1 Grand Prix bid proposal.

Cape Town Grand Prix Bid Proposal

In order to have informed and meaningful discussions on the merit of Cape Town hosting a Formula 1 Grand Prix, the following documents are required:
- ❏ Environmental impact assessment;
- ❏ Economic impact assessment;
- ❏ Tourism impact report;
- ❏ Comprehensive financial report;
- ❏ Social and economic investment report;
- ❏ Cost analysis for infrastructural upgrades and proposed infrastructural changes;
- ❏ Federation Internationale Automobile's (FIA) safety requirements;
- ❏ Analysis report on the revitalisation of the Killarney track; and
- ❏ Sport development report.

Source: Swart (2009)

For events that do not require a bidding process, an informal and a formal appraisal (i.e. feasibility study) of hosting the sport event are still required. The sport event manager must still be 100% sure that he or she will be able to organise the specific event in mind before embarking upon it.

It has often happened that attempts to organise a sports event have failed because the organiser chose the wrong event to promote, had too many other things to do, or was unable to organise the event due to lack of knowledge, skills, etc.

Before the sport event manager attempts to organise a specific tournament or special event, the following key factors should be considered:
- ❏ Is this event a good idea?
- ❏ Are the right skills available?
- ❏ Will the community accept this event – who are the role players?
- ❏ Who will participate/be a spectator?
- ❏ What class of athlete will take part?
- ❏ Do we have the right infrastructure (e.g. facilities, equipment, emergency services)?
- ❏ Where will it be held?
- ❏ Will we be able to attract players and spectators?
- ❏ Will we attract media support?
- ❏ Who will support us (sponsors, etc.)?
- ❏ If there are costs involved, will we be able to cover them?

If unsure how successful the proposed sport event will be, try the following:
- ❏ Consult another area where such an event has taken place;
- ❏ Find out how successful it was;
- ❏ Ask about the problems;
- ❏ Check the costs and profits, if any; and
- ❏ Ask if you would have the same problems in your region

Once a feasibility study has been conducted, it is necessary to develop a comprehensive business plan for your event. Getz (1997: 92–93) identified the following as key aspects to include in the business plan:
- ❏ Background on the organisation and the sport event;

- Explanation of the sport event's purpose, programme and its benefits; if relevant, highlight its uniqueness and tourist appeal;
- Outline the marketing and communications goals, objectives and strategies;
- Specify the financial management policies and procedures to be implemented;
- Include a summary and request financial assistance, if required; and
- Attach relevant appendices, e.g. highlighting successes and uniqueness by supplying photos and other tangible evidence of the event and the organisation, an organisational chart and résumés of key staff, etc.

Event evaluation is another critical component of event administration as it allows the sport event manager to make informed decisions about the success of the event or identify areas for improvement for future editions. The sport event manager can also use the evaluation to justify resources and could further assist with raising future sponsorship and general support.

Turco et al. (2002) assert that there are four themes of research that should be considered timely to sport event managers, namely:
- customer satisfaction research;
- sponsorship evaluations;
- economic impact assessments; and
- host perceptions of events.

Table 20.1 is an example of sport event research conducted at the 2006 Old Mutual Two Oceans Marathon in Cape Town, which illustrates motivations for participation by both participants and spectators.

Table 20.1 Identification of the top three reasons for participating in the 2006 Old Mutual Two Oceans Marathon (in %)

Reason	Total ($n = 200$)
No response	10.5
To improve my physical fitness	67
I enjoy the challenge	65.5
To compete	62.5
To have fun	29.5
To see the location where the event is being held	1.5

Mallen and Adams (2008) identified a series of questions to assist in conducting the evaluation:
- Who are the key stakeholders of the evaluation?
- What are the questions or issues driving the evaluation?
- What is the purpose of the evaluation?
- What resources are available to evaluate the event?
- Which research design strategies are best suitable?

It is further noted that the purpose of the study, nature of the sport event, time, and human and financial resources of the event organisation dictate the most practical data collection methods (Turco et al., 2002). At a minimum a post-match evaluation should consider the following:
- Consult your planning check list to ascertain which tasks were performed incorrectly or not at all, and try to rectify for future reference;
- Try to establish from players and spectators which aspects can be improved upon so that you can do better when organising future games;
- Keep a record of all incidents, both

Sport events **411**

good and bad, in order to formulate a comprehensive evaluation report; and

❑ For major national and international sport events, an official impact study conducted by an independent party can also assist in the organisational improvement of future events. This report is important for sponsors, federations and all role players as the report can confirm the success or failure of an event with respect to the return on investment (ROI). However, a cautionary note should be heeded that since stakeholders may have different objectives, it may not be practical to address all their specific objectives in an event evaluation. Moreover, depending on the objectives, ROIs could produce different results (e.g. an event may be financially profitable but residents may be negatively impacted by major traffic congestion, noise and disorderly behaviour, etc.).

20.2.2 Financial

The sports event manager will have to organise:

❑ ordinary games, e.g. league games from week to week; or

❑ special events, e.g. a one-day or week-long tournament.

On a local level, these events are usually organised to generate funds, market the team or club, and/or to create community involvement. On a national or international level, they are generally organised to meet the same type of requirements but for more professional reasons. Events have become big business, thus the value of the event from a sponsor's perspective is increasingly important. It is not therefore surprising that raising sponsorship for sport events is a critical management skill.

As highlighted in the sport event business plan above, financial management is critical to the success of the sport event. The following questions should be raised as a first step of financial management (Van der Wagen, 2005):

❑ Is the aim to make profit? (Many local sport events are not for profit.)

❑ How much will the event cost?

❑ What are the revenue sources?

❑ If it is a ticketed event, how many tickets must be sold to break even?

❑ What is the cash flow situation?

❑ What control systems are required to prevent fraud?

❑ How will legal and taxation obligations be met?

According to Pike Masteralexis et al. (998: 333), '[b]udgeting is the process of developing a written plan of revenues and expenses for the next accounting cycle' (which refers to the time taken to plan, organise and operate the event). They add that depending on the type of event, it can be very short or, as observed for mega-events, can take several years. The sport event manager should be familiar with zero-based as well as cash flow budgeting. Zero-based budgeting entails all projected revenues and expenses to be justified prior to becoming part of the overall budget (Pike Masteralexis et al., 1998). This type of budgeting forces the sport event manager never to take aspects of the budget for granted, and contributes to looking for ways to become more effective and efficient. Cash flow budgeting depicts 'accounting for the receipt and timing of all sources and cash expenditure' (Pike Masteralexis et al., 1998: 334). Cash flow budgeting allows the sport event manager to pay expenses at predetermined times throughout the accounting cycle. Planning carefully to avoid cash shortfalls, especially since events expend sizable amounts in the initial phases before receiving cash, is critically important.

It is necessary to consider event income strategies for both smaller and larger sport events. Event income can come from a variety of sources, as listed below (Van der Wagen, 2005: 129; Shone & Parry, 2004: 112):

❏ Broadcasting rights (generally major sport events only);
❏ Corporate hospitality areas;
❏ Entry tickets (for ticketed events);
❏ Licensing and merchandising;
❏ Parking fees/transport services;
❏ Photography charges;
❏ Raffles/lottery;
❏ Rental for stalls and exhibitors;
❏ Sale of event programmes;
❏ Sale of food and beverages; and
❏ Sponsorship or grants.

In terms of sponsorship, sport events can offer the sponsor various benefits and are highlighted in table 20.2. Exclusivity is an important consideration; however, sponsors also associate themselves with a range of sport events, depending on their sponsorship objectives.

There are six steps to sport sponsorship, which include the following:

1 Design the sport event with sponsorship opportunities;
2 Secure media sponsors;
3 Define the sponsorship levels;
4 Develop a sponsorship proposal;
5 Identify and target prospective sponsors; and
6 Sign the sponsorship contract.

Many sport organisations that organise sport events are not-for-profit organisations and will generally rely on grants for funding. Similarly to the sponsorship process, successful grant writing includes the following (Smith & McClean, 1998, as cited by Turco et al., 2002: 18):

❏ Idea formulation;
❏ Selection of eternal funding source;
❏ Proposal preparation;
❏ Proposal submission;
❏ Proposal acceptance or rejection; and
❏ Grant administration, or proposal revision and resubmission.

Shone and Parry (2004) note that the generation of additional revenue is a key failure for many events, especially for volunteer events where it is not seen as important as financial control. In today's global economic climate it is particularly important to explore additional revenue streams.

Upon completion of the sport event, a list of the organisation's revenue, expenditure and net profit (or loss) is prepared as per table 20.3. Gross revenue is the total revenue before any deductions,

Table 20.2 Corporate benefits of sport sponsorship

❏ Media exposure ❏ Direct media coverage ❏ Media mentions	❏ Product sampling ❏ Merchandising opportunities (product sales)
❏ Signage	❏ Affiliation with other sponsors
❏ Hospitality opportunities	❏ Community pride/involvement (especially relevant to smaller community sport events)
❏ Name association/lifestyle identification	

Source: Adapted from Turco et al. (2002: 169)

whereas gross profit is determined after direct costs have been deducted. Overhead costs are then deducted to determine the operating profit, and finally net profit is left after taxes are deducted.

Table 20.3 Profit and loss statement

Profit and loss statement as at 30 June 2007	
Gross revenue	R700 000
Less cost of goods sold	R500 000
Gross profit	**R200 000**
Less administrative and other overhead costs	R150 000
Operating profit	**R50 000**
Less other income expenses (such as interest)	R5 000
Profit before tax	R45 000
Less tax	R10 000
Net profit for the event	**R35 000**

Source: Adapted from Van der Wagen (2005)

Event structures are used to aid the governance of an event. For sport events, many organisational structures include volunteers, and hence will be discussed further in the next section below. When forming an organising committee it is necessary to consider the following:

❏ It is important for the sport event manager not to attempt to do everything. The involvement of other players, officials, parents and/ or friends is important. Here is the perfect opportunity to involve them by forming an organising committee. The key players should have a mix of the following skills: financial, marketing, operational and legal. Through the delegation of tasks it will be easier to complete the arrangements in time. This

is of particular importance with special events. The organising committee should be set up well in advance of the event.

❏ Terms of reference for the organising committee should be set up, e.g. to whom they are responsible, duties they are to undertake, specific reporting dates, etc.

❏ It is necessary to list the names and addresses of the committee members and to have regular status meetings. The progress of various sport event organisational aspects will be tracked during these meetings. Figure 20.1 is an example of a checklist for championships, tournaments and courses.

❏ It is necessary to appoint a sport event manager who will be responsible for the overall planning, coordination and evaluation of the sport event. The sport event manager should liaise with the organising committee, the community and the officials. Depending on the level of the event, a professional event management company may be employed to organise it.

❏ Third-party contracting is an essential part of sport event management, as one particular company does not supply all the elements to make an event happen. The most common third-party contracts include the following:
  • Catering;
  • Scaffolding;
  • Sound equipment;
  • Sport-specific technical equipment (beach volleyball area, boxing ring, etc.); and
  • Stage and lighting

As mentioned previously, volunteers play a critical role in the hosting of sport events.

1	Type of sport ....
2	Name of organising official ....
3	Type of competition/championship ....
4	Venue ....
5	Amount granted by committee ....

6 First organising committee meeting
   Place .... Date .... Time...........

7 Members of organising committee
   Chairperson: Tel (w) .... (h) ....
   Secretary: Tel (w) .... (h) ....
   Treasurer: Tel (w) .... (h) ....

8 Meetings held to control the organisation
   Date .... Place .... Time ....
   Date .... Place .... Time ....
   Date .... Place .... Time ....

Figure 20.1 Sport event checklist
Source: Getz (1997: 92–93)

Volunteers can be involved in the short-term pre-event preparation or during event servicing (Mallen & Adams, 2008). Human resources development becomes especially important for sport events due to the high level of volunteers involved. An event may be volunteer managed through an executive committee; however, a professional event organiser could be employed to plan and manage the event (Shone & Parry, 2004). The volunteer management process as outlined in the hallmark and mega-event chapter is applicable to other multi-sport and single sport events, although the timeframe for recruiting and training may be shorter. Figure 20.2 summarises the volunteer life cycle for events. The sport event manager plays an essential role in developing a positive volunteer culture within the event organisation (Mallen & Adams, 2008).

Mallen and Adams (2008) add that in order to manage an effective volunteer programme, consideration of the following is required:

❐ What are the responsibilities of the volunteer (job description)?
❐ What type of work is required (short or long term)?
❐ When and how will the organisation benefit from a volunteer?
❐ Where is the volunteer required?

20.2.3 Design

The design of the events includes consideration for the content, theme, programme, production and catering. The

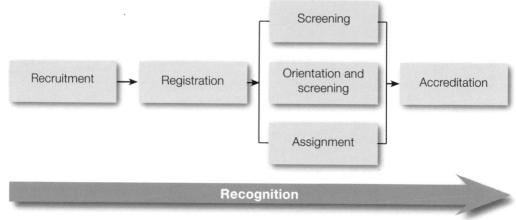

Figure 20.2 Volunteer life cycle for events

Source: Mallen & Adams (2008: 58)

same considerations need to apply as per a mega-event; however, a few more are highlighted in this section. Before deciding on the content, theme or programme, set the objectives of the sport event. For example, it could be only to provide exercise for your players, to promote goodwill between different teams or, in the case of special events, to promote the club, to generate funds, or increase brand awareness and drive sales for the sponsors.

When selecting a sport event, cognisance of the following is required:

❐ Identify who your target market for the sport event will be (e.g. youth, seniors, etc.). This is a significant factor in determining all the other elements of the sport event. If your audience is not reached by all aspects of your sport event, it could be a terrible flop.

❐ Allow sufficient time to organise the sport event. Generally, two to four months is required for a community sport event, while larger sport events require planning for more than a year.

❐ In terms of timing of the sport event, avoid clashes with other tournaments and fixtures and try to ensure that it fits into the school, provincial, regional and/or national calendar. One would also need to consider a possible clash with non-sport events in your community (e.g. a Youth Day celebration) or an event television broadcast (e.g. Manchester United versus Barcelona). Stipulate or estimate the number of entrants or teams, and allocate enough time to complete the sport event, allowing for unforeseen problems such as adverse weather conditions. It is also necessary to consider set-up and breakdown times required, the sport event schedule of the participating sports federation, and the arrival and departure times of participants.

❐ Venue capacity, location, facilities and fit all influence the choice of the venue for the sport event. The size of the venue should be suitable to accommodate the technical requirements of the competition. The venue should be accessible to the public from a transportation perspective. The venue should also have facilities suitable for the scale of the event being staged, e.g. ablution facilities, access for the disabled, catering facilities, etc. In addition, the

Case study 20.1 Volunteer programme of the ICC Cricket World Cup

Two thousand seven hundred and ten (2 710) volunteers were utilised for the ICC Cricket World Cup 2003 (ICC CWC 2003) hosted by South Africa. The volunteer database contains the details of every individual that volunteered for, and participated in, the ICC CWC 2003. A full-time volunteer manager, along with a national committee, was responsible for the overseeing of the project, including:

- ❑ the development of the event-specific unit standards (a unit standard is a registered statement of desired education and training outcomes and its associated assessment criteria together with administrative and other information as specified in the regulations, SAQA, 2006);
- ❑ the setting of criteria for the day-to-day management of the volunteers at the respective stadiums;
- ❑ the development of the recruitment criteria for volunteers;
- ❑ the development of the curriculum and training schedule for the training of volunteers; and
- ❑ the selection of training facilitators.

The national committee is comprised of representatives from within the sporting fraternity, THETA (the hospitality and education training authority) and other relevant bodies.

Volunteers were selected countrywide to act, among others, as ushers, car park attendants, information kiosk attendants, VIP assistants, media and media accreditation assistants; queue busters and magnetometer attendants. The scale of the ICC CWC 2003 demanded a thorough training programme. Topics such as 'Functioning in a Team', 'Organising Oneself in a Workplace', 'Occupational Health and Safety' and most significantly 'Customer Care' all formed part of the curriculum.

In addition, the volunteers were exposed to cricket matches at various venues around the country, for practical, hands-on experience. In so doing, the volunteers not only had an opportunity to implement the theory learnt, but it also provided them with the occasion to familiarise themselves with the venue where each would be stationed. It further allowed them to assess their readiness for the actual World Cup, and to improve on areas that still required further training and development.

'We specifically designed the programme to include customer care because of the anticipated numbers of international guests and tourists that would flock to South Africa for the Cricket World Cup. As South Africa's ambassadors, we acknowledged the key role that our volunteers would play, and thus believed that it was our responsibility to sufficiently empower them so that they would reflect our country's robust hospitality, and showcase our ability to host international events of this magnitude,' said Dr Bacher.

Source: South African Sports Commission (2003)

venue has to fit the profile of the sport event being staged, e.g. the fit with the sponsor's brand and objectives require consideration. Finally, sticking to the design capacity in terms of the number of attendees permitted will also assist in crowd management (Getz, 2007).

When designing an event it is also necessary to consider the format of the competition. The event format looks at the duration of the sport event and the schedule that will be used during that time. Is it a normal game or, in the case of special events, a tournament in the form of a round robin or knockout? Moreover, creative elements to be considered when designing a sport event include the following (adapted from Van der Wagen, 2005: 26–28):

❑ *Theme.* This depends on the type of sport event (regular or extreme, single or multi-sport, one-day or several days, youth or masters' sport, etc.);

❑ *Layout.* Depending on the type of sport, the layout may vary;

❑ *Decor.* Hospitality areas must have suitable decor;

❑ *Suppliers.* Maintain good relations to endure quality service and products;

❑ *Technical requirements.* Use an experienced technical contractor, have a backup system and test new technology;

❑ *Staging.* This is necessary for a winner's podium and/or stage if entertainment is required;

❑ *Entertainment.* This is peripheral

to sport events but nevertheless an important component; and

❑ *Catering.* Quality service delivery and food are critical both for participants and for spectators.

It is also important to note that while sport events usually consist of a game or competition, they are generally packaged as a festival to expand their appeal and generate additional business. The box bottom left describes the *Cape Argus* Pick n Pay Cycle Tour, which takes place annually in Cape Town, South Africa. It has evolved from a road race to several cycling races and is packaged as a lifestyle event.

When catering for VIPs and players for local events, involve club and/or family members in preparations. Ensure that dietary requirements are met, e.g. vegetarian, halaal, kosher, etc. For spectators, ensure that sufficient products are available to sell to raise funds for the club as well as sufficient variety to meet the needs of spectators.

An aspect of event design that has become extremely important for sport events is that of the environment. Getz (2007) advises that, at the minimum, events should meet the RRR standards (reduce, re-use and recycle). It will be necessary to ensure that both the sport event manager and the subcontractors take steps to minimise the impact of the event on the environment. There is a demand for 'green' events with participants and spectators becoming more environmentally conscious. Examples of 'green' events include the Indy 500, the FIFA World Cup, the Olympic Games, the FBR Phoenix Open (PGA event), X Games (extreme sport) and football college games, among others (Davidson, 2007; AZ_Sun, 2008; Greenwatch, 2009). These sport events have introduced a number of

Cape Argus Cycle Tour Lifestyle Week Events

❑ Mountain Bike Challenge – 4 200 cyclists participated

❑ Cape Argus Pick n Pay Tricycle and Junior Tours – 2 400 kids participated

❑ Cape Argus Rotary Pedal Power Association Lifecycle Expo – 350 exhibitors, only registration venue for all participants and estimated 79 000 visitors in 2008

❑ Giro del Capo – a five-day stage race with the 5th and final stage incorporated into the Cape Argus Pick n Pay Cycle Tour (the main event), which will see the Giro lead 35 000 cyclists around the picturesque Cape Peninsula.

Source: Cape Argus Pick n Pay Cycle Tour (2009)

measures to reduce environmental impacts such as the use of recyclable containers, rewarding spectators with tokens for recycling their garbage, disposable food utensils that were recycled and are made of renewable and composite materials, and minimising energy usage. A more in-depth case study of the Super Bowl is presented as an example of how to 'green' an event. Davidson (2007) concludes that sport events are becoming fertile testing grounds for new environmental practices, and leave lasting examples of how events can change practices for the better.

20.2.4 Marketing

There are many similarities for marketing for a mega-event and a major international sport event, therefore consideration should be given to marketing covered in the mega-event section. In addition, a few marketing suggestions for a smaller, community-based sport event are outlined below.

Sport event marketing is concerned with enhancing the profile of the event, meeting the needs of the target audience and generating revenue (Van der Wagen, 2005). Even if a sport event is government funded, it is still necessary to attract a high level of attendance. Pricing and ticketing are important considerations. If it is necessary and possible, try to attract the local media, e.g. the local community newspaper, radio, etc., to promote the event. Market it through applying advertising, personal selling, sales promotion and publicity-creation techniques, and ensure that they are packaged for effective communication. Before approaching a sponsor, identify the benefits, ascertain exposure to be generated and check for compatibility with the sport event. Case study 20.3 highlights the importance of brand fit and also the increase in corporate community investment.

Hollebeek (2009) contends that recently marketing practitioners have come under increasing pressure to account for their marketing expenditure and the extent to which they meet the financial corporate

Case study 20.3 Sport sponsorship – the risk of marketing own goals

Sport is a valuable element in corporate community investment because of associations with fair play, health and community and its ability to reach a wide range of consumers. Sport clubs and organisers are waking up to the funding opportunities corporate community investment programmes offer, particularly as the recession hits sponsorship budgets. However, funding sport has pitfalls for brands. For example, while sport has proved attractive to fast-food, soft drinks and confectionery companies, campaigners suggest the association of such products with sport is contradictory. Companies respond that links with sports underline the message that their products can be part of a balanced diet and what matters is a healthy lifestyle.

Grassroots work is key to effective corporate community investment programmes in sport. Brands such as Coca-Cola incorporate community sport initiatives into big-money sponsorship of major sporting events such as the Olympics or a UK football league. Steve Hemsley, author of the April report, warns that brands can easily be accused of cynically exploiting links with sports but 'eyebrow-raising' is less likely if the aim is seen as genuinely philanthropic. 'There is a marketing benefit,' Hemsley says, 'but that mustn't be your reason for doing it.'

Hugh Milward, head of public affairs for McDonald's in the UK, agrees. He cites the company's football in the community initiatives in the UK as a goodwill gesture, saying: 'It is a demonstration of our commitment to giving back to the communities in which we serve.' McDonald's has helped put in place 13 000 football coaches in the UK since 2000 with the aim of coaching one million children by 2010.

Critics, however, argue that if brands such as McDonald's are not investing money in sport for commercial reasons then they would leave their logos at the door, and not have any branding on show at programmes.

Corporate responsibility consultant John Luff suggests sponsorship strategies are more likely to be trusted by consumers if they tie in with what the company does. Banks sponsoring playing fields may be very laudable, but supporting initiatives to improve numeracy skills may be more coherent, and strike a chord with consumers.

Yet the temptation for brands to jump on the mass appeal of sport will always prove too strong to resist. In this context, the trend for rolling community investment into major sponsorship deals is welcome.

Source: Ethical Corporation (n.d.)

objectives. Hollebeek adds that return on marketing investment (ROMI) has tended to conform to the relatively short-term accounting valuation period which has led to inconsistent valuation of marketing resources and investments. A longer-term and a more holistic approach are therefore required. However it is further underscored that when evaluating the impact of sponsorship at a specific event, it is difficult to isolate other marketing impacts taking place simultaneously via other media channels.

Technology is evolving rapidly every day, and sport event managers have to be aware of how technology influences how they run their daily business operations (Pike Masteralexis et al., 1998). One area in which technology impacts on event organisation to a significant extent is that of media relations. Email, the World Wide Web, fax on demand and fax back have contributed to almost instantaneous information regarding the particular sporting event. It is important for home pages to be updated continuously so that media have the most current material. News releases are now made available via the website or fax on demand. Turco et al. (2002) add that communication via the internet has become a popular means of advertising and providing information about one's event. The following examples provide online registration, travel packages and other pertinent event information, and are worth having a look at.

- ❏ *Cape Argus* Pick n Pay Cycle Tour: http://www.cycletour.org.za
- ❏ British and Irish Lions Tour, South Africa 2009: http://www.lionsrugby.com/home.php
- ❏ Association of Surfing Professionals (ASP) World Tour: http://www.aspworldtour.com/2009/

20.2.5 Operations

There are many operational details that need to be finalised before the sport event. It refers to all the systems that must be in place and the actions that have to be taken to produce the event (Getz, 2007). Once the event has been identified, the checklist should be set up containing *all* the activities that need to be completed in order for the game to be hosted. The checklist should also include a space for the person responsible, as well as a D-day for that specific activity. The checklist must be continuously controlled to ensure that assignments are carried out. A control checklist should also be prepared and can be adapted for a specific sport event. It outlines to whom the activity has been assigned, the control and when it has been completed. This is the most important

document in a sport event manager's life, and should be so detailed that in the event of someone else having to take over the project, the process occurs without a hitch. Proper operational planning can ensure that the organisation of the sport event runs smoothly, without the event manager having to deal with surprises and mishaps. For example, protocol should be established for honorary guests as players. Honorary guests like sponsors and local leaders are very important, and special attention should be paid to the care of these VIPs. It is important that the person assigned to do so is aware of who the dignitaries are in order to prevent embarrassment. This person should also be sufficiently skilled in terms of protocol, such as the manner in which invitations are addressed, seating arrangements, etc. Players should be made as comfortable as possible (e.g. change rooms should be clean, and transport should be arranged if necessary).

As previously mentioned, technological development has a profound impact on sport event management. Another important aspect to consider is that of transportation. Turco et al. (2002: 243) note that 'the ease of transportation will enable participants and spectators to engage in non-native sports as effortlessly as sports in their own areas', adding that major sports will become more globalised, and professional leagues will spread across continents. A case in point is the Super 14 rugby series which takes place in Australia, South Africa and New Zealand, and the DLF Indian Premier League (IPL) cricket. The DLF IPL involves a number of top international cricketers from all over the world playing against each other in eight different teams. It was scheduled to take place in India in 2009 and within

Extract of an event plan for the All Blacks (New Zealand) vs France

Introduction
Event: All Blacks vs France
Crowd estimate: Capacity crowd
Date: 2 June 2007

Preparation – to pre-event brief (24 May 2007)
❒ Development of overall event plan

Phase 1 – pre-event (24 May 2007)
❒ Presentation of event management plan
❒ Completion of all plans and execution as required
  • Corporate hospitality
  • Event security
  • Transport management plan (TMP) and signage completed
  • Communications plans
  • Detailed fine-tuning as required

Phase 2 – Event 2–3 June 2007
❒ Execution of all plans as confirmed in event management plan

Phase 3 – Post Event 3 June 2007
❒ De-rig west lounge
❒ De-rig media
❒ Identify and repair damages
❒ Security to cover activities

Situation – important stakeholders for event:
❒ Patrons (3 000 corporate and 40 000 non-corporate patrons)
❒ Staff/officials (800 catering staff, 300 patron management staff, 100 media and 200–300 officials)
❒ Neighbours (local residents)
❒ NZRU (New Zealand Rugby Union – a critical stakeholder)
❒ Auckland City Council (compliance officers checking noise, light spill, liquor licence, transport management plan and crowd management)

Opportunities/constraints
❒ National/international recognition for Eden Park Trust Board's future development of Eden Park
❒ Revenue opportunities for commercial stakeholders and region as a whole
❒ Opportunity to create firm impression that Eden Park is a valuable national and regional asset

Aim
❒ Create a safe and enjoyable environment in which to experience rugby

four weeks of the tournament commencing it was relocated to South Africa due to security concerns. In just under a month, officials scheduled the 59 matches in 37 days at eight venues, made 40 000 hotel bookings and purchased 10 000 plane tickets (BBC Sport, 2009). Careful consideration to logistical and operational requirements had to be considered when making this decision.

Another way in which technological innovations affect event organisation is that of security. The following case study details some of the state-of-the-art security measures that were implemented for the ICC Cricket World Cup in South Africa. Security will be discussed further in the risk management section below. It is evident that the successful sport event manager will have to keep abreast of technological changes in all aspects of event organisation, particularly with regard to how these developments impact daily operations.

20.2.6 Risk

All events carry an element of risk, and sport events have the additional risk of danger to sportspersons and, in some instances, the attendees as well. For example, motor-sport racing has more inherent dangers for the participants and spectators, while cliff diving or big-wave surfing have intrinsic risks for these extreme athletes. Another significant risk for sport event managers is that of temporary fencing and seating (Van der Wagen, 2005). When venues are stretched to capacity or tickets are oversold, it can lead to fatalities as witnessed in the many soccer disasters (see an example in case study 20.4 below). Van der wagen adds that the challenge for sport event managers is to reduce risk to an acceptable level by careful planning and by introducing new procedures and technologies. An effective crowd management system can prevent or lessen disasters at sport events.

Case study 20.4 Safety and security at the ICC Cricket World Cup 2003

One of the fundamental components which underscored the success of safety and security delivery during the tournament was the countrywide host venue deployment of metal detectors and highly sophisticated digital CCTV installations. The installation design called for no less than 53 PTZ Dome Cameras, integrated with remote-control units, system controllers, 14-inch colour monitors, 24-hour time-lapse VCRs, input digital recorders and matrix switchers. The equipment was installed at all 12 local host cricket grounds. Pilot tests were mostly conducted during the Sri Lanka and Pakistan tours between October 2002 and January 2003. The technicians were present at every pilot and Cricket World Cup match to confirm 100% performance. Upon reviewing the tournament at its completion, Bacher said, 'When I first proposed the comprehensive safety and security measures recommended by the Security Directorate, incorporating the use of state-of-the-art electronic security measures, many people felt I was way over the top. But so successful did our measures prove to be that I would be very surprised if the International Cricket Council does not make them mandatory for future Cricket World Cup tournaments as well as all One Day international matches. Such a development would be yet another first for South Africa.'

Source: Blick South Africa (2003)

Levine (1988, cited by Turco et al., 2002) notes that a comprehensive risk management plan will take the following into consideration:

❏ Identify all areas of potential risk (risk analysis);
❏ Exclude or reduce risk by conducting training programmes, safety programmes and inspection procedures;
❏ Establish protective funds for risks that cannot be eliminated; and
❏ Implement a risk management plan.

Rossouw (2000) reports that the plan will involve not only those who plan the methods that help to ensure a safe sports event but will also include comments from the beneficiaries of the planning: the participants and spectators, as well as sponsors and other guests. These key groups must be involved in the planning to make certain that as many safety hazards as possible have been considered and that the final plan is practical and can be easily used by the participants and spectators. The internal planning team may select a seemingly perfect location for the first-aid station only to find out that neither the participants nor the spectators elected to use it because of its inconvenient location. Their input is essential in creating a workable safety plan.

The following general pointers provided by Rossouw (2000) should be considered when dealing with the risk management plan:

❏ Use a focus group comprised of event staff to help identify a wide range of potential threats and plan for their efficient management;
❏ Provide effective oral, visual and physical communications so that employees, spectators and participants will know what to do in an emergency. Use one central control centre for emergency medical services (EMS) so that miscommunication will not occur and radio lines are left open. Write a

report after each incident for litigation and evaluation purposes;

☐ Select an insurance broker knowledgeable in the sports event field who can advise wisely about the amount and type of coverage required; and

☐ Involve external groups such as athletes and spectators in the safety review process to ensure overall acceptance and usage.

Crowd management strategies are critical to a smooth-running event. Preventative measures such as clearly marked exits, and staff training with regard to alcohol policies, etc. should be in place. It is important to recognise that the risk management plan does not exonerate the sport event manager from all responsibility and liability regarding the event (Turco et al., 2002). If the sport event is not organised in a safe and responsible manner, the event manager may be held liable for any injuries or problems that may arise (Pike Masteralexis et al., 1998). They conclude that the sports event manager should acknowledge the importance of addressing risk management concerns related to the event in order to confine legal liability.

Case study 20.5 The 2001 Ellis Park soccer stadium disaster

A commission of inquiry into the Ellis Park soccer stadium disaster in Johannesburg, South Africa, was released in 2002. The report chronicles South Africa's worst sporting crowd disaster. On 11 April 2001, at a high-profile match between Kaizer Chiefs and Orlando Pirates at Ellis Park, 43 people were killed and more than 150 were injured. The following 14 factors were identified as contributing to the crowd crush tragedy and mismanagement:

1 Poor forecast of match attendance;
2 Failure to learn from the lessons of the past;
3 Failure by the role players to clearly identify and designate areas of responsibility;
4 Absence of overall command of the joint operation centre;
5 The inappropriate and untimely announcement that tickets were sold out;
6 Failure to adhere to FIFA (international controlling body) and SAFA (national controlling body) guidelines;
7 Unbecoming spectator behaviour;
8 Sale of tickets at the venue and unreserved seating;
9 The use of teargas or a similar substance;
10 Corruption on the part of certain members of security personnel;
11 Dereliction of duty;
12 Failure to use the big screen;
13 Inadequate public address system; and
14 Failure by the public order police unit to react timeously and effectively.

While it is beyond the scope of this case study to list all the recommendations, the following guidelines were highlighted as minimum security enforcement facilities for stadia:

☐ Facilities to carry out a continuous counting of admitted spectators from the opening of the gates;
☐ Crowd monitoring facilities, both inside and outside the stadium;
☐ An effective public address system;
☐ An effective communication system between all the security enforcement agencies

- ❏ Effective evacuation arrangements;
- ❏ Mechanisms, such as the provision of multiple entrances, to avoid the concentration of spectators in one particular area;
- ❏ Proper lighting inside and outside the stadium;
- ❏ Emergency, medical and related facilities;
- ❏ The calculation of stadium capacity;
- ❏ Seat numbering or identification (coding);
- ❏ The demarcation of standing areas where applicable;
- ❏ Demarcated areas for family, children and disabled persons; and
- ❏ Proper signage.

Source: South Africa, Republic of (2002)

Other aspects of risk management related to sport events are further highlighted below.

- ❏ *Liability.* What happens if a player or spectator gets injured at a match and the wrong treatment is administered? Turco et al. (2002) note that while the sport event manager does not have to protect the participant or spectator from every conceivable risk, reasonable care must be taken to protect them from the most serious cases. Thus the sport event manager must be equipped to deal with emergency medical or security problems that may occur in a large public gathering.
- ❏ *Letters of consent and indemnity.* Consent must be obtained from parents or guardians of underage children participating and indemnity forms must be signed by adult participants. Clear notices must be placed at the entrances to the stadium indicating the indemnity from expenses arising from injuries and loss or damage to property of spectators and players. This assists in indemnifying the organisers from claims resulting from the above.
- ❏ *Safety and security.* Local services (e.g. the South African Police Service and ambulance services) should be called upon to assist with these matters.

A safety and security representative could be represented on the organising committee to ensure efficiency with regard to emergency matters. A disaster management plan should also be put in place, with a spokesperson to deal with the media in the event of a major disaster occurring at the event.

It is important for the sport event manager to always make sure that contingency plans as backup for original plans that do not work are in place (e.g. having a referee on standby if the assigned one does not show up).

20.3 Summary

Sport participation and attendance have become increasingly popular in recent years due to increased access to consumer markets via mass information systems and is thus more inclusive to segments previously excluded from participation. It is therefore imperative that sport event managers understand how the knowledge domains can be applied to a range of sport events which occur at different levels. The necessity for educated and trained sport event managers to ensure successful events was underscored.

This chapter elaborated upon how key knowledge domains, namely administration, design, marketing, operations, risk and evaluation, can be used a tool to manage sport events. Best-practice issues in relation to this genre of events were considered, and case studies were used to illustrate key considerations and to further demonstrate some of the typical management challenges in relation to this genre of events. Of significance are challenges related to informal and formal bidding processes, the management of volunteers in the sport sector, the importance of sport event research, and design considerations for various types of sport event including those with respect to a 'green' event. Additional challenges elaborated upon included sponsorship and grant writing, the significance of detailed operation checklists and risk management considerations, both in terms of the spectators and participants.

Questions for research

1 Why is evaluation necessary in sport event management?
2 In order to host a sport festival in your local community, it is necessary to select a site. Develop a checklist for a venue inspection of three potential sites and select the most appropriate one.
3 You have been tasked with 'greening' your event. Outline some measures that you will undertake to achieve this objective.
4 Draw up a checklist of all activities that have to be planned for a sport event in your community.
5 Develop a risk management plan based upon the requirements of a specific sport event/ tournament.

Recommended websites

Browse the following internet sites for interesting and informative information:

International Events Group IEG: http://www.sponsorship.com
Leisure Information Network: http://www.lin.ca
Recreation Management: http://leoisaac.com/sportman/
SPRIG Promoting Information in Leisure Tourism and Sport: http://www.sprig.org.uk

Suggested reading

Getz, D. 2007. *Event Studies: Theory, Research and Policy for Planned Events.* Oxford: Elsevier.
Mallen, C & Adams, LJ. 2008. *Sport, Recreation and Tourism Event Management.* UK: Elsevier.

Photo: EIBTM

Photo: EIBTM

Photo: World Travel Market

Photo: World Travel Market

21

Exhibitions, expositions and fairs

John Knocker, Howard Pell and Dimitri Tassiopoulos

Abstract

Worldwide, exhibitions are growing in numbers as well as in importance, as they effectively become a temporary shop window for different industries. The reason for the growth of the industry is due to the unique feature of catering to the various senses of touch, taste, sight and sound in a manner that no other medium can achieve. As a marketing platform, there is the added benefit of delivering measurable objectives to give immediate feedback to sellers and buyers alike. Exhibitions are not only for product display, they are a place of learning, for customer interaction, and for the exchange of information and ideas. One of their benefits is that they bring people who sell products, systems and services together with buyers and potential buyers who want to buy or learn more about such products. They are used by exhibitors to showcase their companies, their products and their expertise to customers, prospective customers and past customers, and often to the customers of other exhibitors.

Chapter objectives

After you have read this chapter you should be able to:

❏ understand the benefits exhibitions provide;

❏ appreciate the elements required to organise an exhibition; and

❏ have consideration for the practical issues associated with running an exhibition.

21.1 Introduction

Exhibitions have been around for a very long time, dating back as far as the ancient civilisations of the Egyptians, the Phoenicians, the Greeks, the Chinese and the Romans, where tradesmen would travel to see and meet local makers of cloth, dye, silverware, etc., in market squares and bazaars (WEC, 2009). The Romans, states UFI (2009b), began to host fairs ranging from roving locations to permanent venues, thus developing a kind of 'fair industry'. In the Bible, a fair taking place in the town of Zor (now part of Lebanon) is mentioned in the Old Testament (Ezekiel, chapter 27). Herod King of Judea (37–4 BC) was the first to build a permanent fair centre (3 200 m²) with a wall around it, located in the town of Botana, and where archaeologists found evidence (coins mainly) indicating that visitors to this fair centre came from Syria, Egypt, Italy, Greece, Spain and France.

'Over time, as trade expanded from the east Mediterranean across to the west and into the north of Europe, new markets evolved and new distribution routes were essential to meet the growing requests for new and interesting products and services' (WEC, 2009: internet).

The term *fair*, which was only used for the first time in the Middle Ages, according to UFI (2009b), comes from the Latin word *feria* meaning 'religious festival', usually taking place near a convent

---

Exhibitions defined

A simple definition of an exhibition is the 'bringing together in one place for a set period of time, buyers and sellers enabling products to be viewed, handled, demonstrated discussed and purchased', according to Allwood and Montgomery (1989: 14). Stated another way, 'an exhibition is an event bringing buyers and sellers and interested persons together to view or to sell products, services, and other resources to a specific industry or the general public, which can be scheduled alone or in conjunction with other events' (Silvers, 2009b).

Exhibitions are broadly seen as consisting of two categories, namely trade and consumer exhibitions. During recent times, a further category has been established which is known as a confex. These are conferences within an industry or profession with a small number of exhibition stands, and are generally erected in the foyer area of the conference. They tend to be smaller events serving a useful purpose with the conference and meetings being the main focus, majoring on an intellectual theme but also offering suppliers a platform to promote their products and services to a smaller but targeted audience. In this chapter the confex-type event is not being addressed specifically although the organisational side is similar. The promotion of the event tends to be somewhat different.

or a church. The same sense is to be found in the term currently used in German – *Messe* – which derives from the Latin term *Missa*, or 'religious service', at which the priest, on pronouncing the final words '*ite, Missa est*', declared the religious service at an end, thus giving the sign for the opening of the market, usually held in the church square. The first fair of this kind was the 'Foire de Saint Denis' near Paris, founded by King Dagobert in 629, and which by 710 was already attracting more than 700 merchants.

During the Middle Ages, large fairs were held at regular intervals in different parts of Europe. Records found in the archives of the city of Utrecht (the Netherlands) indicate that Bishop Godebald gave the city a charter in 1127, which included the permit to organise 'fairs' outside of the town ramparts. At that time, according to UFI (2009b), the city of Utrecht already organised four fairs annually. Another early example was the Leipzig Fair, which started in 1165, which had not only cash-and-carry products, but also production means.

In the mid- to late-1800s, according to WEC (2009), exhibitions had been extended to include consumers and were considered social outings with many exhibitions focusing on one theme. A landmark event was the Great Exhibition that was held in the Crystal Palace in Hyde Park, London, England in 1851, and became the world's first international exhibition. The exhibition showcased the 'Works of Industry of All Nations'. Particularly, it displayed to the world the achievements of British manufacturers and illustrated the industrial predominance of Great Britain at that time. The exhibition remained open for five months and attracted in excess of six million visitors.

Case study 21.1 Exhibitions in South Africa

In 1877 the first recorded exhibition in South Africa was held in Cape Town in the Cape Colony, entitled 'The South African International Exhibition' (Allwood, 1977). Perhaps the best known show in South Africa is the Rand Easter Show that commenced in the early 1900s in Johannesburg. It was the only show in the area, combining agricultural, industrial and consumer exhibitions, and attracting large crowds of visitors over 10–14 days during the Easter period. Farmers also participated, displaying their cattle, pigs and poultry, and the judging of stock was indeed a prestigious event for the community.

Schoolchildren visited during their holidays, enjoying, among other things, the fun fair that was a real attraction for them, and so the whole family looked forward to the annual event. As time progressed, the interests of business were not being best served and entrepreneurs saw an opportunity to develop other exhibitions for mining and building to meet the needs of industry. The show then became a consumer show for the general public and has continued successfully for many years.

Since 1945, exhibition activity has expanded at a tremendous rate throughout the world and currently there are in excess of 8 000 major exhibitions per year (Klein, 2009), with most continents having exhibition halls of high quality (Allwood, 1997). Research conducted by UFI (2009a) among the members of the Union des Foires (UFI) (a global association of the exhibition industry) to determine if an increase of exhibition space was anticipated in venues of 5 000 m² or larger revealed that exhibition venues were anticipating an increase of 13% in additional exhibition space for the foreseeable future.

'Today', states WEC (2009: internet), 'exhibitions are one of the most lively and effective sales and marketing tools.' They offer a unique mixture of information, communication and entertainment, and are a medium that allows the use of all five senses in an atmosphere of face-to-face contact.

21.2 Event fundamentals

The following section examines the aspects of a professional exhibition's management. The topics covered have been arranged according to event domains of staging any type of event professionally. These guidelines are applicable to national and international exhibitions. The basic objective is to plan and mount a successful and profitable event that can become a regular feature on the exhibition calendar.

But events need to be beneficial to visitors and to exhibitors. These, after all, are the stakeholders to whom the organisers have to be accountable if they intend to continue to run subsequent events of a similar nature, and both need to experience value when spending money or time in attending as exhibitors or as visitors.

21.2.1 Administration

Checklist (not in sequential order)
1 Budget
2 Number of names on mailing list
3 Brochure
4 Floor plans
5 Advertising
6 Exhibitor – trade advertising
7 Visitor – trade advertising
8 Road posters
9 Opening and closing times
10 Complimentary tickets
11 Public relations
12 Conferences
13 Catalogue
14 Exhibitor manual
15 Badges and passes
16 Subcontractors
17 Final hall plan
18 Temporary staff
19 Features
20 Sponsorship

21.2.2 Budget

The preparation of an accurate and detailed budget and the subsequent control of expenditure are essential. Only after the budget has been agreed will it become possible to set the selling prices for space at the exhibition.

The following suggested items give an indication of the elements that need to be taken into account for setting out the budget. Depending upon the circumstances, it is probable that additional items may have to be included.

Venue

The venue in this context relates to the variety of elements that have to be included in the physical organisation of an exhibition. Within the budget we take into account the cost of hiring the venue, which includes items the venue owner will require to be included in the contract for the renting of the facility. Naturally the hall rent forms part of the contract, but care needs to be taken to appreciate that the space being used may not be the full venue cost. The owners will more than likely state that the organiser will be billed separately for other charges such as the electricity supply. Should there be machinery on show, electricity will require adequate power for the equipment to operate, which may be at a higher charge than that needed simply for lighting. Other charges may be levied by the venue, but in any event the organiser will have costs associated with the office from where the physical exhibition is to be managed, and such costs must be included in the budget. The same will apply to the price of operating a public address system, and the costs that will be incurred for waste disposal, and for security staff. The other costs that need to be factored in will include a parking area for exhibitors and visitors, signage, temporary staff and telephone rental. Once the organisers have assumed responsibility for the venue, they will be faced with cleaning charges for the offices and the hall, and also need to make provision for the cost of turning an exhibition hall into an upmarket place by adding dressing, such as plants, carpeting, lighting and reception counters. A checklist of the items needed should be created.

Exhibitors

To attract exhibitors to participate in the show, attention has to be paid to the cost of the marketing material, and services that will be employed to carry out this important function. These might require printing of brochures, placing of advertisements, purchasing direct mail advertising lists, and launching the show to attract interest. Having secured exhibitors they need to be contracted to take part, and contract books, exhibitors badges, manuals and regular newsletters need to be written, all of which must be included in the budget. Further costs will be incurred if the decision is taken to run a training seminar, and these must be included in the budget, particularly if there is no cost to the exhibitor.

Visitor promotion

The cost of advertising in trade press and dailies, and on radio and possibly on television has to be paid for, unless the organiser makes use of a contra deal for advertising in exchange for a stand at the show. Such deals, however, do not usually encompass the whole of the advertising programme. Those mentioned above may also need to be included in the cost of attracting visitors. But other costs will be incurred such as complimentary tickets, posters, and public relations and press release service.

Operational costs

There will always be administrative costs to be budgeted for, which may be in the form of consultants' fees, entertainment, hotels and travelling, and commission for salespersons or agents. Remember to provide a small percentage for the provision for bad debts.

Overhead costs

There are ongoing (or fixed) expenses of an exhibit or exhibition which cannot be attributed to any specific activity but are still necessary for the exhibit or exhibition to function. Examples include insurance, salaries, car expenses, office rent and telephones, and any other overheads, including office equipment.

This may or may not include the cost of recovering the expenditure of hiring the exhibition space from exhibitors at the show. In the case where this cost is not recovered from the exhibitors, the total revenue generated by the exhibition show will also have to do so.

Once the total costs have been established, it should be possible to calculate the selling price of space (in m²), to provide an acceptable return on investment (ROI) whereby the first exhibition show should ideally break even in terms of income and expenditure, with subsequent events resulting in increasingly larger returns. Unfortunately, experience shows that first shows usually provide a negative return.

An estimate will have to be made of the space that will be sold on a conservative basis, particularly in the case of a first exhibition. Before setting the selling price it is advisable to determine what the competitive rates per m² are for other exhibitions, and so avoid trying to sell at a rate which is deemed unreasonable for the target market. There are other income streams that an organiser can include in the budget, such as adding a small margin for selling services to exhibitors such as carpets, stand construction, electrical connections, etc. The acceptable margin added is likely to amount to about 10–15%.

21.2.3 Return on investment (ROI)

Planning and attending an exhibition can be a very expensive exercise, according to Access (2009), so accurate calculations must be made before the event to ensure the appropriate return on the investment can be made. If exhibition budget levels are not controlled, costs can spiral and reduce the return on investment (ROI) to zero. Working with an experienced exhibition management company to develop a comprehensive brief and subsequent design can help reduce the risks. While dedicated project management throughout the process can ensure costs are identified and monitored, in the exhibition business today the calculation of ROI is becoming an increasingly important management tool.

The discussion hereafter will focus on the application of ROI in the two key areas of the exhibitions industry: exhibition organisers and exhibitors.

Exhibition organisers

Apart from calculating the ROI for the company as a whole, ROI can also be used for measuring the results of individual events the company is staging. A company's programme of exhibitions can be divided into two main areas – established events and new or first-time events.

It is with new events that ROI plays a most important role. It is a truism in the exhibitions industry that first-time exhibition events will in all probability result in a loss. This is because the research costs in establishing a new show are often quite heavy, and difficulty will be experienced in persuading prospective exhibitors to take part in an event which has not been staged before. Also, visitors are difficult to attract to the show in large numbers, all of which means that promotional expenditure will be high. So for a first event, the ROI will likely be negative. If it is decided to run the event for a second time, the aim should be to break even from a financial viewpoint but the ROI may still be negative as the loss from the first event must be recovered. Thereafter, the show should produce a profit and a positive ROI.

For established exhibitions, the calculation of the ROI should indicate whether the show is increasing, or at least maintaining its profitability. If not, this will indicate the necessity to re-examine the methods of operation, and to discover if changes are necessary.

The actual calculation of the ROI requires a detailed and accurate budget and exact allocation of all the costs involved in the research and actual mounting of the event. The other side of the equation will be the income received from exhibitors' and entrance fees paid by visitors. As indicated above, any losses incurred in the early stages must be carried forward, thus increasing the overall investment upon which the ROI will need to be calculated.

A properly calculated and recorded series of ROIs will act as a barometer to management indicating whether it is worthwhile to carry on with the particular exhibition. Such figures must be considered in conjunction with the research carried out by the organisers among both exhibitors and visitors to determine their reaction to the value of the particular event.

Exhibitors

It is important for exhibitors to calculate their ROI as applied to their participation at an exhibition. This will guide them as to whether it is worthwhile to participate in future events.

The calculation of the costs involved in participating in an exhibition should not be too difficult provided accurate records are kept by exhibitors of all the costs involved. The main items that need to be taken into account are: the cost of hiring the space

from the organisers; the cost of erecting the actual stand; services such as electricity, water, security, etc.; designing and printing of special promotional material; advertising; any research costs; entertainment costs; and costs of all staff manning the stand, etc. In the case of salespeople, a calculation should be made of the value of the sales which would normally be obtained but are foregone due to attendance at the show. The total of these expenditures will provide the value of the investment made in participating at the exhibition.

For exhibitors, the calculation of the ROI for a particular event can be a challenging task. The value of any actual sales made at the exhibition is fairly straightforward, but what about future sales which can be attributed to enquiries/contacts made at the exhibition? This puts a premium on the accurate and detailed recording of all visitors to the stand. Such information provides a valuable prospect list for follow-up action by sales staff after the event. Any sales affected subsequently which can be attributed to contacts made at the exhibition should be added to sales actually made at the exhibition to arrive at the total return. A time limit should be set for taking into account such subsequent sales – depending upon the company's product range, six months is probably a reasonable time.

Consideration must also be taken of the non-tangible benefits resulting from participation at the show, i.e. cementing relationships with existing customers, developing new prospects, projecting a positive image of the company to the market, and possible research of projected new products. Calculating the financial figure for such benefits can be an arbitrary process but should be quantified in some way to arrive at the total value of the return achieved from taking part at the exhibition.

The exhibitors need to establish measurable key indicators for ROI in the following areas:

- ❏ The management of marketing budgets to ensure adequate return on marketing investment (ROMI) from exhibitions;
- ❏ Attaining a higher return on expense (ROE) through identifying leaner exhibiting strategies so as to reduce selling and customer acquisition costs;
- ❏ 'Rightsizing' an exhibit for maximum productivity and profits;
- ❏ Building qualified booth traffic through the utilisation of low-cost, high-impact marketing tools so as to grow sales through fine-tuning promotion messages;
- ❏ Closing more sales at tradeshows and getting higher-quality leads that convert to sales; and
- ❏ Improving ROI through the use of trade-show financial performance metrics.

Carrying out this process and arriving at a reasonably accurate ROI should provide a more businesslike reason for taking part in an exhibition than the reasons which are sometimes given by exhibitors: 'We go there because all our competitors are there' or 'It's a nice jolly for the salesmen'!

21.2.4 Human resources in exhibitions

The onus is on the organiser to ensure that the promises made to exhibitors are delivered and one of the essential elements is the employment of competent persons to carry out the organising function. There could be a need for permanent and temporary staff to be employed, particularly if the organiser only has one or two shows. It would not be an economic proposition to employ a large staff, and temporary personnel may be the best option. Whether the staff is full time or temporary, employees delivering a satisfactory experience for the exhibitor

---

Example 21.1 Center for Exhibition Industry Research ROI Toolkit

The Center for Exhibition Industry Research (CEIR, 2009) has developed a series of simple tools to assist exhibitors in planning for an exhibition and to measure performance in delivering a return on investment (ROI) from exhibiting. The key issues that need to be considered by exhibitors are indicated hereunder:

Pre-event planning	
Potential audience estimator	Should we exhibit?
Exhibit staff estimator	How many staff members are needed to engage our potential audience?
Exhibit space estimator	How much space is required to attract and accommodate our potential audience?
Post-event measurement	
Reach	How many of our potential audience did we reach?
Staff performance	How active was our staff in reaching our potential audience?
Potential ROI estimator	What is the ROI potential from enquiries/leads obtained?

and for the visitor means that meticulous training of all functions is essential. This will require that the recruitment function of competent and effective staff is seriously addressed. In addition to competence, exhibition personnel should be easily identified, and so uniforms become a useful means of corporate identification and add to the image that a good organiser should wish to portray.

21.2.5 Systems management

Many factors contribute to the success of a good organiser, and poor systems management will cause the downfall of an otherwise well-considered event. The system used will need to record all the pertinent details of potential exhibitors. The same applies to the recording of other useful contacts, which are mentioned in the marketing sector. In addition, the recording of customer contracts and the essential attention to detail required in keeping floor plans up to date makes it necessary to employ a system that can handle all aspects of professional organisation.

21.2.6 Training of exhibitors' staff

It is astounding that companies will spend very large sums on their stand at an exhibition but fail to give any specialised training to the staff that will man it. The purpose of training is to ensure that exhibitors are able to take full advantage of the selling and promotional opportunities that will occur. It is for these reasons that some organisers arrange training sessions for the exhibitors' staff to prepare them for the different circumstances that they will encounter at the show. There are some excellent training films covering selling, etc. at exhibitions that can be used with

good effect at such training sessions and can maximise the selling and promotional opportunities.

21.2.7 Stand manager

A stand manager needs to be appointed with the necessary skills and ability to ensure that the company's objectives are attained. Stand managers must also be given the necessary authority to take whatever action is needed before and during the show. The objectives, budget, functions, responsibilities and authority should be drawn up and agreed on with the manager.

21.2.8 Briefing staff

The persons who are going to staff the stand during the exhibition need to be thoroughly briefed as to their duties and the objectives of the company in relation to the show. Selling on an exhibition stand is very different from the normal selling activity, and this needs to be clearly understood. There may be technical staff on the stand and they need to have a clear understanding of what their function and responsibilities are, bearing in mind that they may interact with customers in their normal job function.

In many cases the company and their staff are unaware of what is needed to make a success of their participation at the exhibition. Unless steps are taken to deal with this situation, the company may well come to the conclusion that exhibiting is a waste of time and will not take part in future exhibitions.

21.3 Design

There are considerations that have to be addressed when contemplating the exhibition, which will have direct consequences if appropriate attention is not paid to some hygiene factors. Unless they are given due thought, the exhibition being planned may be unsuccessful for all parties concerned. These will include the following issues:

21.3.1 Time of year

Avoid peak holiday times, which are June and July in the UK and August in Europe. In the southern hemisphere they are likely to be April and December. Many potential visitors will be away over these periods and this will detract from the all-important visitor attendance. When considering dates for a proposed exhibition it is essential to consult both overseas and local exhibition calendars to avoid clashing with competing events (Klein, 2009).

21.3.2 Duration

The advantages and disadvantages of short versus long shows are difficult to evaluate. Except in exceptional circumstances, shows of more than five days should be avoided as the company staff will be taken away from their main task, which causes difficulty in running their business and providing adequate staffing at the exhibition. There are exceptions to this, one example being the Rand Show. The general pattern is tending towards events of a three- to four-day duration.

21.3.3 Frequency

Assuming the exhibition is to be a regular event it is necessary to decide if it should take place annually, biennially or at longer intervals. Take into consideration the rapid technological change that applies to the specific industry and the products being displayed. The electronics and IT industries experience very rapid change for which an annual event becomes necessary and is called for.

In other industries where heavy equipment is required, less-rapid change occurs, and an exhibition usually takes place on a less frequent cycle. The very heavy costs involved in setting up the equipment also detract from more frequent exhibitions.

21.3.4 Venue selection

Usually a number of venues are available in a city or province. The first decision is in which city the exhibition should be held. There will be cases where the industry being served will dictate the location of the exhibition. In the case of an event for the fishing industry, the obvious choice would be at the coast.

If there are several venues available a number of factors need to be considered. The following are some of the main points to consider:

❑ What is the age of the exhibition hall? A newer building will probably have better facilities.
❑ Where is the physical location of the building? Lack of easy access and good parking facilities for visitors could affect attendance.
❑ What is the floor-loading capacity? This is particularly important if heavy equipment or vehicles are to be featured.
❑ Is there an adequate supply of electricity, water, compressed air, etc.?
❑ Are good catering facilities available?
❑ Are there adequate facilities if a conference is being planned to run concurrently with the exhibition?

Case study 21.3 Propak Africa

Propak Africa, a major packaging and processing show, is an example of an exhibition that demonstrates the importance of taking frequency into account. This exhibition had become a very successful and important one for the packaging industry, and was run in Johannesburg every third year. The timing of the exhibition was arranged to ensure that it did not conflict with other major international shows for the packaging industry. After running the exhibition for many years, it became evident that more than 25% of the exhibitors were based in the Western Cape, which is about 1 400 kilometres away from the Johannesburg area where the show was organised. By researching the market it was discovered that there was a large need for packaging in the Western Cape, which was why many of the packaging machine and product suppliers were operating from there. That region grows grapes, deciduous fruit and wheat. All of these agricultural products need to be packaged or processed into consumable food, juices and wine so that they can be exported to the international market or distributed around South Africa.

It was further discovered that some decision makers did not travel to the Propak Africa show in Johannesburg, and research confirmed the need for a regional packaging event in Cape Town. Arrangements were made for Propak Cape to be established and organised but it could not be held in the same year as the existing South African show, so it was billed for 18 months after the Johannesburg event and organised so as not to conflict with the world's largest packaging show, Interpack, held every third year in Düsseldorf, Germany. Propak Cape has also become an important show that attracts exhibitors from other parts of the country as well as from overseas, and does not conflict with the larger South African show.

21.3.5 Exhibition layout

A set of hall plans has to be prepared which will show the layout of the exhibition and the exhibitors' stands in the venue. Careful consideration must be given to stand sizes. The smallest is usually 3m × 3m (i.e. 9m²). Depending upon the products to be displayed, a range of larger stands should be designed into the hall plan. Only one plan should be kept in a central place to ensure that a stand is not sold twice to different exhibitors.

Aspects that must be taken into account when drawing up the plans are the following:

❏ Aisles, an entrance feature, registration area and service areas, etc. must be incorporated into the layout from the beginning. Maximum profit can be achieved through careful planning of the layout. As a rough rule of thumb these elements will use up 40–45% of the total space available in the hall. The smaller the space used for such purposes, the more space available for sales and the higher the income that can be achieved.

❏ Services such as electricity, water and compressed air, etc. will usually be available via underfloor ducts in the hall. Stand layout must take the position of ducting into account. In some older halls these services may be provided from overhead.

21.3.6 Conferences

As indicated previously, a conference is a valuable addition to an exhibition. It adds to the intellectual content, importance and prestige of the event, and ensures that quality visitors attend. Where possible, it is very important and highly desirable for the venue for the conference to be adjacent to the exhibition as this will make it easy for delegates to attend. A complimentary invitation ticket for admission to the show should be given to conference delegates with their conference packs. Allocating reserved parking to delegates can help to cement the relationship with the organisers of the conference.

21.3.7 Setting objectives

Clearly define what objectives can be expected from exhibiting. The objectives should be quantified so that it is possible to measure the degree of success after the exhibition is over. These will not necessarily be the volume of sales, although they might be. Other quantifiable objectives could be a specific number of leads, a specific number of new contacts, meeting a specific number of existing customers, meeting with previous customers, launching a new product, market research and others.

21.3.8 Visiting exhibitions

To obtain the maximum benefit from their visit to an exhibition, visitors need to plan in advance. Setting of objectives will help them to gain the maximum benefit from their visit, which means that they should be clear in their mind about their reasons for visiting an exhibition. This may be to look for a particular product or service, to catch up on the latest developments in the industry, to meet with suppliers who are exhibiting or to look for alternative ones, etc. In many cases the relative trade publication/s will publish a preview of the exhibition in the issue before the exhibition opens. Alternatively, it may be possible for visitors to obtain an advance copy of the catalogue or to ask the organisers for a list of exhibitors, which will enable them to plan a beneficial tour of the show.

Walking around an exhibition is a tiring process and it is often better to make two visits on successive days rather than try to cover the whole show in a single day.

The majority of exhibitors will have available brochures, pamphlets and technical literature about their products that visitors will want to collect for their information or for future decision making. It is advisable to have some sort of bag or container to hold brochures and samples, although often it will be possible to obtain a suitable bag at the exhibition, free of charge.

21.4 Operations

Having taken notice of the aspects leading up to the physical creation of the exhibition, we turn our attention to critical functions which will assist in bringing the final planning stages of the show to a logical conclusion. In this operations section, other practical details have to be arranged in advance of the commencement of the build-up period of the exhibition.

21.4.1 Time management

It is not possible to set out all the elements of running an exhibition in sequence, which makes it important to set out a critical path analysis for all the functions that need to be performed. Many functions overlap other activities, and attention needs to be given to all the elements as the event is set for a date – which is not moveable once this is done. Working back from the exhibition date and working forward from the inception will assist in setting the critical path to incorporate all the activities.

21.4.2 Appointment of contractors

Once an exhibitor has booked a stand there are numerous activities that the organiser has to undertake before the exhibition opens to ensure that it is a success. Most of this work is carried out by outside contractors and the organiser must make certain that those appointed are suitable for the work. The following is a list of the main areas that have to be covered.

❏ *Stand construction.* All the exhibitor gets from the organiser is a number of square metres of unimproved floor space in the hall. To make an effective display it is necessary to have a stand constructed. Smaller stands tend to use a shell scheme which generally consists of back and side walls, a fascia board to feature the exhibitor's name and a stand number. The organiser appoints a contractor to provide a shell scheme to the exhibitors who require this form of stand. For larger and more distinctive stands, a special design is needed and there are specialist companies of stand constructors who carry out this work. Exhibitors will normally appoint their own contractor.

❏ *Electrical fittings.* All stands require light and power points, and there are specialist electrical contractors who carry out this work. It is usual to have one single contractor to carry out this work for the whole show. Stand contractors prefer to appoint an electrical contractor with whom they usually work for the stands they are constructing.

❏ *Plumbing.* Some stands may require a water supply, and a plumbing contractor will need to be appointed. If the industry for which the exhibition is being organised needs water and waste or compressed air on a number of stands, the organiser should appoint a plumber. This may apply in food preparation, machine tools, printing and others. If only one or two stands require water, the stand contractors will be responsible for securing a plumber for their stand.

❏ *Other aspects.* Carpeting, furniture, security, fire prevention and forwarding agents will require contractors to be appointed for the exhibition. There are companies that specialise in contracting to shows. It is not worth it to skimp by handling these responsibilities personally. They require specialised skills, tools and equipment and are worth the cost of using the right suppliers. Products arriving from outside the country need to be cleared through customs, and experts need to be contracted to avoid tarnishing the reputation of the show or the organiser.

As catering at an exhibition frequently becomes an area of complaint from exhibitors and visitors, organisers need to spend time ahead of the event with the company supplying the catering. Often, it will be the venue owner who appoints the catering contractor. Prices, quality and service need to be addressed. Indicate what is expected in terms of the type of food, i.e. quick meals such as curry and rice, or fast foods such as sandwiches and hamburgers, all of which will depend upon the profile of the expected visitors. Ensure that the catering company delivers acceptable food, service and prices.

21.4.3 Other elements

❐ *Electricity, water, compressed air facilities.* At the time of taking over the hall/s, the organiser needs to check with the hall owner that these aspects are of an acceptable standard. Establish what remedial action to take if there is a power failure at any time. For example, are stand-by generators available?

❐ *Signage.* Insufficient signage can often be an irritation to visitors. Look at the venue from the position of people who are coming for the first time to the city where the exhibition is taking place. If they have had difficulty in finding the exhibition venue, they probably will not be in the best frame of mind. It is up to the organiser to make certain that the signage to the venue and at the exhibition (including the parking area) is clear and prominently displayed. Exhibition halls, catering facilities, toilets, the conference venue, banking and postal points, and the way to the exit are all important and must be well signposted. Once visitors have reached the exhibition hall they ought to be able to find the location of any particular stand without difficulty. Both at the entrance and in prominent positions in the hall it is helpful to have display boards indicating the position of all stands within the hall.

❐ *Visitor reception area.* The speedy and efficient registration of visitors is the mark of a professional organiser. At a trade/industrial exhibition, the majority of visitors will probably already be in possession of a complimentary ticket. However, there will be visitors who do not fall into this category but qualify for free entrance. Provision must be made for such people to be able to complete tickets without any difficulty. Pre-registration via the internet relieves the burden at the reception area. Facilities need to be made to make registration as simple and speedy as possible.

❐ *Overall security at the exhibition.* This entails guarding the parking areas, reception, catering and halls. It is the responsibility of the organisers, and entails employing a company which specialises in this type of work. The selected company must be given a clear brief as to the responsibilities that must be agreed and implemented, and regular checks must be carried out to make certain that the work is being done.

❐ *Parking.* This has to be allocated among exhibitors, visitors, press, conference delegates, VIPs and the organiser's staff. Clear signage is necessary to indicate the different areas, and during the exhibition it is advisable to have parking attendants to avoid any confusion.

❐ *Vehicle access.* During the build-up and breakdown periods, provision must be made for access for the various contractors. During the build-up period when contractors and exhibitors are bringing material into the hall/s, care must be taken to avoid aisles and entrances being blocked.

Always take the trouble to check that the toilets are clean and that the catering at the restaurant is of an acceptable standard. These are common areas of complaint from visitors and exhibitors

21.4.4 Assembling the exhibition

All the arrangements have been concluded, the contractors appointed, the exhibitors requirements recorded, floor plans finalised and the orders placed with the show contractors for the delivery of the exhibition. The organisation of the event, which might have taken a year or more to accomplish, has to be delivered in the space of a couple of days. This calls for cool heads and a well-oiled machine to take responsibility for the assembling of the event, as promised to the exhibitors. Contractors will descend on the venue expecting to be able to start their activities, but if the logical procedures have not been carried out, there will be chaos, giving a feeling of total disorganisation.

Organisation and teamwork are essential for an effective delivery. The operations team must ensure that the layout of the show is marked out as quickly as possible so that the official show electrician can lay all the electrical cables in the underfloor ducts. Concurrently, the plumbers have to install their plumbing for water and waste, the suppliers of compressed air must do their work, and any other cabling must be put in the ducts before the carpet layers can start their function, which must be done before the stand erectors begin their construction.

During this build-up period, the exhibitors start to arrive. Most will arrive on the last day, causing unparalleled pressure for the hard-pressed staff in the organisers' office. Because an exhibition is not an everyday occurrence and the setting is somewhat foreign, tempers can be a little frayed. The staff in the organisers' office needs to remain pleasant and calm. Exhibitors believe that having paid the organiser to exhibit, they are entitled to levels of service which are often unrealistic. The organiser needs to deliver good service and a good experience without going to unrealistic lengths. This is a fine line, as exhibitors should not be made to feel unwelcome, particularly as the organiser wants them to return in the future.

It cannot be emphasised enough that the systems employed in the organiser's office for handling exhibitors' requirements have to be highly efficient. Exhibitors must receive a level of service that gives them a feeling of being dealt with in a professional manner. They are in a strange environment and are likely to be quite stressed getting their stands organised. At that time in the overall event there will be many balls that have to be kept in the air at once. There is no room for inefficiency. Preplanning is absolutely essential, and attention to detail must be a reality, not a cliché. Pay attention to the systems used.

21.5 Marketing and sponsorship

Marketing of the show becomes extremely important. It deals with two main elements, namely attracting exhibitors and attracting visitors. Exhibition teams also need to design strategic plans to leverage sponsorship and exhibition sales to maximise revenue for an event. The strategy needs to consist of extensive research and marketing, personal communication and relationship management that delivers outcomes for the sponsors, the exhibitors, the visitors and the organiser.

Sponsorship opportunities for major suppliers are ideal for branding, for showing dominance and for selling products in an industry. Where sponsorship is sold, it provides an excellent, effective and useful method for improving exposure by capitalising on an event and for adding revenue for the organiser, thereby making a contribution to the overall profitably. Sponsorship can be negotiated by including the sponsor's name in the title of the show, or by adding it to advertisements, posters, radio commercials and signage, and any other aspect from which the sponsors believe that they derive benefit from being associated with the exhibition. The perceived benefit will be measured in proportion to the price they pay for being the sponsors.

21.5.1 Collecting and managing leads

It is necessary to carry out market research to ensure that there are potential customers for the product or service proposed. The reason for an event failing to live up to expectations can often be attributed to lack of adequate market research beforehand.

Two main areas to be researched are the number of potential exhibitors and of visitors. For instance while almost everybody uses safety matches for lighting a fire, if there is only one company that manufactures them, there would be not much scope for a match exhibition. There is an obligation on the part of the organiser for exhibitors to meet sufficient visitors and the converse applies for visitors.

21.5.2 Potential exhibitors

There are numerous sources for finding names and addresses, etc. of companies manufacturing and supplying particular products and services, such as trade directories; trade associations; trade publications; catalogues from similar exhibitions; and lists of members of professional bodies. The information obtained from these sources must be systematically recorded for use when the campaign to sell exhibition space to potential exhibitors commences.

21.5.3 Potential visitors

To assess the viability of the event, it is necessary to form as accurate a figure as possible of the number of potential visitors who could visit the exhibition. The reason for exhibiting is to meet sufficient potential customers, and a number of sources can be used to arrive at a conclusion:

1 There may well be professional people who would visit. For example, in the case of a building products exhibition, architects, quantity surveyors and consulting engineers would all be prospects. Their numbers can be obtained from the appropriate professional bodies.
2 The number of readers of trade and technical publications can be regarded as potential visitors.
3 An approach to some prominent potential exhibitors who are au fait with the industry can be a guide as to the number of potential visitors for the industry.
4 Contact with the relative trade association could be valuable. Once an overall total of potential visitors has been calculated, it will be necessary to estimate the percentage who could possibly attend the exhibition.

Once the first event has taken place it will be easier to arrive at the expected number of visitors for future exhibitions. As an indicator, experience in checking the figures of a large number of events locally and abroad shows that for every square metre of space sold on a trade exhibition, one to 1.5 visitors can be expected to attend. Similar information has not been established for a consumer event.

21.5.4 Professional/trade organisations

Apart from providing useful information with regard to potential exhibitors and visitors, establish a good working relationship with such bodies during the research stage. Through these contacts the organisation should be strongly encouraged to hold a conference alongside the exhibition. This adds to the prestige of the exhibition, attracts high-calibre individuals and is a useful publicity platform.

21.5.5 Overseas events

Exhibition organisers need to find out if any similar events have taken place in other countries. If an exhibition of this type has not been staged before, it will be necessary to find out why. This may indicate that the proposed exhibition would not be viable, or it might not have been thought of previously. Industries and products are constantly changing, and opportunities present themselves as a result. As an example, computers and cellphones handle many functions in today's business as well as personal lives, and could present opportunities that were not applicable in the past. On the other hand, if similar events have been held before, this is a positive sign and it would be important to find out as much information as possible about them. If time allows it would be very worthwhile to arrange a visit to such an event. Avoid clashing with overseas events of a similar nature by conducting effective research.

21.5.6 Exhibitor promotion

Unless sufficient exhibitors are present it will be a major disappointment for the

Case study 21.4 Drupa, Düsseldorf, Germany

Drupa in Düsseldorf is the largest printing show in the world, and is held every four years. In South Africa it is regarded as a must for senior technical staff in printing companies to visit. Every time Drupa is held there is an exodus from South Africa of senior people from the printing industry. Because of the importance of this exhibition, printing personnel from around the world attend. In South Africa the local printing show, Print Expo, needed to set dates at a suitable time so that it did not clash with Drupa, otherwise exhibitors would not participate. Many of them as well as their customers would be at Drupa, and a local show at that time would be a disaster from the start. The dates needed to be far enough away to ensure that if new products were being shown and were to be launched in South Africa later, there would be sufficient time to have them shipped and put on display. Equally, the producers would need enough time to be able to supply products, given that they may receive large orders at the overseas show.

visitors. The purpose of the exhibition is to put buyers and sellers together, and if either group is too small, the value of exhibiting and visiting is negated. Promotion of the event is of paramount importance for the current and the future events.

To achieve the budgeted volume of space sales, a carefully coordinated selling campaign must be planned and put into operation. The following indicates the main aspects that need to be covered:

❑ Develop a complete list of prospective exhibitors;

❑ Initiate a direct-mail selling campaign

to all prospects, and repeat at regular intervals throughout the selling campaign; and/or

☐ Make use of an electronic database that covers the industry, and send mail shots to that list at regular intervals. Get professional help as far as the content of the mailer is concerned;

☐ Endeavour to obtain editorial publicity about the exhibition in the appropriate trade/technical publications.

21.5.7 Visitor promotion

As previously mentioned, exhibitors will have signed up for a stand because they want to meet with the maximum number of the right people, and it is mainly the organisers' responsibility to produce this audience. Failure to adequately promote an exhibition is the main reason for an unsuccessful event, causing major dissatisfaction with exhibitors. Having said that it is mainly the organiser's responsibility to produce an audience, exhibitors must play a part in promoting the show in which they will be participating. The joint effort by organisers, exhibitors and associations is the most effective way to promote an exhibition.

It is up to the organisers to decide whether the visitor promotion campaign will be planned and carried out in-house or whether an outside agency will be used. Advertising agencies are often concerned with the promotion of consumer goods by making effective use of the daily press, radio and TV, all of which are expensive. A trade exhibition makes use of below-the-line methods which are less expensive and often more effective for industrial products.

A useful way to undertake the visitor promotion programme is to consider using some or all of the following:

☐ *Complimentary invitation tickets.* This is probably the most effective means of bringing in visitors. Tickets can be distributed in various ways, such as supplying exhibitors with enough to enable them to distribute them to their customers via salespersons, by direct mail, included with monthly statements or through agents. Produce electronic complimentary tickets and send them to customers and make use of databases.

☐ *Trade/technical publications.* They may include a ticket as an insert in the publication before the show takes place or provide the organiser with a subscriber list.

☐ *Professional bodies.* Organisations which are associated with the industry being featured at the exhibition may agree to distribute tickets to their members.

☐ *Trade/technical journals.* Advertisements and editorials may be placed in appropriate journals.

☐ *Supplements.* Trade journals or the daily press may agree to feature a special supplement about the exhibition from which they would derive income from advertising by exhibitors. This can be a good opportunity for publicity.

☐ *Street posters.* Posters create top-of-mind-awareness. If permitted, they are a useful reminder to potential visitors that the exhibition is taking place. It is important to keep the design of the poster simple – the name of the exhibition, venue and dates are all that is required.

☐ *Radio.* This medium is also an excellent reminder. The radio-advertising programme can be commenced shortly before the exhibition starts. If possible, the best time to advertise is when potential visitors are driving to or from work.

- ❏ *Advertisements.* These are expensive in the daily press and on TV. If the budget permits, though, these media can be considered.

21.5.8 Public relations (PR) activities

To ensure success, the maximum PR exposure both to prospective exhibitors and to visitors is required. Unless the organiser has an internal PR department, it is advisable to appoint an outside agency. Such organisations usually have excellent connections with press, radio and TV, and can obtain more exposure than the company itself can. PR to prospective exhibitors should begin as soon as possible, whereas PR to attract visitors should commence closer to the opening of the show. However, no PR exposure is ever wasted.

21.5.9 Exhibitor services manual

This manual is published by the organiser and is issued to all exhibitors well in advance of the exhibition. It is often published in hardcopy and also available to exhibitors on the internet. The organisers issue a unique code to each exhibitor for them to gain access and to place orders electronically. It contains information of a general nature, such as any restrictions imposed by the venue owner that could affect stand construction, and dates and times when the halls will be open for build-up and breakdown. There will be forms by means of which the exhibitor can order requirements for a shell scheme, furniture, carpets, stand cleaning, electrical, telephones, etc. The manual will also contain a section on the exhibition catalogue so that exhibitors can submit the information which is to appear about their company, and if required place an order for advertisements in the catalogue.

In some instances the organisers may issue a set of rules and regulations covering the exhibition.

21.5.10 Show catalogue

The exhibition catalogue is a vital element providing information about the show and the exhibitors. In the case of major events, it acts as a reference book about the show and the industry with an effective lifespan of one or more years. The responsibility for the production of the catalogue rests with the organiser. However, the use of a reputable trade publication to produce a catalogue is the most effective way of producing one. The emphasis is on established publishers because they know the industry and understand publishing, which is a skilled profession. The biggest problem in the compilation of the catalogue is obtaining the necessary information from exhibitors. However, when appointing a publisher, make sure that the end product will be available on time and with the information the organiser requires, such as the full name and address of each exhibitor and their stand location.

The catalogue generally contains the following information:
- ❏ A message from the organiser;
- ❏ Hall plans of the show;
- ❏ An alphabetical listing of exhibitors with brief details of their products on show;
- ❏ A product index;
- ❏ Exhibitor advertisements, which are paid for; and
- ❏ Industry information such as the names of associations and other industry details.

21.5.11 Research at an exhibition

Some organisers will carry out research on the attitudes and opinions of both exhibitors and visitors to a show. For organisers wishing to provide exhibitors with accurate information and visitors' views, it is essential to use professional research organisations. The basic reasons for this are to highlight any problems that occurred during the event so as to avoid a recurrence in the future and to obtain information that can be used to sell the next exhibition. Research is expensive but if the information is used to give valuable information to the exhibitor and thereby grow the event, the money will be well spent. Whether or not this type of research is employed, organisers should create a questionnaire to be sent to exhibitors to get their feedback on the event.

Exhibitor research

The close of the show is not the ideal time to ask exhibitors to fill in a questionnaire. These can be distributed with the request that they be returned to the organiser when completed. Alternatively they can be posted or emailed to exhibitors shortly after the end of the show. Feedback is important and should be encouraged. Following are some aspects of exhibitors' views it may be helpful to get feedback on: whether they will take part in the next exhibition; facilities at the show, i.e. venue; length of the exhibition; opening and closing times; promotion of the show; services provided by contractors; parking; catering facilities; availability and condition of toilets; visitors, i.e. numbers, categories, perceived quality, enquiries and orders obtained, etc.

Visitor research

Information about visitor's attitudes and views are usually obtained by means of an exit interview. The questionnaire used should not be too lengthy as the visitor has probably spent several hours at the exhibition, is tired and wants to get home. The questions asked should cover such aspects as: name; employer; position; professional qualifications; buying authority; views on the venue and facilities; products on display; attitude of exhibitor's staff; orders placed at the exhibition or any that are likely to be placed in the future; how the visitor heard about the exhibition and whether he or she is likely to visit the next one.

As mentioned previously, it is worthwhile employing a professional market research company to carry out visitor research. They will advise and decide how many interviews need to be obtained to get a statistically accurate result.

21.6 Risks in organising exhibitions

With any type of organising there will be risks that have to have special attention paid to them, and exhibitions are no exception. The main matters will relate to security and fire, but other issues are also relevant and attention is drawn to some of these below.

21.6.1 Security

Worldwide, security always remains a risk that has become particularly relevant in the current prevailing circumstances throughout the world. Security is a problem at exhibitions and similar events where large numbers of people are gathered together. Organisers must be aware of this situation and take the necessary measures to protect exhibitors and visitors against potential risks.

Bomb threats have to be taken seriously and the security consultants must be tasked with providing written directions and systems to deal with such hazards. Included in their advice will be access control to the exhibition.

21.6.2 Stand security

The security of exhibitor's stands and equipment is the responsibility of the exhibitor, and this point must be made quite clear right from the beginning. A company appointed by the organisers will be available to provide security on individual stands. Exhibitors are responsible for arranging their own insurance for the products on their stands as well as for the stand construction in cases where a specially constructed stand is erected.

21.6.3 Fire protection

Check with the venue owner that the required standard of fire protection equipment is in place. Record the telephone number of the nearest fire brigade station. Ensure that an evacuation procedure in the event of fire has been given to all exhibitors, and that the organisers' staff is fully aware of the action to be taken in such an eventuality.

21.6.4 Abandonment insurance

An abandonment insurance policy is available from some insurance companies where insurance can be purchased against the show being cancelled due to circumstances beyond the control of the organiser. This might be considered expensive, but will enable the reimbursement for space and other costs to be made to exhibitors. A case in point would be if the exhibition venue burnt down and other arrangements could not be made to stage the show. The organisers may find themselves out of pocket after refunding the exhibitors and paying for promotional and other costs.

21.6.5 General

The capital required for organising an exhibition is relatively low when compared with other businesses, but the risks are high. The organiser is bringing together a new group of people involved in a particular industry and if their objectives and purposes are not met, they may collectively arrange to sue the organiser for non-performance. In most cases of failure, the organiser has usually not carried out an adequate programme to promote the event. If an audience of quality in adequate numbers is not attracted to satisfy most of the exhibitors, fingers will quickly be pointed at the organiser. This is a poor reflection on the exhibition, on the industry being showcased, and on the businesses that have agreed to support the show, as well as for the exhibition industry. Everyone suffers when a poor exhibition is organised. Visitors often become exhibition wary when they see new exhibitions which may apparently relate to their business, but they cannot afford the time or cost to visit another new event that may not justify the effort. It is the organisers' responsibility to do sufficient effective promotion of the event to attract an audience of quality.

21.7 Summary

Many factors have to be considered when organising an exhibition and most of the activities associated with organising have been addressed in this chapter. The order as laid out in this chapter is not necessarily the order in which to organise an exhibition. There will be aspects that need to be done concurrently and in a different sequence. The overriding matter of importance is that attention to detail is critical. Organisers have to do research before they embark on a project, which could entail months of work. It is more effective to delay the staging of an exhibition to produce an outstanding and better event than to hurry it along and run a mediocre or poor event. Payment will come from the marketing budgets of customers and they are looking for a ROI on the time and money they have invested.

Around the world, exhibition organisers of repute belong to an association within their own country, which will practice a code of ethics. Each association and country will require organisers to adhere to their own set of guidelines for their industry. Although differing from association to association, in overall terms they will include principles such as:

❑ ensuring that organisers deal with visitors and exhibitors with professionalism, integrity and courtesy;
❑ fostering mutual respect and trust among individuals and organisations within the exhibition industry with regard to business dealings as members with other members, clients and the public in general;
❑ embracing honesty, integrity, fair dealing, professionalism and accountability;
❑ conducting business in accordance with accepted principles of honesty and speaking truthfully in all business practices to pursue their client's legitimate objectives;
❑ undertaking to treat all knowledge of a client's intentions or business organisation as confidential;
❑ displaying integrity and fair dealing with clients, competitors and vendors to foster healthy competition and the creation of value; and
❑ being accountable and responsible for business dealings.

Throughout the world there are effective exhibition industry associations operating to serve the industry in that country. They watch the industry activities, advise organisers on new developments and carry out research on behalf of exhibitions locally as well as in some cases internationally. Their purpose is to raise the standard of exhibitions and ensure that organisers apply ethical practices. The associations are governing bodies made up of organisers and one of their many functions is to deal with issues that might arise when an exhibitor has had a less-than-acceptable service level from the organiser.

Questions for research

1 Evaluate the purpose that exhibitions strive to achieve.
2 Assess the role timing plays in organising an exhibition.
3 Determine the difference between exhibitor and visitor promotion.
4 Determine how an organiser can ensure that the event provides visitors with the maximum benefit from visiting an exhibition.
5 Critically evaluate the benefits that outside contractors provide in organising an exhibition.
6 Determine the relevance of research before, during and after an exhibition.

Recommended websites

The following internet sites can be browsed for interesting and informative information:

AEO – The Association of Event Organisers Ltd, UK:. http://www.aeo.org

AUMA – Ausstellungs und Messe-Ausschuss der Deutschen Wirtschaft e.V.: http://www.auma.de

CEIR – Center for Exhibition Industry Research, USA: http://www.ceir.org

CEIR – ROI Toolkit: http://roitoolkit.exhibitsurveys.net/Home/Welcome.aspx

EXSA – The Exhibition Association of South Africa: http://www.exsa.co.za

IAEM – The International Association of Exhibition Managers, USA: http://www.iaem.org

UFI – The Global Association of the Exhibition Industry: http://www.ufi.org

Photo: World Travel Market

Photo: Dimitri Tassiopoulos

Photo: EIBTM

Photo: Zoë Moosman

22

Political, civic and government events

Jo-Ansie van Wyk

Abstract

This chapter equips the student and practitioner to plan, manage and evaluate a political, a government and a civic event. Political events are hosted by political actors such as, for example, governments, civil society organisations (such as interest groups and political parties) and inter-governmental organisations in order to commemorate an historical event, inaugurate a public official, celebrate national public holidays, interact with communities on social service delivery, campaign for an election to public office, create awareness of a socio-political issue or negotiate a political decision. Political events require attention to media accreditation, protocol and security. The aim of this chapter is to enable the administration, design, marketing, operations and risk prevention of a political event.

Chapter objectives

After you have read this chapter you should be able to:
- ❐ define political, government and civic events;
- ❐ explain the objectives of political events;
- ❐ discuss the developmental impact of political events;
- ❐ administer tools for political events;
- ❐ design tools for political events;
- ❐ identify and manage all operational aspects of a political event;
- ❐ market aspects of a political event; and
- ❐ identify and manage risks associated with a political event.

22.1 Introduction

This chapter focuses on various aspects related to managing and staging events with a political nature or purpose in order to achieve various political objectives. Furthermore, we introduce you to political events and their significance and objectives; discuss their developmental (tourism and investment) potential; establish a process of planning, decision making, implementing and managing; identify major stakeholders and other participants; determine fundraising and sponsorship needs; go into protocol and accreditation issues; identify the potential security threats of events; plan, and equip you to research, plan, manage and promote events celebrating historically significant political events as tourism attractions.

Staging a political event flawlessly offers noteworthy rewards to the event manager. Some are financial, others are more opportunities and greater prestige. Top political event managers/organisers take a strategic and comprehensive approach by building a solid organisational structure; facilitating collaboration between all stakeholders; managing suppliers, sponsors and donors effectively; communicating often; and tracking all potential security and other risks, and their potential impact

and develop contingency plans (Kearney, 2002: internet).

It is beyond the scope of this chapter to discuss all the relevant knowledge domains. The approach to this chapter will be to highlight specific aspects that are of significance to political event planning and management, and are presented further below.

22.2 Political, civic and government events: definitions and objectives

What constitutes *politics*, or the *political* or a *political event*? Politics can be defined as the process of 'who gets what, when, where and how'. This definition assumes the presence of decision makers (stakeholders); some form of authority (people with a mandate, planners and managers, i.e. *who*); objectives (see below); position, interests or power to be achieved (*what*); a time frame (*when*); events, policies or campaigns (*how*); and at what venue and level, be it governmental, provincial or local (*where*). Whenever there is competition (*get*) in any society for scarce resources (be it water, land, jobs, contracts, social services, power or a political appointment), this competition can be defined as *political*.

Civic and government events are

political events. For this reason, the terms *civic*, *political* and *government events* are sometimes used interchangeably. However, these three types of events correspond and differ in some aspects. General political and civic events fall outside government events as they are often driven by formal and informal organisations in society, and are paid for by private funds. Whereas government events are predominantly aimed at promoting government policies, attracting more votes and maintaining power, political and civic events aim to raise awareness of socio-economic issues and government policy deficiencies such as lack of service delivery, or ultimately to gain power.

Further examples of political, civic and government events are cited in the box below

Civic or civil society refers to associations and other organised bodies which are intermediate between the state and the family (Bealey, 1999: 59). A civic event is a carefully planned, organised, managed and implemented/hosted event by either individual citizens or a community organisation to highlight awareness of a particular socio-political issue of interest to the community, or outsourced to professional event managers (see case study 22.1). Examples of citizens' political participation, and hence political in nature, civic events have a political purpose and message with the intention to create social awareness and to reach as many people as possible by a variety of means, such as hosting an event, marketing and the media, and to reach a specific objective or a number of objectives. Owing to their activist nature, civic events are sometimes associated with conflict and violence. For this reason, even democratic governments have placed some legal restrictions on the hosting of civic

Selected examples of politically related events

- ❏ Political party and non-governmental organisation (NGO) canvassing and/or campaign events;
- ❏ Fundraising activities for political parties, interest groups and NGOs;
- ❏ Political party conventions and conferences;
- ❏ Government-community meetings (so-called town hall meetings);
- ❏ National, provincial and local government elections;
- ❏ Distribution of flyers and pamphlets during elections or awareness campaigns;
- ❏ Protest marches;
- ❏ Political rallies;
- ❏ Public speeches or statements by official office holder;
- ❏ Lobbying;
- ❏ Funeral of a political or public official;
- ❏ Inaugurations and commemorations;
- ❏ Public holiday events;
- ❏ Political road shows;
- ❏ Campaign management and communication;
- ❏ Issue management;
- ❏ Fundraising;
- ❏ Public opinion surveys;
- ❏ Investment and inter-governmental conferences; and
- ❏ Political demonstrations.

events. These restrictions are often enacted in legislation and local government policy papers, and related to, inter alia, the time, location, scope and details of the organisers of the event. Although some of the restrictions are also related to political and government events, civic events such as protests and marches can very often result in violence as they are a more direct mode of expressing grievances.

Case study 22.1 Example of a picket as a civic event: 'Stop French Hijab Ban' picket

3 February 2004
In a great show of anger to the proposed Hijab ban in France, many across the globe observed an International Day of Solidarity with Muslim women of France on 17 January 2004. Islamic Forum Europe once again calls upon all freedom-loving people to picket outside French embassies and diplomatic missions against the proposed ban on 3 February 2004 when the French parliament deliberates on the issue.

We call upon Muslim governments, Islamic leaders, organisations and mosques to raise the issue on the occasion of Eid al-Adha. President Chirac's ban on religious wear deliberately targets Muslim females who wear the headscarf, and signals one of the greatest setbacks for freedom and justice.

Source: Islamic Forum Europe (2004: internet)

The constitutions of most democratic states guarantee all its citizens freedom of speech, association, assembly and expression. The importance and significance of political events lie in expressing these freedoms, achieving a number of political objectives, having some tourism potential, creating employment and generating business opportunities.

Some of the objectives of a political event are to:

❑ promote public policy or to harness public support for a new direction in government policy;

❑ increase political power and influence by, inter alia, winning elections, be it on national, provincial or local level. Political parties canvass for votes and campaign during elections. These campaigns, for example, include a number of events such as political party rallies, various public meetings, and advertisements on the internet (including Facebook), in newspapers, on television and on the radio;

❑ commemorate an event of historical significance such as an election victory and the re-burial of victims of political killings such as the funeral of Saartjie Baartman (the so-called 'Hottentot Venus') in 2003 in the Eastern Cape province in South Africa, Holocaust victims of World War II in Germany and those killed during the Rwanda genocide of 1994;

❑ celebrate and commemorate public holidays with historical political significance;

❑ conclude international treaties, conventions and agreements;

❑ communicate, create awareness of and educate about an issue of public, social or international importance in order to influence government(s) to address the issue. This can include events to campaign to reinstate or abolish the death penalty, to protest against crime in a march by business people, or to create awareness of child abuse. Since 2000, the South African government, for example, has conducted *Izimbizos* (similar to American town hall meetings) with communities. The Izimbizo Programme of the South African Presidency is a political event that includes the President, the deputy president, ministers, provincial premiers, members of provincial executive councils (MECs), mayors, municipal councillors and ordinary South Africans. The purpose of these government-driven events is to facilitate discussions between communities and decision makers (The Presidency, 2009: internet).

22.3 The developmental impact of staged political events

Political events have major development (tourism and investment) potential and impacts – especially when held at historically important locations and venues. A tourist can be described as a person visiting or invited to an area for business, family affairs, political activities, celebrations, education, sport or holiday away from his or her hometown as well as spending money in a location other than the one where he or she earns it. Furthermore, tourism's economic and political dimensions have implications for the allocation of and competition for power (and hence decision making) and resources, and access to these resources (such as budgets) within host communities, cultural representation, socialisation and the income of a particular community or province.

By their nature, governments and their decision makers have the power to decide 'who gets what, where, when and how' in the development of tourism. This is illustrated in government's establishment of tourism ministries and tourism development agencies. Moreover, only governments issue passports to their citizens to travel, governments institute visa requirements, and governments regulate procedures for the conclusion of international agreements and foreign exchange transactions. In undemocratic countries, the government even issues travel documents for its citizens to travel from one of its regions to another as free movement of people is strictly regulated to, inter alia, prevent political events from taking place. It is also often governments that warn their citizens not to visit conflict and war-prone regions.

Major political, government or civic events are globally part of the attraction of a particular tourist destination. Top tourist destinations also include politically relevant sites and locations such as, for example, the Great Wall of China; Gorée Island; the Vatican; Robben Island; Mecca; Jewish concentration camps in, for example, Germany and Poland; and Versailles outside Paris. In 2006, Soweto outside Johannesburg (South Africa), for example, attracted nearly 2 000 tourist visits per day (*Finweek*, 2006: 43–44). Soweto is famous for its uprisings against the apartheid government.

Political campaigns of political parties and civil society organisations are good business. Barack Obama's presidential campaign was reported to have amounted to US$1 billion. It is estimated that the African National Congress (ANC), a political party in South Africa, for example, has spent about R40 million on campaign T-shirts only (*Financial Mail*, 2009: internet).

Globally, governments as political actors regularly host national and international political events. Mega political events include conferences of intergovernmental organisations such as, for example, the

Non-Alignment Movement (NAM), the United Nations (UN), the Group of Eight Industrialised Countries (G8), the African Union (AU) and the Association of Southeast Asian Nations (ASEAN). As governmental events, intergovernmental or multilateral conferences involve delegations for various governments, and focus on issues of mutual interest. Government events also include, among others, state visits, peace negotiations, presidential inaugurations and summits. A summit refers to a meeting between heads of state or heads of government for diplomatic or propaganda purposes (Berridge & James, 2003: 255). South Africa's hosting of the United Nations' World Summit on Sustainable Development (WSSD) in 2002, for example, had a positive impact on the country's economy. The South African government spent R449.8 million on the event, with the private sector and international community's contribution amounting to R474.7 million. Delegates were reported to have spent R1.6 billion, and 13 870 employment opportunities were created (Van der Westhuizen, 2006: 145–146).

The impact of staging and commemorating political events often goes beyond mere investment and tourism. It also stirs so-called 'wars of memories' between political victims, political survivors and political oppressors. One such example is the protest against the opening of the Centre for the French Presence in Algeria in France, which is regarded by some as a one-sided depiction of France's 130 years of colonialism in Algeria (*Sunday Times*, 2009: 9).

Countries that have emerged from a history of violence and war such as, for example, Rwanda and Croatia, have been able to re-interpret, commemorate and commodify these political events. Both these countries experienced 'ethnic cleansing' or genocide during the 1990s. Commenting on Croatia, Goulding and Domic (2009: 99) write:

> In societies that have undergone such turmoil the reification of history and its symbolic meaning goes beyond national identification, it permeates the very essence of selfhood and cannot be divorced from the prevailing economic, political and social conditions. Museums and heritage sites, road names, fountains, festivals and re-enactments become more than a leisure or aesthetic experience, rather they operate as 'sign systems' which reinforce an intense sense of Croatian identity.

The construction of heritage, or the commemoration of a political event, has often been criticised as commodifying a politically relevant site or event. This criticism has often been expressed vis-à-vis Robben Island (off Cape Town) and Cape Town's Victoria and Alfred (V&A) Waterfront in South Africa. With regard to the latter, Worden and Van Heyningen (1996: 215–233) argue that, in this case, the past, heritage or public history can easily be controlled by private companies. The event manager should be sensitive to corporate presentations of historical events. Worden and Van Heyningen (1996: 233) warn that '[h]istory under this kind of control rarely perceived the need to recover and preserve the varieties of human experience, bad as well as good. And heritage is interpreted as aesthetic physical environment rather than as human consciousness'.

22.4 Administration of a political event

Political actors, as clients, often outsource the planning, implementation and management of political events to professional event management companies and/or consultants with a proven track record. Politicians simply either do not have the skills or the time to plan and manage an event. Political event consultancy firms should be able to offer the following political event management services:

- Briefings for political stakeholders;
- Briefings on government tender processes;
- Issue management;
- Government relations;
- Grassroots organising;
- Political fundraising;
- Financial management and reporting;
- Planning, implementing and managing an event with a specific purpose;
- Lobbying;
- Training seminars;
- Public meetings and conferences;
- Acting as political power brokers and creating access to key decision makers;
- Managing election campaigns and election contribution campaigns;
- Organising high-level conferences, commemorations, inaugurations and celebrations;
- Organising celebrity endorsement of a political event;
- Facilitating the attendance of key government officials at major events;
- Finding and managing the venue;
- Arranging accommodation for participants; and
- Conducting evaluations of the event.

The need for a political event (such as those mentioned above) is identified by a political player (the client) who either approaches an events manager in government or an events management company, or institutes a bidding/tendering process. The client identifies the type of event required to be arranged as well as the purpose it aims to achieve. The proposed special political event is researched, budgeted and presented to the highest political authority for consideration. The goal is to receive approval for the organisation to participate or produce the event with a political impact.

One important aspect of managing a political event is regular consultations with various stakeholders (see figure 22.1). Owing to the nature of politics, various political interests are at stake. When stakeholders and their interests are not taken into account, the success of an event can be jeopardised. Governments often makes presentations to parliament or the country's legislature (House of Commons, Senate or National Assembly). Similar consultations are held with local governments, representatives of civil society sectors such as organised labour, business, academia, the media, agriculture, religious groups and diplomatic missions. These representatives were required to consult with their constituencies and give feedback at subsequent meetings of this nature.

Personnel are appointed or assigned by advertising, screening, appointing and training (if needed). Other members of the planning team such as those responsible for finances, marketing, logistics, client relations, operations and legal matters are appointed. A task team is usually appointed by cabinet, consisting of government ministers and directors-general of the government departments responsible for supervising the planning and staging the presidential inauguration. Next, the assignment of an event manager and committee as well as which departments or sectors will participate in and coordinate the event occurs. This is often identified by a government's communications institution

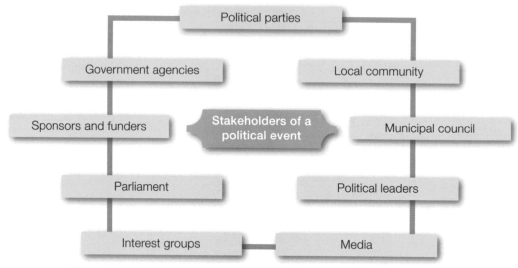

Figure 22.1 Political stakeholders and actors involved in political events

and the victorious political party, who jointly appoints one or more project managers. Event planning starts months prior to the event, including the publication of event-related publications outlining the purpose, challenges, structures, processes, phases and themes for the event.

Whether a bidding process is required or not, the event manager is expected to present preliminary bid proposals to the organising committee. Once the organising committee has evaluated the proposal, consultations with the event manager take place in order to reach an agreement on matters such as the scope, impact, budget and nature of the event. Approval of the proposal means that the event manager can now plan the event in greater detail.

22.5 Design of a political event

When designing a political event, the following aspects should be addressed: catering, content, entertainment, environment, production, programme and theme.

Case studies 22.2 and 22.3 include details of events related to a presidential inauguration and the celebration of national public holidays.

Political celebrations often include entertainment such as the performance of top recording artists, bands and mass choirs. This requires the identification of artists in line with the event theme, signing contracts with artists and appointing choreographers.

An internet site of the event should be constructed as well as a media and marketing campaign initiated. Media operations such as accreditation, a media centre, licensing of broadcast rights, as well as regular press statements and conferences about the event should be organised during this phase. In the run-up to the main events, the Department of Foreign Affairs markets the country abroad, and stages events in foreign countries where the country has diplomatic representation.

Case study 22.4 contains a generic guide to organising a picket line as an example of a civic event. Note the important aspects of civic events.

22.6 Marketing of a political event

The 'political marketplace' has undergone several changes, including a decline in political party membership and registered support; a decline in party identification; global lower voter turnout; the increased importance of television, and information and communications technology; a proliferation of political issues and actors; and the erosion of traditional bases of segmentation or cleavages in the electorate and supporters such as class and geography, while complex new segments – based on religion, race, class and lifestyle – have become increasingly more important (Lees-Marshment, 2009: 6).

The objective of marketing of a political event is, among others, to drive public opinion, create awareness, advance a particular political ideology, win elections, pass legislation, and celebrate a historical event. In order to achieve these and other politically relevant objectives, the event manager has to market the event. Examples of political event-related marketing include public opinion polling, campaigning through SMS, Twitter, email and Facebook, telephone campaigns, political fundraising campaigns and candidate introduction advertisements.

The marketing knowledge domain of a political event includes various functional units, which are discussed below. In the case of governmental political events, the event manager in consultation with government's communication services will plan and execute marketing of an event. Most civic and political actors also have a communications department responsible for media and marketing.

❑ Prior to the conceptualisation and staging of a political event, research should be conducted on the objective of the event, the intended target audience, and its demographics and needs. Once a profile of the target audience has been developed marketing plans focusing on difference market segmentation (the youth, elderly, women, etc.) should be developed. For each of these segments, different marketing messages and mediums should be employed.

❑ Materials management includes the design and distribution of flyers, brochures, invitations, tickets and programmes. Banners, billboards, posters, blogging, CD-ROMs, DVDs and MP3s are other types of marketing materials that can be distributed to the target audience.

❑ Political actors such as organisations, governments, political parties and community organisations often develop a unique identity. These actors make use of political merchandise such as commemorative T-shirts, buttons, caps, flags, banners and umbrellas. Merchandising management includes the design, manufacture, packaging and distribution of this merchandise. Ambush marketing should be prevented by issuing licences to print and distribute these items.

❑ The promotion management of a political event can include advertising, digital and television broadcasting, internet, ceremonies and celebrity endorsement of the event.

❑ Public relations management includes the compilation of media contact lists and media liaison. The latter includes media conferences on the political event where media kits are distributed, interviews with relevant decision makers are conducted and media releases are issued. Public relations management can also include a media preview related to an event. For this reason, spokespersons for each event should be appointed and introduced to the media as a contact person.

❑ Most political events tend to be free or by invitation only. Sales management of a political event is related merchandise sales, access to the venue and sponsorship sales.

❑ Securing funds for any political event often determines its scope. In order to address this need, sponsors and donors are often approached. The benefits for companies that sponsor an event include contributions to the event programme, marketing, networking opportunities and privileged access to main stakeholders of the event. Sponsoring political events is a controversial issue as the sponsor is perceived to be receiving influence, access and special treatment in return. In most countries, sponsoring political events is regulated by law and official codes of practice, which requires sponsors and recipients to declare this, none more so that the presidential elections in the US. For the 2008 US elections, for example, the John McCain campaign received sponsorships from Fortune 500 companies including Merrill Lynch, Citigroup Inc, Morgan

Stanley and Goldman Sacs (Centre for Responsive Politics, 2009: internet). In undemocratic countries such as, for example, Ethiopia (Alliance, 2009: internet) and Zimbabwe (*IRIN News*, 2008: internet), sponsoring political events is sometimes limited, banned, prevented or criminalised. Once funds are secured, stakeholder management becomes more important. Managing and executing political events is costly, and if unregulated and not transparent, may compromise democratic values such as equality and transparency.

22.7 Operation of a political event

Hosts of political events often require media accreditation, which refers to complying with the event host's access requirements for the sole purpose of covering the event for a specified media outlet. Whether on local, state, national or international level, proper protocol is vital in assuring that relations between the officials of organisations and governments (be it at local, provincial, national or international level) are conducted with minimum friction and maximum efficiency. Protocol prescribes the forms and procedures that constitute acceptable and efficient relations and conduct. It provides information on the order of precedence, ranking officials every level from the president down; on titles and forms of address to be used in written and oral communications; on calling cards, invitations and replies; on official entertaining and private parties; on table seating arrangements; on flag etiquette; and much more (McCaffree, Innis & Sand, 2002: internet).

Protocol arrangements for inter-governmental events include, for example, travel arrangements of heads of state and government, reception at the state protocol lounge at the airport of arrival, a guard of honour, transport and motorcades, clearance of private aircraft, accommodation and the provision of VIP security (DFA, 2009: 1–10).

Media accreditation is strictly reserved for members of the press – print, photographic, radio, television, film, news agencies and online media – who represent a bona fide media organisation. In the case of United Nations events, for example, only media professionals of countries recognised by the UN General Assembly are accredited on proof of a track record of reporting for media organisations on international affairs. The UN does not accredit media professionals of the information outlets of non-governmental organisations. Moreover, media organisations whose activities run counter to the principles of the Charter of the United Nations are not accredited (UN (n.d.): internet).

Event managers should establish a media centre, which is a central location for the dissemination of event-related information prior to the event day. On event day the media centre should be run by the political actors' communications and media team staffed with specialist media practitioners including media and event professionals. Media workspaces should include internet-enabled desktop computers, desks and tables, power supply, a reception and enquiries desk, technological support staff, video and sound feeds, photographic pool pictures, and screens to monitor the pools. The media centre has to operate from early until the close of proceedings. Media statements and speeches delivered should be distributed to accredited media representatives.

Political events are sometimes staged at historically significant venues, buildings or areas. A venue should be able to house the expected number of people from a logistical point of view. Venues such as, for example, Robben Island (off Cape Town), Red Square (Moscow), Ground Zero (New York), Tiananmen Square (Beijing) and the pyramids at Giza (Cairo) are often used for major political events.

The scope of the event determines which technology should be made available. Event support systems, computer hardware and software programs, media information systems, internet, and ticketing/access should be determined, as well as contingency plans. During the 2008 US presidential campaign, for example, parties cited the major role played by the internet in their campaign. Political event managers were quick to harness the power of technology, and made use of Facebook, Twitter, SMSs, internet and their websites.

Computer software programs enable event managers to distribute information and analyses as well as to execute management functions electronically. Examples of these include automated invitations to and attendance of political events, surveying the benefits and costs from attending and managing a particular event, as well as conducting online public opinion polls on issues which, inter alia, track political risk management. Events information technology (IT) corporations often apply call-centre technology in managing political events and use political message dialling systems through which they broadcast and market upcoming political events, as well as party positions on issues and related news to targeted audiences. Event managers use this system, for example, to play a particular political message, introduce candidates and/or issues, promote an upcoming political event, conduct political surveys and touch-phone responses, and political fundraising. Lastly, state-of-the-art software has the ability to generate real-time reports, graphs and statistics, an important evaluating service to measure the effectiveness and impact of the political event or campaign. This includes all the physical requirements such as audiovisual equipment, seating arrangements, signs and table settings.

When deciding on a venue, a number of important aspects related to the smooth running of the event are important to consider. Some of the services that should be offered by a venue should include:

- access to airports, bus and railway stations, and taxi stands;
- access to accommodation facilities (if required);
- a business centre with telephones, fax, postal, internet and courier services;
- facilities for physically challenged persons;
- a computerised message service;
- catering facilities;
- medical services;
- secure parking;
- suites for private meetings;
- security teams and surveillance cameras;
- automatic fire detection and sprinkler systems; and
- banking and foreign exchange facilities.

Case study 22.5 includes an operations checklist that can be applied to political events.

Case study 22.5 A summarised operations checklist for a generic political event

- ❐ *What is the purpose of the event?*
- ❐ *Who will be involved in the planning, management and staging of the event?*
- ❐ *What is the programme for the event?*
- ❐ *What are the requirements pertaining to the management of this event?*
- ❐ *Where will the event take place? What locations were identified?*
- ❐ *What are the requirements for ticketing, sales and access to the event?*
- ❐ *Will any procession, parades, crowd control, seating and staging of an activity be required? Should open spaces be left to allow for the free movement of people?*
- ❐ *What decorations and/or décor (such as flags, banners and posters) will be required and allowed?*
- ❐ *Should any special provision be made for animals (dogs and/or horses) for crowd control, or facilities for use by disabled persons?*
- ❐ *What assistance is provided for disabled individuals?*
- ❐ *What are the infrastructure and transport requirements for the event? What provision should be made for infrastructure? Who will manage and set these up?*
- ❐ *What power needs exist? Should power generators, phone lines and computer access be organised?*
- ❐ *What special equipment is required for, for example, medical emergencies, access control, security and vehicles? Who will supply these?*
- ❐ *What equipment, tools and supplies are needed during the planning process as well as on the event day?*
- ❐ *What security risks may arise? What type of access control will be followed?*
- ❐ *What command and communications functions should be catered for? Who is responsible for specific functions on the day of the event?*
- ❐ *What programmes and activities should be planned for and compiled?*
- ❐ *Are volunteers going to assist in the event?* If so, advertising, screening, appointing, training, clothing and scheduling of staff will be required. Furthermore, identification and access control should be arranged for.
- ❐ *What directions, parking, loading zones and signage are needed?* Adequate and secure parking; access control with clear directions and seating arrangements; public transportation; and transportation of event organisers, the general public, VIPs and equipment, as well as the transportation of materials is needed. Arrangements should also be made for the transportation of materials after the event.
- ❐ *What guidelines should be followed during accreditation? Who should be accredited? How should accreditation be indicated?*
- ❐ *What arrangements should be made for safety, security and medical needs during the event?* These arrangements should include first aid, emergency response and accessibility, comfort stations such as ablution facilities, shelters from the weather, security force presence and waste disposal.
- ❐ *What provision should be made for hospitality and refreshments?*
- ❐ *What diplomatic protocol should be followed?*
- ❐ *What command and operations facilities should be in place?*
- ❐ *How will communications be managed before, during and after the event? Will any celebrities and artists be appearing?*

IIII➡

❐ *What kind of technical facilities are needed?* These could include electricity, communications systems, media liaison, sound systems, public address systems, video screens, computer screens, audiovisual equipment and those relating to broadcasting. Furthermore, determine capacity requirements such as cables and power sources, an event network, network equipment and cabling, public announcement system, telephones and fax machines, and wireless systems (such as walkie-talkies and cell phones). By applying various instruments and types of technology, the event manager can provide high volume contacts and notifications, extend business hours, cut costs, provide multilingual support, and efficiently plan, market and manage a political event.

❐ *What contingency plans are in place? Has insurance been taken out?*

Sources: Adapted from Kearney (2002: 1–12); Getz, (1997: 89–93)

22.8 Risks associated with political, civic and government events

Some of the risks associated with events include accidents, injuries, security breaches, event interruptions, theft, construction failures, threatened claims of disruption and litigation (Catherwood & Van Kirk, 1992: 188). Another risk can be the outbreak of an epidemic such as swine flu, Ebola fever or an increase in the risk of contracting malaria. Even if no such risks exist, contingency planning should include the presence of medical personnel at the event, alerting hospitals near the event location of the event, as well as the training of volunteers in basic first aid.

Perpetrators of politically related violence or those posing a risk to political events often target public political events in order 'to achieve maximum publicity for explicit aims' (Whittaker, 2004: 50). Assassinations, violence, kidnapping, 'tiger kidnapping' (using the threat of violence against a person as a leverage to force another to participate in a crime) or attacks at political events are often premeditated and politically motivated, and are applied to threaten and/or intimidate government or the general public (Control Risks Group,

2007: 2). Threats or occurrences of protest marches, bomb threats and explosions at politically related events have in the past included the disruption of several annual meetings of the World Bank, the World Trade Organization (WTO), the G8 (Group of Eight Industrialised Countries) and the International Monetary Fund (IMF). In the past, a number of Olympic Games were also used for political purposes. For example, in 1936 Nazi Germany staged the Olympic Games in Berlin in such a way as to glorify Adolf Hitler's ideas about national socialism. In 1980, the US boycotted the Moscow Olympic Games, and in 1984 the then USSR boycotted the Los Angeles Olympic Games, both states using it as a political instrument against one another during the height of the Cold War. In the build-up to the Beijing Olympic Games in 2008, the Chinese government employed the latest surveillance equipment from companies such as General Electric, Honeywell, Panasonic and Siemens, staged anti-terrorism drills and sought advice from the world's top law-enforcement agencies. The Chinese government is reported to have spent US$300m (£150m) on security at Olympic venues. Olympic sites also had airport-style security checks, with X-ray machines, metal detectors and scanners for body searches, and surveillance cameras installed throughout Beijing, China's capital city (BBC News, 2008: internet).

Security and risks are some of the main concerns on the part of the client and the event managers that need to be addressed early in event management process as well as during the planning and hosting process (Poirier, 1997: 675). In the wake of 11 September 2001, a greater awareness exists with regard to the potential risks for attacks on major public and/or international venues and meetings with historical and/or political significance.

> Event security risks can be defined as any event, action or individual that could disrupt the managing and staging of an event, pose safety and security hazards, or cause reputation damage. Event risk management entails an analysis of crowd management systems, command and control assessments, contingency plans, incident management training of all relevant staff, emergency evacuation, risk assessment before, during and after an event, security procedure development, site safety, access control, and a comprehensive search of venue prior to an event.
>
> *Control Risks Group, (2003: 1)*

Four broad areas with regard to security management of a political event need to be considered and implemented. These are professional security management; threat assessment; security objectives and plan; and post-event assessment. Threat assessment includes the assessment of safety risks associated with a particular event, venue and/or person. An assessment of the venue, the significance of the event, the event theme and the expected attendees/audience are factors to consider.

Security for political events is provided either by volunteers associated with the political organisation, government security forces and/or private security providers. Most often political events necessitate the involvement of metropolitan and national police services and the national defence force. Once the security provider (a private firm or a government security agency) has been appointed, security objectives can be identified and a security plan and protocol developed. This should be done in consultation with the event management team. Security deployment should include security inspections at entrances, explosive-detection dogs and equipment, metal detection technology, uniformed and undercover guard placement, searches, radio equipment, vendor accreditation and crowd-control plans. Security services should already be operational during the event set-up phase. In order to pre-empt any unwanted events hijacking the main day, rehearsing the day or event is of major importance. Service providers as well as guest accreditation, clearance and ticketing should be done during this phase. Lastly, security services offered during an event should be assessed after the event by both the security company and the event managers (Shaw, 2008: internet).

Political events have to comply with legislation (including those relating to freedom of assembly and speech, and property rights) as well as local government requirements pertaining to the public marketing, such as posters and billboards. The event should have insurance against loss, liability, coverage requirements and policy management. All contracts and negotiations should be legalised.

Emergency management for political events should provide for on-site medical services, evacuation procedures, and crisis and disaster management. Moreover, health and safety concerns should also include fire safety, the deployment of additional fire personnel and vehicles, and officers to manage crowd behaviour and control. Dedicated disaster management personnel should also be deployed, and evacuation sites should be identified and indicated clearly. During the 2009 presidential inauguration in South Africa, for example, 360 Peace and Development Project (PDP) officers were deployed in and around the Union Buildings, the venue for the event. PDPs were young people with basic training in road traffic control and crime prevention who were responsible for identifying possible threats and alerting the metro police (*BuaNews Online*, 2009: internet).

22.9 Summary

Government, civic and political events include a wide variety of events, which have political as well as tourism significance. The aim of this chapter was to enable the planning, management and evaluation of political, government and civic events. The chapter defined and identified political, government and civic events; explained the objectives of political events; identified major stakeholders and other participants, and protocol and media accreditation associated with such events; and described the potential security threats to a political event.

Questions for research

1 Critically evaluate the concept *political event*.
2 Choose one of the official public holidays of historical significance in any country of your choice, write analytical notes on its background and draft a plan for a political event to commemorate the day.
3 Your events management company was awarded a contract to stage an event to commemorate *any* politically significant incident, event or day. Your client requested the details as outlined in table 22.1. Choose any politically significant incident, event or day, and compile the following details:

Table 22.1 Research requested to manage and stage an event

Client information and contact details	Research proposal, problem and background
Main aim and objectives of research	Event stakeholders
Title of research or event	Branding of event
Preliminary programme and entertainment	Target group/audience
Vendor contracts	Marketing strategy
Celebrity endorsement	Identification of resources
Budget and funding required	Communication of results (internet, media statements)
Briefings (by whom, to whom?)	Time frames for event planning and event day
Details of project leader	

Source: Adapted from Goldblatt, (2004a; 2004b)

4   Explain the developmental benefits of staging a political event.
5   Case study 22.6 includes an example of a political event. Discuss it within each of the domains referred to in this chapter.

Case study 22.6 An example of a political event

The national conference and the election campaign of a political party

Globally, political parties regularly convene their national conference, which is often their highest decision-making event attended by delegates from national, provincial and local party structures prior to national elections. These national conferences aim to assess and formulate the party's policies and election manifestos, as well as electing parties' leaders and officials. These conferences are often held at politically historically relevant locations.

Political parties often accredit journalists to attend the open sessions of their conferences. The infrastructure for these events often also includes restaurant facilities, smoking lounges and reception areas.

Events management companies are often contracted to manage the event and maintain the infrastructure during the conference.

Access to conference venues is by accreditation only and security is either provided by the party's officials or by police services. In order to address security concerns of the event security officers including trained marshals are often deployed in joint operations overseeing safety and security, by the police services.

Political parties run their campaigns from their party headquarters. Elections campaign teams are assembled several months before the announcement of the election.

During the election campaign, party structures are complemented by volunteers who campaigned for the party. Other political events include door-to-door campaigning, celebrity endorsements of the party's campaign at rallies and social events.

Political party rallies are major political events. Depending on the size of the party, these are held in large stadia and are often broadcast via television or to other party venues. Rallies are a show of strength for parties and are often attended by the party's top leadership and its most well-known supporters in business or entertainment. Business corporations, political parties and interest groups often use celebrities extensively to increase the support for their ideas and policies, and appeal and promotion of their products and/or services. Celebrity endorsement done by sports personalities, actors, figures in the entertainment industry, and leading church and business figures in the society is increasingly becoming a powerful business, political, advertising and communication instrument. A celebrity or public figure's status, prestige, legitimacy and credibility can by his or her political endorsement create 'positive effects' in the minds of supporters, donors, sponsors, tourists, voters, taxpayers and consumers.

---

6   Identify an example of a civic event. Discuss it within each of the domains referred to in this chapter, and identify the challenges and opportunities associated with the staging of a civic event.

Recommended websites

Browse the following internet sites for interesting and informative information:

An example of commemorating a political event such as the 1972 Olympic Games: http://www.hurryupharry.org/2008/10/27/commemorating-40-years-on-from-munich-a-threat-to-national-security http://en.wikipedia.org/wiki/Munich_massacre http://www.palestinefacts.org/pf_1967to1991_munich.php

An example of a code of practice for a civic event such as a picket: www.berr.gov.uk/files/file23914.pdf

General information on how to manage a civic event such as a political rally: http://www.howcast.com/guides/2112-How-To-Stage-a-Political-Rally

General information on managing a government event such as a donor conference: http://ww.undg.org/docs/7540/Donor-Conference---quick-how-to-guide.doc

General information on managing political events against racism: http://www.unitedagainstracism.org/pages/info26.htm

General information on the South African presidential inauguration in 2009, and protocol guidelines and administrative arrangements: http://www.dfa.gov.za/protocol/pres%20inaug.html

23 Banqueting

Malcolm Ellis

Abstract

The aim of this chapter is to introduce the reader to the concept of 'banqueting'. The chapter deals with a brief history of banqueting to provide a background to the way banqueting events are handled in the current era, and so provide a framework of knowledge of this sector of the events industry. This chapter furthermore examines the management and provision of banqueting as an integral part of the events management field.

Chapter objectives

After you have read this chapter you should be able to:

- ❏ understand and explain the background of 'banqueting' as opposed to 'dining';
- ❏ understand how banqueting fits into the events management process;
- ❏ describe a number of different types of banquets and the reasons behind the choice of each;
- ❏ understand the concept of 'service' as it applies to the banqueting field;
- ❏ understand the key success criteria in managing the provision of banquets;
- ❏ recognise the increasing importance of technology to the banquet provider;
- ❏ recognise the key importance of after-event evaluations; and
- ❏ be able to apply the foregoing within the overarching criterion of achieving a return on investment for the originator of the banquet.

Banquets generally consisted of two courses, each made up of a variety of dishes, anything from 10 to 40 in number.

Lillicrap & Cousins (2008: 70)

23.1 Introduction

Banquets are variously defined as follows:
'banquet n. 1 a lavish and sumptuous meal; feast. 2 a ceremonial meal for many people, often followed by speeches ...', while 'banqueting' can be defined as 'to hold or take part in a banquet'
Collins English Dictionary (1994: 122)

'A banquet is a large public meal or feast, complete with main courses and desserts. It usually serves a purpose, such as a charitable gathering, a ceremony, or a celebration, often preceded or followed by speeches in honour of someone'.
Wikipedia (2009a: internet)

So what then is the difference between banqueting and dining? Is there a difference? Even if there is, why the differentiation between two names for what is, after all, the provision of food and beverages to people eating?

In the first instance, dining may be taken as the provision of food and beverages to diners or people dining. Strictly speaking, as the etymological root of the word comes from the Latin *disjejunuare* via Norman-French *disner* into English 'dinner', the meaning is actually to 'break the fast' (Collins, 1994). So perhaps those 'diners' who ask for fried eggs and bacon in the evening are not so far off the mark after all. Similarly, the ubiquitous 'diner', taken here to mean a place where ready-for-consumption food can be bought, found all over the North American continent, is absolutely accurately named as being a place where a fast, or period without food, can be broken. However, for many people, the term 'dining' will be taken as meaning merely 'eating', whether or not a fast is being broken.

'Banqueting', on the other hand, finds its root in *banco* from the Old German meaning 'a table' (Collins, 1994). In modern usage, the word has come to imply a highly structured meal – one that has a degree of formality.

From the aspect of events, it may be taken that 'dining' refers to any form of eating, any meal or any type of service, whereas the term 'banquet' refers to the more formal occasion, and one that is frequently the high point of the event from a food service point of view.

23.2 The place of banqueting in event management

Structured and planned events should have aims or objectives. Often the aims culminate with the celebration of the achievement of those aims, and as seen previously, celebration frequently involves food. But here the provision of food is required to be memorable to impress the celebration of the event upon the minds of the participants. One way that achieves the aims of celebration while simultaneously creating a memorable occasion is by offering a formal banquet to the event participants.

> *The enjoyment of food and wine is very much a matter of personal taste. Today there is a relaxed attitude. People have broken away from the very rigid approach to the marriage of food and wine. People tend to drink what they like, when they like, and tend to be more open and honest about their wine preferences*
>
> Kinton, Ceserani & Foskett, (2004: 364)

There is a degree of formality when banquets are considered. The meal has a formal structure, i.e. it will follow the classical menu order in terms of what is happening during the meal, and in terms of the way the event itself is conducted. It is not without reason that the person in charge of the banquet, as far as the banquet guests are concerned, is referred to as the Master of Ceremonies (MC).

> *There are two main types of function: Formal meals (sometimes called banquets) … [and] buffet receptions.*
>
> Lillicrap & Cousins, (2008: 358)

23.3 Banqueting and design

Banquets have come a long way from the type of event held indoors in a medieval castle or hall. They are formal occasions and, as such, their design follows a formal structure. This is true even when they become extremely large events, perhaps even held outdoors if there is no indoor venue large enough at the event site. On some occasions, banquets have been held simultaneously at a number of widely scattered venues, linked by television cameras and screens, to accommodate the number of guests that have to be seated.

The design of a banquet comprises a number of elements that must all work together seamlessly to provide the total event the organiser is seeking. These elements will include the following:

23.3.1 The venue

The venue where the banquet is to be held is the first of the factors that limit the design of the banquet. The size of the venue determines the upper limit of the numbers that may be catered for. If the venue is out of doors, then the weather becomes a factor. If the banquet is to be held under canvas, the fire hazard must be factored in. Is the banqueting room close to the kitchen? Can food be transported, stored, plated *and* kept warm? If not, alternative arrangements have to be made. The permutations are innumerable. Experience will guide the banqueting manager to direct the event designer to the most practical choice.

Case study 23.1 Congress banquet luncheon, Victoria Falls, Zimbabwe

Unusually, a banquet luncheon was to be held as the final event for a congress. As the luncheon was the last act of the outgoing congress after the election of a new association president, the luncheon banquet had to not only welcome the new president, but also honour the former president who had served the association well for many years. In addition, there were a number of ministers of state in attendance and it was rumoured that the state president would also make an unscheduled appearance.

The venue could seat 600 people conference style in the largest indoor venue available. The banquet could not be held out of doors for security reasons. The challenge was to change the venue from a conference-style 600-seater to 650 places at banqueting tables. After some discussion, it was believed that this could be achieved if the casino tables in the room next door could be removed to make space for the banqueting tables, and the casino tables could be replaced before the casino opened that evening.

The menu had to be such that it could be plated in a hurry. The venue had no facilities for keeping such large quantities of plates warm, so an assembly line had to be formed, starting with the empty plates at one end, and in very short order, full plates out at the other end and into the venue. The food had to be such that it could be kept hot in large quantities without losing quality, brought quickly to the assembly line, placed rapidly but neatly on a plate and garnished, then rushed into the banquet room.

Service was going to be an issue. Even by using every member of waiting staff it employed, cross-trained bedroom staff and every spare pair of hands available, there was still a shortfall of about 30 members of serving staff. The solution was to 'borrow' service staff from other hotels in Victoria Falls. The guests at the banquet had, in any case, just checked out from the other hotels, and their restaurants would largely be empty. By emphasising the benefits for the town as a whole, the management of the other hotels were persuaded to loan their staff members.

Scheduling was going to be a major trial. The final plenary was scheduled to finish at around 11:00. The luncheon was scheduled to start at 13:00. The guests would leave the conference room, go to their hotel rooms to change, check out if necessary, and return to the congress hotel for lunch. After lunch, they would be bussed to the airport where a fleet of aircraft was waiting to take them back to their home country. Effectively, that gave the staff a mere two hours to change from a conference-style venue of 600 to a banquet venue for 650 in the same venue. A major task indeed.

The staff of the host hotel worked through the night to make every preparation they could to simplify things on the morrow. Finally, the big day dawned. After the guests left the dining room after breakfast, the staff stripped it of all the equipment required and stacked it ready for use near the conference venue. The bar staff were opening hundreds of bottles of wine, crating them and sending them to the walk-in refrigerators of the main stores to be cooled.

After tea had been served mid-morning to the congress delegates, the outdoor pool venue was first stripped of chairs and tables and then laid out as a pre-luncheon drinks venue. The intention of this was two-fold: firstly, to give the delegates time to gather after returning from their hotels and, secondly, to welcome those dignitaries who had not been part of the plenary. A third, and unspoken, reason was to keep the delegates 'happily' occupied should there be a delay in preparing the banquet venue.

The executive members of the association were very well aware of the challenges. They finished the plenary a mere 10 minutes late, which in itself was some form of record. As the delegates left through the front doors of the conference room, the sliding doors to the casino were being opened and the staff members were starting to dismantle the conference venue and its tables and chairs. Narrow baize-covered conference tables were placed side by side to be used as broader dining tables. Drawings of the place settings were placed temporarily on the walls so that staff unfamiliar with the items could also help lay tables. More chairs were carried in by the bedroom staff. Dining-room chairs were brought in to be used at the top table.

The pace heated up. Guests were arriving at the drinks venue, but the banquet room was still unready. It was confirmed that the state president was not attending, so the lay-up of the top table had to be amended. The band that was to play background music had arrived but needed extension cords to take power to the corner where they were to play. Final touches were being put on the tables under the supervision of the executive housekeeper. Flowers and greenery stripped from the resort's gardens (and from those of the hotel next door, if rumour was to be believed) decorated the tables. Just 10 minutes before the start, and as some of the guests were starting to drift towards the luncheon venue, the executive members of the association were advised that all was ready. Strictly speaking, it was not, for as the guests walked through the doors to the banquet room, the general manager of the congress hotel was seen to be polishing the wine glasses of the top table.

As far as the members of the association were concerned, the banquet went without a hitch. Behind the scenes out of the public eye, it was another matter. Each of the waiters from other hotels was paired with a waiter from the host hotel so that they had someone they could follow if they became confused. The chef was plating food, ably assisted by his kitchen brigade. The groundsman was ensuring that the wine was cold and left the service area as fast as it was needed. His staff was busy running backwards and forwards from the stores area carrying box after box of wine and minerals. The accountant was standing inside the kitchen door with a roll of paper towels checking each plate to make sure that it was presented without drips or spills. The general manager and the assistant manager were inside the venue guiding the servers to the right places, answering questions from the guests (thankfully very few), and ensuring that everything went according to plan – or, if not, correcting whatever was wrong as fast as possible – this while supervising the service at the top table to ensure the dignitaries were served accordingly. The speeches were made as scheduled. The longest was made immediately after the main course was cleared away, thus giving the staff a small breather – and the chef a chance to start plating 650 desserts. A gesture that was very well received was when the outgoing president of the association insisted that all the staff involved be brought into the venue so that the delegates could applaud them.

By 14:30, the banquet guests were leaving. Compliments were lavished on the general manager, who was quick to point out that it had been a team effort and that even hotels normally seen as 'competition' had played their part. The general feeling was that things had gone very well indeed. On the following days, the event designer, who had stayed behind to recover from the strain of organising the event, repeatedly remarked that she had had her expectations exceeded, to the extent that the new chairman of the association had already commissioned her to organise the following year's general meeting – in Mauritius.

23.3.2 The décor

Once the venue has been chosen, then the design of the décor can be finalised. Although the décor is often chosen with some or other theme in mind, it should complement the banquet as an event and not dominate it. Particularly with banquets held at resort complexes, there is often a wealth of décor and themed material available for the banquet designer. Nevertheless, the purpose of the banquet should always be kept in mind. For example, if the banquet was to honour the outgoing president of a turf club, it would be possible, and would remain in keeping with a possible theme of 'A Night at the Races', to have live racehorses with jockeys in racing silks circling the venue. However, this may draw attention away from the guest of honour and the speeches made honouring him. Here again, an experienced banqueting manager will be able to guide the event designer.

23.3.3 The menu

The menu is usually the relatively easiest part of the event to plan. The event organiser at least has an idea of what is wanted, and the caterer has a very good idea of what can be provided, so the two become an easy match. The caterer will be very conscious of the neecessity to cater well to the needs and wants of the banquet, and will be just as aware of the limitations of his or her staff. In some cases, a compromise has to be reached between the caterer and the event designer. Fortunately, the banquet is often the culminating event of a conference or convention and, as such, there is frequently a most generous food budget to work with. Under circumstances such as those, the very finest of meals can be prepared.

23.3.4 The beverages

Beverages are frequently a source of concern to both the banquet manager and the event designer. The event designer does not wish to appear stingy or mean, while at the same time the banqueting manager (at the very least!) is aware of the real dangers of providing the guests with an oversupply of alcoholic beverages.

In countries where alcohol is forbidden, this concern is taken care of by legislation. However, in such cases, there are often special licences that may be extended to banquet organisers under very controlled circumstances.

The issue really affects those countries where alcohol is permitted. The challenge is always to prevent some guests from overindulging while appearing attentive and generous to all. No one wishes banquet guests who may have dined well but not wisely to clamber behind the wheel of a vehicle to drive themselves home.

Well-trained wine waiters are very aware of these concerns of management. Glasses should never be filled to the brim. In some instances, particularly where a large number of wines are to be served, it may be sensible to downsize the glasses used, i.e. serve red wine in a white-wine glass, and so forth.

23.3.5 The speeches

Speeches are often held during the course of the meal service. Many banqueting managers will attempt to persuade the event organiser to have just a welcoming speech at the beginning of the banquet and then to hold the rest until the coffee and perhaps liqueurs are on the table. From a service point of view this is a very desirable practice as once the tables have been cleared of plates and cutlery, the MC has a clear field, as it were, to meet the purpose of the evening. The disadvantage is that the banquet guests may be too well wined and dined to give as much attention to the proceedings as they perhaps should.

23.3.6 The entertainment

Entertainment at banquets is often a cause of headaches for the banquet supervisor, particularly when the entertainment takes place during the service of the meal. It cannot be emphasised enough that the careful banqueting supervisor will ensure that the entertainment takes place after the meal has been served when there is no time pressure at all on the service staff.

23.4 Common banqueting table arrangements

There are a number of classic arrangements for the seating arrangements. In every case, the intention is that the attention of the guests is easily attracted to, and can remain focused upon, either the top table or the places of honour. Traditionally, the centre of the top table is where the host of the event sits, with the guests of honour seated adjacent, and this protocol still remains. The MC will be positioned such that attention is not drawn away from the top table. To this end, the MC will usually place him- or herself to the side or end of the top table, nearest the service entrance, from which discreet entrances and exits may be occasioned, and where communication with the service staff is facilitated.

This arrangement is, of course, the original banqueting set-up. The honoured people sat on the outside of the top table. The less honoured sat further down the legs of the 'U'. In some cases, the legs became very long indeed to cater for a long and narrow room. It was not unusual to see a third, fourth or even fifth leg being added to accommodate larger numbers. (In this event, the arrangement became known as a 'comb' rather than a 'U' table). But in each case, it was relatively easy for the guests to turn, at least partially, to face the top table and give their attention to the speakers. A disadvantage of this arrangement is that communication with guests other than those immediately to the left and right of one's seat and immediately across the leg of the 'U' becomes quite difficult.

The hollow square table is best suited to relatively small numbers as the numbers that can be accommodated in any given space are very limited using this arrangement. The advantage, however, is that everyone, without moving their position, can face the speaker. Depending on the size of the square, it might be very difficult to talk to

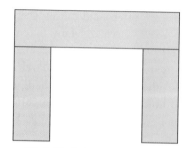

Figure 23.1 U-shaped table arrangement

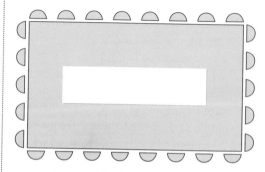

Figure 23.2 Hollow square table

anyone other than the guests on either side of the seat occupied.

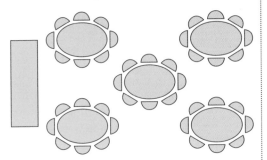

Figure 23.3 Oval table arrangement

Oval or, more usually, round tables were designed to allow everyone at the table to communicate with everyone else at the table with relative ease. Unfortunately, as the diameter of the tables became bigger and the centrepieces larger and more ornate, this end was defeated, and the guests were back, more or less, to talking to the guests immediately to their right and left. Once more, the guests were left with their backs to the table of honour and during speeches were almost obliged to present their backs to the other guests at the table at which they were seated in order to face the speaker. In the meantime, because the shape of the tables is inordinately wasteful of space, banquet designers found that they were no longer able to seat as many people at round tables in a given space as they were at a 'U' or a 'comb'-shape arrangement.

Even so, and perhaps because of the trend towards informality in the early 21st century, very many conference designers still choose to fill their venues with round tables. However, for the more formal banquet, rectangular arrangements are still the *sine qua non* of delivery.

The examples given here are by no means the only layouts available to the banqueting organiser. It must be noted that, although there are table layouts and settings that long experience has taught as being well suited to the purpose, the events organiser is the final arbiter. Once again the advice of 'get it in writing' applies, particularly when the events organiser is so ill-advised as to reject the banqueting manager's inputs and select a most impractical table layout.

23.5 Banqueting and service design

> *There are essentially two styles of food service used at functions. The first is the buffet arrangement where the guests will usually serve themselves from a display of food and beverage items. The second is the more formal 'sit-down' function where guests are served at their tables by food service staff; this latter style may be further subdivided into those functions where plated meals are served and those at which silver service is used.*
>
> Davis & Stone (1995: 291)

Care must be exercised when choosing the style of service as each different style has a number of subordinate types of services and each type lends itself to a different level of formality.

23.5.1 French service

As the name indicates, this type of service originated in France. In the culinary field, the French regard themselves as their own arbiter, and therefore like to choose and act in their own way. It is this kind of service that will always be appreciated by the most knowledgeable customer, and by the gastronome or person well versed in food and drink, and it can only be offered at small, more intimate banquets.

The service can be carried out in one of two ways. For one to three persons, the dishes can be placed directly onto the table. The principal dish is placed before the guests who serve themselves from it, the dish cover being close to hand. The other dishes are grouped around the main dish according to the space available. Everything must be arranged on the table with taste. It is usual and recommended that the principal dish be placed on a dish-warmer (*rechaud*). For four or more persons, the waiter has a trolley or small table (*gueridon*) available and passes the dishes from it. Before commencing to serve, he must discreetly ascertain the principal person at the table. He then holds the main dish in his right hand, covered by a folded napkin, and approaches the guest. The guest will then help him- or herself. In very high-class establishments, this type of service will probably be recommended because there will be a variety of guests attending, and the waiters will not know the habits and preferences of each one. However, when attempting to offer this level of service to a large number of people simultaneously, the problems are enormous and may indeed be insurmountable (Ellis, 1974: 15–18).

23.5.2 Russian service

This type of service is very unusual and now almost obsolete. The cost of both labour and ingredients is forbiddingly expensive. Again, it will only be used in small intimate settings where expense is no object. The dishes are presented to the guests in entire pieces on richly garnished platters. After the presentation, the dishes are withdrawn to the side of the room and the meats, etc., carved in view of the guests. The portioned meats are subsequently served to the guests on plates. Accompaniments are served from serving dishes. (The closest resemblance to this style of service now is in very traditional, perhaps old-fashioned, restaurants where a carving trolley is brought to the table and the joint is carved in front of the guest by either a carver (*chef trancheur*), the *maitre d'hôtel*, or frequently, one of the kitchen brigade). Once more, this type of service is unlikely to be used for anything other than the smallest, most intimate of banquets. It is occasionally used now when presenting a chef's table, traditionally served in the kitchen of fine hotels and restaurants to *very* discerning customers (Ellis, 1974: 15–18).

23.5.3 Buffet service

Buffet service is now frequently seen at functions and has, in many cases, become the preferred method of service even though it does not lend itself to formality. A buffet – hot and/or cold and often including a carvery, soups and speciality stations – is presented to the guests, who help themselves from the many foods on offer. A derivative of this style, referred to as a 'carvery buffet', has a chef to carve joints for the guests and perhaps to assist with the service from large, multi-portioned dishes. Where ethnic foods and specialities are on offer, these may be cooked to order by specially trained staff. The biggest advantage of this service is that it is very labour efficient as most of the work is done by the customers. Waiters only have to clear plates and debris, and serve drinks, thus relatively inexperienced, and therefore inexpensive, staff may be used. Again, it must be noted that a degree of formality will be lost. The buffet is also very flexible in that many different styles of foodstuffs can be presented appropriately.

In addition, as the guests help themselves to the foods on offer, the impression is one of munificence. However, this generosity is also the main disadvantage of the buffet, as management has no direct control over the size of portions served. Sometimes, the size of plate available to the guest is made smaller to assist with cost control. The staff, especially the serving staff, should be trained in such a way that they will help to maintain portion control to assist in preventing the food on the buffet running short. The final advantage is that unsophisticated guests will be able to indicate their choice of food by pointing to it rather than by trying to pronounce unfamiliar names or attempting to find their way through the maze of a classical French menu (Ellis, 1974: 15–18).

> Both American (or plated) and Russian (or silver) service lend themselves very well to banquet service.

> Morgan (1974: 324)

23.5.4 English service

According to English tradition, the head of the family had the plates and dishes placed in front of him and he prepared the dishes of each person according to his knowledge of the preferences (or sometimes in spite of them!) of each person. Despite Morgan's opinion (see above), it is more generally accepted that English, or *silver service* as it is has now become, derives from this practice rather than from Russian service.

The dish is prepared, portioned, garnished and decorated in the kitchen. It is presented to the guests, from the left, and served on to their plate using a spoon and fork. The food is lifted off the serving dish, and never slid from service dish to the plate.

Silver service has many advantages. It can be quick and allows for excellent portion control, especially where this must be exercised over expensive or rare meats. The food can be presented properly on the plate to give the most appetising appearance by a properly skilled waiter. The plates will not be overfilled. Unlike French service, the waiter and not the guest is in charge of the size of the portions and may be called upon to utilise his or her skill and discretion to ensure that everyone is served fairly. The presentation itself is largely dependent upon the skill of the waiter and thus, to some extent, will vary. In addition, where many people have to be served by a limited number of staff, service may be relatively slow. Serving directly from a trolley is permissible but in a formal setting for a large number of people may just not be practical. All sauces should be presented separately to the guest, but in a banqueting setting are often served from the main platter by the waiter (Ellis, 1974: 15–18).

23.5.5 American service or plate service

In this style of service, the food is placed on the plate at the kitchen hotplate or 'pass' and is taken by the waiter to the guest. It is then placed appropriately in front of the guest. The arrangement of the food on the plate can be controlled very strictly by the kitchen staff, and thus high levels of presentation and standardisation are maintained. The service itself can be organised with military precision.

The advantages of this style of service are that it is quite rapid and fuss free, which appeals to many people. Portion control can be well maintained, as can standards of presentation. Again, relatively unskilled labour may be used. Care must be taken that special dietary needs are appropriately served (Ellis, 1974: 15–18).

23.6 Speeches and entertainment

As the banquet is an occasion with a degree, and sometimes a high degree, of formality, the structure of the meal itself is highly formalised. Each course and each item on the programme is announced by the MC, and these usually have a time limit. This limit is to enable the caterer to accurately plan when to start putting the food on the plates or serving platters so that it will be served at the appropriate temperature – at the appropriate time.

In modern usage, the MC is often some glib celebrity who believes the purpose of the job is to be an entertainer. This is incorrect and detracts from the purpose of the banquet, which is to celebrate an event, or to honour a guest at the meal. The original purpose of the MC was to ensure that each speaker was introduced with full title and honour. This was in addition to announcing the commencement of service of each course of the meal. The person in charge of the food service must work very closely with the MC to ensure the banquet (the 'ceremony') flows flawlessly according to a set plan.

23.7 Banqueting and operations

Silvers (2004a) suggests that the events operations function concentrates on bringing together the people, products and services that will be to produce the event project, in this case the formal banquet, as well as the roles, responsibilities, applications and manoeuvres associated with each. It is furthermore stated that flawless coordination is required in order to manage this mix of logistical and functional requirements such that the needs and expectations of the banquet organiser are exceeded.

The main requirements of a formal meal are a well-chosen menu, an elegant appearance to the room and to the tables, efficient and unobtrusive service and, quite vital, punctuality on the part of the [event management]. This latter quality, alas, is not always matched by the client and his guests.

Small (1976: 69)

Once again, it must be emphasised that the service must, in all cases, be flawless and unobtrusive. It is a hallmark of the best service that banquet guests are somewhat surprised to find food and drink placed in front of them without a very clear recollection when it arrived – nor when the used crockery from the previous course was taken away.

With any formal, structured banquet, sequence timing is vital. Where speeches, awards or entertainment is scheduled during the service of the meal, both the food production staff and the food service staff are placed under pressure to ensure that neither the quality of the food nor the seamlessness of the service is compromised. Communication between the service leader and the chief caterer must remain absolutely flawless.

An experienced banqueting manager will often be able to determine when an inter-service item is coming to an end, and will be able to advise the caterer accordingly. The guests at the banquet should not be able to tell that the service staff has been waiting impatiently to produce their *piece de resistance*.

Once the [banquet] started, plated works of art begun parading on our table. All

Case study 23.2 Colley's Supper Rooms, UK

'And now, onto the main event! The dessert parade! This was what we all had really been waiting for and we certainly weren't disappointed. First up was a gargantuan steamed syrup pudding which had us all gasping in awe. Seriously, this was the largest steamed pudding I've ever seen. Next in line was an iced passion fruit *parfait* which I'm sorry to say didn't really seem to register with anyone – we were all still reeling from the sight and smell of the steamed pudding! This was rapidly followed by a rather simple but pretty peach jelly. Again, this still didn't register with everyone. I think the next dish to be paraded past us was the Almond Bread and Butter Pudding with Marzipan Nuggets and *Amaretto*. This looked very yummy indeed, almost better than the steamed pudding. Things get a little hazy at this point. In quick succession came a Chocolate Marquise with Caramel Sauce, *Tarte Tatin* with *Calvados* and Cream, and a Cheese Platter with an artfully carved swan adorning the platter' (A Spoonful of Sugar, 2008: internet).

the courses were prepared exquisitely with the freshest ingredients one could ever imagine. The creativity of the chef and his staff was evident with each plate that arrives. The entire meal was like a well-orchestrated concert where each course builds up and prepares your tongue for the crescendo of taste that is yet to come. The dessert parade was like the perfect punctuation to a well thought of [banquet].

Kreez (2008: internet)

It should be understood that the entire menu planning, venue décor planning and, above all, service planning entail a great deal of effort by the event designers and the subordinate team of servers and caterers. To the guests, it must look effortless.

Experience helps. So do routines that have been honed to perfection, and the use of appropriate technology. At one time, 'runners' were employed at large banquets to ensure messages were passed quickly and without too many interruptions. Wireless handsets had their place in facilitating communication between the service staff supervisors and the production

staff, particularly in very large (or outdoor) venues. It can now be seen, perhaps with a degree of wry amusement, that not everyone with an earpiece and a cuff-microphone belongs to the presidential secret service.

In smaller units in smaller venues, the staff will communicate well without too much technology. A simple shake of the head, a pointing finger or a single clap of the hands will suffice to give the correct signal to well-trained and practised staff.

The experienced banquet manager will always leave space – and time – for the unexpected. At one stage, punctuality was, reputedly according to Louis XVIII of France, 'the politeness of kings'. Regrettably, this is no longer the case. One definition of punctuality is 'the art of guessing how late the other person will be'. Unfortunately for the tardy, the cooking of food is a very finely timed art. Leave the food cooking too long while waiting for the guest of honour and the evening can be ruined for all. Every effort should be made to have the banquet start on time. There can be no real reason to reward the lack of punctuality by having everyone else wait for those who cannot arrive on time.

This said, it has now become the norm to offer some form of refreshments prior to the banquet to allow those perhaps unavoidably delayed to arrive before the event starts. Many invitations now offer pre-dinner drinks or cocktails, and invite the guests to arrive 'at' a time 'for' a subsequent time a short while later. The invitation will state, for example, 'Dinner, 18:30 for 19:00', allowing 30 minutes of grace during which welcome drinks can be served and greetings exchanged.

> *Just as with restaurants, where particular consultants deal with specific elements, the planning of the function space may require special consultants, such as acoustic and audiovisual specialists and lighting designers.*
>
> Stipanuk (2002: 463)

Depending on the size and location of the banquet venue, it may well be necessary to call in specialist technologists to assist with acoustics, lighting and sound. Many venues have such specialists on hand, if not on the staff, but there are times when outside experts have to be brought in to supervise a special occasion.

23.8 Banqueting and marketing

> *Some large [hotel] properties offer a ... banquet department, headed by a catering manager who books and sells banquets.*
>
> Powers & Barrows (2006: 313)

In 1972, DeWitt Coffman (1972: preface) said in his book, *Marketing for a Full House*, that marketing was 'all of the planning and action that goes into a) searching out all potential sources of business, b) finding just what it is that these potential customers want and need in the way of facilities and services, c) selling those

potential customers, d) servicing them so that they spend the maximum amount of money, and e) convincing them to return again'. Very little has changed since that was written to make it any less of a good definition.

With reference to banqueting, however, it is parts d) and e) that take priority. Although close liaison with members of the sales team is vital if for no other reason than to ensure they do not 'over-promise', the task of the banqueting department is largely to deliver the goods promised by the sales team. This must be done in such a manner that the event organiser, the guests of honour, the hosts and the other guests at the banquet all believe that they have had a memorable occasion and wish to repeat it.

There are those who would argue that this refers to 'operations' rather than marketing. But then Drucker (1973: 64) said: 'The aim of marketing is to make selling superfluous. The aim is to know and understand customers so well that the product or service fits them and sell itself.' If a banqueting department designs its products and services them so well to the customer that they wish to repeat the experience, then the banqueting department can surely be described as marketing itself.

One *caveat*. As with any hospitality or event business, a reputation can be broken with one poor performance. Just as word-of-mouth advertising is well known as one of the best, and certainly one of the cheapest, sales tools, so too can word-of-mouth disparagement break the reputation of a banqueting provider. This caution, too, may serve as an additional motivator too encourage the banqueting organiser to go the extra mile to ensure complete satisfaction to the banquet guests.

However, when banqueting can be

expected to be done well and is marketed properly, the banquet itself may attract sponsorship. From the banqueting organiser's viewpoint, this is a good thing as it often means that the available budget is expanded and so allows a more luxurious meal to be provided. From the event organiser's point of view, sponsorship is highly desirable as it goes some way toward meeting expenses. Finally, from the sponsor's view, it is a good thing to be associated with the honouring of a worthy person or cause. Not only is the sponsorship (frequently) tax deductible, there is always much goodwill and favourable publicity to be garnered. The only drawback from the banqueting organiser's viewpoint is that sometimes sponsors require their name to be most prominently displayed, which may detract from the dignity of the occasion.

23.9 Banqueting and risk

Appraisal is the action of placing a value on a measurement or collection of measurements. The measurements taken in a food and beverage operation are predominantly concerned with performance and are therefore referred to as 'performance measures'.

Cousins, Foskett and Shortt (1995: 154)

'Risk' in terms of banqueting can perhaps be seen in one of two ways. Primarily there is the risk to the well-being of the organisation, where the 'risk domain deals with the protective obligations, opportunities, and legalities traditionally associated with any enterprise, including an event project. These areas are inextricably linked with every choice made and all activities conducted, and are increasingly mandated by stakeholders ranging from regulatory authorities to discriminating event consumers' (Silvers, 2009). Secondly, there is the potential of physical risk to the guests, the staff or the infrastructure itself. It can, with justification, be argued that there are considerable overlaps between the two categories. This may be true, but for the purposes of this chapter, let them be divided.

23.9.1 Risk to the organisation

This form of risk refers to the risk to the reputation and the profitability of the organisation. A poorly organised, poorly delivered banquet will inevitably lead to a loss of reputation and a loss of business. A loss of business will lead to a loss of profitability. It follows therefore that every effort must be made to ensure that the reputation of the business – and of the event designer – is enhanced. It must be noted that any business which fails to show the event designer in the best possible light is almost certain to be overlooked for further business.

Hotels can spend many months building trust and respect with meeting planners but can lose the confidence of the important individuals quickly because of poor service delivery, broken promises and incidents of inappropriate behaviour on the part of employees ...

Rutherford (2002: 339)

One of the challenges for the banqueting supervisor is to be able to form a balanced and accurate judgement of how the banquet was perceived. Feedback from the guests and organisers is vital, and a system must be in place to obtain this. Where the guests of the banquet are local (say from the same town, city, perhaps even province) then the banqueting supervisor can arrange for telephone canvassing. The omnipresent mobile or cellphone makes this canvassing easy if perhaps a trifle expensive. This presumes, however, that the banqueting supervisor has access to a databank of telephone numbers. Often the event organisers will make this information available from their own records. Unfortunately, sometimes they perceive privacy of their guests as being paramount.

If the guests at the banquet cannot be contacted, then the banqueting supervisor is often dependent on the opinions expressed by the event organiser. It has been known for an unscrupulous event organiser to coerce the banquet provider into agreeing to a substantial discount based on the reported displeasure of the hosting organisation. When the banquet provider later sent an apologetic note with a suitably placatory gift, he was dumbfounded when asked if he had not received the organisation's fulsome thanks for the 'best banquet in their history'.

As might be guessed, the hosting organisation had paid the full quoted price to the event manager who had taken the discount offered by the banquet providers as an additional reward for his own efforts.

23.9.2 Physical risk

The world is becoming increasingly violent. Perhaps it would be more accurate to say that there seem to be increasing numbers of violent incidents. Many of these seem to be aimed not at individuals but at groups of people. From the point of view of gaining publicity, the higher the profile of the groups attacked, the greater the amount of publicity. Almost by definition, a banquet can be seen as a grouping of high-profile persons. What is more, they are likely to

be located in one spot for a lengthy period, and one usually known well in advance. This would seem to be a recipe for a violent disaster.

It is true that certain personages attract high risks, but just as soon as the risk is known, so too can precautions be put into place. These issues are addressed more fully in chapter 17.

23.10 Banqueting and administration

Silvers (2004a) has it that '[t]he Administration domain deals primarily with the proper allocation, direction, and control of the resources used in an event project. Since resources are finite by definition, it is imperative that they be acquired, developed and utilized in the most efficient and effective manner to benefit the event project and limit its risk'.

Of the resources that are used, the one that is of particular concern is staffing. It is generally acknowledged throughout the events and hospitality industry that there is an extremely high turnover of staff, particularly at the lower levels. For the banqueting supervisor, this is particularly problematical as it can mean that a service brigade that had its skills honed to perfection a short time before now has very few of the original, trained members. The training has to be started over, and there are concomitant expenses that obviously have an effect on the bottom line of the project.

This particular issue is somewhat easier to deal with where staff used in a banqueting or events venue is permanently employed elsewhere on the property. Many large resorts cross-train their staff members so that they become multiskilled and so can be used in any number of areas

Case study 23.3 Banquet disaster averted

What caused the problem?

A large resort and casino complex was about to open a new and very large conference centre. As it was the first event in the newly built and furnished centre, a prestigious client had been persuaded to hold the launch of their 'latest and greatest' offering in the venue. The staff was in the process of laying up for 650 guests at round tables of ten. The tables and chairs were in place. All was in process to open the venue with a formal banquet.

Early in the morning, the staff was faced with a potential disaster. During the night, a fire-main water pipe running through the ceiling space had burst and had vented large amounts of water into the venue. It had taken some while for the staff on duty to locate the stopcock and turn the water off. Tables and chairs were damaged, some by soaking, some by falling ceiling tiles. The high-quality, woollen carpet was sodden.

There was no other venue at the resort large enough to seat the expected numbers of guests, and the conference organisers were due to check in to the resort within 48 hours.

What transpired?

Management and staff worked around the clock. Fortunately, the contractors were still on site finishing off other tasks elsewhere in the new building. Ceiling tiles were taken from areas out of the view of the public and used to replace those in the conference venue.

Every carpet-cleaning company that could be found within 300kms was located and hired (expense was not an obstacle at this stage!) to come and extract the water from the carpet, and heaters and fans were hired to dry it out. Unfortunately, however, as the carpet dried, it shrank and pulled away from the fittings at the side of the room. Carpet-fitting contractors were called in and worked non-stop to cut, fit and sew in a border around the edges of the room. New furniture was trucked in overnight. Damaged décor was made good. The catering staff worked long shifts to ensure that the contractors were being fed on the job and so did not lose time taking overly long meal breaks. Overtime payments were liberal.

The only lingering sign of the disaster was a smell of wet carpet, which was countered by the copious use of spray deodoriser.

The room was finished and filled with banqueting furniture, the tables were laid, the decorating was done, and the event went off without a hitch – that the guests were aware of. The event organiser was heard to remark that the venue was the jewel in the crown of the resort.

The financial cost to the resort? Not as expensive as may be thought as the insurance company paid for much of the cost. The benefits? Priceless – over 650 goodwill ambassadors for the resort. The event organiser was still recommending business to the resort many years later.

where they are required. The management of such establishments will usually pay for the extra hours worked, frequently at the level of the job being worked. For example, an employee may be a full-time bedroom cleaner, an entry-level position. During banquets, that same person may be used (after training) as a banqueting waiter, and paid for the hours worked as such. After the banquet is over, the employee reverts to cleaning bedrooms. In general, staff members appreciate the opportunity to earn an additional income. There is also some status to be gained among one's peers, and the very real opportunity of being found suitable for promotion because of diligence demonstrated.

The constant turnover of staff requires a constant reappraisal of security risks, which are not only to the physical well-being of the banquet guests (since 9/11, this is an ever-increasingly serious consideration), but to the security of the assets of the organisers – the fittings and equipment, the food stocks and the liquid (sometimes very liquid) assets. It is not unknown for dishonest staff to hide flexible liquid containers inside their trouser legs to be filled with their employer's best cognac. These risks are often minimised by close supervision, but during service times the supervisor's attention is necessarily focused on the banquet. It does not take very long for a theft to occur.

Another risk that the organisers will wish to minimise is the handling of cash. As soon as cash appears, there are almost inevitable opportunities for a dishonest person to make it disappear. In some cases, there is no choice. If the budget for the banquet does not stretch to the provision of drinks other than the wines on the tables, a cash bar will have to be provided, so someone will be handling cash at the event.

Along with the irksome task of training and retraining comes the necessity to administer the hours worked by the staff. Some countries have very restrictive labour legislation regulating the number of hours that, particularly, casual staff may be employed. It follows that a close watch will need to be kept on the hours worked and subsequently paid. Once again, technology is proving a boon in this respect. Not only are computers used to determine the wages due, they are being increasingly used to both monitor and control the access to the venue from the service areas. With the ease of availability to radio frequency identification (RFID) hardware, it is now easy to determine quite accurately who is where at any given time. The detection equipment can be mounted subsurface and the passer-by may not even know that their movements are being monitored. It goes without saying that there are expenses to be covered if these chips are used, but circumstances may make them a viable and affordable option.

23.11 Return on investment

The return on investment (ROI) is sometimes referred to as the return on owner's equity, and is a key profitability ratio (Schmidgall, 1997: 212). The ROI ratio compares the profits of the enterprise to the owner's investment.

The question in every owner's mind is usually, 'Can I earn more by using my capital elsewhere?' Sometimes there is an element of sentimentality that clouds the judgement; and sometimes it is an element of pride. Perhaps the investment has belonged to the family for a period of time and is regarded as 'part of the family'; perhaps capital has been invested poorly, but the investor is unwilling to admit this. But the fundamental question remains the same, 'Can I earn more somewhere else?' This is the question that the banqueting manager has to answer when called to account. Has the banqueting business been operated in the most profitable manner?

The banqueting manager will always be conscious of this overriding priority. Sometimes it will be necessary to make short-term losses (perhaps offering services at cost or break even), knowing that this tactic will bring rewards in the end. Nevertheless, the decision must be a calculated risk, one made while knowing all the factors involved. An effective banqueting manager does not take leaps of faith based on little more that educated guesswork. The responsibility of assuring the required ROI does not allow for this.

23.12 Summary

[Banquets] may be routine to professional function caterers [and planners] but every function is a special occasion to the host and the client, and probably to many of the guests too.

Small (1976: 83)

There are undoubtedly many items that can be regarded as important by the people involved. The caterer will regard the provision of outstanding food from a well-planned and prepared menu as vital. The service provider will regard the prompt and flawless service of that food to the customer as paramount. The *sommelier* or wine butler will regard the provision of well-chosen wines that complement the food as being foundational to the evening. The MC may regard the witty introduction of the guest of honour as being an integral part of the success of the event. To some extent, they are all correct. However, it must never be forgotten that above all else, the guests at the banquet must walk away believing that they have had a wonderful and memorable evening, and that the banquet organiser must be congratulated. Not the staff, not the event manager – the person in whose name the invitations were sent.

It must never be forgotten by the management and staff of a banquet that their purpose there is to facilitate the giving of honour to the guests of honour. Lao Tzu, the Chinese philosopher, is quoted as having said: 'The great leader is one who lets the people say, we did it ourselves'. This can also be applied to the banqueting sector of the events industry.

Questions for research

1 Many banquets will be required to accommodate interruptions to food service by speakers and entertainers. These items are usually programmed to take a specific time. Entertainers are prone to extend the time schedule, particularly if they believe their act is being well received by the banquet guests. How would you deal with a situation of this nature?

2 The classical banqueting menu offered up to 16 different courses. Is this still usual in modern times? If not, why not? If so, why? Consider at least three reasons why this number of courses would be problematical for the banquet service manager.

3 How best can technology be used to facilitate banqueting management? Can the ubiquitous mobile phone be used to assist in banquet service?

4 There are a number of common banquet service styles. The organiser of your event believes that offering a Russian service would be offensive to his North American clients. How would you advise him?

5 You are serving a banquet of 200 people. Speeches by a very important political person are scheduled. Two minutes into the speech, he is repeatedly interrupted by a heckler seated at a table near the rear of the room. What should you do?

6   What roles do function areas play in a hotel? Why is it highly desirable that they be multifunctional rather than specialised to one role? How does this assist the banqueting management?

Recommended websites

Browse the following internet sites for interesting and informative information:

An America version of banqueting halls: http://www.dinolfosbanquets.com/

Google™ images of banquets and banqueting. A wonderful resource to see what other organisers have arranged for their banquets: http://images.google.co.za/images?hl=en&client=firefox-a&rls=org.mozilla:en-GB:official&hs=NBS&q=banquets&um=1&ie=UTF-8&ei=rqOJSrHYAYqhjAebi-miCw&sa=X&oi=image_result_group&ct=title&resnum=4

The Expo Centre, Johannesburg, South Africa, boasts of being a 'one-stop' centre: http://www.expocentre.co.za/component/content/article/5-yoocarouselexpo/31-cocktails-buffets-a-themed

The International Asia Pacific Convention Center Hna Resort Sanya promotes itself through its website at: http://www.wego.com/hotels/china/sanya/international-asiapacific-conventioncenter-hna-resort-sanya

What better place to hold a banquet than a cCastle? Visit the website of Schloss Mittersill at: http://ztrio.com/joomla/index.php?option=com_content&task=blogcategory&id=28&Itemid=94

Suggested reading

Conway, DG. 2004. *The Event Manager's Bible: The Complete Guide to Planning and Organising a Voluntary or Public Event*. Oxford: How to Books.

Friedman, S. 2003. *Meeting and Events Planning for Dummies*. New York: John Wiley & Sons.

LaFleur, T & Hyten, C. 1995. Improving the quality of hotel banquet staff performance. *Journal of Organizational Behaviour Management*, 15(1) 69–93.

Raj, R, Walters, P & Rashid, T. 2009. *Events Management: An Integrated and Practical Approach*. New Delhi: Sage Publications India (Pvt) Ltd.

Turn, J, Norton, P & Nevan Wright, J. 2006. *Management of Events Operations*. Oxford: Elsevier Butterworth-Heinemann.

Photo: World Travel Market

Photo: Dimitri Tassiopoulos

Photo: Juta

Photo: World Travel Market

24

Corporate events

Paul Walters and Razaq Raj

Abstract

The purpose of this chapter is to explain and discuss the importance of corporate events within the events industry. Corporate events activities are organised for the benefit of companies who want to entertain clients, prospective clients or employees at the company's expense. A variety of options for entertaining is available, including evening receptions and dinners with a private view of current exhibitions.

Chapter objectives

After you have read this chapter you should be able to:

☐ examine the impact of corporate events on organisations and the reasons why more and more companies are interested in hosting corporate events;

☐ provide an international context for the appreciation of conferences within a venue setting;

☐ identify the differing internal roles in the mounting/staging/hosting of a corporate event; and

☐ explain the essential unfolding operation from decision to delivery.

24.1 Introduction

The corporate events market, as a generic term, has many distinct platforms of delivery. Those platforms are the cornerstone to understanding how corporate events can ultimately meet all their respective client, partner, sponsor, customer and stakeholder requirements. It can be said that this market has a wide selection of events that meet the corporate event definition. Corporate events can also be classed as business entertaining, a way in which major organisations can achieve growth by 'communication, sales, marketing and public relations strategy' (Allen, 2007).

Corporate events are highly complex and play a major part in the overall events industry. Corporate events and corporate entertainment often involve the exploitation of major sporting and cultural events, as described by Rogers (1998), to strengthen the links between an organisation, usually a corporate one, and its clients or potential clients.

Another way of illustrating the message at corporate events is holding team-building days, which are usually organised by corporate hospitality/entertainment companies. Team-building activities can range from go-carting to paint-balling,

> ### Case study 24.1 British Grand Prix Silverstone Formula 1 hospitality
>
> Formula 1 racing can be very exciting for delegates who are anticipating first-class hospitality for both days of the British Grand Prix staged at Silverstone, the only hospitality complex available close to the start of the race.
>
> An organisation may invite its clients to be wined and dined at the British Grand Prix, Silverstone. There may be a short presentation or an informal message announced on stage so that the company also has the chance to get its message or mission across.

and with locations worldwide for some companies it may also involve flying clients abroad and taking part in such exercises in international locations.

This chapter will present the various types of corporate events and explain, using case study examples, the range, scope and growth of the market. With the growth identified, this chapter will draw upon the ever-changing requirements from facility owners as a delivery, after platform to client expectation, and thus customer satisfaction.

24.2 The corporate events industry

The events industry is fast moving and very competitive, and is based on the needs and demands of consumers of various ages. The industry is continuously expanding in trying to meet the needs of small to very large-scale international companies. As technology is continuously advancing, events organisers are under continuous pressure to keep up to date with new advances.

Corporate events are more effective and better value for money than advertising and other types of marketing. One of the most important benefits is the face-to-face contact with customers, which, it can be argued, is a difficult task to achieve through indirect marketing. The following establish the industry acceptance terms within the corporate event market:

❑ *Incentive travel.* These are exceptional travel experiences to motivate, recognise superior performance, get buyers together and thank customers;

❑ *Motivational meetings.* These encompass any perceived motivational element to include recreation, motivational speeches, awards and team-building activities. Attendance is a function of the position or role of the participant, not as a reward from an incentive programme; and

❑ *Business events.* These are activities that include sales meetings, conventions, business meetings and social gatherings (banquets, theatre or sporting events).

The industry can be split into many sections: the corporate, charity and volunteer sectors;

Case study 24.2 British conference market trends

Conferences and meetings are estimated to be worth £11.7 billion annually by the British Conference Market Trends Survey 2005, exhibitions and trade fairs over £9.3 billion annually, and corporate events between £700 million and £1 billion annually.

The British Conference Market Trends Survey 2008, produced by the British Association of Conference Destinations, highlighted the importance of public-sector, and association conferences, now accounting for 52% of all meetings and conferences. By contrast, the number of corporate meetings and conferences forms just 48% of all events.

The UK corporate events market is continuously growing, and sporting events such as the 2006 World Cup are one way in which the market is progressing. Such events are reviving the UK tourism industry. 'With the new Wembley stadium recently opened in 2007, with a capacity of over 18 000 corporate seats, it is expected to boost demand for corporate hospitality during the year' (Market Review, 2002).

With events such as the 2012 Olympics due to take place in London, the corporate events market is growing at a fast pace, allowing tourism activity to increase and the economy to grow. From an economic perspective, companies hosting corporate events, are 'place marketing', trying to create that positive image and attract investors to their company. Corporate events organised by tourist destinations such as the London Tourist Board are aiming to attract quality tourists, spread the demand across the economy, and increase visitor spend and length of stay. Attractions holding corporate events for consumers are trying to encourage repeat visits at facilities, resorts and attractions. They are all ways of communication between the companies and its investors and customers.

central and local government; profit-making events, associations and institutes; and many more.

24.3 The impact of corporate events

An event can have an enormous fiscal impact on a host destination, with political and pharmaceutical conferences being some of the biggest. The UK National Tourist Board's Delegate Expenditure Survey 2006 highlights that corporate multi-day events have a delegate spend of £459 per day, without applying the multiplier effect.

The MPI Foundation (2006: 2) states in the *Economic Impact of Meetings and Events White Paper*:

> With 450 000 square feet of meeting space and 6 600 available hotel rooms, Winnipeg (Canada) usually hosts six to eight city–wide conventions and 200 meetings per year. The community typically draws more than 50 000

Case study 24.3 Destination management and incentive events in Sydney, Australia

Sydney hosted the annual conference of a major Chinese pharmaceutical company in November 2007, according to Business Events Sydney (BESydney, 2008). The city catered for 2 200 delegates, who all pursued both business and leisure activities.

The company's managing director said staff members agreed that the Sydney event was the best conference they had ever attended. The congress culminated in a gala awards ceremony, a glittering event featuring Olympic gold medallist, Ian Thorpe, as guest presenter.

Business Events Sydney helping at every point
BESydney supported the company at every stage of the event including:
❑ assisting delegates with the visa application process;
❑ organising value-added duty-free shopping and welcome banners; and
❑ arranging for Olympian Ian Thorpe to attend the gala ceremony.

International bidding partners
Throughout the bid process, members of the BESydney office in Hong Kong worked closely with the China-based client to create a tailor-made proposal that would address all of the conference requirements.

Taking care of all incentive delegates' needs
In its final presentation to the company, BESydney outlined a detailed itinerary and destination information, as well as value-added services and a video showcasing Sydney and welcoming the conference delegates. Representatives from the Australian embassy and Qantas also gave a professional presentation, furthering Chinese confidence in Sydney's ability to deliver a premium result.

In the end, Sydney won the event over competitors Bali and Bangkok because of its beautiful harbour setting, cosmopolitan lifestyle, world-famous attractions and ability to put together the best possible conference and incentive package.

The managing director of the Chinese pharmaceutical company said, 'The success of our annual conference was a result of the strong support from Business Events Sydney.'

delegates for stays of three to four days, generating $40 to $45 million in direct expenditure. In 2006, the community hosted 13 city-wide meetings or events, including the Grey Cup and the Aboriginal Music Awards.

24.4 Corporate hospitality events

Corporate events within the sports and leisure market are considered to be one of the biggest growth areas.

24.5 Venues and event planning for corporate events

Planning for corporate events carries with it long-term negotiations with venue suppliers and contractors. The conference industry has a history of creating long lead times for securing venues. On average, corporate events begin the planning two to three years in advance. This process is commonly experienced with large multinational companies. The conference is more than a business trip – it is also a destination event.

The planning process requires more than just the typical understanding of setting out all deliverables and attributing tasks and activities with milestones as key indicators for assessing the overall status of the plan. Project planning within this type of sphere requires international language and cultural understanding to obtain external activities that meet customer needs.

Case study 24.4 Corporate events, UK

The premier and prestigious events such as Royal Ascot, Wimbledon, Lords Cricket and the Open Golf Championship are some of the most desired events to incorporate corporate hospitality.

'According to figures from research firm Market & Business Development (MBD), the UK market was worth £765m last year. The sector has grown year on year since 1999, although the 10% growth at the beginning of the period slowed to 1% in both 2002 and 2003, owing to a scaling down of projects and hospitality budgets. However, positive growth is set to continue – even accelerate' (Caterersearch, 2004).

This is complemented by two of the biggest corporate hospitality suppliers in the UK – Sodexho Prestige and Compass Group.

'In a recent NOP survey of companies which buy corporate hospitality commissioned by Sodexho Prestige, the food service giant Sodexho's corporate hospitality arm, one-third of respondents (34%) said that they had increased their spending in 2003, while almost half (44%) felt that corporate hospitality was now an essential part of doing business' (Caterersearch, 2004).

Ascot, Henley, Glyndebourne, Cheltenham, Lord's, Twickenham – the names of the most prestigious events in the British corporate and social calendar – are prominent in the lists of hospitality opportunities on offer to companies. Corporate hospitality is now re-emerging as an important communication tool; however, there are clear and prominent changes taking place that will inevitably alter how corporate hospitality is conceived and perceived. The elite listings within the social calendar reflect some natural biases in the market, with its leanings to the very largest public companies with head offices in London and boardrooms. Corporate hospitality is essentially a tactical way for companies to drive themselves forward, although its impact on the bottom line is often difficult to measure.

A great deal of the planning process can be negotiated and developed within the host destination, therefore, consultation with the client through this early stage is essential. The development of a full itinerary that covers not only the main purpose of the conference, but will entice international delegates to attend on a regular basis is also essential. This ultimately leads to the area of marketing. Delegates will make a decision to attend a conference based on a number of aspects: the destination, the key speakers selected to address the audience throughout the conference, and the external activities arranged as part of the conference entertainment.

Acquiring key speakers for the conference can be part of the organiser's responsibility. If individuals of that stature are a late addition to the conference portfolio, then marketing will need special attention to entice delegates to sign up early. Where a conference has a stable history and a regular client base, early sign-up of delegates is a major advantage within the planning process. Armed with this information, an organiser can give early indicators to contractors and suppliers. This will reduce the financial risk and secure venues without the possibility of losing deposits. Where this is not the case and delegates are expected to make a decision to attend a conference once they have received a full itinerary and the cost attributed, this brings with it higher financial risk to the organiser with project planning brought together early and a dormant period within the planning stage before the event set-up and delivery.

As stated earlier, this type of planning differs in many aspects to other type of events. Within the planning stage there may be a requirement to test many of the elements booked. Planning within other sectors of the event industry only allows for direct testing and sampling at the event delivery stage. Monitoring and controlling a plan over a long period requires a project manager that can motivate team members and maintain a consistent level of commitment.

24.6 Corporate marketing strategies

Marketing corporate events is more than just an internal business arrangement with the intended delegates and the organisation. It is now part of the marketing mix for host destinations on a global scale. Local tourism boards can highlight the type of corporate exposure to the local area. Government departments can also show in their internal and external publications the level to which corporate events are a significant part of the business mix within a region or nation, thus encouraging other potential organisations to book their next corporate conference/meeting. The venues may also illustrate through their website and printed material the type of events hosted at their venue.

Corporate marketing can also take on another dimension. Within a business sector, it is essential to demonstrate that a business is buoyant and fruitful. This communicates a positive message to employees, investors, shareholders and competitors. An external strategy to market a corporate event looks at the wider business market and places it firmly within its sector. Individual organisations will undertake all forms of marketing throughout a fiscal year; international conferences will bring together each one in the same location under one roof. The potential marketing benefits derived from that amalgamation of industry professionals and organisations represented is potentially unquantifiable in fiscal terms. However, the marketing benefits are not only immediate but long-lasting. Corporate events such as expos and G8 summits are continually communicated through numerous channels years after the event.

24.7 Corporate sponsorship

Historically, naming rights within the UK market are more aligned to sport stadiums and live-music venues, for example Emirates Stadium Arsenal Football Club named after Emirates Airlines and now called Emirates Stadium (based in Holloway, North London) and the recent O_2 naming rights on the 11 Academy Music Group (AMG) venues which as from 1 January 2009, were renamed O_2 Academy. The deal removes this existing incumbent Carling Lager, a UK beer brand.

Sponsorship has become a major means of marketing communication for many corporations and public-sector organisations.

Case study 24.5 Manchester 2002 Commonwealth Games

When organising the Manchester 2002 Commonwealth Games, the organising committee approached Microsoft UK to become a primary sponsor. In return, Microsoft would gain valued image and reputation but also an opportunity to showcase technology and entertain customers. This was a high-profile event for Microsoft and possibly the highest attracting media event for the company.

Skinner and Rukavina (2003) believe that an event that is well sponsored creates a good image; sees through the eyes of the sponsor; networks, which opens doors; stays in touch with sponsors; gives added value to sponsors; is perceived as the best; has outstanding staff; and gives sponsors results.

For this reason, large companies sponsor corporate events to gain all these benefits, and those events like exhibitions and large conferences to allow the right image and impression to be distributed to the right channel. Some companies acquire naming rights, which refers to the right to name a venue or an event, and events are usually granted in exchange for financial considerations (such as sponsorship). Securing the naming rights for stadia, theatres and other public gathering places is seen by such companies as a form of promotion.

24.8 Developing customer loyalty through corporate events

A successful corporate event will create a positive lasting impression on the customer and potentially differentiate the company from its competitors. An advertising campaign can reach millions of consumers yet generate many sales, whereas a corporate event may target fewer customers providing an opportunity to distribute important information, for example at a product launch.

One of the most important aspects of organising corporate events is that they are generally informal and face to face. It makes customers feel valued and important allowing a company representative to listen and respond to their individual questions and issues raised. Customers feel they are receiving instant and reliable feedback.

'Every day, trade shows, training, marketing, human resources development, sport and athletic, and other corporate events are held throughout the world' (O'Toole

& Mikolaitis, 2002: 1). Companies may choose to employ an external company to organise an exhibition for them.

For instance, Ferrari may hold a special exhibition in the *Galleria Ferrari* museum in Italy. The event is an overview of the Ferrari heritage and may attract thousands of visitors from all over the world. An entrance fee is payable, and there will be a selection of shops and a café area for refreshments, generating an income for Ferrari. But that is not the only reason to hold such a worldwide attraction event. It is also about improving the Ferrari image, developing the brand and sustaining relationships with customers and other corporate stakeholders.

'World's Fairs, or Expos, represent national marketing and foster international trade and tourism. Meetings and conventions are mostly related to the affairs of associations and corporations and might involve learning, morale-building and making policies' (Getz, 2007: 8).

Case study 24.6 Macworld, US

Macworld is holding the next edition of the World Expo event in the Moscone Center in San Francisco. It will be a five-day celebration in which they aim to educate, entertain and immerse the entire MAC community. The exhibition will also have conferences, special presentations, exhibit-hall highlights and experiences that meet their customers' needs. MAC will be spending thousands if not millions on one event but the return will be incredible to the company, especially for its reputation. World's fairs are almost all controversial as their large costs, and social and environmental impacts raise concern among political bodies.

24.9 Corporate event operations

Event operations within a venue setting have the added advantage of working to specific policies and procedures already in place. Apart from policies and procedures, legal commitments must also take precedence when planning operational delivery. Many international conference venues are affiliated to associations that also govern and stipulate benchmark standards on service quality for delegates, standard equipment, employment rights, regulations, etc. It is vital before booking a conference venue to undertake a visit to ensure that working policies and procedures are acceptable to meet operational success. Where the venue is in an international destination, contractual and legal requirements including insurance, should not only follow international law on human rights but also the home destination legal framework. This will ultimately take precedence in any negotiation, therefore seeking out legal representation within the host nation is an essential requirement to ensure all legal aspects are covered.

For any operation to run successfully, human resources must demonstrate competent and qualified individuals if required. To source local employees is sometimes cost effective but not always operationally expedient. Staff may need particular training and cultural awareness. If this option becomes a necessity for the organising team, the operational manager must engage with all local human resource suppliers to assess level of competence before agreements are signed off. Therefore, within the planning stage it is essential operational lead time to work with indigenous employees from the host community. In many international destinations, locally acquired employees who meet universal operational standards are readily available and can be sourced through contacts with international venues.

Quality always remains the main focus for any operational manager, and consistent monitoring of the operation, and not just at high-demand time, will help to ensure customer satisfaction is given full consideration. Where customer demand is higher than anticipated, the operational manager must have flexibility to bring about changes to staffing levels or increase the number of consumable products. All operations go through various levels of demand fluctuation over a given period. It is the skill of the operational manager that anticipates the fluctuations and makes necessary adjustments when required.

While delegates are seated for a time as part of the conference, the 'lean' period can be best exploited to brief staff and check that all items are working and ready for intended use. Within the operational delivery, other stakeholders may also have a specific operational need. Vendors/point-of-sale operators and sponsors have a clear marketing agenda to meet. Locations within the venue should allow for increased sales through customer footfall without infringing fire safety law or disrupting the operational flow of the event.

24.10 Corporate event risk management

Risk assessment as a business function follows a basic methodology wherever it is applied. The health and safety executive gives a working model that has applicability to many business situations. The five steps to risk assessment – identify, decide, evaluate, record and review – become the foundation for assessing many events.

Some corporate events, however, have significant risk assessment as part of their procedure, which sometimes requires specialist personnel and equipment. Corporate events that have a political content with VIP or political delegates require a different level of police assessment. The bomb squad plays a significant role in determining the safety of the buildings and immediate location. Special detachments within the police will also, if deemed necessary, interview individuals who work at the venue. The proximity to which an individual has contact with delegates could determine how stringent a risk assessment is carried out.

> ### Case study 24.7 First political conference, UK
>
> In 2006, the UK Labour Party had its first political conference in Manchester, the first time it was not held at a seaside destination. Security was key and security clearance for staff meant regular briefings between Labour, Manchester Central, the police and private security firm, Group 4, seven months ahead of the event. Owing to the high level of security, access to the venue for delegates required a lengthy lead time because of major security concerns, according to *Manchester Evening News (2006)*.

Pharmaceutical companies that have corporate conferences must also develop a risk assessment that looks at politically motivated organisations. Animal rights movements and their affiliated members around the world carry out their agenda with various degrees of potential impact. Individual members and groups should be given the highest priority when developing a risk assessment that will protect delegates and remove potential disruption to the event. Corporate and political conferences come with a strategy of risk assessment to meet customer satisfaction and event delivery. Therefore, developing working relationships with external agencies – government or otherwise – must become a significant part of the risk assessment. Where potential situations such as the ones mentioned above are not given significant attention, the negative impact on a conference or meeting goes beyond any fiscal loss to the organisation or host destination, and it has a ripple effect that can reverberate throughout the industry.

Case study 24.8 Manchester Museum of Science and Industry (MOSI), UK

MOSI aims to be a world-class cultural attraction, and in striving to do so it is supported by the Department for Culture, Media and Sport (DCMS), Heritage Lottery Fund, North West Development Agency, Investors in People, and the Charity Commission. MOSI is a facility that celebrates Manchester's industrial heritage in science and industry.

MOSI is structured in two parts: it has a commercial trading arm, and a charitable status which is independent of the commercial company. The charitable status deals primarily with running the museum. This acts as a tax advantage, where the museum can claim back tax on some exhibitions. The commercial arm contracted the Compass Group, who installed Milburn on 8 May 2006 to deliver corporate hospitality. (Milburn is a company owned by Compass Group delivering corporate hospitality service throughout the UK.)

The museum also undertakes corporate hospitality events with its contracted service supplier, the Compass Group. The DCMS is the main benefactor in terms of revenue; however, this financial assistance does not cover all expenditure. The baseline cost for running the venue is also supplemented by additional income streams – conferences and banqueting, business dinners, product launches, networking and award dinners.

The food provision, which is a major feature within the museum under the Compass umbrella, also doubles as the corporate hospitality for all events attached to the venue. The conference and banqueting side offered within the museum is jointly delivered by way of the museum staff and the Compass Group.

The full capital cost implication for supplying corporate hospitality and banqueting comes entirely from the contracted service supplier, Compass. Milburn, part of the Compass Group, delivers the full package in terms of banqueting and corporate hospitality. Human resource issues for Milburn in terms of food for daytime visitors and banqueting remain with Milburn. This type of business arrangement is a franchise concession. The revenue and service agreements are set by the museum. The service agreement operates on a three-year cycle, and the revenue targets are set on a yearly basis. The full contract operates on a five-year time scale, with formal tenders received after the contractual period. Prior to the late 2000s world recession, the revenue was set on a 10% yearly growth rate.

Where a financial and contractual arrangement requires the service provider to outlay the capital cost for securing a deal this potentially leaves the service provider with a period to recoup costs and make a profit before the end of the five-year tenure. If the deal is severed prior to the five-year window, the capital equipment must be purchased by the museum. This financial outlay only takes place if the museum terminates the contract before full term.

The five-year contract has within it performance related targets, undertaken by an independent research company. This looks at service quality through mystery shopping and customer feedback. (Mystery shopping is an activity employed predominantly by service providers to test the level of service quality given to customers, which in turn is feedback to the company.) The service-level agreement is synergised and benchmarked against external competitors, which extends to the museum and Milburn.

Client concession partnerships require continual review to ensure a strategic push year on year so that complacency does not become a business impediment.

Within the Milburn set-up for securing and producing corporate events, a sales office is situated within the business profile. The salespeople seek out sales opportunities and convert them into tangible events within the museum facility.

Utilisation and penetration of the marketing spend for Milburn, including the software and hardware capability, must be linked directly with the museum's internal IT provision – an end-to-end system that looks at sales enquiries, conversion rates from clients and repeat bookings.

The model of a franchise provision for corporate catering within MOSI is similar for 90% of the museums in Manchester. The difference with this model as with other provisions is that sales and banqueting are entirely given over to Milburn. With this proficiency comes an increase in sales – double that when under the control of the museum – which gives a wider customer base that was previously Manchester centric.

Going beyond that, we look at international corporate events as a new market and approached by two factors – a partnership approach with Manchester Art Gallery, Chill Factor and the Imperial War Museum, which all have a similar Milburn contractual set-up. An international event can then have cross-fertilisation between venues where facilities are not available or do not meet the required standard. A formal dinner for 300 is physically unsuitable for MOSI but can fit within the Imperial War Museum. The greater sales push for international events comes with the bidding unit within the marketing of Manchester. This relationship has been in place for approximately five years; however, the benefits of that relationship can only bear fruit if the bidding unit has a clear understanding of what the museum offers to corporate clients.

The marketing difference for corporate clients for attending events at MOSI is the museum itself. This alone is not sufficient because quality in service provision is a key driving factor for clients and customers. The benchmark where standard equipment is a basic requirement is measured against hotels and conference venues.

Food provision and the preparation area must also be in proximity to the event within the facility. Therefore long-term structural development is part of the museum's strategic goal. Along with this contractual business arrangement comes a more proactive approach to managing situations on behalf of the client or customer. Staff members are empowered to deal with situations on the spot, rather than within the museum's standard working philosophy. This method/approach is standard with successful service suppliers. To extend the service offer to customers and clients, resource purchasing must increase and staff mindset must change, thus customer satisfaction and repeat business become the business norm.

World-class service is a standard set by the chief executive of The Bridge Water Hall. This is a standard that looks at the best hotel provision in Manchester, and each hotel is audited against it. To achieve the benchmark standard, a unit must maintain a minimum of 85%. In customer quality and service provision, this audit is undertaken in part by mystery shopping.

To continually improve quality and standards, the model above has been replicated as a world-class standard for museums in Manchester. It includes meet-and-greet training along with customer-facing training. Alongside that, the museum is also accredited with a Charter Mark and visitor attraction accreditation, a national standard which leads to Investing In People. Investing In People is a government organisation set up to improve training and education across a multitude of industries.

The Manchester Museum of Science and Industry was the first museum in the UK to have a Charter Mark and visitor attraction accreditation.

Customers who attend the museum or MOSI corporate events have no knowledge that two separate provisions are supplying a professional service. This seamless approach is a necessity to maintain customer satisfaction and repeat business. Therefore, Milburn must also include staff training and development within their business profile that meets with the approval of MOSI.

Service provision for food at corporate events within MOSI remains with Milburn. Staffing for entrance and security is managed by MOSI. Major events, for instance paying host to Tony Blair, the former leader of the Labour Party, require greater synchronisation between both providers. This has become a common feature on how the joint collaboration drives operational requirements for corporate events.

Team building and business events are two types of events that operate within MOSI (events of this type operate on a two- to three-hour window). The key marketing pull for these organisations is removing themselves from their natural environment, mostly legal. Many companies find it beneficial to undertake business meetings outside of their formal setting, allowing for free thinking and a focused approach to finding business solutions. These events are more frequent in number, but financial spend is not comparable with frequency. Large-scale award dinners bring in a better financial return due to similar labour outlay but with a higher unit spend per customer.

24.11 Summary

This chapter showed us that corporate events are the current motivational strategy that is used to motivate employees, and is known as a non-financial reward. Nevertheless, corporate events are also a marketing tool for companies, a communication tool and, most of all, a way in which they can promote goods and services.

Corporate events are highly complex and play a major part in the overall events industry. Hosting corporate events is a modern approach used by organisations to award, reward, motivate and incentivise to their employees, clients and customers.

The impact of corporate events on tourist destinations demonstrates that they are vital in ensuring the growth of the economy for a particular region. Corporate events that have a political content by way of delegates attending require a different level of police assessment. Having the council and government on board, representing the event brings the tourism sector closer together, working on events that can boost the re-spend in one sector. Marketing Manchester has a remit to engage with conferences that have a tourism impact within the region. This approach ensures a level of partnership communication across all potential media, thus encouraging further business opportunities in conferencing.

Questions for further research

1 Examine the impact of corporate events on organisations and why companies are more and more interested in hosting corporate events.
2 Critically analyse and discuss the role that corporate events play in the development of commercial festivals.
3 Evaluate the importance of corporate events in the events industry.

Recommended websites

Browse the following internet sites for interesting and informative information:

Asia-Pacific Incentives & Meetings Expo (AIME): http://www.aime.com.au/
British Association of Conference Destinations: http://www.bacd.biz/files/ BCVS2008orderform.pdf
Business Events Sydney (BESydney): http://www.businesseventssydney.com.au/plan-an-event/event-planning-toolkit/preparation/preparation_home.cfm
Commonwealth Games Federation: http://www.thecgf.com/games/intro.asp?yr=2002
DRM Associates: http://www.npd-solutions.com/launchcons.html
EIBTM – the leading global event for the meetings and incentive industry: http://www. eibtm.ch/
IMEX – the worldwide exhibition for meetings and incentive travel: http://www.imex-frankfurt.com/
Incentives and Meetings International (I&MI) – the worldwide network for professional buyers and planners of international meetings, incentive travel programmes, congresses and corporate events: http://www.i-mi.com/
Market review: http://www.myvenues.co.uk/news/Industry/Uk-corporate-hospitality-set-to-grow/559/

Photo: World Travel Market

Photo: IMEX

Photo: IMEX

Photo: World Travel Market

25 *Meetings*

Deborah Johnson

Abstract

The meeting industry today is complex and challenging. Meetings have become big business and thus represent major economic gain for the host community and facilities where the meeting is being staged. The society of today is an information society. This implies that information is transferred, and meetings provide a platform for this to occur. Meetings have become a medium for communication. It is contended that meetings can also be regarded as a form of training and education. As stated by Wright (2005), 'on any given day there are more adult learners sitting in hotel meeting rooms than in all the universities in the nation'. Wright (2005) points out that those meeting delegates are focused on programme content and determine their attendance on the basis of value expectations in terms of their own professional, social or business benefits. An information society allows for asynchronous learning for people to become proficient in their field by attending virtual classes through distance-learning programmes and through the medium of web meetings. Meetings can

be held without moving away from the computer (Wright, 2005). However, this does not imply that fewer meetings will be held as technology cannot replace the dynamics of human interaction. On the contrary, the meetings industry is a growing one, and the expanded emphasis on international meetings with aspects such as esoteric logistics and dynamics, simultaneous interpretation, protocol and cross-cultural sensitivity places a great demand on the meeting manager. This will require that meeting managers become more knowledgeable and professional in the approach, planning and implementation of their meetings.

Chapter objectives

After you have read this chapter you should be able to:
- ❏ appreciate the size, scope and growth of the meeting industry; and
- ❏ conceptualise, plan, organise, manage and stage a meeting professionally.

25.1 Preface

Meeting professionals are highly skilled specialists who are thoroughly versed in the techniques of international meeting management. They further interface between corporations, associations or societies sponsoring the meeting as well as the service providers to the meeting. Their professionalism, knowledge, attention to detail and management skills assure the client of a successful, well-run event that achieves its goal. The position of the meeting manager has emerged as a management role.

25.1.1 Introduction

Astroff and Abbey (2002) note that three decades ago the hospitality industry looked at servicing the meeting market as an evil, and the meeting business was regarded as an insignificant market segment. The meeting industry is different today. The average meeting delegate spends approximately $250 per day, according to the Convention Industry Council (CIC), generating nearly over $122 billion. Within the hospitality industry, leisure travellers represent large numbers; however, meeting attendees bring in the majority of the revenue earned for this industry (Astroff & Abbey, 2002). Managing meetings is an art, focusing on competencies such as identifying suitable venues, negotiating rebated accommodation rates, pricing and quoting delegate fees, lining up keynote speakers and finding suitable sponsors. The complexity of arranging meetings on behalf of other people can be very challenging. To be successful, stamina, a positive frame of mind at all times, effective administration as well as a practical approach are required. As a meeting manager, values are important, in particular those relating to services offered, time and resources, the manner in which business is conducted, and the manner in which meeting managers will present themselves. To be successful, meeting management knowledge to stay ahead in the industry is required, as is hard work, sacrifice of personal time on occasion and a positive attitude. The purpose of this chapter is to provide some fundamental principles and techniques to enable the meeting manager to manage meetings in a professional manner.

25.1.2 Meetings, a global perspective

Although rising costs for transportation and hospitality services have been noted within the meetings sector, meetings are still being held. However, according to De Lollis (2008) this market is under threat due to the global economic crisis. Leaders from the CIC met during 2008 to deal with a strategy to promote the positive impact of face-to-face meetings in doing business, employing workers and sustaining communities, as media reports perceived conferences, business meetings and events to be wasteful. (Kotowski, 2008). Kotowski (2008: 1) further states that '[w]hat is missing from the current debate is the value that conferences and events bring to business. Conferences provide the necessary business education and exhibitions provide industry information and support the sales efforts critical to driving revenue to companies'.

Despite the threat to the meeting market, the market is lucrative and the demand for services is high. Astroff and Abbey (2002) posit that smaller meetings are more in demand and so is the training activity associated with them. The meeting industry is highly cyclical, and competition between service providers such as hotels is evident. Contract and negotiation issues favour hotels, and meeting planners also continue to face higher rates, longer lead times, reduced flexibility with dates and stiffer penalties if they are not successful in filling the space (Astroff & Abbey, 2002). It is contended that workers and managers in their respective fields will always require constant upgrading of skills and knowledge thus meetings will provide the platform for the various markets to conduct training.

25.2 What is a meeting?

A professional meeting is a gathering of people at a specified time and place for the purpose of communicating specific information. The meeting can also be regarded as a planned communication encounter between two or more persons for a common purpose (Landey, 2008). Further, the Meetings Industry Association (1996: 1) defines a meeting as '[a]n event involving ten or more people for a minimum of four hours during one day or more, frequently held outside the company's own premises'.

25.2.1 The reasons for staging meetings

Astroff and Abbey (2002: 7) state that 'meetings are held for a variety of purposes such as to keep abreast of today's ever-changing technology, to keep sales goals on track, to meet for group motivation and rewards and many more'. The CIC also acknowledges that meetings can provide very necessary business education (Kotowski, 2008). It is thus contended that a meeting becomes the communication of intellectual and emotional stimuli to accomplish a common purpose.

25.2.2 Types of meetings

The meeting spectrum is very broad and incorporates many types of meetings. It would simplify the focus if all of these events could be referred to as 'meetings'; however this is not the case as there are many synonyms for this term with various nuances. The following depicts the type and extent of meetings in the industry today. These can be regarded as business or educational events, and take place on a global scale.

- **Clinic.** This type of meeting is limited to small groups interacting with each other on an individual basis. It is normally used for training activities and is particularly focused on specific topics.
- **Colloquium.** This is an academic meeting where one or more academics present lectures on specific topics and then answer questions.
- **Conference.** A conference involves much discussion and participation. It is a term that is used in technical and scientific as well as trade areas. A conference programme deals with specific challenges or developments, and could involve smaller breakaway meetings. They can also be small or large in attendance.
- **Congress.** A congress is a gathering held at regular intervals for a formal exchange of views and information. Attendance is generally large, and the purpose is often to resolve current issues or challenges.
- **Convention.** A convention generally consists of informative sessions with a specific theme or topic which can be linked to politics, trade, science or technology, among others. Conventions can involve general sessions and supplementary smaller meetings, and are produced with and without exhibits. They have a repetitive cycle, the most common of which is annual. The general sessions normally require large venues for the whole group, and where specific issues are discussed in smaller groups, breakaway rooms are used.
- **Exhibitions/trade shows.** An exhibition is an event held in conjunction with another meeting such as a conference or convention. The exhibition format will normally be used for display by vendors of goods and services. The trade show, on the other hand, is a show that is held for its own sake and is normally not open to the general public. If it is open to the general public it is known as a consumer show, and a nominal entrance fee is charged.
- **Forum.** This is a meeting that involves back-and-forth discussion, which is led by presenters or panellists. Audience participation is normally expected, and a moderator will summarise points of view and lead the discussion.
- **Institute.** Conferences, seminars and workshops are often offered by an institute which is normally established within a trade or profession to offer extended educational and training opportunities. These terms further suggest continuing training programmes every quarter of the year.
- **Lecture.** The lecture is a formal or structured individual presentation, often done by one expert.
- **Meetings.** If there is no term to apply to an event it is simply referred to as a meeting. This is applicable when the participants are members of a single organisation discussing aspects such as organisational affairs.
- **Retreat.** A retreat implies a small meeting in a remote location with the purpose of bonding and intensive planning sessions.
- **Seminar.** A seminar involves participation and a sharing of knowledge by all. It is managed under the supervision of a discussion leader. The format is small groups, but as it grows it will change format to become a forum or symposium.
- **Symposium.** A symposium is similar to a forum, except that conduct is more formal. The method used is by presentation.

- *Web conferencing.* Web conferencing is used to conduct live meetings or presentations via the internet.
- *Workshop.* The workshop format involves general sessions with small groups that deal with specific challenges or assignments. It is normally used by training directors for skills training (Astroff & Abbey, 2002).

25.2.3 Who holds meetings?

As there are various reasons for holding meetings, there are also various businesses, corporations and people that will hold a meeting. For convenience and to conceptualise who holds meetings, the meeting business of today can be grouped into the following categories:
- Corporations;
- Associations; and
- Non-profit organisations.

Although meetings can be very costly to organise, they play a critical role in fostering education and training, and provide a platform for the meeting holders to network and share issues of mutual interest.

25.3 Conceptualisation of the meeting

The following section examines the aspects of professional meeting management. The topics covered have been arranged according to event domains of staging any type of event professionally, and these guidelines are applicable to national and international meetings. No meeting will be successful without thorough planning. Planning will provide an appropriate timeframe to follow and result in the setting of specific goals and objectives for the meeting. The need for a meeting will be identified by the meeting owner, and the meeting will be organised either by an in-house meeting manager or outsourced to a professional meeting manager. In either scenario, the same amount of work and planning will be involved. Each meeting is unique and requires proper planning. The two case studies 25.1 and 25.2 provide an overview of the organising of specific meetings.

25.3.1 Meeting administration and management

Organising a meeting is a process which is integrated and complex. There are many aspects to consider and to remember. The meeting manager identifies, determines and examines the many factors that will shape the design and the production of the meeting. This is applicable to any type and size of meeting. Factors that will guide the meeting process of planning include the needs of the stakeholders, the practicality of the logistics, the availability of resources, and the vision, mission and goals of the meeting. Further policies for meeting managers in terms of sustainability ('greening' their meetings) were established in 2004 by the CIC's Green Meetings Task Force. This implies that meeting managers are required to be mindful of the environmental considerations of their event and should implement the minimum best practices for organising their meeting (CIC, 2004).

Goldblatt (2002) states that there is a process to follow when creating and producing a professional meeting. This process includes five specific phases:
- Concept of the meeting;
- Researching the requirements of the meeting;
- Planning the meeting;

Case study 25.1 Saudi Arabia: The 3rd Saudi International Banking & Investment Conference, 9–10 May 2009, Jeddah Hilton Hotel

Website: http://www.xs-conferences.com

'It is no secret that Saudi Arabia is a favourite choice for those who are seeking good investment opportunities. This reputation is due to many factors. To name but a few; the political stability this country enjoys plus the pro investment strategy that the leadership is adopting. This of course will give more strength to the national economy and will create more job opportunities on both long and short terms. The 3rd Saudi International Banking & Investment Conference (SIBIC, 2009), comes in a time when economic & investment issues make headlines locally, regionally and globally. Therefore this conference is at the centre of attention and interest of banks, stock establishments, brokers, economists and all those with interest in economical issues. Moreover, the huge banking industry in Saudi Arabia is racing time to improve and develop its performance in order to be able to reserve a seat in the front rows of completion both regionally and on a global level.'

The meeting was sponsored and supported by the Financial Stock Committee of the Jeddah Chamber of Commerce and Industry and the Prince Sultan College for Tourism and Business, Jeddah. Over 500 delegates attended the prestigious meeting.

The conference was planned in accordance with the five EMBOK domains, namely administration, design, marketing, operations and risk. In terms of adhering to the EMBOK procedures, the following was used as a guideline to execute the conference successfully:

Administration. This entailed financial management, human resource management, information management, procurement procedures, management of stakeholders, database management and effective time control of the process;

Design. As the conference took place within the Jeddah Hilton Hotel, the hotel provided assistance with the site design of the conference environment. Further, the hotel also assisted with the food and beverage requirements, technical aspects and the theme.

Marketing. For this conference, a marketing plan was developed, as was in place a year prior to the execution of the meeting. Further materials were developed that were used for the public relations and promotional aspects of the event. Sponsorships were also secured successfully, which included Bank Aljazira, the Saudi Research and Marketing Group, Banque Saudi Fransi and the Alhamrani Group of Companies.

Operations. As the conference took place in a secured venue, much assistance was provided by the venue in terms of operational matters. The registration of delegates took place online prior to the conference; however, a registration area was set up to deal with any errors and late registrations. Protocol was adhered to in terms of receiving royal dignitaries and guests, and hosts were used to assist with ushering the audience during the meeting proceedings. Further aspects such as logistics, site management, technical matters and communication were dealt with very smoothly on site and no challenges were reported.

Risk. A thorough risk assessment was conducted as royal guests were present at the conference. Strict security measures were in force and executed successfully. Special insurances were secured for any incidents. The safety and security aspect was outsourced. The service provider and meeting organiser worked together to ensure that a safety and security plan was in place for the event. Security staff was on site all the time, and also assigned to deal with any type of challenge.

The overall feedback regarding the conference was that is was very professionally organised. Specific mention was made to the choice of venue, which was rated as excellent, and the smooth operational flow of all aspects related to the conference.

❑ Coordinating the meeting; and
❑ Evaluating the meeting.

It is an art to put together a meeting. Creativity is essential and is required when dealing with each new meeting. The meeting environment becomes the STAGE for the meeting manager, who will play a large role in the production of the meeting to ensure that the meeting is memorable for the client, stakeholders and the participants:

S	– Satisfy the needs
T	– Tantalise the senses
A	– Analyse the site
G	– Guide guest impressions
E	– Establish the atmosphere

The nature of the meeting will determine its design and the theme. It is advisable to conduct a brainstorming session which will enable the sharing of creative ideas and concepts without criticism. Brainstorming produces IDEAS:

I	– Include your ideas
D	– Develop exercises
E	– Encourage creativity
A	– Accept all suggestions
S	– Select the best components

Source: Tassiopoulos (2005)

It is advisable to always work from checklists in planning the meeting. The following are examples of checklists for a meeting; however these can be adapted to the nature of the meeting that is being organised.

Financial management

Responsible fiscal management is essential to any meeting and is among the meeting manager's most important responsibilities. Staying within the budget is evidence of the meeting manager's competence, and

budgeting to generate revenue is a measure of success. At a Meeting Professionals International (MPI) conference held in Turin during March 2009, findings were shared with the industry regarding the return on investment (ROI) of meetings. The research indicated that meetings provide the highest return on investment with 23% of the respondents choosing events marketing as the discipline that provided the greatest return on investment (Gantrygroup, 2009). Further ROI, in particular for meetings, is focused in bringing in a profit for the meeting. ROI for meetings can be approached in two ways, firstly in terms of the profit the meeting will bring in for the meeting manager and, secondly, the publicity of the meeting for the client. When a meeting brings in a profit it can be regarded as a quantitative measurement on the ROI as it can actually be determined. If a meeting is well organised the word-of-mouth aspect becomes a positive ROI for the meeting manager and the meeting owner. The focus again can be regarded as a qualitative ROI, but is more difficult to determine quantitatively.

Long-term financial results are an important consideration in meeting management. Meetings can be non-profit and profit making. Goldblatt (2002) posits that there are three categories of meeting budgets:

❑ Profit-oriented meetings, where the revenue will exceed the expenses;
❑ Breakeven meetings where the revenue is equal to the expenses; and
❑ Hosted meetings, where the client will cover the cost of the event.

ROI determination for a meeting is important. It is a performance measure that can be used to evaluate the efficiency of an investment or to compare the efficiency of a number of different investments.

Example 25.1 Example of a checklist

ALL PURPOSE CHECK LIST FOR MEETINGS/EVENTS
....
....
....

Actions	Responsible person	Completion date		Completed	Comments
		Anticipate date	True date		

However, the meeting manager should keep in mind that the calculation for ROI can be modified to suit the situation – it depends on what is included as returns and costs. The term in the broadest sense attempts to measure the profitability of an investment.

It is important to estimate how much a meeting will cost and to keep track of the actual expenses incurred. With every

Example 25.2 Example of a meeting checklist

Item description	Jan				Feb				March				April				May*			
	1	2	3	4	1	2	3	4	1	2	3	4	1	2	3	4	1	2	3	4
MEETING TIMETABLE																				
Transport																				
❏ Finalise transport contributor																				
❏ Plan logistics movements																				

meeting, money that changes hands must be documented and the financial records need to reflect this accordingly. Estimated costs can be determined by considering the following:

❏ Is the aim of the meeting to make a profit?
❏ How much will the meeting cost?
❏ What are the types of revenue sources?
❏ What items for selling are required in order to break even?
❏ What will the cash flow process be?
❏ What control systems should be in place to avoid fraud?
❏ How will the legal and taxation obligations be met?

Preparing a meeting budget becomes part of the initial planning phase. The budget will include the projected revenue and expenditure from which the net profit or loss is determined. The meeting budget further becomes a plan that is based upon quotes from vendors, contractors and suppliers. This involves research to ensure that no expenses have been overlooked.

The meeting budget further provides a guideline for expenditure approval and ensuring that financial aspects of the meeting remain on track (Van der Wagen, 2005). The meeting budget should include the meeting management fee and a contingency for unexpected expenses, which can range from 5-10% of the costs. The following budget process, according to Van der Wagen (2005), is advisable:

❏ Draft the meeting budget, based on an analysis of all available meeting information, ensuring that the income and expenditure estimates are clearly identified and supported by valid, reliable and relevant information;
❏ Research the internal and external environments for potential impacts on the meeting budget;
❏ Assess and present alternative approaches to the budget;
❏ Ensure that the draft meeting budget reflects the meeting objectives;
❏ Circulate the draft meeting budget to the meeting team for comments, input and broader discussion;

- Negotiate the meeting budget with the relevant stakeholders, including the meeting client where relevant;
- Be agreeable, and incorporate modifications to the meeting budget;
- Complete the final meeting budget in the required format within the designated time;
- Inform colleagues of the final meeting budget in a timely manner;
- Review the meeting budget regularly to assess performance against estimates;
- Analyse and investigate any deviations; and
- Collect the necessary information for future budget preparation.

Capital is required to set up a meeting. A meeting could take a year to plan in which period costs can be incurred, all which have to be paid in advance. In instances where the client is paying for a meeting, a deposit can be negotiated; however, payment of the balance may not be paid to the meeting manager until at least one month after the completion of the event. Adequate planning of cash is thus necessary. Ideally an establishment fee should be negotiated to alleviate any cash flow challenges. Monthly expenses and projected revenue need to be documented to establish how cash flow can be managed effectively. Cash handling refers to dealing with cash relating to aspects of the meeting. Specific people should be appointed with the meeting manager as overseers of cash handling. Whoever handles an amount of cash needs to sign for it in order to take full responsibility for it. It is advisable that staff assigned with the responsibility of cash handling receive a special clearance. Receipts need to be retained and effectively documented in the case of expenses. A form of financial control also needs to be established. All purchases must be approved, and the use of requisition forms are encouraged.

Regular and detailed budget reports are necessary as they provide the client with information on the performance measured in terms of the meeting budget. Apart from the preparation of the meeting budget, financial reporting is the most important phase of the system of meeting budget control. Financial reporting entails not only external but also internal reports. The following requirements are suggested for financial meeting reports:

- Reports must contain the phases of the meeting in order to exercise effective control at all levels:
- They must be compiled in accordance with the needs of the users;
- They must be as simple as possible;
- The necessary information must be conveyed accurately and reliably; and
- In order to ensure the greatest possible utility, reports must be completed easily, quickly and in time.

Human resource management

Human resource management is an important function that must be carried out in order to achieve the aims of the meeting successfully. A common denominator for meetings is their reliance on quality staff in order to deliver the necessary services. Wiersma and Strolberg (2003) state that no matter what meeting is being planned, a good team is required to make it happen.

Organisation planning for meetings can be complex, and generally will require a variety of charts suitable for each stage of the meeting. These charts can include pre-meeting charts, charts for during the meeting and post-meeting charts. Staff orientation and training are essential to the success of any meeting. Meeting staff and volunteers need to be trained in the objectives of the meeting, the actual venue of the meeting and their specific duties as they relate to the meeting. All staff members must be provided with a general outline of the meeting, its objectives and its organisational structure. The following provides an example of meeting organisational structures:

Familiarisation tours of the meeting venues for the staff are necessary as this will acquaint them with the location of facilities, the functional areas and departments, the spectator services that are provided and emergency procedures. They also need to know their duties and what is expected of them, and how to perform their duties. Maps and checklists are useful tools for training staff as are special manuals developed by the meeting manager regarding meeting policies and procedures. Customer service orientation is essential, and staff members need to know how to deal with customers. Training days need to be organised, and briefing sessions need to be part of the meeting process with the commencement of the meeting. Meeting management training manuals, according to Van der Wagen (2005), should include information on shift routine and specific tasks, venue operations and general meeting information.

Employment regulations refer to those specifically developed in relation to the meeting. Conditions and factors are to be discussed with staff members and reflected in their respective contracts. Such regulations, however, must be within the boundaries of legal requirements. All paid staff and volunteers should be remunerated according to the set labour agreement. Workplace agreements can be developed with the staff. It is necessary to have professional legal advice with regard to aspects concerning staff and their rights. Recognition of the work of both paid and

volunteer staff can have a great impact on motivation. An effective strategy for staff is to set realistic goals – this will allow them to experience how their work contributed to the success of the meeting. Staffing policies should also be developed as part of the human resource planning strategy for the meeting. These policies should cover focus areas such as health and safety, misconduct, poor performance, sexual harassment and contravention of safety procedures.

Procurement management

Procurement in the meeting scenario implies a method by which items necessary to stage and host the meeting are purchased from external suppliers. The procurement management process for meetings would involve managing the ordering, receipt, review and approval of items from the suppliers. Specific systems would need to be set up to manage this process, and it is recommendable to have a procurement division that can manage this function. A procurement policy is important to the meeting manager as this is the guideline to be followed in terms of how the supplier relationship will be managed and to ensure that a high level of service is received from the suppliers. Further, the procurement policy will assist in identifying the goods and services set within a specific framework and methodology. The policy will also identify rules and regulations related to purchase orders and issues to suppliers, delivery timeframes from suppliers, methods of receiving goods and services, and relevant documentation of the process. How to approve supplier payments will also form part of the policy.

Bid solicitations imply receiving extensive quotes from service suppliers to supply services that are linked to the planned meeting. These quotes can take

Example 25.3 Example of the composition of a meeting organising

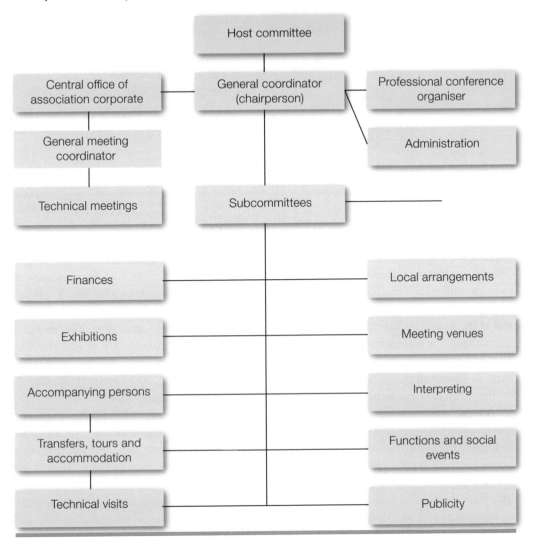

the form of a bid from the providers. The meeting manager needs to determine the criteria for bid solicitations. A bid is a document that covers concepts and services that can be supplied, and is a comprehensive document of what can be offered with the relevant pricing, as well as the capabilities of the providers. It can also include previous references. The meeting manager can also have criteria for the bid development and invite service providers to bid in terms of providing services to the meeting.

Purchasing procedures are required for the meeting. This will ensure that a system is followed allowing for adequate documentation of what services and items are being purchased. It further allows for people to take responsibility and accountability for purchasing set within a system. Purchasing procedures would

Example 25.4 Example of a simple organisational structure for a meeting

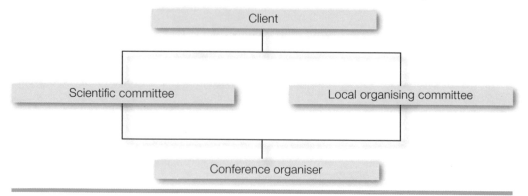

include identifying the supplier contracts that are required. Planned purchases and acquisitions would be followed as this will determine what services and items need to be purchased for the meeting. Relevant documentation such as orders, invoices and receipts will be kept to document the relevant process and to track all purchases. This will indicate what has been paid and what is outstanding, as well as what has been and what is still to be supplied.

A total quality management system will enforce a system approach to purchasing and a tracking of all purchasing. It will allow for people to be in positions of responsibility and accountability in terms of purchases for the meeting. The quality of the system will be monitored, as well as the quality of services and items required for the meeting. Further quality control will allow an approach to deal with services and items that do not meet the required benchmark of quality set for the meeting and how to alleviate these challenges. Ultimately, it provides for a form of financial management as this is a cost to the meeting.

Stakeholder management

Stakeholders include the meeting client, meeting participant, any other person or company that can be linked to the meeting, and service providers to the meeting. They are actively involved in the project and whose interests may be positively or negatively affected as a result of project execution or completion. Further, they could exert influence over the meeting and the end result. These stakeholders become an important part of the success of the meeting. The relationship that is created with these stakeholders becomes a vehicle to achieving meeting goals and objectives. Having a positive relationship with stakeholders can be regarded as a social ROI for the meeting. This is an approach to understanding and managing the impacts of a meeting or similar project. Further, it is based on stakeholders, and places financial values on the important impacts identified by stakeholders who do not have market value. The aim is to include the value of people in order to give them a voice in resource-allocation decisions. The key components to stakeholder partnerships and their management is to define the roles, to understand the type of communication that will be directed to each, to listen to each stakeholder and to always acknowledge their involvement to the meeting.

Accountability in the meeting scenario will refer to the accountability towards stakeholders in the meeting process. The meeting manager with the core management team is accountable in terms of ensuring effective relationships with stakeholders.

Systems management

Systems management for meetings basic-ally involves the implementation and the coordination of database, knowledge management and knowledge transfer systems using suitable technology applications and equipment to integrate the needs and requirements of the meeting. There are many methods for effective communication within the meeting setup and the focus is to make it as effective as possible. Decisions would need to be made regarding what the most effective methods would be, and this will be determined by the nature of the specific meeting. There are also various database systems to manage running the meeting effectively. These systems assist in the management of information regarding the participants and speakers and various aspects related to the meeting. For example, Summit Pro is a software system that assists with providing meeting management variables and managing data back to back. Again, the nature of the meeting will determine which system is most suitable.

Time management for meetings

Outstanding time management skills are required to gain the maximum benefit from planning the meeting. An ability to develop an instant rapport with staff and in particular new staff becomes essential, specifically when time is limited.

Case study 25.2 Saudi Arabia: Government and Corporate Social Responsibility Forum, Marbia Conference Hall, Makkah, 8 March 2009, under the patronage of His Royal Highness Prince Khaled Al Faisal

Website: http://www.xs-conferences.com

The key focus of the event was on community-based projects and corporate social responsibilities within the Kingdom of Saudi Arabia. It was a one-day event, comprising a short programme with four sessions linked to social responsibility. The key focus of the meeting was to promote trends in developing social responsibility and the role of government in this. Professional meeting principles were adhered to in terms of organising the meeting. As there were royal dignitaries in attendance, strict protocol was adhered to. The location was in one of the Holy Cities of Saudi Arabia, Makkah, thus access to the meeting was only for people of the Muslim faith. The feedback regarding the meeting was that it was professionally organised.

25.3.2 Meeting design

Meeting design focuses on the artistic interpretation of the meeting. It also incorporates its the vision, mission and goals. The key element is to create a positive experience at the meeting. Designing a meeting requires creativity so that those attending feel they have experienced a special moment. Design is mostly seen, therefore, as a skilled action or an act of creativity that gives something a visual identity or recognition. Meeting design is the creation, according to Brown (2005), of conceptual development and design to maximise the positive and meaningful impact for the meeting participants. Further, the world is changing and is making meeting managers rethink the way they produce their meetings. Environmental and social issues combined with the current state of the global economy presents new challenges in meeting design. Meetings thus need to adapt and evolve to produce cost-effective, relevant and meaningful events that are fiscally, socially and environmentally responsible. To assist with meeting design it is advisable to work from a client discussion sheet when meeting clients. This ultimately provides specific information that can be used in determining the design of the meeting. Below is an example that can be adapted to the nature of the meeting.

Content design

Content design of the meeting will incorporate selecting the most appropriate topics, formats and presenters to achieve the key focus of the meeting. The nature of the meeting will determine these selections. It will involve the meeting manager and organising team to discuss matters and to reach consensus.

Entertainment design

Entertainment design for the meeting will focus on the identification and selection of the type of entertainment suitable to the meeting. It can include social entertainment, ancillary programmes and recreational activities for the participants.

Environment design

Besides the meeting following a specific programme format, it will be taking form within a specific environment. The nature of the meeting will influence the setting of the environment. Aspects that would be considered in terms of designing the environment include the arrangement of specific décor, furniture and signage. Another consideration is the way rooms are set up, the way the tables and chairs are arranged. The type of meeting will determine these setups. Figure 25.1 and 25.2 illustrates just a few examples of room setups that you could consider.

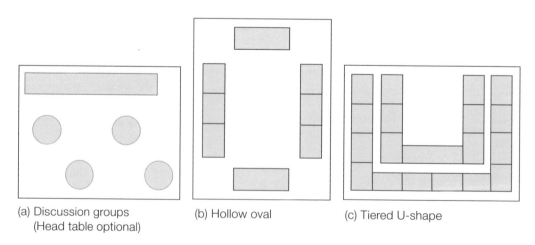

(a) Discussion groups
(Head table optional)

(b) Hollow oval

(c) Tiered U-shape

Figure 25.1 Meeting rooms setups (adapted from Pain, 1979: 41–43)

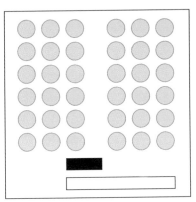

(a) Theatre arangement

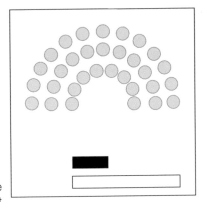

(b) Amphitheatre arrangement

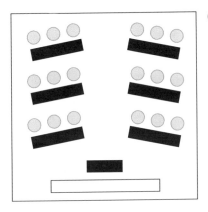

(c) Classroom arrangement

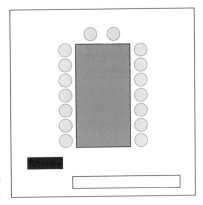

(d) Centre table arrangement

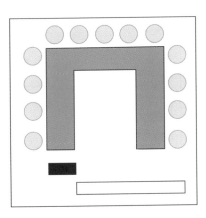

(e) U-shaped table arrangement

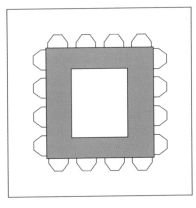

(f) Hollow square arrangement

Figure 25.2 (a) to (f) Meeting venue setups (adapted from Pain, 1979: 41–43)

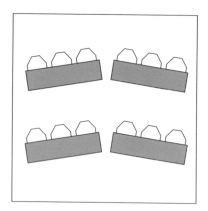

(g) Herringbone arrangement

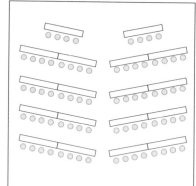

(h) V-shaped classroom arrangement

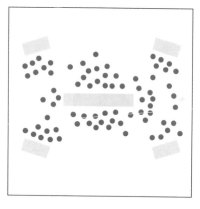

(i) Reception arrangement

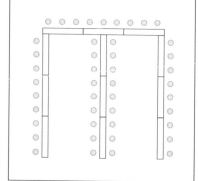

(j) E-shaped arrangement

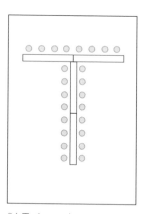

(k) T-shaped arrangement

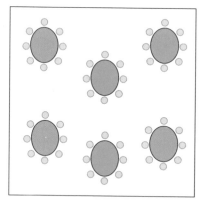

(l) Banquet arrangement

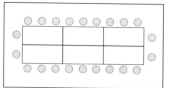

(m) Board of directors arrangement

Figure 25.2 (g) to (m) Meeting venue setups (adapted from Pain, 1979: 41–43)

Food and beverage design

In planning food and beverages for meetings, it is necessary to have a basic understanding of different foods as participants are likely to be health conscious and demand healthy foods. The food and beverage design will also involve the development of a plan that will link to the focus point and theme of the meeting. This will further impact the selection of menus, the style of serving and requirements associated with the serving of alcohol. It is very important to make sure about what cultural requirements are part of the meeting. Further, it is advisable to develop a catering process for the meeting detailing all the necessary steps, activities, sequences and responsibilities. Measures for safety and health also need to be adhered to.

Production and technical design

This aspect provides an important focus to the meeting. It involves the selection of appropriate sound, lighting, visual projection, multimedia, special effects and other elements required to meet the desired impression of the meeting. The type of meeting will determine the relevant selection.

Programme design

Clearly defined goals are essential to meeting programme design. Articulated by management, the meeting goals and objectives are to serve as the formal criteria against which all elements are judged before the programme is accepted. Aspects such as a timeframe, for example how much time is available for the selected programme (five

Example 25.5 Example of a client discussion sheet in view of planning a meeting

WESTERN CAPE MEETING CONSULTING SERVICES CC

(in small letters your address, tel, fax, cell and email)

CLIENT DISCUSSION FORM

Name of client	
Address	
Tel/fax	
Email	
Cell	
Contact person	

What is the theme of the meeting?...

Who are the organisers?...

Others involved with the organisation? ....

Has the organising committee held any meetings to date?..

When? ....

What commitments have been made/discussed? ....

How many main organising committee meetings do you envisage holding? ....

How many members on the organising committee? ....

Have the site and venue been decided? ....

Is it a national or international meeting? ....

How many delegates to attend? ....

Fixed ideas on the format of the meeting? ....

Will there be an exhibition complementing the meeting? ....

Will there be a technical programme coordinator/committee and will the services
of a meeting organiser be required? ....

Are presenters being invited? ....

Will presenters be offered perks? ....

Are you going to call for papers, select presenters and edit papers? ....

Will you publish proceedings? ....

Will VIPs and government or others be involved? ....

Will you require interpreters? ....

Are social/entertainment events to be offered?...

Will a separate 'partners' programme' be offered? (selecting a DMC for this) ....

Child-care programmes? ....

How many announcements do you envisage? ....

Will you want a separate printed programme? ....

Will pre- and post tours be offered? ....

Will technical excursions be part of the meeting? ....

Who will be responsible for the finances? ....

Is basic support funding available? ....

Will you be seeking sponsorship? ....

Who will manage the finances? ....

Who handles registration? ....

Housing arrangements for delegates? ....

Transportation? ....

Audiovisual aids? ....

Legal issues considered? ....

Space use and set-up design? ....

On site communications? ....

Meeting wrap-up? ....

hours to four days), and content become important in the design of the programme. It further includes all activities that influence the shape of the meeting.

Theme design

The key focus of the meeting will determine the selection of the theme for the meeting such as a sporting focused meeting, medical meeting or cosmetics meeting. It would need to communicate the purpose of the meeting, the message, the image and branding of the meeting.

Marketing for meetings

Marketing for a meeting is the process of planning and executing the conception, pricing, promotion and distribution of ideas, goods and services to create exchanges that satisfy individual and organisational goals (Van der Wagen, 2005).

Return on marketing investment (ROMI) is a metric used to measure the overall effectiveness of a marketing campaign to assist meeting managers to make better decisions regarding allocating future investments linked to their meetings. Furthermore, ROMI can be defined as the optimisation of marketing spend for the short and long term in support of the brand strategy by using valid, objective marketing metrics, creating increased revenue and profit for the meeting.

Marketing plan

A marketing plan can be developed for a single meeting, and follows the same guidelines as developing one for a business. In terms of the meeting, the following process would be applicable, namely to analyse the internal business environment, analyse the external business environment, identify target markets, develop products and prices,

plan the distribution system, develop the meeting marketing objectives, develop action plans and budgets, and monitor success (Van der Wagen, 2005).

Materials management

Materials management for meetings involves the design and delivery of printed materials that will be used to support the marketing of the meeting, and operational activities that are required for the meeting. Specific aspects would include advertising, delegate tags, speaker tags, brochures, flyers, forms, invitations, media kits, posters, printing, programmes, registration packs and DVDs.

Merchandise management

In terms of the meeting, this function will involve overseeing the product development, manufacture and distribution of retail merchandise associated with the meeting. Specific elements for the meeting would involve customer service, licensing, logo wear and brand management.

Promotion management

When it comes to successfully promoting the meeting, there is no 'one size fits all' plan or magic formula that works every time. Every meeting is different. The audience the promotion is aimed at, the location, the agenda, the season and the economy can play a critical role in the success or the failure of a meeting. Promotion management further involves the actions of procurement and organising advertising campaigns, promotional events, cross-promotion alliances and activities to generate attention and interest for the meeting.

Public relations management

Public relations will assist in communicating the meeting message to the audience and publics of the meeting. Publicity is a cost-effective manner in relaying the meeting message to the target audience. Further, public relations management deals with the formulation and execution of tactics capable of generating publicity coverage for the meeting. Prior to soliciting publicity it becomes important for the meeting manager to establish the target market and the media. It is also important to know the meeting and to conceptualise it.

Sales management

Sales management for meetings involves the action of supervising procedures, platforms and transaction processes for the on-site, remote and electronic sales activities connected to the meeting. This can include registration operations, concessions, special rebates and other retail endeavours to achieve profit outcomes for the meeting.

Sponsorship management

Finding sponsors to support the meeting not only assists with the bottom line, but can also bring new resources and energy to the meeting. Sponsorship involves the exchange of value for value. Sponsorship can further be regarded as a strategic partnership with commitment to actions and support from both sides. The goal is to create a win-win relationship that will assist the meeting and the sponsor. The steps of sponsorship management would include auditing specific opportunities, targeting sponsors, developing a sponsorship package, assigning value to the package, agreement with the meeting team on documentation, legal contracts and having a follow-up report.

25.3.3 Meeting operations

A meeting manager needs to plan the implementation of the meeting at micro level with attention to detail. Meeting operations further involves the people, products and services that are brought to the meeting site. It also includes allocating the roles and responsibilities of staff to ensure that operations and logistics run smoothly.

Attendee management

Attendee management for meetings focuses on the actual control systems for participants such as the registration process and access process to the meeting. It is an operational and logistical function that will make use of information technology systems, and requires dedicated staff to manage and control the process. Specific actions will include access control, group movements, guest relations, registration systems and ushering systems. The set-up of such a control system would be in a dedicated meetings operation venue.

Communication management

Communication is an important feature for the management of a meeting, which will start early in the planning phase of the meeting, continue during the building and running of the meeting, to post-meeting evaluations. Depending on the type of meeting, it will involve information technology systems as relevant tools to execute the communication process. Communication structures that are highly productive and that avoid confusion need to be set up. Further it will involve a communication plan and the relevant equipment to ensure that communication takes place effectively. It includes all the stakeholders to the meeting as well as the preparation and incorporation of documentation and contact information, presented in an accessible format.

Infrastructure management

The infrastructure linked to a meeting includes the equipment and services to ensure that the functional elements of the meeting are met. This further involves the actual implementation of emergency services, maintenance, lighting systems, medical services and parking.

Logistics management

Meeting logistics will focus on the analysis, sequencing and supervision of the tasks of the move-in and move-out activities of the meeting, such as action plans, ceremonial protocol, contractors, installations and dismantling.

Participant management

Participants linked to the meeting need to be managed, and their specific functions need to be verified and tracked. Functions will include accountability, facility personnel, media, providers of services and meeting committees.

Site management

In terms of a meeting, site management will involve the inspection and the selection of locations and facilities that will serve the requirements of the meeting. The actions of site management will include accessibility matters, maps, relevant furnishings, signage, site facilities, site inspections, site personnel, site plans, equipment and storage.

Technical management

For meetings, technical aspects are very important. These will include the necessary and appropriate staging and equipment, and supervision of their installation and operation, and, most importantly, the attendant technical personnel to be on site. For meetings the following actions are relevant: audiovisual services, equipment, projection systems, sound distribution, sound equipment and technicians.

25.3.4 Meeting risk management

All meeting managers face a range of risks. It is impossible for a meeting manager to fully understand all laws that are pertinent to their industry. Risk is the chance that something will go wrong. It further involves the process of identifying such risks, assessing them and managing them. It becomes a part of good management practice (Van der Wagen, 2005).

Compliance management

Meeting compliance includes all the necessary permissions required for a variety of aspects linked to the meeting, which includes alcohol laws, consent forms, fire safety, food inspections, intellectual property, licences, music licensing, permits, safety inspections, waivers and visas. It is the responsibility of the event manager to ensure that compliances are met and adhered to.

Decision management

Decision management involves the actions of approval and consultation. It stipulates who has the authority to deal with matters and to make decisions regarding them. Further it is the establishment of practical decision-making systems for the meeting that include the accurate framing of decisions, the application of relevant resources, criteria, rules and regulations, and granting the necessary authority. Specific actions will focus on contingency plans, crisis plans, incident reporting, risk analysis, risk avoidance, risk control, risk diffusion, risk documentation, risk fields, risk identification, risk mitigation, risk monitoring, risk resilience and risk retention.

Emergency management

Emergency management will involve the identification of the relevant authorities, medical services and other emergency responders that can be liaised with should any emergencies occur linked to the meeting.

Health and safety management

Health and safety aspects for meetings involve the establishment and the implementation of fire safety, life safety, occupational safety and policies linked to control of audiences and procedures that ensure the health and welfare of each individual involved or in attendance at the meeting. Particular areas of importance to meetings are equipment training, fall protection, fire safety systems, lighting, noise levels, occupational hazards, occupational health and safety (OSH) requirements, safety meetings and waste management.

Legal management

It is advisable to have legal advice on hand when staging meetings. It is also important for the meeting manager to remain abreast of general changes to legislation that could impact the daily operations of the meeting. Legal management further implies the negotiation and execution of the contracts and other legal documents associated with acquisitions and matters of the meeting. It also involves overseeing the lawful design and implementation of the policies, procedures and practices of the meeting organisation.

Security management

Security is required for the meeting premises, equipment, cash and other valuables. The meeting manager should have a sound knowledge of what security would incorporate for the meeting; however, the function of security would be outsourced to a professional service provider. The meeting manager will work very closely with the service provider

as the responsibility for a safe and secure meeting environment remains with him or her. Security would also become part of the on-site team of the meeting. An important function of security is to ensure that the correct people have access to areas and to act in a responsible manner in the case of accident or emergency. Security management will also involve the sourcing, selection and deployment of the personnel and equipment to be used to provide protective services and support for the meeting.

25.4 Summary

Successful meeting executives, according to Wright (2005), understand that organisational objectives are only half of the meeting communication process. One of the reasons why a meeting may not be successful is because the meeting manager was not cognisant of the expectations of the audience. Further, the needs of the participants may not have been addressed as they are not always the same as those of the organisation. Wright (2005: 4) states that 'the attention of the delegates must be engaged immediately and then held for as long as the meeting lasts – whether two, three or four days. The prime enemy of good meetings is boredom and planners will do anything to counter it. For that dramatic techniques must be employed, which means that the natural tendency to go for a climax at the end of the meeting must sometimes be sacrificed in order to rivet delegates' attention from the outset'. The meeting manager must be centred on the task of the meeting and ensure an equal balancing of meeting elements. The ultimate goal for the meeting manager is to provide the audience with a seamless meeting without revealing any challenges.

Questions for research

1 Write a short report on the status of meetings today, particularly in view of the current economic global crisis.
2 Explain the role and function of a meeting planner.
3 By means of examples, discuss why meetings are held.
4 Differentiate between the types of meetings that are held in industry.
5 Motivate the importance of protocol at meetings.
6 By using an example, motivate the importance of risk management for any type of meeting.
7 Can design have a positive impact on a meeting? Motivate by providing relevant examples.
8 Using the meeting conceptualisation topics discussed in this chapter, develop a meeting plan for the following events:
  ❒ Annual SAACI conference: http://www.saaci.co.za
  ❒ Annual FEDHASA conference: http://www.fedhasa.co.za
  ❒ Annual IAPCO general assembly: http://www.iapco.org

Recommended websites

Browse the following internet sites for interesting and informative information:
Convention Industry Council: http://www.conventionindustry.org
Information on return on investment: http://www.answers.com/topic/return-on-investment http://whatis.techtarget.com/definition/return-on-marketing-investment--romi-.html
International Congress and Convention Association: http://www.iccaworld.com
Links to information for the events industry professional: http://www.worldofevents.net
Southern African Association for the Conference Industry: http://www.saaci.co.za
Special site to access event information: http://www.blackle.com
The industry meeting network http://www.industrymeetings.com
The International Association of Professional Congress Organisers: http://www.iapco.org

References

2010 FIFA World Cup Organising Committee South Africa. 30 November 2005. *Presentation by Dr Danny Jordaan at the National Communication Partnership Workshop.* Johannesburg.

2010 FIFA World Cup Organising Committee South Africa. 30 September 2008. *SA's first 2010 impression set to count.* Available from: http://www.fifa.com/worldcup/news/newsid=893236.html [accessed on 20 May 2009].

2010 FIFA World Cup Organising Committee South Africa. 11 February 2009. *OC happy with 2010 FIFA World Cup™ budget allocations.* Available from: http://www.fifa.com/worldcup/organisation/media/newsid=1023686.html [accessed on 20 May 2009].

A Spoonful of Sugar. 2008. Available at: http://www.aspoonfulofsugar.net/wp/2004/09/colleys-supper-rooms/ [accessed on 15 August 2009].

Abbott, A. 1988. *The System of Professions: An Essay on the Division of Expert Labor.* Chicago: The University of Chicago Press.

Abelson, J, Forest, PG, Eyles, J, Smith, P, Martin, E & Gauvin, FP. 2001. *Deliberations about Deliberation: Issues in the Design and Evaluation of Public Consultation Processes.* McMaster University Centre for Health Economics and Policy Analysis Research Working Paper 01–04, June 2001. Available from: http://www.vcn.bc.ca/citizens-handbook/compareparticipation.pdf [accessed on 20 May 2009].

Access. 2009. *Exhibition return on investment.* Available from: http://www.accessdisplays.co.uk/exhibition-roi.htm [accessed on 2 July 2009].

Adfocus. 1998. *Sponsors feeling the price pinch.* Supplement to the *Financial Mail:* 117–118, 29 May.

ADTA. 2007. *Abu Dhabi Tourism Authority Entity Plan 2008–2009.* UAE: Abu Dhabi Tourism Authority.

Ahmed, F, Moodley, V & Sookrajh, R. 2008. The environmental impacts of beach sport tourism events: A case study of the Mr Price Pro Surfing Event, Durban, South Africa. *Africa Insight,* 38(3): 73–85.

Allen, J. 2000. *Event Planning: The Ultimate Guide to Successful Meetings, Corporate Events, Fundraising Galas, Conferences, Conventions, Incentives and other Special Events.* Ontario: John Wiley & Sons, Canada Limited.

Allen, J. 2007. *The Executive's Guide to Corporate Events & Business Entertaining.* Canada, John Wiley & Sons.

Allen, J, O'Toole, W, McDonnell, I & Harris, J. 2002. *Festival and Special Event Management,* 2 ed. London: Wiley.

Allen, J, O'Toole, W, McDonnell, I & Harris, J. 2005. *Festival and Special Event Management,* 3 ed. London: Wiley.

Allen, J, O'Toole, W, McDonnell, I & Harris, R. 2008. *Festival and Special Event Management,* 4 ed. John Wiley & Sons Australia, Ltd.

Alliance. 2009. *Ethiopian NGO law will ban foreign organisations from funding pro-democracy activities.* Available at: http://www.alliancemagazine.org/en/content/ethiopian-ngo-law-will-ban-foreign-organizations-funding-pro-democracy-activities [accessed on 24 July 2009].

Allmers, S & Maennig, W. 2008. South Africa 2010: Economic scope and limits. *Hamburg Contemporary Economic Discussions*, 21: 1–33.

Allwood, J & Montgomery, B. 1989. *Exhibition Planning and Design.* Londra: BT Batsford Ltd.

Allwood, J. 1977. *The Great Exhibitions – 150 years.* USA: Cassell & Collier Macmillan Publishers.

Arab News. 2008. *Souk Festival Planned for July.* Available from: http://www.saudigazette.com.sa [accessed on 7 June 2009].

Archer, B. 1973. *The Need for Design Education.* London: Royal College of Art.

ASOM, 1997. *Association of Marketers' sponsorship guidelines.* [Unpublished trade report].

Astroff, MT & Abbey, JR. 2002. *Convention Sales and Services.* Las Vegas: Waterbury Press.

Athens. 2004a. Company structure. In *Athens 2004.* Available from: htpp:www.athens2004.com/athens2004/page/legacy?lang=en&cid=3358470429149VgnVCMServer28130b0aRCRD [accessed on 22 June 2004].

Athens. 2004b. Logistics. In *Athens 2004.* Available from: htpp://www.athens2004.com/athens2004/page/legacy?lang=dd0847044291f00VgnVCMServer28130b0aRCRD [accessed on 22 June 2004].

Auld, T & McArthur, S. 2003. Does event-driven tourism provide economic benefits? A case study from the Manawatu Region of New Zealand. *Tourism Economics*, 9(2): 191–201.

AZ_Sun. Two big green sporting events happening in the 'Valley of the sun'. *11th Hour Action.* Available from: http://11thhouraction.com/node/1273 [accessed on 29 May 2009].

Bale, J. 2003. *Sport, Space and the City,* 2 ed. Blackburn: Blackburn Press.

Banks, G. 2002 *Inter-State Bidding Wars: Calling a Truce.* Australia: Productivity Commission.

Bayley, S (Ed.). 1985. *The Conran Directory of Design.* London: Conran Octopus Limited.

BBC News. 2008. *China's Olympic security dilemma.* 12 March. Available at: http://www.news.bbc.co.uk/1/hi/world/asia-pacific/7292025.stm [accessed on 29 April 2009].

BBC Sport. 18 April 2009. *IPL action begins in South Africa.* Available from: http://www.news.bbc.co.uk/sport1/hi/cricket/8002936.stm [accessed on 29 May 2009].

Bealey, F. 1999. *The Blackwell Dictionary of Political Science.* Oxford: Blackwell Publishers.

Becatti, F. 2006. Show me the money. *Marketing Mix*, 24(6): 18–19.

Becker, H & Vanclay, F (Eds). 2006. *The International Handbook of Social Impact Assessment.* Cheltenham: Edward Elgar.

Beijing Olympic Committee of the Olympic Games (BOCOG). 2007. *Beijing 2008 Olympic Games – An environmental review.* Available from: http://www.unep.org/downloads/BeijingReport.pdf [accessed on 20 July 2008].

Beijing. 2008. *9 August 2008. Beijing welcomes world to 2008 Olympic Games.* Available from: http://www.en.beijing2008.cn/ceremonies/headlines/n214519367.shtml [accessed on 27 May 2009].

BEISG. 2008. *The Business Events Industry Strategy Group 2008 – a National Business Events Strategy for Australia 202.* Australia.

Bell, RA & Vazquez, IJ. 1996. Planning for competitive strategy in declining industry. In *Practising Responsible Tourism,* LC Harrison & W Husbands, W (Eds). New York: John Wiley & Sons.

Berg, J. 2008. A Night at the Museum. In *BizBash Media Inc.* Available at: http://www.bizbash.com/chicago/content/editorial/12883_columbian_ball_reaches_fund-raising_goals_despite_lower_attendance.php [accessed on 14 August 2009].

Berridge, G. 2007. *Events Design and Experience.* Oxford: Elsevier Butterworth-Heinemann.

Berridge, GR & James, A. 2003. *A Dictionary of Diplomacy,* 2 ed. New York: Palgrave Macmillan.

BIE. n.d. (a). *The theme makes the Expo.* Available from: http://www.bie-paris.org/tme/ [accessed on 21 June 2009].

BIE. n.d. (b). *International Exhibitions Bureau Regulation of International Exhibitions.* Available from: http://www.bie-paris.org/main/index.php?p=214&m2=227 [accessed on 21 June 2009].

Bitner, Mary Jo. 1995. Building service relationships: It's all about promises. *Journal of the Academy of Marketing Science,* 23(4): 246–251.

Blick South Africa. 2003. Surveillance a success at sporting event. *Technews.* Available from: http://securitysa.com/article.asp?pklArticleid=2405&pklIssueID=325&pklCategoryID=3 [accessed on 12 May 2004].

BMI Sport Info. 1999. *Sponsortrack.* October. [Unpublished trade report].

BMI Sport Info. 2004. *Sponsorwatch.* [Unpublished trade report].

Boehme, AJ. 1999. *Planning Successful Meetings and Events.* New York: American Management Association.

Bohlmann, HR. 2006. *Predicting the economic impact of the 2010 FIFA World Cup on South Africa.* University of Pretoria Department of Economics Working Paper Series: 2006–11.

Boo, S & Busser, JA. 2006. Impact analysis of a tourism festival on tourist destination images. *Event Management,* 9(4): 223–237.

Bovey, P. 2006. Solving outstanding mega-event transport challenges: The Olympic experience. *Public Transport International,* 6: 32–34. Available from: http://www.rand.org/pubs/technical_reports/2007/RAND_TR516.meta-analysis.pdf [accessed on 19 June 2009].

Bowdin, G, McDonnell, I, Allen, J & O'Toole, B. 2006. *Events Management.* Oxford: Butterworth-Heinemann.

Breeden, T. 2008. *Motivation and Employee Appreciation Events.* [internet]. Available from: http://www.officearrow.com/forums/organizing-corporate-events/396-motivation-employee-appreciation-events.html [accessed on 21 June 2009].

Brett, B. 2009. Bryan Brett Associates: Personal interview, 29 April.

British Association of Conference Destinations. 2008. *British Conference Market Trends Survey (BCMTS)* [internet]. Birmingham, BACD. Available from: http://www.bacd. biz/files/BCVS2008orderform.pdf [accessed on 20 June 2009].

Brown, G, Chalip, L, Jago, L & Mules, T. 2002. *The Sydney Olympics and Brand Australia in Destination Building: Creating the Unique Destination Proposition.* Oxford: Butterworth-Heinemann.

Brown, S. 2005. *Event Design – An Australian Perspective.* Second International Event Management Body of Knowledge Global Alignment Summit, Johannesburg.

Brown, S & James, S. 2004. Event design and management: Ritual sacrifice. In *Festival and Special Events Management*, Yeoman, I (Ed.) Oxford: Elsevier.

BuaNews Online. 2009. *Pretoria residents reminded of road closures.* 8 May. Available at: http://www.buanews.gov.za/news/09/09050812051001 [accessed on 8 May 2009].

Buchholz, S & Roth, T. 1987. *Creating the High-Performance Team.* New York: John Wiley & Sons, Inc.

Burke, R. 2007. *Project Management Techniques* (college edition). UK: Burke Publishing.

Business Events Sydney (BESydney). 2008. *Sydney incentive meeting case study: Chinese pharmaceutical company conference.* Available from: http://www.businesseventssydney. com.au/bid-for-an-event/incentives-events-in-sydney/incentive-case-study/incentive-case-study.cfm [accessed on 16 August 2009].

Canadian Tourism Human Resource Council. 2008. International event management standard (IEMS) draft. Available from: http://www.saaci.co.za/downloads/IEMS_Draft_1_Standard_06_june.pdf [accessed on 19 June 2009].

Cape Argus Pick n Pay Cycle Tour. 2009. *Cape Argus Cycle Tour Lifestyle Week Events.* Available from: http://www.cycletour.co.za/ [accessed on 29 May 2009].

Carnival in Rio. n.d. *The Rio Carnival Guide.* Available from: http://www.rio-carnival.net/ [accessed on 29 May 2009].

Casey, D. 2008. *The impact of mega events.* Presentation at the International Symposium on the Impact of Mega Sports Events on Developmental Goals. Hosted by the University of the Western Cape, the Flemish government and the Inter-University Council (VLIR-DBBS), 5–7 March 2008, Stellenbosch, South Africa. Available from: http://www.toolkitsportdevelopment.org/html/resources/B2/B29EBF4A-92C0-4C7F-A06C-910F1ACB7D40/Casey.ppt [accessed on 6 June 2009].

Caterersearch (2004) Available from: http://www.caterersearch.com/Articles/2004/06/24/53954/corporate-hospitality-is-more-than-just-the-ticket.html [accessed on 20 June 2009].

Catherwood, DW & Van Kirk, RL. 1992. *The Complete Guide to Special Event Management.* New York: John Wiley & Sons.

CCT. 2008. *City of Cape Town Events Policy* (April 2008). The City of Cape Town, South Africa.

CEIR (Center for Exhibition Industry Research). 2009. *ROI Toolkit.* Available from: http://roitoolkit.exhibitsurveys.net/Home/Welcome.aspx [accessed on 2 July 2009].

Centre for Responsive Politics. 2009. *Top 20 contributors: Senator John McCain 2005–2010.*

Available at: http://www.opensecrets.org/politicians/contrib.php?cycle=2010&cid=N00 006424&type=I&mem= [accessed on 24 July 2009].

Centre on Housing Rights and Evictions (COHRE). 2007. *Fair Play for Housing Rights: Mega-Events, Olympic Games and Housing Rights – Opportunities for the Olympic Movement and Others.* Geneva: COHRE.

Centre on Housing Rights and Evictions (COHRE). 2007. *Fair play for housing rights: Mega-events, Olympic Games and housing rights.* Available from: htpp://cohre.org/mega-event [accessed on 19 June 2009].

Chalip, L 2004. Beyond impact: A general model for host community event leverage. In *Sports Tourism: Interrelationships, Impacts and Issues,* Ritchie, BW & Adair, D (Eds). Clevedon: Channel View Publications.

Chappelet, J & Junod, T. 2006. A Tale of 3 Olympic Cities: What can Turin learn from the Olympic legacy of other Alpine cities? In *Major Sport Events as Opportunity for Development,* Torres, D.Valencia: Instituto Nóos, 83–90.

Chernuschenko, D. 1994a. *Greening our Games: Running Sports Events and Facilities that Won't Cost the Earth.* Ottawa: Centurion.

Chernuschenko, D. 1994b. *Sports Tourism goes Sustainable: The Lillehammer Experience.* Visions in Leisure and Business.

Chicago Tribune. 2008. *Testament to progress atrophies after Games.* Available from: http://www.archives.chicagotribune.com/2008/aug/05/sports/chi-05-athens-olympicsaug05 [accessed on 6 June 2009].

Chilwane, T. 2009. Hardcore by-laws for World Cup host cities. *The Weekender,* 9–10 May, 3.

Chinese pharmaceutical company [internet]. Available from: http://www.businesseventssydney.com.au/bid-for-an-event/incentives-events-in-sydney/incentive-case-study/incentive-case-study.cfm [accessed on 16 August 2009]

Chislett, D. 1998. The smart money's on sport. *Marketing Mix,* 16(11): 53–62.

Citrine, K.1997. Site planning for events. In *Event Operations.* Washington: International Festivals and Events Association (IFEA).

City of Melbourne. 2009. *Event Partnership Program.* Available from: http://www.melbourne.vic.gov.au/info.cfm?top=77&pa=4482&pg=4487 [accessed on 16 June 2009].

City of Port Phillip. n.d. *Waste-wise events.* Available from: http://www.portphillip.vic.gov.au/waste_wise_events.html [accessed on 24 May 2009].

Cleland, DT. 1999. *Project Management,* 3 ed. New York: McGraw-Hill.

Collins, J. 2001. *Good to Great.* New York: HarperCollins Publishers, Inc.

Collins, J & Porras, J I. 1994. *Built to Last: Successful Habits of Visionary Companies.* New York: HarperCollins Publishers, Inc.

Commonwealth Games Delhi 2010. *Position description summary – legacy.* Available from: http://www.cwgdelhi2010.org/cwgCareer/2nd%20Bucket/Legacy-CGKMP-DIR-D2010.pdf [accessed on 27 May 2009].

Commonwealth Games Federation. 2008. Commonwealth Games Federation [internet]. Available from: http://www.thecgf.com/games/intro.asp?yr=2002 [accessed on 20 June 2009].

Comrades Marathon. 2009. *20 Facts about the Comrades Marathon You Might not Know.* Available from: http://www.runner.co.za/2009/04/04/20-facts-about-the-comrades-marathon-you-might-not-know/ [accessed on 6 June 2009].

Conferences and Incentives Management (I) Pvt Ltd [internet]. Available from: http://www.thehindubusinessline.com/2009/01/09/stories/2009010950660700.htm [accessed on 20 July 2009].

Contact Publications. 1998. *1998–2007 SA Conference & Exhibition Calendar.* Durban.

Contact Publications. 1999. *1999–2008 SA Conference & Exhibition Calendar.* Durban.

Contact Publications. 2000. *2000–2009 SA Conference & Exhibition Calendar.* Durban.

Contact Publications. 2001. *2001–2008 SA Conference & Exhibition Calendar.* Durban.

Contact Publications. 2002. *2002–2008 SA Conference & Exhibition Calendar.* Durban.

Contact Publications. 2003. *2003–2008 SA Conference & Exhibition Calendar.* Durban.

Contact Publications. 2004. *2004–2008 SA Conference & Exhibition Calendar.* Durban.

Contact Publications. 2005. *2005–2009 SA Conference & Exhibition Calendar.* Durban.

Contact Publications. 2006. *2006–2010 SA Conference & Exhibition Calendar.* Durban.

Contact Publications. 2007. *2007–2011 SA Conference & Exhibition Calendar.* Durban.

Contact Publications. 2008. *2008–2012 SA Conference & Exhibition Calendar.* Durban.

Contact Publications. 2009. *2009–2013 SA Conference & Exhibition Calendar.* Durban.

Control Risks Group. 2003. *Event security.* Available at: http://www.crg.com [accessed on 11 November 2003].

Control Risks Group. 2007. *Tiger kidnap: The threat to the UK banking sector.* Available at: http://www.controlrisks.com/pdf/tiger_kidnap_report_LR.pdf [accessed on 29 April 2009].

Convention Industry Council. 2004. *Green Meetings Report.* USA.

Convention Industry Council. 2005. *Professional Meetings Management: Comprehensive Strategies for Meetings, Conventions and Events,* 5 ed. Available from: http://www.conventionindustry.org [accessed on 11 July 2009].

Cooper, C, Fletcher, J, Gilbert, D, Shepherd, R & Wanhill, S. 1999. *Tourism: Principles and Practice,* 2 ed. Essex: Addison Wesley Longman Ltd.

Cornelissen, S. 2005. *The Global Tourism System. Governance, Development and Lessons from South Africa.* UK: Ashgate.

Cornelissen, S. 2007. Crafting legacies: The changing political economy of global sport and the 2010 FIFA World Cup. *Politikon,* 34(3): 249–259.

Cornelissen, S & Swart, K. 2006. The 2010 Football World Cup as a political construct: The challenge of making good on an African promise. In *Sports Mega-events – Social Scientific Analyses of a Global Phenomenon,* Horne, J & Manzenreiter, W (Eds). Oxford, UK: Blackwell Publishing.

Council Report. 2007. *Impacts of events on parks: Sustainability.* Available from: Available from: http://www.melbourne.vic.gov.au/opm/bc/CTEE/meetings/C3_331_20070125.pdf. [accessed on 23 June 2009].

Cousins J, Foskett D & Shortt, D. 1995. *Food and Beverage Management.* Harlow: Longman Group Ltd.

Crayton, C. 1997. Managing volunteers. In *Event Operations.* Washington: IFEA.

Crompton, J. 1995. Economic impact analysis of sports facilities and events: Eleven sources of misapplication. *Journal of Sport Management,* 9: 14–35.

CSR Europe. 2009. *Sustainable marketing guide.* Available from: http://www.csreurope.org/ [accessed on 25 July 2009].

CSRwire. 2009. *Socially responsible investing.* Available from: http://www.csrwire.com/ eventss?category=20 [accessed on 6 June 2009].

David Suzuki Foundation. 2009. *Sydney sets Precedence with Green Games.* Available from: http://www.davidsuzuki.org/About_us/Dr_David_Suzuki/Article_Archives/ weekly09200001.asp [accessed on 23 June 2009].

Davidson, A. 19 January 2007. *Greening the Superbowl.* Available from: http://www.forbes. com/2007/01/19/super-bowl-green-sports-biz-cz_ad_0119green.html [accessed on 29 May 2009].

Davidson, R. 2003. *Marketing Destinations and Venues for Conferences, Conventions and Business Events.* Oxford: Elsevier Butterworth-Heinemann.

Davidson, R & Rogers, T. 2006. *Marketing Destinations and Venues for Conferences Conventions and Business Events.* Oxford: Butterworth-Heinemann.

Davis, B & Stone, S. 1995. *Food and Beverage Management,* 2 ed. Oxford: Butterworth-Heinemann.

Davis, D & Tisdell, C. 1995. Recreational scuba-diving and carrying capacity in marine protected areas. *Ocean & Coastal Management,* 26(1): 19–40.

De Lollis, B. 2008. Business meetings could get smaller if economy falters. *USA Today.* (8 September). Available from: http://www.usatoday.com/travel/news/2008-09-08conventions_n.htm [accessed on 1 May 2009].

De Tolly, P. 1992. Cape Town's central Waterfront. *Architecture SA,* May–June, 23–26.

DEAT. 2003. *Responsible Tourism Handbook.* Pretoria: SA Government (Department of Environmental Affairs & Tourism).

DEAT & SAT. 2005. *Overview of South African Sport Industry Competitiveness* (October). Pretoria: Department of Environmental Affairs and Tourism (DEAT) & South African Tourism (SAT).

DeWitt Coffman, C. 1972. *Marketing for a Full House.* Ithaca: Cornell University.

DFA (South African Department of Foreign Affairs). 2009. *Presidential Inauguration 2009. Protocol guidelines and administrative arrangements.* Pretoria: DFA. Available at: http://www.dfa.gov.za/protocol/pres%20inaug.html [accessed on 28 April 2009].

DMAI. 2009. *About the industry.* Available from: http://www.destinationmarketing.org/ page.asp?pid=21 [accessed on 13 July 2009].

DRM Associates. 2002. DRM Associates [internet]. Available from: http://www.npd-solutions.com/launchcons.html [accessed on 20 June 2009].

Drucker, PF. 1973. *Management: Tasks, Responsibility, Practices.* New York: Harper & Row.

Du Toit, 2009. How will the credit crunch affect sponsors? *Your Sport. Sport & Recreation South Africa,* 2nd quarter.

Duffy, N. 2003. *Passion Branding.* Chichester: John Wiley.

East of England Tourism. 2006. *The Value of 'V'*. [online]. Available from: http://www.eet. org.uk/doclib/ECONOMIC_IMPACT_OF_THE_V_Festival___Summary_Report. pdf [accessed on 11 July 2009].

Eden Park Trust Board. n.d. *Event Management at Eden Park*. Available from: http://www. aucklandcity.govt.nz/Council/projects/edenpark/docs/event.pdf [accessed on 29 May 2009].

Edinburgh Convention Bureau (ECB). 2009. Available from: http://www. conventionedinburgh.com/ [accessed on 21 March 2009].

Edinburgh festivals. 2009. Available from: http://www.edinburgh-festivals.com/ [accessed on 21 March 2009].

Eisinger, PK. 2000. The politics of bread and circuses: Building the city for the visitor class. *Urban Affairs Review*, 35(3): 316–333.

Ellis, M. 1974. *A Waiter's Vade Mecum*. [Unpublished.]

EMBOK. 2009. *Risk – domains and processes*. Available from: http://www.embok.org [accessed on 28 July 2009].

Emery, PR. 2002. Bidding to host a major sports event: The local organising committee perspective. *International Journal of Public Sector Management*, 15(20).

EPMS CD-ROM. 2009. *Event project management system*. Bondi Beach, NSW, Australia. Available from: http://www.epms.net

Erdogan, BZ & Kitchen, PJ. 1998. Managerial mindsets and the symbiotic relationship between sponsorship and advertising. *Marketing Intelligence and Planning*, 16(6): 369–374.

Escoffier, A. 1965. *Ma Cuisine*. London: Paul Hamlyn Ltd.

Espejo, R. 2003. *The Viable System Model: A Briefing about Organisational Structure*. Available from: http://www.synch.com [accessed on 20 November 2008].

ESPN. 30 October 2007. *FA to meet over 2018 World Cup bid*. Available from: http:// soccernet.espn.go.com/news/story?id=477184&&cc=3888 [accessed on 3 April 2009].

Ethical Corporation. n.d. *Sports sponsorship – The risk of marketing own-goals*. Available from: http://www.ethicalcorp.com/content.asp?contentid=6477 [accessed on 29 May 2009].

eTurboNews, Inc. 2009. *Kingdom of Saudi Arabia records 1 344 tourism events in 2008*. Available from: http://www.eturbonews.com/7527/kingdom-saudi-arabia-records-1344-tourism-events-2008 [accessed on 9 June 2009].

eTurboNews, Inc. 2009a. *New program promotes local small businesses*. Available from: http://www.eturbonews.com:80/10140/new-program-promotes-local-small-businesses [accessed on 4 July 2009].

European Commissions/7 Framework programme/theme: Capacities/research infrastructures. 2009. *Global Project*. Available from: http://www.global-project.eu/ [accessed on 10 July 2009].

Evans, M, Jamal, A & Foxhall, G. 2009. *Consumer Behaviour*, 2 ed. West Sussex. John Wiley & Sons.

Events Research International (ERi). 2008. *About Responsible Events*. Available from: http://www.eventsresearch.org/index.php?id=164 [accessed on 6 June 2009].

HSE. 2002. *Event safety guide,* 3 ed. Crown copyright.

EventScotland. 2008. *Scotland the Perfect Stage: A Strategy for the Events Industry in Scotland 2009–2020.* Scotland.

EventView. 2008. North America. Connecticut. Event Marketing Institute. Available from: http://www.eventmarketing.com/emi/ [accessed on 10 April 2009].

EventView. 2009. *MPI Unveils 2009 Trends for Event Marketing in Europe.* United Kingdom: Cut Communications.

Faul, MA, Pistorius, CWI, Van Vuuren, LM & De Beer, CS. 1993. *Accounting: An Introduction,* 4 ed. Durban: Butterworths.

Fayol, H. 1949. General principles of management. Chapter 4 in *General Industrial Management.* Pitman & Sons, Ltd. [See Pugh, 1971].

FIFA World Cup 2006. 2003. *Volunteers.* Available from: http://fifaworldcup.yahoo.com/06/en/o/octeam/volunteers.html [accessed on 27 June 2004].

FIFA. 2004. *Host nation of the 2010 FIFA World Cup – South Africa.* Available from: http://www.fifa.com/en/media/index/0,1369,101476,00.htmlcomp=2010&artcileid=101476 [accessed on 27 June 2004].

FIFA. 2008. *Volunteers will be the lifeblood of 2010.* Available from: http://www.fifa.com/confederationscup/news/newsid=817589.html [accessed on 20 May 2009].

FIFA. n.d. *Host broadcasting.* Available from: http://www.fifa.com/aboutfifa/tv/hostbroadcasting.html [accessed on 20 May 2009].

Financial Mail. 2009. Elections good for large and small. 17 April. Available at: http://www.biz-community.com/Article/196/73/35109.html [accessed on 20 April 2009].

Finweek. 2006. From derelict township to vibrant city. Can Soweto become Joburg's next Sandton? 31 August, 43–44.

Fredline, L. 2004. Host community reactions to motorsport events: The perception of impact on quality of life. In *Sport Tourism – Interrelationships, Impacts and Issues,* Ritchie, BW & Adair, D (Eds). Clevedon Hall, UK: Channel View Publications.

Freidson, E. 1986. *Professional Powers: A Study of the Institutionalization of Formal Knowledge.* Chicago: The University of Chicago Press.

Fullerton, S. 2007. *Sports Marketing.* New York: McGraw-Hill Irwin.

GamesBid.com. 2009. *Security a concern for Delhi.* Available from: http://www.gamesbids.com/eng/other_news/1216134381.html [accessed on 20 May 2009].

Gantrygroup. 2009. *Is ROI in the eye of the beholder?* Available from: http://www.gantrygroup.com/images/Newsletter/News15.html

Garrigos, SFJ, Narangajavanab, Y & Marques, DP. 2004. Carrying capacity in the tourism industry: A case study of Hengistbury Head. *Tourism Management,* 25(2): 275–283.

Gerber, ME. 1995. *The E-Myth Revisited: Why Small Businesses Don't Work and What To Do About It.* New York: HarperCollins Publishers, Inc.

Getz, D. 1991. Special events. In *Managing Tourism,* Medelik, S (Ed.). Oxford: Butterworth-Heinemann.

Getz, D. 1994a. Event tourism and the authenticity dilemma. In *Global Tourism – The Next Decade,* Theobald, WF (Ed.). Oxford: Butterworth-Heinemann.

Getz, D. 1994b. Event tourism: Evaluating the impacts. In *Travel, Tourism and Hospitality Research – A Handbook for Managers and Professionals.* Brent Ritchie, JR & Goeldner, CR (Eds), 2 ed. New York: John Wiley & Sons.

Getz, D. 1995. Island competitiveness through festivals and special events: The case of Newfoundland. In *Island Tourism: Management, Principles and Practice,* Conlin, MC & Baum, T (Eds). Chichester: John Wiley & Sons.

Getz, D. 1997. *Event Management & Event Tourism.* New York: Cognizant Communication Corporation.

Getz, D. 2007. *Event Studies: Theory, Research and Policy for Planned Events.* Oxford, Butterworth-Heinemann.

Getz, D. 2008. *Event Studies.* Oxford: Elsevier.

Getz, D, O'Neil, M & Carlsen, J. 2001. Service quality evaluation at events through service mapping. *Journal of Travel Research,* 39(4): 380–390.

Gladwell, M. 2005. *Blink: The Power of Thinking Without Thinking.* New York: Little, Brown & Company.

Glasson, J, Thérivel, R & Chadwick, A. 1999. *Introduction to Environmental Impact Assessment,* 2 ed. London: Spon Press.

Gold , JR & Ward, SV. 1994. *Place Promotion: The Use of Publicity and Marketing to Sell Towns and Regions.* Chichester: Wiley.

Goldblatt, JJ. 1990. *Special Events: The Art and Science of Celebration.* New York: Van Nostrand Reinhold.

Goldblatt, JJ. 1997. *Special Events: Best Practices in Modern Event Management.* UK: John Wiley & Sons.

Goldblatt, JJ. 2002a. *Special Events: Best Practices in Modern Event Management,* 3 ed. New York: International Thompson Publishing Company.

Goldblatt, JJ. 2002b. *Special Events: Twenty-first Century Global Event Management,* 3 ed. New York: John Wiley & Sons, Inc.

Goldblatt, JJ. 2004. *Special Events: Event Leadership for a New World.* Hoboken, USA: John Wiley & Sons.

Goldblatt, JJ. 2008. *Special Events: The Roots and Wings of Celebration,* 5 ed. New Jersey: John Wiley & Sons.

Goldblatt, J & Supovitz, F. 1999. *Dollars and Cents: How to Succeed in the Special Events Business.* New York: John Wiley & Sons, Inc.

Golusin, M & Ivanovic, OM. 2009. Definitions, characteristics, and state of the indicators of sustainable development in countries of south-eastern Europe. *Agriculture, Ecosystems & Environment,* 130(1–2): 67–74.

Gossling, SG. 2002. Global environmental consequences of tourism. *Global Environmental Change,* 12(4): 283–302.

Goulding, C & Domic, D. 2009. Heritage, identity and ideological manipulation: The case of Croatia. *Annals of Tourism Research,* 36/1: 86–102.

Gratton, C & Henry, I (Eds). 2001. *Sport in the City: The Role of Sport in Economic and Social Regeneration.* London: Routledge.

Gratton, C, Dobson, N & Shibli, S. 2001. The role of major sports events in the economic regeneration of cities. In *Sport in the City: The Role of Sport in Economic and Social Regeneration,* Gratton, C & Henry, I. (Eds). London: Routledge.

Gratton, C, Shibli, S & Coleman, R. 2006. The economic impact of major sports events: A review of ten events in the UK. In *Sports Mega-events – Social Scientific Analyses of a Global Phenomenon,* Horne J & Manzreiter, W (Eds), 41–58.

Greater Manchester Destination Management Plan. 2007/2008. Available from: www.worldclassservice.co.uk/site/display.php? [accessed on 25 June 2009].

Greene, SJ. 2003. Staged cities: Mega-events, slum clearances and global capital. *Yale Human Rights and Development Law Journal,* 6: 161–187. Available from: http://islandia.law.yale.edu/yhrdlj/PDF/Vol%206/greene.pdf [accessed on 20 May 2009].

Greenwatch. 29 January 2009. *Sporting events going green.* Available from: http://www.green-watch.org/view-news-article.cfm?newsID=47 [accessed on 29 May 2009].

GTBS. 2009. *Green Tourism Business Scheme (GTBS), United Kingdom.* Available from: http://www.green-business.co.uk/index.asp [accessed on 21 June 2009].

Gursoy, D, Kim, K & Uysal, M. 2004. Perceived impacts of festivals and special events by organisers: An extension and validation. *Tourism Management,* 25(2): 171–181.

Gwinner, K (1997) A model of image creation and image transfer in event sponsorship. *International Marketing Review.* University Press,14(3).

Halbwirth, S & Toohey, K. 2001. The Olympic Games and knowledge management: A case study of the Sydney Organising Committee of the Olympic Games. *European Sport Management Quarterly,* 1: 91–111.

Halbwirth, S & Toohey, K. 2005. *Sport event management and knowledge management: A useful partnership.* Proceedings of the event management research conference, Sydney, 13–14 July 2005. Sydney: Centre for Tourism, Sport and Service Innovation.

Hall, CM. 1992a. Adventure, sport and health tourism. In *Special Interest Tourism,* Weiler, B & Hall, CM (Eds). London: Belhaven Press.

Hall, CM. 1992b. *Hallmark Tourist Events.* London: Belhaven Press.

Hall, CM. 1997. *Hallmark Tourist Events: Impacts, Management and Planning.* London: Belhaven Press.

Hall, CM. 2004. Sport tourism and urban regeneration. In *Sport Tourism: Interrelationships, Impacts and Issues,* Ritchie, BW & Adair, D (Eds). Clevedon (UK): Channel View Publications.

Hansen, B. 1995. *Off-premises Catering Management.* New York: John Wiley & Sons.

Harris, EJ. 1998. *Advanced Project Management: MS Project.* Bisho: Fort Hare Institute of Government, Information Technology and Management Centre.

Haughey, D. 2009. *The Project Management Body of Knowledge (PMBOK). Available from :* http://www.projectsmart.co.uk/pmbok.html [accessed on 2 July 2009].

Head, D. 2009. *Slip and fall precautions vital for businesses.* Available from: http://www.accidentsdirect.com/public-liability/slip-and-fall-precautions-vital-for-businesses.aspx [accessed on 6 June 2009].

Henley Royal Regatta. 2009. *History.* Available at: http://www.hrr.co.uk/pdisp.php?pid=5 [accessed on 25 June 2009].

Herzberg, F. 1966. The motivation-hygiene theory. Chapter 6 in *Work and the Nature of Man*. World Publishing Co. [See Pugh, 1971].

Higham, J & Ritchie, B. 2001. *Niche Tourism*. Oxford: Butterworth-Heinemann.

Hildreth, RA. 1990. *The Essentials of Meeting Management*. Englewood Cliffs: Prentice Hall.

Hiller, H. 2000. Mega-events, urban boosterism and growth strategies: an analysis of the objectives and legitimations of the Cape Town 2004 Olympic bid. *International Journal of Urban and Regional Research*, 24(2): 439–458.

Hollebeek, L. *Return on marketing investment: Towards a development of a new metric*. Available from: http://www.docstoc.com/docs/1024706/Return-on-Marketing-Investment [accessed on 29 June 2009].

Hooper, J. 2003. *Octagon – ahead of its game*. [Unpublished trade report].

Hoyle, HJ. 2002. *Event Marketing: How to Successfully Promote Events, Festivals, Conventions, and Expositions*. New York: John Wiley & Sons.

HSE, GB. 1996. *Managing Crowds Safely*. Suffolk: HSE Books.

HSE, GB. 1999. *The Event Safety Guide: A Guide to Health, Safety and Welfare at Music and Similar Events*. Suffolk: HSE Books.

Huggins, A. 2003. *The greening of sporting events: Production of environmental management guidelines for eventing*. Unpublished PhD thesis, University of East Anglia.

Hunsaker, PL & Alessandra, AJ. 1980. *The Art of Managing People*. New York: Simon & Schuster, Inc.

i wireless Center. No author. Available from: http://www.iwirelesscenter.com/ pdf/ suggseating.pdf [accessed 13 August 2009].

Institution of Structural Engineers (ISE). 2007. *Temporary demountable structures: Guidance on design, procurement and use*, 3 ed. ISE.

International Association for Public Participation. 2005. *Spectrum of public participation*. Available from: http://www.iap2.org/associations/4748/files/spectrum.pdf [accessed on 23 March 2009].

International Festival Audience Research. 2002. [internet] Available from: http://www. edinburgh-festivals.com/festivals.cfm?id=International [accessed on 18 June 2009].

International Olympic Committee (IOC). 2008. *2016 Candidature procedure and questionnaire*. Available from: http://www.multimedia.olympic.org/pdf/en_ report_1318.pdf [accessed on 20 May 2009].

International Symposium on Green Events. 2004. *Greening events and leaving positive legacies*. Results of conference on Local Governments Implementing Sustainability Principles as Hosts of International Events held in Barcelona, Spain. Available from: http://www.iclei-europe.org/index.php?id=1012 [accessed on 20 July 2008].

Ioannides, D. 1995. Planning for international tourism in less developed countries: Towards sustainability. *Journal of Planning Literature*, 9(3): 236–242.

IOC Beijing 2008. *Marketing media guide*. Available from: http://multimedia.olympic.org/ pdf/en_report_1329.pdf [accessed on 20 May 2009].

IOC. 2008. *Games of the XXXI Olympiad 2016 Working Group Report*. Lausanne, Switzerland.

IOC. 2008. *Opening ceremony of the summer Olympics,* February. Available from: http://www.multimedia.olympic.org/pdf/en_report_1134.pdf [accessed on 20 May 2009].

IOC. n.d. *Objectives of Olympic marketing* . Available from: http://www.olympic.org/uk/organisation/facts/introduction/objectives_uk.asp [accessed on 20 May 2009].

IRIN News. 2008. *Zimbabwe: NGO ban starting to bite,* 7 July. Available from: http://www.irinnews.org/report.aspx?ReportID=79127 [accessed on 24 July 2009].

Islamic Forum Europe, 2004. *'Stop French Hijab Ban' picket,* 3 February. Available from: http://www.mcb.org.uk/features/features.php?ann_id=211 [accessed on 20 July 2009].

Ives, V. 1998. Media as your scrumhalf. *Marketing Mix,* 16(11): 60–62.

Jago, LK & Shaw, RN. 1998. Special events: A conceptual and definitional framework. *Festival Management & Event Tourism,* 5(1/2): 21–33.

Jefkins, F. 1994. *Advertising,* 3 ed. London: Pitman.

Johnson, G, Scholes, K & Wittington, R. 2008. *Exploring Corporate Strategy,* 8 ed. London: FT Prentice Hall.

Johnson, O. n.d. *The Munich Beer Festival.* Available from: http://ezinearticles.com/?The-Munich-Beer-Festival&id=634886 [accessed on 27 May 2009].

Jordaan, MJS. 1994. *Career Guide to the Tourist Industry in SA.* Pretoria: SATOUR.

JOWSCO. 2002. *What is the World Summit on Sustainable Development?* Department of Environmental Affairs & Tourism South Africa. Available from: http://www.environment.gov.za/sustdev/jowsco/jowsco_index.html [accessed on 27 June 2004].

Kearney, AT. 2002. *The main event. Best practices for managing mega-sports events.* Available from: http://www.atkearney.com [accessed on 20 April 2004].

Kerzner, H. 1998. *Project Management,* 6 ed. New York: John Wiley & Sons.

Key Leisure Markets (2001) *Tourism in the UK.* London: MarketScape Ltd

King, I. 2009. *Music festivals prove to be recession proof* [online], *The Times,* 11 June. Available from: http://www.business.timesonline.co.uk/tol/business/industry_ sectors/media/article6474017.ece [accessed on 12 July 2009].

Kinton, R, Ceserani V & Foskett D. 2004. *The Theory of Catering,* 9 ed. London: Hodder & Stoughton Educational.

Kirkup, N & Major, B. 2007. Doctoral Foundation paper: The reliability of economic impact studies of the Olympic Games: A post-Games study of Sydney 2000 and considerations for London 2012. *Journal of Sport and Tourism,* 11(3–4): 275–296.

Klein, J-M. 2009. *EventsEye: Trade shows, exhibitions, conferences and business events worldwide.* Available from: http://www.eventseye.com/ [accessed on 2 July 2009].

Kloot, L. 1999. Admonitor: Sponsorship or advertising? The debate rages. *The Weekend Argus*: Saturday Business Report: 15, 8 May.

Koekemoer, H. 2009. *Training Material.* Alex Gintan Associates.

Koenderman, T. 2009. *Ad Review.* Sandton: Finweek.

Kolah, A. 2007. *Sponsorship Works: A Brand Marketer's Casebook.* London: SportBusiness.

Kotowski, K. 2008. *CIC Member Organisations meet to create action plan to counter negative media regarding legitimate meetings and events.* Alexandria: Convention Industry Council.

Kreez. 2008. *Intricate thoughts blog-spot.* Available from: http://www.intricate-thoughts. blogspot.com/2009/07/94th-mensiversary-ron-blaauw-restaurant.html [accessed 18 August 2009].

Krugman, C & Wright, R. 2007. *Global Meetings and Exhibitions.* Ontario: John Wiley & Sons, Canada Limited.

Landey, J. 2008. *Special Events Toolkit, Services SETA.* Johannesburg: Services SETA.

Leavitt, HJ. 1951. Some effects of certain communication patterns on group performance. *Journal of Abnormal and Social Psychology,* January, 46: 38–50. [See Pugh, 1971].

Lees-Marshment, J. 2009. *Political Marketing. Principles and Applications.* London: Routledge.

Leibold, M. 1990. *Tourism Marketing and Publicity.* Cape Town: SAPTO.

Lenhart, M. 1998. Taking up space. *Meetings & Conventions,* December, 55–61.

Lillicrap, DR. 1971. *Food and Beverage Service.* London: Edward Arnold (Publishers) Ltd.

Lillicrap, DR & Cousins, J. 2008. *Food and Beverage Service,* 7 ed. London: Hodder Education.

Lindberg, K, McCool, PF, Brown, K, Turner, RK, Hameed, H & Bateman, I. 1998. A critique of environmental carrying capacity as a means of managing the effects of tourism development: A comment. *Environmental Conservation,* 25(4): 291–294.

Local Organising Committee (LOC). 2006. *Green Goal: Legacy Report. FIFA LOC Germany.* Available from: http://www.oeko.de/oekodoc/292/2006-011-en.pdf [accessed on 20 July 2008].

Longnecker, JG, Moore, CW & Petty, JW. 2006. *Small Business Management: An Entrepreneurial Emphasis,* 10 ed. South Western College Publishing.

MacKenzie, A. 2004. Mice industry welcomes grading scheme. *Southern African Tourism Update* (May).

Macworld [internet]. Available from: http://www.macworld.com/article/139713/2009/03/macworldexpo2010.html [accessed on 2 July 2009]

Mallen, C & Adams, LJ. 2008. *Sport, Recreation and Tourism Event Management.* UK: Elsevier.

Malouf, L. 1999. *Behind the Scenes at Special Events.* Hoboken: Wiley.

Manchester Evening News. 2006. [internet]. Available from: http://www.manchestereveningnews.co.uk/.../1131380_labour_party_conference_will_return_to_manchester_[accessed on 20 June 2009].

Mann, P. 2008. Legacy best practice. An introduction and global review. *Legacy Lives 2008 Conference Report,* 28–30 January. Pmp Legacy: UK.

Maralack, D & Lloyd, N. 2005. Bidding for major events. In *Event Management,* 2 ed., Tassiopoulos, D (Ed.). Lansdowne: Juta Academic.

March, JG & Simon, HA. 1958. *Organizations.* Wiley. [See Pugh, 1971].

Market Association. 1998. *Corporate Hospitality.* MAPS: Market Assessment Publications Ltd.

Markus, GH. 2002. *What is Design Today?* New York: HN Abrams.

Maslow, AH. 1943. A theory of human motivation. *Psychological Review,* 50(4), 370–396.

Masterman, G. 2004. *Strategic Sports Event Management*. Oxford: Elsevier Butterworth-Heinemann.

Masterman, G & Wood, E. 2006. *Innovative Marketing Communications: Strategies for the Events Industry*. Oxford: Butterworth-Heinemann.

Matthews, D. 2007. *Special Event Production: The Process*. Oxford: Elsevier.

Matthews, D. 2008. *Special Event Production: The Process*. Amsterdam: Butterworth-Heinemann.

McCaffree, JM, Innis, P & Sand, RM. 2002. *Protocol: The Complete Handbook of Diplomatic, Official and Social Usage*, 25 ed. Dallas: Durban House Publishing Company Inc. Available from: http://www.usaprotocol.com/about.html [accessed on 29 April 2009].

McDonald, D. 1991. Sponsorship and the image of the sponsor. *European Journal of Marketing*, 25(11): 31–38.

McDonnell, I, Allen, J & O'Toole, W. 1999. *Festival and Special Event Management*. Brisbane: John Wiley & Sons Australia Ltd.

Mean Fiddler. 2001. *Carling Weekend*. [internet]. Available from: http://www.meanfiddler.com [accessed on 20 April 2009].

Media Forum: Get with the game. 1999. *Marketing Mix*, 17(6): 63–65.

Meenaghan, T. 1983. Commercial sponsorship. *European Journal of Marketing*, 17(7): 5–67.

Meenaghan, T. 1991. The sponsorship medium. *European Journal of Marketing*, 25(11): 5–10.

Meenaghan, T. & Shipley, D. 1999. Media effect in commercial sponsorship. *European Journal of Marketing*, 33(3): 328–348.

Meerabeau, E, Gillett, R, Kennedy, M, Adeoba, J, Byass, M & Tabi, K. 1991. Sponsorship in the alcoholic drinks industry in the 1990s. *European Journal of Marketing*, 25(11): 39–56.

Meeting Professionals International (MPI). 2009a. *EventView 2009*. Available from: http://www.mpiweb.org [accessed on 6 June 2009].

Meeting Professionals International (MPI). 2009b. *FutureWatch 2009*. Available from: http://www.mpiweb.org [accessed on 6 June 2009].

Meetings Industry Association of Australia. 1996. *The MIAA Guide to Design and Operation of Meetings and Exhibition Venues*. Sydney: Meetings Industry Association of Australia.

Melbourne Victoria. 2009. *Multicultural Events*. Available from: http://www.visitvictoria.com/displayobject.cfm/objectid.0007C337-47CA-1A83-846A80C476A901EF/ [accessed on 16 June 2009].

Middlebury College. 2009. *Corporate Social Responsibility Speaker Series*. Available from: http://www.middlebury.edu/academics/ump/majors/es/eventss/csrss/ [accessed on 6 June 2009].

Mintel International Group Ltd (2002) *Sponsorship*. [internet]. Available from: http://www.lmu.ac.uk/learningcentre/mintel [accessed on 29 June 2009].

Mintzberg, H. 1994. *The Rise and Fall of Strategic Planning*. New York: The Free Press.

Mintzberg, H. 2005. *Managers not MBAs: A Hard Look at the Soft Practice of Managing and Management Development*. San Francisco: Berrett-Koehler Publishers, Inc.

Mlangeni, M. 1999. Sport is becoming big business in SA. *Business Day*: 16, 12 April.

Moesch, C & Muller, H. 2008. UEFA Euro 2008™ evaluation and impacts on sustainable development. *Challenges facing football in the 21st Century*, 15–17 May. University of Berne: Switzerland.

Monroe, JC. 2006. *Art of the Event: Complete Guide to Designing and Decorating Special Events*. Oxford: Wiley.

Montreal Jazz Festival. 2009. Available from: http://www.montrealjazzfestival.com/ [accessed on 20 April 2009].

Moon, G. 2007. *Social Impact Assessments*. Available from: http://www.enviropaedia.com/topic/default.php?topic_id=216 [accessed on 20 May 2009].

Morello, A. 2000. Design predicts the future when it anticipates experience. *Design Issues*, 16: 35–44.

Morgan, WJ. 1974. *Supervision and Management of Quantity Food Preparation*. Berkley: McCutcheon Publishing Corporation.

Morris, D. 2008. Tomorrow's sponsorship is all in the mind. *SportBusiness International*. Available from: http://www.sportbusiness.com/britsport/167820/tomorrow-s-sponsorship-is-all-in-the-mind [accessed on 6 March 2009].

Moxley, J. 1995. *Advanced Co-ordination Manual*. Boulder, Colorado: Zone Interactive.

MPI. 1996. Meetings Industry Association. UK Conference Market Survey.

MPI Foundation. 2006. *The economic impact of meetings and events*. An MPI Foundation Canada White Paper. Available from: http://www.mpiweb.org/...Whitepapers/MPI_NMID%20Economic%20Impact%20White%20Paper.pdf [accessed on 2 July 2009].

MPI. 2008. *Meetings Activity in 2006: A Portrait of the Canadian Sector*. Dallas: Meeting Professionals International.

Mules, T & Faulkner, B. 1996. An economic perspective on special events. *Tourism Economics*, 2(2): 107–117.

Munich Beer Festival: Oktoberfest. 9 March 2009. Available from: http://www.munichbeerfestival.com [accessed on 27 May 2009].

Nelson, KB. 2004. *Sociological theories of career choice: A study of workers in the special events industry*. Unpublished manuscript. University of Nevada, Las Vegas.

Nelson, KB, Silvers, JR & Park, M. 2005. *Developing an event management curriculum: An important step towards professionalization*. Conference proceedings, Second International EMBOK Imbizo Global Alignment Summit. Johannesburg: Institute of Event Management.

North East England Festivals and Events Toolkit. *Working with volunteers*. Available from: http://www.tourismnortheast.co.uk [accessed on 21 June 2009].

Notting Hill Carnival (2001). Available from: http://www.mynottinghill.co.uk/nottinghilltv/carnival-countdown.htm [accessed on 20 March 2009].

NSC. 2008. *North Shore City Events Strategy* (draft June 2008). New Zealand.

NZ Major Events. 2006. *The National Events Strategy: Taking Our Place on the World Stage*. New Zealand.

O'Neill, J. 2007. *Review into a Possible Events Corporation for New South Wales for the Premier of New South Wales, the Hon. Morris Iemm, MP*. Australia.

O'Toole, W & Mikolaitis, P. 2002. *Corporate Event Project Management.* Canada: John Wiley & Sons.

Ohmann, S, Jones, I & Wilkes, K. 2006. The perceived social impacts of the 2006 Football World Cup on Munich residents. *Journal of Sport and Tourism,* 11(2): 129–152.

O'Reilly, T. 2008. *Branson's V Festival comes to SA.* Available from: http://www.mediaclubsouthafrica.com/index.php?option=com_content&view=article&id=735:v-festival-spread-its-wings&catid=43:culture_news&Itemid=112 [accessed on 29 April 2009].

O'Sullivan, EL & Spangler, KJ. 1999. *Experience Marketing,* PA: Venture Publishing.

O'Toole, WJ. 2006. *Event risk management* Available from: http://www-personal.usyd.edu.au/~wotoole/EPMS_Control/Control_Areas/Risk/risks.html [accessed on March 2009].

Paul, D. 2002. Moving the money. *SA Sports Illustrated,* 109–115, November.

Percy, L & Elliott, R. 2009. *Strategic Advertisement Management,* 3 ed. Oxford: Oxford University Press.

Pereira, L. 2009. *Global tourism: Special focus on business travel.* Presentation at the Cape Town and Western Cape Destination Conference, 5–6 March. Victoria & Alfred Waterfront, Cape Town: Department of Economic Development and Tourism, Western Cape Province.

Pike Masteralexis, L, Barr, CA & Hums, MA. 1998. *Principles and Practice of Sport Management.* Aspen: Gaithersburg, MA.

Pine, J & Gilmore, BH. 1999. *The Experience Economy: Work is Theatre & Every Business a Stage.* Boston: Harvard Business School.

Pink, DH. 2006. *A Whole New Mind: Why Right-brainers will Rule the Future.* New York: Riverhead Books.

PMI. 2000. *A Guide to the Project Management Body of Knowledge.* Newton Square, Pennsylvania: Project Management Institute.

Poirier, RA. 1997. Political risk analysis and tourism. *Annals of Tourism Research,* 24(3): 675–686.

Polivka, EG. 1996. *Professional Meeting Management,* 3 ed. Alabama: PCMA.

Powers, T & Barrows, CW. 2006. *Hospitality Industry,* 6 ed. Hoboken: John Wiley & Sons.

Proctor, T. 2005. *Essentials of Marketing Research,* 4 ed. FT Prentice Hall.

Public and Commercial Services Union, 2007. *Ten point guide to organising a picket line.* Available from: http://www.pcs.org.uk/en/resources/activists_toolkit/ten-point-guide-to-organising-a-picket-line.cfm [accessed on 21 July 2009].

Public Safety Canada. 2008. *Best practice guidelines for screening volunteers.* Available from: http://www.publicsafety.gc.ca/res/cor/rep/vol-ben-eng.aspx [accessed on 20 May 2009].

Pugh, C & Wood, EH. 2004. The strategic use of events within local government: A study of London Borough Councils [electronic version]. *Event Management,* 9: 61–71.

Pugh, CWE. 2004. The strategic use of events within local government: A study of London borough councils. *Event Management,* 9: 61–71.

Pugh, DS (Ed.). 1971. *Organization Theory: Selected Readings.* Harmondsworth, Middlesex: Penguin Education.

Quester, P & Farelly, F. 1998. Brand association and memory decay effects of sponsorship: The case of the Australian Formula 1 Grand Prix. *Journal of Product and Brand Management,* 7(6): 539–556.

Raj, R, Walters, P & Rashid, T. 2009. *Advanced Event Management: An Integrated and Practical Approach*: Sage.

Remarkable Productions. 2007. *Stoke-on-Trent City Council, Festivals and Events Strategy Summary Report 2007.* UK.

Render, B & Heizer, J. 1997. *Principles of Operations Management,* 2 ed. New Jersey: Prentice Hall.

Republic of South Africa. 1993. *Occupational Health and Safety Act 85 of 1993* (S1 read with S8). Pretoria: Government Printer.

Republic of South Africa. 2002. *Disaster Risk Management Act 57 of 2002.* Pretoria: Government Printer.

Richards, B. 1992. *How to Market Tourist Attractions, Festivals and Special Events.* Essex: Longman.

Ritchie, BW. 1996. How special are special events? The economic impact and strategic development of the New Zealand Masters Game. *Festival Management & Event Tourism,* 4: 117–126.

Ritchie, JRB & Smith, BH. 1991. The impact of mega events on host region awareness: A longitudinal study. *Journal of Travel Research,* 30(1): 3–10.

Rogers, T. 1998. *Conferences– A 21st Century Industry.* United States of America: Addison Wesley Longman Limited.

Rogers, T. 2003a. *Business Tourism Briefing: An Overview of the UK's Business Tourism Industry.* UK: Business Tourism Partnership.

Rogers, T. 2003b. *Conferences and Conventions: A Global Industry.* Oxford: Elsevier Butterworth-Heinemann.

Rossmann, JR & Schlatter, BE. 2003. *Recreation Programming: Designing Leisure Experiences,* 3 ed. Champaign, IL: Sagamore Publishing.

Rossouw, J. 2000. Sports event management. In *Event Management: A Professional and Developmental Approach,* 1 ed., Tassiopoulos, D (Ed.). Lansdowne: Juta Academic.

Russell, M. 2006. *PCMA REPORT: Crisis planning for the meeting, planning and convention industry.* Available from: http://www.pcma.org/Convene/Issue_Archives/December_2006/PCMA_Report_(Crisis).htm

Rutherford Silvers, J. 2004. *Professional Event Co-ordination.* Ontario: John Wiley & Sons, Canada Limited.

Rutherford Silvers, J. 2009. *Updated EMBOK Structure as a Risk Management Framework for Events.* Available from: http://www.juliasilvers.com/embok/EMBOK_structure_update.htm [accessed on 6 July 2009].

Rutherford, DG. 2002. *Hotel Management and Operations,* 3 ed. New York: John Wiley & Sons.

SA Tourism & DEAT. 2002. *Towards a National Event Strategy for South Africa: Final Report* (October). Pretoria: SA Government (Department of Environmental Affairs and Tourism and South African Tourism).

Saayman, M. 2002. *Hospitality, Leisure and Tourism Management.* Potchefstroom: Leisure Consultants & Publications.

Saayman, M & Rossouw, R. 2008. The economic value of the 2010 Soccer World Cup. *Acta Commercii*, 8: 1–13.

Saget, A. 2006. *Event Marketing beyond Logistics and Planning.* Chicago: Kaplan.

SAQA. 2006. *Glossary of terms.* Available from: http://www.saqa.org.za/ [accessed on 20 May 2009].

Saveriades, A. 2000. Establishing the social tourism carrying capacity for the tourist resorts of the east coast of the Republic of Cyprus. *Tourism Management*, 21(2): 147–156.

Schaaf, P. 1995. *Sports Marketing.* New York: Prometheus Books.

Schmader, SW. 1997. From the flow chart to action. In *Event Operations.* Washington: International Festivals and Events Association.

Schmidgall, RS. 1997. *Hospitality Industry Management Accounting.* East Lansing: Educational Institute, American Hotel and Lodging Association.

Schmied, M, Stahh, H, Roth, R, Armbruster, F, Turk, S & Friedel, C. 2007. *Green champions in sport and environment: Guide to environmentally sound large sporting events.* Berlin: Federal Ministry for the Environment, Nature, Conservation and Nuclear Safety.

Schmitt, B. 1999. *Experiential Marketing: How to Get Customers to Sense, Feel, Think, Act and Relate to your Company.* New York: Free Press.

Scholtes, PR. 1998. *The Leader's Handbook.* New York: McGraw-Hill.

Sen, P. 2008. *Olympic Volunteer Roundup.* 2008. Available from: http://www.worldvolunteerweb.org [accessed on 21 June 2009].

Senge, PM. 1990. *The Fifth Discipline: The Art and Practice of the Learning Organization.* New York: Currency Doubleday.

Shaw, E. 2008. Maximum security. *Event Solutions.* March. Available from: http://www.event-solutions.com/magazine/march_2008/maxium_security [accessed on 29 April 2009].

Shaw, G & Williams, AM. 2002. *Critical Issues in Tourism: A Geographical Perspective*, 2 ed. Oxford: Blackwell Publishing.

Shibli, S & Gratton, P. 2001. The economic impact of two major sporting events in two of the UK's 'National Cities of Sport'. In *Sport in the City: The Role of Sport in Eonomic and Social Regeneration*, Gratton, C & Henry, I (Eds). London: Routledge.

Shock, PJ & Stefanelli, JM. 1992. *Hotel Catering.* New York: John Wiley & Sons.

Shone, A & Parry, B. 2004. *Successful Event Management: A Practical Handbook*, 2 ed. London: Thompson Press.

Shukla, N & Nuntsu, N. 2005. Event marketing. In *Event Management*, 2 ed., Tassiopoulos, D (Ed.). Cape Town: Juta Academic.

Silvers, JR. 2004. *Updated EMBOK Structure as a Risk Management Framework for Events.* Available from: http://www.juliasilvers.com/embok/EMBOK_structure_update.htm#HumanResources [accessed on 1 August 2009].

Silvers, JR. 2004a. *Global knowledge domain structure for event management*. Conference proceedings, 2004 Las Vegas International Hospitality and Convention Summit, Gu, Z (Ed.), 228–245. University of Nevada, Las Vegas.

Silvers, JR. 2004b. *Professional Event Coordination*. Hoboken, NJ: John Wiley & Sons, Inc.

Silvers, JR. 2005. *The potential of the EMBOK as a risk management framework for Events*. Conference Proceedings, 2005 Las Vegas International Hospitality and Convention Summit. University of Nevada Las Vegas.

Silvers, JR. 2006. *An EMBOK Research Menu. The EMBOK Project*. [internet]. http://www.juliasilvers.com/embok/Research_Menu.htm

Silvers, JR. 2008. *Risk Management for Meetings and Events*. Oxford: Butterworth-Heinemann.

Silvers, JR. 2009a. *Decision management: Are your decisions brilliant or blundering?* Presentation at Catersource/Event Solutions 2009 Conference, Las Vegas, NV.

Silvers, JR. 2009b. *Event management body of knowledge project*. Available from: http://www.juliasilvers.com/embok/EMBOK_structure_update.htm#HumanResources [accessed on 2 July 2009].

Silvers, JR, Bowdin, GAJ, O'Toole, WJ, & Nelson, KB. 2006. Towards an international event management body of knowledge (EMBOK). *Event Management*, 9(4), 185–198. New York: Cognizant Communications.

Silvers, JR & Nelson, K. 2005. *Introduction to Meeting and Event Management*. Albuquerque, NM: Speaking of Events.

Simon, HA. 1960. Decision making and organizational design. In *The New Science of Management Decision*. Harper & Row. [See Pugh, 1971].

Sinclair, JM (Ed). 1994. *Collins English Dictionary*. Glasgow: HarperCollins Publishers.

Singh, RK, Murty, HR, Gupta, SK & Dikshit, AK. 2008. An overview of sustainability assessment methodologies. *Ecological Indicators*, 9(2): 189–212.

Sivek, R. 1996. Working with unions at facilities. In *ISES Gold*, 2 ed. Arlington, Virginia: International Special Events Society (Educational Services Institute).

Skinner, BE & Rukavina, V. 2003. *Event Sponsorship*. Canada, John Wiley & Sons.

Skinner, C, Von Essen, G & Mesham, L. 2001. *Handbook of Public Relations*, 6 ed. Cape Town: Oxford University Press.

Small, K, Edwards, D & Sheridan, L. 2005. A flexible framework for evaluating the socio-cultural impacts of a (small) festival. *International Journal of Event Management Research*, 1(1): 66–76.

Small, M. 1976. *Catering for Functions*. London: Barrie & Jenkins Ltd.

Smith, A. 2001. Sporting a new image? Sport-based regeneration strategies as a means of enhancing the image of the city tourist destination. In *Sport in the City: The Role of Sport in Economic and Social Regeneration*, Gratton, C & Henry, I (Eds). London: Routledge.

Smith, K. 2008. The information mix for events: A comparison of multiple channels used by event organisers and visitors. *International Journal of Event Management Research*, 4(1). Available from: http://www.ijemr.org/index.html?page=25580 [accessed on 21 July 2009].

Smuts, D & Westcott, S. 1991. *The Purple shall Govern. A South African A to Z of Nonviolent Action*. Cape Town: Oxford University Press.

Sonder, M. 2004. *Event Entertainment and Production.* Hoboken: Wiley.

Sookrajh, R. 2008. Nature-based sport events and the physical environment: A case study of the Halfway-Telkom Midmar Mile. *Alternation,* 15(1): 66–86.

South Africa, Republic of. 2002. *Commission of inquiry into the Ellis Park Stadium disaster of 11 April 2001.* Available from: http://www.info.gov.za/view/DownloadFileAction?id=70241 [accessed on 20 May 2009].

South Africa, *The Good News.* 25 March 2009. *MTN to build world class media centre.* Available from: http://www.sagoodnews.co.za/countdown_to_2010/mtn_to_build_the_world_cup_2010_media_centre.html [accessed on 20 May 2009].

South African Sports Commission. 2003. *Bidding to Host Sport and Recreation Events in South Africa.* Centurion: South African Sports Commission.

South African Tourism. 2007. *Event Tourism Growth Strategy 2007–2010* (August). Johannesburg: South African Tourism.

SouthAfrica.info. 1 September 2009a. *Calling all 2009, 2010 volunteers!* Available from: htpp://www.southafrica.info/2010/volunteers.htm [accessed on 20 May 2009].

SouthAfrica.info. 1 September 2009b. *Thousands put up hands for 2009.* Available from: htpp://www.southafrica.info/2010/confed-volunteers.htm [accessed on 20 May 2009].

Spilling, OR. 1998. Beyond intermezzo? On the long-term industrial impacts of mega-events: The case of Lillehammer 1994. *Festival Management & Event Tourism,* 5, 101–122.

Spilling, OR. 2000. Beyond intermezzo? On the long term industrial impacts of mega-events: The case of Lillehammer 1994. In *Evaluation of Events: Scandinavian Experiences,* Mossberg, L (Ed.). NY: Cognizant Communication Corp.

Spirit of Vancouver. 12 February 2008. *Vancouver 2010 volunteer programme launched.* Available from: http://www.spiritofvanocuver/spiritof/vancouver_2010/79/1 [accessed on 22 May 2009].

SportBusiness International. 2001. *Sport business information resources.* [Unpublished trade report].

Sports Marketing Surveys. 2005. *The world sponsorship monitor.* [Unpublished trade report].

Srinivas, H. 2009. *Urban environmental management, the sustainable tourism gateway – tourism destination management.* Available from: http://www.gdrc.org/uem/eco-tour/destination-mgmt.html [accessed on 19 June 2009].

Staging Connections. 2008. *Staging Connections and Telstra create industry first: Beams executive via live hologram.* (May press release). Available from: http://www.stagingconnections.com/media/aav/news_releases/StagingConnections_Telstra%20Hologram%20PR_30May08.pdf [accessed on 10 July 2009].

Stair, RM. 1996. *Principles of Information Systems: A Managerial Approach,* 2 ed. London: International Thomson Publishing Europe.

STB. 2009. *Singapore Tourism Board –Tourism 2015.* Available from: http://app-stg.stb.gov.sg/asp/abo/abo08.asp [accessed on 15 May 2009].

Stiernstrand, J. 1996. *The Nordic Model: A Theoretical Model for Economic Impact Analysis of Event Tourism Festival Management & Event Tourism,* 3: 165–174.

Stinchcombe, K & Gibson, RB. 2001. Strategic Environmental assessment as a means of pursuing sustainability: Ten advantages and ten challenges. *Journal of Environmental Assessment Policy Management*, 3(3): 343–372.

Stipanuk, DM. 2002. *Hospitality Facilities Management and Design*, 2nd ed. East Lansing: Educational Institute, American Hotel and Lodging Association.

Stokes, R. 2008. *E-marketing, the Essential Guide to Online Marketing*, 2 ed. Available from: http://www.quirk.biz/emarketingtextbook [accessed on 10 June 2009].

Sunday Times (Travel & Food), 2009. *The war of memories*. 5 April, 9.

Swart, K. 2005. Mega-event management. In *Event Management: A Professional and Developmental Approach*, 2 ed. Tassiopoulos, D. (Ed.). Lansdowne: Juta.

Swart. R. 2009. Personal communication. 20 May.

Sydney Olympic Park Authority. 2009. *A living legacy, transformed into a major urban centre*. Available from: http://www.sydneyolympicpark.com.au/corporate/about_us/olympic_legacy [accessed on 6 June 2009].

Tassiopoulos, D. 2005. *Event Management: A Professional and Developmental Approach*, 2 ed. Lansdowne: Juta Academic.

Tassiopoulos, D & Haydam, N. 2008. Golf tourists in South Africa: A demographic and psychographic study of a niche market in sports tourism. *Tourism Management*, 29(5), 870–882.

Tassiopoulos, D & Johnson, D. 2009. Chapter 8: Social impact of events. In *Event Management and Sustainability*. Raj, R & Musgrave, J (Eds). United Kingdom: CABI.

Temkin, S. 2009. FIFA is giving the red card to ambush tactics. *Business Day: Business Law & Tax Review*, 11 May, 1–2.

The Daily Dispatch online. 2003. *Boy, 5, dies from food poisoning*. Available at http://www.dispatch.co.za/2003/08/07/easterncape/aameat.html [accessed on 14 August 2009].

The Football Licensing Authority, GB. 2008. *Guide to Safety at Sports Grounds*, 5 ed. UK: TSO (The Stationery Office).

The Herald online. 2003. *14 hit by food poisoning at popular restaurant*. Available from: http://www.theherald.co.za/herald/2003/01/07/news/n03_07012003.htm [accessed on 14 August 2009].

The Leeds Festival. 2002. [internet]. Available from: http://www.leedsmusicfestival.co.uk/ [accessed on 20 April 2009].

The Munich Beer Festival. Available from: http://ezinearticles.com/?The-Munich-Beer-Festival&id=634886 [accessed on 27 May 2009].

The Munich Beer Festival: Oktoberfest! March 2009. *Welcome to Munich Beer Festival.com* Available from: http://munichbeerfestival.com/content.php?article.1.255 [accessed on 27 May 2009].

The Presidency (of South Africa). 2009. *Izimbizo*. Available at: http://www.thepresidency.gov.za/main.asp?include=izimbizo/main.html [accessed on 21 April 2009].

Thérivel, R. & Partidário, MR. 1996. *The Practice of Strategic Environmental Assessment*. London: Earthscan Publications.

Thomas, PH. 2009. *Postgraduate Diploma in Management Practice (Events): Module 4*. Cape Town: University of Cape Town Business School.

Thwaites, D. 1994. Corporate sponsorship by the financial services industry. *Journal of Marketing Management,* 10: 743–763.

Times-7 Sport. 2007. *Levene Half Marathon Timed by World-leading Technology* (August media release). Available from: http://www.times-7sport.com/levene-half-marathon-uses-times-7-solutions [accessed on 10 July 2009].

Tricker, R. 2001. *ISO 9001:2000 for Small Businesses,* 2 ed. Oxford: Butterworth-Heinemann.

Trigg, P. 1995. *Leisure and Tourism GNVQ: Intermediate.* Oxford: Butterworth-Heinemann.

Trotter, C. 1999. *Lessons in Excellence.* Berkley: Ten Speed Press.

Tuckman, BW. 1965. Developmental sequence in small groups. *Psychological Bulletin,* 63, 384–399. Washington, DC: American Psychological Association.

Tum, J, Norton, P & Wright, JN. 2005. *Management of Event Operations (Events Management).* Oxford: Butterworth-Heinemann Ltd.

Turco, DM, Riley, R & Swart, K. 2002. *Sport Tourism.* FIT: Morgantown, WV.

Turco, DM, Swart, K, Bob, U & Moodley, V. 2003. Socio-economic impacts of sport tourism in the Durban Unicity, South Africa. *Journal of Sport Tourism,* 8(4): 223–239.

Two Oceans Expo. 2008. *Old Mutual Two Oceans Marathon* Available from: http://www.oldmutual.co.za/about-us/sponsorship/sport/two-oceans-marathon/training-centre/expo.aspx [accessed on 6 June 2009].

UFI. 2009a. *Global economic crisis barometer research.* Available from: http://www.ufi.org/media/publicationspress/2009_economic_crisis_barometer_may_2009.pdf [accessed on 2 July 2009].

UFI. 2009b. *Background and fundamentals.* Available from: http://www.ufi.org/pages/thetradefairsector/basicknowledge.aspx#1.1 [accessed on 2 July 2009].

UN (United Nations). n.d. *Accreditation Requirements.* New York: UN Media Accreditation and Liaison Unit. Available from: http://www.un.org/media/accreditation/form/myform.asp [accessed on 29 April 2009].

UNEP. 2002. [internet] Available from: http://www.uneptie.org/pc/tourism [accessed on 29 June 2009].

United Nations Environmental Programme (UNEP) 2007. *Sports and Sustainable Development.* Available from: http://unesdoc.unesco.org/images/0015/001508/150845e.pdf [accessed on 20 July 2008].

United Nations. 2000. Press release ENV/DEV/557 PI/1318. *United Nations to Hold 2002 World Summit on Sustainable Development in Johannesburg, South Africa.* 21 December.

United Nations. 2003. *Environmental impact assessment principles and process.* Available from: http://www.unescap.org/drpad/vc/orientation/M8_1.htm [accessed on 12 May 2009].

Van Aardt, I & Van Aardt, C. 1997. *Entrepreneurship and New Venture Management.* Johannesburg: International Thomson Publishing.

Van der Wagen, L. 2005. *Event Management for Tourism, Cultural, Business and Sporting Events,* 2 ed. Australia: Pearson.

Van der Wagen, L. 2007. *Event Management.* Sydney: Pearson.

Van der Wagen, L & Carlos, BR. 2005. *Event Management for Tourism, Cultural, Business, and Sporting Events.* Upper Saddle River, NJ: Pearson Education, Inc.

Van der Westhuizen, J. 2006. Pretoria and the global conference circuit: Hot air, or hot stuff? In *In Full Flight. South African Foreign Policy after Apartheid,* Carlsnaes, W & Nel, P (Eds). Midrand, Johannesburg: Institute for Global Dialogue.

Van Wyk, JA & Tassiopoulos, D. 2009. *Policy, Politics and Events: A Case Study of South Africa's 2010 FIFA World Cup™: Managing International Sports Events in Sustainable Political Context.* Conference proceedings of paper presented at the 6th International Conference for Consumer Behaviour and Retailing Research, Vorarlberg University of Applied Sciences, Dornbirn, Austria, 16–18 April 2009.

Vanclay, F. 2003. International principles for social impact assessment. *Impact Assessment and Project Appraisal,* 21(1): 5–11.

VANOC, October 2007. *Vancouver 2010 Olympic Games Impact Program Baseline Report.* Available from: http://www.vancouver2010.com/dl/00/35/13/-/35136/prop=data/tzomid/35136.pdf [accessed on 20 May 2009].

Venø Thesburg, M. 2007. *Environmental group opposes 2010 Football World Cup.* Available from: http://www.playthegame.org/news/detailed/environmental-group-opposes-2010-football-world-cup.html [accessed on 22 May 2009].

Verheem, R & Tonk, JAMN. 2000. Strategic environmental assessment: One concept, multiple forms. *Impact Assessment Project Appraisal* 19(3): 177–182.

Wallbank, T. 2002. *Market review.* [internet]. Manchester. Available from: http://www.myvenues.co.uk/news/Industry/Uk-corporate-hospitality-set-to-grow/559/ [accessed on 2 July 2009].

Walmsley, D. 2008. *Sports Event Bidding: A Strategic Guide for Sports Property Owners and Event Bidders.* London: Sport Business.

Walters, G. 2008. *Bidding for major sporting events: Key issues and challenges faced by sports governing bodies in the UK.* A report for the Central Council of Physical Recreation. London: CCP.

Wanklin, T. 2005. Organisations and organising events. In *Event Management,* 2 ed. Tassiopoulos, D. (Ed.). Cape Town: Juta Academic.

Warren, K. 2008. *Strategic Marketing Dynamics.* Chichester: John Wiley & Sons, Ltd.

Watt, DC. 1998. *Event Management in Leisure and Tourism.* New York: Addison Wesley Longman.

WBPDC. 2008. *Western Bay of Plenty District Council Events Strategy 2009–2012.* New Zealand.

Webster's New World College Dictionary. 2009. *Grunt.* Available from: http://www.yourdictionary.com/grunt [accessed on 3 July 2009].

WEC (World Exhibitions Club). 2009. *History of Exhibitions.* Available from: http://www.wecexhibitions.com/historyexhibitions.php [accessed on 2 July 2009].

Weed, M & Bull, C. 2004. *Sports Tourism: Participants, Policy and Providers.* Oxford: Elsevier Butterworth.

Westerbeek, HM, Turner, P & Ingerson, L. 2002. Key success factors in bidding for hallmark sporting events. *International Marketing Review,* 19(3): 303–322.

Western Cape Department of Cultural Affairs and Sport. 2009. *Fanjol News*. March/April.

Weyers, M. 2009. Alex Gintan Associates, personal interview (12 March).

Whale, M. 1997. *ABC of Event Management*. Bedfordview: Dictum Publishers.

Whitelegg, D. 2000. Going for gold: Atlanta's bid for fame. *International Journal of Urban and Regional Research*, 24: 801–817.

Whittaker, DJ. 2004. *Terrorists and Terrorism in the Contemporary World*. London: Routledge.

Wiersma, EA & Strolberg, KE. 2003. *Exceptional Events, Concept to Completion*, 2 ed. Texas: Chips Books.

Wikipedia. 2009a. *Banquet*. Available from: http://en.wikipedia.org/wiki/Banqueting [accessed 14 August 2009].

Wikipedia. 2009c. *Gap analysis*. Available from: http://en.wikipedia.org/wiki/Gap_analysis [accessed on 15 July 2009].

Wikipedia. 2009c. *Indian Premier League – television rights and sponsorships*. Available from: http://en.wikipedia.org/wiki/Indian_Premier_League#Television_rights_and_sponsorships [accessed on 10 July 2009].

Wikipedia. 2009d. *Web 2.0*. Available from: http://en.wikipedia.org/wiki/Web_2.0 [accessed on 15 July 2009].

Williams, E. *CSR Europe's Sustainable Marketing Guide*. Available from: http://www.csreurope.org [accessed on 25 July 2009].

Worden, N & Van Heyningen, E. 1996. Signs of the times: Tourism and public history at Cape Town's Victoria and Alfred Waterfront. *Cahiers d'Études Africaines*, 36(141/142): 215–236.

Wright, R. 2005. *The Meeting Spectrum*. Canada: HRD Press.

Wycoff, J. 1991. *Mind Mapping: Your Personal Guide to Exploring Creativity and Problem Solving*. New York: Berkley Books.

Xinhuanet. 2008. *NBC: Beijing Olympic opening ceremony draws record ratings for non-US games*. Available from: http://news.xinhuanet.com/english/2008-08/10/content_9125816.htm [accessed on 22 May 2009].

Yates, JF. 2003. *Decision Management: How to Assure Better Decisions in Your Company*. San Francisco: Jossey-Bass.

Yeoman, I, Robertson, M, Ali-Knight, J, Drum mond, S & McMahon-Beattie, U. 2004. *Festival and Events Management*. Oxford: Elsevier Butterworth-Heinemann.

Yorkshire Evening Post. 2002. [internet]. Available from: http://www.thisisleeds.co.uK/> [accessed on 29 April 2009].

Yorkshire Post Newspaper. 2002. [internet]. Available from: http://www.ypn.co.uK/. [accessed on 29 April 2009].

Youell, R. 1995. *Leisure & Tourism – Advanced GNVQ*, 2 ed. Harlow: Longman.

YouTube™. 2009. *Search words: 'event' 'invitation'*. Available from: http://www.YouTube.com [accessed on 10 July 2009].

Yunus, E. 2004. *Indicators to measure sustainability in tourism.* Paper presented at the 7th International Forum on Tourism Statistics (9–11 June 2004), World Tourism Organisation, Stockholm, Sweden.

Zevin, R. 2003. *An Exploratory Study of the Special Events Industry: Developing a Skill Set.* Unpublished manuscript. University of Nevada, Las Vegas.

Index

Entries are listed in letter-by-letter alphabetical order. Page references in *italic* indicate where you can find a figure or table relating to the index entry term.

A

Abu Dhabi, United Arab Emirates 37
accountability 19, 133-134
accounting see financial management
acid-test ratio 173-174
advertising 262
affinity diagrams 321-322, *322*
agencies 79-84
agendas see programme design
alcoholic beverages 234, 277, 350, 475, 519
ambush marketing 287-288, 386
animation 203-204
art events 14-15
articles of organisations 132-133
assets
      events as 35-37
      management of 172, 178
association buyers 72-74
associations not for gain 130
attendee management 307-313
auditing 156, 178-179
authenticity 7-8

B

balance sheets 172, 173
Balloon Glow, Albuquerque, NM 53
banqueting 470-488
    administration 484-486
    case studies 473-474, 481, 485
    definition of 471-472
    design management 472-476
    entertainment 480
    human resource management 484-486
    marketing management 482-483
    operations management 480-482
    recommended websites 488
    return on investment (ROI) 486-487
    risk management 483-484
    service design 477-480
    speeches 480
    sponsorships 483
    table arrangements 476-477, *476*, *477*
    venues for 472
bar charts 150, *150*
benefits of events 6-8
beverages see alcoholic beverages

bidding 87-107
    case studies 91, 93, 96, 98, 101, 104-105
    checklists 98-101, *99-100*
    critical path documents 101-102
    definition of 88-91
    destination image 94-95
    documents for 95-102
    economic issues 92-93, 97-98
    environmental issues 92-94, 97-98
    factors to consider 91-97
    hallmark and mega-events 368-370, *369*
    meetings 515
    pitching 90-91
    process of 88-91, 95, 102-105
    procurement 89-90
    recommended websites 107
    request for proposals (RFPs) 96, 101
    social issues 92-93, 97-98
    sport events 409-410
    tendering 90
    timeframes 101-102
BlackOut Dining Experience, UK 197
boards of directors 134
body of knowledge 53-56
Bonnaroo Music and Arts Festival, US 392, 402
brainstorming 121, 339, 508
brand value 36-37
breakeven point 179, *180*
British Grand Prix, Silverstone 490
budgeting 163-167, 412, 431-433, 510-511
business events see corporate events
business plans 410-411
business travel agencies 79
buyers 70-74
'buy in' events 41-42
by-laws 386

C

capacity 26, 219, 308-309, *310*
Cape Argus Pick n Pay Cycle Tour 418
Cape Town, South Africa 37, 410
capital expenditure (CAPEX) budgets 165
carrying capacity see capacity
cash flow management 165, 167-169, 177, 371-372
caterers, working relationships with 228-236
catering design 186, 197-198, 201, 225-248

case studies 227, 232, 237, 238, 240, 242, 244, 245
controlled-access events 243-245
experiential dimensions 227-228
food production 245-247
food trends 233-236
health and safety concerns 230-232
planning stages *235*
recommended websites 248
record keeping 228, 230, 235
religious and cultural diversity 245
sporting events 231-232
uncontrolled-access events 236-242
wedding receptions 244
working relationship with caterers 228-236
cellular messaging 332
Championchips 22, 33
charitable donations 276
CHCs *see* corporate hospitality companies (CHCs)
checklists 98-101, *99-100, 415*, 508, 512
chief executive officers 135-136
civic centres 77
civic events 453-454, 460 *see also* political events
clinics 505
close corporations (CC) 129
closure of events 148-149
code of ethics 449
Colley's Supper Rooms, UK 481
colloquiums 505
commercial returns 36
committees 131-132
Commonwealth Games 380, 495
communication channels 332-333
communications management 295-299
communications mix 261-266
community development 8-9
compliance management 349-350
concept of event 112
concessions 176
conferences 438-439, 491, 505
confex events 429
congresses 505
consortiums 129
consultants 84
consumer shows 14, 505
content design 186, 202
continual event improvement process 294, *295*
contract planners *see* professional conference organisers (PCOs)
controlled-access events 243-245
convention and visitor bureaux (CVBs) 79-81
conventions 505

coordination *see* planning and coordination
copyright 267
corporate buyers 70-72
corporate companies 129
corporate events 489-501
    case studies 490, 491, 492, 493, 495, 496, 497, 498-500
    customer loyalty 495-496
    definition of 14
    hospitality events 283, 493
    human resource management 496-497
    impact of 492-493
    industry of 491-492
    marketing strategies 494-495
    operations management 496-497
    planning 493-494
    recommended websites 501
    risk management 497-498
    sponsorships 495
    venues 493-494
corporate hospitality 283, 493
corporate hospitality companies (CHCs) 81
corporate philanthropy 276
corporate social responsibility (CSR) 23, 515
cost accounting 163
cost-benefit analysis 215
cost cutting 171-172
CPA *see* critical path analysis (CPA)
crashing 155-156
creativity 188, 192-198, *193*
Cricket World Cup 424
critical path analysis (CPA) 152
critical path documents 101-102
crowd management 307-313, *310, 311*
CSR *see* corporate social responsibility (CSR)
cultural diversity 23-25, 245
cultural events 13-14
customer loyalty 495-496
CVBs *see* convention and visitor bureaux (CVBs)

D
databases 27, 326-328, *326, 327*
decision criteria 44, *45*
decision making 60-61, *60*, 354-355
décor 307
demographic interests 21
design management 185-206
    banqueting 472-477
    case studies 187, 189, 195, 197, 203-204
    communication 198
    creativity 188, 192-198, *193*
    definition of 186-188

elements of 190-191, *190*
exhibitions 436-439
festivals 399-400, *400*
hallmark and mega-events 375-379, *375*
meetings 515-522
pitching 192
planned-event experiences 198-205
political events 458-459
recommended websites 206
role of 189-192
sport events 415-419
tools for 200-202, *200*
destination image 26, 78-79, 94-95, 492
destination management companies (DMCs) 81-82
destination management organisations (DMOs) 78, 79-80
Destination Marketing Association International (DMAI) 80
development *see* community development
development of events 37-39, *38, 39*, 146-147, *147*
dining 471-472 *see also* banqueting
discretionary time 20-21
DMAI *see* Destination Marketing Association International (DMAI)
DMCs *see* destination management companies (DMCs)
DMOs *see* destination management organisations (DMOs)
donated goods 176
Drupa, Düsseldorf, Germany 444
duration of events 153-154, *154*

E
economic forces 20
economic impacts 92-93, 97-98, 214-215, *221*
Edinburgh Festival, UK 394-395
educational events 14
EIAs *see* environmental impact assessments (EIAs)
electronic marketing 262-264, *265-266*
Ellis Park soccer stadium disaster 425-426
email 332-333
EMBOK *see* Event Management Body of Knowledge (EMBOK)
emergency management 304, 352-354, *352 see also* risk management
employees *see* human resource management
entertainment design 186, 202
environmental education 219-220
environmental impact assessments (EIAs) 220-221
environmental impacts 92-94, 97-98, 197, 216-222, *221*, 269-270, 418-419
environment design 186

essential services 304
ethical issues 269-270, *271*, 350-352, 449
Euro 2008 Impact Model 387
evaluation
exhibitions 447
hallmark and mega-events 387-388
information technology (IT) 337-338
operations management 313
project management 156-158, *157*
sponsorships 285-287
sport events 411-412, *411*
event administrators 135-136
Event ConneQion Expo (2008) 189
Event Management Body of Knowledge (EMBOK) 54-56, 64
events, definition of 5-8, *7*, 9-15, *10*, 69
events corporations 46-47
events production houses 82
events sector 4-5, *10*, 15, 17-19, 20-25
in South Africa 4, 28-32
events tourism 5-6
event triangle model 68-70, *69*
exchange of views 121
exhibitions 82, 428-450
administration 431
budgeting 431-433
case studies 332, 430, 431, 438, 444
definition of 429, 505
design management 436-439
ethical issues 449
history of 429-431
human resource management 435-436
information technology (IT) 330, 332
marketing management 442-447
operations management 439-442
recommended websites 450
return on investment (ROI) 433-435, *435*
risk management 447-448
sponsorships 442-447
stand managers 436
systems management 436
experiential marketing 267
expositions *see* exhibitions

F
Facebook *see* Web 2.0 technology
facilities 120-121
fairs *see* exhibitions
feasibility studies 114
festivals 390-407
administration 395
advantages of 391-393

case studies 392, 393, 394-395, 399, 401-402, 403, 404
definition of 13-14
design management 399-400, *400*
marketing management 401-404
operations management 404-405
programme of 398-401
project management 395-397
recommended websites 406-407
risk management 405-406
role of 393-395
sponsorships 403
stakeholders 397-398
FIFA World Cup 75-76, 202, 215, 216-217, 368, 371, 373
financial management 161-182
accounting 162-163
auditing 178-179
bidding 97
breakeven point 179, *180*
budgeting 163-167
cash flow management 167-169
challenges 179-181
controls 164, 176-178
hallmark and mega-events 370-372, *371*
measuring performance 172-174
meetings 508-511
price administration 174-176
profit 174-176
recommended websites 181
sport events 412-415, *413, 414, 415*
statements 169-172
fire safety 349, 357, 358, 448 *see also* risk management
five Ws 253-254
food and beverages *see* catering design
food poisoning 231, 232
forums 505
founding members of organisations 132
four As 78
framework plans 114-115
function sheets 155
fundraising 276 *see also* sponsorships
Future of Event Management Charter, The xvi-xviii

G

GAAP *see* generally accepted accounting practices (GAAP)
Gantt charts 102, 150, *150*
gap analysis 334-336
generally accepted accounting practices (GAAP) 162
global economic downturn 287
goodwill 36-37

government buyers 74
government events *see* political events
governments 35, 39-42, *39, 40-41*, 131, 288
grading 75
Grahamstown National Arts Festival 237, 238
Grand Prix 410, 490
grants 276, 413
Green Tourism Business Scheme (GTBS) 77
growth in events industry 19
'grunt' events market 72-74
GTBS *see* Green Tourism Business Scheme (GTBS)

H

hallmark and mega-events 365-389
administration 367-375, *367, 369, 371*
bidding 368-370, *369*
case studies 371, 373, 374, 376, 377, 378, 379, 380, 382, 384, 385, 386, 387
definition of 11-13
design management 375-379, *375*
evaluation 387-388
financial management 370-372, *371*
human resource management 372-375
legacy *373*, 377-379
marketing management 379-385, *380*
operations management 382-385, *383*
recommended websites 389
risk management 385-386
health and safety management 98, 230-232, 355-357
see also risk management
Henley Festival, UK 308
Henley Royal Regatta 111
heritage events 13-14, 456
hierarchical structure in organisations 139, *139, 140*
hologram attendees 334
hotels 74-75
HSBC Global Education Challenge 279
hub organisational structure 57-58, *57*
Hugo Boss fashion show, Berlin 187
human resource management 134-140
banqueting 484-486
corporate events 496-497
exhibitions 435-436
hallmark and mega-events 372-375
meetings 511

I

IACVB *see* International Association of Convention and Visitor Bureaux (IACVB)
IAPCO *see* International Association of Professional Congress Organisers (IAPCO)
IBC *see* International Broadcast Centre (IBC)

incentive travel houses 83
income and expenditure budgets 165
income statements 169-172
incorporated partnership (Inc) 129
information technology (IT) 317-339
    case studies 319-320, 325, 330, 331, 332, 333,
        334, 335, 336
    communication channels 332-333
    databases 326-328, *326, 327*
    evaluation 337-338
    exhibitions 330, 332
    global participation 333-336
    language interpretation 330, 331
    planning 318-326, *321, 322*
    political events 463
    recommended websites 338-339
    registration systems 329-330
    return on investment (ROI) 334-335, 336
    transcription 330, 331
    translation 330, 331
    websites 328
infrastructure 214-215, 302-305
institutes 505
institutions 131
insurance management 360, 448
Interbou, South Africa 431
intermediaries 79-85
International Association of Convention and Visitor
    Bureaux (IACVB) 81
International Association of Professional Congress
    Organisers (IAPCO) 83
International Broadcast Centre (IBC) 384
internet promotions 262-264, 328, 420-421
interpretation *see* language interpretation
interpretive vision 52
IT *see* information technology (IT)

K
knowledge management (KM) 388

L
language interpretation 330, 331
layout plans 116-117
leadership 25-26, 59-62
lead system 81
learning 62
lectures 505
Leeds West Indian Carnival 401-402
legacy of events 16, 17-19, 28, *373*, 377-379, 380
legal aspects of bidding 97
liabilities 172
licensing 267

lifelong learning 62
lighting systems 304, 306
liquidity ratio 173
local tourist office (LTO) 73
logical examination 51
logistics management 294-295, 383-384
logos 267
LTO *see* local tourist office (LTO)

M
Macworld, US 496
major events 11 *see also* hallmark and mega-events
management 49-64
    body of knowledge 53-56
    case studies 53, 55, 62
    context of 55-56
    decision making 60-61, *60*
    definition of 50-53
    interpretive vision 52
    leadership 59-62
    lifelong learning 62
    logical examination 51
    motivation 61
    organisational structures 56-59, *57*
    practical wisdom 52-53
    professionalism 59-62
    recommended websites 64
    soft skills *60*
    styles of 56
    volunteers 58, *59*
Manchester City 393, 399, 495, 498-500
marketing management 26, 251-272
    banqueting 482-483
    communications 260-266, *263, 265-266*
    corporate events 494-495
    definition of 252
    environmental issues 269-270
    ethical issues 269-270, *271*
    evaluation 267-269
    exhibitions 442-447
    experiential marketing 267
    festivals 401-404
    hallmark and mega-events 380, *380*
    marketing materials *263*, 264, 266
    marketing mix 258-260, *271*
    marketing plans 256-258, *257*
    market research 253-254
    market segmentation *10*, 255, *255*
    meetings 521
    merchandising 266-267
    political events 460-462
    recommended websites 271-272

return on marketing investment (ROMI) 267-269
six Ps 258-260
social issues 269-270
sport events 419-421
SWOT analysis 255-256, *256*
marketing materials *263, 264, 266*
marketing mix 258-260, *271*
marketing plans 256-258, *257*
market research 253-254
market segmentation *10*, 255, *255*
market sub-groups 74
mascots 267
matrix structure 128-129, *128*, 135
media relations 262, 336, 462
medical services 98, 304
meetings 502-525, *514, 516-518*
    administration 506-515
    bidding 515
    case studies 507, 515
    characteristics of meeting managers 503
    checklists 508, 512
    client discussion sheet 519-520
    definition of 14, 504, 505
    design of 515-522
    environmental issues 510
    financial management 508-511
    global perspective on 504
    holders of 506
    human resource management 511
    management of 506-515
    marketing management 521
    operations management 522-523
    procurement management 512-514
    reasons for 504
    recommended websites 525
    return on investment (ROI) 508-511
    risk management 523-524
    stakeholder management 514-515
    systems management 515
    table arrangements *516-518*
    time management 515
    types of 504-506
mega-events *see* hallmark and mega-events
memorandum and articles of association 132-133
merchandising 266-267, 283
mind mapping 121
monitoring *see* evaluation
motivation 61
MTN 278, 384
Munich Oktoberfest 242
Museum of Science and Industry 227

N
national tourism organisations (NTOs) 84
network scheduling 150-152, *151*
nomological structure of events 10-11, *11*
non-profit organisations 130
North East England Festivals and Events Toolkit 136-137
North Shore City, New Zealand 37
NTOs *see* national tourism organisations (NTOs)

O
objectives of events 114
OGI programme *see* Olympic Games Impact (OGI) programme
Olympic Games
    ambush marketing 287
    costs of 93
    decision criteria 44
    legacy 16, 17
    opening ceremony 376, 382
    security management 465-466
    sustainability 216-217, 378
    volunteers 137
Olympic Games Impact (OGI) programme 216-217, 378
operations management 293-316, *297*
    attendee management 307-313, *310, 311*
    banqueting 480-482
    case studies 308, 314-315
    communications management 295-299, *296*
    continual event improvement process 294, *295*
    corporate events 496-497
    evaluation 313
    exhibitions 439-442
    festivals 404-405
    hallmark and mega-events 382-385, *383*
    infrastructure management 302-305
    logistics management 294-295, *296*
    meetings 522-523
    plans 297-299, *298*
    political events 462-465
    recommended websites 315
    scheduling 302-305
    site management 299-302
    sport events 421-423
    technical management 305-307
operations plans 297-299, *298*
organisations
    articles of 132-133
    culture of 139-140
    structures of 56-59, *57*, 126, 128-129, *128*, 514
    types of 127-131, *127, 128*

organising 125-142
    case studies 132, 137
    critical success factors 140-141
    human resource management 134-138
    organisational structures 128-129, *128, 139, 140*
    recommended websites 141
    setting up event organisations 132-134, *133*
    stakeholder management 139-140
    types of organisations 127-131, *127, 128*
outsourced events 41-42
owner's equity 172

P

parking 118, 303-304 *see also* transport
participant management 307-313
partnerships 129
patronage 276
payroll budgets 165
PCOs *see* professional conference organisers (PCOs)
people with disabilities 304
personnel budgets 165
PERT *see* programme evaluation review technique
    (PERT)
petty cash 178
picketing 460 *see also* political events
pitching 90-91, 192
planning and coordination 108-124
    case studies 111
    catering design *235*
    compliance 122
    corporate events 493-494
    definition of 109
    financial management 163-164
    incremental approach 112
    recommended websites 123
    responsibility for 109-111
    steps in *110*, 111-121
    success factors for 122-123
    systematic approach 112
    tools for 121-122
PLC *see* product life cycle (PLC)
political events 451-469
    administration 456-458
    case studies 454, 459, 460, 464-465, 468, 497
    definition of 452-455
    design management 458-459
    developmental impact of 455-456
    marketing management 460-462
    objectives of 454-455
    operations management 462-465
    recommended websites 469
    risk management 465-467

stakeholders 457, *458*
political forces 21-22
population interests 21
PR *see* public relations (PR)
practical wisdom 52-53
presidential inaugurations 459
price administration 174-176
private limited companies 129
procurement 89-90, 514-516
production design 186, 187, 201-202
product life cycle (PLC) 45-46
professional conference organisers (PCOs) 79, 83
professionalism 59-62
profit and loss statements *414*
profits 174-176
programme design 118-120, 186, 201
programme evaluation review technique (PERT)
    152-153, *152*
project auditing 156
project management 143-160
    activities of 146-149
    critical factors 159
    definition of 144-146, *145*
    festivals 395-397
    financial management 153-156, 163
    monitoring 156-158, *157*
    project teams 130-131
    qualities of project managers 147-148
    reasons projects fail 145-146
    recommended websites 160
    time management 153-156, *154*
    tools and techniques 149-153
project managers, qualities of 147-148
project teams 130-131
Propak Africa 438
proposals 284-285
public companies 129
publicity 262
public participation *211*, 212-213
public relations (PR) 259-260, 446, 461, 521
public transport *see* transport

Q
quality 25
questionnaires *157, 158*, 244, 447 *see also* surveys
quick ratio 173

R
radio frequency identification (RFID) tags 330,
    335-336
record keeping 227, 228, 235
recycling 304-305

Red Nose Day 240
regeneration 21, 93
registration systems 329-330
religious diversity 245
request for proposals (RFPs) 96, 101, 104-105
research at exhibitions 447
Responsible Tourism Guidelines 24, 33
retreats 505
return on expenses (ROE) 174-176, *175*
return on investment (ROI) 19, 33, 36-37, 72
    banqueting 486-487
    bidding 92
    case studies 37, 91, 319-320, 336
    exhibitions 433-435, *435*
    financial management 174-176, *175*
    hallmark and mega-events 387-388
    information technology (IT) 334-335
    meetings 508-511
    planning and coordination 115
    sponsorships 285-286
    sport events 412
return on marketing investment (ROMI) 267-269,
    420, 521
revenue management 175-176
RFID tags 330, 335-336
RFPs *see* request for proposals (RFPs)
rich pictures 320-321, *321*
risk management 343-362
    banqueting 483-484
    case studies 349, 356, 358, 360, 424
    compliance management 349-350
    corporate events 497-498
    decision management 354-355
    definition of 344-349, *345*, *347*, *348*
    emergency management 352-354, *352*
    ethics management 351-352
    exhibitions 447-448
    festivals 405-406
    hallmark and mega-events 385-386
    health and safety management 355-357
    insurance management 360
    legal management 350-351
    meetings 523-524
    political events 465-467
    recommended websites 361-362
    security management 357-360
    sport events 423-426
ROE *see* return on expenses (ROE)
ROI *see* return on investment (ROI)
role players 67-86
    agencies 79-84
    buyers 70-74
    case studies 75-76, 77, 80, 81, 83
    important organisations 84-85
    recommended websites 86
    suppliers 74-79
    triangle model 68-70, *69*
ROMI *see* return on marketing investment (ROMI)
Roswell Convention and Visitors Bureau, Georgia,
    USA 80
Rugby World Cup 98, 282

S

SA Conferences and Exhibitions Calendar 29-31
safety and security *see* risk management
sales promotions 261-262
Samba Parade Guide, Brazil 377
SA Tourism 29
Saudi Arabia 507, 515
SBNAF *see* Standard Bank National Arts Festival
    (SBNAF)
scheduling 150-152, *151*, 302-305, 401
SEAs *see* strategic environmental assessments (SEAs)
section 20 companies 129
section 21 companies 130
security management 357-360 *see also* risk
    management
    bidding 98
    case studies 385
    design management 197
    exhibitions 447-448
    meetings 524
    Olympic Games 465-466
segmenting markets *10*, 255, *255*
selection of venues 112-114
seminars 505
service design 477-480
service level agreements (SLA) 351
SIAs *see* social impact assessments (SIAs)
signage 283-284, 303
site management 299-302
situational analysis 255-256, *256*
six Ps 258-260
SLA *see* service level agreements (SLA)
SMERF market 72-74
SMSs 332
social capital 36
social impact assessments (SIAs) 212-214
social impacts 92-93, 97-98, 210-214, *211*, *221*,
    269-270
social life-cycle events 15
socially responsible investing (SRI) 23
social systems 58-59, *59*
soft skills *60*

sole proprietors 129
solvency 172-174
Souk festival 132
sound systems 306
South African Tourism 29
spaces for events 115-117
speaker management 324, 325
special effects 306-307
special events planners 83-84
special-purpose events venues 17-19
speeches at banquets 480
sponsorships 17, 273-290
    activation and leverage of 283-284
    approaching potential sponsors 284-285
    banqueting 483
    case studies 278, 279, 280, 282, 287, 403, 420
    challenges 287-289
    corporate events 495
    definition of 275-276
    evaluation 285-286
    exhibitions 442-447
    festivals 403
    future developments 287-289
    levels and opportunities of 281-282
    meetings 522
    objectives of sponsors 278-281
    political events 461-462
    proposals 284-285
    reasons for favour and growth of 276-278
    reciprocal event–sponsor relationship *274*
    recommended websites 290
    return on investment (ROI) 285-286
    sport events 413, *413*, 420
    types of *275*
sport events 408-427
    administration 409-412
    bidding 409-410
    case studies 417, 419, 420, 422-423, 424,
        425-426
    catering design 231-232
    checklists *415*
    definition of 14
    design management 415-419, *415*
    environmental issues 418-419
    evaluation 411-412, *411*
    financial management 412-415, *413, 414*
    marketing management 419-421
    operations management 421-423
    recommended websites 427
    return on investment (ROI) 412
    risk management 423-426
    volunteers 415, *416*

SRI *see* socially responsible investing (SRI)
staged authenticity 14
stakeholders 139-140, 147-148, 397-398, 457, *458*,
    514-515
Standard Bank National Arts Festival (SBNAF) 237,
    238
stand managers 436
statistics of SA events sector 28-32, *31, 32*
stock control 177-178
strategic development 34-48
    case studies 37, 41, 44, 46, 47
    decision criteria 44
    development of events 37-39, *38*, 44-46
    events as assets 35-37
    events corporations 46-47
    procurement of events 39-42, *40-41*
    recommended websites 48
    support process 42-44, *43, 45*
strategic environmental assessments (SEAs) 220-221
Super Bowl 419
suppliers 74-79
support process 42-44, *43, 45*
surveys 335 *see also* questionnaires
sustainability 23, 207-224
    case studies 24, 216-217, 218, 222
    economic considerations 214-215, *221*
    environmental issues 216-222, *221*
    recommended websites 223-224
    social issues 210-214, *211, 221*
SWOT analysis 255-256, *256*
symposiums 505
systems management 436, 517-518

T
TA *see* tourism authority (TA)
table arrangements 476-477, *476, 477, 516-518*
Tall Ships, Liverpool, UK 314-315
tangible products of events 6
targeted benefits of events 6
TBL *see* triple bottom line (TBL)
teamwork 59, 130-131
technical management 305-307
technological forces 22-23
telecommunications infrastructure 98
temporary structures 305-306
tendering 90
Ten Ugly Men Festival 62
termination strategies 148-149
theme of events 6, 154, 187, 194, 197, *375*
tickets 178
time management 518
total quality management (TQM) 153, 514

tourism authority (TA) 43-44, *43*
tourism industry *5*
tourism organisations 84
TQM *see* total quality management (TQM)
trade associations 84
trade events *see* corporate events
trade media 84-85
trade shows 14, 505
traffic 98, 303 *see also* transport
training 137-138, 436
transcription 330, 331
translation 330, 331
transport 76, 82-83, 98, 117-118, 384-385
triangle model 68-70, *69*
triple bottom line (TBL) 23, 209, *221*, 269-270
trusts 130
Twitter *see* Web 2.0 technology

U
uncontrolled-access events 236-242
UNEP *see* United Nations Environmental Programme (UNEP)
unions 138
United Nations Environmental Programme (UNEP) 217
unregistered partnerships 129
urban regeneration 21, 93
utility companies 130

V
values 23
venue-finding agencies 84
venues 17-19, 74-78, 472, 493-494
V Festival 392, 404
virtual meetings 333-334
visitor experiences 6-8
Vodafone Live Music, UK 280
volunteers 8, 59, *59*, 136-137, 171-172, 373-375, 415, *416*, 417
voting 335

W
waste management 219, 221-222, 304-305
WBS *see* work breakdown schedules (WBS)
Web 2.0 technology 148, 336, *337*
web conferencing 334, 506
web marketing *see* websites
web organisational structure 57-58, *57*
websites 262-264, 328, 420-421
wedding receptions 244
work breakdown schedules (WBS) 149-150
workshops 506

Y
yield management 175-176

Z
zero-based budgeting 165, 412